Communications in Computer and Information Science 1525

More information about this series at https://link.springer.com/bookseries/7899

Michael Kamp · Irena Koprinska · Adrien Bibal ·
Tassadit Bouadi · Benoît Frénay · Luis Galárraga ·
José Oramas · Linara Adilova et al. (Eds.)

Machine Learning and Principles and Practice of Knowledge Discovery in Databases

International Workshops of ECML PKDD 2021
Virtual Event, September 13–17, 2021
Proceedings, Part II

Springer

For the full list of editors *see next page*

ISSN 1865-0929   ISSN 1865-0937 (electronic)
Communications in Computer and Information Science
ISBN 978-3-030-93732-4   ISBN 978-3-030-93733-1 (eBook)
https://doi.org/10.1007/978-3-030-93733-1

This Springer imprint is published by the registered company Springer Nature Switzerland AG
The registered company address is: Gewerbestrasse 11, 6330 Cham, Switzerland

Editors

Michael Kamp (iD)
IKIM, Ruhr-University Bochum
Bochum, Germany

Monash University
Melbourne, Australia

Adrien Bibal (iD)
University of Namur
Namur, Belgium

Benoît Frénay (iD)
University of Namur
Namur, Belgium

José Oramas (iD)
University of Antwerp
Antwerp, Belgium

Yamuna Krishnamurthy (iD)
Royal Holloway University of London
Egham, UK

Christine Largeron
Université Jean Monnet
Saint-Etienne cedex 2, France

Tiphaine Viard
Telecom Paris
Paris, France

Massimiliano Ruocco
Norwegian Univesity of Science
and Technology
Trondheim, Norway

Claudio Gallicchio
University of Pisa
Pisa, Italy

Franz Pernkopf (iD)
Graz University of Technology
Graz, Austria

Holger Fröning (iD)
Heidelberg University
Heidelberg, Germany

Riccardo Guidotti (iD)
University of Pisa
Pisa, Italy

Irena Koprinska (iD)
University of Sydney
Sydney, NSW, Australia

Tassadit Bouadi (iD)
University of Rennes 1
Rennes, France

Luis Galárraga (iD)
Inria
Rennes, France

Linara Adilova
Ruhr University Bochum
Bochum, Germany

Bo Kang (iD)
Ghent University
Ghent, Belgium

Jefrey Lijffijt (iD)
Ghent University
Gent, Belgium

Pascal Welke (iD)
University of Bonn
Bonn, Germany

Erlend Aune
BI Norwegian Business School
Oslo, Norway

Gregor Schiele (iD)
University of Duisburg-Essen
Essen, Germany

Michaela Blott (iD)
Xilinx Research
Dublin, Ireland

Günther Schindler
Heidelberg University
Heidelberg, Germany

Anna Monreale (iD)
University of Pisa
Pisa, Italy

Salvatore Rinzivillo (ID)
ISTI-CNR
Pisa, Italy

Eirini Ntoutsi (ID)
Freie Universität Berlin
Berlin, Germany

Bodo Rosenhahn (ID)
Leibniz University Hannover
Hannover, Germany

Daniela Cialfi (ID)
University of Chieti-Pescara
Chieti, Italy

Maxwell Ramstead (ID)
McGill University
Montreal, Canada

Pedro M. Ferreira (ID)
University of Lisbon
Lisboa, Portugal

Donato Malerba (ID)
Universita di Bari Aldo Moro
Bari, Italy

Philippe Fournier-Viger (ID)
Shenzhen University
Shenzhen, China

Sebastian Ventura (ID)
University of Córdoba
Córdoba, Spain

Min Zhou (ID)
Noah's Ark Lab, Huawei
Beijing, China

Ilaria Bordino
UniCredit
Rome, Italy

Francesco Gullo (ID)
Unicredit
Rome, Italy

Lorenzo Severini
Unicredit
Rome, Italy

Przemyslaw Biecek (ID)
Warsaw University of Technology
Warsaw, Poland

Mykola Pechenizkiy (ID)
Eindhoven University of Technology
Eindhoven, The Netherlands

Christopher Buckley (ID)
University of Sussex
Brighton, UK

Pablo Lanillos (ID)
Radboud University Nijmegen
Nijmegen, The Netherlands

Tim Verbelen (ID)
Ghent University
Ghent, Belgium

Giuseppina Andresini (ID)
University of Bari Aldo Moro
Bari, Italy

Ibéria Medeiros (ID)
University of Lisbon
Lisbon, Portugal

M. Saqib Nawaz (ID)
Harbin Institute of Technology
Harbin, China

Meng Sun (ID)
Peking University
Beijing, China

Valerio Bitetta
UniCredit
Milan, Italy

Andrea Ferretti
UniCredit
Milan, Italy

Giovanni Ponti
ENEA Headquarters
Portici, Italy

Rita Ribeiro (ID)
University of Porto
Porto, Portugal

João Gama (iD)
University of Porto
Porto, Portugal

Lee Cooper (iD)
Northwestern University
Chicago, IL, USA

Jonas Richiardi (iD)
University of Lausanne
Lausanne, Switzerland

Diego Saldana Miranda (iD)
F. Hoffmann–La Roche Ltd
Basel, Switzerland

Guilherme Graça (iD)
University of Lisbon
Lisbon, Portugal

Ricard Gavaldà (iD)
UPC BarcelonaTech
Barcelona, Spain

Naghmeh Ghazaleh (iD)
PD Personalised Healthcare
Basel, Switzerland

Damian Roqueiro (iD)
ETH Zurich
Basel, Switzerland

Konstantinos Sechidis (iD)
Novartis Pharma AG
Basel, Switzerland

Preface

The European Conference on Machine Learning and Principles and Practice of Knowledge Discovery in Databases (ECML PKDD) is the premier European conference on machine learning and data mining. In 2021, ECML PKDD was held virtually during September 13–17 due to the COVID-19 pandemic.

The program included workshops on specialized topics held during the first and last day of the conference. This two-volume set includes the proceedings of the following workshops:

1. Workshop on Advances in Interpretable Machine Learning and Artificial Intelligence (AIMLAI 2021)
2. Workshop on Parallel, Distributed, and Federated Learning (PDFL 2021)
3. Workshop on Graph Embedding and Mining (GEM 2021)
4. Workshop on Machine Learning for Irregular Time Series (ML4ITS 2021)
5. Workshop on IoT, Edge, and Mobile for Embedded Machine Learning (ITEM 2021)
6. Workshop on eXplainable Knowledge Discovery in Data Mining (XKDD 2021)
7. Workshop on Bias and Fairness in Artificial Intelligence (BIAS 2021)
8. Workshop on Workshop on Active Inference (IWAI 2021)
9. Workshop on Machine Learning for Cybersecurity (MLCS 2021)
10. Workshop on Machine Learning in Software Engineering (MLiSE 2021)
11. Workshop on Mining Data for Financial Applications (MIDAS 2021)
12. Workshop on Data Science for Social Good (SoGood 2021)
13. Workshop on Machine Learning for Pharma and Healthcare Applications (PharML 2021)
14. Workshop on Machine Learning for Buildings Energy Management (MLBEM 2021)

Each workshop section contains the papers from the workshop and a preface from the organizers.

We would like to thank all participants and invited speakers, the Program Committees and reviewers, and the ECML PKDD conference and workshop chairs – thank you for making the workshops a successful event. We are also grateful to Springer for their help in publishing this volume.

October 2021

Michael Kamp
on behalf of the volume editors

Organization

Workshop Chairs

AIMLAI 2021

Adrien Bibal	University of Namur, Belgium
Tassadit Bouadi	University of Rennes, France
Benoît Frénay	University of Namur, Belgium
Luis Galárraga	Inria, France
José Oramas	University of Antwerp, Belgium

PDFL 2021

Michael Kamp	IKIM, Ruhr-University Bochum, Germany/Monash University, Australia
Linara Adilova	Ruhr-University Bochum and Fraunhofer IAIS, Germany
Yamuna Krishnamurthy	Royal Holloway, University of London, UK

GEM 2021

Bo Kang	Ghent University, Belgium
Christine Largeron	Université Jean Monnet, France
Jefrey Lijffijt	Ghent University, Belgium
Tiphaine Viard	Telecom Paris, France
Pascal Welke	University of Bonn, Germany

ML4ITS 2021

Massimiliano Ruocco	Norwegian University of Science and Technology, Norway
Erlend Aune	BI Norwegian Business School, Norway
Claudio Gallicchio	University of Pisa, Italy

ITEM 2021

Gregor Schiele	University of Duisburg-Essen, Germany
Franz Pernkopf	Graz University of Technology, Austria
Michaela Blott	Xilinx Research, Ireland
Holger Fröning	Heidelberg University, Germany
Günther Schindler	Heidelberg University, Germany

XKDD 2021
Riccardo Guidotti   University of Pisa, Italy
Anna Monreale   University of Pisa, Italy
Salvatore Rinzivillo   ISTI-CNR, Italy
Przemyslaw Biecek   Warsaw University of Technology, Poland

BIAS 2021
Eirini Ntoutsi   Freie Universität Berlin, Germany
Mykola Pechenizkiy   Eindhoven University of Technology,
                            The Netherlands
Bodo Rosenhahn   Leibniz Universität Hannover, Germany

IWAI 2021
Christopher Buckley   University of Sussex, UK
Daniela Cialfi   University of Chieti-Pescara, Italy
Pablo Lanillos   Donders Institute, The Netherlands
Maxwell Ramstead   McGill University, Canada
Tim Verbelen   Ghent University, Belgium

MLCS 2021
Pedro Ferreira   University of Lisbon, Portugal
Michael Kamp   IKIM, Ruhr-University Bochum,
                            Germany/Monash University, Australia
Giuseppina Andresini   University of Bari Aldo Moro, Italy
Donato Malerba   University of Bari Aldo Moro, Italy
Ibéria Medeiros   University of Lisbon, Portugal

MLiSE 2021
Philippe Fournier-Viger   Shenzhen University, China
M. Saqib Nawaz   Harbin Institute of Technology, China
Sebastian Ventura   University of Cordoba, Spain
Meng Sun   Peking University, China
Min Zhou   Huawei, China

MIDAS 2021
Valerio Bitetta   Unicredit, Italy
Ilaria Bordino   Unicredit, Italy
Andrea Ferretti   Unicredit, Italy
Francesco Gullo   Unicredit, Italy
Giovanni Ponti   ENEA, Italy
Lorenzo Severini   Unicredit, Italy

SoGood 2021

Ricard Gavaldà	UPC BarcelonaTech, Spain
Irena Koprinska	University of Sydney, Australia
João Gama	University of Porto, Portugal
Rita P. Ribeiro	University of Porto, Portugal

PharML 2021

Lee Cooper	Northwestern University, USA
Naghmeh Ghazaleh	F. Hoffmann–La Roche Ltd., Switzerland
Jonas Richiardi	Lausanne University Hospital and University of Lausanne, Switzerland
Damian Roqueiro	ETH Zurich and D-BSSE, Switzerland
Diego Saldana	F. Hoffmann–La Roche Ltd., Switzerland
Konstantinos Sechidis	Novartis Pharma AG, Switzerland

MLBEM 2021

Pedro Ferreira	University of Lisbon, Portugal
Guilherme Graça	University of Lisbon, Portugal

Contents – Part II

MIning DAta for financial applicationS

Sixth Workshop on Data Science for Social Good (SoGood 2021)

Machine Learning for Pharma and Healthcare Applications

Machine Learning for Buildings Energy Management

Contents – Part I

Parallel, Distributed, and Federated Learning

Graph Embedding and Mining

International Workshop on Active Inference

Machine Learning for CyberSecurity

Workshop on Machine Learning for Cybersecurity (MLCS 2021)

The last decade has been a critical one regarding cybersecurity, with studies estimating the cost of cybercrime to be up to 1 percent of the global GDP in 2020. The capability to detect, analyze, and defend against threats in (near) real-time conditions is not possible without employing machine learning techniques and big data infrastructures. This gives rise to cyberthreat intelligence and analytic solutions, such as (informed) machine learning on big data and open-source intelligence, to perceive, reason, learn, and act against cyber adversary techniques and actions. Moreover, organizations' security analysts have to manage and protect systems and deal with the privacy and security of all personal and institutional data under their control. The aim of this workshop was to provide researchers with a forum to exchange and discuss scientific contributions, open challenges, and recent achievements in machine learning and their role in the development of secure systems.

Cybersecurity is of the utmost importance for computing systems. The ethics guidelines for trustworthy artificial intelligence authored by the European Commission's Independent High Level Expert Group on Artificial Intelligence in April 2019 have highlighted that machine learning-based artificial intelligence developments in various fields, including cybersecurity, are improving the quality of our lives every day, that AI systems should be resilient to attacks and security, and that they should consider security-by-design principles.

Due to the scale and complexity of current systems, cybersecurity is a permanent and growing concern in industry and academia. On the one hand, the volume and diversity of functional and non-functional data, including open source information, along with increasingly dynamical operating environments, create additional obstacles to the security of systems and to the privacy and security of data. On the other hand, it creates an information rich environment that, leveraged by techniques at the intersection of modern machine learning, data science and visualization fields, will contribute to improve systems and data security and privacy.

This poses significant, industry relevant, challenges to the machine learning and cybersecurity communities, as the main problems arise in contexts of dynamic operating environments and unexpected operating conditions, motivating the demand for production-ready systems able to improve and, adaptively, maintain the security of computing systems as well as the security and privacy of data.

Based on the recent history, we organized this workshop as a European forum for cybersecurity researchers and practitioners wishing to discuss the recent developments of machine learning for developing cybersecurity, by paying special attention to solutions rooted in adversarial learning, pattern mining, neural networks and deep learning, probabilistic inference, anomaly detection, stream learning and mining, and big data analytics.

Cyberthreats have increased dramatically, exposing sensitive personal and business information, disrupting critical operations, and imposing high costs on the economy. The number, frequency, and sophistication of threats will only increase and will become more targeted in nature. Furthermore, today's computing systems operate under increasing scales and dynamic environments, ingesting and generating more and more functional and non-functional data. This calls for tools and solutions combining the latest advances in areas such as data science, visualization, and machine learning. We strongly believe that the significant advance of the state of the art in machine learning over the last few years has not been fully exploited to harness the potential of available data, for the benefit of systems-and-data security and privacy. In fact, while machine learning algorithms have been already proven beneficial for the cybersecurity industry, they have also highlighted a number of shortcomings. Traditional machine algorithms are often vulnerable to attacks, known as adversarial learning attacks, which can cause the algorithms to misbehave or reveal information about their inner workings. As machine learning-based capabilities become incorporated into cyber assets, the need to understand adversarial learning and address it becomes clear. On the other hand, when a significant amount of data is collected from or generated by different security monitoring solutions, big-data analytical techniques are necessary to mine, interpret, and extract knowledge of these big data.

This year's workshop followed the success of the two previous editions (MLCS 2019 and MLCS 2020) co-located with ECML PKDD 2019 and ECML PKDD 2020 - in both editions the workshop gained strong interest, with an attendance of between 30 and 40 participants, lively discussions after the talks, and a vibrant panel discussion in the 2019 edition. MLCS 2021 also aimed at providing researchers with a forum to exchange and discuss scientific contributions and open challenges, both theoretical and practical, related to the use of machine-learning approaches in cybersecurity. We wanted to foster joint work and knowledge exchange between the cybersecurity community, and researchers and practitioners from the machine learning area, and its intersection with big data, data science, and visualization. The workshop provided a forum for discussing novel trends and achievements in machine learning and their role in the development of secure systems. It aimed to highlight the latest research trends in machine learning, privacy of data, big data, deep learning, incremental and stream learning, and adversarial learning. In particular, it aimed to promote the application of these emerging techniques to cybersecurity and measure the success of these less-traditional algorithms.

We hope that the workshop contributed to identifying new application areas as well as open and future research problems related to the application of machine-learning in the cybersecurity field.

Donato Malerba
Giuseppina Andresini
Ibria Medeiros
Michael Kamp
Pedro M. Ferreira

Organization

MLCS 2021 Chairs

Donato Malerba — Università degli Studi di Bari Aldo Moro, Italy
Giuseppina Andresini — Università degli Studi di Bari Aldo Moro, Italy
Ibéria Medeiros — Universidade de Lisboa, Portugal
Michael Kamp — CISPA Helmholtz Center for Information Security, Germany, and Monash University, Australia
Pedro M. Ferreira — Universidade de Lisboa, Portugal

Program Committee

Aikaterini Mitrokotsa — Chalmers University of Technology, Sweden
Gennady Andrienko — Fraunhofer IAIS, Germany
Gianluigi Folino — National Research Council of Italy, Italy
Leonardo Aniello — University of Southampton, UK
Marc Dacier — Eurecom, France
Marco Vieira — University of Coimbra, Portugal
Miguel Correia — University of Lisbon, Portugal
Mihalis Nicolaou — Cyprus Institute, Cyprus
Rogério de Lemos — University of Kent, UK
Tommaso Zoppi — University of Florence, Italy
Vasileios Mavroeidis — University of Oslo, Norway

Dealing with Imbalanced Data in Multi-class Network Intrusion Detection Systems Using XGBoost

Malik AL-Essa[1]([⊠]) [iD] and Annalisa Appice[1,2] [iD]

[1] Dipartimento di Informatica, Università degli Studi di Bari Aldo Moro,
via Orabona, 4, 70126 Bari, Italy
{malik.alessa,annalisa.appice}@uniba.it
[2] Consorzio Interuniversitario Nazionale per lInformatica - CINI, Bari, Italy

Abstract. Network intrusion detection is a crucial cyber-security problem, where machine learning is recognised as a relevant approach to detect signs of malicious activity in the network traffic. However, intrusion detection patterns learned with imbalanced network traffic data often fail in recognizing rare attacks. One way to address this issue is to use oversampling before learning, in order to adjust the ratio between the different classes and make the traffic data more balanced. This paper investigates the effect of oversampling coupled to feature selection, in order to understand how the feature relevance may change due to the creation of artificial rare samples. We perform this study using XGBoost for the network traffic classification. The experiments are performed with two benchmark multi-class network intrusion detection problems.

Keywords: Network intrusion detection · Imbalanced classification · Oversampling · Feature selection · Multi-class classification

1 Introduction

With the rapid advances in the internet and communication fields, network security has emerged as a vital research domain. An intrusion detection system (IDS) is a mandatory line of the network defence process to preventing the network from possible intrusions by continuously inspecting the network traffic, in order to ensure its confidentiality, integrity and availability. Nowadays, the most promising IDSs analyse historical network flows created based on source/destination IP, source/destination port, protocol and timestamp looking for signs of malicious activity. They commonly learn intrusion detection to map network flows to classes. The flow classification is done by analysing flow-based characteristics (e.g., the duration of a flow, the protocol type and the total number of forwarding and backwarding packets transmitted between two hosts), which are more stable than the byte or packet-based characteristics to track long-term changes in network behaviour [30].

© Springer Nature Switzerland AG 2021
M. Kamp et al. (Eds.): ECML PKDD 2021 Workshops, CCIS 1525, pp. 5–21, 2021.
https://doi.org/10.1007/978-3-030-93733-1_1

With the recent boom of artificial intelligence in cybersecurity, the use of machine learning (ML) [16] and, more recently, deep learning (DL) methods [1, 6, 7] has definitely emerged as relevant approach to accurately detect intrusions across the network traffic data. However, ML (as well DL) methods yield very accurate classifications when trained on a large amount of data that are equally distributed among different classes. Instead, their performance declines significantly in the case of learning from imbalanced data [12]. In the imbalanced scenario, the target classes having a dominant share in the imbalanced dataset are known as majority classes, while the classes which are outweighed by majority classes are known as minority (or rare) classes. The presence of rare attack classes is very common in network intrusion detection datasets.

Benchmark network intrusion detection datasets like NSL-KDD [29] and CICIDS17 [27] are examples of imbalanced datasets, where the normal samples represent the largest majority class, while attack categories such as Remote to Local (R2L) and User to Root (U2R) in NSL-KDD, as well as Web Attack-Brute Force, Web Attack-XSS, Web Attack-Sql Injection, Infiltration and Heartbleed in CICIDS17 represent rare classes. As the number of rare attacks represents less than 1% of the training datasets of both NSL-KDD and CICIDS17, ML (or DL) methods trained on the imbalanced training sets of these datasets may perform poorly when classifying minority attack classes. The problem is even more complex in NSL-KDD where the testing data commonly used in the experimental studies also cover examples of zero-day attacks in the rare categories. Zero-day attacks represent security vulnerabilities that have been developed recently and can be used to successfully attack a system. They take place as the hackers develop the threat and the developers have zero-day to fix it [20]. Nowadays, they represent one of the biggest threat to any organisation.

Up to now various resampling approaches have been already investigated in combination with ML (and DL) methods, in order to deal with the imbalanced scenario of the network traffic. In particular, various oversampling methods (e.g., Generative Adversarial Networks (GAN) or Synthetic Minority Oversampling Technique (SMOTE)) have been tested to generate artificial samples of the minority class [8, 26], while downsampling methods have been tested to reduce the amount of samples of the majority class [26]. A recent study [9] has compared the performance of various methods for resampling imbalanced data in network intrusion detection datasets by concluding that resampling, mostly oversampling, aids in improving the accuracy in recognising attacks of minority categories. The study of [8] has also shown that generating artificial attacks may improve the generality of intrusion detection patterns learned with augmented traffic data by allowing us to detect zero-day attacks appearing in the testing set. The study of [8] has been conducted in the binary scenario, in order to disentangle normal data from attacks without providing any classification of the attack categories. However, we believe that similar conclusions can be generalised to the multi-class scenario.

In this paper, we also explore the use of oversampling in multi-class intrusion detection. We use eXtreme Gradient Boostin (XGBoost) [15] as a classification algorithm. This decision is supported by recent studies using XGBoost for attack detection and classification (e.g. [12,13,21,24]). In addition, we couple the study of the performance of oversampling to that of feature selection, in order to explore how both approaches can gain accuracy in recognising unseen and/or rare attacks. As a further contribution, we perform a preliminary investigation to verify how the relevance of features for classification can be conditioned through the generation of artificial rare attacks. This information may provide useful insights for identifying more robust features for improving the zero-day attack detection ability.

This paper is organised as follows. The related works are presented in Sect. 2. The materials and methods are described Sect. 3. The findings in the evaluation are discussed in Sect. 4. Finally, Sect. 5 refocuses on the purpose of the research, draws conclusions and proposes future developments.

2   Related Work

Despite the recent boom of DL in cybersecurity, a wide amount of research in network intrusion detection is still focused on fitting traditional ML methods to classify network traffic data. In particular, many recent studies have bet on XGBoost [15] as an effective classification technology for detecting and classifying attacks in network traffic [13,21,24]. The use of this algorithm is well supported by the systematic study illustrated in [11] that has shown how XGBoost performs efficiently and in robust manner to find a network attack by outperforming various classification algorithms like AdaBoost, Naïve Bayes, Multi-layer perceptron and K-Nearest Neighbour. On the other hand, a few recent studies [5,12] have started the investigation of sophisticated pipelines that cascade deep neural networks (i.e. a Siamese network in [12] and a Triplet network in [5]) trained for the attack detection and XGBoost trained for the attack classification.

In addition, various studies investigate resampling solutions for mitigating the effect of the skewed attack class distribution and provide the evidence of the potential of multiclass classification algorithms for network intrusion detection. In [9], both oversampling and downsampling techniques are evaluated in the Big Data framework by using the Spark's ANN multi-class classifier. The study has shown that oversampling increases the training time, but improves the ability of detecting minority attacks. In [24], oversampling (based on Adaptive Synthetic (ADASYN)) is combined with XGBoost, while the principal component analysis (PCA) algorithm is used to reduce the redundancy features of the data. In [23], oversampling (based on SMOTE) is combined with reinforcement learning to learn intrusion detection patterns, which are less vulnerable to various types of attacks. SMOTE is combined with Random Forest in [28] to avoid overfitting. A similar idea is also investigated in [8], where the authors address the binary intrusion detection problem (attack detection without attack family classification) by applying generative adversarial learning for resampling rare data.

Finally, feature selection plays a crucial role in building effective network intrusion detection systems. It allows us to reduce the data dimensionality by

removing noisy and irrelevant features that may cause overfitting or be susceptible to adversarial manipulations. In [24], PCA is used as an alternative to feature
selection. However, PCA constructs new features, i.e. the principal components
of the original dataset, while the feature selection selects a subset of the original
features without any transformation of the traffic data. A recent summary of
feature selection algorithms for intrusion detection system has been illustrated
in [2]. In [17], XGBoost is adopted for the feature selection task followed by a
deep neural network for the classification of the network traffic.

Similarly to the studies reported above, in this paper, we also adopt feature selection for reducing the dimensionality of the network traffic data. In
addition, we investigate how feature selection may contribute to make XGBoost
an effective and robust classification technology for detecting and classifying
unseen attacks in network traffic. As we couple feature selection to oversampling, we conduct an ablation study to verify how both components can actually
contribute to the gain in accuracy. Finally, we perform a further step in this
direction by exploring the effect of oversampling on the relevance of features in
the rare attack classification task. This analysis paves the way for explaining
how artificial samples generated through oversampling can contribute to make
an intrusion detection pattern more robust to the presence of zero-day attacks.

3   Materials and Methods

In this Section, we briefly revise the ML methods that we have combined to
define the network intrusion detection configurations evaluated in this study.

3.1   Oversampling

Oversampling of rare data before learning is a traditional solution that can be
used to handle the attack imbalance, in order to achieve the balanced condition
[9]. In this study, we use SMOTE [14] that is a well known heuristic oversampling method widely used in ML applications. The core idea of SMOTE is to
insert new, synthetic samples that are generated randomly between minority
class samples and their neighbours. To this aim, it first searches for the K nearest neighbours for each data sample in the minority class. Based upon the idea
that the neighbour features and their class labels are correlated, it performs the
linear interpolation operation. In particular, the interpolation step applies the
correlation formula between neighbour features and class to obtain the interpo-
lated synthetic samples. Experiments in [23,28] show as SMOTE can improve
the situation of overfitting when generating artificial samples of rare attacks.

3.2   Feature Selection

Feature selection consists of detecting relevant features and discarding irrelevant
ones with the goal of obtaining a subset of features that describe properly the
given problem with a negligible degradation of performance [33]. This stage is

performed according to various literature studies [2, 4, 34] that have identified feature selection as a pre-processing phase in attack defence, which can increase classification accuracy and reduce computational complexity. In this study, we rank features according to how they potentially gain in classification accuracy. Similarly to [8], we compute the Mutual Info (MI) [31], in order to measure the worth of every input feature. The MI quantifies the amount of information obtained about the class through observing each feature to be analyzed. A feature that does not have much effect on the data classification has very small MI and it can be ignored without affecting the accuracy of a classifier. Based upon this consideration, features are ranked into the training set according to the MI measure so that the top-k features can be retained.

3.3 XGBoost

XGBoost [15] is one of the most popular machine learning algorithms (outside deep learning) used in the network traffic classification [13, 21, 24]. It is a highly flexible and versatile algorithm that learns a decision tree-based ensemble using a gradient boosting framework to minimise the error of sequential models. In particular, XGBoost is efficient as the process of sequential tree building is performed using parallelized implementation. It is designed to make efficient use of hardware resources and it is implemented with the depth-first approach that contributes to improve computational performance significantly. In addition, XGBoost is able to penalise more complex models through, backward tree pruning, LASSO (L1) and Ridge (L2) regularization to prevent overfitting. Finally, it employs the distributed weighted Quantile Sketch algorithm to effectively find the optimal split points among weighted datasets.

3.4 OneVsOne and OneVsRest

OneVsOne (OVO) and OneVsRest (OVR) are two ML combination strategies [22] to decompose a multi-class problem into binary (simpler) sub-problems. Both are used in [5] to perform multi-class classification of attacks.

OVO performs the training stage of binary classification on $(n-1)n$ trials—one trial for each pair of classes in the dataset. n denotes the number of distinct classes in the original training set. In each trial we consider a subset of the training set, comprising the samples labelled with the two selected classes, and generate a binary classification model for the selected classes. In the testing stage each binary classifier is used to predict a class. Hence, we assign a testing sample to the class with the majority counts.

OVR performs the binary training stage of binary classification on n trials—one trial for each category in the multi-class dataset. In each trial, the entire training set is considered with the selected class as the positive class and the left-out classes assigned to the negative class. The classification of a testing sample requires that each model predicts a class membership probability. The argmax of these scores (class index with the largest score) is then used to predict a class.

Note that compared with the OVO strategy, the number of binary classifiers which we have to train is quite small.

In OVO the number of classifiers is quadratic with the number of classes, while in OVR it is linear with the number of classes. One advantage of the OVR strategy is its interpretability. Since each class is represented by one and only one classifier, it is possible to gain knowledge about the class by inspecting its corresponding classifier. On the other hand, although OVO requires more classifiers, each classifier built by OVO only needs to distinguish any two classes in the original multi-class problem. Thus, each classifier processes fewer samples, and the problems to be learned by each classifier are usually simpler compared with the original multi-class problem and the OVR strategy. In addition, the class-imbalanced problem that is necessarily introduced in OVR strategy does not exist in the OVO strategy.

3.5   Implementation Details

The code used in the experimental study is written in Python 3.8 by importing:

1. SMOTE from imblearn.over_sampling.SMOTE;
2. feature selection with Mutual Info from sklearn.feature_selection.SelectKBest;
3. XGBoost from xgboost.XGBoostClassifier;
4. both OVO and OVR from sklearn.multiclass. OneVs OneClassifier and sklearn.multiclass.OneVs RestClassifier, respectively
5. StandardScaler from sklearn.preprocessing.

The numeric features are scaled. The categorical features are pre-processed using the one-hot-encoder technique. The number of features k for the feature selection step is chosen exploring the range of possible values between 10 and the maximum number of features with step equal to 10. The tree depth is selected among 6, 9 and 12. The sub-sample size is selected among 0.5, 0.75 and 1.0. The remaining parameters of the methods listed above are set by adopting the default parameter set-up reported in the documentation. We use the grid search performed on a 5-fold stratified cross-validation of the training set to automatically choose the number of features in the feature selection, as well the tree depth and the sub-sample size in the binary classification. We import sklearn.model_selection.GridSearchCV and sklearn.model_selection.StratifiedKFold as implementations of the grid search and the stratified cross validation, respectively.

4   Evaluation Study

We use two benchmark datasets in our evaluation. The datasets are described in Sect. 4.1. The evaluation metrics are described in Sect. 4.2, while the experimental results are discussed in Sects. 4.3–4.5.

Table 1. Number of samples per category in both the training set and testing set of NSL-KDD (0: DoS, 1: Probe, 2: U2R, 3: R2L, 4: Normal) and CICIDS17 (0: DoS Hulk, 1: DoS GoldenEye, 2: DoS Slowloris, 3: DoS Slowhttptes, 4: DDoS, 5: PortScan, 6: FTP Patator, 7: SSH-Patator, 8: Bot, 9: Web Attack Brute Force, 10: Web Attack-XSS, 11: Web Attack SQL Injection, 12: Infiltration, 13: HeartBleed, 14: Normal)

	Total	0	1	2	3	4	5	6	7	8	9	10	11	12	13	14
NSL-KDD Train	25192	9234	2289	11	209	13449										
NSL-KDD Test	22544	7458	2421	200	2754	9711										
CICIDS17 Train	44854	8413	2296	1131	2045	4738	6039	3233	2347	772	614	256	6	4	5	12955
CICIDS 17Test	67289	12475	3548	1710	3187	7111	9055	4705	3550	1194	893	396	15	27	6	19417

4.1 Dataset Description

We use two benchmark datasets, that is, NSL-KDD and CICIDS 2017. A summary of the characteristics of both datasets is reported in Table 1. NSL-KDD [29] is a revised version of the KDDCUP99 that is obtained by removing the duplicate samples from KDDCUP99. For this experiment we adopt the data setting that includes KDDTrain$^+$_20Percent and KDDTest$^+$ as the testing set.[1]. We select this dataset as it has been recently used in the evaluation of various multi-class intrusion detection methods. CICIDS 2017[27] was collected by the Canadian Institute for Cybersecurity in 2017. The original dataset is a 5-day log collected from Monday July 3, 2017 to Friday July 7, 2017. In our experimental study, we consider the training and testing sets of CICIDS2017, built according to the strategy described by [25]. We note that both U2R(denoted as 2 in Table 1) and R2L(denoted as 3 in Table 1) are rare attacks in NSL-KDD, while Bot (denoted as 8 in Table 1), Web Attack Brute Force (denoted as 9 in Table 1), Web Attack-XSS (denoted as 10 in Table 1), Web Attack SQL Injection (denoted as 11 in Table 1), Infiltration (denoted as 12 in Table 1) and HeartBleed (denoted as 13 in Table 1) are rare attacks in CICIDS17.

4.2 Experimental Setting and Evaluation Metrics

We perform an experimental study to analyse the performance of various intrusion detection configurations defined by training the multi-class classification model with multi-class XGBoost, OVO and OVR, respectively. We run both OVO and OVR by training the binary XGBoost model in each binary sub-task. We perform an ablation study exploring the effect of oversampling (SMOTE) and/or feature selection (FS) in combination with XGBoost, OVO and OVR, respectively. This corresponds to evaluate the accuracy performance of twelve configurations. To evaluate the accuracy of the defined configurations, we analyse the F1 score per class. In addition, we consider the overall metrics like overall accuracy, micro F1, weighted F1 and macro F1.

---

[1] https://www.unb.ca/cic/datasets/nsl.html.

Table 2. F1 Score for each class in the testing set of NSL-KDD (0: DoS, 1: Probe, 2: U2R, 3: R2L, 4: Normal). The best results per each class are in bold.

	0	1	2	3	4
XGBoost	0.90	0.67	0.44	0.11	0.83
FS+XGBoost	0.90	0.67	0.40	0.09	0.83
SMOTE+XGBoost	**0.91**	0.69	0.42	0.18	0.84
SMOTE+FS+XGBoost	0.90	0.7	0.46	0.17	0.85
OVO	**0.91**	0.69	0.44	0.13	0.84
FS+OVO	**0.91**	0.66	0.45	0.10	0.85
SMOTE+OVO	**0.91**	0.74	0.56	0.13	**0.86**
SMOTE+FS+OVO	**0.91**	**0.75**	**0.57**	0.14	**0.86**
OVR	**0.91**	0.69	0.37	0.08	0.82
FS+OVR	0.90	0.68	0.40	**0.22**	0.82
SMOTE+OVR	0.90	0.72	0.46	**0.22**	0.84
SMOTE+FS+OVR	0.90	0.72	0.46	0.21	0.84

Table 3. F1 Score for each class in the testing set of CICIDS17 (0: DoS Hulk, 1: DoS GoldenEye, 2: DoS Slowloris, 3: DoS Slowhttptes, 4: DDoS, 5: PortScan, 6: FTP Patator, 7: SSH-Patator, 8: Bot, 9: Web Attack Brute Force, 10: Web Attack-XSS, 11: Web Attack SQL Injection, 12: Infiltration, 13: HeartBleed, 14: Normal). The best results per each class are in bold.

	0	1	2	3	4	5	6	7	8	9	10	11	12	13	14
XGBoost	1	1	**0.99**	0.99	1	1	1	1	**0.99**	0.77	0.43	0.22	0.62	0.67	1
FS+XGBoost	1	1	**0.99**	0.99	1	1	1	1	**0.99**	0.77	0.43	0.36	0.62	0.67	1
SMOTE+XGBoost	1	1	**0.99**	0.99	1	1	1	1	**0.99**	0.74	**0.48**	0.18	0.62	0.29	1
SMOTE+FS+XGBoost	1	1	**0.99**	0.99	1	1	1	1	**0.99**	0.75	0.47	0.37	0.71	0.29	1
OVO	1	1	**0.99**	0.99	1	1	1	1	**0.99**	0.76	0.41	0.12	0.0	0.91	1
FS+OVO	1	1	**0.99**	0.99	1	1	1	1	**0.99**	0.76	0.41	0.12	0.0	0.91	1
SMOTE+OVO	1	1	**0.99**	0.99	1	1	1	1	**0.99**	0.73	0.44	0.10	0.53	0.91	1
SMOTE+FS+OVO	1	1	**0.99**	0.99	1	1	1	1	**0.99**	0.73	0.44	0.10	0.58	0.91	1
OVR	1	1	**0.99**	1	1	1	1	1	**0.99**	0.77	0.41	0.24	0.5	0.91	1
FS+OVR	1	1	**0.99**	1	1	1	1	1	**0.99**	0.77	0.41	0.24	0.5	0.91	1
SMOTE+OVR	1	1	**0.99**	0.99	1	1	1	1	**0.99**	0.74	0.46	**0.52**	0.68	0.67	1
SMOTE+FS+OVR	1	1	**0.99**	0.99	1	1	1	1	**0.99**	0.74	0.46	**0.52**	0.71	0.67	1

4.3   Pipeline Analysis

We start analysing the F1 score measured per class for the tested configurations. Tables 2 and 3 report the F1 score measured on the classes of the testing sets of NSL-KDD and CICIDS17, respectively. We note that, in NSL-KDD, the highest F1 score is commonly achieved by training the configuration that couples the oversampling to both the feature selection and the multi-class strategy OVO (SMOTE+FS+OVO in Table 2). In CICIDS17, the highest F1 score is commonly achieved by training the configuration that couples the oversampling to the multi-class strategy OVR (SMOTE+OVR in Table 3). We also note that the

Table 4. Accuracy, micro F1, weighted F1, macro F1 of the compared pipelines on NSL-KDD and CICIDS17. For each metric the best results are in bold.

	NSL-KDD				CICIDS17			
	Accuracy	MicroF1	WeightedF1	MacroF1	Accuracy	MicroF1	WeightedF1	MacroF1
XGBoost	0.798	0.80	0.78	0.59	**0.991**	0.99	0.99	0.84
FS+XGBoost	0.794	0.79	0.77	0.58	**0.991**	0.99	0.99	0.85
SMOTE+XGBoost	0.806	0.81	0.79	0.61	**0.991**	0.99	0.99	0.82
SMOTE+FS+XGBoost	0.811	0.81	0.8	0.61	0.990	0.99	0.99	0.84
OVO	0.810	0.81	0.79	0.6	0.990	0.99	0.99	0.81
FS+OVO	0.810	0.81	0.79	0.59	0.990	0.99	0.99	0.81
SMOTE+OVO	0.830	**0.83**	**0.82**	**0.64**	0.990	0.99	0.99	0.84
SMOTE+FS+OVO	**0.831**	**0.83**	**0.82**	**0.64**	0.990	0.99	0.99	0.85
OVR	0.797	0.80	0.77	0.57	**0.991**	0.99	0.99	0.85
FS+OVR	0.794	0.79	0.77	0.6	**0.991**	0.99	0.99	0.85
SMOTE+OVR	0.808	0.81	0.79	0.63	**0.991**	0.99	0.99	**0.87**
SMOTE+FS+OVR	0.810	0.81	0.79	0.63	**0.991**	0.99	0.99	**0.87**

top-ranked configuration gains F1 score in almost all the classes of NSL-KDD, while it commonly gains in F1 score in the minority classes of CICIDS17 (e.g. in Web Attack SQL Injection that is a very challenging attack to detect). In both datasets, the performance of the multi-class XGBoost is outperformed by using a multi-class strategy (OVO or OVR) to decompose the multi-class problem into binary sub-tasks. In particular, OVO is the most effective multi-class strategy in NSL-KDD, where samples belong to 5 classes only, while OVR is the most effective strategy in CICIDS17, where samples belong to 15 different classes. This is an expected outcome as the performance of OVO may decrease in presence of a large amount of distinct categories [22]. The overall metrics (accuracy, micro F1, weighted F1 and macro F1) reported in Table 4 also confirm conclusions drawn above. In addition, we note that while all the overall metrics are improved in the top-ranked configuration (SMOTE+FS+OVO) of NSL-KDD, only the macro F1 is really improved in the top-ranked configuration (SMOTE+OVR) of CICIDS17. The remaining overall metrics do not change significantly in this CICIDS17. As macro F1 is computed giving the same importance to all the classes, this result shows that SMOTE+OVR is improving the ability of detecting rare classes, without significantly changing the performance achieved on the majority classes of CICIDS17. Additional considerations concern the fact that the oversampling procedure is a crucial step in both datasets, while the feature selection actually contributes to gain in accuracy in NSL-KDD dataset only. We recall that the testing set of NSL-KDD comprises several samples of zero-day attacks (also in the rare classes). So, our interpretation of this result is that the feature selection coupled to the oversampling may be a valid means to identify the more robust features to detect unseen attacks. Learning an intrusion detection model with these features may aid in avoiding the possible artifacts of overfitting the training data.

4.4   Oversampling Versus Feature Relevance Analysis

Deepening the analysis of the performance achieved with the use of feature selection, we proceed this study by analysing the effect of oversampling on feature relevance in NSL-KDD. We perform this analysis exploring the relevance of features in terms of MI. In addition, we leverage an explainable artificial intelligence method, in order to explain how the effect of the traffic data features on the classification of the new traffic data may change due to the addition of artificial training samples, which possibly resemble unseen, upcoming attacks. We perform this study by using the moDel Agnostic Language for Exploration and eXplanation (DALEX) [10].[2] DALEX is a framework for explaining predictive black-box models. It implements techniques for understanding both the global and local structure of a black-box model. In this study, we use the global explanation methodology of DALEX, which allows us to explain the behaviour of the XGBoost classification model by measuring the global relevance of different features. In particular, DALEX uses a permutation-based variable-importance measure to quantify the relevance of each feature [18]. For each feature, its effect is removed by resampling or permuting the values of the feature and a loss function compares the performance before and after. Intuitively, if a feature is important, randomly permuting its values will cause the loss to increase. By inspecting how the feature importance ranks of decision yielded with a classification model changes from the training to the testing set, we can understand how the model learned on the training set fits well to the testing set also.

Table 5. MI of the top-20 features of NSL-KDD selected on the original training set and the oversampled training set. Features that do not appear in both rankings are in bold.

Original			
(1) duration	(2) src_bytes	(3) dst_bytes	(4) hot
(5) logged_in	(6) num_compromised	(7) count	(8) srv_count
(9) serror_rate	(10) srv_serror_rate	(11) rerror_rate	(12) srv_rerror_rate
(13) same_srv_rate	(14) diff_srv_rate	(15) srv_diff_host_rate	(16) dst_host_count
(17) dst_host_srv_count	(18) dst_host_same_srv_rate	(19) dst_host_diff_srv_rate	(20) dst_host_same_src_port_rate
Oversampled			
(1) duration	(2)src_bytes	(3) dst_bytes	(4) **land**
(5) **wrong_format**	(6) **urgent**	(7) **hot**	(8) **num_failed_login**
(9) logged_in	(10) num_compromised	(11) **root_shell**	(12) **num_root**
(13) **num_file_creations**	(14) **num_shells**	(15) **num_access_files**	(16) **is_guest_login**
(17) count	(18) srv_count	(19) serror_rate	(20) srv_serror_rate

Mutual Info Analysis. Table 5 reports the top-20 ranked features that are selected with the MI measured on both the original training set and the oversampled training set, respectively. This analysis highlights that adding synthetic samples to the training step changes the relevance of features. In particular,

---

[2] https://github.com/ModelOriented/DALEX.

some features (that are evaluated less relevant for the classification on the original data) grow in relevance as synthetic attacks have been generated for the training step. As these synthetic attacks contribute to resemble possible unseen attacks in the training set, it is plausible that they also improve the relevance of features that are actually more robust to the upcoming unseen attacks.

Explainable Artificial Intelligence Analysis. Tables 6 and 7 report the top-20 relevant features identified with DALEX for the classification models trained with OVO and SMOTE+OVO, respectively. The feature relevance is computed on both the original training set (NSL-KDDTrain) and the original testing set (NSL-KDDTest), respectively. We note that SMOTE+OVO exhibits 10 features that appear simultaneously in the list of the top-20 features identified as relevant

Table 6. Top-10 relevant features identified with DALEX for the classification models trained with OVO and evaluated on NSL-KDDTrain and NSL-KDDTest. Features ranked in the top-20 list of both NSL-KDDTrain and NSL-KDDTest are in bold.

Feature rank	OVO+KDDTrain	OVO+NSL-KDDTest
1	src_bytes	**logged_in**
2	count	**flag_S0**
3	num_learners	service_private
4	service_ecr_i	service_smtp
5	service_http	service_domain
6	protocol_type_udp	service_domain_u
7	wrong_format	service_echo
8	diff_srv_rate	flag_RSTR
9	dst_host_serror_rate	urgent
10	dst_host_diff_srv_rate	service_efs
11	dst_host_same_src_port_rate	service_exec
12	**logged_in**	flag_RSTOS0
13	dst_host_same_srv_rate	service_finger
14	**flag_S0**	service_discard
15	hot	flag_RSTO
16	dst_host_srv_diff_host_rate	service_gopher
17	dst_host_srv_serror_rate	service_hostnames
18	dst_host_rerror_rate	flag_REJ
19	duration	service_http_443
20	same_srv_rate	service_http_8001

by DALEX, in order to explain the predictions yielded on both NSL-KDDTrain and NSL-KDDTest. Instead, OVO exhibits only 2 features that appear simultaneously in the list of the top-20 features identified as relevant by DALEX, in order to explain the predictions yielded on both NSL-KDDTrain and NSL-KDDTest.

For a quantitative analysis, we also compute the Euclidean distance (sum of squared difference) between the ranks that DALEX assigns to all the features involved in the classification models trained with both OVO and SMOTE+OVO, respectively. The top-relevant feature is assigned to rank 1 and so on. In particular, we compute the Euclidean distance between the two DALEX rank feature vectors associated with OVO and computed on NSL-KDDTrain and NSL-KDDTest, respectively, as well as the Euclidean distance between the two DALEX rank feature vectors associated with SMOTE+OVO and computed on NSL-KDDTrain and NSL-KDDTest, respectively. Both Euclidean distances, reported in Fig. 1, confirm that the training set and the testing set move close in terms of explanation of classifications once synthetic data have been generated to train the classification model. This can be seen as a further evidence that oversampling has improved the relevance of the traffic data features that are presumably more robust to the zero-day attacks.

4.5   Related Method Analysis

At the completion of this study, we compare the accuracy performance that we have achieved with the best configurations tested in this study for both NSL-KDD and CICIDS17 to that of several related methods selected from the recent state-of-the-art literature. For the methods in this comparative study, we collect the overall accuracy, since this metric is commonly provided in the reference studies. The collected results are reported in Table 8 for the two datasets. For CICIDS17, we report the results of a single related method that has been evaluated with the training set and the testing extracted using the same strategy adopted in this study. Various studies analyse CICIDS17 data in the literature, however they are tested with experimental settings that are very different from the one used in this study. Therefore, they cannot be reasonably included in this comparative study. Collected results show that we are able to achieve accuracy values in both datasets, which are comparable to that reported in the literature. This analysis highlights that promising results are also achieved in the recent literature by leveraging ensemble learning. This may also represent a useful suggestion for the future work.

Table 7. Top-20 relevant features identified with DALEX for the classification models trained with SMOTE+OVO and evaluated on NSL-KDDTrain and NSL-KDDTest. Features ranked in the top-20 list of both NSL-KDDTrain and NSL-KDDTest are in bold.

Feature rank	SMOTE+OVO+NSL-KDDTrain	SMOTE+OVO+NSL-KDDTest
1	**service_hostnames**	service_ftp_data
2	service_bgp	service_telnet
3	service_csnet_ns	rerror_rate
4	service_ctf	**dst_host_count**
5	**service_daytime**	service_auth
6	service_discard	srv_diff_host_rate
7	service_domain	**flag_S1**
8	service_domain_u	flag_REJ
9	service_echo	flag_RSTO
10	service_eco_i	duration
11	urgent	num_root
12	**service_efs**	service_gopher
13	**service_exec**	**service_http_443**
14	**service_ftp**	service_daytime
15	**service_gopher**	**service_http_8001**
16	dst_host_srv_rerror_rate	**service_ftp**
17	**dst_host_count**	service_imap4
18	**service_http_443**	**service_hostnames**
19	**service_http_8001**	**service_exec**
20	**flag_S1**	**service_efs**

Table 8. Comparison of related methods

Method	Dataset	Accuracy
SMOTE+FS+OVO	**NSL-KDD**	**0.83**
Triplet network+XGBoost [5]	NSL-KDD	0.83
Smote+Adversarial Reinforcement Learning [23]	NSL-KDD	0.82
Adaptive ensemble learning [19]	NSL-KDD	0.85
DNN [3]	NSL-KDD	0.73
Feature selection + DNN [32]	NSL-KDD	0.78
SMOTE+OVR	**CICIDS17**	**0.99**
Feature selection + Ensemble learning [25]	CICIDS17	0.98

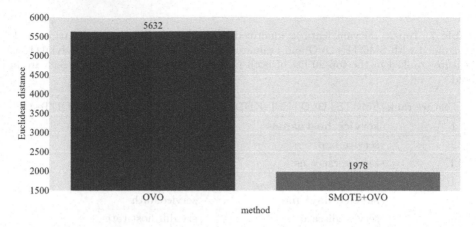

Fig. 1. The Euclidean distances computed for the feature rankings computed with DALEX for OVO and SMOTE+OVO, respectively. The Euclidean distance is computed between the two rank feature vectors that DALEX computes for each classification model evaluated on both NSL-KDDTrain and NSL-KDDTest.

5   Conclusion

Although several ML approaches have been proposed in the recent literature to increase the effectiveness of the intrusion detection systems, still there are problems with algorithms handling the multi-class intrusion detection task, especially, when the learning step is conducted with rare attack samples and predictions are requested for unseen attack patterns. In this paper, we perform a systematic investigation of how we can deal with the imbalanced learning issue in multi-class intrusion detection model by coupling oversampling, feature selection, and multi-class strategies. The key idea investigated in this paper is that coupling oversampling to feature selection may aid in improving the ability of correctly detecting rare and/or unseen attacks by also avoiding artifacts due to training data overfitting. As we use XGBoost as a base classification algorithm, we also verify that using a multi-class strategy as OVO or OVR to decompose the multi-class problem into binary sub-tasks may contribute to achieve a gain in accuracy. Experiments performed using two benchmark datasets (NSL-KDD and CICIDS17) allow us to achieve promising accuracy in both datasets (0.83 in NSL-KDD and 0.99 in CICIDS2017). Results are also promising compared to various, recent, related methods. In addition, the analysis of the feature relevance conducted in NSL-KDD paves the way for understanding how the oversampling strategy may aid in identifying robust, network traffic features that may better contribute to improve the ability of recognizing both rare and unseen attacks (zero-day attacks). As future work, we intend to investigate the performance of deep learning algorithms (e.g. Generative Adversarial Networks (GANs) for the data generation, Deep Neural Networks (DNNs) for the classification), in order to improve the accuracy of the described IDS pipeline. In addition, we plan to explore autoencoders as a data compression technique to reduce the effect of possible heavy-tail distributions in traffic data features.

Acknowledgments. The research of Malik AL-Essa is funded by PON RI 2014-2020 - Machine Learning per l'Investigazione di Cyber-minacce e la Cyber-difesa - CUP H98B20000970007. We acknowledge the support of the project "Modelli e tecniche di data science per la analisi di dati strutturati" funded by the University of Bari "Aldo Moro".

References

1. Ahmad, Z., Shahid Khan, A., Wai Shiang, C., Abdullah, J., Ahmad, F.: Network intrusion detection system: a systematic study of machine learning and deep learning approaches. Trans. Emerg. Telecommun. Technol. **32**(1), e4150 (2021). https://doi.org/10.1002/ett.4150
2. Alazzam, H., Sharieh, A., Sabri, K.E.: A feature selection algorithm for intrusion detection system based on pigeon inspired optimizer. Expert Syst. Appl. **148**, 113249 (2020). https://doi.org/10.1016/j.eswa.2020.113249
3. Alin, F., Chemchem, A., Nolot, F., Flauzac, O., Krajecki, M.: Towards a hierarchical deep learning approach for intrusion detection. In: Boumerdassi, S., Renault, É., Mühlethaler, P. (eds.) MLN 2019. LNCS, vol. 12081, pp. 15–27. Springer, Cham (2020). https://doi.org/10.1007/978-3-030-45778-5_2
4. Andresini, G., Appice, A., Di Mauro, N., Loglisci, C., Malerba, D.: Exploiting the auto-encoder residual error for intrusion detection. In: 2019 IEEE European Symposium on Security and Privacy Workshops (EuroS PW), pp. 281–290. IEEE (2019)
5. Andresini, G., Appice, A., Malerba, D.: Autoencoder-based deep metric learning for network intrusion detection. Inf. Sci. **569**, 706–727 (2021). https://doi.org/10.1016/j.ins.2021.05.016
6. Andresini, G., Appice, A., Malerba, D.: Nearest cluster-based intrusion detection through convolutional neural networks. Knowl.-Based Syst. **216**, 106798 (2021). https://doi.org/10.1016/j.knosys.2021.106798
7. Andresini, G., Appice, A., Mauro, N.D., Loglisci, C., Malerba, D.: Multi-channel deep feature learning for intrusion detection. IEEE Access **8**, 53346–53359 (2020)
8. Andresini, G., Appice, A., Rose, L.D., Malerba, D.: Gan augmentation to deal with imbalance in imaging-based intrusion detection. Futur. Gener. Comput. Syst. **123**, 108–127 (2021)
9. Bagui, S., Li, K.: Resampling imbalanced data for network intrusion detection datasets. J. Big Data **8**(1), 1–41 (2021). https://doi.org/10.1186/s40537-020-00390-x
10. Baniecki, H., Kretowicz, W., Piatyszek, P., Wisniewski, J., Biecek, P.: dalex: Responsible Machine Learning with Interactive Explainability and Fairness in Python. arXiv:2012.14406 (2020). https://arxiv.org/abs/2012.14406
11. Bansal, A., Kaur, S.: Extreme gradient boosting based tuning for classification in intrusion detection systems. In: Singh, M., Gupta, P.K., Tyagi, V., Flusser, J., Ören, T. (eds.) ICACDS 2018. CCIS, vol. 905, pp. 372–380. Springer, Singapore (2018). https://doi.org/10.1007/978-981-13-1810-8_37
12. Bedi, P., Gupta, N., Jindal, V.: I-SiamIDS: an improved Siam-IDS for handling class imbalance in network-based intrusion detection systems. Appl. Intell. **51**, 1133–1151 (2021)

13. Bhati, B.S., Chugh, G., Al-Turjman, F., Bhati, N.S.: An improved ensemble based intrusion detection technique using XGBoost. Trans. Emerg. Telecommun. Technol. 1–15 (2020). https://doi.org/10.1002/ett.4076
14. Chawla, N., Bowyer, K., Hall, L., Kegelmeyer, W.: Smote: synthetic minority oversampling technique. J. Artif. Intell. Res. (JAIR) **16**, 321–357 (2002)
15. Chen, T., Guestrin, C.: Xgboost: a scalable tree boosting system. In: Proceedings of the 22nd ACM SIGKDD International Conference on Knowledge Discovery and Data Mining, KDD 2016, pp. 785–794. Association for Computing Machinery, New York (2016). https://doi.org/10.1145/2939672.2939785
16. da Costa, K.A., Papa, J.P., Lisboa, C.O., Munoz, R., de Albuquerque, V.H.C.: Internet of things: a survey on machine learning-based intrusion detection approaches. Comput. Netw. **151**, 147–157 (2019). https://doi.org/10.1016/j.comnet.2019.01.023
17. Devan, P., Khare, N.: An efficient XGBoost–DNN-based classification model for network intrusion detection system. Neural Comput. Appl. **32**(16), 12499–12514 (2020). https://doi.org/10.1007/s00521-020-04708-x
18. Fisher, A., Rudin, C., Dominici, F.: All models are wrong, but many are useful: learning a variable's importance by studying an entire class of prediction models simultaneously. J. Mach. Learn. Res. **20**(177), 1–81 (2019)
19. Gao, X., Shan, C., Hu, C., Niu, Z., Liu, Z.: An adaptive ensemble machine learning model for intrusion detection. IEEE Access **7**, 82512–82521 (2019). https://doi.org/10.1109/ACCESS.2019.2923640
20. Inzimam, M., Yongle, C., Zhang, Z.: An efficient approach towards assessment of zero-day attacks. Int. J. Comput. Appl. **975**, 8887 (2019)
21. Jiang, H., He, Z., Ye, G., Zhang, H.: Network intrusion detection based on PSO-Xgboost model. IEEE Access **8**, 58392–58401 (2020). https://doi.org/10.1109/ACCESS.2020.2982418
22. Lorena, A.C., de Leon Ferreira de Carvalho, A.C.P., Gama, J.: A review on the combination of binary classifiers in multiclass problems. Artif. Intell. Rev. **30**(1–4), 19–37 (2008). https://doi.org/10.1007/s10462-009-9114-9
23. Ma, X., Shi, W.: AESMOTE: adversarial reinforcement learning with SMOTE for anomaly detection. IEEE Trans. Netw. Sci. Eng. **8**(2), 943–956 (2021). https://doi.org/10.1109/TNSE.2020.3004312
24. Pan, L., Xie, X.: Network intrusion detection model based on PCA + ADASYN and XGBoost. In: 3rd International Conference on E-Business, Information Management and Computer Science, EBIMCS 2020, pp. 44–48. Association for Computing Machinery (2020)
25. Rajagopal, S., Kundapur, P.P., Hareesha, K.S.: Towards effective network intrusion detection: from concept to creation on azure cloud. IEEE Access **9**, 19723–19742 (2021). https://doi.org/10.1109/ACCESS.2021.3054688
26. Sapre, S., Islam, K., Ahmadi, P.: A comprehensive data sampling analysis applied to the classification of rare IoT network intrusion types. In: IEEE 18th Annual Consumer Communications Networking Conference, CCNC 2021, pp. 1–2 (2021). https://doi.org/10.1109/CCNC49032.2021.9369617
27. Sharafaldin, I., Habibi Lashkari, A., Ghorbani, A.: Toward generating a new intrusion detection dataset and intrusion traffic characterization, pp. 108–116 (2018). https://doi.org/10.5220/0006639801080116
28. Tan, X., et al.: Wireless sensor networks intrusion detection based on smote and the random forest algorithm. Sensors **19**(1), 203 (2019). https://doi.org/10.3390/s19010203

29. Tavallaee, M., Bagheri, E., Lu, W., Ghorbani, A.A.: A detailed analysis of the KDD CUP 99 data set. In: CISDA, pp. 1–6 (2009)
30. Velan, P., Medková, J., Jirsík, T., Čeleda, P.: Network traffic characterisation using flow-based statistics. In: NOMS 2016–2016 IEEE/IFIP Network Operations and Management Symposium, pp. 907–912 (2016)
31. Vergara, J.R., Estévez, P.A.: A review of feature selection methods based on mutual information. Neural Comput. Appl. **24**(1), 175–186 (2013). https://doi.org/10.1007/s00521-013-1368-0
32. Vinayakumar, R., Alazab, M., Soman, K.P., Poornachandran, P., Al-Nemrat, A., Venkatraman, S.: Deep learning approach for intelligent intrusion detection system. IEEE Access **7**, 41525–41550 (2019)
33. Yu, L., Liu, H.: Feature selection for high-dimensional data: A fast correlation-based filter solution. In: Proceedings, Twentieth International Conference on Machine Learning, vol. 2, pp. 856–863 (2003)
34. Zuech, R., Khoshgoftaar, T.: A survey on feature selection for intrusion detection. In: ISSAT International Conference on Reliability and Quality in Design, pp. 150–155 (2015)

Adversarial Robustness of Probabilistic Network Embedding for Link Prediction

Xi Chen[(✉)], Bo Kang, Jefrey Lijffijt, and Tijl De Bie

IDLab, Department of Electronics and Information Systems, Ghent University,
Technologiepark-Zwijnaarde 122, 9052 Ghent, Belgium
{xi.chen,bo.kang,jefrey.lijffijt,tijl.debie}@ugent.be

Abstract. In today's networked society, many real-world problems can be formalized as predicting links in networks, such as Facebook friendship suggestions, e-commerce recommendations, and the prediction of scientific collaborations in citation networks. Increasingly often, link prediction problem is tackled by means of network embedding methods, owing to their state-of-the-art performance. However, these methods lack transparency when compared to simpler baselines, and as a result their robustness against adversarial attacks is a possible point of concern: could one or a few small adversarial modifications to the network have a large impact on the link prediction performance when using a network embedding model? Prior research has already investigated adversarial robustness for network embedding models, focused on classification at the node and graph level. Robustness with respect to the link prediction downstream task, on the other hand, has been explored much less.

This paper contributes to filling this gap, by studying adversarial robustness of Conditional Network Embedding (CNE), a state-of-the-art probabilistic network embedding model, for link prediction. More specifically, given CNE and a network, we measure the sensitivity of the link predictions of the model to small adversarial perturbations of the network, namely changes of the link status of a node pair. Thus, our approach allows one to identify the links and non-links in the network that are most vulnerable to such perturbations, for further investigation by an analyst. We analyze the characteristics of the most and least sensitive perturbations, and empirically confirm that our approach not only succeeds in identifying the most vulnerable links and non-links, but also that it does so in a time-efficient manner thanks to an effective approximation.

Keywords: Adversarial robustness · Network embedding · Link prediction

1 Introduction

Networks are used to model entities and the relations among them, so they are capable of describing a wide range of data in real world, such as social

© Springer Nature Switzerland AG 2021
M. Kamp et al. (Eds.): ECML PKDD 2021 Workshops, CCIS 1525, pp. 22–38, 2021.
https://doi.org/10.1007/978-3-030-93733-1_2

networks, citation networks, and networks of neurons. The recently proposed Network Embedding (NE) methods can be used to learn representations of the non-iid network data such that networks are transformed into the tabular form. The tabular data can then be fed to solve several network tasks, such as visualization, node classification, recommendation, and link prediction. We focus on link prediction that aims to predict future or currently missing links [25] as it has been widely applied in our lives. Examples include Facebook friendship suggestions, Netflix recommendations, predictions of protein-protein interactions, etc.

Many traditional link prediction approaches have been proposed [31], but the task is tackled increasingly often by the NE methods due to their state-of-the-art performance [30]. However, the NE methods lack transparency, e.g., Graph Neural Networks (GNNs) [14], when compared to simpler baselines. Thus, similar to many other machine learning algorithms [13], they could be vulnerable to adversarial attacks. It has been shown that simple imperceptible changes of the node attribute or the network topology can result in wrongly predicted node labels, especially for GNNs [7,56]. Meanwhile, adversarial attacks are easy to be found in our daily *online* lives, such as in recommender systems [28,47,50].

Robustness of NE methods for link prediction is important. Attacking link prediction methods can be used to hide sensitive links, while defending can help identify the interactions hidden intentionally, e.g., important connections in crime networks. Moreover, as links in online social networks represent the information sources and exposures, from the dynamic perspective, manipulations of network topology can be used to affect the formation of public opinions on certain topics, e.g., via exposing a targeted group of individuals to certain information sources, which is risky. The problem we want to investigate is: *Could one or a few small adversarial modifications to the network topology have a large impact on the link prediction performance when using a network embedding model?*

Existing adversarial robustness studies for NE methods mainly consider classification at the node and graph level, which investigates whether the labels will be wrongly predicted due to adversarial perturbations. It includes semi-supervised node classification [3,11,40,45,46,55–60], and graph classification [7,20,29]. Only a few works consider the link-level task [2,4,9,26], leaving robustness of NE methods for link prediction insufficiently explored.

To fill the gap, we study the adversarial robustness of Conditional Network Embedding (CNE) [22] for the link prediction task. CNE is a state-of-the-art probabilistic NE model that preserves the first-order proximity, of which the objective function is expressed analytically. Therefore, it provides mathematically principled explainability [23]. Moreover, comparing to other NE models, such as those based on random walks [15,35], CNE is more friendly to link prediction because the link probabilities follow directly from the model so there is no need to further train a classifier for links with the node embeddings. However, there has been no study on the adversarial robustness of CNE for link prediction.

In our work, we consider only the network topology as input, meaning that there is no node attribute. More specifically, given CNE and a network, we measure the sensitivity of the link predictions of the model to small adversarial perturbations of the network, i.e., the changes of the link status of a node pair. The sensitivity is measured as the impact of the perturbation on the link predictions. Intuitively, we quantify the impact as the KL-divergence between the two link probability distributions learned by the model from the clean and the corrupted network through re-training. While the re-training can be expensive, we develop effective and efficient approximations based on the gradient information, which is similar to the computation of the regularizer in Virtual Adversarial Training (VAT) [33]. Our main contributions are:

- We propose to study the adversarial robustness of a probabilistic network embedding model CNE for link prediction;
- Our approach allows us to identify the links and non-links in the network that are most vulnerable to adversarial perturbations for further investigation;
- With two case studies, we explain the robustness of CNE for link prediction through (a) illustrating how structural perturbations affect the link predictions; (b) analyzing the characteristics of the most and least sensitive perturbations, providing insights for adversarial learning for link prediction.
- We show empirically that our gradient-based approximation for measuring the sensitivity of CNE for link prediction to small structural perturbations is not only time-efficient but also significantly effective.

2 Related Work

Robustness in machine learning means that a method can function correctly with erroneous inputs [18]. The input data may contain random noise embedded, or adversarial noise injected intentionally. The topic became a point of concern when the addition of noise to an image, which is imperceptible to human eyes, resulted in a totally irrelevant prediction label [13]. Robustness of models against noisy input has been investigated in many works [8,32,52], while adversarial robustness usually deals with the worst-case perturbations on the input data.

Network tasks at the node, link, and graph level are increasingly done by network embedding methods, which include shallow models and GNNs [27]. Shallow models either preserve the proximities between nodes (e.g., DeepWalk [35], LINE [39], and node2vec [15]) or factorize matrices containing graph information [36,41] to effectively represent the nodes as vectors. GNNs use deep structure to extract node features by iteratively aggregating their neighborhood information, e.g., Graph Convolutional Networks (GCNs) [24] and GraphSAGE [16].

Adversarial learning for networks includes three types of studies: attack, defense, and certifiable robustness [5,21,37]. Adversarial attacks aim to maximally degrade the model performance through perturbing the input data, which include the modifications of node attributes or changes of the network topology. Examples of attacking strategies for GNNs include the non-gradient based NETTACK [56], Mettack using meta learning [58], SL-S2V with reinforcement learning [7], and attacks by rewiring for graph classification [29]. The defense strategies are designed to protect the models from being attacked in many different ways, e.g., by detecting and recovering the perturbations [45], applying adversarial training [13] to resist the worst-case perturbation [11], or transferring the ability to discriminate adversarial edges from exploring clean graphs [40]. Certifiable robustness is similar in essence to adversarial defense, but it focuses on guaranteeing the reliability of the predictions under certain amounts of attacks. The first provable robustness for GNNs was proposed to certify if a node label will be changed under a bounded attack on node attributes [59], and later a similar certificate for structural attack was proposed [60]. There are also robustness certifications for graph classification [12,20] and community detection [19]. The most popular combination is GNNs for node or graph classification, while the link-level tasks has been explored much less.

Early studies on robustness for link-level tasks usually target traditional link prediction approaches. That includes link prediction attacks that aim to solve specific problems in the social context, e.g., to hide relationships [10,43] or to disguise communities [42], and works that restrict the perturbation type to only adding or only deleting edges [48,53,54], which could result in less efficient attacks or defenses. The robustness for NE based link prediction is much less investigated than classification, and is considered more often as a way to evaluate the robustness of the NE method, such as in [2,34,38]. To the best of our knowledge, there are only two works on adversarial attacks for link prediction based on NE: one targeting the GNN-based SEAL [51] with structural perturbations and one targeting GCN with iterative gradient attack [4].

3 Preliminaries

In this section, we provide the preliminaries of our work, including the notations, the probabilistic network embedding model CNE that we use for link prediction, and the virtual adversarial training method to which the our idea is similar.

3.1 Link Prediction with Probabilistic Network Embedding

Network embedding methods map nodes in a network onto a lower dimensional space as real vectors or distributions, and we work with the former type. Given a network $G = (V, E)$, where V and E are the node and edge set, respectively, a network embedding model finds a mapping $f : V \rightarrow \mathbb{R}^d$ for all nodes as $X = [x_1, x_2, ...x_n]^T \in \mathbb{R}^{n \times d}$. Those embeddings X can be used to visualize the network in the d-dimensional space; classify nodes based on the similarity between vector pairs; and predict link probabilities between any node pair.

To do link prediction, a network embedding model requires a function g of vectors x_i and x_j to calculate the probability of nodes i and j being linked. This can be done by training a classifier with the links and non-links, or the function follows naturally from the model. Conditional Network Embedding (CNE) is the probabilistic model on which our work is based, and of which the function g directly follows [22]. Suppose there is an undirected network $G = (V, E)$ with its adjacency matrix A, where $a_{ij} = 1$ if $(i, j) \in E$ and 0 otherwise, CNE finds an optimal embedding X^* that maximizes the probability of the graph conditioned on that embedding. It maximizes its objective function:

$$P(G|X) = \prod_{(i,j)\in E} P(a_{ij} = 1|X) \prod_{(k,l)\notin E} P(a_{kl} = 0|X). \tag{1}$$

To guarantee that the connected nodes are embedded closer and otherwise farther, the method uses two half normal distributions for the distance d_{ij} between nodes i and j conditioned on their connectivity. By optimizing the objective in Eq. (1), CNE finds the most informative embedding X^* and the probability distribution $P(G|X^*)$ that defines the link predictor $g(x_i, x_j) = P(a_{ij} = 1|X^*)$.

Many network embedding methods purely map nodes into vectors of lower dimensions and focus on node classification, such as the random-walk based ones [15,35,39] and GCNs [24]. Those methods require an extra step to measure the similarities between the pairs of node embeddings for link prediction. Comparing to them, CNE is a better option for link prediction. Moreover, CNE provides good explainability for link predictions as g can be expressed analytically [23].

3.2   Virtual Adversarial Attack

Adversarial training achieved great performance for the supervised classification problem [13], and virtual adversarial training (VAT) is better for the semi-supervised setting [33]. By identifying the most sensitive 'virtual' direction for the classifier, VAT uses regularization to smooth the output distribution. The regularization term is based on the virtual adversarial loss of possible local perturbations on the input data point. Let $x \in \mathbb{R}^d$ and $y \in Q$ denote the input data vector of dimension d and the output label in the space of Q, respectively. The labeled data is defined as $\mathcal{D}_l = \left\{ x_l^{(n)}, y_l^{(n)} | n = 1, ..., N_l \right\}$, the unlabeled data as $\mathcal{D}_{ul} = \left\{ x_{ul}^{(m)} | m = 1, ..., N_{ul} \right\}$, and the output distribution as $p(y|x, \theta)$ parametrized by θ. To quantify the influence of any local perturbation on x_* (either x_l or x_{ul}), VAT has the Local Distribution Smoothness (LDS),

$$\text{LDS}(x_*, \theta) := D\left[p(y|x_*, \hat{\theta}), p(y|x_* + r_{vadv}, \theta) \right] \tag{2}$$

$$r_{vadv} := \text{argmax}_{r; ||r||_2 \le \epsilon} D\left[p(y|x_*, \hat{\theta}), p(y|x_* + r, \theta) \right], \tag{3}$$

where D can be any non-negative function that measures the divergence between two distributions, and $p(y|x, \hat{\theta})$ is the current estimate of the true output distribution $q(y|x)$. The regularization term is the average LDS for all data points.

Although VAT was designed for classification with tabular data, the idea of it is essentially similar to our work, i.e., we both quantify the influence of local virtual adversarial perturbations. For us, that is the link status of a node pair. As we have not yet included the training with a regularization term in this work, we now focus on finding the r_{vadv} in Eq. (3). That is to identify the most sensitive perturbations that will change the link probabilities the most.

4   Quantifying the Sensitivity to Small Perturbations

With the preliminaries, we now formally introduce the specific problem we study in this paper. That is, to investigate if there is any small perturbations to the network that have large impact on the link prediction performance. The small perturbations we look into are the edge flips, which represent either the deletion of an existing edge or the addition of a non-edge. It means that we do not restrict the structural perturbations to merely addition or merely deletion of edges.

Intuitively, that impact of any small virtual adversarial perturbation can be measured by re-training the model. But re-training, namely re-embedding the network using CNE, can be computationally expensive. Therefore, we also investigate on approximating the impact both practically with incremental partial re-embedding, and theoretically with the gradient information.

4.1   Problem Statement and Re-Embedding (RE)

The study of the adversarial robustness for link prediction involves identifying the worst-case perturbations on the network topology, namely the changes of the network topology that influence the link prediction results the most. For imperceptibility, we focus on the small structural perturbation of individual edge flip in this work. Thus, our specific problem is defined as

Problem 1 (Impact of a Structural Perturbation). Given a network $G = (V, E)$, a network embedding model, how can we measure the impact of each edge flip in the input network on the link prediction results of the model?

Intuitively, the impact can be measured by assuming the edge flip as a virtual attack, flip the edge and retrain the model with the virtually corrupted network, after which we know how serious the attack is. That means we train CNE with the clean graph $G = (V, E)$ to obtain the link probability distribution $P^* = P(G|\boldsymbol{X}^*(\boldsymbol{A}))$. After flipping one edge, we get the corrupted graph $G' = (V, E')$, retrain the model, and obtain a different link probability $Q^* = Q(G'|\boldsymbol{X}^*(\boldsymbol{A}'))$. Then we measure the impact of the edge flip as the KL-divergence between P^* and Q^*. In this way, we also know how the small perturbation changes the node embeddings, which helps explain the influence of the virtual attack.

If the virtual edge flip is on node pair (i, j), $a'_{ij} = 1 - a_{ij}$ where a_{ij} is the corresponding entry in the adjacency matrix of the clean graph $\boldsymbol{A}$ and a'_{ij} of the corrupted graph $\boldsymbol{A}'$. Re-embedding G' with CNE results in probability $Q^*(i, j)$, then the impact of flipping (i, j), which we consider as the sensitivity of the model to the perturbation on that node pair, denoted as $s(i, j)$, is:

$$s(i, j) = KL\left[P^* \| Q^*(i, j)\right]. \tag{4}$$

Measured practically, this KL-divergence is the actual impact for each possible edge flip on the predictions. The optimal embeddings $\boldsymbol{X}^*(\boldsymbol{A})$ and $\boldsymbol{X}^*(\boldsymbol{A}')$ not only explain the influenced link predictions but also exhibit the result of the flip.

Ranking the node pairs in the network by the sensitivity measure for all node pairs allows us to identify the most and least sensitive links and non-links for further investigation. However, re-embedding the entire network can be computationally expensive, especially for large networks. The sensitivity measure can be approximated both empirically and theoretically, and we will show how this can be done in the rest of this section.

4.2 Incremental Partial Re-Embedding (IPRE)

Empirically, one way to decrease the computational cost is to incrementally re-embed only the two corresponding nodes of the flipped edge. In this case, our assumption is that the embeddings of all nodes except the two connecting the flipped edge (i.e., node i and j) will stay unchanged since the perturbation is small and local. We call it Incremental Partial Re-Embedding (IPRE), which allows only the changes of x_i and x_j if (i, j) is flipped. It means that the impact of the small perturbation on the link probabilities is restricted within the one-hop neighborhood of the two nodes, resulting in the changed link predictions between node i and j with the rest of the nodes. The definition of the impact in Eq. (4) still holds and only the ith and jth columns and rows in the link probability matrix have non-zero values. Comparing to RE, IPRE turns out to be a faster and effective approximation, which we will show with experiments.

4.3 Theoretical Approximation of the KL-Divergence

Incrementally re-embedding only the two nodes of the flipped edge is faster but it is still re-training of the model. Although our input is non-iid, in contrast to the tabular data used in VAT [33], we can form our problem as in Eq. (5), of which the solution is the most sensitive structural perturbation for link prediction.

$$\Delta A := \operatorname{argmax}_{\Delta A; ||\Delta A||=2} KL\left[P(G|X^*(\hat{A})), P(G|X^*(\hat{A} + \Delta A))\right]. \quad (5)$$

CNE has its link probability distribution expressed analytically, so the impact of changing the link status of node pair (i, j), represented by the KL-divergence in Eq. (4) can be approximated theoretically. Given the clean graph G, CNE learns the optimal link probability distribution $P^* = P(G|X^*(A))$ whose entry is $P_{kl}^* = P(a_{kl} = 1|X^*)$. Let $Q^*(i, j)$ be the optimal link probability distribution of the corrupted graph G' with only (i, j) flipped from the clean graph. The impact of the flip $s(i, j)$ can be decomposed as,

$$s(i, j) = KL\left[P^*||Q^*(i, j)\right] = \sum \left[p \log \frac{p}{q} + (1 - p) \log \frac{1 - p}{1 - q}\right], \quad (6)$$

where p and q are entries of P^* and $Q^*(i, j)$ respectively. We can approximate $s(i, j)$ at G, or equivalently, at P^*, as G is close to G' thus P^* is close to $Q^*(i, j)$.

The first-order approximation of $s(i, j)$ is a constant because at G its gradient $\frac{\partial KL[P^*||Q^*(i,j)]}{\partial a_{ij}} = 0$, so we turn to the second-order approximation in Eq. (7), which, evaluated at G, is $\tilde{s}(i,j)$ in Eq. (8). That requires the gradient of each link probability w.r.t the edge flip, i.e., $\frac{\partial p}{\partial a_{ij}} = \frac{\partial P_{kl}^*}{\partial a_{ij}}$. Now we will show how to compute it with CNE.

$$s(i,j) \approx \frac{\partial KL\left[P^* \| Q^*(i,j)\right]}{\partial a_{ij}} \Delta A + \frac{1}{2} \frac{\partial^2 KL\left[P^* \| Q^*(i,j)\right]}{\partial a_{ij}^2} \Delta A^2, \qquad (7)$$

$$\tilde{s}(i,j) = \frac{1}{2} \sum \frac{1}{p(1-p)} \left[\frac{\partial p}{\partial a_{ij}}\right]^2. \qquad (8)$$

The Gradient. At the graph level, the gradient of a link probability P_{kl}^* for node pair (k,l) w.r.t the input graph A is $\frac{\partial P_{kl}^*}{\partial A} = \frac{\partial P_{kl}^*}{\partial X^*(A)} \frac{\partial X^*(A)}{\partial A}$. While at the node pair level, the gradient of P_{kl}^* w.r.t. a_{ij} is

$$\frac{\partial P_{kl}^*}{\partial a_{ij}} = \frac{\partial P_{kl}^*}{\partial x^*(A)} \frac{\partial x^*(A)}{\partial a_{ij}} \qquad (9)$$

$$= x^{*T}(A) E_{kl} E_{kl}^T \left[\frac{-H}{\gamma^2 P_{kl}^*(1-P_{kl}^*)}\right]^{-1} E_{ij} E_{ij}^T x^*(A), \qquad (10)$$

where for clearer presentation we flatten the matrix X to a vector x that is $nd \times 1$, E_{kl} is a column block matrix consisting of n blocks of size $d \times d$ where the k-th and l-th block are positive and negative identity matrix I and $-I$ of the right size respectively and 0s elsewhere, and H is the full Hessian below

$$H = \gamma \sum_{u \neq v} \left[(P_{uv}^* - a_{uv}) E_{uv} E_{uv}^T - \gamma P_{uv}^*(1-P_{uv}^*) E_{uv} E_{uv}^T x^*(A) x^{*T}(A) E_{uv} E_{uv}^T\right].$$

The gradient reflects the fact that the change of a link status in the network influences the embeddings x^*, and then the impact is transferred through x^* to the link probabilities of the entire graph. In other words, if an important relation (in a relatively small network) is perturbed, it could cause large changes in many P_{kl}^*s, deviating them from their predicted values with the clean graph.

The gradient in Eq. (10) is exact and measures the impact all over the network. However, the computation of the inverse of the full Hessian can be expensive when the network size is large. But fortunately, H can be well approximated with its diagonal blocks [23], which are of size $d \times d$ each block. So we can approximate the impact of individual edge flip with $\tilde{s}(i,j)$ at a very low cost using

$$\frac{\partial P_{kl}^*}{\partial a_{ki}} = (x_k^* - x_l^*)^T \left[\frac{-H_k}{\gamma^2 P_{kl}^*(1-P_{kl}^*)}\right]^{-1} (x_k^* - x_i^*), \qquad (11)$$

where $H_k = \gamma \sum_{l:l \neq k} \left[(P_{kl}^* - a_{kl})I - \gamma P_{kl}^*(1-P_{kl}^*)(x_k^* - x_l^*)(x_k^* - x_l^*)^T\right]$ is the kth diagonal block of H. Here P_{kl}^* is assumed to be influenced only by x_k and x_l, thus only the edge flips involving node k or l will result in non-zero gradient for P_{kl}^*. It essentially corresponds to IPRE, where only the attacked nodes are allowed to move in the embedding space. In fact, as the network size grows, local perturbations are not likely to spread the influence broadly. We will show empirically this theoretical approximation is both efficient and effective.

5   Experiments

For the purpose of evaluating our work, we first focus on illustrating the robustness of CNE for link prediction with two case studies, using two networks of relatively small sizes. Then we evaluate the approximated sensitivity for node pairs on larger networks. The research questions we want to investigate are:

- How to understand the sensitivity of CNE to an edge flip for link prediction?
- What are the characteristics of the most and least sensitive perturbations for link prediction using CNE?
- What are the quality and the runtime performance of the approximations?

Data. The data we use includes six real world networks of varying sizes. **Karate** is a social network of 34 members in a university karate club, which has 78 friendship connections [49]. **Polbooks** network describes 441 Amazon co-purchasing relations among 105 books about US politics [1]. **C.elegans** is a neural network of the nematode C.elegans with 297 neurons linked by 2148 synapses [44]. **USAir** is a transportation network of 332 airports as nodes and 2126 airlines connecting them as links [17]. **MP** is the largest connected part of a Twitter friendship network for the Members of Parliament (MP) in the UK during April 2019, having 567 nodes and 49631 edges [6]. **Polblogs** is a network with 1222 political blogs as nodes and 16714 hyperlinks as undirected edges, which is the largest connected part of the US political blogs network from [1].

Setup. We do not have train-test split, because we want to measure the sensitivity of *all* link probabilities of CNE to *all* small perturbations of the network. The CNE parameters are $\sigma_2 = 2$, $d = 2$ for the case studies, $d = 8$ for evaluating the approximation quality, learning rate is 0.2, max_iter $= 2k$, and ftol $= 1e - 7$.

5.1   Case Studies

The first two research questions will be answered with the case studies on Karate and Polbooks, which are relatively small thus can be visualized clearly. Both networks also have ground-truth communities, which contributes to our analysis. With Karate, we show how the small perturbations influence link probabilities via node embeddings. On Polbooks, we analyze the characteristics of the most and least sensitive perturbations. Note that we use the dimension 2 for both the visualization of CNE embeddings and the calculation of the sensitively.

Karate. To show the process of attacking CNE link prediction on Karate, we illustrate and analyze how the most sensitive edge deletion and addition affect the model in predicting links. With the RE approach, we measure the model sensitivity to single edge flip and find the top 5 sensitive perturbations in Table 1. The most sensitive deletion of link $(1, 12)$ disconnects the network, and we do not consider this type of perturbation in our work because it is obvious and easy to be detected. We see the other top sensitive perturbations are all cross-community, and we pick node pairs $(1, 32)$ and $(6, 30)$ for further study.

Table 1. The top 5 sensitive perturbations

Rank	Node Pair	s(i, j)	A[i, j]	Community?
1	(1, 12)	12.30	1	Within
2	(1, 32)	2.52	1	Cross
3	(20, 34)	1.96	1	Cross
4	(6, 30)	1.75	0	Cross
5	(7, 30)	1.75	0	Cross

Table 2. Runtime in seconds

	RE	IPRE	Approx
Polbooks	0.889	0.117	0.00012
C.elegans	2.819	0.568	0.00045
USAir	6.206	0.781	0.00043
MP	8.539	2.289	0.00116
Polblogs	45.456	27.648	0.00124

Figure 1 shows the CNE embeddings of the clean Karate and the perturbed graphs, where the communities are differentiated with green and red color. CNE embeddings might have nodes overlap when $d = 2$, such as node 6 and 7, because they have the same neighbors, but this will not be a problem if d is higher.

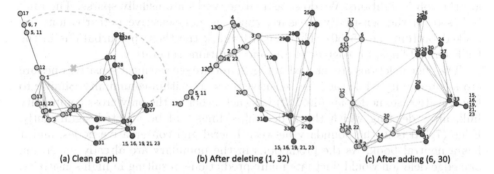

(a) Clean graph   (b) After deleting (1, 32)   (c) After adding (6, 30)

Fig. 1. Case study on Karate with the most sensitive perturbations.

The deletion of edge $(1, 32)$ is marked with a cross in Fig. 1(a), after which the changed node embeddings are shown in Fig. 1(b). Although being rotated, the relative locations of the nodes change a lot, especially node 1, 32, and those in the boundary between the communities, e.g., node 3 and 10. Node 1 is pushed away from the red nodes, and as the center of the green nodes, it plays an essential role in affecting many other link probabilities. Comparing to other cross-community edges, $(1, 32)$ is the most sensitive because both nodes have each other as the only cross-community link. So the deletion largely decreases the probability of their neighbors connecting to the other community. Moreover, node 1 has a high degree. Therefore, it makes sense that this is the most sensitive edge deletion.

The addition of edge $(6, 30)$ is marked as a dashed arc in Fig. 1(a), and the case is similar for $(7, 30)$. Adding the edge changes the node locations as shown in Fig. 1(c). The distant tail in green that ends with node 17 moves closer to the red community. Note that both node 6 and 30 had only the within-community

Table 3. The top sensitive and non-sensitive perturbations

Edge deletion - S				Edge addition - S				Edge addition - Non-S			
Rank	Node pair	s(i, j)	Community	Rank	Node pair	s(i, j)	Community	Rank	Node pair	s(i, j)	Community
1	(46, 102)	16.91	N-L	2	(3, 98)	15.53	C-L	5458	(37, 39)	0.035	C-C
15	(7, 58)	14.64	N-C	3	(3, 87)	15.42	C-L	5454	(8, 47)	0.036	C-C
Edge deletion - Non-S				4	(28, 33)	14.98	N-C	5451	(33, 35)	0.038	C-C
5460	(72, 75)	0.033	L-L	5	(25, 98)	14.96	C-L	5449	(30, 71)	0.039	L-L
5459	(8, 12)	0.034	C-C	6	(25, 91)	14.92	C-L	5438	(66, 75)	0.042	L-L

links before the perturbation. Even though their degrees are not very high, the added edge changes the probabilities of many cross-community links from almost zero to some degree of existence, pulling nodes to the other community.

Polbooks. Polbooks has three types of political books, which are liberal (L), neutral (N), and conservative (C), marked with colors red, purple, and blue, respectively. Shown in Table 3 are the most and least sensitive perturbations, where the left column are the Top 2 deletions and the middle and right columns are the top 5 additions. We do so as real networks are usually sparse. The rank is based on the sensitivity measure, thus the non-sensitive perturbations are ranked bottom (i.e., 5460). Then we will mark the those perturbations in the CNE embeddings, for edge deletions and additions separately.

The edge deletions are marked in Fig. 2, and we see the most sensitive ones are cross-community while the least sensitive ones are within-community. Similar to the Karate case, node pair $(46, 102)$ has each other as the only cross-community link, after deleting which the node embeddings will be affected significantly. Edge $(7, 58)$ is in the boundary between liberal and conservative nodes, and it has a neutral book. As the predictions in the boundary are already uncertain, one edge deletion would fluctuate many predictions, resulting in high sensitivity. The least-sensitive edge deletions are not only within-community, but are also between high-degree nodes, i.e., $d_{72} = 22$, $d_{75} = 16$, $d_8 = d_{12} = 25$. These nodes have already been well connected to nodes of the same type, thus they have stable embeddings and the deletions have little influence on relevant predictions.

We mark the edge additions separately for the sensitive and non-sensitive perturbations in Fig. 3, to contrast their difference. The left Fig. 3(a) shows the top 5 sensitive edge additions are all cross-community, and all include at least one node at the distant place from the opposing community, i.e., nodes 33, 91, 87, 98. Being distant means those nodes have only the within-community connections, while adding a cross-community link would confuse the link predictor on the predictions for many relevant node pairs. Meanwhile, as the sensitive perturbations involve low-degree nodes, they are usually unnoticeable while weighted highly by those nodes. The non-sensitive edge additions are similar to the non-sensitive deletions in the sense that both have the pair of nodes embedded closely. As long as the two nodes are mapped closely in the embedding space, it makes little difference if they are connected and the node degree does not matter much.

Interestingly, our observations in the case studies agree only partially with a heuristic community detection attack strategy called DICE [42], which has been used as a baseline for attacking link prediction in [4]. Inspired by modularity, DICE randomly disconnect internally and connect externally [42], of which the goal is to hide the a group of nodes from being detected as a community. Our analysis agrees with connecting externally, while for link prediction the disconnection should also be *external*, meaning that disconnecting internally might not work for link prediction. If the internal disconnection are sampled to node pairs that are closely positioned, the attack will have the little influence. Therefore, it might not be suitable to use DICE for link prediction attacks.

5.2 Quality and Runtime of Approximations

We use the sensitivity measured by re-embedding (RE) as the ground truth impact of the small perturbations. The quality of an approximation is determined by how close it is to the ground truth. As the sensitivity is a ranked measure, we use the normalized discounted cumulative gain (NDCG) to evaluate the quality of the empirical approximation IPRE and the theoretical approximation with the diagonal Hessian blocks Approx. The closer the NDCG value is to 1, the better. We do not include the theoretical approximation with the exact Hessian because it can be more computationally expensive than RE for large networks. To show the significance, the p-value of each NDCG is found with randomization test of 1,000 samples. The runtime for computing the sensitivity of one edge flip is recorded on a server with Intel Xeon Gold CPU 3.00 GHz and 1024 GB RAM.

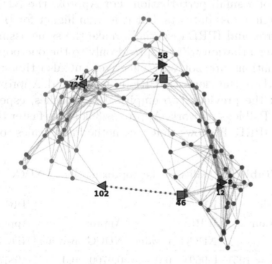

Fig. 2. Case study on Polbooks with the most and least sensitive edge deletion.

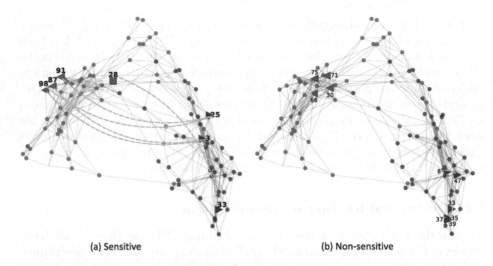

(a) Sensitive   (b) Non-sensitive

Fig. 3. Case study on Polbooks with the most and least sensitive edge addition.

Shown in Table 4 are the quality of the approximations on five real-world networks. The first two columns show how well IPRE and Approx approximate RE, and the third column shows how well Approx approximates IPRE. We see the NDCG values in the table are all significantly high. Comparing to Approx, IPRE better approximates RE, and as the network size gets relatively large, the NDCG is alway larger than 0.99, indicating that the larger the network, the more local the impact of a small perturbation. For Approx, the NDCG for approximating RE are high across datasets, but it is even higher for IPRE. The reason is that both Approx and IPRE essentially make the same assumption that the influence of the perturbation will be spread only to the one-hop neighborhood.

The approximations are not only effective, but also time-efficient. We see in Table 2 that RE is the slowest, IPRE is faster, and Approx is significantly much faster than the previous two empirical approaches, especially for larger networks. On the Polblogs network, Approx is 36k times faster than RE and 22k times faster than IPRE. It shows that our method also scales to large networks.

Table 4. Quality of the approximations - NDCG

Ground truth	RE				IPRE	
Approximation	IPRE		Approx		Approx	
	NDCG	p-value	NDCG	p-value	NDCG	p-value
Polbooks ($n = 105$)	0.9691	0.0	0.9700	0.0	0.9873	0.0
C.elegans ($n = 297$)	0.9977	0.0	0.9880	0.0	0.9905	0.0
USAir ($n = 332$)	0.9902	0.0	0.9697	0.0	0.9771	0.0
MP ($n = 567$)	0.9985	0.0	0.9961	0.0	0.9960	0.0
Polblogs ($n = 1222$)	0.9962	0.0	0.9897	0.0	0.9899	0.0

6   Conclusion

In this work we study the adversarial robustness of a probabilistic network embedding model CNE for the link prediction task by measuring the sensitivity of the link predictions of the model to small adversarial perturbations of the network. Our approach allows us to identify the most vulnerable links and non-links that if perturbed will have large impact on the model's link prediction performance, which can be used for further investigation, such as defending attacks by protecting those. With two case studies, we analyze the characteristics of the most and least sensitive perturbations for link prediction with CNE. Then we empirically confirm that our theoretical approximation of the sensitivity measure is both effective and efficient, meaning that the worst-case perturbations for link prediction using CNE can be identified successfully in a time-efficient manner with our method. For future work, we plan to explore the potential of our theoretical approximation to construct a regularizer for adversarially robust network embedding and to develop certifiable robustness for link prediction.

Acknowledgements. The research leading to these results has received funding from the European Research Council under the European Union's Seventh Framework Programme (FP7/2007-2013) (ERC Grant Agreement no. 615517), and under the European Union's Horizon 2020 research and innovation's programme (ERC Grant Agreement no. 963924), from the Flemish Government under the "Onderzoeksprogramma Artificiële Intelligentie (AI) Vlaanderen" programme, and from the FWO (project no. G091017N, G0F9816N, 3G042220).

References

1. Adamic, L.A., Glance, N.: The political blogosphere and the 2004 U.S. election: divided they blog. In: Proceedings of LinkKDD 2005, pp. 36–43 (2005)
2. Bojchevski, A., Günnemann, S.: Adversarial attacks on node embeddings via graph poisoning. In: Proceedings of the 36th ICML, pp. 695–704 (2019)
3. Bojchevski, A., Günnemann, S.: Certifiable robustness to graph perturbations. In: Proceedings of the 33rd NeurIPS, vol. 32 (2019)
4. Chen, J., Lin, X., Shi, Z., Liu, Y.: Link prediction adversarial attack via iterative gradient attack. IEEE Trans. Comput. Soc. Syst. **7**(4), 1081–1094 (2020)
5. Chen, L., et al.: A Survey of Adversarial Learning on Graphs. arXiv preprint arXiv:2003.05730 (2020)
6. Chen, X., Kang, B., Lijffijt, J., De Bie, T.: ALPINE: active link prediction using network embedding. Appl. Sci. **11**(11), 5043 (2021)
7. Dai, H., et al.: Adversarial attack on graph structured data. In: Proceedings of the 35th ICML, pp. 1115–1124 (2018)
8. Dai, Q., Li, Q., Tang, J., Wang, D.: Adversarial network embedding. In: Proceedings of the 32nd AAAI, vol. 32 (2018)
9. Dai, Q., Shen, X., Zhang, L., Li, Q., Wang, D.: Adversarial training methods for network embedding. In: Proceedings of the 28th WWW, pp. 329–339 (2019)
10. Fard, A.M., Wang, K.: Neighborhood randomization for link privacy in social network analysis. World Wide Web **18**(1), 9–32 (2015)

11. Feng, F., He, X., Tang, J., Chua, T.-S.: Graph adversarial training: dynamically regularizing based on graph structure. IEEE Trans. Knowl. Data Eng. **33**(6), 2493–2504 (2021)
12. Gao, Z., Hu, R., Gong, Y.: Certified robustness of graph classification against topology attack with randomized smoothing. In: Proceedings of the GLOBECOM 2020, pp. 1–6 (2020)
13. Goodfellow, I.J., Shlens, J., Szegedy, C.: Explaining and harnessing adversarial examples. In: Proceedings of the 3rd ICLR (2015)
14. Gori, M., Monfardini, G., Scarselli, F.: A new model for learning in graph domains. In: Proceedings of 2005 IEEE IJCNN, vol. 2, pp. 729–734 (2005)
15. Grover, A., Leskovec, J.: node2vec: scalable feature learning for networks. In: Proceedings of the 22nd ACM SIGKDD, pp. 855–864 (2016)
16. Hamilton, W., Ying, Z., Leskovec, J.: Inductive representation learning on large graphs. In: Proceedings of the 31st NeurIPS, vol. 30 (2017)
17. Handcock, M.S., Hunter, D.R., Butts, C.T., Goodreau, S.M., Morris, M.: statnet: An R package for the Statistical Modeling of Social Networks (2003). http://www.csde.washington.edu/statnet
18. IEEE: IEEE Standard Glossary of Software Engineering Terminology. IEEE STD 610.12-1990, pp. 1–84 (1990). https://doi.org/10.1109/IEEESTD.1990.101064
19. Jia, J., Wang, B., Cao, X., Gong, N.Z.: Certified robustness of community detection against adversarial structural perturbation via randomized smoothing. In: Proceedings of the 29th WWW, pp. 2718–2724 (2020)
20. Jin, H., Shi, Z., Peruri, V.J.S.A., Zhang, X.: Certified robustness of graph convolution networks for graph classification under topological attacks. In: Proceedings of the 34th NeurIPS, vol. 33, pp. 8463–8474 (2020)
21. Jin, W., Li, Y., Xu, H., Wang, Y., Tang, J.: Adversarial attacks and defenses on graphs: a review and empirical study. arXiv preprint arXiv:2003.00653 (2020)
22. Kang, B., Lijffijt, J., De Bie, T.: Conditional network embeddings. In: Proceedings of the 7th ICLR (2019)
23. Kang, B., Lijffijt, J., De Bie, T.: ExplaiNE: An Approach for Explaining Network Embedding-based Link Predictions. arXiv preprint arXiv:1904.12694 (2019)
24. Kipf, T.N., Welling, M.: Semi-supervised classification with graph convolutional networks. In: Proceedings of the 5th ICLR (2017)
25. Liben-Nowell, D., Kleinberg, J.: The link-prediction problem for social networks. J. Am. Soc. Inf. Sci. Technol. **58**(7), 1019–1031 (2007)
26. Lin, W., Ji, S., Li, B.: Adversarial attacks on link prediction algorithms based on graph neural networks. In: Proceedings of the 15th ACM AsiaCCS, pp. 370–380 (2020)
27. Liu, X., Tang, J.: Network representation learning: a macro and micro view. AI Open **2**, 43–64 (2021)
28. Liu, Z., Larson, M.: Adversarial item promotion: vulnerabilities at the core of top-N recommenders that use images to address cold start. In: Proceedings of the 30th WWW, pp. 3590–3602 (2021)
29. Ma, Y., Wang, S., Derr, T., Wu, L., Tang, J.: Attacking Graph Convolutional Networks via Rewiring. arXiv preprint arXiv:1906.03750 (2019)
30. Mara, A.C., Lijffijt, J., De Bie, T.: Benchmarking network embedding models for link prediction: are we making progress? In: Proceedings of the 7th IEEE DSAA, pp. 138–147 (2020)
31. Martínez, V., Berzal, F., Cubero, J.C.: A survey of link prediction in complex networks. ACM Comput. Surv. **49**(4), 1–33 (2016)

32. Mirzasoleiman, B., Cao, K., Leskovec, J.: Coresets for robust training of deep neural networks against noisy labels. In: Proceedings of the 34th NeurIPS, vol. 33, pp. 11465–11477 (2020)
33. Miyato, T., Maeda, S.I., Koyama, M., Ishii, S.: Virtual adversarial training: a regularization method for supervised and semi-supervised learning. IEEE PAMI **41**(8), 1979–1993 (2018)
34. Pan, S., Hu, R., Long, G., Jiang, J., Yao, L., Zhang, C.: Adversarially regularized graph autoencoder for graph embedding. In: Proceedings of the 27th IJCAI, pp. 2609–2615 (2018)
35. Perozzi, B., Al-Rfou, R., Skiena, S.: DeepWalk: online learning of social representations. In: Proceedings of the 20th ACM SIGKDD, pp. 701–710 (2014)
36. Qiu, J., Dong, Y., Ma, H., Li, J., Wang, K., Tang, J.: Network embedding as matrix factorization: unifying DeepWalk, LINE, PTE, and node2vec. In: Proceedings of the 11th ACM WSDM, pp. 459–467 (2018)
37. Sun, L., et al.: Adversarial attack and defense on graph data: a survey. arXiv preprint arXiv:1812.10528 (2018)
38. Sun, M., et al.: Data poisoning attack against unsupervised node embedding methods. arXiv preprint arXiv:1810.12881 (2018)
39. Tang, J., Qu, M., Wang, M., Zhang, M., Yan, J., Mei, Q.: LINE: large-scale information network embedding. In: Proceedings of the 24th WWW, pp. 1067–1077 (2015)
40. Tang, X., Li, Y., Sun, Y., Yao, H., Mitra, P., Wang, S.: Transferring robustness for graph neural network against poisoning attacks. In: Proceedings of the 13th WSDM, pp. 600–608 (2020)
41. Wang, X., Cui, P., Wang, J., Pei, J., Zhu, W., Yang, S.: Community preserving network embedding. In: Proceedings of the 31st AAAI, vol. 31 (2017)
42. Waniek, M., Michalak, T.P., Wooldridge, M.J., Rahwan, T.: Hiding individuals and communities in a social network. Nat. Hum. Behav. **2**(2), 139–147 (2018)
43. Waniek, M., Zhou, K., Vorobeychik, Y., Moro, E., Michalak, T.P., Rahwan, T.: How to hide one's relationships from link prediction algorithms. Sci. Rep. **9**(1), 1–10 (2019)
44. Watts, D.J., Strogatz, S.H.: Collective dynamics of 'small-world' networks. Nature **393**(6684), 440–442 (1998)
45. Wu, H., Wang, C., Tyshetskiy, Y., Docherty, A., Lu, K., Zhu, L.: Adversarial examples for graph data: deep insights into attack and defense. In: Proceedings of the 28th IJCAI, pp. 4816–4823 (2019)
46. Xu, K., et al.: Topology attack and defense for graph neural networks: an optimization perspective. In: Proceedings of the 28th IJCAI, pp. 3961–3967 (2019)
47. Yang, G., Gong, N.Z., Cai, Y.: Fake co-visitation injection attacks to recommender systems. In: Proceedings of the 24th NDSS (2017)
48. Yu, S., et al.: Target defense against link-prediction-based attacks via evolutionary perturbations. IEEE Trans. Knowl. Data Eng. **33**(2), 754–767 (2021)
49. Zachary, W.W.: An information flow model for conflict and fission in small groups. J. Anthropol. Res. **33**(4), 452–473 (1977)
50. Zhang, H., Li, Y., Ding, B., Gao, J.: Practical data poisoning attack against next-item recommendation. In: Proceedings of the 29th WWW, pp. 2458–2464 (2020)
51. Zhang, M., Chen, Y.: Link prediction based on graph neural networks. In: Proceedings of the 32nd NeurIPS, vol. 31 (2018)
52. Zheng, C., et al.: Robust graph representation learning via neural sparsification. In: Proceedings of the 37th ICML, pp. 11458–11468 (2020)

53. Zhou, K., Michalak, T.P., Vorobeychik, Y.: Adversarial robustness of similarity-based link prediction. In: Proceedings of the 19th IEEE ICDM, pp. 926–935 (2019)
54. Zhou, K., Michalak, T.P., Waniek, M., Rahwan, T., Vorobeychik, Y.: Attacking similarity-based link prediction in social networks. In: Proceedings of the 18th AAMAS, pp. 305–313 (2019)
55. Zhu, D., Zhang, Z., Cui, P., Zhu, W.: Robust graph convolutional networks against adversarial attacks. In: Proceedings of the 25th ACM SIGKDD, pp. 1399–1407 (2019)
56. Zügner, D., Akbarnejad, A., Günnemann, S.: Adversarial attacks on neural networks for graph data. In: Proceedings of the 24th ACM SIGKDD, pp. 2847–2856 (2018)
57. Zügner, D., Borchert, O., Akbarnejad, A., Guennemann, S.: Adversarial attacks on graph neural networks: perturbations and their patterns. ACM Trans. Knowl. Discov. Data **14**(5), 1–31 (2020)
58. Zügner, D., Günnemann, S.: Adversarial attacks on graph neural networks via meta learning. In: Proceedings of the 7th ICLR (2019)
59. Zügner, D., Günnemann, S.: Certifiable robustness and robust training for graph convolutional networks. In: Proceedings of the 25th ACM SIGKDD, pp. 246–256 (2019)
60. Zügner, D., Günnemann, S.: Certifiable robustness of graph convolutional networks under structure perturbations. In: Proceedings of the 26th ACM SIGKDD, pp. 1656–1665 (2020)

Practical Black Box Model Inversion Attacks Against Neural Nets

Thomas Bekman[✉], Masoumeh Abolfathi, Haadi Jafarian, Ashis Biswas,
Farnoush Banaei-Kashani, and Kuntal Das

University of Colorado, Denver, Denver, CO 80204, USA

Abstract. Adversarial machine learning is a set of malicious techniques
that aim to exploit machine learning's underlying mathematics. Model
inversion is a particular type of adversarial machine learning attack where
an adversary attempts to reconstruct the target model's private training data. Specifically, given black box access to a target classifier, the
attacker aims to recreate a particular class sample with just the ability to query the model. Traditionally, these attacks have depended on
the target classifier returning a confidence vector. The process of model
inversion iteratively creates an image to maximize the target model's
confidence of a particular class. Our technique allows the attack to be
performed with only a one-hot-encoded confidence vector from the target. The approach begins with performing model extraction, e.g. training
a local model to mimic the behavior of a target model. Then we perform
inversion on the local model within our control. Through this combination, we introduce the first model inversion attack that can be performed in a true black box setting; i.e. without knowledge of the target
model's architecture, and by only using outputted class labels. This is
possible due to transferability properties inherent in our model extraction approach known as Jacobian Dataset Augmentation. Throughout
this work, we will train shallow Artificial Neural Nets (ANNs) to mimic
deeper ANNs, and CNNs. These shallow local models allow us to extend
Fredrikson et al.'s inversion attack to invert more complex models than
previously thought possible.

Keywords: Black box model inversion attacks · Adversarial machine
learning

1 Introduction

As machine learning advances its usage is becoming increasingly common. It is
being used in a wide range of problems such as: predicting lifestyle choices, medical diagnosis and facial recognition [1–3]. Often times, these machine learning
models can be queried via publicly available APIs. A good example is Amazon's

---

Supported by University of Colorado, Denver.

M. Kamp et al. (Eds.): ECML PKDD 2021 Workshops, CCIS 1525, pp. 39–54, 2021.
https://doi.org/10.1007/978-3-030-93733-1_3

Rekognition API, which uses deep learning to help developers do a wide range of image recognition tasks, including facial recognition [4]. Another example is Google's Cloud Healthcare API which automates the process of building models for healthcare purposes [5]. It is clear that the privacy of the training data is essential for these two services, and for many others.

For many years, there was this underlying assumption that a machine learning model alone could not expose its training data. But it has been shown that a malicious entity with just the ability to query a model can reverse engineer its training data, in an attack known as model inversion [17]. There are two main classes of model inversion, black box and white box attacks. The first assumes you have no knowledge of the target model (the model being attacked), while the latter assumes you have full access to the trained model including its underlying architectural information and gradient at any given point. The attack discussed in this work will be of the former category.

Moreover, there are two general approaches used in this area. The first optimization-based approach uses gradient descent to iteratively improve, and eventually recreate training data [6–10]. For example the original model inversion attack (MIA) [17] cast the inversion task as an optimization problem. It aims to optimize the returned class confidence for an input image, and in the process it iteratively updates an image so that an initial black image is turned into a representative sample of a given class. Unfortunately this approach has been found both in the literature and in our experiments to be ineffective against deeper ANN's and CNN's [11–14].

Another approach exists for model inversion as well. They are known as training based approaches, and were developed by Yang et al. [14]. Their attack works by training a model that acts as an inverse of the target model. They first query a set of images against the target model in order to collect a confidence vector for each image. They then train their inversion model to produce an image from an input confidence vector. Their work significantly outperforms the original MIA approach, in that they are capable of inverting more complex models, and produce images that are much more faithful to the original training images.

The problem with both of these approaches is that they require confidence vectors from a target model. This makes these attacks less reasonable in a real-life setting, as a privacy-conscious machine learning service would most likely only return class labels, or they would add noise or round off the confidence vectors in order to prevent adversarial machine learning attacks [16,17]. Our approach allows for only the use of class labels in order to perform model inversion, thus overcoming any manipulation of the output confidence vector that maintains the accuracy of the prediction. Although this is not the first approach that allows for only the use of class labels to perform model inversion, our approach allows for significantly fewer queries to the target model in order to work, thus making it a more discrete route for an adversary [15].

Our approach to solving this problem involves first performing model extraction. This is the process by which a local model is trained to mimic the behavior of a target model. This allows one to use the local "substitute" model as a white box to perform model inversion. We performed model extraction by training a local model on a synthetic dataset generated via Jacobian Dataset Augmentation (which will be discussed in greater detail below) [18]. The use of this technique over previous model extraction techniques allows our attack to easily transfer between different model types (therefore eliminating the need to know the architecture of the target model), and enables a local model to be trained on very few queries to a target model [15]. After training the local model, we then perform the white box model inversion attack outlined in the original MIA paper [17]. By using a simple substitute ANN to mimic more complex target ANN's, we are capable of performing the original MIA attack against complex neural nets that previously could not be inverted using this approach.

Contributions. The contributions this work makes to the community could be summarized as follows:

1. We propose an approach that allows accurate black box model inversion with high dimensional image data, without making use of confidence vectors.
   (a) Our approach is very generalizable allowing a local model (of a single architecture) to mimic the behavior of any number of target models; this removes the assumption of any knowledge of the target model's architecture.
2. Our model inversion approach significantly reduces the number of queries required to perform the attack.
3. We also show how white box attacks can be converted into black box attacks through the use of model extraction. This will be a promising research direction for future model inversion work.

The rest of this paper is organized as follows. In Sect. 2, we review the background knowledge needed to establish an understanding of the problem domain. We then present our proposed model inversion approach in Sect. 3. Experimental results are discussed in Sect. 4. Section 5 discusses the related work followed by discussion and conclusion in Sect. 6 and 7 respectively.

2   Background

This section presents a brief overview of essential information about adversarial machine learning, particularly model inversion. The goal is to put our research in the context of the current state of the field and explain the mathematical background of related approaches.

2.1   The Fredrikson et al. Attack

Fredrikson et al. were the first to perform a model inversion attack with the goal of stealing high dimensional data, in their case images of faces. Their attack was framed as an optimization problem. They made the assumption that the target model returns a class label, along with the associated confidence value. So they update their desired data iteratively with the goal of optimizing the confidence value for the class label they are attempting to reverse-engineer.

They start the process with access to a white box target model, and a black image. After querying the white box model with an image x they now have the gradient of the cost function (evaluated at the image) corresponding to the desired label Y, represented by the equation:

$$c(x) = 1 - f_{label}(x) \tag{1}$$

the function evaluated at the label Y is represented as:

$$c(x)[Y] \tag{2}$$

The gradient is then used to update the image using standard gradient descent, where λ is the learning rate:

$$x_i = x_{i-1} - \lambda * \nabla c(x_{i-1})[Y] \tag{3}$$

This is then used as the starting point for the subsequent iteration. If the returned confidence value is high enough the process will stop and the image will be returned. Conversely if the gradient fails to improve after so many iterations the process is stopped, and the highest confidence image generated is returned. Below is the algorithm used for this process:

Algorithm 1. Inversion attack for facial recognition models [17]

1: **function** MI-FACE($Y, \alpha, \beta, \gamma, \lambda$)
2:      $c(x) = 1 - f_Y(x)$
3:      $x_0 \leftarrow 0$
4:      **for** $i \leftarrow 1...\alpha$ **do**
5:          $x_i \leftarrow x_{i-1} - \lambda * \nabla c(x_{i-1})$
6:          **if** $c(x_i) \geq max(c(x_{i-1}), ..., c(x_{i-\beta}))$ **then**
7:              **break**
8:          **if** $c(x_i) \leq \gamma$ **then**
9:              **break**
10:     **return** $[argmin_{x_i}(c(x_i)), min_{x_i}(c(x_i))]$

2.2 Jacobian Dataset Augmentation

Jacobian Dataset Augmentation is a synthetic dataset generation technique that aims to create samples that best represent the decision boundary of some target model with minimal label queries. To best understand this approach it is worthwhile to discuss alternative techniques.

The naive approach would be to make an infinite number of queries to the target model. This way we would know the entire output of the model for any input x belonging to the entire input domain. This would give us a copy of the target model. Unfortunately, this method is not tractable. Consider a model with Z input components, each with Y possible discrete values. This gives Y^Z possible input queries. Now imagine the number of queries required for a continuous domain. Such a large number of queries would be easy to detect. It has also been found that using a Gaussian noise to select points results in a local model that does not mimic the target [18].

The heuristic used to create synthetic training data is based on identifying the directions in which the target model output is changing around an initial set of training data. Intuitively identifying the directions of change requires more input-output pairs to capture the output fluctuations of the target model. Thus, to get a local model to approximate the decision boundary of a target model this method attempts create data points that repeatedly cross the decision boundary.

These directions are identified by the Jacobian matrix (JF) of the local model. Specifically, the sign of the Jacobian matrix corresponding to the label assigned to the input x by the target model (O). This is defined as (where lambda is the modification rate):

$$\lambda * sgn(J_F(x)[O(x)]) \tag{4}$$

Below is a more detailed description of the multiple steps of the Jacobian Augmentation process along with the steps to train the substitute model.

1. An initial set of data is collected that is representative of the training data domain. Throughout this work we use a facial recognition model; so for this step we collect images of faces. Moreover, we run various experiments where we use a mix of images from both the AT&T face dataset and the Facescrub dataset.
2. The architecture of the local model must be selected. In our case we train local ANNs to mimic the behavior of various different models. We show that by using a simple ANN as the local model we are capable of overcoming the original MIA attacks deficiencies against more complex models like CNNs.
3. Substitute Training, the subheadings below are done iteratively:
   (a) Labeling: The local dataset is used to query the target model and obtain labels. In the first iteration this is just the initial dataset.
   (b) Training: The local model selected in step 2 is trained using traditional training techniques.
   (c) Augmentation: Jacobian Augmentation as described by the equation above is applied to the initial training set S_P. The augmented images are then concatenated to S_P to create S_{P+1}. For further iterations steps a, b and c are repeated with the newly augmented set S_{P+1}.

Step 3 is repeated multiple times in order to improve the performance of the local model. The sequence of operations are more formally noted in Algorithm 2 below.

Algorithm 2. Substitute Model Training: for oracle O, a maximum number of substitute max_p of substitute training epochs, a substitute model architecture F, and an initial training set S_0 [18]

```
1: Input: O, max_p, S_0, λ
2: Define architecture F
3: for  p ∈ 0..max_p − 1 do
4:      // Label the substitute training set
5:      D ← {(x, O(x)) : x ∈ S_p}
6:      // Train F on D to evaluate parameters θ_F
7:      θ_F ← train(F, D)
8:      // Perform Jacobian-based dataset augmentation
9:      S_{p+1} ← {x + λ * sgn(J_F(x)[O(x)]) : x ∈ S_p} ∪ S_p
10: return θ_F
```

3 Methodology

This section presents the main methodology proposed in this research work. Two subsections describe the threat model and attack pipeline, respectively.

3.1 Threat Model

The goal of our threat model is to mimic real-life scenarios where an adversary would actually try to perform a black box model inversion attack. We make the assumption that an adversary has no specific knowledge of a target model's architecture. However, we do assume an adversary knows the purpose of a given target model, e.g. they may know it takes an input image, and then returns the name of the person in the image. With this knowledge we can use some basic understanding of machine learning to make educated guesses about the type of model being employed by our desired target. For example, it is well known that CNNs are used for image recognition tasks, while RNNs and LSTMs are used for analyzing time series data.

Our testing was done against various facial recognition models trained on the AT&T face dataset. Unlike other model inversion attacks, we assume the adversary only has access to the output class label. Therefore, if a query has a confidence value below 0.7 for any given query, then no output label is returned. This confidence cutoff is necessary as without giving the confidence values, it is not possible for an end user of the model to know if the output classification has any validity.

Our attack involves training a local substitute model to mimic the behavior of a target model using the Jacobian Dataset Augmentation technique. This technique requires an initial dataset in order to begin the process. The initial dataset consisted of faces from the Facescrub dataset, along with images from the AT&T face dataset. It is important to note that the images from the AT&T face dataset were never the same as those used to train the target model. Various experiments were performed with different percentages of the AT&T faces compromising the initial Jacobian dataset, these percentages ranged from 50% to 1% [20]. Moreover, we also adopted the assumption from the original model inversion work, and that is the adversary knows the desired class label. In our case we are trying to invert a face, so we assume we know the name of that particular individual. By knowing an individual's name, along with other auxiliary information (like place of work, email, or place of residence), it is possible to scrap their personal photos from social media sites [21]. The initial dataset for the Jacobian Augmentation process aims to mimic what this sort of dataset would look like.

3.2 Attack Pipeline

The attack pipeline is composed of the following steps, listed sequentially in the order they are performed.

1. Determine what type of data was used to train the target model. In our experiments, we knew the target model was a facial recognition model, so the training data must have been faces.
2. Scrap the appropriate data based on your assumptions of the training data. For our experiments, we would have scrapped Facebook for pictures of faces.
3. Perform Jacobian Dataset Augmentation using the scrapped images. After this step, the adversary has a fully trained local model that mimics the behavior of the target.
4. For each class (or just the desired class of interest), perform white box model inversion (using the technique laid out in Fredrikson et al.) on the local model.
5. The output of step 4 should be a recognizable face. If it's just noise, then the inversion failed.

The first step listed is just a research step. Our attack is based on the assumption that an adversary can figure out what type of training data is used to train a target model. Often, it is trivial for an adversary to know the purpose of a target model, so one can easily extrapolate from there. Once they see the type of data, the attacker must then determine a good source for it.

The second step involves building a scraper to obtain the data necessary from Step 1. The goal here is to get data as close as possible to the data used to train the target model. For example, if the target model is a facial recognition model that only identifies males, one should obtain men's images exclusively.

In step three, the adversary takes all of their scrapped data and uses it as the initial seed dataset within Jacobian Dataset Augmentation. This initial seed dataset is iteratively modified each iteration of Jacobian Dataset Augmentation. It is used to teach the local substitute model to mimic the target model's decision boundary. The process is explained in much greater detail in Sect. 2.1

At the start of step 4, you now have a local model that mimics the target model's behavior. Using this local model, the adversary then performs a white box optimization-based model inversion attack, as described in Sect. 2.2.

The final step (step 5) is just a check. The result of step 4 should be an image that is recognizable as a person. If the image appears as noise, the adversary should know the attack failed to converge. In none of our experiments did an inversion converge to the wrong person; the only failure was lack of convergence, where only noise was returned.

4 Experimental Evaluation

This work consists of three sets of experiments. The first set explores how the initial composition of "seed" data for Jacobian Augmentation affects the resulting model inversion attack. The next set of experiments explores how transferable this attack is between different local and target models. And finally, we compare this approach to the original Fredrikson et al. model inversion attack.

4.1 Experimental Set up

Throughout this paper we have referred to both a local and target model. The local model is the one the adversary has complete control over, while the target model is considered a black box. The only ability the adversary has is to query the target model, and have class labels returned.

The target model is trained with 8 out of 10 faces for each of the 40 classes in the AT&T face dataset. The remaining 2/10 faces are used as a portion of the initial augmentation dataset used as the beginning of our model inversion process. These 2/10 faces are also mixed with faces from the Facescrub dataset. The ratio between Facescrub and AT&T faces is described in greater detail below. It is important to note that local and target model never see the exact same piece of training data.

As of now there is no widely accepted metric for the success of a model inversion attack. So, to assess our work we calculate the Mean Squared Error (MSE) between a ground truth face (in the target model training data) and the inverted image. Moreover, we compare the results of our class-label-free black box attack to the Fredrikson et al. white box attack. The logic is that we want our black box approach to match, or exceed what is possible in the white box case.

4.2 Effects of Training Data Composition

The goal of this set of experiments is to find out what portion of disjoint AT&T face data is ideal for performing model inversion. As described previously our initial "seed" dataset is a mixture of AT&T faces (not used for training the target model), and faces from the Facescrub dataset. We create various ratios to test (50%, 20%, 10%, 5%, 1%). For example, the 50% dataset has 2 AT&T faces, and 2 faces from the Facescrub dataset. Moreover, the 1% dataset has 2 AT&T faces and 98 faces from the Facescrub dataset. The number of faces from the AT&T dataset is always constant (2), but to achieve the desired ratio more faces from the Facescrub dataset are added. It should be noted that the adversary has no way of knowing which faces actually represent classes from the target model, thus the Facescrub faces are selected randomly.

Figure 1 represents how the percentage of AT&T face data affects the final inversion result. At first we ran a set of experiments where the local and target model were the same. This was to verify that our attack model works under the best possible scenario, where the adversary is lucky enough to determine the exact architecture of the target model. In this case both the target and local model are an ANN with a single hidden layer using the sigmoid activation function and having 3000 nodes. The output layer has 40 nodes, and has the softmax function associated with it.

It is clear that the smaller percentage of AT&T faces (and greater number of total images) lead to a better inversion result. This is probably due to a greater portion of the input domain being represented (due to a larger number of Facescrub images) in the initial Jacobian dataset.

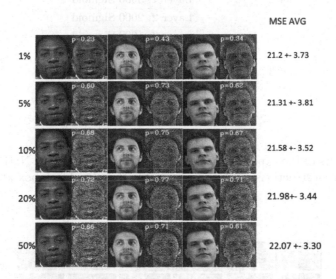

Fig. 1. Displayed are the inversion results based on percentage of AT&T faces. The left-hand column displays the percentage of AT&T faces, and the right-hand column displays the MSE between the ground truth and inverted image. The MSE is displayed as the average MSE across all 40 AT&T faces, and the standard deviation between faces. The number inside of the images, is the model's confidence for the associated class label. It is apparent that the smaller percentage of AT&T faces and the larger dataset clearly led to improved inversion results.

4.3 Realistic Scenario: Where the Target and Substitute Models Are Different

The next set of experiments more accurately emulate a model inversion attack in a real-life scenario. In each case the target model varied, but the local substitute model was an ANN with a single layer of 3000 nodes and a sigmoid activation. A simple substitute model was chosen as the Fredrikson et al. approach performs better on simpler models.

Table 1 defines the target model architectures for each test. In all cases the local substitute model was trained with the 1% face dataset described previously.

Table 1. The target model architecture for various experiments. The text describes the number of nodes in each layer, along with the activation function.

ANN architectures	
Experiment name	Target model architecture
Set 1	Layer 1: 3500 Sigmoid
	Layer 2: 500 Sigmoid
Set 2	Layer 1: 3500 Sigmoid
	Layer 2: 2000 Sigmoid
	Layer 3: 1000 Sigmoid
	Layer 4: 5000 Sigmoid
Set 3	Layer 1: 2000 Relu
	Layer 2: 1000 Relu
	Layer 3: 500 Relu

The results of the experiment are shown in the figure below. Notice how the white box reconstructions are less recognizable than the black box attacks.

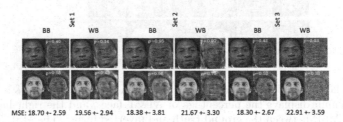

Fig. 2. This shows the final results of model inversion for each set. The MSE shown is the average result after inverting all 40 faces in the AT&T dataset.

In all cases shown in Fig. 2 the black box attack was able to create a recognizable face. Moreover, the black box inversion recreated all the faces in set 1 and 3. But in set two only 37/40 faces resulted in a recognizable inversion. Moreover, it is clear the black box attack outperforms the white box attack.

4.4 Inverting a CNN

Generally Convolution Neural Nets (CNNs) are used in image recognition tasks. It has been shown that Fredrikson et al.'s attack does not work on CNNs in the white box or original black box setting. In this experiment we used a local substitute ANN with 1 hidden layer, using the sigmoid activation function (3000 nodes). The target CNN consisted of 3 convolutional layers (each with a relu activation function), the first layer contained 64 8×8 kernels, while the second had 128 6×6 kernels, and the final layer had 128 5×5 kernels. The last convolutional layer fed into a dense output layer with 40 nodes.

Our black box substitution approach (using the 1% dataset) inverted 28/40 AT&T faces (achieving a 21.4 ± 4.1 MSE), while the white box attack directly on the CNN inverted 0/40 AT&T faces and achieved an MSE of: 24.3 ± 1.6. An example of the inversion results are displayed in Fig. 3 below.

Fig. 3. A few examples of successfully inverted black box images, compared to the outputs of the white box attack. It is clear from the results shown below that using our substitution approach, it is possible to invert the training data of a CNN.

4.5 Numerical Approximation

Previous approaches were able to successfully perform model inversion by maximizing the desired class probability. It was shown that the less information provided by the confidence vector, the worse the inversion results become [17]. We attempted to perform Fredrikson et al.'s numerical approximation approach (which was the black box approach they proposed in their work) with just class labels. In this approach the confidence vector was all zero's with the predicted class having a 1. As expected the output of the model inversion is a solid black image, which was the starting point of the attack. This fails as numerical approximation can only change a pixel value if the perturbation in a given pixel alters the predicted class. Individual pixel changes from the black image are unlikely to change the target model's output class label. Therefore, it gets stuck at the initial black image after every iteration of the inversion algorithm.

5   Related Work

Our work is related to cutting edge research in membership inference, model extraction and model inversion. Within a membership inference attack one starts with a piece of data that is believed to be in the training dataset of a target model. Then using this approach one can determine if that piece of data was truly in the training data. This is very similar to model inversion, except in model inversion one starts out with some auxiliary knowledge of the training data, and the goal is to reproduce recognizable pieces of training data, not exact replications. This approach was first introduced by [13]. Multiple defenses have been suggested against this attack such as adding drop out, stacking target models, and distributed training of target models with noisy parameter sharing [13, 22, 23].

Moreover, our work adopts approaches from model extraction. Our model extraction approach was developed in [18] with the goal of using a local model to produce adversarial inputs for target models. In their work they aim to create a local model that mimics the decision boundaries of a target model, but unlike [15] may not have it mimic predictions for every possible input. The Jacobian Augmentation approach requires significantly fewer queries than [15] to create a local model sufficient to perform their attack. Pavel et al. also explored a method for training a substitute model to create adversarial input [24]. But their approach requires a large amount of labeled data, which is expensive to collect. In fact their work is only evaluated against Random Forests and SVM's.

Model inversion was first introduced in [2], where they aimed to extract sensitive medical data from a linear model. This work was then followed by [17] where they developed a gradient descent-based technique to invert target model training data. Our technique for inverting data is from their work, but they applied the algorithm directly to the target model. Unlike our work, their attack required confidence scores in order to perform inversion. Our work also follows in the footsteps of [15] where they first perform model extraction to create a local model, and then perform model inversion. Unfortunately, their equation solving approach does not scale up to DNNs in practice. In order to recover 2225 parameters of a shallow network (one hidden layer with 20 nodes) they had to make 108,200 label queries. Moreover, they define their query budget as 100 * k, where k is the number of parameters. Finally, they don't address how they would attack deeper networks without knowledge of their architecture. Like Tramer et al. our attack allows model inversion with just class labels, but we are capable of doing it with fewer queries, and we have a scheme for inverting deeper models without having any knowledge of their architecture. For example, our attack needed 24,768 queries to invert a 4-layer ANN (With 45,591,040 parameters) with a 1% dataset. In our approach the number of queries in our model is independent of the target model, and dependent on the size of the initial scrapped dataset, and the number of data augmentation rounds. Although we drastically decreased the required queries compared to this work, the success of our lower query budget should be compared to a greater number of studies to assess the efficacy of our technique compared to cutting-edge work. We leave this for future studies.

Recently, deep learning has been used to perform novel model inversion attacks. In [24], the authors used an autoencoder to learn the mappings between the target model's output and the associated training image. The inversion results are impressive, but they depend on the target model outputting a confidence vector. Another recent approach involved using GAN's to recreate training data [25]. Their input begins as a distorted version of the training data, or a piece of training data with a portion removed. Their technique borrows from inpainting to recreate recognizable images. But unlike our approach they require white box access to the model, as they need the output loss for a given class as part of their discriminator's loss function.

6 Discussion

Throughout this work we present one of the first (to our knowledge) practical black box model inversion attacks that can work with no knowledge of the target model and with only class labels as outputs. The only other work to use class labels for model inversion is Tramer et al., but their attack is not practical for complex target models, as described previously.

Our attack heavily depended on the transferability property of Jacobian Dataset Augmentation described in [19]. In their work they used Jacobian Dataset Augmentation to train a local model, which they then used to craft adversarial samples. In their best case they found that 75% of adversarial samples were misclassified when the local DNN and target DNN had different architectures. This implies their technique allows the local model to adequately mimic the decision boundary of the target model. Unlike Tramer et al., the local and target models do not necessarily have the same predictions for all inputs [15]. In our work the target models achieved 95% accuracy on the training data, but our local model generally achieved an accuracy of 75%–80% on the original AT&T Data. But, we were still able to achieve inversion. This shows that full model extraction is not necessary if you have access to some auxiliary knowledge (in our case a large amount of faces), and a small percentage of images from the same distribution as the target models training data. Throughout our work we intentionally choose a shallow local model to mimic the behavior of more complex local models. If one observes the white box results, it is clear that Fredrikson et al.'s technique performs poorly on complex models. But by exploiting the transferability property of Jacobian dataset augmentation, we are able to successfully perform inversion on simple models that have mimicked the decision boundary of more complex models.

Moreover, our attack is able to perform inversion in a realistic scenario. The idea is an adversary begins the attack by scraping images from social media, with the goal of possibly obtaining a photo of an individual that is a member of the training data (although it is unlikely there will be many of these images). In our attack we mimicked this by using AT&T faces as a small percentage of the substitute model's training data. It is important to note the faces used in the substitute models training data were not part of the target model's training data. Interestingly, the smaller the percentage of AT&T faces in the local model's data the greater the inversion result. This is most likely due to the fact that the smaller percentage data had a larger amount of face images. Having a larger number of faces allows the substitute model to better understand the underlying distribution of training data in the target model. A similar result was observed in [19] where a large semantically similar dataset of images improved model inversion results.

A concession that had to be made is the 70% cutoff. We attempted experiments without the 70% cutoff, and we were incapable of achieving model extraction and therefore inversion. In those experiments every image was assigned a class even if the confidence was extremely low, therefore the training data used for the local model had too much noise for it to converge to a meaningful solution. With the 1% dataset the local model had an accuracy of 2.5% for the AT&T face dataset (the same as random guessing). Although this could be used as a defense against this attack, it would also render the target model useless for any practical purposes. Therefore, some version of the cutoff would likely be used for class-only models in the wild.

We believe this work shows that a powerful approach for model inversion is to first attempt model extraction. We show that model extraction as the first step of model inversion actually minimizes the number of queries to the target model. Moreover, using model extraction first has been the only method shown to allow model inversion on complex models where the target model only outputs class labels.

7   Conclusion and Future Work

In conclusion we demonstrated a novel combination of model extraction and model inversion. We found that by using Jacobian Dataset Augmentation to train a substitute model we were able to invert models previously thought impossible using Fredriskon's et al.'s approach [14,25]. Moreover, we show that by using Jacobian Augmentation one can actually transfer the decision boundary of deeper ANNs and CNNs to single layer ANN.

By using this combination of techniques, we were able to successfully invert recognizable images under a realistic attack scenario, where no knowledge of the target model is assumed, and only class labels are outputted. Moreover, we explored the concept of using semantically similar data to improve training the local model, and therefore improve inversion. We found that indeed the greater the amount of auxiliary data the better the final inversion result. This is ideal as auxiliary data is often easy to find if one knows the purpose of the target model.

Future work could further explore how various model extraction techniques can be combined with model inversion approaches to improve model inversion results. It is also worth exploring as there are model extraction approaches that require confidence scores, or white box access to target models. It would be interesting to see if a substitute model could replace the target model in those instances. Finally, our work shows that defensive techniques that modify output confidence vectors are not secure, as we only require class labels. Therefore, future defensive techniques should concentrate on modifying the internals of a model, or performing input validation.

References

1. Chi, C.-L., et al.: Individualized patient-centered lifestyle recommendations: an expert system for communicating patient specific cardiovascular risk information and prioritizing lifestyle options. J. Biomed. Inform. **45**(6), 1164–1174 (2012)
2. International Warfarin Pharmacogenetics Consortium: Estimation of the warfarin dose with clinical and pharmacogenetic data. N. Engl. J. Med. **360**(8), 753–764 (2009)
3. Taigman, Y., Yang, M., Ranzato, M.A., Wolf, L.: Deepface: closing the gap to human-level performance in face verification. In: Proceedings of the IEEE Conference on Computer Vision and Pattern Recognition, pp. 1701–1708 (2014)
4. AWS. https://aws.amazon.com/rekognition/
5. Google Cloud. https://cloud.google.com/healthcare/
6. Fredrikson, M., et al.: Privacy in pharmacogenetics: an end-to-end case study of personalized warfarin dosing. In: 23rd USENIX Security Symposium (USENIX Security 2014) (2014)
7. Jensen, C.A., et al.: Inversion of feedforward neural networks: algorithms and applications. Proc. IEEE **87**(9), 1536–1549 (1999)
8. Lee, S., Kil, R.M.: Inverse mapping of continuous functions using local and global information. IEEE Trans. Neural Netw. **5**(3), 409–423 (1994)
9. Mahendran, A., Vedaldi, A.: Understanding deep image representations by inverting them. In: Proceedings of the IEEE Conference on Computer Vision and Pattern Recognition (2015)
10. Várkonyi-Kóczy, A.R.: Observer-based iterative fuzzy and neural network model inversion for measurement and control applications. In: Rudas, I.J., Fodor, J., Kacprzyk, J. (eds.) Towards Intelligent Engineering and Information Technology, pp. 681–702. Springer, Heidelberg (2009). https://doi.org/10.1007/978-3-642-03737-5_49
11. Hitaj, B., Ateniese, G., Perez-Cruz, F.: Deep models under the GAN: information leakage from collaborative deep learning. In: Proceedings of the 2017 ACM SIGSAC Conference on Computer and Communications Security (2017)
12. Papernot, N., et al.: SoK: security and privacy in machine learning. In: 2018 IEEE European Symposium on Security and Privacy (EuroS&P). IEEE (2018)
13. Shokri, R., et al.: Membership inference attacks against machine learning models. In: 2017 IEEE Symposium on Security and Privacy (SP). IEEE (2017)
14. Yang, Z., et al.: Neural network inversion in adversarial setting via background knowledge alignment. In: Proceedings of the 2019 ACM SIGSAC Conference on Computer and Communications Security (2019)
15. Tramèr, F., et al.: Stealing machine learning models via prediction APIs. In: 25th USENIX Security Symposium (USENIX Security 2016) (2016)
16. Jia, J., et al.: Memguard: defending against black-box membership inference attacks via adversarial examples. In: Proceedings of the 2019 ACM SIGSAC Conference on Computer and Communications Security (2019)

17. Fredrikson, M., Jha, S., Ristenpart, T.: Model inversion attacks that exploit confidence information and basic countermeasures. In: Proceedings of the 22nd ACM SIGSAC Conference on Computer and Communications Security (2015)
18. Papernot, N., et al.: Practical black-box attacks against machine learning. In: Proceedings of the 2017 ACM on Asia Conference on Computer and Communications Security (2017)
19. Papernot, N., McDaniel, P., Goodfellow, I.: Transferability in machine learning: from phenomena to black-box attacks using adversarial samples. arXiv preprint arXiv:1605.07277 (2016)
20. Ng, H.-W., Winkler, S.: A data-driven approach to cleaning large face datasets. In: 2014 IEEE International Conference on Image Processing (ICIP). IEEE (2014)
21. Batrinca, B., Treleaven, P.C.: Social media analytics: a survey of techniques, tools and platforms. AI Soc. **30**(1), 89–116 (2014). https://doi.org/10.1007/s00146-014-0549-4
22. Salem, A., et al.: ML-leaks: model and data independent membership inference attacks and defenses on machine learning models. arXiv preprint arXiv:1806.01246 (2018)
23. Hayes, J., et al.: Logan: membership inference attacks against generative models. arXiv preprint arXiv:1705.07663 (2017)
24. Laskov, P.: Practical evasion of a learning-based classifier: a case study. In: 2014 IEEE Symposium on Security and Privacy. IEEE (2014)
25. Zhang, Y., et al.: The secret revealer: generative model-inversion attacks against deep neural networks. In: Proceedings of the IEEE/CVF Conference on Computer Vision and Pattern Recognition (2020)

NBcoded: Network Attack Classifiers Based on Encoder and Naive Bayes Model for Resource Limited Devices

Lander Segurola-Gil[1]([✉]), Francesco Zola[1,2], Xabier Echeberria-Barrio[1], and Raul Orduna-Urrutia[1]

[1] Vicomtech Foundation, Basque Research and Technology Alliance (BRTA), Donostia, Spain
{lsegurola,fzola,xetxeberria,rorduna}@vicomtech.org
[2] Institute of Smart Cities, Public University of Navarre, 31006 Pamplona, Spain

Abstract. In the recent years, cybersecurity has gained high relevance, converting the detection of attacks or intrusions into a key task. In fact, a small breach in a system, application, or network, can cause huge damage for the companies. However, when this attack detection encounters the Artificial Intelligence paradigm, it can be addressed using high-quality classifiers which often need high resource demands in terms of computation or memory usage. This situation has a high impact when the attack classifiers need to be used with limited resourced devices or without overloading the performance of the devices, as it happens for example in IoT devices, or in industrial systems. For overcoming this issue, NBcoded, a novel light attack classification tool is proposed in this work. NBcoded works in a pipeline combining the removal of noisy data properties of the encoders with the low resources and timing consuming obtained by the Naive Bayes classifier. This work compares three different NBcoded implementations based on three different Naive Bayes likelihood distribution assumptions (Gaussian, Complement and Bernoulli). Then, the best NBcoded is compared with state of the art classifiers like Multilayer Perceptron and Random Forest. Our implementation shows to be the best model reducing the impact of training time and disk usage, even if it is outperformed by the other two in terms of Accuracy and F1-score (~2%).

Keywords: Cybersecurity · Attack classification · Bayesian system · Autoencoder · Network traffic

1 Introduction

In the midst of the era of the Internet of Things (IoT), cybersecurity is becoming a field with strong importance in the daily life. In fact, cyber-attacks are evolving incredibly fast, making them more sophisticated [31] as time goes by. Not only that, the domain where these can be deployed is increasing at a significant velocity due to the fast growth of devices connecting to the internet [20]. According

© Springer Nature Switzerland AG 2021
M. Kamp et al. (Eds.): ECML PKDD 2021 Workshops, CCIS 1525, pp. 55–70, 2021.
https://doi.org/10.1007/978-3-030-93733-1_4

to [20], there are about 20 billion devices connected to the global net. These are not only composed of wearables; appliances from medical devices to automotive control units are part of the huge net thanks to the Industry 4.0 paradigm, the Smart Factory and the Industrial IoT (IIoT). In fact, many industries and critical infrastructures have now many devices connected to the internet [8]. Therefore, the consequences of a cyber-attack are not only limited to digital leak or losses, hijacking, Denial of Service (DoS) or ransom, but a much larger scope, affecting in economical, reputational, psychological and societal terms too [1].

Due to the need of confronting these cyber-threats, cybersecurity has evolved too. Many approaches have been proposed in order to avoid or alert when a cyber-attack is going on. Initially, static rule based solutions could work, but as it is mentioned, with the evolution of the cyber-threads, Artificial Intelligence (AI) based solutions [38] burst strongly. When trying to detect or predict anomalous situations, Machine Learning (ML) techniques, a branch of AI, can provide specially interesting approaches [34]. These algorithms allow network suitable tools that may learn specific patterns.

When talking about limited resourced environments, these may not be capable of assuming the requirements that many of these AI algorithms need, in terms of resources and time consumption [17]. For example, in some IoT devices and Industrial systems, several problems might end up being faced when trying to implement one of these AI based solutions, with regard to the need of huge computational power, lack of enough RAM, or even lack of disk space for saving models. This scenario is not an appropriate one to deploy a high demanding Deep Learning (a branch of ML) model, and there will be the need of a trade off resources for accuracy. In fact, this will become a challenge for the AI systems [17].

This problem should be tackled by the creation of light learning models, in spite of making sacrifices in terms of performance, while trying to maintain it as much as possible, in exchange of a low resource usage. For this reason, in this work, we present a novel light and fast attack classification system, with the name of NBcoded. The main idea is to exploit the lightness and fastness of the Naive Bayes (NB) classifiers, while exploiting the autoencoders abilities to deconstruct and construct the initial data, in order to reduce the noisy data and get more clear patterns of it. This, enhances the classification task for the NB classifiers, preserving its lightness. NBcoded works by combining autoencoder and NB technologies, aiming to classify network traffic into attack/unexpected or normal traffic.

The main goals of this work are:

- Compare Naive Bayes classifiers assuming different distributions, comprising Gaussian, Complement and Bernoulli, in a network traffic classification task.
- Improve the Naive Bayes classification quality by adding an extra-layer based on Autoencoder information.
- Compare the best results of the previous experiments with state of the art techniques, in terms of quality, training time and disk usage.

The rest of the paper is divided as follows: in Sect. 2, general concepts as well as state of the art are introduced. Section 3 explains the proposed approach for attack classification, detailing each member composing the NBcoded. In Sect. 4, the used dataset as well as the selected evaluation metrics are introduced. Section 5 presents the performed experiments and Sect. 6 illustrates the results obtained in those. Finally, Sect. 7 presents the conclusions of this work as well as the guidelines for future works are drawn.

2 Background

In this section, several general concepts are introduced, in particular in Sect. 2.1 and Sect. 2.2, the main concepts of the Naive Bayes classifier and Autoencoders (AE) are introduced respectively, and in Sect. 2.3 the state of the art is presented.

2.1 The Naive Bayes Classifier

The Naive Bayes (NB) classifier [27] is a probabilistic classifier based on the Bayes theorem [5], together with the next assumption; Let $(X_1, ..., X_n)$ be a vector of variables and let C be a dependant variable on X_i for $i = 1, .., n$. Then the NB classifiers naively assumes the conditional independence for all X_i with $i = 1, ..., n$ related to C. In other words,

$$P(C|X_1, ..., X_n) = \frac{P(X_1, ..., X_n|C)P(C)}{P(X_1, ..., X_n)} = \frac{P(C)\Pi_{i=1}^n P(X_i|C)}{P(X_1, ..., X_n)}, \quad (1)$$

where $P(C|X_1, ..., X_n)$ is called the posterior probability, $P(C)$ is the prior probability, and $P(X_1, ..., X_n)$ is the evidence. This last part, is a constant that can be calculated by the provided evidence or data, so

$$P(C|X_1, ..., X_n) \propto P(C)\Pi_{i=1}^n P(X_i|C).$$

Then, basically, given an observation $(x_1, ..., x_n)$ and a NB classifier f, for a set of classes C, f will make the prediction by using the Maximum a posteriori (MAP) estimation, by

$$f(x_1, ..., x_n) = \arg \max_c P(C = c)\Pi_{i=1}^n P(X_i = x_i|C = c).$$

To completely define the NB classifier, it is needed to determine $P(X_i|C)$ distributions. For this, many distribution can be assumed, such as the Gaussian distribution, Bernoulli distribution [22] or Multinomial distribution [28]. From this procedure the NB learning algorithm is created, and from this point and for the rest of the paper, depending on the chosen distribution, the model will be called the Gaussian NB (GNB), Bernoulli NB (BNB) or Complement NB (CNB) [28], where the last one is a derivation of the Multinomial distribution for imbalanced datasets.

2.2 Autoencoders

The idea of autoencoder was firstly introduced in [7]. These learning algorithms are a kind of Neural Networks (NN), created with the aim of encoding or representing data, commonly for dimension reduction. The architecture of an autoencoder may differ depending on the amount of hidden layers, but basically they all have the same structure. They are compounded by an input layer, gradually smaller hidden layers (where the last one is called the bottleneck), gradually bigger hidden layers and the output layer, which has the same size as the input layer (Fig. 1).

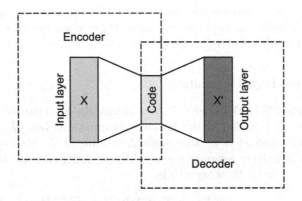

Fig. 1. Autoencoder basic structure

In the training phase, the model learns to compress the data and to decompress it. Thus, the *encoder* component (Fig. 1) learns to condense the data, maintaining the relevant information, so the *decoder* component (Fig. 1) can recover the original data. Once the model is trained, the encoder component reduces the dimension of the data, compressing the relevant information and removing the noise of the data, i.e., the irrelevant or duplicated information.

2.3 Related Work

The AI, in particular, the ML branch, has been widely studied in the recent years. For example, in [9,40] a One-class Supported Vector Machine (SVM) for malware detection and for brain tumor detection respectively is used, in [16] some problems related to partial differential equations are solved using Artificial Neural Networks (ANN), in [33] sleep classification is performed by the application of Random Forest (RF). Related to cybersecurity, in [32], a review where different ML techniques composed by the ones mentioned above and other such as the Naive Bayes (NB), are compared against different tasks like intrusion, malware and spam detection. Last years Deep Learning (DL) architectures have provided a great leap forward in ML field. Many DL techniques have been studied in [13] in attack detection tasks.

In particular, the NB classifier is widely studied on many fields. For example, in medicine for the detection of cerebral infarction [29], or for coronary heart disease, breast cancer and diabetes [15]. Research in many other fields can be found too; in [36], for predicting water floods, or in [23], for earthquake predictions. Another interesting study is presented in [18], where they propose an automatic bridge crack recognition tool based on CNN and NB.

Regarding cybersecurity, in [6] NB along with other ML algorithms are tested against the UNSW-NB15 dataset. In [12], they propose an Intrusion Detection System (IDS), using the NB and SVM as reference models with which to test against, using the NSLKDDCup1999 [35] dataset.

For Autoencoders, in [24], this technology is used for prediction of hearth disease, in [21] for the prediction of $C\alpha$ angles and dihedrals from protein sequences or in [30] for explosion and earthquake classification.

In the cybersecurity field, autoencoders are used in [2] for mitigating covert cyber attacks in smart grids, or fooling IDS like in [11]. In particular, for attack detection, in [10] autoencoders are used for Distributed Denial of Service (DDoS) detection or in [3], where they combine it with a SVM for a binary and five different attack class classification.

3   Proposal

In this section, the NBcoded pipeline is presented. In particular, in Sect. 3.1, the architecture of the presented classifier is presented and in Sect. 3.2 the learning process is clarified.

3.1   NBcoded Architecture

The family of NB algorithms is a technology that has been widely studied in the state-of-the-art as for example in [12,35]. They bring light and fast classification models, but they often do not get high performance when compared to some other state-of-the-art methods. In some cases, this might be due to the incapacity of these naive methods to reach deeper patterns, despite having the advantage of being very light and needing a minimum request of resources for the processing, particularly when they face other training models. The main idea of this work is to present NBcoded, a light, and fast attack classification tool, which combines the lightness of the NB models with an enhanced performance given by the autoencoders, preserving the need for a limited quantity of resources, but bringing a competitive performance.

As shown in Fig. 2, NBcoded consists of two parts; the data encoder part and the NB based attack classification part. The introduced model works by analyzing data flows in two steps: firstly, the flows given data is encoded into a less dimensional space. Then, the codification is given to the NB algorithms to be classified. The idea of applying an encoder is making an improvement in classification tasks for the NB classifiers, making data less noisy and projecting data to get fewer features.

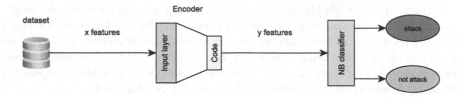

Fig. 2. NBcoded architecture

For the first part, the creation of the encoder, an autoencoder is created first. For this task, a multilayer autoencoder is choosen, that is, an autoencoder with more than one hidden layer. More specifically, the chosen architecture is constructed as it follows; due to the selected features, the input layer consists of 9 features. Then, it is followed by a 8 neuron hidden layer, to end descending into a 6 neuron layer. Symmetrically, it ascends until the output layer is reached. The chosen optimizer has been the *Adam* optimizer, with the mean absolute error loss and an l2 regularizer with a factor of 0.001. With regard to the activation function, the *tanh* has been the one choosen for every layer. From this structure, the encoder layers of an autoencoder are taken, that is, the 9 neuron, 8 neurons and the 6 neurons layers. The task of this part will be to encode data of dimension 9, to a dimension of 6, depicting the most representative patterns in the new space, cleaning it from noisy points.

For the second part, the output of the first part will be taken as the input of the classifier with the task of classifying attacks. For this, the NB classifier is proposed.

The composition of these two technologies results in a light and fast classifier. In fact, the selected autoencoder structure is composed by a little amount of layers/neurons, what makes the encoder even lighter. The Naive Bayes classifiers are well known by their lightness and fastness too.

3.2 NBcoded Learning

In this architecture, a 9 neurons input layered autoencoder will receive a 9 featured dataset for the training phase. The training set will be split into two same sized parts. One of both will be used in the mentioned training phase of the autoencoder. Once the training is done, the trained encoder will be subtracted from it. At this point, the encoder will receive the other part with the task of encoding it.

For the second part, the NB classifier will receive the output of the encoder, comprising 6 featured points, so it can be trained. In this case, an assumption between Gaussian, Complement and Bernoulli distributions will be done. Firstly, the prior is calculated from the data points, getting the probability of a given random point belonging to one class or the other. Then, the prior will be updated as it follows; In a first step, the assumed likelihood distributions parameters will be fitted by the provided encoded data, and then the prior will be updated following the Eq. 1, resulting in the a posteriori distribution. Once the training is done, the new distribution will remain static with no updates.

Following with the real scenario case, once the proposed tool is ready for classification, it will receive 9 featured data points as input, that will be projected into a 6 dimensional space. Then the encoded data points will be classified into a normal class (0) or attack/unexpected class (1), giving a binary classification of each point as the output.

4   Experimental Framework

In this section, an explanation of the used dataset is given, as well as the evaluation metrics selected. In Sect. 4.1, the used dataset is explained, in Sect. 4.2, the selected features together with the carried preprocess are presented, in Sect. 4.3 the evaluation metrics are explained, and finally, in Sect. 4.4, the chosen ML parameters, as well as used computer characteristics, are shown.

4.1   Dataset Overview

The experiments drawn in this research are implemented using the UNSW-NB15 dataset[1], a complete network flows dataset created with the aim of covering some gaps found in other benchmark datasets [26]. This dataset is widely used in cybersecurity, for example for creating a deep learning binomial classifier based on neural networks for implementing an intrusion detection system [4]; for presenting a framework that combines linear and learning algorithms to create a Hybrid Anomaly Detection Model (HADM) [25] or to introduce a Deep Feature Embedding Learning (DFEL) framework for anomaly prediction which combines neural networks for feature embedding and making predictions [41]. It is also used for extracting temporal graph information that is then used for classifying network behaviours, as introduced in [43].

The UNSW-NB15 dataset contains real normal and synthetic abnormal network traffic, generated in the University of New South Wales (UNSW) cybersecurity lab. In particular, the abnormal traffic is generated by deploying 9 different attack families, which are Fuzzers, Analysis, Backdoors, Denial-of-Service (DoS), Exploits, Generic, Reconnaissance, Shellcode and Worms. The whole dataset is generated and divided into two separated captures, the first one of 16 h, and the second of 15 h. Then, the whole data traffic is preprocessed using tools like Argus, and Bro-IDSArgus[2] and Bro-IDS[3] for aggregating similar flows into unique records defined by 47 features and two labels fields, one for indicating normal/attack flows (binary label), and the other one for specifying the attack family among the 9 available. This aggregation reduces the two capture days

---

[1] https://www.unsw.adfa.edu.au/unsw-canberra-cyber/cybersecurity/ADFA-NB15-Datasets/.

[2] https://qosient.com/argus/index.shtml.

[3] https://zeek.org/.

up to 12 h and 12 h and a half, respectively, with $2,540,044$ number of samples of which $2,218,761$ labelled as normal connections and $321,283$ labelled as attack connections.

4.2   Dataset Preprocess and Feature Selection

Even if the selected dataset was made with the aim of covering limitations, several studies, as [42] have shown that it has some gaps related to class overlap and class imbalance. For this reason, the need of data transformation along with the selection of representative features is needed.

Data Normalization. The high variability of the dataset values can be a huge problem that affects the quality of the ML models since it can introduce biasing [14], which can lead to skewed learning algorithms. This may happen by the fact that these outliers may grab the attention disproportionately. To avoid this, a common solution is normalizing data. For this, normalization with the rule indicated in Expression 2 is performed in this work.

$$\frac{X - X_{\min}}{X_{\max} - X_{\min}} \tag{2}$$

In this case, normalization is applied to each particular feature, in order to give the same representation to each.

Feature Selection. As it is proposed in [39], the selected features for this study have been *sload, dload, dmeansz, smeansz, stcpb, dtcpb, sttl, djit* and *trans-depth* and the dataset has been filtered by the feature *service*, taking into account only the *unknown, ftp* and *dns* services. Before this process is done, the dataset has $2,540,044$ samples, and after the whole process, $2,045,019$ are left.

4.3   Evaluation Metrics

For evaluating our solution and in order to compare the results with other state of the art technologies, several metrics are extracted in terms of performance, as well as disk usage and training time. The time is measured by capturing the needed time for the model to finish the training phase. This might be particularly interesting in a scenario in which the training is done in place, i.e. directly in the limited resource device. When talking about the NBcoded pipeline, the training time for the autoencoder is measured, as well as the training time for the NB. Then both times are summed up to measure the training time of the proposed architecture. In terms of disk usage, once the models are trained, they are saved as binary files in disk to measure the disk usage. Once again, to measure the disk usage of the NBcoded, the disk usage of the trained encoder is summed with the disk usage of a trained NB.

The metrics related to the performance are the ones derived from the confusion matrix (Fig. 3) related to binary classification.

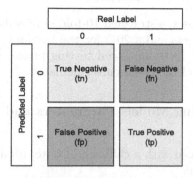

Fig. 3. Feature matrix

These can be interpreted as it follows:

- True Negative (tn): This is the case when the predicted value and the real value equals 0.
- False Negative (fn): This is the case when the predicted value is 0 but the real value equals 1.
- False Positive (fp): This one occurs when the predicted value is 1 but the real value equals 0.
- True Positive (tp): This one happens when both values equal 1.

From these values, some interesting metrics can be extracted, which represent well the performance of the models, that are

- Precision: This measures the relative success rate of the model referred to the total amount of real positives. It is calculated by

$$\frac{tp}{tp + fn}.$$

- Recall: This measures the relative success rate of the model referred to the total amount of predicted positives. It is calculated by

$$\frac{tp}{tp + fp}.$$

- Accuracy: This one measures the relative success rate of the model for the whole set. It can be computed by

$$\frac{tp + tn}{tp + fp + tn + fn}.$$

– F1-score: The harmonic mean of the precision and recall. It is computed by

$$2 \cdot \frac{precision \cdot recall}{precision + recall}.$$

For the testing purposes, a stratified 10-fold cross-validation is used, in splits of 80% for the training sets and a 20% for the tests sets which allows similarly balanced sets. Once the 10 training and testing phases are completed, a mean and standard deviation of the results are calculated.

4.4   Machine Learning Models Parameters and Computer Characteristics

The autoencoder is trained with a callback of 5 iterations is established for 100 epochs, in batches of 250.

For the other state-of-the-art methods, a 100 treed [19] Random forest is chosen, with no limit of node expansion. Concerning the MLP, a two hidden layered model is chosen, where each of the layers is composed of 100 neurons. This one is trained with an early stop of 5 iterations within 100 epochs, in batches of 250. The experiments where carried on a Windows 10 machine, with 8 GB of RAM and 4 CPUs of 3.40 GHz

5   Experimental Study

In this section, the main concepts of the experiments carried in this study are exposed. Those are comprised by three experiments, where the aim of the first one is to create baseline values, the second one is to prove an optimization of these values and the third one aims to show a competitive performance of the proposed model in comparison with other state-of-the-art methods.

Experiment 1. The aim of this first experiment is to compare different Gaussian NB, Complement NB, and Bernoulli NB models, in order to create baseline values and see the improvements of these in the next experiments. For this purpose, the three different NB classifiers are trained with the same training data and tested using the same test data, only in terms of *precision, recall, accuracy* and *F1*-score. As the experiment aims to establish baseline values for the three different NB classifiers, no metrics related to time and resource usage are taken into account.

Experiment 2. The aim of this second experiment is to demonstrate the improvement of the previously tested algorithms when applying an encoding layer first. For this, the same 3 NB models are studied again, in a stratified 10-fold cross-validation, but in this case, 2 training sets are subtracted, where each has 40% of the total dataset (and again a 20% for the testing sets). In this split, an AE is trained with one of the training sets and then, encoder layers are subtracted from it. For the next step, the other training set is given to the encoder for the generation of the less dimensional dataset. Once the encoding is done, the 6 featured dataset is used to feed the three NB models, in order to demonstrate an improvement of these, as well as to select the most competitive one. For the complement case, the dataset is translated to get positive values. Finally, the test set is given to the encoder, and the output of it is given to the NB models to classify samples into the attack or normal class.

Experiment 3. Finally, in this third experiment, the model obtaining the best performance in the previous experiment is compared with state of the art technologies like RF and MLP, which are frequently used as a baseline [37], and with the augmented version of their architecture, i.e. when they use an encoder layer as input. In this way, it is possible to get deeper in the autoencoders role. As the aim of this experiment is to compare not only the general performance of these models, but the resource and time usage too, in this last experiment an evaluation not only measuring the *precision, recall, accuracy* and *F1*-score is carried, but also resource and time consumption are reported in terms of disk usage and training time.

6   Results

In this section, the results of the previously described experiments are presented.

Experiment 1. These results will establish the starting point and the reference which with to compare when performing the experiments with the proposed tool. As it can be seen in Table 1, the one getting better results is the Gaussian NB, which gets quite competitive results when this particular preprocess of the data is carried out, even without the application of an encoder layer.

Table 1. Different NB results

Models	Precision	Recall	Accuracy	F1
GNB	0.88 ± 0.01	0.98 ± 0	0.98 ± 0	$92.8\% \pm 0\%$
CNB	0.46 ± 0.03	0.92 ± 0	0.84 ± 0.01	$61.4\% \pm 2.7\%$
BNB	0.50 ± 0	0.88 ± 0	0.87 ± 0	$64.2\% \pm 0\%$

Experiment 2. In this experiment, the results of the NBcoded tool are shown, assuming Gaussian, Complement and Bernoulli distributions.

As it can be seen in Table 2, the three models have had an improvement when classifying over the baseline values established in the first experiment. As it can be observed, the one getting better results has been the GNB. In comparison with the first experiment, the Gaussian NB has gotten an improvement of 1.5% in the F1-score, whereas the Complement NB and the Bernoulli NB, have gotten an improvement of 28.2% and 30% in the F1-score respectively, making the BNB the one with the most improvement, although the GNB is the one with the best performance.

Table 2. Results of different NB priors combined with an encoder layer

Models	Precision	Recall	Accuracy	F1
Gaussian NBcoded	0.91 ± 0	0.98 ± 0	0.98 ± 0	$94.3\% \pm 0\%$
Complement NBcoded	0.85 ± 0.18	0.98 ± 0.01	0.96 ± 0.08	$89.6\% \pm 14.3\%$
Bernoulli NBcoded	0.92 ± 0.01	0.97 ± 0.01	0.98 ± 0	$94.2\% \pm 0\%$

Experiment 3. For this last experiment, the comparison between the Gaussian NBcoded and the other state of the art technologies, in terms of the used 4 metrics, time and disk usage.

Table 3. Comparison of the Gaussian NBcoded, the MLP and the RF

Models	Precision	Recall	Accuracy	F1
Gaussian NBcoded	0.91 ± 0	0.98 ± 0	0.98 ± 0	$94.3\% \pm 0\%$
Multi Layer Perceptron	0.92 ± 0.01	0.99 ± 0.01	0.99 ± 0	$95.2\% \pm 0.01\%$
Random Forest	0.94 ± 0.01	0.99 ± 0.01	0.99 ± 0	$96.5\% \pm 0\%$
Encoder + MLP	0.95 ± 0.02	0.95 ± 0.03	0.99 ± 0	$94.9\% \pm 0\%$
Encoder + RF	0.96 ± 0	0.94 ± 0.03	0.99 ± 0	$94.6\% \pm 0.02\%$

Firstly, as it is shown in Table 3, it is possible to see that the application of an encoder layer generates an improvement in terms of precision, but it worsens the recall and F1, in the case of MLP and RF classifiers. Secondly, the results obtained by the Gaussian NBcoded can compete in terms of precision, recall accuracy, and F1-score against the MLP and the RF. Furthermore, in terms of training time and disk usage, the Gaussian NBcoded outperforms the two others, as it can be observed in Table 4. As the results obtained for the MLP and RF with the encoder do not provide any improvement for the F1, the results in terms of disk usage and training time, which of course will be more higher since we have added a new layer in the implementation, are omitted.

Table 4. Needed time in seconds for training, and disk usage in kilobytes.

Models	Training time	Disk usage
Gaussian NBcoded	169.15 ± 23.92	15.41 ± 0
MLP	282.89 ± 182.36	45.62 ± 0.16
RF	217.97 ± 18.83	$94,047.34 \pm 541.95$

6.1 Discussion

As it can be observed in the first experiment, the GNB gets quite good results detecting attacks when this particular selection of features is performed. However, the CNB and GNB do not fit well with the data. Even the recall and accuracy can be quite good in both cases, the remaining two measures are far from being competitive. In fact, due to the class imbalance found in the UNSW-NB15, this can be explained straightforwardly; the Bernoulli and Complement NB models classify in a high rate attacks as normal behaviour. However, this scenario changes when the encoder comes into play. This might be due to firstly, the noise reduction in the data. Secondly, the encoder might model well the dependency between variables printing those in a less dimensional space. This may help the NB classifiers in their task, by the fact that the error given by the assumption of independence between variables might be reduced. This last statement could be reinforced due to the fact that using the encoder with the MLP and RF does not provide any advantage. In terms of training time, the Gaussian NBcoded seems to be the fastest one, even if this phase might be performed "outside" of the limited system, i.e. in a more suitable one, and finally transferring the trained model.

7 Conclusions and Future Works

In this work, the idea was to create a novel attack classifier that can be used in limited resourced scenarios and without affecting the performance of small devices, as for example the ones used in IoT or Industry process. The classifier is tested against the UNSW-NB15 dataset, obtaining an F1-score of 94.3%, while maintaining a low 15.41 kb disk usage and a low 169.15 s of training time, which demonstrates the viability of the proposed classifier in attack classification tasks for low resourced devices. Future works can compress the testing of the model in IoT devices, to ensure that the models do not interfere with their functionalities. Another interesting future approach might be to stack autoencoders to try to clean the data even more. This would add some training time, while keeping the disk usage, due to the fixed architecture of the encoder.

Acknowledgements. This work has been partially supported by the Spanish Centre for the Development of Industrial Technology (CDTI) under the project ÉGIDA (EXP 00122721/CER-20191012) - RED DE EXCELENCIA EN TECNOLOGIAS DE SEGURIDAD Y PRIVACIDAD and by the Basque Country Government under the ELKARTEK program, project TRUSTIND (KK-2020/00054).

References

1. Agrafiotis, I., Nurse, J.R.C., Goldsmith, M., Creese, S., Upton, D.: A taxonomy of cyber-harms: defining the impacts of cyber-attacks and understanding how they propagate. J. Cybersecur. 4, tyy006 (2018)

2. Ahmed, S., Lee, Y., Hyun, S.H., Koo, I.: Mitigating the impacts of covert cyber attacks in smart grids via reconstruction of measurement data utilizing deep denoising autoencoders. Energies **12**(16), 3091 (2019)
3. Al-Qatf, M., Lasheng, Y., Al-Habib, M., Al-Sabahi, K.: Deep learning approach combining sparse autoencoder with SVM for network intrusion detection. IEEE Access **6**, 52843–52856 (2018)
4. Al-Zewairi, M., Almajali, S., Awajan, A.: Experimental evaluation of a multi-layer feed-forward artificial neural network classifier for network intrusion detection system. In: 2017 International Conference on New Trends in Computing Sciences (ICTCS), pp. 167–172. IEEE (2017)
5. Bayes, T.: LII. An essay towards solving a problem in the doctrine of chances. By the late rev. Mr. Bayes, FRS communicated by MR. price, in a letter to John Canton, AMFR S. Philos. Trans. R. Soc. Lond. **53**(53), 370–418 (1763)
6. Belouch, M., El Hadaj, S., Idhammad, M.: Performance evaluation of intrusion detection based on machine learning using apache spark. Procedia Comput. Sci. **127**, 1–6 (2018)
7. Bourlard, H., Kamp, Y.: Auto-association by multilayer perceptrons and singular value decomposition. Biol. Cybern. **59**(4), 291–294 (1988)
8. Boyes, H., Hallaq, B., Cunningham, J., Watson, T.: The industrial internet of things (IIoT): an analysis framework. Comput. Ind. **101**, 1–12 (2018)
9. Burnaev, E., Smolyakov, D.: One-class SVM with privileged information and its application to malware detection. In: 2016 IEEE 16th International Conference on Data Mining Workshops (ICDMW), pp. 273–280. IEEE (2016)
10. Catak, F.O., Mustacoglu, A.F.: Distributed denial of service attack detection using autoencoder and deep neural networks. J. Intell. Fuzzy Syst. **37**(3), 3969–3979 (2019)
11. Chen, J., Wu, D., Zhao, Y., Sharma, N., Blumenstein, M., Yu, S.: Fooling intrusion detection systems using adversarially autoencoder. Digit. Commun. Netw. **7**(3), 453–460 (2020)
12. David, A.O., Joseph, U.J.: A novel immune inspaired concept with neural network for intrusion detection in cybersecurity (2020)
13. Dixit, P., Silakari, S.: Deep learning algorithms for cybersecurity applications: a technological and status review. Comput. Sci. Rev. **39**, 100317 (2021)
14. Fernández, A., García, S., Galar, M., Prati, R.C., Krawczyk, B., Herrera, F.: Learning from Imbalanced Data Sets, vol. 11. Springer, Cham (2018). https://doi.org/10.1007/978-3-319-98074-4
15. Jackins, V., Vimal, S., Kaliappan, M., Lee, M.Y.: Ai-based smart prediction of clinical disease using random forest classifier and naive bayes. J. Supercomput. **77**(5), 5198–5219 (2021)
16. Khoo, Y., Lu, J., Ying, L.: Solving parametric PDE problems with artificial neural networks. Eur. J. Appl. Math. **32**(3), 421–435 (2021)
17. Krishnan, S., et al.: Artificial intelligence in resource-constrained and shared environments. ACM SIGOPS Oper. Syst. Rev. **53**(1), 1–6 (2019)
18. Li, G., Liu, Q., Zhao, S., Qiao, W., Ren, X.: Automatic crack recognition for concrete bridges using a fully convolutional neural network and Naive Bayes data fusion based on a visual detection system. Meas. Sci. Technol. **31**(7), 075403 (2020)
19. Liu, M., Lang, R., Cao, Y.: Number of trees in random forest. Comput. Eng. Appl. **51**(5), 126–131 (2015)
20. Lombardi, M., Pascale, F., Santaniello, D.: Internet of things: a general overview between architectures, protocols and applications. Information **12**(2), 87 (2021)

21. Lyons, J., et al.: Predicting backbone $c\alpha$ angles and dihedrals from protein sequences by stacked sparse auto-encoder deep neural network. J. Comput. Chem. **35**(28), 2040–2046 (2014)
22. McCallum, A., Nigam, K., et al.: A comparison of event models for Naive Bayes text classification. In: AAAI 1998 Workshop on Learning for Text Categorization, vol. 752, pp. 41–48. Citeseer (1998)
23. Menon, A.P., Varghese, A., Joseph, J.P., Sajan, J., Francis, N.: Performance analysis of different classifiers for earthquake prediction: PACE (2020)
24. Mienye, I.D., Sun, Y., Wang, Z.: Improved sparse autoencoder based artificial neural network approach for prediction of heart disease. Inform. Med. Unlocked **18**, 100307 (2020)
25. Monshizadeh, M., Khatri, V., Atli, B.G., Kantola, R., Yan, Z.: Performance evaluation of a combined anomaly detection platform. IEEE Access **7**, 100964–100978 (2019)
26. Moustafa, N., Slay, J.: UNSW-NB15: a comprehensive data set for network intrusion detection systems (UNSW-NB15 network data set). In: 2015 Military Communications and Information Systems Conference (MILCIS), pp. 1–6. IEEE (2015)
27. Murphy, K.P., et al.: Naive Bayes classifiers. Univ. Br. Columbia **18**(60), 1–8 (2006)
28. Rennie, J.D., Shih, L., Teevan, J., Karger, D.R.: Tackling the poor assumptions of Naive Bayes text classifiers. In: Proceedings of the 20th International Conference on Machine Learning (ICML 2003), pp. 616–623 (2003)
29. Rukmawan, S., Aszhari, F., Rustam, Z., Pandelaki, J.: Cerebral infarction classification using the k-nearest neighbor and Naive Bayes classifier. In: Journal of Physics: Conference Series, vol. 1752, p. 012045. IOP Publishing (2021)
30. Saad, O.M., Inoue, K., Shalaby, A., Sarny, L., Sayed, M.S.: Autoencoder based features extraction for automatic classification of earthquakes and explosions. In: ICIS, pp. 445–450 (2018)
31. Sallinen, M.: Weaponized malware, physical damage, zero casualties-what informal norms are emerging in targeted state sponsored cyber-attacks?: the dynamics beyond causation: an interpretivist-constructivist analysis of the us media discourse regarding offensive cyber operations and cyber weapons between 2010 and 2020 (2021)
32. Shaukat, K., et al.: Performance comparison and current challenges of using machine learning techniques in cybersecurity. Energies **13**(10), 2509 (2020)
33. Sundararajan, K., et al.: Sleep classification from wrist-worn accelerometer data using random forests. Sci. Rep. **11**(1), 1–10 (2021)
34. Verbraeken, J., Wolting, M., Katzy, J., Kloppenburg, J., Verbelen, T., Rellermeyer, J.S.: A survey on distributed machine learning. ACM Comput. Surv. (CSUR) **53**(2), 1–33 (2020)
35. Verma, J., Bhandari, A., Singh, G.: Review of existing data sets for network intrusion detection system. Adv. Math. **9**(6), 3849–3854 (2020)
36. Wang, H., Wang, H., Wu, Z., Zhou, Y.: Using multi-factor analysis to predict urban flood depth based on Naive Bayes. Water **13**(4), 432 (2021)
37. Wankhede, S., Kshirsagar, D.: DoS attack detection using machine learning and neural network. In: 2018 Fourth International Conference on Computing Communication Control and Automation (ICCUBEA), pp. 1–5. IEEE (2018)
38. Wirkuttis, N., Klein, H.: Artificial intelligence in cybersecurity. Cyber Intell. Secur. J. **1**(1), 21–23 (2017)
39. Zhang, H., Wu, C.Q., Gao, S., Wang, Z., Xu, Y., Liu, Y.: An effective deep learning based scheme for network intrusion detection. In: 2018 24th International Conference on Pattern Recognition (ICPR), pp. 682–687. IEEE (2018)

40. Zhou, J., Chan, K., Chong, V., Krishnan, S.M.: Extraction of brain tumor from MR images using one-class support vector machine. In: 2005 IEEE Engineering in Medicine and Biology 27th Annual Conference, pp. 6411–6414. IEEE (2006)
41. Zhou, Y., Han, M., Liu, L., He, J.S., Wang, Y.: Deep learning approach for cyber-attack detection. In: IEEE INFOCOM 2018-IEEE Conference on Computer Communications Workshops (INFOCOM WKSHPS), pp. 262–267. IEEE (2018)
42. Zoghi, Z., Serpen, G.: UNSW-NB15 computer security dataset: analysis through visualization. arXiv preprint arXiv:2101.05067 (2021)
43. Zola, F., Segurola, L., Bruse, J.L., Idoate, M.G.: Temporal graph-based approach for behavioural entity classification. arXiv preprint arXiv:2105.04798 (2021)

Workshop on Machine Learning
in Software Engineering

1st Workshop on Machine Learning in Software Engineering (MLiSE 2021)

Software engineering (SE) is about methodologies and techniques for building high-quality software systems. However, modern software systems are becoming larger and more complex. Many of these systems are distributed and contain hundreds or even thousands of individual components that interact and communicate with each other through various interfaces. This not only complicates the process of software development, but also makes it more difficult and challenging to ensure their correctness and reliability.

On the other hand, recent advances and novel machine learning (ML) techniques deal with the development of methods that can automatically or semi-automatically infer models from data. Although, ML has already revolutionized numerous domains such as image recognition, translation, and healthcare, it is not yet extensively used in SE. The increasing demand and interest in SE to improve quality, reliability, cost-effectiveness, and the ability to solve complex problems has led researchers to explore the potential and applicability of ML in SE. For example, some emerging applications of ML for SE are source code generation from requirements, automatically proving the correctness of software specifications, and providing intelligent assistance to developers. Moreover, SE techniques and methodologies can be used to improve the ML process (SE for ML).The interest in ML in SE is evident from the exponential growth in the number of articles published on ML for SE in recent years.

The first international Workshop on Machine Learning in Software Engineering (MLiSE 2021) brought together the SE, ML, and data mining communities to work toward novel ML for SE methods, and their underlying assumptions and guarantees, to allow researchers, practitioners, and software engineers to identify and adopt the suitable ML methods to improve SE processes and software itself.

MLiSE 2021 was held online in conjunction with the European Conference on Machine Learning and Principles and Practice of Knowledge Discovery in Databases (ECML PKDD 2021). The 13 papers submitted to this workshop were evaluated using double-blind peer review by at least three reviewers. Based on the evaluation, a total of seven papers were accepted for presentation. Moreover, Zhi Jin from Peking University, China, accepted our invitation to give a keynote talk about "Deep learning enabled program understanding", as well as Atif Mashkoor from Johannes Kepler University who spoke about "The Relationship Between Machine Learning and Software Engineering Life Cycle Stages".

The organizers would like to thank the authors, keynote speakers, and Program Committee members for their contributions to the workshop.

November 2021

Philippe Fournier-Viger
M. Saqib Nawaz
Sebastian Ventura
Meng Sun
Ming Zhou

Organization

Organizing Committee

Philippe Fournier-Viger	Shenzhen University, China
M. Saqib Nawaz	Harbin Institute of Technology, China
Sebastian Ventura	University of Cordoba, Spain
Meng Sun	Peking University, China
Min Zhou	Huawei Noah's Ark Lab, China

Program Committee

Moulay Akhloufi	University of Moncton, Canada
Guangdong Bai	University of Queensland, Australia
Mustapha Bouakkaz	Université de Laghouat, Algeria
Tin Truong Chi	University of Dalat, Vietnam
Wensheng Gan	Jinan University, China
Osman Hasan	National University of Science and Technology, Pakistan
Tzung-Pei Hong	National University of Kaohsiung, Taiwan
Rage Uday Kiran	University of Aizu, Japan
M. Ikram Ullah Lali	University of Education, Pakistan
Pinar Karagoz	Middle East Technical University, Turkey
Bac Le	Ho Chi Minh City University of Science, Vietnam
Jerry Chun-Wei Lin	Western Norway University of Applied Sciences, Norway
Ai Liu	Hiroshima University, Japan
Wanwei Liu	NUDT, China
Jose Maria Luna	University of Cordoba, Spain
João Mendes-Moreira	University of Porto, Portugal
Engelbert Mephu Nguifo	Université Blaise Pascal, France
Farid Nouioua	University of Bordj Bou Arreridj, Algeria
José Proença	ISEP, Portugal
Wei Song	North China University of Technology, China
Bay Vo	Ho Chi Minh City University of Technology, Vietnam
Cheng-Wei Wu	National Ilan University, Taiwan
Youxi Wu	Hebei University of Technology, China
Unil Yun	Sejong University, South Korea
Xiyue Zhang	Peking University, China

A Stacked Bidirectional LSTM Model for Classifying Source Codes Built in MPLs

Md. Mostafizer Rahman[1,2](✉) 🆔, Yutaka Watanobe[1] 🆔, Rage Uday Kiran[1] 🆔, and Raihan Kabir[1] 🆔

[1] Graduate Department of Computer Science and Engineering,
The University of Aizu, Aizu-Wakamatsu, Fukushima, Japan
{d8212103,yutaka,udayrage}@u-aizu.ac.jp
[2] Department of Computer Science and Engineering,
Dhaka University of Engineering & Technology, Gazipur, Bangladesh

Abstract. Over the years, programmers have improved their programming skills and can now write code in many different languages to solve problems. A lot of new code is being generated all over the world regularly. Since a programming problem can be solved in many different languages, it is quite difficult to identify the problem from the written source code. Therefore, a classification model is needed to help programmers identify the problems built (written/developed) in Multi-Programming Languages (MPLs). This classification model can help programmers learn better programming. However, source code classification models based on deep learning are still lacking in the field of programming education and software engineering. To address this gap, we propose a stacked Bidirectional Long Short-Term Memory (Bi-LSTM) neural network-based model for classifying source codes developed in MPLs. To accomplish this research, we collect a large number of real-world source codes from the Aizu Online Judge (AOJ) system. The proposed model is trained, validated, and tested on the AOJ dataset. Various hyperparameters are fine-tuned to improve the performance of the model. Based on the experimental results, the proposed model achieves an accuracy of about 93% and an F1-score of 89.24%. Moreover, the proposed model outperforms the state-of-the-art models in terms of other evaluation matrices such as precision (90.12%) and recall (89.48%).

Keywords: Deep learning · Classification · Source code classification · Stacked Bi-LSTM · LSTM · Programming education · Software engineering

1 Introduction

Programming is one of the most creative and important skills in the development of Information and Communication Technology. Many types of researches have been dedicated to modeling and understanding the program code better [1].

© Springer Nature Switzerland AG 2021
M. Kamp et al. (Eds.): ECML PKDD 2021 Workshops, CCIS 1525, pp. 75–89, 2021.
https://doi.org/10.1007/978-3-030-93733-1_5

The outcomes of these researches are supporting core software engineering and programming education endeavors such as code classification, error detection, finding error locations, prediction, snippet suggestion, code patch generation, and developer modeling [1]. Since programmers are creating new programs to facilitate our lives, and they also can solve a problem in different programming languages. As a result, a huge amount of source code written in various languages is regularly pushed to the Cloud repositories [2]. However, due to the large size of source code repositories, manual classification of source code is quite expensive and time-consuming [2]. In a study [3], a convolutional neural network was used to classify the source codes based on the algorithms used in codes. In [3], experiments conducted using source codes were written in the C++ programming language. Rahman et al. [4] proposed a bidirectional long short-term memory (Bi-LSTM) neural network to classify the source codes written in C programming language. Similarly, an attention-based LSTM language model has been applied to classify the programming codes [5,6].

In addition to programming, multilingual applications are spreading in a variety of fields, including social media, audio, video, text, business, and medicine. Machine learning algorithms are increasingly being applied to classify multilingual data resources, such as sentiment analysis [7] and texts related to medicine [8]. In [9], the single-layer Bi-LSTM model used for sentiment classification, and three different movie review databases consisting of public opinions about movies were used in the experiment. The experimental results show that the single-layer Bi-LSTM model was better than the other models compared.

Over the past few years, programmers have been upgrading themselves in terms of skills, applications, and adaptation to new programming environments and languages. As a result, the nature of source code archives has become more heterogeneous and challenging for researchers. Nowadays, novice programmers spend a lot of time identifying problems in source code that are solved using Multi-Programming Languages (MPLs) (e.g., C, C++, Java, Python, Python3, etc.). This is a hindrance to learning programming, not only for novice programmers but also for experienced programmers.

In this research, we present a stacked Bi-LSTM model for classifying source codes developed in MPLs. Since methods, classes, variables, tokens, and keywords have both short-term and long-term dependencies, the stacked Bi-LSTM layers make the model deeper and provide a better understanding of the context of the codes. Using a large number of real-world source codes, we trained LSTM, Bi-LSTM, and stacked Bi-LSTM models. We tweak various hyperparameters and observe the performance of the models. The main contributions of the proposed research are as follows:

- The proposed model classifies the source codes developed in different programming languages
- The model helps both novice and experienced programmers identify problem's theme/title/name from the source code. By identifying the problem, they can understand the code better
- This model can be useful to detect algorithm in the source codes

- The proposed model can be deployed in the field of software engineering to recognize code in the large code archives
- The stacked Bi-LSTM neural network generate better classification results than other state-of-the-art models

The remainder of the paper is structured as follows. In Sect. 2, we present related works. In Sect. 3, we discuss our proposed approach. Section 4 presents the dataset and data preprocessing steps. Section 5 shows the experimental results. Lastly, in Sect. 6, we conclude this research.

2 Related Work

Various research methodologies have been introduced and proposed for classification in different domains. In addition to traditional classification methods, machine learning-based models have recently been effectively employed for classification tasks. In [10], three well-known classifiers such as k-nearest neighbor, relevance feedback, and Bayesian independence were combined to classify medical texts. Different combinations of these classifiers yielded better results than the single classifier. On the other hand, the uni-gram language model was used to classify text [11]. Recently, many supervised and unsupervised classification models such as artificial neural networks (ANNs), support vector machines (SVMs), and random forest (RF) trees have been applied to various classification tasks. Meanwhile, in [12], a large number of source codes were classified based on SVM, the model correctly classified the source code into topics and languages.

Despite the use of traditional classification methods, deep learning-based models have recently been used moderately in code-related classification tasks. In the last few years, techniques based on machine learning (e.g., neural networks) have shown promising results for text processing and classification, especially deep learning techniques (e.g., RNN, CNN, LSTM, Bi-LSTM). A single-layered Bi-LSTM model used for binary (0 or 1) sentiment classification, Bi-LSTM model was reported to be computationally efficient than other models [9].

In [13], an LSTM neural network-based model was proposed for automatic classification of source code archives based on programming languages. The recurrent neural network model gave more significant results than the Naive Bayes classifier. In [3–6], CNN, LSTM, and Bi-LSTM based models were used to classify source code, and these models yielded significant results compared to supervised classification methods, but all of them used source codes written on a specific programming language (such as C or C++). Since it is difficult to explain which model is better, but the proposed source code classification model using stacked Bi-LSTM neural network is different from the existing models.

3 Proposed Approach

In this research, we design an efficient deep neural network model to improve classification performance, and this model focuses on source code related classification tasks. The source code consists of various classes, methods, keywords, variables, operators, and other operations, which vary from programming language to programming language. Therefore, it is important for a neural network-based model to understand the features, characteristics, and semantics of the code. Considering this point, we proposed an efficient stacked Bi-LSTM neural network-based model for source code classification. Figure 1 shows the workflow of our proposed classification model, which consists of several steps from data collection to classification.

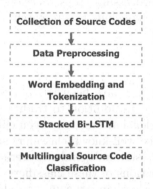

Fig. 1. Workflow of the proposed classification model

3.1 Bi-LSTM Neural Network

The concept of Bi-LSTM was first introduced in research [14], which processes data sequences in both directions (e.g., forward and backward). The Bi-LSTM model consists of two independent hidden layers connected to the same output layer, as shown in Fig. 2. The forward hidden layer (h_t^{fwrd}) receives input in ascending order (1, 2, 3,...,T), while the backward hidden layer (h_t^{bkwrd}) receives the input sequence in descending order (T,...,3, 2, 1). Finally, the results of the forward and backward hidden layers are summed to produce an output. The mathematical expressions for the forward, backward, and output layers are

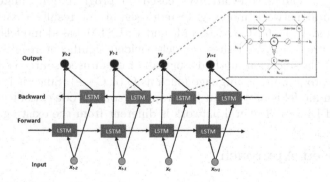

Fig. 2. An unfolded architecture of Bi-LSTM neural network [4]

shown in Eqs. (1)–(3). Over the past few years, Bi-LSTM networks have shown substantially better performance in real-world applications compared to unidirectional LSTM.

$$h_t^{fwrd} = tanh(W_{xh}^{fwrd}x_t + W_{hh}^{fwrd}h_{t-1}^{fwrd} + b_h^{fwrd}) \tag{1}$$

$$h_t^{bkwrd} = tanh(W_{xh}^{bkwrd}x_t + W_{hh}^{bkwrd}h_{t+1}^{bkwrd} + b_h^{bkwrd}) \tag{2}$$

$$y_t = W_{hy}^{fwrd}h_t^{fwrd} + W_{hy}^{bkwrd}h_t^{bkwrd} + b_y \tag{3}$$

where h_t^{fwrd}, h_t^{bkwrd}, and y_t are forward hidden layer vector, backward hidden layer vector and output layer respectively.

3.2 Stacked Bi-LSTM

One variation of the Bi-LSTM model is stacked Bi-LSTM, which uses several Bi-LSTM layers to train the neural network with better contextual information. Stacked Bi-LSTM uses the same update formula as Bi-LSTM. In this model, we have used a two-layer Bi-LSTM neural network. In stacked Bi-LSTM, the output of hidden state of each Bi-LSTM layer is given as input to the next Bi-LSTM layer. The stacked Bi-LSTM architecture improves the ability of neural networks to learn more contextual information and has been used effectively in various applications [15].

The stacked recurrent neural network had achieved state-of-art performance for a language modeling tasks [16]. Figure 3 shows the overall network architecture using the stacked Bi-LSTM that employs in this study.

4 Dataset and Preprocessing

In this study, we collected a real-world dataset from the Aizu Online Judge (AOJ) system [17,18]. AOJ is a well-known online judging system, which is used for programming practice and academic courses. It has a huge number of source code archives and logs (about 5.5 million). Currently, the AOJ has about 90,000 registered users and 2,500 interesting problem sets that are systematically categorized for easy understanding [19]. Furthermore, various educational institutions and organizations use the AOJ system to organize programming contests. Recently, IBM used the AOJ dataset for a research called "Project CodeNet" [20]. However, in this study, we collected about 35,000 source codes written in MPLs for our experiments. Each source code belong to a specific problem title (e.g., insertion sort, bubble sort, stack, 15-puzzle, graph, etc.). A summary source codes with problem's title shown in Table 1. According to Table 1, the source codes are distributed among 25 unique classes.

The statistics for each programming language in the dataset are shown in Fig. 4. In the experiment, source codes written in about 14 different languages are used. The diversity of the dataset is shown by these statistics.

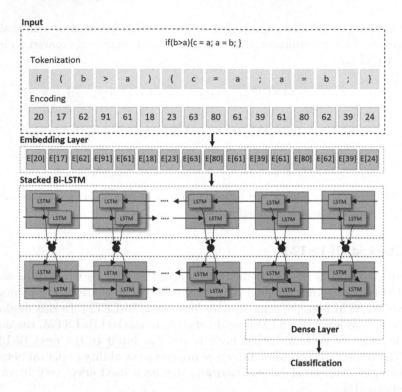

Fig. 3. Architectural overview of the proposed stacked Bi-LSTM network

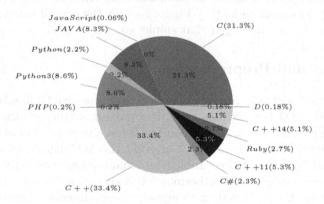

Fig. 4. Statistical overview of the programming languages based on source codes

Data preprocessing is one of the most important steps in machine learning. The irrelevant and irrational information can cause the poor results in any machine learning model. In order to get better performance from the machine learning model, data preprocessing is considered as a major step. However, when writing code, irrelevant information such as comments, line breaks, tabs, and spaces are

Table 1. A summary of source codes with problem title

Sl.	Problem title	Number of codes
1	Insertion Sort	4208
2	Greatest Common Divisor (GCD)	3054
3	Prime Numbers	2907
4	Bubble Sort	3381
5	Selection Sort	2945
6	Stable Sort	1545
7	Fibonacci Number	1750
8	Longest Common Subsequence (LCS)	1257
9	Matrix Chain Multiplication	1090
10	Graph	1410
11	Breadth First Search (BFS)	1006
12	Depth First Search (DFS)	1300
13	Minimum Spanning Tree	1077
14	Single Source Shortest Path I	957
15	Single Source Shortest Path II	615
16	Maximum Profit	3255
17	Shell Sort	1309
18	8 Puzzle	198
19	Connected Components	613
20	8 Queens Problem	309
21	15 Puzzle	146
22	Naive String Search	263
23	String Search	206
24	Pattern Search	67
25	Multiple String Matching	131

included in the code. Therefore, we have removed all unnecessary information from the source codes. The Natural Language Toolkit (NLTK) [21] is used to preprocess the data. We considered each keyword, token, variable, function, class, operator, operand, etc. in the source code as a normal word. First, we created a vocabulary list containing the unique words and assigned a natural number to each unique word. This process is called tokenization and encoding, as shown in Fig. 5.

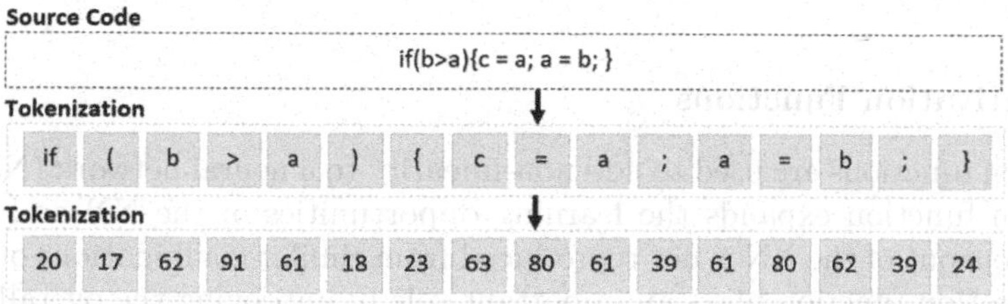

Fig. 5. Tokenization and encoding

5   Experimental Results

In this section, we present the network hyperparameters, activation functions, evaluation methods, and empirical results of the proposed stacked Bi-LSTM model and other state-of-the-art models.

5.1   Hyperparameters

Source code is a complex collection of statements such as variables, keywords, tokens, functions, classes, and mathematical operations. These statements are highly dependent on each other. Therefore, neural networks, especially deep neural networks, have the ability to learn the complex context of the source code and solve various tasks associated with the source code. Neural networks can also learn the complex relationships between the inputs and outputs of source code [22]. However, the training and performance of a neural network is highly dependent on the selection of optimal hyperparameters. We have fine-tuned the hyperparameters for our proposed model to obtain better performance. The values of the hyperparameters are shown in Table 2.

Table 2. List of the hyperparameters and settings used in the proposed model

Name of the hyperparameter	Values
Vocabulary size (v)	10000
Maximum sequence length (m)	500
Embedding Size (e)	64
Truncating type ($trunc\_type$)	post
Padding type ($padding\_type$)	post
Out of vocabulary token (oov_tok)	$<OOV>$
Optimizer	Adam
Loss function ($cross\_entropy$)	sparse_categorical_crossentropy
Activation functions	ReLU and Tanh
Epochs ($epoch$)	25, 50, 100, and 150
Bi-LSTM nodes	128
Training portion of the dataset	80%
Validation portion of the dataset	15%
Testing portion of the dataset	5%

5.2   Activation Functions

Activation functions are used to add non-linearity to a neural network (NN). The activation function expands the learning opportunities of the NN and ensures that the output of the NN is not reproduced from similar combinations of inputs. The activation function plays an important role in improving the overall performance of the network [23]. In the absence of activation functions, each layer of the NN behaves like a single layer perceptron or simple linear regression model; the activation functions of the NN include Linear, Sigmoid, Tanh, Rectified linear unit (ReLU), Leaky ReLU, and so on [23]. In this paper, we used tanh and ReLU activation functions separately and the performance of both functions is investigated.

Hyperbolic Tangent or Tanh: The Tanh function takes any real number from NN as input and produces an output in the range of -1 to 1 [23]. The Tanh function outputs 1 for large values and -1 for small values according to the following Eq. (4).

$$\sigma(x) = \frac{1 - e^{-2x}}{1 + e^{-2x}} \tag{4}$$

ReLU: In Deep Neural Networks (DNNs), the ReLU activation layer has a positive impact on the performance of the network. The ReLU activation function is used to avoid the gradient vanishing problem in DNNs. If the value of the input is less than 0, ReLU generates 0, and if it is greater than 0, it generates the same value [23]. In this way, ReLU speeds up the network compared to other activation functions. The following Eq. (5) is used in the ReLU layer.

$$\sigma(x) = max(0, x) \tag{5}$$

Softmax: The Softmax function is used for multi-class classification. The Softmax function takes a vector of real values from the NN and converts it into a vector of probabilities that sum to 1. This is used as the output layer for multi-class classification of the DNN model [23]. To calculate the probability, the following Softmax formula (6) is used.

$$\sigma(\vec{X})_i = \frac{e^{X_i}}{\sum_{j=1}^{Z} e^{X_j}} \tag{6}$$

where X is the input vector received from the NN, X_i is the elements of the input vector X, e^{X_i} is the exponential function applied to each element of X, and the $\sum_{j=1}^{Z} e^{X_j}$ term ensures that the probability of each element is in the range of 0 to 1, and the sum of the probabilities of all elements is 1, and Z is the number of class.

5.3   Evaluation Methods

The performance of a classification model using neural network depends on the elements of the confusion matrix. The confusion matrix has four elements: precision, recall, F1-score, and accuracy. Each element is evaluated based on four terms: true positive (T_P), false positive (F_P), true negative (T_N), and false negative (F_N). For example, c is the true class for a given problem p, and $\bar{c}$ is the opposite of the true class of c. T_P classifies problems in class c as class c, $(c \longrightarrow c)$, while F_P classifies problems in class $\bar{c}$ as incorrect class c, $(\bar{c} \longrightarrow c)$. On the other hand, T_N classifies problems in class $\bar{c}$ as class $\bar{c}$, $(\bar{c} \longrightarrow \bar{c})$, and F_N classifies problems in class c as incorrect class $\bar{c}$, $(c \longrightarrow \bar{c})$.

Precision (P)**:** It is used to measure the correctness of a classification model. It indicates how many of the positive classifications are correct.

$$Precision(P) = \frac{T_P}{T_P + F_P} \tag{7}$$

Recall (R)**:** This is used to measure the completeness of a classification model and is calculated as the ratio of T_P to the total number of actual classes $(T_P + F_N)$.

$$Recall(R) = \frac{T_P}{T_P + F_N} \tag{8}$$

F1-score: It is calculated using the scores of P and R and is the harmonic mean of P and R. The F1-score is useful when the distribution of F_P and F_N is uneven.

$$F1 - score = \frac{2 * (P * R)}{P + R} \tag{9}$$

Accuracy: It is an important metric to measure the performance of a model. The accuracy of a model is evaluated by the ratio of the total number of correct predictions to the total number of predictions.

$$Accuracy = \frac{T_P + T_N}{T_P + T_N + F_P + F_N} \tag{10}$$

5.4 Results

In this section, we show the experimental results generated based on different hyperparameter settings. In addition to the proposed stacked Bi-LSTM model, several state-of-the-art models such as LSMT and Bi-LSTM were trained and validated to compare the performance of the proposed model.

Figures 6, 7, and 8 show the accuracy and loss per epoch for the LSTM, Bi-LSTM, and stacked Bi-LSTM model during training and validation, respectively. We trained the models with different numbers of epochs and activation functions such as ReLU and tanh, and most of the models performed best when 150 epochs and ReLU activation function were used.

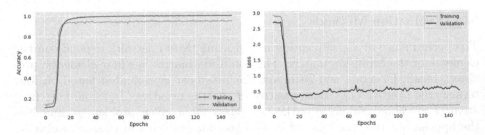

Fig. 6. Accuracy and loss per epoch during training and validation for the LSTM model

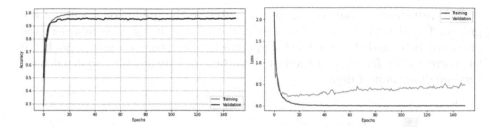

Fig. 7. Accuracy and loss per epoch during training and validation for the Bi-LSTM model

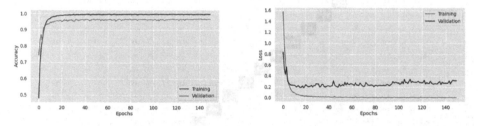

Fig. 8. Accuracy and loss per epoch during training and validation for the stacked Bi-LSTM model

The following observations can be drawn from these above figures: (i) the proposed model obtained higher training and validation accuracy than the LSTM and Bi-LSTM models and (ii) the proposed model has less loss than other two comparative models.

Considering these evaluation metrics, i.e., precision, recall, and F1 score, we compared the classification results with other state-of-the-art models. The results show that the proposed stacked Bi-LSTM model significantly outperforms the other models. Table 3 shows the average precision, recall, and F1 scores of all the models considering the epoch number 150 and the activation function ReLU. It can be seen that the proposed stacked Bi-LSTM model outperforms the other state-of-the-art models in all three evaluation metrics.

Table 3. Average precision, recall, and F1-score of all models

Model	Precision	Recall	F1-score
LSTM	0.8248	0.8380	0.8116
Bi-LSTM	0.8456	0.8508	0.8348
Stacked Bi-LSTM	0.9012	0.8948	0.8924

Figure 9 shows a confusion matrix to visualize the prediction results of the proposed model. In the confusion matrix, the $x-$axis and $y-$axis represent the predicted label and the true label, respectively. The proposed model predicted the correct class for most of the test data, but misclassification occurred for a very small amount of data.

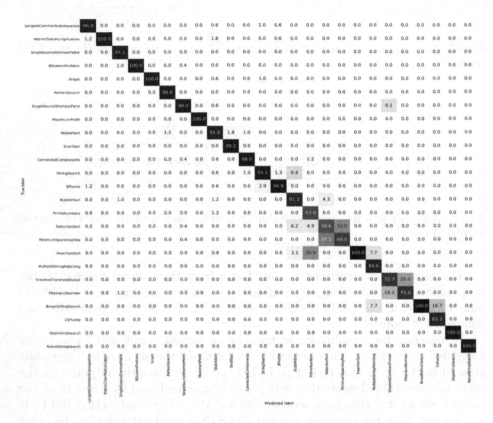

Fig. 9. Confusion matrix for all classes using the stacked Bi-LSTM model

The accuracy of all the models was also calculated considering the different number of epochs and activation functions as shown in Tables 4 and 5, respectively. The proposed stacked Bi-LSTM model achieved better accuracy with both activation functions at different epochs.

Table 4. Average accuracy of the models using ReLU activation function

Epochs	Models		
	LSTM	Bi-LSTM	Stacked Bi-LSTM
25	0.89	0.89	0.91
50	0.90	0.90	0.91
100	0.88	0.92	0.93
150	0.91	0.91	0.93

Table 5. Average accuracy of the models using Tanh activation function

Epochs	Models		
	LSTM	Bi-LSTM	Stacked Bi-LSTM
25	0.88	0.87	0.92
50	0.89	0.91	0.92
100	0.89	0.91	0.93
150	0.90	0.90	0.93

In summary, our proposed stacked Bi-LSTM model produced satisfactory results compared to other state-of-the-art models. The model is applied to classify multilingual real-world source codes using various hyperparameters. The proposed model outperforms the other models in each evaluation matrix such as precision, recall, F1 score, and accuracy. These results indicate that the proposed model has the potential to learn complex contexts of source codes of different programming languages. All the experimental suggests that the proposed model can be applied to other purposes of complex task classification.

6   Conclusion

In this research, we presented a deep learning classification model based on a stacked Bi-LSTM neural network. The architecture of the stacked Bi-LSTM neural network enables learning more complex features from the source codes for the classification task. In our experiments, we collected 35,000 real-world source codes written in different languages and classified them into about 25 classes. The proposed model and other state-of-the-art models were trained on these codes for the source code classification task. In the proposed model, the hyperparameters of the network were fine-tuned to achieve optimal results. The proposed model showed relatively good performance in terms of various evaluation metrics. The average precision, recall, F1-score, and accuracy of the proposed model are 0.9012, 0.8948, 0.8924, and 0.93, respectively, which are better than other state-of-the-art models such as LSTM and Bi-LSTM. Moreover, the performance of the proposed model was evaluated for each class, and significant classification results were achieved.

For the future work, we plan to consider different stack layers (e.g., 3-layer Bi-LSTM, 4-layer Bi-LSTM, etc.) and hyperparameters for this model. We also plan to perform extensive experiments on a large number of MPLs-based source codes to evaluate the performance of the model.

Acknowledgement. This research was supported by the Japan Society for the Promotion of Science (JSPS) under KAKENHI (Grant Number 19K12252).

Conflict of Interest. The authors declare that they have no conflict of interests.

References

1. Dam, H.K., Tran, T., Pham, T.: A deep language model for software code, ArXiv abs/1608.02715 (2016)
2. Gilda, S.: Source code classification using neural networks. In: 2017 14th International Joint Conference on Computer Science and Software Engineering (JCSSE), pp. 1–6 (2017)
3. Ohashi, H., Watanobe, Y.: Convolutional neural network for classification of source codes. In: 2019 IEEE 13th International Symposium on Embedded Multicore/Many-Core Systems-on-Chip (MCSoC), pp. 194–200 (2019)
4. Rahman, M.M., Watanobe, Y., Nakamura, K.: A bidirectional LSTM language model for code evaluation and repair. Symmetry **13**(2), 247 (2021)
5. Rahman, M.M., Watanobe, Y., Nakamura, K.: Source code assessment and classification based on estimated error probability using attentive LSTM language model and its application in programming education. Appl. Sci. **10**(8), 2973 (2020)
6. Rahman, M.M., Watanobe, Y., Nakamura, K.: A neural network based intelligent support model for program code completion. Sci. Program. **2020**, 1–18 (2020)
7. Attia, M., Samih, Y., Elkahky, A., Kallmeyer, L.: Multilingual multi-class sentiment classification using convolutional neural networks. In: The Proceedings of the Eleventh International Conference on Language Resources and Evaluation (LREC 2018), Miyazaki, Japan (2018)
8. Mutuvi, S., Boros, E., Doucet, A., Jatowt, A., Lejeune, G., Odeo, M.: Multilingual epidemiological text classification: a comparative study. In: The Proceedings of the 28th International Conference on Computational Linguistics, Barcelona, Spain (2020)
9. Hameed, Z., Garcia-Zapirain, B.: Sentiment classification using a single-layered BiLSTM model. IEEE Access **8**, 73992–74001 (2020)
10. Larkey, L. S., Croft, W. B.: Combining classifiers in text categorization. In: Proceedings of the 19th Annual International ACM SIGIR Conference on Research and Development in Information Retrieval, ser. SIGIR 1996, Zurich, Switzerland, pp. 289–297. ACM (1996)
11. Lewis, D.D., Gale, W.A.: A sequential algorithm for training text classifiers. In: Croft, B.W., van Rijsbergen, C.J. (eds.) Proceedings of the 17th Annual International ACM SIGIR Conference on Research and Development in Information Retrieval, ser. SIGIR 1994, Dublin, Ireland, pp. 3–12. Springer, New York (1994). https://doi.org/10.1007/978-1-4471-2099-5_1
12. Ugurel, S., Krovetz, R., Giles, C. L.: What's the code? Automatic classification of source code archives. In: Proceedings of the Eighth ACM SIGKDD International Conference on Knowledge Discovery and Data Mining, ser. KDD 2002, Edmonton, Alberta, Canada, pp. 632–638. ACM (2002)

13. Reyes, J., Ramírez, D., Paciello, J.: Automatic classification of source code archives by programming language: a deep learning approach. In: 2016 International Conference on Computational Science and Computational Intelligence (CSCI), pp. 514–519 (2016)
14. Schuster, M., Paliwal, K.K.: Bidirectional recurrent neural networks. IEEE Trans. Signal Process. **45**(11), 2673–2681 (1997)
15. Cui, Z., Ke, R., Pu, Z., Wang, Y.: Stacked bidirectional and unidirectional LSTM recurrent neural network for forecasting network-wide traffic state with missing values. arXiv:2005.11627 (2020)
16. Hermans, M., Schrauwen, B.: Training and analyzing deep recurrent neural networks. In: Proceedings of the 26th International Conference on Neural Information Processing Systems (NIPS 2013), vol. 1, pp. 190–198. Curran Associates Inc., Red Hook, NY, USA (2013)
17. Watanobe, Y.: Aizu online judge [Online] (2018). https://onlinejudge.u-aizu.ac
18. Aizu online judge: Developers site (API) [Online]. http://developers.u-aizu.ac.jp/index
19. Intisar, C. M., Watanobe, Y., Poudel, M., Bhalla, S.: Classification of programming problems based on topic modeling. In Proceedings of the 2019 7th International Conference on Information and Education Technology (ICIET 2019). Association for Computing Machinery, New York, NY, USA, pp. 275–283 (2019)
20. International Business Machines (IBM): Project CodeNet (2021). https://github.com/IBM/Project_CodeNet
21. Loper, E., Bird, S.: NLTK: the natural language toolkit. In: Proceedings of ACL Workshop Effective Tools Methodologies Teaching Natural Languages Processing and Computational Linguistics, Philadelphia, PA, USA, pp. 1–8 (2002)
22. Goodfellow, I., Bengio, Y., Courville, A.: Deep Learning. MIT Press, Cambridge (2016)
23. Szandała, T.: Review and comparison of commonly used activation functions for deep neural networks. In: Bhoi, A., Mallick, P., Liu, C.M., Balas, V. (eds.) Bio-inspired Neurocomputing. Studies in Computational Intelligence, vol. 903. Springer, Singapore (2021). https://doi.org/10.1007/978-981-15-5495-7_11

Metamorphic Malware Behavior Analysis Using Sequential Pattern Mining

M. Saqib Nawaz[1](ID), Philippe Fournier-Viger[1(✉)](ID), M. Zohaib Nawaz[2](ID), Guoting Chen[3](ID), and Youxi Wu[4](ID)

[1] School of Humanities and Social Sciences, Harbin Institute of Technology (Shenzhen), Shenzhen, China
{msaqibnawaz,philfv}@hit.edu.cn
[2] Department of Computer Science and IT, University of Sargodha, Sargodha, Pakistan
zohaib.nawaz@uos.edu.pk
[3] School of Science, Harbin Institute of Technology (Shenzhen), Shenzhen, China
chenguoting@hit.edu.cn
[4] Department of Computer Science and Engineering, Hebei University of Technology, Tianjin, China

Abstract. Application Programming Interface (API) calls in windows operating system (OS) is an attractive feature for malware analysis and detection as they can properly reflect the actions of portable executable (PE) files. In this paper, we provide an approach based on sequential pattern mining (SPM) for the analysis of malware behavior during executions. A dataset that contains sequences of API calls made by different malware on Windows OS is first abstracted into a suitable format (sequences of integers). SPM algorithms are then used on the corpus to find frequent API calls and their patterns. Moreover, sequential rules between API calls patterns as well as maximal and closed frequent API calls are discovered. Obtained preliminary results suggest that discovered frequent patterns of API calls and sequential rules between them can be used in the development of malware detection and classification techniques.

Keywords: Malware analysis · Sequential pattern mining · API calls · Frequent patterns · Sequential rules

1 Introduction

The name malware (malicious software) is used collectively for a number of software that is designed primarily to access restricted data, block data to get ransom and damage or destruct computers and mobile devices without owners' knowledge or permission [7,32]. Since their emergence in the late 1980s, malware pose a serious threat to computing systems and networks. Although computing devises have become more secure with each new Operating System (OS) update, attackers can still bypass these security components by using different methods. Due to COVID-19, cybercrime is up 600%, and in the last ten years, there has

© Springer Nature Switzerland AG 2021
M. Kamp et al. (Eds.): ECML PKDD 2021 Workshops, CCIS 1525, pp. 90–103, 2021.
https://doi.org/10.1007/978-3-030-93733-1_6

been an 87% increase in malware infections. Moreover, malware attacks in 2019 have costed the average US company an average of $2.4 million per year[1].

As malware can cause enormous loss and adverse effects, its analysis and detection is an important research topic in cybersecurity. Anti-malware software [16] that provides protection against malware mainly use signature-based method for malware detection. During the scanning process, these tools search for unique signatures (short and unique strings set) that are already extracted from known malicious files. An executable file is identified as a malicious code if its signature matches with the list of available signatures. This approach is fast in identifying known malware. However, extracting signature is a tedious and time consuming activity and requires funds and expertise. Moreover, signature-based method looks for already known malicious patterns, thus it is unreliable and ineffective against the new malicious codes [7]. Nowadays, new malware samples are created at a high speed. For example, recent McAfee report[2] says that approximately 77 M new malicious activities were detected in Q1 2021.

To overcome aforementioned drawbacks, data mining and machine learning techniques are now used for the analysis of malware and in the development of efficient malware classification and detection techniques. In this study, we focus on Windows based-malware as this OS is by far the most popular desktop OS with a market share of about 72.98%[3]. On Windows OS, a malware needs to use some of the OS's services. The entire set of requests made by malware to get these services through application programming interface (API) calls creates malicious behaviour. We believe that sequential pattern mining (SPM) [13] is well suited to analyse sequences of API calls made by malware. SPM, a special case of structured data mining, is used to discover meaningful and hidden knowledge in large sequential datasets. SPM has been used extensively in the past in various applications such as bioinformatics [1,20], market basket analysis [23], text analysis [19,25], energy reduction in smarthomes [29], webpage click-stream analysis [10] and proof sequences [21,22].

In this study, the focus is on metamorphic malware. An SPM-based approach is presented for the analysis of API calls sequences made by malware that were run in an isolated secured environment. The basic idea of the approach is to first convert the API calls sequences into a corpus that is suitable for learning, where each API call is converted into an integer. SPM techniques are then used on the corpus to find frequent API calls and their patterns. Moreover, sequential rules between API calls patterns as well as maximal and closed frequent API calls are discovered. We believe that obtained results can be used in the development of malware detection and classification techniques, where frequent patterns of API calls and the sequential rules between them can be used for the classification and detection process.

The remainder of this paper is organized as follows. Section 2 describes the related work on using data mining and machine learning in the analysis of

---

[1] http://www.legaljobs.io/blog/malware-statistics.

[2] http://mcafee.com/enterprise/en-us/lp/threats-reports/apr-2021.html.

[3] http://gs.statcounter.com/os-market-share/desktop/worldwide.

malware API calls. The details of the dataset that we used in this work is provided in Sect. 3, followed by the proposed SPM-based approach that is used for the analysis of API calls in Sect. 4. Section 5 presents and discusses the obtained results. Finally, Sect. 6 concludes the paper with some future research directions.

2   Related Work

API was used first as a feature of program in [17] where a method was developed for anomaly intrusion detection based on sequences of system calls. API calls were also used in [33] for the development of an intelligence malware detection system (IMDS). IMDS performance was much better than signature-based and other data mining-based methods in terms of detection rate and classification accuracy. A dynamic malware detection system was developed in [3] that was also based on API calls of malware. The work [31] used the call grams and odds ratio selection to discover the distinct API sequences. These sequences were then used as inputs to the classifiers to categorize malware and benign samples. API call sequences were transformed into byte-based sequential data in [26] that was used later in the detection process. The malware detection approach in [30] used text mining and topic modeling for feature extraction and selection based on the API call sequences.

To capture the common API sequence among different malware types, the longest common sequence (LCS) algorithm was used in [18] and multiple sequence alignment (MSA) algorithms were used in [6] to find common API calls sequences and their classification into different malware families. Frequent API names and their arguments were used in [27] to represent the behaviour of a malware. The Apriori algorithm [2] was used to mine frequent itemsets composed of API names and/or API arguments. However, the Apriori algorithm does not take into account the sequential ordering of events, such as API calls. Thus, it fails to discover important patterns and also ignore the sequential relationship between events. Moreover, the malware detection method in [24] used one SPM algorithm to discover frequent API call patterns of malware. Three classifiers were then used on the patterns for the classification of malware samples. Authors claim that they discovered discriminative frequent API call patterns. However, the algorithm that they used was CM-SPAM which is generally used to find common sequential patterns, not discriminative patterns. Moreover, the dataset is not discussed in detail and no link is provided to download the dataset.

Compared to previous works, we used a dataset for API calls of metamorphic malware. Moreover, not one but various SPM algorithms are used on the dataset to discover not only frequent API calls and their patterns, but also the sequential rules between discovered patterns as well as closed and maximal sequential patterns of API calls. Using more than one SPM algorithm also allowed us to check their effectiveness on the dataset of API calls sequence of malware that we discuss in the next section.

3   Dataset

The benchmark dataset [4,5] contains Windows API calls of various metamorphic malware such as WannaCry and Zeus. An application running on Windows uses APIs to utilize a function that the OS provides. The use of an OS functions is called an API call. During execution, an application can makes many API calls. For example, to create a file, an application calls the *CreateFileA* API. Similarly, the API call *DeviceIoControl* is used by an application to perform direct input and output operations on, or retrieve information about, a specified device driver. Thus, API calls are generally used in dynamic malware analysis. A metamorphic malware can change its structure continuously by making changes in their source code and signature patterns with each iteration.

In the dataset [4,5], approximately 20,000 malware were collected from GitHub and their MD5 (Message-Digest algorithm 5) hash values were obtained. Cuckoo Sandbox Environment was then used to check the behavior of each malware separately in an isolated environment. The final data in the dataset contains all Windows API call requests made by the malware on Windows 7 OS. The API calls sequences are further filtered and those rows in the sequences were discarded that did not contain at least 10 different API calls. The hash values of malware were searched with the VirusTotal service and the analysis results from the VirusTotal service was stored in a database. Each malware's families was identified by using each analysis result that was obtained with VirusTotal.

The final dataset contains 8 different leading malware families, which are: *Trojan, Backdoor, Downloader, Worms, Spyware, Adware, Dropper* and *Virus*. Table 1 shows the number of malware belonging to malware families in the whole dataset.

Table 1. Malware distribution according to their families

Malware family	Samples	Considered
Spyware	832	21
Downloader	1001	91
Trojan	1001	585
Worms	1001	92
Adware	379	9
Dropper	891	19
Virus	1001	36
Backdoor	1001	147
Total	7101	1000

The whole dataset contains 7,101 sequences in total. In this work, we considered the first 1000 sequences from the dataset. Considered sequences belonged to different malware types and the detail of the sequences belonging to which malware type is provided in Table 1. In the first 1000 sequences, approximately 60% of sequences belonged to the *Trojan* family.

4   Analyzing API Calls with SPM

The structure of the SPM-based approach for the analysis of API calls made by different malware is shown in Fig. 1. It consists of two main parts:

1. *Converting different malware API calls dataset into a suitable format for SPM*: The sequences of API calls made by malware are transformed in a suitable abstraction, so that no meaningful information from the sequences are left out. For this, we use the *"API calls sequences to integers"* abstraction, where each API call type is converted into a distinct positive integer. Such abstraction allows wide diversity and makes the approach more general in nature.
2. *Learning through SPM*: SPM algorithms are used on the corpus to discover the common API calls and their frequent sequences, sequential relationships of frequent API calls and their patterns with each other and frequent closed and maximal frequent API calls.

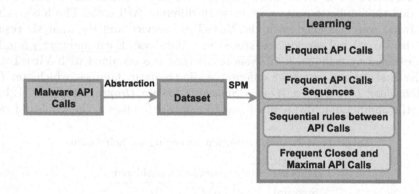

Fig. 1. Proposed SPM-based approach

In the following we present some concepts related to sequences in the context of this work for better understanding.

Let $AC = \{ac_1, ac_2, ..., ac_m\}$ represent the set of API calls. An *API calls set ACS* is a set of API calls such that $ACS \subseteq AC$. $|ACS|$ denotes the set cardinality. An *ACS* has a length k (called k-*ACS*) if it contains k API calls, i.e., $|ACS| = k$. For example, consider the set of API calls $PS = \{LdrLoadDll, NtOpenKey, CopyFileA, FindResourceA, GetFileSize, Exception\}$. The following set $\{LdrLoadDll, NtOpenKey, Exception\}$ is an API calls set that contains three API calls. An order relation on API calls is defined by assuming that there exists a total order on API calls $\prec$ such as the lexicographical order.

An API calls sequence is a list of API calls sets $S = \langle ACS_1, ACS_2, ..., ACS_n \rangle$, such that $ACS_i \subseteq ACS$ $(1 \leq i \leq n)$. An *API calls corpus ACC* is a list of API calls sequences $ACC = \langle S_1, S_2, ..., S_n \rangle$, where each sequence has an identifier (ID). For example, Table 2 shows an *ACC* that has four API calls sequences with IDs 1, 2, 3 and 4.

Table 2. A sample of an API calls corpus

ID	API calls sequence
1	$\langle\{LdrLoadDll,\ RegOpenKeyExA,\ NtOpenKey,\ NtQueryValueKey\}\rangle$
2	$\langle\{NtClose,\ DeviceIoControl,\ NtClose,\ NtClose,\ NtReadFile,\ WSAStartup\}\rangle$
3	$\langle\{NtCreateFile,\ GetFileSize,\ NtClose,\ NtReadFile,\ DrawTextExA,$ $NtDelayExecution,\ NtClose,\ GetKeyState\}\rangle$
4	$\langle\{FindWindowExW,\ FindFirstFileExA,\ OpenKey,\ NtClose,\ NtClose,$ $NtCreateFile,\ LdrGetProcedureAddress,\ GetAsyncKeyState,\ GetKeyState,$ $DeviceIoControl,\ NtClose,\ NtDelayExecution\}\rangle$

The final step is to convert the API calls into sequences of integers to bring the dataset in a more suitable format for SPM techniques. In the final corpus, each line represents an API calls sequence for a malware. Each API call in the sequence is replaced by a positive integer. For example, the API call *NtClose* is replaced with 6. Moreover, API calls are separated with a single space followed by a negative integer -1. Negative integer -2 appears at the end of each line that shows the end of a sequence. The four API calls sequences in Table 2 are converted into the integer sequences shown in Table 3.

Table 3. Conversion of API calls sequences into integer sequences

ID	API call sequence
1	1 -1 3 -1 4 -1 5 -1 -2
2	6 -1 12 -1 6 -1 6 -1 32 -1 23 -1 -2
3	7 -1 11 -1 6 -1 32 -1 15 -1 18 -1 6 -1 22 -1 -2
4	19 -1 22 -1 14 -1 6 -1 6 -1 7 -1 19 -1 31 -1 22 -1 12 -1 6 -1 18 -1 -2

An API calls sequence $S_\alpha = \langle \alpha_1, \alpha_2, ..., \alpha_n \rangle$ is present or contained in another API calls sequence $S_\beta = \langle \beta_1, \beta_1, ..., \beta_m \rangle$ iff there exist integers $1 \le i_1 < i_2 < ... <$ $i_n \le m$, such that $\alpha_1 \subseteq \beta_{i1}, \alpha_2 \subseteq \beta_{i2}, ..., \alpha_n \subseteq \beta_{im}$ (denoted as $S_\alpha \sqsubseteq S_\beta$). If S_α is present in S_β, then S_α is a *subsequence* of S_β. In SPM, various measures are used to investigate the importance and interestingness of a subsequence. The *support* measure is used by most SPM techniques. The *support* of S_α in *ACC* is the total number of sequences (S) that contain S_α, and is represented by $sup(S_\alpha)$:

$$sup(S_\alpha) = |\{S|S_\alpha \sqsubseteq S \land S \in ACC\}|$$

SPM is an enumeration problem that aims to find all the *frequent subsequences* in a sequential dataset. S is a *frequent sequence* (also called *sequential pattern*) iff $sup(S) \geq minsup$, where $minsup$ (minimum support) is the threshold being determined by the user. A sequence containing n items (API calls in this work) in a corpus can have up to $2^n - 1$ distinct subsequences. This makes the naive approach to calculate the support of all possible subsequences infeasible for most corpora. Several efficient algorithms have been developed in recent years that do not explore all the search space for all possible subsequences.

All SPM algorithms investigate the patterns search space with two operations: *s-extensions* and *i-extensions*. A sequence $S_\alpha = \langle \alpha_1, \alpha_2, ..., \alpha_n \rangle$ is a *prefix* of another sequence $S_\beta = \langle \beta_1, \beta_1, ..., \beta_m \rangle$, if $n < m$, $\alpha_1 = \beta_1$, $\alpha_2 = \beta_2$, ..., $\alpha_{n-1} = \beta_{n-1}$, where α_n is equal to the first $|\alpha_n|$ items of β_n according to the $\prec$ order. Note that SPM algorithms follow a specific order $\prec$ so that the same potential patterns are not considered twice and the choice of the order $\prec$ does not affect the final result produced by SPM algorithms. A sequence S_β is an *s-extension* of a sequence S_α for an item x if $S_\beta = \langle \alpha_1, \alpha_2, ..., \alpha_n, \{x\} \rangle$. Similarly, for an item x, a sequence S_γ is an *i-extension* of S_α if $S_\gamma = \langle \alpha_1, \alpha_2, ..., \alpha_n \cup \{x\} \rangle$. SPM algorithms either employ breadth-first search or depth-first search algorithms. In the following, a brief description of state-of-the-art SPM algorithms is presented.

In frequent itemset mining (FIM), the first and most famous algorithm is the Apriori algorithm [2]. It can find frequent itemsets in large databases. It proceeds by discovering common items that can be extended to larger itemsets that appear sufficiently often. Itemsets (ACS in this work) extracted by Apriori can also be used to identify association rules (relationships) between items. Over the years, several fast and memory efficient FIM algorithms have been proposed.

The TKS (Top-k Sequential) algorithm finds the top-k sequential patterns in a corpus, where k is set by the user and it represents the number of sequential patterns to be discovered by the algorithm. TKS employs the basic candidate generation procedure of SPAM and vertical database representation. With vertical representation, support for patterns can be calculated without performing costly database scans. This makes vertical algorithms to perform better on dense or long sequences. TKS also uses several strategies for search space pruning and depends on the PMAP (Precedence Map) data structure to avoid costly operations of bit vector intersection. Another SPM algorithm is the CM-SPAM algorithm that examines the whole search space to discover frequent sequential patterns in the corpus. The CMAP (Co-occurrence MAP) data structure is used in CM-SPAM to store co-occurrence of item information. A generic pruning mechanism that is based on CMAP is used for pruning the search space with vertical database representation, to efficiently discover sequential patterns. More detail on TKS and CM-SPAM can be found in [9] and [8] respectively.

However, one main drawback of aforementioned algorithms is that they may find too many sequential patterns for users. The complexity and generated patterns can be reduced by mining closed and maximal sequential patterns. A sequential pattern s_a is said to be *closed* if there is no other sequential pattern s_b, such that s_b is a superpattern of s_a, $s_a \sqsubseteq s_b$, and their supports are equal. A sequential pattern s_a is said to be *maximal* if there is no other sequential pattern s_b, such that s_b is a superpattern of s_a, $s_a \sqsubseteq s_b$. The problem of mining closed (maximal) sequential patterns is to discover the set of closed (maximal) sequential patterns. CloFAST (Closed FAST sequence mining algorithm based on sparse id-lists) [15] and VMSP (Vertical mining of Maximal Sequential Patterns) [14] are the two algorithms used for finding closed and maximal sequential patterns, respectively, in large databases.

Sequential patterns that appear frequently in a corpus with low confidence are worthless for decision making or prediction. Sequential rules discover patterns by considering not only their support but also their confidence. A sequential rule $X \rightarrow Y$ is a relationship between two $ACSs$ $X, Y \subseteq AC$, such that $X \cap Y = \emptyset$ and $X, Y \neq \emptyset$. The rule $r : X \rightarrow Y$ means that if items of X occur in a sequence, items of Y will occur afterward in the same sequence. X is contained in S_α (written as $X \sqsubseteq S_\alpha$) iff $X \subseteq \bigcup_{i=1}^{n} \alpha_i$. A rule $r : X \rightarrow Y$ is contained in S_α ($r \sqsubseteq S_\alpha$) iff there exists an integer k such that $1 \le k < n$, $X \subseteq \bigcup_{i=1}^{k} \alpha_i$ and $Y \subseteq \bigcup_{i=k+1}^{n} \alpha_i$. The confidence of r in ACC is defined as:

$$conf_{ACC}(r) = \frac{|\{S | r \sqsubseteq S \wedge S \in ACC\}|}{|\{S | X \sqsubseteq S \wedge S \in ACC\}|}$$

The support of r in ACC is defined as:

$$sup_{ACC}(r) = \frac{|\{S | r \sqsubseteq S \wedge S \in ACC\}|}{|ACC|}$$

A rule r is a *frequent sequential rule* iff $sup_{ACC}(r) \ge minsup$ and r is a *valid sequential rule* iff it is frequent and $conf_{ACC}(r) \ge minconf$, where the thresholds $minsup, minconf \in [0, 1]$ are set by the user. Mining sequential rules in a corpus deals with finding all the valid sequential rules. For this, the ERMiner (Equivalence class based sequential Rule Miner) algorithm [11] is used. It relies on a vertical database representation and the search space of rules is explored using the equivalence classes of rules with the same antecedent and consequent. It employs two operations (left and right merges) to explore the search space of frequent sequential rules, where the search space is pruned with the Sparse Count Matrix (SCM) technique, which makes ERMiner more efficient than other sequential rule finding algorithms.

5   Results and Discussion

All the following experiments are performed on an HP laptop with a fifth generation Core i5 processor and 4 GB RAM. SPMF data mining library, developed in JAVA, is used to analyze the API calls corpus. It is an open-source and cross-platform framework that is specialized in pattern mining tasks. SPMF offers implementations for more than 180 data mining algorithms. More detail on SPMF can be found in [12].

We first used SPMF to convert the API calls sequences into integer sequences that is suitable for SPM algorithms. The first 1000 sequences contain 254 distinct API calls in total and on average, each sequence contains approximately

11,502 API calls. Results obtained by applying SPM algorithms on the corpus are discussed next. Interested readers can find the converted dataset used in this work at: github.com/saqibdola/MBAwSPM.

The Apriori algorithm was first applied on the corpus to find the frequently occurring API calls. Apriori takes a corpus and a *minsup* threshold as input and outputs the frequent API calls. The sets extracted by Apriori are listed in Table 4. For high *minsup* values, Apriori generated less frequent patterns. By decreasing *minsup* to 10%, Apriori generated 274 patterns. The top five freuquent API calls in 1000 sequences were *GetAsyncKeyState*, *GetKeyState*, *DeviceIoControl*, *NtClose* and *NtDelayExecution* with 2,343,660, 1,103,492, 800,088, 680,206 and 573,625 occurrences, respectively.

Table 4. Frequent API calls extracted by Apriori

Frequent API calls count	Min. Sup
117	100%
118	90%
120	80%
123	70%
127	60%
135	50%
141	40%
155	30%
170	20%
274	10%

The frequent API calls sets obtained with Apriori are uninteresting in the sense that they are unordered as they do not follow any specific order. Moreover, Apriori does not ensure that API calls from a API calls set appear contiguously in the sequence. Apriori fails to discover important sequential patterns and also ignore the sequential relationship between API calls. Next, we present the results from the application of SPM algorithms that overcome the drawbacks of Apriori. Thus they reveal more meaningful patterns and information.

The TKS algorithm is applied on the corpus to find top-k sequential patterns of API calls. TKS takes a corpus and a user specified parameter k as input and returns the top-k most frequent patterns as output. Some API calls frequent patterns discovered by the TKS algorithm with varying length are shown in Table 5. Note that the column **Sup** indicates the occurrence count of each pattern in the corpus. Table 5 provides some useful information related to frequent occurrences of API calls and patterns in the sequences. The second last column shows that the same API call *NtClose* as a sequence of six occurred 920 times in the corpus. Similarly, the API call in the last column *LdrGetProcedureAddress* occurred as a sequence of ten 880 times in the corpus.

Unlike TKS, the CM-SPAM algorithm offers the *minsup* threshold. Table 6 lists some of the most useful frequent API calls patterns in the corpus which are

Table 5. Extracted API calls patterns with TKS algorithm

Pattern	Sup
NtClose, NtQueryValueKey, NtClose	919
LdrLoadDll, LdrGetProcedureAddress, NtClose	904
NtClose, NtOpenKey, NtQueryValueKey, NtClose	915
NtClose, NtOpenKey, NtClose, NtClose, NtClose	916
NtClose, NtOpenKey, NtClose, NtClose, NtClose, NtClose	916
NtAllocateVirtualMemory, NtClose, NtClose	882
6 × NtClose	920
10 × LdrGetProcedureAddress	880

extracted with the CM-SPAM algorithm. The first four API calls patterns appear in at least 90% of the sequences in the corpus. The next four patterns appear in at least 80% of the sequences. Discovered patterns with the CM-SPAM algorithm are almost similar to the results obtained with the TKS algorithm. It was found that API call *NtClose* appeared in almost every frequent patterns discovered using TKS and CM-SPAM. Moreover, in 254 total API calls, approximately 15 API calls appeared mostly in frequent patterns.

Table 6. Frequent API calls patterns extracted with CM-SPAM

Pattern	Min. Sup	Sup
NtClose, NtQueryvalueKey, NtClose	0.9	919
NtClose, NtQueryValueKey, NtqueryValueKey, NtClose	0.9	915
NtOpenKey, NtClose, NtClose, NtClose	0.9	934
7 × NtClose	0.9	900
NtCreateFile, NtClose, NtClose	0.8	803
LdrGetDllHandle, LdrGetDllHandle, NtClose, NtClose	0.8	841
NtFreeVirtualMemory, NtClose, NtClose	0.8	803
12 × NtClose	0.8	816

Table 7 shows the relationships between frequent API calls that are discovered through sequential rule mining with the ERMiner algorithm. The confidence (*misconf*) threshold is set to 80%, which means that rules have a confidence of at least 80% (a rule $X \to Y$ has a confidence of 80% if the set of API calls in X is followed by the set of API calls in Y at least 80% of the times when X appears in a sequence). For example, the first rule in Table 7 indicates that 94.5% of the time, the API call *LdrLoadDll* is followed after *LdrGetProcedureAddress* and this rule has occurred 898 times in the corpus. Similarly, the second rule is the opposite of the first rule: 98.9% of the time, the API call *LdrGetProcedureAddress* is followed after *LdrLoadDll* 917 times in the corpus. With ERminer, we found some interesting relationships and dependencies between frequent API calls.

Table 7. Discovered sequential rules

Rule	Sup	Conf
$LdrGetProcedureAddress \rightarrow LLdrLoadDll$	898	0.945
$LdrLoadDll \rightarrow LdrGetProcedureAddress$	917	0.989
$NtClose \rightarrow LdrLoadDll$	859	0.86
$LdrLoadDll \rightarrow NtClose$	913	0.98
$LdrLoadDll, NtAllocateVirtualMemory \rightarrow LdrGetProcedureAddress$	859	0.97
$LdrLoadDll, LdrGetProcedureAddress \rightarrow NtAllocateVirtualMemory$	841	0.91
$LdrLoadDll, NtAllocateVirtualMemory \rightarrow NtClose$	871	0.98
$LdrLoadDll, NtClose \rightarrow NtAllocateVirtualMemory$	810	0.88
$LdrLoadDll, LdrGetProcedureAddress, NtQueryValueKey \rightarrow NtClose$	855	0.99
$NtClose \rightarrow LdrLoadDll, LdrGetProcedureAddress, NtQueryValueKey$	808	0.81
$LdrGetProcedureAddress, NtClose \rightarrow NtOpenKey, NtQueryValueKey$	834	0.88
$LdrGetProcedureAddress, NtOpenKey \rightarrow NtQueryValueKey, NtClose$	840	0.93
$LdrLoadDll, NtOpenKey, NtQueryValueKey, LdrGetDllHandle \rightarrow NtClose$	808	0.991

Some of the discovered closed and maximal sequential API calls patterns are
listed in Table 8. The closed sequential patterns provide a lossless representation
of all sequential patterns and they represent the largest subsequences common
to sets of sequences. For example, if each sequence represents the behavior of a
malware, the closed patterns represent the largest patterns common to groups of
malware sequences. Whereas the maximal API calls patterns are not loseless and
is always not larger than the set of closed sequential patterns and all sequential
patterns. Note that in maximal sequential API patterns, the *max gap* is set to
1. This means that no gap is allowed and each consecutive API call of a pattern
appears consecutively in a sequence.

Table 8. Closed (C) and Maximal (M) frequent sequential API patterns

Closed	Sup
$NtAllocateVirtualMemory, NtAllocateVirtualMemory$	729
$NtClose, NtOpenKey, NtQueryValueKey$	755
$NtFreeVirtualMemory, NtClose, NtClose$	803
$NtOpenKey, NtQueryValueKey, NtClose, NtClose$	700
$LdrGetDllHandle, 4 \times LdrGetProcedureAddress$	702
$16 \times LdrGetProcedureAddress$	702
Maximal	**Sup**
$LdrLoadDll, LdrGetDllHandle$	842
$LdrLoadDll, LdrLoadDll, LdrGetDllHandle$	814
$LdrGetDllHandle, LdrGetProcedureAddress, NtOpenKey$	806
$LdrLoadDll, NtClose, NtOpenKey$	817
$3 \times LdrGetProcedureAddress, LdrLoadDll, LdrGetDllHandle$	807
$36 \times LdrGetProcedureAddress$	801

During execution, we found that all the algorithms worked efficiently on the corpus and results obtained indicated that the total number of API calls in each sequence (abstraction simplicity) has a direct correlation on the efficiency of SPM algorithms.

6   Conclusion

In this paper, sequential pattern mining (SPM) algorithms were used to analyse malware behavior, which is an important research topic in cybersecurity. A dataset that contain API calls sequences of various metamorphic malware was first converted into a suitable format. Various SPM algorithms were then used on the abstracted dataset to find frequent API calls, frequent API calls sequences, the sequential relationships between frequent patterns as well as closed and maximal frequent API calls patterns. All the algorithms performed efficiently on the dataset and some interesting patterns were found with SPM. There are several directions for future work, some of which are:

- Applying SPM algorithms on the whole dataset and also on each malware types. This will allow us to discover frequent patterns of each malware and also investigate their behavior separately.
- Predicting the next API calls in a sequence using prediction models offered by SPMF.
- Using emerging patterns mining or contrast set mining techniques [28] on the API calls of various malware to discover emerging (or contrasting) trends that show a clear and useful difference (or contrast) between various malware behavior.
- Taking the frequent patterns of API calls discovered by TKS, CM-SPAM and sequential rules between frequent API calls discovered by ERMiner as features for the development of malware samples classification and detection.

References

1. Abouelhoda, M., Ghanem, M.: String mining in bioinformatics. In: Gaber, M. (ed.) Scientific Data Mining and Knowledge Discovery, pp. 207–247. Springer, Heidelberg (2009). https://doi.org/10.1007/978-3-642-02788-8_9
2. Agrawal, R., Srikant, R.: Fast algorithms for mining association rules in large databases. In: Proceedings of VLDB, pp. 487–499 (1994)
3. Ahmadi, M., Sami, A., Rahimi, H., Yadegari, B.: Malware detection by behavioural sequential patterns. Comput. Fraud Secur. **2013**(8), 11–19 (2013)
4. Çatak, F.Ö., Yazi, A.F.: A benchmark API call dataset for windows PE malware classification. CoRR, abs/1905.01999 (2019)
5. Çatak, F.Ö., Yazi, A.F., Elezaj, O., Ahmed, J.: Deep learning based sequential model for malware analysis using Windows exe API calls. Peer J. Comput. Sci. **6**, e285 (2020)
6. Cho, I.K., Im, E.G.: Extracting representative API patterns of malware families using multiple sequence alignments. In: Proceedings of RACS, pp. 308–313 (2015)

7. Fan, Y., Ye, Y., Chen, L.: Malicious sequential pattern mining for automatic malware detection. Expert Syst. Appl. **52**, 16–25 (2016)
8. Fournier-Viger, P., Gomariz, A., Campos, M., Thomas, R.: Fast vertical mining of sequential patterns using co-occurrence information. In: Tseng, V.S., Ho, T.B., Zhou, Z.-H., Chen, A.L.P., Kao, H.-Y. (eds.) PAKDD 2014. LNCS (LNAI), vol. 8443, pp. 40–52. Springer, Cham (2014). https://doi.org/10.1007/978-3-319-06608-0_4
9. Fournier-Viger, P., Gomariz, A., Gueniche, T., Mwamikazi, E., Thomas, R.: TKS: efficient mining of Top-K sequential patterns. In: Motoda, H., Wu, Z., Cao, L., Zaiane, O., Yao, M., Wang, W. (eds.) ADMA 2013. LNCS (LNAI), vol. 8346, pp. 109–120. Springer, Heidelberg (2013). https://doi.org/10.1007/978-3-642-53914-5_10
10. Fournier-Viger, P., Gueniche, T., Tseng, V.S.: Using partially-ordered sequential rules to generate more accurate sequence prediction. In: Zhou, S., Zhang, S., Karypis, G. (eds.) ADMA 2012. LNCS (LNAI), vol. 7713, pp. 431–442. Springer, Heidelberg (2012). https://doi.org/10.1007/978-3-642-35527-1_36
11. Fournier-Viger, P., Gueniche, T., Zida, S., Tseng, V.S.: ERMiner: sequential rule mining using equivalence classes. In: Blockeel, H., van Leeuwen, M., Vinciotti, V. (eds.) IDA 2014. LNCS, vol. 8819, pp. 108–119. Springer, Cham (2014). https://doi.org/10.1007/978-3-319-12571-8_10
12. Fournier-Viger, P., et al.: The SPMF open-source data mining library version 2. In: Berendt, B., et al. (eds.) ECML PKDD 2016. LNCS (LNAI), vol. 9853, pp. 36–40. Springer, Cham (2016). https://doi.org/10.1007/978-3-319-46131-1_8
13. Fournier-Viger, P., Lin, J.C.W., Kiran, R.U., Koh, Y.S., Thomas, R.: A survey of sequential pattern mining. Data Sci. Pattern Recogn. **1**(1), 54–77 (2017)
14. Fournier-Viger, P., Wu, C.-W., Gomariz, A., Tseng, V.S.: VMSP: efficient vertical mining of maximal sequential patterns. In: Sokolova, M., van Beek, P. (eds.) AI 2014. LNCS (LNAI), vol. 8436, pp. 83–94. Springer, Cham (2014). https://doi.org/10.1007/978-3-319-06483-3_8
15. Fumarola, F., Lanotte, P.F., Ceci, M., Malerba, D.: CloFAST: closed sequential pattern mining using sparse and vertical id-lists. Knowl. Inf. Syst. **48**(2), 429–463 (2016)
16. Griffin, K., Schneider, S., Hu, X., Chiueh, T.: Automatic generation of string signatures for malware detection. In: Kirda, E., Jha, S., Balzarotti, D. (eds.) RAID 2009. LNCS, vol. 5758, pp. 101–120. Springer, Heidelberg (2009). https://doi.org/10.1007/978-3-642-04342-0_6
17. Hofmeyr, S.A., Forrest, S., Somayaji, A.: Intrusion detection using sequences of system calls. J. Comput. Secur. **6**(3), 151–180 (1998)
18. Ki, Y., Kim, E., Kim, H.K.: A novel approach to detect malware based on API call sequence analysis. Int. J. Distrib. Sens. Netw. **11**, 659101:1–659101:9 (2015)
19. Mustafa, R.U., Nawaz, M.S., Ferzund, J., Lali, M.I.U., Shahzad, B., Fournier-Viger, P.: Early detection of controversial Urdu speeches from social media. Data Sci. Pattern Recogn. **1**(2), 26–42 (2017)
20. Nawaz, M.S., Fournier-Viger, P., Shojaee, A., Fujita, H.: Using artificial intelligence techniques for COVID-19 genome analysis. Appl. Intell. **51**(5), 3086–3103 (2021)
21. Nawaz, M.S., Fournier-Viger, P., Zhang, J.: Proof learning in PVS with utility pattern mining. IEEE Access **8**, 119806–119818 (2020)
22. Nawaz, M.S., Sun, M., Fournier-Viger, P.: Proof guidance in PVS with sequential pattern mining. In: Hojjat, H., Massink, M. (eds.) FSEN 2019. LNCS, vol. 11761, pp. 45–60. Springer, Cham (2019). https://doi.org/10.1007/978-3-030-31517-7_4

23. Ni, L., Luo, W., Lu, N., Zhu, W.: Mining the local dependency itemset in a products network. ACM Trans. Manage. Inf. Syst. **11**(1), 3:1–3:31 (2020)
24. Pektas, A., Pektas, E.N., Acarman, T.: Mining patterns of sequential malicious APIs to detect malware. Int. J. Netw. Secur. Appl. **10**(4), 1–9 (2018)
25. Pokou, Y.J.M., Fournier-Viger, P., Moghrabi, C.: Authorship attribution using small sets of frequent part-of-speech skip-grams. In: Proceedings of FLAIRS, pp. 86–91 (2016)
26. Qiao, Y., Yang, Y., He, J., Tang, C., Liu, Z.: CBM: free, automatic malware analysis framework using API call sequences. In: Sun, F., Li, T., Li, H. (eds.) Knowledge Engineering and Management. AISC, vol. 214, pp. 225–236. Springer, Heidelberg (2014). https://doi.org/10.1007/978-3-642-37832-4_21
27. Qiao, Y., Yang, Y., Ji, L., He, J.: Analyzing malware by abstracting the frequent itemsets in API call sequences. In: Proceedings of TrustCom, pp. 265–270 (2013)
28. Ventura, S., Luna, J.M.: Supervised Descriptive Pattern Mining. Springer, Cham (2018). https://doi.org/10.1007/978-3-319-98140-6
29. Schweizer, D., Zehnder, M., Wache, H., Witschel, H.F., Zanatta, D., Rodriguez, M.: Using consumer behavior data to reduce energy consumption in smart homes: applying machine learning to save energy without lowering comfort of inhabitants. In: Proceedings of ICMLA, pp. 1123–1129 (2015)
30. Sundarkumar, G.G., Ravi, V., Nwogu, I., Govindaraju, V.: Malware detection via API calls, topic models and machine learning. In: Proceedings of CASE, pp. 1212–1217 (2015)
31. Uppal, D., Sinha, R., Mehra, V., Jain, V.: Malware detection and classification based on extraction of API sequences. In: Proceedings of ICACCI, pp. 2337–2342 (2014)
32. Ye, Y., Li, T., Adjeroh, D.A., Iyengar, S.S.: A survey on malware detection using data mining techniques. ACM Comput. Surv. **50**(3), 41:1–41:40 (2017)
33. Ye, Y., Wang, D., Li, T., Ye, D., Jiang, Q.: An intelligent PE-malware detection system based on association mining. J. Comput. Virol. **4**(4), 323–334 (2008)

Applying Machine Learning to Risk Assessment in Software Projects

André Sousa[1]([✉])⬥, João Pascoal Faria[1]⬥, João Mendes-Moreira[1]⬥,
Duarte Gomes[2]⬥, Pedro Castro Henriques[2]⬥, and Ricardo Graça[3]⬥

[1] Faculty of Engineering, University of Porto, Porto, Portugal
{up201902618,jpf,jmoreira}@fe.up.pt
[2] Strongstep, Porto, Portugal
{duarte.gomes,pedroch}@strongstep.pt
[3] Fraunhofer AICOS, Porto, Portugal
ricardo.graca@fraunhofer.pt

Abstract. Risk management is one of the ten knowledge areas discussed in the Project Management Body of Knowledge (PMBOK), which serves as a guide that should be followed to increase the chances of project success. The popularity of research regarding the application of risk management in software projects has been consistently growing in recent years, especially with the application of machine learning techniques to help identify risk levels of risk factors of a project before its development begins, with the goal of improving the likelihood of success of these projects. This paper presents the results of the application of machine learning techniques for risk assessment in software projects. A Python application was developed and, using Scikit-learn, two machine learning models, trained using software project risk data shared by a partner company of this project, were created to predict risk impact and likelihood levels on a scale of 1 to 3.

Different algorithms were tested to compare the results obtained by high performance but non-interpretable algorithms (*e.g.*, Support Vector Machine) and the ones obtained by interpretable algorithms (*e.g.*, Random Forest), whose performance tends to be lower than their non-interpretable counterparts. The results showed that Support Vector Machine and Naive Bayes were the best performing algorithms. Support Vector Machine had an accuracy of 69% in predicting impact levels, and Naive Bayes had an accuracy of 63% in predicting likelihood levels, but the results presented in other evaluation metrics (*e.g.*, AUC, Precision) show the potential of the approach presented in this use case.

Keywords: Risk management · Risk assessment · Software projects · Machine learning · Classification

This article is a result of the project PROMESSA - NORTE-01-0247-FEDER-039887, supported by Norte Portugal Regional Operational Programme (NORTE 2020), under the PORTUGAL 2020 Partnership Agreement, through the European Regional Development Fund (ERDF).

M. Kamp et al. (Eds.): ECML PKDD 2021 Workshops, CCIS 1525, pp. 104–118, 2021.
https://doi.org/10.1007/978-3-030-93733-1_7

1 Introduction

According to the Project Management Body of Knowledge, a project risk is "an uncertain event which, if it occurs, has a positive or negative effect on one or more project objectives" [16]. Software projects are notoriously complex development activities, and thus the concept of risk cannot be ignored when considering this type of projects. Software projects can encounter various types of risks, such as technical, management, financial, contractual/legal, personnel, and related to other resources [19].

In 2015, the Standish Group International's CHAOS Report [9], a study of the success of software projects throughout the year, reported a 29% success rate for the roughly 5000 projects investigated. A project is considered successful if it is completed within its allocated budget, its original delivery deadline, and with all of the features that were planned at the start of its development life cycle [10]. The same study reported a 19% failure rate for the set of projects investigated, meaning the projects suffered from cost overruns, time overruns, or lacking content that was initially specified.

However, it is in the category of challenged projects that we can find the largest percentage of projects. As can be seen in Table 1, from 2011 to 2015, 49%, 56%, 50%, 55%, and 52% of the software projects, respectively, were considered challenged, meaning they were completed but either over-budget, over the allocated time estimates, or offering fewer features than originally planned. While there has always been a larger percentage of successful projects compared to the percentage of failed ones in this period, the extremely high percentage of challenged projects indicates that there is definitely a possibility to improve the success rate of a large amount of these projects. This is where the concept of risk, and more importantly, risk management needs to be considered.

Table 1. Results of the Standish Group's CHAOS report [9]

	2011	2012	2013	2014	2015
Challenged projects	49%	56%	50%	55%	52%
Successful projects	29%	27%	31%	28%	29%
Failed projects	22%	17%	19%	17%	19%

Identifying and preparing mitigation strategies to deal with the possible risks in a software project is an important task to reduce the chances of failure during the development of a software project. More often than not, this is done when the development of the project is already underway. Instead, it should be performed before development begins. This way, the team gains more time to prepare mitigation plans to deal with risks that might happen as the project is being developed and does not become overwhelmed with the risks if they occur.

However, the process of identifying risks, their probability of occurrence, and their possible impact before development begins is not an easy task. After all, there is already so much to consider before developing a new software project in an organizational environment, and some factors will inevitably be overlooked.

Considering the problem described above, a software module aimed at accurately predicting the impact and likelihood of risks of a new software project before development begins using machine learning techniques was developed. The module is part of a larger project: the PROject ManagEment Intelligent aSSistAnt, or PROMESSA for short, which will aid in tasks such as project prioritization, optimization and recommendation of resources, delivery date estimates, and analysis of risk and their related management actions through the use of machine learning techniques. The software module described in this paper tackles the risk management tasks of this project.

The purpose of this paper is to present the results obtained with the application developed and, more specifically, the comparison between the algorithms tested, some of which focus on interpretability, and others which focus on the best predictive performance possible. The remaining sections of this paper are structured as follows. An overview of the concepts of risk and risk management in software projects is presented in Sect. 2. In Sect. 3, the data used to train the models is described, and the tools used to create the models and the application are presented. Section 4 presents the results of the algorithms tested before choosing which would be used for the final models. Lastly, Sect. 5 presents the conclusions extracted based on the work developed and the results obtained, and lists the next steps for future work and improvements in this application.

2 Risk and Risk Management in Software Projects

Risk in software projects can be seen as "the potential that a chosen action or activity will lead to a loss or an undesirable outcome" [5]; "a set of factors or conditions that can pose a serious threat to the successful completion of a software project" [18]; or "the probability and impact of an event on a project" [2]. From these definitions, it is possible to identify some common themes, such as a risk possibly leading to a loss. In a software project, a loss can manifest itself through lower quality of the final product, increased costs, changes to the release date of the product, or, in a worst-case scenario, failure and cancellation [20].

Software projects can be impacted by various types of risks, such as technical, management, financial, contractual, legal, personnel, or related to other resources, which are generally situations that are not a direct responsibility of the project team, such as the unavailability of computer resources or equipment [19].

In a software development project, risks can be influenced by the business domain, the business style, culture of the organization, and characteristics of the members involved in the project [12], so it is important to identify risks according to the environment in which the project is being developed. To facilitate this process, risk factor and item classifications found in the literature can be used. These classifications usually list the most frequent risk items that can affect a project's path towards success, and teams can use these to evaluate if there is a possibility of any of those risks occurring during the development of their own projects, and if so, what could be their impact on the project. Essentially, those are the 2 parts that make up a risk: the likelihood of the risk happening, and the degree of impact it has on the project if it does occur.

Wallace's categorization [18] of risk items according to six risk dimensions (Team, Organizational Environment, Requirements, Planning and Control, User, and Complexity) is still widely used in this research area. This categorization presents common risk items in software projects. By grouping them according to the areas that project managers must consider in the development of a software project, it makes it so they can identify what areas are more likely to be problematic throughout the course of the development of the project and prepare their risk management strategies accordingly.

Those are just some examples of risk classifications that can negatively affect specific areas during the development of a software project. There are a lot more risks that can be identified and doing it at an early stage of the project (ideally before development starts) is crucial for a successful development life cycle, as it means the project manager as well as the development team can start to plan actions to take if these risks materialize during the project development.

Identifying, classifying, and prioritizing actions for risks according to their priority are just some of the phases of a process called risk management, which is defined by Standard ISO/IEC/IEEE 24765:2010 as "an organized process for" identifying and handling risk factors; assessing and quantifying the identified risks; and developing plans to deal with the identified risks [6].

In a very simplified way, the goal of risk management is to increase the probability of positive events on a software project, while at the same time decreasing the probability of negative events on the same project [3]. To do that, risk management is often divided into two key activities: risk assessment and risk control, which are composed of more specific steps.

3   Data and Methods

The data set used for this application was provided by Strongstep, one of the project's partner companies. It consists of 140 samples related to risks in 18 projects, and 11 variables, where the first three variables are used only to identify the projects and respective risks in the data set and are not used when training the models. The data available was divided into three different sets: training (75 samples), test (25 samples), and validation (40 samples). The validation set was used during parameter optimization and, due to the limited number of samples available, it was also added to the training set used to train the models, with the goal of maximizing the amount of training samples available to train the models without compromising processes such as parameter optimization and the tests performed on the test set.

The complete set of variables is as follows:

– **Project ID** - unique ID of the project. This is an incrementing quantitative value used as an identifier of the project and is not used for training.

- **Project Name** - name of the project. As with Project ID, this is a qualitative variable that is not used for training, and only serves as an identifier of the project.
- **Risk Description** - description of the risk. Similarly to the previous two variables, this is a field that is not used for training, and only serves as an identifier of the risk.
- **Project Type** - this is a categorical variable that represents the type of project in the platform.
- **Project Manager Profile** - this variable indicates the profile of the manager of the project. It is also a categorical variable with possible values being Junior and Senior.
- **Number of Team Members** - quantitative value indicating the number of team members involved in the project.
- **Project Duration** - quantitative value indicating the duration of the project in hours.
- **Budget** - budget allocated to the project. This is a categorical variable with values that describe the budget allocated to the project based on the numeric amount. Possible values are Very Low, Low, Medium, or High.
- **Risk Category** - this is a categorical variable indicating the category of a risk that was added for a given project. The categories in this variable are very close to the most frequent risk categorizations that are found in the literature, and includes risk categories such as Project Complexity, Management, Planning and Control, among others.
- **Risk Impact** - impact of the risk on a scale from 1 to 3, indicating a low, medium, or high impact on the project, respectively.
- **Risk Likelihood** - likelihood of the risk occurring during project development on a scale from 1 to 3, indicating a low, medium, or high likelihood of occurrence, respectively.

As for data preprocessing tasks, categorical variables were encoded through one-hot encoding, which represents each class through a new attribute with either a 0 or 1, where 0 indicates the absence of that class, and 1 indicates its presence. This was used in the Project Type, Budget, and Risk Category variables.

Additionally, feature scaling was used to scale the range of the values of the quantitative independent variables. This is an important step because if one attribute's range of values varies significantly more than the range of values of another attribute, the former will become dominant in the data set, resulting in an anomaly and a decrease in the predictive performance of the models. For the purposes of this application, min-max scaling was used through Scikit-learn's MinMaxScaler.

Feature selection was performed to detect if any of the independent variables had a variance of 30% or below, which were considered to be low variance features, and thus would be removed from the training set. This was the case with the Project Manager Profile and Number of Team Members variables, with Project Manager Profile value "Senior" and Number of Team Members value "2" found in over 70% of the data set risks. After this process, the independent variables that were used in training were Project Type, Project Duration, Budget, and Risk Category.

In an attempt to tackle the class imbalance problem in the data set, where risks with impact level 2 are almost twice as frequent as risks with impact level 3, and four times as much when compared to risks with impact level 1, oversampling was also tested. Oversampling increases the number of samples of the minority classes either through data replication or by generating new data to improve the imbalance detected in the data set. A drawback of this technique is the fact that it increases the chances of overfitting occurring [11], as it replicates instances that are already found in the data set.

Before testing the algorithms, hyperparameter tuning was performed to obtain the best set of hyperparameters for each algorithm. Hyperparameters are used in machine learning to improve the learning process and differ from an algorithm's internal parameters in that they cannot be learned from the data during the training phase [21]. Using a Neural Network as an example, the weights of its hidden layers are internal parameters, whereas the activation function is a hyperparameter.

This process was performed over the validation set, together with the use of stratified K-fold cross-validation (with $k = 4$) to improve the efficiency of this process. After the execution of this process, the ideal set of hyperparameters for the algorithms selected for testing were saved to be used during the testing phase.

To assess the quality of the models, various evaluation metrics were used: accuracy, AUC, F-measure, precision, and recall. These metrics provide different information so analysing their results can provide a lot of insight into the quality of the predictions made by the models. Additionally, confusion matrices were used to analyse what the models were predicting and, more importantly, where they could be failing in some predictions.

Stratified K-fold cross-validation (with $k = 4$) was also used to obtain the results presented. The 40 data samples used for validation are set aside temporarily, and the remaining 100 data samples are used in the Stratified K-Fold instance which, with $k = 4$, splits these samples into 4 different groups of 75 training and 25 test samples. As this is a small data set with few samples to train the models, the remaining 40 validation data samples are added to the 75 training samples on each cross-validation group. That way, 115 isolated data samples are fitted to train the model, and tests are performed on the remaining 25 test samples on each group.

The tests were performed on 6 different machine learning algorithms, 3 considered interpretable (Gradient Boosted Trees [7], Random Forest [4], and Naive Bayes [17]), and 3 considered non-interpretable (Neural Network [8], Support Vector Machine [15], and K-Nearest Neighbours [1]). Interpretability in machine learning is defined as "the degree to which a human can understand the cause of a decision" [13].

Interpretable machine learning algorithms make it easier to understand not only the prediction made by the model, but more importantly why that prediction was made. If a prediction that does not exactly correspond to what was expected occurs, developers can use this information to identify possible problems in the data set, the model, or possibly both. An example of the information that these algorithms can provide is, in the case of tree or estimator-based algorithms, the possibility to visualize the decision tree used by the algorithm to make its prediction. However, there is a trade-off involved with interpretable machine learning algorithms, namely the fact that predictive performance tends to drop in these algorithms.

The goal was to compare their results and make a decision regarding whether the common performance trade-offs in non-interpretable algorithms were worth the reduced amount of information that can be obtained from these. The tests were run 10 times for each algorithm, and the results presented are the average of the results of those runs.

The machine learning models were created using Python and the Scikit-learn package. Additionally, the imbalanced-learn package was used as it provides methods for oversampling, which was one of the approaches used to try to maximize the results of the models, as previously mentioned. Lastly, in order to integrate with the project's main modules, which enables the different services developed by the partner companies' own tools, the Flask web framework was used to develop a REST API that receives the information used to predict the impact and likelihood levels of risks in a new project.

4   Results and Discussion

4.1   Risk Impact

Table 2 shows the results of the tests performed for the risk impact model, which makes predictions on the risk impact target variable. An example of a confusion matrix made by one of the algorithms tested for this target variable is shown in Fig. 1.

As expected, based on the analysis of interpretable algorithms and the trade-offs associated with them, the interpretable algorithms display mostly worse results than their non-interpretable counterparts, except for Random Forest.

Table 2. Results of the risk impact model evaluation with different algorithms

Algorithm	Accuracy	AUC	F-Measure	Precision	Recall
Gradient Boosted Trees	0.54	0.64	0.52	0.55	0.54
Random Forest	0.63	0.69	0.57	0.55	0.63
Multinomial Naive Bayes	0.54	0.67	0.50	0.50	0.54
Neural Network	0.62	**0.71**	0.58	0.58	0.62
Support Vector Machine	**0.69**	0.68	**0.64**	**0.60**	**0.69**
K-Nearest Neighbours	0.68	0.64	0.63	0.59	0.68

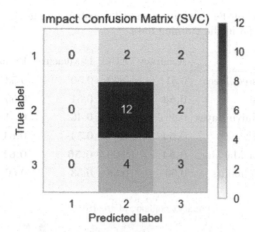

Fig. 1. Example of a confusion matrix of predictions made by the risk impact model (Support Vector Machine)

While the Random Forest algorithm presents strong results in most metrics (particularly accuracy, AUC, and recall), the overall best results still come from a non-interpretable algorithm: Support Vector Machine, with the highest value for accuracy (69%), F-Measure (0.64), precision (0.60), and recall (0.69), surpassed only by two algorithms in AUC score: Neural Network and Random Forest. Another non-interpretable algorithm - K-Nearest Neighbours - presents the next highest scores for accuracy (68%), F-Measure (0.63), and recall (0.68).

As was previously mentioned, oversampling was used to try to improve the model's predictions in this unbalanced data set. SVMSMOTE [14] was applied on the minority class (impact level 1) rather than all classes except the majority one (impact levels 1 and 3), as while there was some discrepancy between the number of risks with impact levels 2 and 3, that problem was considerably worse when comparing risks with impact levels 1 and 2. Figure 3 shows the original risk impact class distribution (left) and the risk impact class distribution after the use of SVMSMOTE on the training data (right), respectively.

Unfortunately, as the results in Table 3 show, oversampling did not manage to improve the results on the evaluation metrics used, returning mostly worse results all around with some exceptions (*e.g.*, minor differences in Random Forest and Support Vector Machine's AUC, 0.03 higher precision in Neural Network). However, by analysing the confusion matrix of the risk impact model trained with the original data set (shown in Fig. 1) and the confusion matrix of the risk impact model trained with oversampling applied to the training data (shown in Fig. 2), it becomes clear where the latter model is failing.

Risk impact level 3 is predicted 7 times in the tests performed without over-sampling, and 6 times in the tests performed with oversampling applied to the training data, but the majority class (risk impact level 2) is no longer the only other class predicted by the model, with 4 predictions of risk impact level 1 when oversampling is applied to the training data. This is the expected behaviour with

Table 3. Comparison of the risk impact model's evaluation metrics with oversampling applied (SVMSMOTE) in the training data

Algorithm	Accuracy	AUC	F-Measure	Precision	Recall
Gradient Boosted Trees	0.51	0.62	0.50	0.53	0.51
Random Forest	**0.54**	**0.70**	0.51	0.53	**0.54**
Multinomial Naive Bayes	0.46	0.66	0.46	0.54	0.46
Neural Network	**0.54**	**0.70**	0.54	**0.61**	**0.54**
Support Vector Machine	**0.54**	0.69	**0.56**	**0.61**	**0.54**
K-Nearest Neighbours	0.50	0.66	0.53	0.60	0.50

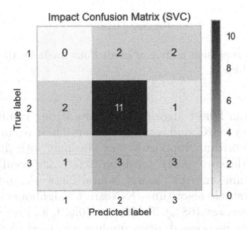

Fig. 2. Example of a confusion matrix of predictions made by the risk impact model (Support Vector Machine) with oversampling applied to the training data

the more balanced class distribution that is obtained with the use of oversampling, but it did not improve the results for any algorithm tested, aside from the previously mentioned exceptions.

Despite overall worse results compared to the tests performed for the risk impact model (without oversampling), it is interesting to note the proximity when comparing the results of the interpretable algorithms with the results of the non-interpretable algorithms. The results of the interpretable algorithms are now closer to the results of the non-interpretable algorithms, mostly due to the considerable drop in results obtained by the non-interpretable algorithms, particularly Support Vector Machine and K-Nearest Neighbours.

As for the best overall results, it is a mix between interpretable and non-interpretable algorithms: Random Forest matched the best scores in accuracy (54%), AUC score (0.70) and recall (0.54), while Support Vector Machine and Neural Network equalled those results. Additionally, Neural Network and Support Vector Machine obtained the highest score in precision (0.61), while the latter had the best overall score in F-Measure (0.56).

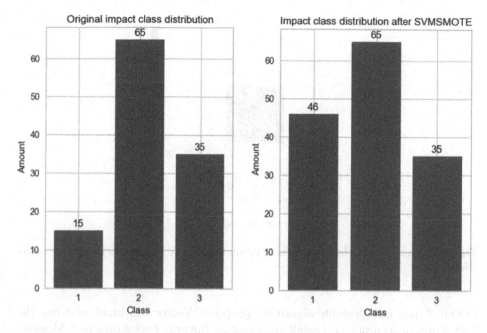

Fig. 3. Risk impact class distribution without (left) and with oversampling applied to the training data (right)

4.2   Risk Likelihood

The tests for the risk likelihood model followed the same workflow as the tests for the risk impact model, and the results of these are shown in Table 4, together with an example of a confusion matrix made by one of the tested algorithms, which is shown in Fig. 4.

Table 4. Results of the risk likelihood model evaluation with different algorithms

Algorithm	Accuracy	AUC	F-Measure	Precision	Recall
Gradient Boosted Trees	0.52	0.55	0.49	0.48	0.52
Random Forest	0.58	**0.62**	0.53	0.52	0.58
Complement Naive Bayes	**0.61**	**0.62**	**0.56**	**0.58**	**0.61**
Neural Network	0.57	0.61	0.50	0.47	0.57
Support Vector Machine	**0.61**	0.59	0.53	0.53	**0.61**
K-Nearest Neighbours	0.56	0.58	0.50	0.50	0.56

Complement Naive Bayes stands out as the overall best performing algorithm when it comes to predicting risk likelihood levels, with the highest value for accuracy (61%), AUC score (0.62), F-Measure (0.56), precision (0.58) and recall

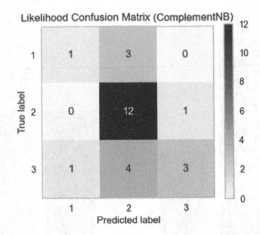

Fig. 4. Example of a confusion matrix of predictions made by the risk likelihood model (Naive Bayes)

(0.61). A non-interpretable algorithm (Support Vector Machine) matches the best scores in accuracy and recall and presents the next best scores in F-Measure (0.53, also obtained by Random Forest) and Precision (0.53).

Aside from Gradient Boosted Trees, which presents the lowest scores in all metrics except precision, the difference between the results of the interpretable and non-interpretable algorithms is not as obvious in predictions for the risk likelihood target variable compared to what was seen in the predictions for the risk impact target variable. In fact, two interpretable algorithms (Random Forest and Complement Naive Bayes) outperform the remaining non-interpretable algorithms (Neural Network and K-Nearest Neighbours), in a clear contrast to what was seen in the results of the risk impact predictions.

As with the risk impact model, oversampling was also used to try to improve the model's predictions regarding risk likelihood, which also has an imbalanced class distribution. SVMSMOTE was applied only on the minority class (likelihood level 1). Figure 6 shows the original risk likelihood class distribution (left) and the risk likelihood class distribution after the use of SVMSMOTE on the training data (right), respectively.

As was the case with the tests performed for the risk impact model, the results in Table 5 show that, in most cases, the use of oversampling did not improve the results on the metrics used to evaluate the risk likelihood model. By analysing the confusion matrix of the risk likelihood model trained with the original data set (shown in Fig. 4) and the confusion matrix of the risk likelihood model trained with oversampling applied to the training data (shown in Fig. 5), it becomes easier to understand this drop in the evaluation metrics scores obtained with oversampling applied. There are less predictions made for the majority class (risk likelihood level 2) and more predictions are made for minority class (risk likelihood level 1), to which oversampling was applied. It is the expected behaviour and is confirmed by the differences seen in the aforementioned confusion matrices.

Table 5. Comparison of the risk likelihood model's evaluation metrics with oversampling applied (SVMSMOTE) in the training data

Algorithm	Accuracy	AUC	F-Measure	Precision	Recall
Gradient Boosted Trees	0.52	0.45	0.49	0.48	0.52
Random Forest	0.56	0.59	0.53	0.54	0.56
Complement Naive Bayes	**0.63**	**0.61**	**0.59**	**0.62**	**0.63**
Neural Network	0.51	0.60	0.50	0.51	0.51
Support Vector Machine	0.55	0.54	0.51	0.59	0.55
K-Nearest Neighbours	0.42	0.56	0.41	0.43	0.42

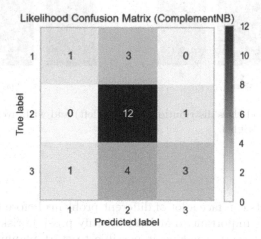

Fig. 5. Example of a confusion matrix made by the risk likelihood model (Naive Bayes) with oversampling applied to the training data

Although the overall scores are worse when comparing to the tests performed in the risk likelihood model without oversampling, the differences here are not as high when compared to the differences seen in the risk impact model's results with and without oversampling applied to the training data. The interpretable algorithms mostly keep similar scores while improving on them in a few cases (most noticeably Naive Bayes' results), while the results of the non-interpretable algorithms drop more significantly in comparison to the results without oversampling, particularly in the case of the K-Nearest Neighbours algorithm.

Complement Naive Bayes stands out again as the overall best performing algorithm in the tests for the risk likelihood model, with the highest value for accuracy (63%), AUC score (0.61), F-Measure (0.59), precision (0.62) and recall (0.63). As for the next best scores, it is a mix between both types of algorithms, with Random Forest having the next highest accuracy (56%), F-Measure (0.53) and recall (0.56), and Support Vector Machine obtaining the next highest overall value of AUC score (0.60) and precision (0.59).

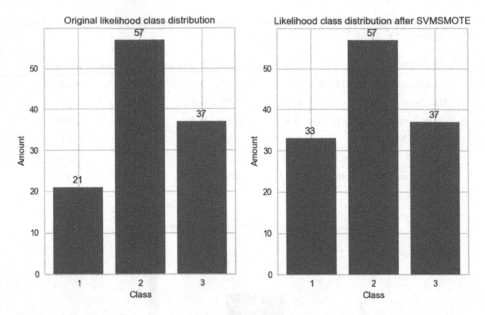

Fig. 6. Risk likelihood class distribution without (left) and with oversampling applied to the training data (right)

5   Conclusion

As software projects can face a lot of different problems before they are released to the market, it is important to at least identify possible risks that can occur before development starts, making it possible to start planning risk management and mitigation strategies if the risks materialize, rather than dealing with the problems as they appear. Risk management in software projects is a research area with consistently growing popularity, especially when combined with machine learning approaches to create models that can identify or predict risks before project development starts, with the goal of identifying risks in a software project, and ultimately develop and implement strategies to prevent or limit the impact of the identified risks if they materialize during development.

With the goal of facilitating the use of risk management approaches for software project development, a software module aimed at accurately classifying risk impact and likelihood levels in different risk categories of new software development projects was developed. Two models were trained with real project data and risks from one of the project's partner companies - one to predict risk impact levels, the other to predict risk likelihood levels.

Different algorithms were tested with the goal of understanding the performance trade-offs typically involved in interpretable algorithms (*e.g.*, Random Forest, Naive Bayes) and whether those trade-offs were worth the different type of information these algorithms can return, such as general information like feature importance or more specific information such as the flow taken by a

Random Forest estimator to generate a prediction. In the end, the Support Vector Machine and Complement Naive Bayes algorithms were chosen for the risk impact and risk likelihood models, respectively.

These algorithms obtained 69% and 63% accuracy, respectively, but more importantly, their results in other metrics show that this is not a situation where the algorithms are obtaining a higher accuracy score by just predicting the majority class and can distinguish between the three classes available with a reasonable degree of confidence. Both algorithms obtained the highest result in accuracy, F-Measure, precision, and recall, with Support Vector Machine being surpassed by Neural Network in AUC score for the risk impact target variable, while Naive Bayes had the highest AUC score for the risk likelihood target variable.

In terms of new approaches in this research area, the comparison of interpretable algorithms with their non-interpretable counterparts was relevant to assess the differences in their predictions. Additionally, the integration with project management tools as part of the PROMESSA project brings the opportunity to facilitate the use of risk management processes by different organizations.

As for future improvements, the focus should be on obtaining more quality data to continuously improve the models' understanding of the relationships between the attributes of a project and the risk impact and likelihood level associated with the risk categories that can have an effect on the development of a new software project, and consequently improve on the results presented.

Notice the focus on **quality** data, as just integrating with any data source, and increasing the amount of data samples to train the models is sometimes not enough. As was seen, the data set for this project started with 6 training features, but two of them were removed as they had very low variance and were having a negative effect on the predictions of the models instead. It is then important to find more data that can be used, but also analyse the importance and variance of any new features that are added to the data set and assess if they have a positive or negative effect on the models' predictions.

References

1. Altman, N.: An introduction to kernel and nearest-neighbor nonparametric regression. Am. Stat. **46**, 175–185 (1992)
2. Boehm, B.: Software risk management: principles and practices. IEEE Softw. **8**, 32–41 (1991)
3. Boehm, B.: Software project risk and opportunity management. In: Ruhe, G., Wohlin, C. (eds.) Software Project Management in a Changing World, pp. 107–121. Springer, Heidelberg (2014). https://doi.org/10.1007/978-3-642-55035-5_5
4. Breiman, L.: Random forests. Mach. Learn. **45**(1), 5–32 (2001). https://doi.org/10.1023/A:1010933404324
5. Chawan, P., Patil, J., Naik, R.: Software risk management. Int. J. Comput. Technol. **6**, 60–66 (2013)
6. Felderer, M., Auer, F., Bergsmann, J.: Risk management during software development: results of a survey in software houses from Germany, Austria and Switzerland. In: Großmann, J., Felderer, M., Seehusen, F. (eds.) RISK 2016. LNCS, vol. 10224, pp. 143–155. Springer, Cham (2017). https://doi.org/10.1007/978-3-319-57858-3_11

118   A. Sousa et al.

7. Friedman, J.: Greedy function approximation: a gradient boosting machine. Ann. Stat. **29**, 1189–1232 (2001)
8. Glorot, X., Bengio, Y.: Understanding the difficulty of training deep feedforward neural networks. In: AISTATS (2010)
9. Group, T.S.: Chaos report 2015 (2015). https://standishgroup.com/sample_research_files/CHAOSReport2015-Final.pdf
10. Hsieh, M.Y., Hsu, Y.C., Lin, C.T.: Risk assessment in new software development projects at the front end: a fuzzy logic approach. J. Ambient Intell. Humanized Comput. **9** (2016). https://doi.org/10.1007/s12652-016-0372-5
11. Kaur, P., Gosain, A.: Comparing the behavior of oversampling and undersampling approach of class imbalance learning by combining class imbalance problem with noise. In: Saini, A.K., Nayak, A.K., Vyas, R.K. (eds.) ICT Based Innovations. AISC, vol. 653, pp. 23–30. Springer, Singapore (2018). https://doi.org/10.1007/978-981-10-6602-3_3
12. Mizuno, O., Hamasaki, T., Takagi, Y., Kikuno, T.: An empirical evaluation of predicting runaway software projects using Bayesian classification. In: Bomarius, F., Iida, H. (eds.) Product Focused Software Process Improvement, pp. 263–273. Springer, Heidelberg (2004)
13. Molnar, C.: Interpretable machine learning (2019). https://christophm.github.io/interpretable-ml-book/
14. Nguyen, H.M., Cooper, E., Kamei, K.: Borderline over-sampling for imbalanced data classification. Int. J. Knowl. Eng. Soft Data Paradigms **3**, 4–21 (2011)
15. Platt, J.C.: Probabilistic outputs for support vector machines and comparisons to regularized likelihood methods. In: Advances in Large Margin Classifiers, pp. 61–74. MIT Press (1999)
16. PMI: A Guide to the Project Management Body of Knowledge (PMBOK Guide), 4th Edn. Project Management Institute (2008)
17. Rennie, J.D.M., Shih, L., Teevan, J., Karger, D.: Tackling the poor assumptions of Naive Bayes text classifiers. In: ICML (2003)
18. Wallace, L., Keil, M., Rai, A.: Understanding software project risk: a cluster analysis. Inf. Manage. **42**(1), 115–125 (2004). https://doi.org/10.1016/j.im.2003.12.007, http://www.sciencedirect.com/science/article/pii/S0378720604000102
19. Westfall, L.: Defining software risk management (2001). http://www.westfallteam.com/sites/default/files/papers/risk_management_paper.pdf
20. Williams, R.C., Pandelios, G.J., Behrens, S.: Software risk evaluation (SRE) method description (version 2.0) (2000)
21. Wu, J., Chen, X.Y., Zhang, H., Xiong, L.D., Lei, H., Deng, S.H.: Hyperparameter optimization for machine learning models based on bayesian optimization. J. Electron. Sci. Technol. **17**(1), 26 – 40 (2019). https://doi.org/10.11989/JEST.1674-862X.80904120, http://www.sciencedirect.com/science/article/pii/S1674862X19300047

SampleFix: Learning to Generate Functionally Diverse Fixes

Hossein Hajipour[1]([⊠]) [iD], Apratim Bhattacharyya[2] [iD],
Cristian-Alexandru Staicu[1] [iD], and Mario Fritz[1] [iD]

[1] CISPA Helmholtz Center for Information Security, Saarbrücken, Germany
hossein.hajipour@cispa.saarland
[2] Max Planck Institute for Informatics, Saarbrücken, Germany

Abstract. Automatic program repair holds the potential of dramatically improving the productivity of programmers during the software development process and correctness of software in general. Recent advances in machine learning, deep learning, and NLP have rekindled the hope to eventually fully automate the process of repairing programs. However, previous approaches that aim to predict a single fix are prone to fail due to uncertainty about the true intend of the programmer. Therefore, we propose a generative model that learns a *distribution* over potential fixes. Our model is formulated as a deep conditional variational autoencoder that can efficiently sample fixes for a given erroneous program. In order to ensure *diverse* solutions, we propose a novel regularizer that encourages diversity over a semantic embedding space. Our evaluations on common programming errors show for the first time the generation of diverse fixes and strong improvements over the state-of-the-art approaches by fixing up to 45% of the erroneous programs. We additionally show that for the 65% of the repaired programs, our approach was able to generate multiple programs with diverse functionalities.

Keywords: Program repair · Generative models · Conditional variational autoencoder

1 Introduction

Software development is a time-consuming and expensive process. Unfortunately, programs written by humans typically come with bugs, so significant effort needs to be invested to obtain code that is only likely to be correct. Debugging is also typically performed by humans and can contain mistakes. This is neither desirable nor acceptable in many critical applications. Therefore, automatically locating and correcting program errors [11] offers the potential to increase productivity as well as improve the correctness of software.

Advances in deep learning [17,18], computer vision [9,26], and NLP [3,30] have dramatically boosted the machine's ability to automatically learn representations of natural data such as images and natural language contents for various tasks. Deep learning models also have been successful in learning the distribution

M. Kamp et al. (Eds.): ECML PKDD 2021 Workshops, CCIS 1525, pp. 119–133, 2021.
https://doi.org/10.1007/978-3-030-93733-1_8

over continuous [16,29] and discrete data [14,21], to generate new and diverse data points [10]. These advances in machine learning and the advent of large corpora of source code [1] provide new opportunities toward harnessing deep learning methods to understand, generate, or debug programs.

Prior works in automatic program repair predominantly rely on expert-designed rules and error models that describe the space of the potential fixes [8,27]. Such hand-designed rules and error models are not easily adaptable to the new domains and require a time-consuming process.

In contrast, learning-based approaches provide an opportunity to adapt such models to the new domain of errors. Therefore, there has been an increasing interest to carry over the success stories of deep learning in NLP and related techniques to employ learning-based approaches to tackle the "common programming errors" problem [12,13].

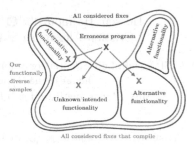

Fig. 1. Our SampleFix approach with diversity regularizer promotes sampling of diverse fixes, that account for the inherent uncertainty in the automated debugging task.

Such investigations have included compile-time errors such as missing scope delimiters, adding extraneous symbols, using incompatible operators. Novice programmers and even experienced developers often struggled with these types of errors [25], which is usually due to lack of attention to the details of programs and/or programmer's inexperience.

Recently, Gupta et al. [13] proposed a deep sequence to sequence model called DeepFix where, given an erroneous program, the model predicts the locations of the errors and a potential fix for each predicted location. The problem is formulated as a deterministic task, where the model is trained to predict a single fix for each error. However, different programs – and therefore also their fixes – can express the same functionality. Besides, there is also uncertainty about the intention of the programmer. Figure 1 illustrates the issue. Given an erroneous program (buggy program), there is a large number of programs within a certain edit distance. A subset of these, will result in successful compilation. The remaining programs will still implement different functionalities and – without additional information or assumptions – it is impossible to tell which program-/functionality was intended. In addition, previous work [28] also identified overfitting as one of the major challenges for learning-based automatic program repair. We believe that one of the culprits for this is the poor objectives used in the training process, e.g., training a model to generate a particular target fix.

Let us consider the example in Fig. 2 from the dataset of DeepFix [13]. This example program is incorrect due to the imbalanced number of curly brackets. In a traditional scenario, a compiler would warn the developer about this error. For example, when trying to compile this code with GCC, the compiler terminates with the error "expected declaration or statement at end of input", indicating

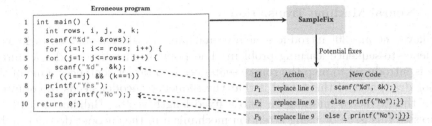

Fig. 2. SampleFix captures the inherent ambiguity of the possible fixes by sampling multiple potential fixes for the given erroneous real-world program. Potential fixes with the same functionality are highlighted with the same color and the newly added tokens are underlined.

line 10 as the error location. Experienced developers would be able to understand this cryptic message and proceed to fixing the program. Based on their intention, they can decide to add a curly bracket either at line 6 (patch P_1) or at line 9 (patch P_2). Both these solutions would fix the compilation error in the erroneous program, but the resulting solutions have different semantics.

Hence, we propose a deep generative framework to automatically correct programming errors by learning the distribution of potential fixes. We investigate different solutions to model the distribution of the fixes and sample multiple fixes, including different variants of Conditional Variation Autoencoders (CVAE) and beam search decoding. It turns out (as we will also show in our experiments) CVAE and beam search decoding are complementary, while CVAE is computationally more efficient in comparison to beam search decoding. Furthermore, we encourage diversity in the candidate fixes through a novel regularizer which penalizes similar fixes for an identical erroneous program and significantly increases the effectiveness of our approach. The candidate fixes in Fig. 2 are generate by our approach, illustrating its potential for generating both diverse and correct fixes. For a given erroneous program, our approach is capable of generating diverse fixes to resolve the syntax errors.

To summarize, the contributions of this paper are as follows, 1. We propose an efficient generative method to automatically correct common programming errors by learning the distribution over potential fixes. 2. We propose a novel regularizer to encourage the model to generate diverse fixes. 3. Our generative model together with the diversity regularizer shows an increase in the diversity and accuracy of fixes, and a strong improvement over the state-of-the-art approaches.

2   Related Work

Our work builds on the general idea of sequence-to-sequence models as well as ideas from neural machine translation. We phrase our approach as a variational auto-encoder and compare it to prior learning-based program repair approaches. We review the related work in order below.

2.1 Neural Machine Translation

Sutskever et al. [30] introduces neural machine translation and casts it as a sequence-to-sequence learning problem. The popular encoder-decoder architecture is introduced to map the source sentences into target sentences. One of the major drawbacks of this model is that the sequence encoder needs to compress all of the extracted information into a fixed-length vector. Bahdanau et al. [3] addresses this issue by using attention mechanism in the encoder-decoder architecture, where it focuses on the most relevant part of encoded information by learning to search over the encoded vector. In our work, we employ a sequence-to-sequence model with attention to parameterize our generative model. This model gets an incorrect program as input and maps it to many potential fixes by drawing samples on the estimated distribution of the fixes.

2.2 Variational Autoencoders

The variational autoencoders [16,24] is a generative model designed to learn deep directed latent variable based graphical models of large datasets. The model is trained on the data distribution by maximizing the variational lower bound of the log-likelihood as the objective function. Bowman et al. [5] extend this framework by introducing an RNN-based variational autoencoder to enable the learning of latent variable based generative models on text data. The proposed model is successful in generating diverse and coherent sentences. To model conditional distributions for the structured output representation Sohn et al. [29] extended variational autoencoders by introducing an objective that maximizes the conditional data log-likelihood. In our approach, we employ an RNN-based conditional variational autoencoder to model the distribution of the potential fixes given erroneous programs. Variational autoencoder approaches enable the efficient sampling of accurate and diverse fixes.

2.3 Learning-Based Program Repair

Recently there has been a growing interest in using learning-based approaches to automatically repair the programs [22]. Long and Rinard [20] proposed a probabilistic model by designing code features to rank potential fixes for a given program. Pu et al. [23] employ an encoder-decoder neural architecture to automatically correct programs. In these works and many learning-based programming repair approaches, enumerative search over programs is required to resolve all errors. However, our proposed framework is capable of predicting the location and potential fixes by passing the whole program to the model. Besides this, unlike our approach, which only generates fixes for the given erroneous program, Pu et al. [23] need to predict whole program statements to resolve the errors.

There are two important program repair tasks explored in the literature: fixing syntactic errors and fixing semantic ones. While in the current work we propose a technique for fixing syntactic errors, we believe that our observation about the diversity of the fix has implications for the approaches aimed at repairing semantic bugs as well. Most of the recent work in this domain aim to predict a unique fix, often extracted from a real-world repository. For example, Getafix [2], a recent approach for automatically repairing six types of semantic bugs, is evaluated on a set of 1,268 unique fixes written by developers. Similarly, DLfix [19] considers a bug to be fixed only if it exactly matches a patch provided by the developer. While this is an improved methodology in the spirit of our proposal it is highly dependent on the performance of the test suite oracle which may not always capture the developer's intent.

DeepFix [13], RLAssist [12], and DrRepair [32] uses neural representations to repair syntax errors in programs. In detail, DeepFix [13] uses a sequence-to-sequence model to directly predict a fix for incorrect programs. In contrast, our generative framework is able to generate multiple fixes by learning the distribution of potential correctness. Therefore, our model does not penalize, but rather encourages diverse fixes. RLAssist [12] repairs the programs by employing a reinforcement learning approach. They train an agent that navigate over the program to locate and resolve the syntax errors. In this work, they only address the typographic errors, rely on a hand-designed action space, and meet problems due to the increasing size of the action space. In contrast, our method shows improved performance on typographic errors and also generalizes to issues with missing variable declaration errors by generating diverse fixes.

In a recent work, Yasunaga and Liang [32] proposed DrRepair to resolve the syntax error by introducing a program feedback graph. They connect the relevant symbols in the source code and the compile error messages and employ the graph neural network on top to model the process of the program repair. In this work, they rely on the compiler error messages which can be helpful, but it also limits the generality of the method. However, our proposed approach does not rely on additional information such as compiler error messages, and it resolves the errors by directly modeling the underlying distribution of the potential correct fixes.

3   SampleFix: Generative Model for Diversified Code Fixes

Repairing the common program errors is a challenging task due to ambiguity in potential corrections and lack of representative data. Given a single erroneous program and a certain number of allowed changes, there are multiple ways to fix the program resulting in different styles and functionality. Without further information, the true, intended style and/or functionality remains unknown. In order to account for this inherent ambiguity, we propose a deep generative model to learn a distribution over potential fixes given the erroneous program – in contrast to predicting a single fix. We frame this challenging learning problem as a conditional variational autoencoders (CVAE). However, standard sampling procedures and limitations of datasets and their construction make learning and generation of diverse samples a challenge. We address this issue by a beam

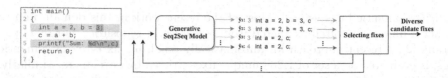

Fig. 3. Overview of SampleFix at inference time, highlighting the generation of diverse fixes.

search decoding scheme in combination with a novel regularizer that encourages diversity of the samples in the embedding space of the CVAE.

Figure 3 provides an overview of our proposed approach at inference time. For a given erroneous program, the generative model draws T intermediate, candidate fixes $\hat{y}$ from the learned conditional distribution. We use a compiler to select a subset of promising intermediate candidate fixes based on the number of remaining errors. This procedure is applied iteratively until arrive at a set of candidate fixes within the maximum number of prescribed changes. We then select a final set of candidate fixes that compile, have unique syntax according to our measure described below (Subsect. 3.5).

In the following, we formulate our proposed generative model with the diversity regularizer and provide details of our training and inference process.

3.1   Conditional Variational Autoencoders for Generating Fixes

Conditional Variational Autoencoders (CVAE) [29], model conditional distributions $p_\theta(\mathbf{y}|\mathbf{x})$ using latent variables $\mathbf{z}$. The conditioning introduced through $\mathbf{z}$ enables the modelling of complex multi-modal distributions. As powerful transformations can be learned using neural networks, $\mathbf{z}$ itself can have a simple distribution which allows for efficient sampling. This model allows for sampling from $p_\theta(\mathbf{y}|\mathbf{x})$ given an input sequence $\mathbf{x}$, by first sampling latent variables $\hat{\mathbf{z}}$ from the prior distribution $p(\mathbf{z})$. During training, amortized variational inference is used and the latent variables $\mathbf{z}$ are learned using a recognition network $q_\phi(\mathbf{z}|\mathbf{x},\mathbf{y})$, parametrized by ϕ. In detail, the variational lower bound of the model (Eq. 1) is maximized,

$$\log(p(\mathbf{y}|\mathbf{x})) \geq \mathbb{E}_{q_\phi(\mathbf{z}|\mathbf{x},\mathbf{y})} \log(p_\theta(\mathbf{y}|\mathbf{z},\mathbf{x})) \\ - D_{\mathrm{KL}}(q_\phi(\mathbf{z}|\mathbf{x},\mathbf{y}), p(\mathbf{z}|\mathbf{x})). \tag{1}$$

Penalizing the divergence of $q_\phi(\mathbf{z}|\mathbf{x},\mathbf{y})$ to the prior in Eq. 1 allows for sampling from the prior $p(\mathbf{z})$ during inference. In practice, the variational lower bound is estimated using Monte-Carlo integration,

$$\hat{\mathcal{L}}_{\mathrm{CVAE}} = \frac{1}{T} \sum_{i=1}^{T} \log(p_\theta(\mathbf{y}|\hat{\mathbf{z}}_i, \mathbf{x})) \\ - D_{\mathrm{KL}}(q_\phi(\mathbf{z}|\mathbf{x},\mathbf{y}), p(\mathbf{z}|\mathbf{x})). \tag{2}$$

where, $\hat{\mathbf{z}}_i \sim q_\phi(\mathbf{z}|\mathbf{x}, \mathbf{y})$, and T is the number of samples. We cast our model for resolving program errors in the Conditional Variational Autoencoder framework. Here, the input $\mathbf{x}$ is the erroneous program and $\mathbf{y}$ is the fix.

However, the plain CVAE as described in [29] suffers from diversity issues. Usually, the drawn samples do not reflect the true variance of the posterior $p(\mathbf{y}|\mathbf{x})$. This would amount to the correct fix potentially missing from our candidate fixes. To mitigate this problem, next we introduce an objective that aims to enhance the diversity of our candidate fixes.

3.2 Enabling Diverse Samples Using a Best of Many Objective

Here, we introduce the diversity enhancing objective that we use. Casting our model in the Conditional Variational Autoencoder framework would enable us to sample a set of candidate fixes for a given erroneous program. However, the standard variational lower bound objective does not encourage diversity in the candidate fixes. This is because the average likelihood of the candidate fixes is considered. In detail, as the average likelihood is considered, all candidate fixes must explain the "true" fix in training set well. This discourages diversity and constrains the recognition network, which is already constrained to maintain a Gaussian latent variable distribution. In practice, the learned distribution fails to fully capture the variance of the true distribution. To encourage diversity, we employ "Many Samples" (MS) objective proposed by Bhattacharyya et al. [4],

$$\hat{\mathcal{L}}_{\mathrm{MS}} = \log\Big(\frac{1}{T}\sum_{i=1}^{T} p_\theta(\mathbf{y}|\hat{\mathbf{z}}_i, \mathbf{x})\Big) \\ - D_{\mathrm{KL}}(q_\phi(\mathbf{z}|\mathbf{x}, \mathbf{y}), p(\mathbf{z}|\mathbf{x})). \tag{3}$$

In comparison to Eq. 2, this objective (Eq. 3) encourages diversity in the model by allowing for multiple chances to draw highly likely candidate fixes. This enables the model to generate diverse candidate fixes, while maintaining high likelihood. In practice, due to numerical stability issues, we use "Best of Many Samples" (BMS) objective, which is an approximation of 3. This objective retains the diversity enhancing nature of Eq. 3 while being easy to train,

$$\hat{\mathcal{L}}_{\mathrm{BMS}} = \max_i \big(\log(p_\theta(\mathbf{y}|\hat{\mathbf{z}}_i, \mathbf{x}))\big) \\ - D_{\mathrm{KL}}(q_\phi(\mathbf{z}|\mathbf{x}, \mathbf{y}), p(\mathbf{z}|\mathbf{x})). \tag{4}$$

3.3 DS-SampleFix: Encouraging Diversity with a Diversity-Sensitive Regularizer

To increase the diversity using Eq. 4 we need to use a substantial number of samples during training. This is computationally prohibitive especially for large models, as memory requirements and computation time increases linearly in the number of such samples. On the other hand, for a small number of samples, the objective behaves similarly to the standard CVAE objective as the recognition network has fewer and fewer chances to draw highly likely samples/candidate fixes, thus limiting diversity. Therefore, in order to encourage the model to generate diverse fixes even with a limited number of samples, we propose a novel regularizer that aims to increase the distance between the two closest candidate fixes (Eq. 5). This penalizes generating similar candidate fixes for a given erroneous program and thus encourages diversity in the set of candidate fixes. In comparison to Eq. 4, we observe considerable gains even with the use of only $T = 2$ candidate fixes. In detail, we maximize the following objective

$$\hat{\mathcal{L}}_{\text{DS-BMS}} = \max_i \left(\log(p_\theta(\mathbf{y}|\hat{\mathbf{z}}_i, \mathbf{x})) \right) + \min_{i,j} d(\hat{\mathbf{y}}^i, \hat{\mathbf{y}}^j)$$
$$- D_{\text{KL}}(q_\phi(\mathbf{z}|\mathbf{x}, \mathbf{y}), p(\mathbf{z}|\mathbf{x})). \tag{5}$$

Distance Metric. Here, we discuss the distance metric d in Eq. 5. Note, that the samples $\left\{ \hat{\mathbf{y}}^i, \hat{\mathbf{y}}^j \right\}$ can be of different lengths. Therefore, we first pad the shorter sample to equalize lengths. Empirically, we find that the Euclidean distance performs best. This is mainly because, in practice, Euclidean distance is easier to optimize.

3.4 Beam Search Decoding for Generating Fixes

Beam search decoding is a classical model to generate multiple outputs from a sequence-to-sequence model [7,31]. Given the distributions $p_\theta(\mathbf{y}|\mathbf{x})$ of a sequence-to-sequence model we can generate multiple outputs by unrolling the model in time and keeping the top-K tokens at each time step, where K is the beam width. In our generative model, we employ beam search algorithm to sample multiple fixes. In detail, we decode with beam width of size K for each sample $\mathbf{z}$ and in total for T samples from $p(\mathbf{z})$. We set $T = 100$ during inference.

3.5 Selecting Diverse Candidate Fixes

We extend the iterative repair procedure introduced by Gupta et al. [13] in the context of our proposed generative model, where the iterative procedure now leverages multiple candidate fixes. Given an erroneous program, the generative model outputs T candidate fixes. Each fix contains a potential erroneous line with the corresponding fix. So in each iteration we only edit one line of the given program. To select the best fixes, we take the candidate fixes and the input erroneous program, reconcile them to create T updated programs. We evaluate these fixes using a compiler, and select up to the best N fixes, where $N \leq T$. We only select the unique fixes which do not introduce any additional error messages. In the next iterations, we feed up to N programs back to the model. These programs are updated based on the selected fixes of the previous iteration. We keep up to N programs with the lower number of error messages over the iterations. At the end of the repairing procedure, we obtain multiple potential candidate fixes. In the experiments where we are interested in a single repaired program, we pick the best fix with the highest probability score according to our deep generative model.

3.6   Model Architecture and Implementation Details

To ensure a fair comparison, our generative model is based on the sequence-to-sequence architecture, similar to Gupta et al. [13]. Figure 4 shows the architecture of our approach in detail. Note that the recognition network is available to encode the fixes to latent variables z only during training. All of the networks in our framework consists of 4-layers of LSTM cells with 300 units. The network is optimized using Adam optimizer [15] with the default setting. We use $T = 2$ samples to train our models, and $T = 100$ samples during inference. To process the program through the networks, we tokenize the programs similar to the setting used by Gupta et al. [13].

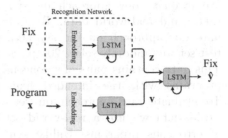

Fig. 4. Overview of network architecture.

During inference, the conditioning erroneous program x is input to the encoder, which encodes the program to the vector v. To generate multiple fixes using our decoder, the code vector v along with a sample of z from the prior $p(z)$ is input to the decoder. For simplicity, we use a standard Gaussian $\mathcal{N}(0, I)$ prior, although more complex priors can be easily leveraged. The decoder is unrolled in time and output logits $(p_\theta(y|\hat{z}_i, x))$.

4   Experiments

We evaluate our approach on the task of repairing common programming errors. We evaluate the diversity and accuracy of our sampled error corrections as well as compare our proposed method with the state of the art.

4.1   Dataset

We use the dataset published by Gupta et al. [13] as it's sizable and includes real-world data. It contains C programs written by students in an introductory programming course. The dataset consists of 93 different tasks that were written by students in an introductory programming course. The programs were collected using a web-based system [6]. These programs have token lengths in the range [75, 450], and contain typographic and missing variable declaration errors. To tokenize the programs and generate training and test data different type of tokens, such as types, keywords, special characters, functions, literals and variables are used. The dataset contains two sets of data which are called synthetic and real-world data. The synthetic data contains the erroneous programs which are synthesized by mutating correct programs written by students. The real-world data contains 6975 erroneous programs with 16766 error messages.

4.2 Evaluation

We evaluate our approach on synthetic and real-world data. To evaluate our approach on the synthetic test set we randomly select 20k pairs. This data contains pairs of erroneous programs with the intended fixes. To evaluate our approach on real-world data we use a real-world set of erroneous programs. Unlike synthetic test set, we don't have access to the intended fix(es) in the real-world data. However, we can check the correctness of the program using the evaluator (compiler). Following the

Table 1. Results of performance comparison of DeepFix, Beam search (BS), SampleFix, and DS-SampleFix on synthetic data. Typo, Miss Dec, and All refer to typographic, missing variable declarations, and all of the errors respectively.

Models	Typo	Miss Dec	All
DeepFix	84.7%	78.8%	82.0%
Beam search (BS)	91.8%	89.5%	90.7%
SampleFix	86.8%	86.5%	86.6%
DS-SampleFix	95.6%	88.1%	92.2%

prior work, we train two networks, one for typographic errors and another to fix missing variables declaration errors. Note that there might be an overlap between the error resolved by the network for typographic errors and the network for missing variables declaration errors, so we also provide the overall results of the resolved error messages.

Table 2. Results of performance comparison of DeepFix, RLAssist, DrRepair, Beam search (BS), SampleFix, DS-SampleFix, and DS-SampleFix + BS. Typo, Miss Dec, and All refer to typographic, missing variable declarations, and all of the error messages respectively. Speed denotes computational time for sampling 100 fixes. ✔ denotes successfully compiled programs, while 🕮 refers to resolved error messages.

Models	Typo		Miss Dec		All		Speed (s)
	✔	🕮	✔	🕮	✔	🕮	
DeepFix [13]	23.3%	30.8%	10.1%	12.9%	33.4%	40.8%	–
RLAssist [12]	*26.6%*	*39.7%*	–	–	–	–	–
DrRepair [32]	–	–	–	–	34.0%	–	–
Beam search (BS)	25.9%	42.2%	**20.3%**	47.0%	44.7%	63.9%	4.82
SampleFix	24.8%	38.8%	16.1%	22.8%	40.9%	56.3%	0.88
DS-SampleFix	27.7%	40.9%	16.7%	24.7%	44.4%	61.0%	0.88
DS-SampleFix+ BS	**27.8%**	**45.6%**	19.2%	**47.9%**	**45.2%**	**65.2%**	1.17

Synthetic Data. Table 1 shows the comparison of our proposed approaches, Beam search (BS), SampleFix and DS-SampleFix, with DeepFix [13] on the synthetic data in the first iteration. In this table (Table 1), we can see that our approaches outperform DeepFix in generating intended fixes for the typographic and missing variable declaration errors. Beam search (BS), SampleFix and DS-SampleFix generate 90.7%, 86.6%, and 92.2% of the intended fixes respectively.

Real-World Data. In Table 2 we compare our approaches, with state-of-the-art approaches (DeepFix [13], RLAssist [12], and DrRepair [32]) on the real-world data. In our experiments (Table 2) we show the performance of beam search decoding, CVAEs (SampleFix), and our proposed diversity-sensitive regularizer (DS-SampleFix). Furthermore, we show that DS-SampleFix can still take advantage of beam search algorithm (DS-SampleFix + BS). To do that, for each sample z we decode with beam width of size 5, and to sample 100 fixes we draw 20 samples from $p(z)$. We also provide the sampling speed in terms of sampling 100 fixes for a given program using an average over 100 runs. The running time results show that CVAE-based models are at least 4× faster than beam search in sampling the fixes. In this experiment, we feed the programs up to 5 iterations.

Table 2 shows that our approaches outperform DeepFix [13], RLAssist [12], and DrRepair [32] in resolving the error messages. This shows that generating multiple diverse fixes can lead to substantial improvement in performance. Beam search, SampleFix, DS-SampleFix, and DS-SampleFix + BS resolve 63.9%, 56.3%, 61.0%, and 65.2% of the error messages respectively. Overall, our DS-SampleFix + BS is able to resolve all compile-time errors of the 45.2% of the programs - around 12% points improvement over DeepFix and 11% points improvement over DrRepair. Furthermore, the performance advantage of DS-SampleFix over SampleFix shows the effectiveness of our novel regularizer.

Note that DrRepair [32] has achieved further improvements by relying on the compiler. While utilizing the compiler output seems to be beneficial, it also limits the generality of the approach. For a fair comparison, we report the performance of DrRepair without the compiler output, but consider informing our model by the compiler output an interesting avenue of future work.

Erroneous program

```
1   #include <stdio.h>
2   int main (){
3     int a, i;
4     scanf("%d\n", &a);
5     int s[a], p[a], g[a];
6     for (i = 0; i < a; i++){
7       scanf("%d", &s[i]);}
8     for (i = 0; i < a; i++){
9       scanf("%d", &p[i]);}
10    for (i = 0; i < a; i++){
11      g[p[i]] = s[i];}
12    for (i = 0; i < a; i++){
13      printf("%d", g[i]);
14    printf("end");
15    return 0 ;}
```

Id	Action	New Code
P_1	replace line 13	printf("%d", g[i]);}
P_2	replace line 14	printf("end");}

Fig. 5. An example illustrating that our DS-SampleFix can generate diverse fixes. Left: Example of a program with a typographic error. The error, i.e., missing bracket, is highlighted at line 13. Right: Our DS-SampleFix proposes multiple fixes for the given error (line number with the corresponding fix), highlighting the ability of DS-SampleFix to generate diverse and accurate fixes.

Qualitative Example. We illustrate diverse fixes generated by our DS-SampleFix in Fig. 5 using a code example with typographic errors, with the corresponding two output samples of DS-SampleFix. In the examples given in Fig. 5, there is a missing closing curly bracket after line 13. We can see that DS-SampleFix generates multiple correct fixes to resolve the error in the given program. This indicates that our approach is capable of handling the inherent ambiguity and uncertainty in predicting fixes for the erroneous programs. The two fixes in Fig. 5 are unique and compileable fixes that implement different functionalities for the given erroneous program. Note that generating multiple diverse fixes gives the programmers the opportunity of choosing the desired fix(es) among the compileable ones, based on their intention.

Generating Functionally Diverse Programs. Given an erroneous program, our approach can generate multiple potential fixes that result in a successful compilation. Since we do not have access to the user's intention, it is desirable to suggest multiple potential fixes with diverse functionalities. Here, we evaluate our approach in generating multiple programs with different functionalities.

In order to assess different functionalities, we use the following approach based on tests. The dataset of Gupta et al. [13] consists of 93 different tasks. The description of each task, including the input/output format, is provided in the dataset. Based on the input/output format, we can provide input examples for each task. To measure the diversity in functionality of the programs in each task, we generate 10 input examples. For instance, given a group of programs for a specific task, we can run each program using the input examples and get the outputs. We consider two programs to have different functionalities if they return different outputs given the same input example(s).

In order to generate multiple programs we use our iterative selecting strategy (Subsect. 3.5). In each iteration, we keep up to N programs with the less number of error messages over the iterations. At the end of the repairing procedure, we obtain multiple repaired programs. As discussed (Fig. 1), a subset of these programs will successfully compile. In this experiment, we use the real-world test set, and we set $N = 50$ as this number is large enough to allow us to study the diversity of the fixes, without incurring an unnecessarily large load on our infrastructure. Our goals in the remaining of this section are: 1. For each erroneous program, to measure the number of generated unique fixes that successfully compile. 2. For each erroneous program, to measure the number of generated programs with different functionalities.

Figure 6a and Fig. 6b show the syntactic diversity of the generated programs, and the diversity in functionality of these programs, respectively. In Fig. 6a we show the percentage of the successfully compiled programs with unique fixes for a given erroneous program. The x-axis refers to the number of generated and successfully compiled unique programs, and y-axis to the percentage of repaired programs for which these many unique fixes were generated. For example, for almost 20% of the repaired programs, DS-SampleFix + BS generates two unique

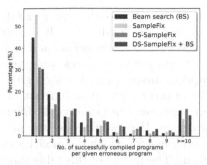 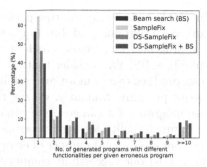

(a) Diversity of the generated programs.   (b) Diversity of the functionality of the generated programs.

Fig. 6. The results show the performance of Beam search (BS), SampleFix, DS-SampleFix, and DS-SampleFix + BS. (a) Percentage of the number of the generated successfully compiled, unique programs for the given erroneous programs. (b) Percentage of the successfully compiled programs with different functionalities for the given erroneous programs.

fixes. Overall, we can see that DS-SampleFix and DS-SampleFix + BS generate more diverse programs in comparison to the other approaches.

Figure 6b shows the percentage of the successfully compiled programs with different functionalities, for a given erroneous program. Here, the x-axis refers to the number of the generated functionally different programs, and y-axis refers to the percentage of erroneous programs with at least one fix, for which we could generate that many diverse fixes. One can observe that in many cases, e.g., up to 60% of the times for SampleFix, the methods generate programs corresponding to a single functionality. However, in

Table 3. Results of performance comparison of Beam Search (BS), SampleFix, DS-SampleFix, and DS-SampleFix +BS on generating diverse programs. Diverse Prog refers to the percentage of cases where the models generate at least two or more successfully compiled unique programs. Diverse Func denotes the percentage of cases where the models generate at least two or more programs with different functionalities.

Models	Diverse Prog	Diverse Func
Beam search	55.6%	45.1%
SampleFix	44.6%	34.9%
DS-SampleFix	68.8%	53.4%
DS-SampleFix + BS	**69.5%**	**60.4%**

many other cases they generate functionally diverse fixes. For example, in almost 10% of the cases, DS-SampleFix generate 10 or more fixes with different functionalities. In Fig. 6b we can see that all of the approaches have higher percentage for generating program with the same functionality in comparison to the results in Fig. 6a. This indicates that for some of the given erroneous programs, we generate multiple unique programs with approximately the same functionality. These results show that DS-SampleFix and DS-SampleFix + BS generate programs with more diverse functionalities in comparison to the other approaches.

In Table 3 we compare the performance of our approaches in generating diverse programs and functionalities. We provide results for all of our four approaches, i.e., Beam search (BS), SampleFix, DS-SampleFix, and DS-SampleFix + BS. We consider that an approach can generate diverse programs if it can produce two or more successfully compiled, unique programs for a given erroneous program. Similarly, we say that the approach produces functionally diverse programs if it can generate two or more programs with observable differences in functionality for a given erroneous program. Here we consider the percentage out of the total number of erroneous programs for which the model generates at least one successfully compiled program. The results of this table show that our DS-SampleFix + BS approach generates programs with more diverse functionalities in comparison to the other approaches.

5   Conclusion

We propose a novel approach to correct common programming errors. We recognize and model the inherent ambiguity and uncertainty when predicting multiple fixes. In contrast to previous approaches, our approach is able to learn the distribution over candidate fixes rather than the most likely fix. We achieve increased diversity of the sampled fixes by a novel diversity-sensitive regularizer. We show that our approach is capable of generating multiple diverse fixes with different functionalities. Furthermore, our evaluations on synthetic and real-world data show improvements over state-of-the-art methods.

References

1. Allamanis, M., Barr, E.T., Devanbu, P., Sutton, C.: A survey of machine learning for big code and naturalness. ACM Comput. Surv. (CSUR) **51**, 1–37 (2018)
2. Bader, J., Scott, A., Pradel, M., Chandra, S.: Getafix: learning to fix bugs automatically. Proc. ACM Program. Lang. **3**(OOPSLA), 1–27 (2019)
3. Bahdanau, D., Cho, K., Bengio, Y.: Neural machine translation by jointly learning to align and translate (2015)
4. Bhattacharyya, A., Schiele, B., Fritz, M.: Accurate and diverse sampling of sequences based on a "best of many" sample objective. In: CVPR (2018)
5. Bowman, S.R., Vilnis, L., Vinyals, O., Dai, A.M., Jozefowicz, R., Bengio, S.: Generating sentences from a continuous space. In: SIGNLL Conference on Computational Natural Language Learning (CoNLL) (2016)
6. Das, R., Ahmed, U.Z., Karkare, A., Gulwani, S.: Prutor: a system for tutoring CS1 and collecting student programs for analysis (2016)
7. Deshpande, A., Aneja, J., Wang, L., Schwing, A.G., Forsyth, D.: Fast, diverse and accurate image captioning guided by part-of-speech. In: CVPR (2019)
8. D'Antoni, L., Samanta, R., Singh, R.: QLOSE: program repair with quantitative objectives. In: Chaudhuri, S., Farzan, A. (eds.) CAV 2016. LNCS, vol. 9780, pp. 383–401. Springer, Cham (2016). https://doi.org/10.1007/978-3-319-41540-6_21
9. Girshick, R.: Fast R-CNN. In: ICCV (2015)
10. Gottschlich, J., et al.: The three pillars of machine programming. In: MAPL (2018)

11. Goues, C.L., Pradel, M., Roychoudhury, A.: Automated program repair. Commun. ACM **62**(12), 56–65 (2019)
12. Gupta, R., Kanade, A., Shevade, S.: Deep reinforcement learning for programming language correction. In: AAAI (2019)
13. Gupta, R.R., Pal, S., Kanade, A., Shevade, S.K.: DeepFix: fixing common C language errors by deep learning. In: AAAI (2017)
14. Jang, E., Gu, S., Poole, B.: Categorical reparameterization with Gumbel-Softmax. In: ICLR (2017)
15. Kingma, D.P., Ba, J.: Adam: a method for stochastic optimization. In: ICLR (2015)
16. Kingma, D.P., Welling, M.: Auto-encoding variational Bayes. In: ICLR (2014)
17. Krizhevsky, A., Sutskever, I., Hinton, G.E.: ImageNet classification with deep convolutional neural networks. In: NIPS (2012)
18. Lee, H., Grosse, R., Ranganath, R., Ng, A.Y.: Unsupervised learning of hierarchical representations with convolutional deep belief networks. Commun. ACM **54**, 95–103 (2011)
19. Li, Y., Wang, S., Nguyen, T.N.: DLFix: context-based code transformation learning for automated program repair. In: International Conference on Software Engineering (ICSE) (2020)
20. Long, F., Rinard, M.: Automatic patch generation by learning correct code. In: ACM SIGPLAN Notices (2016)
21. Maddison, C.J., Mnih, A., Teh, Y.W.: The concrete distribution: a continuous relaxation of discrete random variables (2016)
22. Monperrus, M.: Automatic software repair: a bibliography. ACM Comput. Surv. (CSUR) **51**, 1–24 (2018)
23. Pu, Y., Narasimhan, K., Solar-Lezama, A., Barzilay, R.: sk_p: a neural program corrector for MOOCs. In: ACM SIGPLAN (2016)
24. Rezende, D.J., Mohamed, S.: Variational inference with normalizing flows. In: ICML (2015)
25. Seo, H., Sadowski, C., Elbaum, S., Aftandilian, E., Bowdidge, R.: Programmers' build errors: a case study (at google). In: ICSE (2014)
26. Simonyan, K., Zisserman, A.: Very deep convolutional networks for large-scale image recognition. In: ICLR (2015)
27. Singh, R., Gulwani, S., Solar-Lezama, A.: Automated feedback generation for introductory programming assignments. In: PLDI (2013)
28. Smith, E.K., Barr, E.T., Goues, C.L., Brun, Y.: Is the cure worse than the disease? Overfitting in automated program repair. In: Foundations of Software Engineering (ESEC/FSE) (2015)
29. Sohn, K., Lee, H., Yan, X.: Learning structured output representation using deep conditional generative models. In: NIPS (2015)
30. Sutskever, I., Vinyals, O., Le, Q.V.: Sequence to sequence learning with neural networks. In: NIPS (2014)
31. Wang, L., Schwing, A., Lazebnik, S.: Diverse and accurate image description using a variational auto-encoder with an additive gaussian encoding space. In: NIPS (2017)
32. Yasunaga, M., Liang, P.: Graph-based, self-supervised program repair from diagnostic feedback. In: ICML (2020)

Linguistic Analysis of Stack Overflow Data: Native English vs Non-native English Speakers

Janneke Morin[ID] and Krishnendu Ghosh[✉][ID]

Department of Computer Science, College of Charleston, Charleston, USA
morinja@g.cofc.edu, ghoshk@cofc.edu

Abstract. Collaborative projects in software engineering span globally. English is the primary language for interaction in software development. Native English speakers can adapt to the rigors of software engineering projects because of their familiarity with the language in code development and communications related to software development. We analyze the communications related to software collaboration using linguistic features. We mine data from online question-answer forum, Stack Overflow and evaluate machine learning approaches to classify contributors as native English speakers *vs* non-native English speakers.

Keywords: Linguistic features · Stack Overflow · Native English speakers · Software developers · Machine learning · Word2Vec

1 Introduction

Software projects are developed globally. A team is often spread around different time zones and countries. English is the language for communication during the conceptual development of software. The source code development, though in high level computer language is also, in English. It is natural that the developers who are non-native English speakers face language barriers in software development, which could potentially lead to inefficiency in the process of creation of software. However, more than 60% of the global population is non-native English speaker [1]. English is the primary language used in the internet. It is critical to address the need for linguistic diversity in software development projects. Studies have indicated computer programming have motivated non-native English speaker to learn English and non-native English speakers seek instructional materials in simplified English [2]. Therefore, it is important to evaluate the conversation of native English speakers *vs* non-native English speakers.

Organizations need a better decision making in software development and reducing inefficiencies in software. We address the problem of language barrier in the software community by posing the problem of identifying the linguistic features that potentially, can lead to identification fluency (or lack thereof) in English. An empirical study of online communication is anticipated to provide intricate details about the linguistic features as in the cases of native English speakers and non-native English speakers. Global collaboration in software development projects has been growing at a rapid pace, online Q&A forums such as Stack Overflow have become hubs for millions of budding

© Springer Nature Switzerland AG 2021
M. Kamp et al. (Eds.): ECML PKDD 2021 Workshops, CCIS 1525, pp. 134–142, 2021.
https://doi.org/10.1007/978-3-030-93733-1_9

and seasoned developers alike to exchange knowledge and ideas. `Stack Overflow` is an open source platform and is contributed by users globally. The contents of `Stack Overflow` data is generated by users who are native English speakers or non-native English speakers. Also, the data forms the corpus of linguistic analysis of publicly available attributes of users, such as geographic location in the form of country, and statements in English. There is no explicit way to know if a user of `Stack Overflow` is a native English speaker or otherwise. It becomes challenging to know because the geographical location of the contributors is not very helpful. Clearly, there are countries whose primary medium of instruction is English but can have a subpopulation of non-native English speakers. For example, in the United States, there are subpopulations that are non-native English speaker. Similarly, there are countries whose primary medium of instruction is a non-native English language but a subpopulation is native English speaker. Diversity and inclusion in software projects have been well studied [3,4]. Linguistic diversity connected with cultural and ethnic diversity in software engineering has not been studied in details. This study is timely in understanding linguistic diversity in the software development. In this work, we aim to study one of the challenges embedded in linguistic diversity, native English speakers versus non-native English speakers through the following research questions:

RQ1: *Is the tone of posts authored by native English speakers different than that of non-native English speakers?*

RQ2: *Does positive (or negative language) identify - native English speakers or non-native English speakers?*

The aforementioned research questions is expected to provide some unique characteristics of native and non-native English speakers. Finally, we apply machine learning algorithms on data from *Stack Overflow* to classify communications between native and non-native English speakers.

2 Related Work

Our study is in the intersection on linguistic analysis of `Stack Overflow` and diversity in open source forums. Recent literature have studied different aspects of software engineering-such as diversity [5], geolocation [6], user-behavior [7], age related programming experience [8] and developer interactions [9]. Gender and tenure diversity amongst team members in software projects in GitHub [5]. There is published literature that have demonstrated that there are certain words that cannot be translated to a different language. A study [10] of multilingual corpus of Facebook texts written primarily in German, Italian, and English by users in South Tyrol, Italy. The methodology creates an untranslatable dialect lexicon to process encountered words of this type and to post-process out-of-vocabulary (OOV) tokens in the corpus. The lack of *untranslatable* words leads to selection of words that are likely to express emotionally strong words. For example, a non-native English speaker may use the word *happy* when there is no single English word that express *mildly happy*. Often, there are cultural aspects that are influenced in expressing emotions [11]. Developers tended to answer impolite/negative comments with a positive/negative comment with higher probability than impolite/negative comments [12]. The study found that negative emotions such as sadness and anger tend to be followed by negative emotions more than positive emotion are followed by positive emotions. The researchers built their dataset from fifteen open-source, publicly available projects with a high number of comments from a dataset [13]. Relationship between gender and sentiment in code reviews [14] have been studied. The study was based on mining code reviews of 12 popular OSS projects, eventually reduced to six and stored the data in a MySQL database. This project leveraged SentiWordNet 3.0 [15] to compile words expressing positive and negative sentiments and evaluate these against the dataset. This methodology could be followed for other factors such as location and reputation. The research found that male developers were significantly more likely to author review comments expressing positive/negative sentiments and expletives than females. Often, non-native English speaker express using words that are positive, neutral and negative sentiments than the native English speakers.

Senti4SD [16] presents a classifier for sentiment analysis. The classifier was trained and evaluation on Stack Overflow questions, answers, and comments. The model was built upon a dataset of an even distribution of positive, negative, and neutral text from StackOverflow that included manual annotation for polarity. After extracting features from the texts, the authors used Support Vector Machines (SVM) to train their model. The technology observes a 19% improvement in precision for the negative class and a 25% improvement in recall for the neutral class with respect to the baseline represented by SentiStrength [17]. Wang et al. [18] found that 86 to 96% of the accepted answers are written by frequent contributors on the platform. This paper also explores the time taken to answer questions and its relationship to the frequency that the contributor uses the platform. The study found that questions which were answered by non-frequent contributors are significantly longer than those that were answered by frequent contributors. When considering reputation score, this study also did not directly use reputation score due to the possible difference between score at the time of posting and the time of the data dump.

Geographical connection with developer in GitHub was reported [19]. Geographical information is critical in order to identify- language, cultural and ethnicity of the software developers. Machine learning of Stack Overflow been studied [20] and analyzed [21,22], extensively.

3   Methodology

The StackExchange Data Explorer aggregates data from numerous question-and-answer sites, including Stack Overflow.com. The raw data for this study was collected [23]. The data contained 50,000 comments, the reputation score of the user who made the comment, and his/her location (if included on profile).

Data Preparation: The raw data from StackExchange Data Explorer was processed to extract the geographical location of the users in Stack Overflow. The user location (geocoding) was extracted in the following way: The user locations in the initial dataset were inconsistent- several profiles' specified only the user's country, others a country and city, others no location at all. In order to these geographical location consistent, we used the reverse geocoder package from PyPi. We first geocoded each location, then extracted latitude and longitude values from the result, and searched for the country corresponding to those points. We returned a two-letter code for this country as the final location. The labeling of users as 'native' English speakers were derived from the country code that had listed English as a primary language.

Data was preprocessed with tokenization, stemming and lemmatization. The standard list of English stopwords were removed from each document. For example, the original sentence was *It will help if you give some details of which database you are using as techniques vary.* After preprocessing, the following list of words was the output, ['help', 'give', 'detail', 'database', 'use', 'technique', 'vary'].

Linguistic Features: The following features were extracted from the set of tokens associated with each text: text length, unique tokens, punctuation density, question density, average word length, noun density, pronoun density, verb density, adjective density, adverb density, document cluster determined by K-Means clustering analysis and top five tokens in native and nonnative texts. Here the word *density* meant weighted with the number of tokens. For example, punctuation density is the ration of punctuation tokens with total tokens. The ratio kept these features from being correlated with the size of the document, which was also used as a feature. During extraction of aforementioned features, we found the fifty most frequent words excluding stopwords in the native English speaker and non-native English subsets of the dataset. Then, we created features for the frequency of:

- The top five words in the top fifty for the native but not non-native subset: **'file'**, **'right'**, **'see'**, **'chang'**, **'run'**
- The top five words in the top fifty for the non-native but not native subset: **'version'**, **'return'**, **'post'**, **'even'**, **'run'**

The full feature set included a total of twenty-one features. We performed sequential feature selection on the full feature set including all of the data with the Sequential FeatureSelector from mlxtend. It found the following features the most informative to predicting whether a user was labeled a native English speaker or not: Neutrality score, verb usage, frequency of the following words: Punctuation usage, question usage, and frequency of the following words: 'solut', 'thing', 'chang', 'great', 'without', 'though', 'right', 'post'.

4 Results

We performed classification using machine learning algorithms by phrasing the classification problem as a two-class problem, native English speakers vs non-native English speaker. In addition to identifying the most informative features through sequential feature selection, we manually added features to machine learning models to determine which had the greatest impact on model performance. The technique begins with a feature-set containing a single feature. Then, it trains the model with a feature-set containing one additional feature. If adding that feature increases the performance of the model, then it is kept in the feature-set. Otherwise, it is removed from the set. We used this manual technique to tune our models as described.

We used the following machine learning models with five-fold cross-validation for analysis: Decision Tree, Random Forest, and Logistic Regression. Each model was trained and tested with randomly generated subsets created with 75:25 train:test ratio. Cross validation was performed with the use of *cross_val_score* method from sklearn. Sklearn was also the source of our base models.

We created a function which trains a random forest model with five-fold cross validation on the full list of features, beginning with one feature and adding one at a time, only if it increases model accuracy. The following lists the results of each feature that increased the accuracy:

- Neg: 0.68. The feature, 'Neg' is the ratio for the proportion of text that falls in the negative category, as determined by the Vader Sentiment [24] package for Python.
- Compound: 0.69 The feature, 'Compound', as determined by the VaderSentiment package for Python, is the normalized, weighted composite score of the text. It ranges from −1, the most negative, to +1, the most positive.
- Unique Words (percent of total tokens): 0.69
- Punctuation (percent of total tokens): 0.70
- Question Mark Usage: 0.72
- Adjective Usage: 0.72
- Pronoun usage: 0.73
- Use of the word 'version': 0.74

In the machine learning process, we used five-fold cross validation. The dataset of filtered features was split into five sections/folds. Each individual section took a turn as the test data while the rest of the sections were used together as training data for that iteration. This process helps reduce bias from a single particular train-test split as we used the average accuracy of all five iterations. We also implemented a word embeddings technique through Word2Vec with the Gensim package for Python. Through a multi-layer neural net, Word2Vec converts words to numerical representations, allowing for their use as features which train machine learning models. The model makes use of context of past appearances of a word and cosine similarity to predict its meaning and create associations to other words, represented by dimensions of a vector (neural word embedding) attached to each item in the vocabulary. For example, the dimension of the "good" vector which represents its relationship with "great" should have a high value on the 0–1 scale given the two words' similar meaning. We input the vectors of unseen test data into each of the below models to produce the accuracy metrics.

Figure 1(a) illustrates the receiver operating characteristics (ROC) of the machine learning algorithms that were used for experiments for 75:25 training:test ratio. The Logistic Regression model produced the best results on all metrics given by the classification report, with an average accuracy of about 75% compared to the 70% average accuracy of the Random Forest Model. These were the average accuracy after performing five-fold cross-validation. Figure 1(b) and Fig. 1(c) demonstrates the ROC curves for 80:20 and 90:10 training: test ratio, respectively. The performance of word2Vec is the best among the machine learning algorithms.

The linguistic features used in the classifier were effective to classify the native English speakers versus non-native English speakers. In particular, the performance of

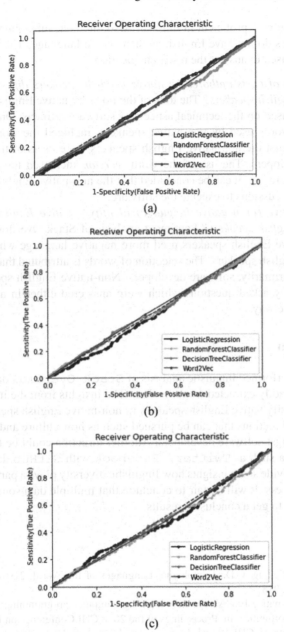

Fig. 1. ROC curves for Logistic Regression, Random Forest, Decision Tree and Word2Vec for Training/Test data (a) 75/25 (b) 80/20 (c) 90/10

Word2Vec when compared with other algorithms, was the best. The feature, of geographical location was not as informative when compared to the linguistic features. It could have been the user claiming from a country were English is not the native language but were very proficient in English. Also, the fact, subpopulation of English-speaking countries do not have English as their native language. The results from the experiments are used to answer the research questions.

RQ1: *Is the tone of posts authored by native English speakers different than that of non-native English speakers?* The tone of the posts by native English speakers were primarily focused on the technical aspects of software artifacts, On the other hand, the top five words used by non-native speakers, included the words version provide insights that the non-native English speakers were users of the software than software developers. The use of the word, *version* increased the accuracy of the classifiers. Therefore, it can be concluded that the non-native English speakers were looking for discussions to execute the software.

RQ2: *Does positive (or negative language) identify - native English speakers and non-native English speakers?* Sentiment analysis of Stack Overflow data provided insights. Native English speakers used more negative language when compared to non-native English speakers. The selection of words is attributed that native-English speakers are primarily, software developers. Non-native English speakers are users and hence, they asked questions which were answered either in an affirmative or non-affirmative way.

5   Conclusion

In the study we performed linguistic analysis of `Stack Overflow` data. The linguistic features are readily extracted from the data. The insights from the interactions were promising to classify native English speakers *vs* non-native English speakers. There are other promising directions that can be pursued such as how culture and ethnicity affect interactions amongst software developers. Another direction could be to integrate data from social media such as `Twitter, Facebook` with `GitHub` data. The experimental results provide some insights how linguistic diversity plays a part in the software development process. It will be fair to conclude that multiple data sources needs to be analyzed in order to get a conclusive results.

References

1. Simons, G.F., Fennig, C.D.: Ethnologue: Languages of the World, 21st edn. SIL International, Dallas (2018)
2. Guo, P.J.: Non-native English speakers learning computer programming: barriers, desires, and design opportunities. In: Proceedings of the 2018 CHI Conference on Human Factors in Computing Systems, CHI'18, vol. 14, pp. 1–14. ACM, New York (2018)
3. Bosu, A., Sultana, K.Z.: Diversity and inclusion in open source software (OSS) projects: where do we stand? In: 2019 ACM/IEEE International Symposium on Empirical Software Engineering and Measurement (ESEM), pp. 1–11. IEEE (2019)
4. Lin, B., Serebrenik, A.: Recognizing gender of stack overflow users. In: Proceedings of the 13th International Conference on Mining Software Repositories, pp. 425–429 (2016)
5. Vasilescu, B., et al.: Gender and tenure diversity in GitHub teams. In: Proceedings of the 33rd Annual ACM Conference on Human Factors in Computing Systems, pp. 3789–3798 (2015)

6. Schenk, D., Lungu, M.: Geo-locating the knowledge transfer in StackOverflow. In: Proceedings of the 2013 International Workshop on Social Software Engineering, pp. 21–24 (2013)
7. Marder, A.: Stack overflow badges and user behavior: an econometric approach. In: 2015 IEEE/ACM 12th Working Conference on Mining Software Repositories, pp. 450–453. IEEE (2015)
8. Morrison, P., Murphy-Hill, E.: Is programming knowledge related to age? An exploration of stack overflow. In: 2013 10th Working Conference on Mining Software Repositories (MSR), pp. 69–72. IEEE (2013)
9. Wang, S., Lo, D., Jiang, L.: An empirical study on developer interactions in StackOverflow. In: Proceedings of the 28th Annual ACM Symposium on Applied Computing, pp. 1019–1024 (2013)
10. Frey, J.-C., Glaznieks, A., Stemle, E.W.: The DiDi corpus of South Tyrolean CMC data: a multilingual corpus of facebook texts. In: CLIC-it (2016)
11. Lomas, T.: Towards a positive cross-cultural lexicography: enriching our emotional landscape through 216 'untranslatable' words pertaining to well-being. J. Posit. Psychol. **11**(5), 546–558 (2016)
12. Ortu, M., Destefanis, G., Counsell, S., Swift, S., Tonelli, R., Marchesi, M.: Arsonists or firefighters? Affectiveness in Agile software development. In: Sharp, H., Hall, T. (eds.) XP 2016. LNBIP, vol. 251, pp. 144–155. Springer, Cham (2016). https://doi.org/10.1007/978-3-319-33515-5_12
13. Ortu, M., Adams, B., Destefanis, G., Tourani, P., Marchesi, M., Tonelli, R.: Are bullies more productive? Empirical study of affectiveness vs. issue fixing time. In: 12th Working Conference on Mining Software Repositories, pp. 303–313. IEEE (2015)
14. Paul, R., Bosu, A., Sultana, K.Z.: Expressions of sentiments during code reviews: male vs. female. In: 2019 IEEE 26th International Conference on Software Analysis, Evolution and Reengineering (SANER), pp. 26–37. IEEE (2019)
15. Baccianella, S., Esuli, A., Sebastiani, F.: SentiWordNet 3.0: an enhanced lexical resource for sentiment analysis and opinion mining. In: Lrec, vol. 10, pp. 2200–2204 (2010)
16. Calefato, F., Lanubile, F., Maiorano, F., Novielli, N.: Sentiment polarity detection for software development. Empir. Softw. Eng. **23**(3), 1352–1382 (2018). https://doi.org/10.1007/s10664-017-9546-9
17. Thelwall, M., Buckley, K., Paltoglou, G., Cai, C., Kappas, A.: SentiStrength (2014). http://sentistrength.wlv.ac.uk
18. Wang, S., Chen, T.-H., Hassan, A.E.: Understanding the factors for fast answers in technical Q&A websites. Empir. Softw. Eng. **23**(3), 1552–1593 (2017). https://doi.org/10.1007/s10664-017-9558-5
19. Rastogi, A., Nagappan, N., Gousios, G., van der Hoek, A.: Relationship between geographical location and evaluation of developer contributions in GitHub. In: Proceedings of the 12th ACM/IEEE International Symposium on Empirical Software Engineering and Measurement, p. 22. ACM (2018)
20. Menzies, T., Majumder, S., Balaji, N., Brey, K., Fu, W.: 500+ times faster than deep learning: (a case study exploring faster methods for text mining StackOverflow). In: 2018 IEEE/ACM 15th International Conference on Mining Software Repositories (MSR), pp. 554–563. IEEE (2018)
21. Allamanis, M., Sutton, C.: Why, when, and what: analyzing stack overflow questions by topic, type, and code. In: 2013 10th Working Conference on Mining Software Repositories (MSR), pp. 53–56. IEEE (2013)
22. Baltes, S., Dumani, L., Treude, C., Diehl, S.: SOTorrent: reconstructing and analyzing the evolution of stack overflow posts. In: Proceedings of the 15th International Conference on Mining Software Repositories, pp. 319–330 (2018)

23. Stack Overflow. https://data.stackexchange.com/. Accessed 21 Jan 2020
24. Hutto, C., Gilbert, E.: VADER: a parsimonious rule-based model for sentiment analysis of social media text. In: Proceedings of the International AAAI Conference on Web and Social Media, vol. 8 (2014)

IReEn: Reverse-Engineering of Black-Box Functions via Iterative Neural Program Synthesis

Hossein Hajipour[1(✉)] , Mateusz Malinowski[2] , and Mario Fritz[1]

[1] CISPA Helmholtz Center for Information Security, Saarbrücken, Germany
hossein.hajipour@cispa.saarland
[2] DeepMind, London, UK

Abstract. In this work, we investigate the problem of revealing the functionality of a black-box agent. Notably, we are interested in the interpretable and formal description of the behavior of such an agent. Ideally, this description would take the form of a program written in a high-level language. This task is also known as *reverse engineering* and plays a pivotal role in software engineering, computer security, but also most recently in interpretability. In contrast to prior work, we do not rely on privileged information on the black box, but rather investigate the problem under a weaker assumption of having only access to inputs and outputs of the program. We approach this problem by iteratively refining a candidate set using a generative neural program synthesis approach until we arrive at a functionally equivalent program. We assess the performance of our approach on the Karel dataset. Our results show that the proposed approach outperforms the state-of-the-art on this challenge by finding an approximately functional equivalent program in 78% of cases – even exceeding prior work that had privileged information on the black-box.

Keywords: Reverse-engineering · Program synthesis · Neural program synthesis · Iterative program synthesis

1 Introduction

Reverse-engineering (RE) is about gaining insights into the inner workings of a mechanism, which often results in the capability of reproducing the associated functionality. In our work, we consider a program to be a black-box function that we have no insights into its internal mechanism, and we can only interface with it through

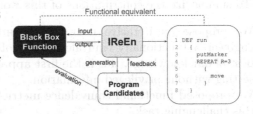

Fig. 1. An example of revealing the functionality of a black-box function using only input-output interactions.

M. Kamp et al. (Eds.): ECML PKDD 2021 Workshops, CCIS 1525, pp. 143–157, 2021.
https://doi.org/10.1007/978-3-030-93733-1_10

inputs and the program generated outputs. This is a desired scenario in software engineering [9,15], or security, where we reverse-engineer, e.g., binary executables for analysis and for finding potential vulnerabilities [14,25]. Similar principles have been applied in the program synthesis domain to understand the functionality of the given program [11,22]. Furthermore, a similar paradigm is used to reverse-engineer the brain to advance knowledge in various brain-related disciplines [17] or seeking interpretation for reinforcement learning agents [23] (Fig. 1).

Despite all of the progress in reverse-engineering the software and machine learning models, there are typical limitations in the proposed works. E.g., in the decompilation task, one of the assumptions is to have access to the assembly code of the black-box programs or other privileged information, which is a significant information leak about the black-box function. In program synthesis, a common issue is that the problem is considered in a relaxed setting, where they only synthesize loop-free or conditional-free programming languages [11]. Furthermore, in deep learning, a common issue is that the reverse-engineered models usually are not represented in an interpretable and human-readable form.

In recent work, neural program synthesizers are employed to recover a functional and interpretable form of a black-box program that is generated based only on I/Os examples [4]. On close inspection, however, it turns out, that these approaches also leverage privileged information, by relying on a biased sampling strategy of I/Os that was obtained under the knowledge of the black-box function.

In contrast to prior work, we propose an iterative neural program synthesis scheme which is the first to tackle the task of reveres-engineering in a black-box setting without any access to privileged information. Despite the weaker assumptions and hence the possibility to use our method broadly in other fields, we show that in many cases it is possible to reverse engineer approximately functionally equivalent programs on the Karel dataset benchmark. We even achieve better results than prior work that has access to privileged information.

We achieve this by an iterative reverse-engineering approach. We query a black-box function using random inputs to obtain a set of I/Os, and refine the candidate set by an iterative neural program synthesis scheme. This neural program synthesis is trained with pairs of I/Os and target programs. To adapt our program synthesize to the domain of random I/Os we fine-tune our neural program synthesize using random I/Os and the corresponding target program.

To summarize the contributions of this work are as follow:

1. We propose an iterative neural program synthesizer scheme to reverse-engineer a functionally equivalent form of the black-box program. To the best of our knowledge, this is the first approach that operates in a black-box setting without privileged information.
2. We proposed functional equivalence metric in order to quantify progress on this challenging task.
3. We evaluate our approach on Karel dataset, where our approach successfully revealed the underlying programs of 78% of the black-box programs. Our approach outperforms prior work despite having access to less information due to weaker assumptions.

2   Related Work

Reverse-Engineering of Programs. Decompilation is the task of translating a low-level program into a human-readable high-level language. Phoenix [3] and Hex-Rays [1] are conventional decompilers. These decompilers are relying on pattern matching and hand-crafted rules, and often fail to decompile non-trivial codes with conditional structures. Fu et al. [9] proposed a deep-learning-based approach to decompile the low-level codes in an end-to-end fashion. In the decompilation task, the main assumption is to have access to a low-level code of the program. However, in our approach, our goal is to represent a black-box function in a high-level program language only by relying on input-output interactions.

Reverse-Engineering of Neural Networks. Reverse-engineering neural network recently has gained popularity. Oh et al. [18] proposed a meta-model to predict the attributes of the black-box neural network models, such as architecture and optimization process. Orekondy et al. [19] investigate how to steal the functionality of the black-box model only based on image query interactions. While these works try to duplicate the functionality of a black-box function, in this work our goal is to represent the functionality of the black-box function in a human-readable program language.

Reverse-Engineering for Interpretability. In another line of work, Verma et al. [23] and Bastani et al. [2] proposed different approaches to have interpretable and verifiable reinforcement learning. Verma et al. [23] designed a reinforcement learning framework to represent the policy network using human-readable domain-specific language, and Bastani et al. [2] represent policy network by a training decision tree. Both of these works are designed for a small set of RL problems with a simple program structure. However, in our work, we consider reverse-engineer a wide range of programs with complex structures.

Program Synthesis. Program synthesis is a classic task which has been studied since the early days of Artificial Intelligence [16,24]. Recently there has been a lot of recent progress in employing the neural-networks-based approaches to do the task of program synthesis. One type of these approaches called *neural program induction* involves learning a machine learning model to mimic the behavior of the target program [6,10,12]. Another type of approach is *neural program synthesis*, where the goal is to learn to generate an explicit discrete program in a domain-specific program language. Devlin et al. [7] proposed an encoder-decoder neural network style to learn to synthesize programs from input-output examples. Bunel et al. [4] synthesizing Karel programs from examples, where they learn to generate program using a deep-learning-based model by leveraging the syntax constraints and reinforcement learning. Shin et al. [21] and Chen et al. [5] leverage the semantic information of execution trace of the programs to generate more accurate programs. These works assume that they have access to the crafted I/O examples. However, in this work, we proposed an iterative program synthesis scheme to deal with the task of black-box program synthesis, where we only have access to the random I/O examples.

3   Problem Overview

In this section, we formulate the problem description and our method. We base our notation on [4,5,21].

Program Synthesis. Program synthesis deals with the problem of deriving a program in a specified programming language that satisfies the given specification. We treat input-output pairs $I/O = \left\{(I^k, O^k)\right\}_{k=1}^{K}$ as a form of specifying the functionality of the program. This problem can be formalized as finding a solution to the following optimization problem:

$$\underset{p \in \mathcal{P}}{\arg\min} \quad \Omega(p) \tag{1}$$

$$\text{s.t. } p(I^k) = O^k \forall k \in \{1, \ldots, K\} \tag{2}$$

where $\mathcal{P}$ is the space of all possible programs written in the given language, and Ω is some measure of the program. For instance, Ω can be a cost function that chooses the shortest program.

The situation is illustrated in Fig. 2. For many applications – also the one we are interested in – there is a true underlying black-box program that satisfies all the input-output pairs. As most practical languages do not have a unique representation for certain functionality or behavior, a certain set of functionally equivalent programs will remain indistinguishable even given an arbitrary large number of input-output observations and respective constraints in our optimization problem. Naturally, by adding more constraints, we obtain a nested constraint set that converges towards the feasible set of functionally equivalent programs.

Program Synthesis with Privileged Information. Recent works implicitly or explicitly incorporates insider information on the function to reverse-engineer. This can come in the form of a binary of the compiled code or an informed sampling strategy of the input-output pairs. It turns out that the majority of recent research implicitly uses privileged information via biased sampling scheme in terms of *crafted* specifications [4,5,20,21]. Note that in order to arrive at

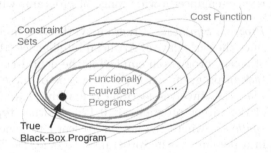

Fig. 2. Illustration of the optimization problem, functional equivalence, and feasible sets w.r.t. nested constraint sets.

these specifications, one has to have access to the program P under the question as they are designed to capture e.g. all branches of the program. We call these crafted specifications *crafted I/Os* and will investigate later in detail how much information they leak about the black-box program.

Black-Box Program Synthesis. In our work, we focus on a black-box setting, where no such side or privileged information is available. Hence, we will have to defer initially to randomly generate K inputs $\{I^k\}_{k=1}^K$ and next query the program p to obtain the corresponding outputs $\{O^k\}_{k=1}^K$. Such generated input-output pairs become our specification that we use to synthesize programs. Note that, unlike the previous setting, here we take advantage of querying the black-box program p in an active way, even though the whole procedure remains automatic. To generate random inputs we follow the procedure proposed by Bunel et al. [4]. We call the obtained I/Os in the black-box setting *random I/Os*. It turns out (as we will also show in our experiments), that indeed such random, uninformed input queries yield significantly less information than the *crafted I/Os* used in prior work. Hence, to arrive at an effective and black-box approach, in the following we propose an iterative reverse-engineering scheme, that gradually queries more relevant inputs.

4   IReEn: Iterative Reverse-Engineering of Black-Box Functions

Reverse-engineering a black-box function and representing it in a high-level language is a challenging task. The main reason is that we can only interact with the black-box function using input-output examples. In addition, solving the above constraint optimization problem is intractable. Therefore, in the following, we relax the optimization problem to a Bayesian inference problem and show how to iteratively incorporate additional constraints in order to arrive at a functional equivalent program with respect to the black-box function.

Figure 3 provides an overview of our iterative neural program synthesis scheme to reverse-engineer the given black-box function. In the first step, we obtain the I/Os by querying the black-box function using random inputs drawn from a distribution of inputs. We condition the neural program synthesizer on the obtained I/Os. Neural program synthesizer outputs the potential program candidate(s), and then we use a scoring system to score the generated candidates. For example, in this figure "program candidate 1" satisfied two out of four sample I/Os, so its score will be 2. If the best candidate does not cover all of the I/Os, we select a subset of I/Os which were not covered by the best candidate program to condition them on the program synthesizer for the next iteration.

4.1   Finding Programs Given Input-Output Constraints

Even for a small set of input-output constraints, finding the feasible set of programs that satisfies these I/Os is not tractable due to the discrete and compositional nature of programs. We approach this challenging problem by relaxing the constraint optimization problem to a Bayesian Inference problem. In this way, samples of the model are solutions to the constraint optimization problem. In order to train such a generative model, we directly optimize the Neural Program

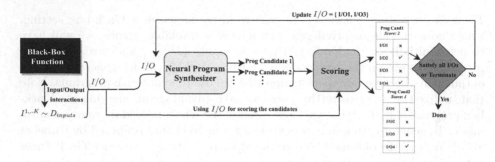

Fig. 3. Overview of the proposed iterative neural program synthesis approach.

Synthesis approach based on Bunel et al. [4]. This is a conditional generative model that samples candidate programs by conditioning on the input-output information.

$$\hat{P} \sim \Psi(I/O). \tag{3}$$

where $\hat{P}$ is a set of sampled solutions that are program candidate(s) $\{\hat{p}_1, ..., \hat{p}_C\} \in \hat{P}$ and $C \geq 1$.

In detail, we train a recurrent encoder and decoder for program synthesis on a set of ground-truth programs $\{p_i\}_i$ and specifications $\{I/O_i\}_i$. Each specification is a set of K pairs $I/O_i = \{(I_i^k, O_i^k)\}_{k=1}^K$ where the program needs to be consistent with, that is, $p_i(I_i^k) = O_i^k$ for all $k \in \{1, ..., K\}$. In our work, we pre-train the program synthesis proposed by Bunel et al. [4], where they use encoder-decoder neural networks to generate the desired program given input-output specifications. Note that the synthesizer is dependent on the input specification, that is, different I/O_a and I/O_b may produce different programs through the synthesis, i.e., $\Psi(I/O_a) = p_a$ and $\Psi(I/O_b) = p_b$. For a detailed discussion, e.g. of the I/O encodings, we refer to Bunel et al. [4].

4.2   Sample Rejection Strategy

Naturally, we expect approximation errors of the optimization problem by the generative model. Two main sources of error are (1) challenges to approximate the discontinuous target distribution (2) only a limited number of constraints can be incorporated in the conditional generative model. In order to correct for these errors, we follow up with a sample rejection stage based on a scoring of the generated program candidates. We use random I/Os obtained from interacting with black-box function to evaluate the generated programs, and score them based on the number of the I/Os which were covered by the programs (See Fig. 3). While in principle, any failed I/O should lead to rejecting a candidate, empirically, we find that keeping the highest scoring samples turns out to be advantageous and prevents situations where no candidates would remain.

4.3   Iterative Refinement

We are still facing two major issues: (1) As we have motivated before and also our experiments will show, querying for certain I/O pairs is more informative than others. Hence, we seek an iterative approach that yields more informative queries to the black box. (2) Due to the computational bottleneck, the conditional generative model only takes a small number of constraints, while it is unclear which constraints to use in order to arrive at the "functional equivalent" feasible set.

Similar problems have been encountered in constraint optimization, where *column generation algorithms/delayed constraint generation* techniques have been employed to deal with large number of constraints [8]. Motivated by these ideas, we propose an iterative strategy, where we condition in each step on a set of violated constraints that we find.

In detail, we present the algorithm of the proposed method in Algorithm 1. Iterative synthesis function takes synthesizer Ψ and a set of I/Os (line 1). In line 2 we initial the s_{best} to zero. Note that we use p_{best} to store the best candidate, and s_{best} to store the score of the best candidate. In the iterative loop, we first condition the program synthesizer on the given I/O set to get the program candidates $\hat{P}$ (line 5). Then we call *Scoring* function to score the program candidates in line 6. The scoring function returns the best program candidate, the score of that candidate, and the new set of I/O where the new I/Os are the one which were not satisfied by $\hat{p}_{best}$. Note that $\hat{p}_{best}$, and $\hat{s}_{best}$ store the best candidate and the score of it for the current iteration. Then at line 7, we check if $\hat{s}_{best}$ for the current iteration is larger than the global score s_{best}, if the condition satisfies we update the global p_{best}, and s_{best} (line 8–9). In line 12 we return the best candidate p_{best} after searching for it for n iterations.

4.4   Fine-Tuning

The goal of synthesizer Ψ is to generate a program for the given I/Os, so it is not desirable to generate a program that contains not-used statements (e.g. a while statement which never hit by the given I/Os). However, in the black-box setting, we only have access to the random I/Os, and there is no guarantee if these I/Os represent all details of the black-box program. So the synthesizer might need to generate a statement in the program which was not represented in the given I/Os. The question is how we can have a synthesizer that makes a balance between these two contradictory situations. To address this issue, we first train synthesizer Ψ on the crafted I/Os and then fine-tune it on the random I/Os. Please note that we only use the crafted I/Os during training. We get the data for fine-tuning by pairing random I/Os with the target programs. We empirically find that fine-tuning the synthesizer can lead to better performance than training it using only random I/Os.

5   Experiments

In this section, we show the effectiveness of our proposed approach for the task of black-box program synthesis. We consider Karel dataset [4, 6] in a strict black-box setting, where we can only have access to I/Os by querying the black-box functions without any privileged information or informed sampling scheme.

Algorithm 1: Iterative Algorithms

---

1 **Function** IterativeSynthesis(Ψ, I/O):

2     $s_{best} = 0$ // To keep the best score.

3   n = $constant$ // e.g., n=10

4   **for** $i \leftarrow 1$ **to** n **do**

5        $\hat{P} = \Psi(I/O)$

6        $\hat{p}_{best}, \hat{s}_{best}, I/O = Scoring(\hat{P})$

7   **if** s_{best} ¡ $\hat{s}_{best}$ **then**

8           $p_{best} = \hat{p}_{best}$

9           $s_{best} = \hat{s}_{best}$

10   **end**

11   **end**

12   **return** p_{best}

13 **End Function**

5.1   The Karel Task and Dataset

To evaluate our proposed approach, we consider Karel programming language. Karel featured a robot agent in a grid world, where this robot can move inside the grid world and modify the state of the world using a set of predefined functions and control flow structures. Recently it has been used as a benchmark in several neural program synthesis works [4,5,21]. Figure 4 shows the grammar specification of this programming language [4]. Using control flow structures such as condition and loop in the grammar of Karel makes this DSL a challenging language for the task of program synthesis. Figure 5 demonstrates an example of the Karel task with two I/O examples and the corresponding program.

Bunel et al. [4] defined a dataset to train and evaluate neural program synthesis approaches by randomly sampling programs from the Karel's DSL. In this dataset, for each program, there is 5 I/Os as specification, and one is the held-out test sample. In this work, we consider the Karel's programs as black-box agent's task, and our goal is to reveal the underlying functionality of this black-box function by solely using input-output interactions. This dataset contains 1,116,854 pairs of I/Os and programs, 2,500 for validations, and 2,500 for testing the models. Note that, to fine-tune the synthesizer to the domain of random I/Os, we used 100,000 pairs of random I/Os and target program for training and 2,500 for validation.

5.2   Training and Inference

We train the neural program synthesizer using the Karel Dataset. To train this synthesizer we employ the neural networks architecture proposed by Bunel et al. [4], and use that in our iterative refinement approach as the synthesizer. Note that, to fine-tune the synthesizer model on random I/Os we use Adam optimizer [13] and the learning rate 10^{-5}. We fine-tune the synthesizer model for 10 epochs. During inference, we use beam search algorithm with beam width 64 and select top-k program candidates.

Prog $p := \text{def } \texttt{run}() \; : \; s$

Stmt $s := \texttt{while}(b) : s \mid \texttt{repeat}(r) : s \mid s_1; s_2 \mid a$
$\quad\quad\quad \mid \texttt{if}(b) : s \mid \texttt{ifelse}(b) : s_1 \texttt{ else} : s_2$

Cond $b := \texttt{frontIsClear}() \mid \texttt{leftIsClear}() \mid \texttt{rightIsClear}()$
$\quad\quad\quad \mid \texttt{markersPresent}() \mid \texttt{noMarkersPresent}() \mid \texttt{not } b$

Action $a := \texttt{move}() \mid \texttt{turnRight}() \mid \texttt{turnLeft}()$
$\quad\quad\quad \mid \texttt{pickMarker}() \mid \texttt{putMarker}()$

Cste $r := 0 \mid 1 \mid \cdots \mid 19$

Fig. 4. The grammar for the Karel programming language.

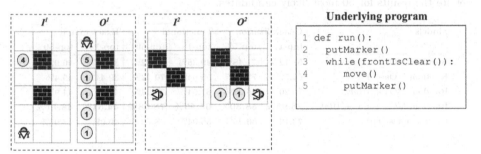

Underlying program

```
1  def run():
2      putMarker()
3      while(frontIsClear()):
4          move()
5          putMarker()
```

Fig. 5. Example of two I/Os of a Karel task with the corresponding underlying program. The robot is Karel, the brick walls represent obstacles, and markers are represented with circles.

5.3 Functional Equivalence Metric

In [4,21], two metrics have been used to evaluate the trained neural program synthesizer. 1. Exact Match: A predicted program is an exact match of the target if it is the same as the target program in terms of tokens. 2. Generalization: A predicted program is a generalization of the target if it satisfies the I/Os of the specification set and the held-out example. Both of these metrics have some drawbacks. A predicted program might be functionally equivalent to the target program but not be the exact match. On the other side, a program can be a generalization of the target program by satisfying a small set of I/Os (in Bunel et al. [4] 5 I/Os has been used as specification and 1 I/O is considered as held-out). However, it might not cover a larger set of I/Os for that target program. To overcome this issue, in this work we proposed the Functional Equivalence metric, where we consider a predicted program as an approximately functional equivalent to the target program if it covers a large set of I/Os which were not been used as the specification in the synthesizing time. To get the set of I/Os, we generate the inputs randomly and query the program to get the outputs. We check if these inputs hit all of the branches of the target program. In our experiments, we found that with using more I/Os the more predicted programs we discover to not be functionally equivalent to the target programs. We found 100 number of I/Os as a point where the number of approximately functional equivalent programs stay stable in the evaluations.

5.4 Evaluation

Table 1. Top: Results of performance comparison of our approach in different settings using random I/Os for black-box program synthesis. Random I/Os mean that we use randomly obtained I/Os in the black-box setting, FT refers to fine-tuned model, and IReEn denote to our iterative approach. Bottom: Results of Bunel et al. [4] when we use crafted I/Os. top-1 denote the results for the most likely candidate, and top-50 denote the results for 50 most likely candidates.

Models	Generalization		Functional		Exact match	
	top-1	top-50	top-1	top-50	top-1	top-50
Random I/Os	57.12%	71.48%	49.36%	63.72%	34.96%	40.92%
Random I/Os + FT	64.72%	77.64%	55.64%	70.12%	39.44%	45.4%
Random I/Os + IReEn	76.20%	85.28%	61.64%	73.24%	40.95%	44.99%
Random I/Os + FT + IReEn	**78.96%**	**88.39%**	**65.55%**	**78.08%**	**44.51%**	**48.11%**
Crafted I/Os ([4])	73.12%	86.28%	55.04%	68.72%	40.08%	43.08%

We investigate the performance of our approach in different settings to do the task of black-box program synthesis. To evaluate our approach we query each black-box program in the test set with 50 valid inputs to get the corresponding outputs. Using the obtained 50 I/Os we synthesize the target program, where we use 5 out of 50 I/Os to conditions on the synthesizer and use 50 I/Os to score the generated candidate and find the best one based on sample rejection strategy. In our iterative approach in each iteration, using sample rejection strategy we find a new 5 I/Os among the 50 I/Os to condition on the synthesizer for the next iteration. To evaluate the generated programs, in addition to generalization and exact match accuracy, we also consider our proposed metric called Functional Equivalence (Subsect. 5.3). To compute the functional equivalency we use 100 I/Os which were not seen by the model. If the generated program satisfies all of 100 I/Os we consider it as a program which approximately functional equivalent to the target program. In all of the results top-k means that we use the given I/Os to find the best candidate among the "k" top candidates. For computing the results for all of the metrics we evaluate the best candidate among top-k.

Table 2. Top: Functional equivalence results of our approaches in synthesizing black-box programs with different complexity. Random I/Os means that we use randomly obtained I/Os in the black-box setting, FT refers to fine-tuned model, and IReEn denotes to our iterative approach. Bottom: Results of Bunel et al. [4] when we use crafted I/Os. Action refers to programs that only contain action functions, Repeat denotes programs with action functions and only a repeat structure, While denotes programs with action functions and only a while control flow, If refers to the programs with action functions and only an if control flow, and Mix denotes programs with more than one control flow structures and action functions. top-1 denotes the results for the most likely candidate, and top-50 denotes the results for 50 most likely candidates.

Models	Action		Repeat		While		If		Mix	
	top-1	top-50	top-1	top-50	top-1	top-50	top-1	top-50	top-1	top-50
Random I/Os	95.59%	99.69%	85.52%	91.44%	26.98%	61.58%	48.88%	72.69%	10.69%	27.12%
Random I/Os + FT	99.39%	99.76%	90.72%	96.38%	56.50%	82.22%	52.06%	77.46%	14.33%	32.19%
Random I/Os + IReEn	**99.84%**	99.84%	**96.38%**	97.36%	60.95%	84.76%	81.26%	89.84%	27.67%	49.94%
Random I/Os + FT + IReEn	**99.84%**	100%	95.39%	**99.64%**	**81.58%**	**93.33%**	**81.52%**	**92.06%**	**32.08%**	**56.22%**
Crafted I/Os	99.08%	100.0%	91.11%	96.71%	54.28%	84.12%	49.20%	79.68%	14.88%	33.84%

Comparison to Baseline and Ablation. Table 1 shows the performance of our approach in different settings in the top, and the results of the neural program synthesizer proposed by Bunel et al. [4] in the bottom. These results show that when we only use random I/Os (first row), there is a huge drop in the accuracy in all of the metrics in comparison to the results of crafted I/Os. However, when we fine-tune the synthesizer the results improve in all of the metrics, especially for the top-1 and top-50 functional equivalence accuracy. Furthermore, when we use our iterative approach for 10 iterations with the fine-tuned model (fourth row), we can see that our approach outperforms even the crafted I/Os in all of the metrics. For example, it outperforms crafted I/Os in functional equivalence and exact match metric by a large margin, 9%, and 5% respectively for top-50 results.

Importance of the Crafted I/Os. In Table 1 in the top first row (Random I/Os) we use random I/Os to condition on the synthesizer, and in the bottom (Crafted I/Os) we use crafted I/Os to condition on the same synthesizer. These results show that using random I/Os on the same synthesizer leads to 15%, and 5% drops in the results for top-50 generalization and functional accuracy respectively. Based on these results we can see that random I/Os contain significantly less information about the target program in comparison to the crafted I/Os.

To further investigate the importance of the crafted I/Os we provide the results of synthesizing programs with different levels of complexity in Table 2. In this table (Table 2) we show the functional equivalency results of simple programs including programs that only contain action functions or *Repeat* structure with action functions, and also complex programs that contain one or multiple conditional control flows.

In Table 2 we can see that for simple programs that only contains action functions or action functions with *Repeat* structure (Note that *Repeat* is like for-loop structure, so any valid input can hit a *Repeat* structure) we have low performance drops in functional equivalence accuracy for Random I/Os in comparison to Crafted I/Os. For example, in the Action column (Table 2) for top-50 accuracy, there is less than 1% points drop for Random I/Os in comparison to the Crafted I/Os results. This is because any I/O examples can represent the functionality of these simple programs. In other words, any I/Os hits all parts of these simple programs. Furthermore, Table 2 shows that for more complex programs we have large drop in functional equivalence accuracy for Random I/Os in comparison to Crafted I/Os. As an example, we can see that for programs with *While* structure in top-1 column, there is more than 27% points drop for Random I/Os in comparison to the Crafted I/Os results. These results indicate that Crafted I/Os contain more informative details about the complex programs in comparison to random I/Os. This is because Crafted I/Os are designed to hit all branches of the programs. However, there is no guarantee if the given Random I/Os hit all of the branches of the complex programs.

Table 2 also provides the results of our iterative approach with and without fine-tuning the model. In this table (Table 2) we can see that for the program with complex control flows our approaches have higher performance gain in comparison to the results for the simple program. This indicates that our iterative refinement approach is capable of generating more accurate programs by iteratively condition the model on informative I/Os. As an example, for the program with multiple control flows (Mix) in the top-1 column, we have around 17% points improvement for Random I/Os + IReEn in comparison to Random I/Os.

Effectiveness of Iterative Refinement. Figure 6a, Fig. 6b, and Fig. 6c show the effectiveness of our proposed iterative approach in 10 iterations. In these figures, x and y axis refer to the number of iterations and the accuracy respectively. Figure 6a shows the generalization accuracy for top-50, in Fig. 6b we can see the results of functional equivalence metric for top-50, and Fig. 6c demonstrates the exact match accuracy for top-50. In these figures, we provide results with and without fine-tuning the synthesizer. Here we can see the improvement of the generalization, functional equivalence, and exact match accuracy over the iterations. We have a margin of 7% improvement in the functional equivalence accuracy for "Random I/Os + FT + IReEn" setting after 10 iterations. In other words, these results show that we can search for better random I/Os and program candidates by iteratively incorporate additional constraints.

Effectiveness of Number of I/Os for Sample Rejection Strategy. In our approach in order to choose one candidate among all of the generated program candidates, we consider a sample rejection strategy. To do that, we use the random I/Os to assign a score to the generated candidates based on the number of satisfied random I/Os. Finally, we consider the candidate with the higher score as the best candidate and reject the rest. Figure 7a, Fig. 7b, and Fig. 7c show the effect of using the different numbers of random I/Os on scoring the candidates and finding the best program candidate. x and y axis in these figures refer to the number of random I/Os, and accuracy of our approaches with and without fine-tuning. In Fig. 7a we show the generalization accuracy, in Fig. 7b we provide functional equivalence results, and Fig. 7c shows the results for exact match accuracy. These figures show that by using more random I/Os in the sample rejection strategy we can find more accurate programs that result to gain better performance in terms of generalization, functional equivalence, and exact match accuracy. In other words, with using more random I/Os for scoring the candidates we can capture more details of the black-box function, and find the best potential candidate among the generated one.

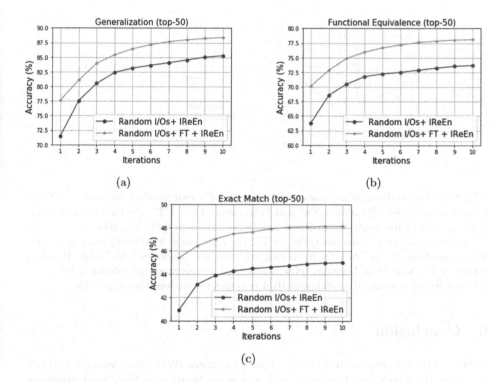

(a)

(b)

(c)

Fig. 6. (a) Generalization accuracy after each iteration for "Random I/Os + IReEn" and "Random I/Os + FT + IReEn". (b) Functional equivalence accuracy after each iteration for "Random I/Os + IReEn" and "Random I/Os + FT + IReEn". (c) Exact match accuracy after each iteration for "Random I/Os + IReEn" and "Random I/Os + FT + IReEn". Note that, Random I/Os means that we use randomly obtained I/Os, FT denotes to the fine-tuned model, and IReEn refers to our iterative approach.

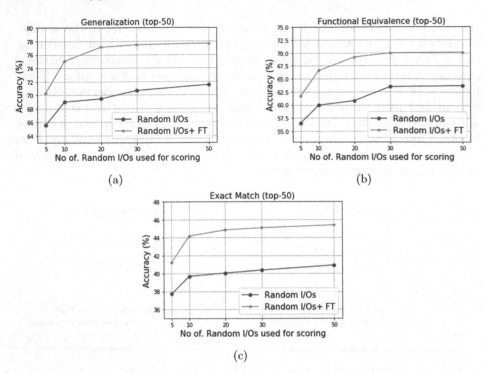

Fig. 7. (a) Generalization accuracy after using the different numbers of random I/Os in scoring strategy for "Random I/Os" and "Random I/Os + FT". (b) Functional equivalence accuracy after using the different numbers of random I/Os in scoring strategy for "Random I/Os" and "Random I/Os + FT". (c) Exact match accuracy after using different numbers of random I/Os in scoring strategy for "Random I/Os" and "Random I/Os + FT". Note that, Random I/Os means that we use randomly obtained I/Os, FT denotes to the fine-tuned model, and IReEn refers to our iterative approach.

6   Conclusion

In this work, we propose an iterative neural program synthesis scheme to reverse-engineer the black-box functions and represent them in a high-level program. In contrast to previous works, where they have access to privileged information, in our problem setting, we only rely on the input-output interactions. To tackle the problem of reverse-engineering the black-box function in this challenging setting, we employ a neural program synthesizer in an iterative scheme. Using this iterative approach we search for the best program candidate in each iteration by conditioning the synthesizer on a set of violated constraints. Our evaluation on the Karel dataset demonstrates the effectiveness of our proposed approach in the reverse-engineering functional equivalent form of the black-box programs. Besides this, the provided results show that our proposed approach even outperforming the previous work that uses privileged information to sample input-output examples.

References

1. Hex-Rays (1998). https://www.hex-rays.com/products/ida/
2. Bastani, O., Pu, Y., Solar-Lezama, A.: Verifiable reinforcement learning via policy extraction. In: NeurIPS (2018)
3. Brumley, D., Lee, J., Schwartz, E.J., Woo, M.: Native x86 decompilation using semantics-preserving structural analysis and iterative control-flow structuring. In: USENIX (2013)
4. Bunel, R., Hausknecht, M., Devlin, J., Singh, R., Kohli, P.: Leveraging grammar and reinforcement learning for neural program synthesis. In: ICLR (2018)
5. Chen, X., Liu, C., Song, D.: Execution-guided neural program synthesis. In: ICLR (2019)
6. Devlin, J., Bunel, R.R., Singh, R., Hausknecht, M., Kohli, P.: Neural program meta-induction. In: NIPS (2017)
7. Devlin, J., Uesato, J., Bhupatiraju, S., Singh, R., Mohamed, A.R., Kohli, P.: RobustFill: neural program learning under noisy I/O. In: ICML (2017)
8. Ford, L.R., Jr., Fulkerson, D.R.: A suggested computation for maximal multi-commodity network flows. Manage. Sci. **5**, 97–101 (1958)
9. Fu, C., et al.: Coda: an end-to-end neural program decompiler. In: NeurIPS (2019)
10. Graves, A., Wayne, G., Danihelka, I.: Neural turing machines. arXiv (2014)
11. Jha, S., Gulwani, S., Seshia, S.A., Tiwari, A.: Oracle-guided component-based program synthesis. In: ICSE (2010)
12. Johnson, J., et al.: Inferring and executing programs for visual reasoning. In: CVPR (2017)
13. Kingma, D.P., Ba, J.: Adam: a method for stochastic optimization. In: ICLR (2015)
14. Kolbitsch, C., Comparetti, P.M., Kruegel, C., Kirda, E., Zhou, X.Y., Wang, X.: Effective and efficient malware detection at the end host. In: USENIX (2009)
15. Lee, J., Avgerinos, T., Brumley, D.: TIE: principled reverse engineering of types in binary programs (2011)
16. Manna, Z., Waldinger, R.: Knowledge and reasoning in program synthesis. Artif. Intell. **6**, 175–208 (1975)
17. Markram, H.: The human brain project. Sci. Am. **306**, 50–55 (2012)
18. Oh, S.J., Schiele, B., Fritz, M.: Towards reverse-engineering black-box neural networks. In: Samek, W., Montavon, G., Vedaldi, A., Hansen, L.K., Müller, K.-R. (eds.) Explainable AI: Interpreting, Explaining and Visualizing Deep Learning. LNCS (LNAI), vol. 11700, pp. 121–144. Springer, Cham (2019). https://doi.org/10.1007/978-3-030-28954-6_7
19. Orekondy, T., Schiele, B., Fritz, M.: Knockoff Nets: stealing functionality of black-box models. In: CVPR (2019)
20. Pattis, R.E.: Karel The Robot: A Gentle Introduction to the Art of Programming. Wiley, Hoboken (1981)
21. Shin, E.C., Polosukhin, I., Song, D.: Improving neural program synthesis with inferred execution traces. In: NeurIPS (2018)
22. Solar-Lezama, A., Tancau, L., Bodik, R., Seshia, S., Saraswat, V.: Combinatorial sketching for finite programs. In: ASPLOS (2006)
23. Verma, A., Murali, V., Singh, R., Kohli, P., Chaudhuri, S.: Programmatically interpretable reinforcement learning. In: ICML (2018)
24. Waldinger, R.J., Lee, R.C.: PROW: a step toward automatic program writing. In: IJCAI (1969)
25. Yakdan, K., Dechand, S., Gerhards-Padilla, E., Smith, M.: Helping Johnny to analyze malware: a usability-optimized decompiler and malware analysis user study. In: Security and Privacy (SP) (2016)

Machine Learning for Intelligent Industrial Design

Philippe Fournier-Viger[1]([✉])(iD), M. Saqib Nawaz[1](iD), Wei Song[2](iD),
and Wensheng Gan[3](iD)

[1] Harbin Institute of Technology (Shenzhen), Shenzhen, China
{philfv,msaqibnawaz}@hit.edu.cn
[2] North China University of Technology, Beijing, China
songwei@ncut.edu.cn
[3] Jinan University, Guangzhou, China
wsgan@jnu.edu.cn

Abstract. Machine learning (ML) techniques have been used to build intelligent software for several domains. This paper reviews and discuss opportunities for using these techniques to build intelligent software for industrial design. Industrial design, sometimes called product design or new product development, is the process of conceiving products to be mass-produced in factories. It consists of several steps such as: analyzing potential customers wants and needs, planning, prototype design, and user evaluation. During each of these steps, data can be collected as documents such as product specifications and feedback forms, or by other means such as using sensors. A promising way of improving these processes to reduce costs (time and investments) and produce better designs, is to analyze data generated or used during product design using ML techniques, and to build intelligent design software. Although several studies have been carried out on this topic, there remains numerous research opportunities. This paper provides a survey of recent studies related to the use of ML in industrial design. The goal is to provide an introduction to this emerging research area and highlight limitations of previous studies and opportunities.

Keywords: Machine learning · Product design · Industrial design · Product users · Review

1 Introduction

Industrial design is the process of designing products that are mass-produced in factories such as smartphones, computers, cars and bags [41]. The process of industrial design is very important as it has a huge impact on the success and profitability of products. Well-designed products may be acclaimed and generate a large amount of profit. On the other hand, ill-designed products may receive poor reviews, have poor sales, and in extreme cases even led to massive product recalls, all of which may lead to huge losses. Besides user satisfaction

© Springer Nature Switzerland AG 2021
M. Kamp et al. (Eds.): ECML PKDD 2021 Workshops, CCIS 1525, pp. 158–172, 2021.
https://doi.org/10.1007/978-3-030-93733-1_11

and profitability, the design of a product must also consider key aspects such as the difficulty of assembling parts in a factory, the type of material/parts to be used and their suppliers, and how the product can be stored, transported, and recycled [28].

Product development is thus an important and complicated process, which must consider numerous constraints. For this reason, there is a lot of interest in improving the process of industrial design to ensure the development of products that meet these requirements. Traditionally, developing new products has been carried out by companies using a more or less methodical approach involving many steps. Some of the key steps of industrial design involves for example to analyze the wants and needs of users, to design product prototype(s), to evaluate the prototype(s), and redesign the prototypes if necessary [17]. Product development can be costly both in terms of time and resources. For example, if user requirements are not taken into account early in the development of a product, multiple prototypes may have to be designed, potentially delaying the launch of the product and resulting in higher development costs. It is thus desirable that product development be performed as efficiently as possible.

To address the issues of developing products that satisfy the above constraints, and improving the efficiency and reducing the costs of product development, an emerging research topic is to use machine learning (ML) techniques to understand or guide the design process. During each step of the product development process, data can be collected. For instance, this can include information about user wants and needs, product feedback from users, information about parts, suppliers and assembly lines, reviews of existing products, and sale data. Using ML techniques to analyze such data can provide major insights for the improvement of products and the process of industrial design. Note that the term ML is used interchangeably with data mining (DM) in this paper.

Several studies [2,7,13–15,25,27,28,44–46] have been published on the use of ML and Artificial Intelligence (AI) in industrial applications, manufacturing, smart production, smart logistics and to improve software for industrial design. However, the studies [14,25,27,28,44,45] are old and hence no longer up-to-date. Moreover, there is a great lack of review in the field of ML in intelligent industrial design. Thus, the contribution of this paper is to provide a clear and concise overview of what has been done through an up-to-date literature review, and hence facilitate the work of researchers in the field of industrial design. The review [44], published in 2007, discussed the application of ML in engineering design, but that discussion is hardly two pages long. Moreover, the study [25], also published in 2007, discussed only the modularity aspect for data-driven design.

Some recent reviews [8,11,43] discussed data-driven design in the product conceptual development phase, the relationship between digitization and its consequences on designers and design processes, and the impact of AI on design and innovation and how modern organization are using and implementing AI-based design practice. In this review, we identified six clusters for the application of ML in industrial design, which are: (1) product acceptability estimation, (2) product development failure prediction. (3) product design as an optimization problem, (4) predictive manufacturing, (5) data-driven design, and (6) design support systems.

The rest of this paper is organized as follows. Section 2 briefly describes the process of industrial design, including the various steps of product development, and the types of data that can be collected. Section 3 presents the methodology used for carrying out the literature review. Then, Sect. 4 reviews studies on the integration of ML in industrial design. Moreover, the types of data and datasets that ML can use in industrial design are discussed. Section 5 provides a discussion of research opportunities. Finally, Sect. 6 draws a conclusion.

2 Industrial Design

Conceiving a product that will be mass-produced in factories is called *industrial design*. The output of this process is documents that can be used to manufacture the product. Industrial design is an activity that is key to the success of a product. Note that in the literature, the terms *product design* and *new product development* are sometimes used with a similar meaning as industrial design. But distinctions are sometimes made between these terms. Do et al. [17] view product development as a five step process:

1. **Product planning**: Learning about the needs of users to write requirements for the design of a novel product.
2. **System design**: Producing a general design of a product as a set of modules, which may correspond to existing product parts.
3. **Detail design**: Producing a detailed design of the product modules by designing its parts, product structure, and creating engineering documents.
4. **Prototyping**: Creating a working prototype of the product based on the detailed design (which may result in redesigning the product).
5. **Preparing the production**: This includes planning required material and resource planning for production.

In this process, the term *product design* refers to steps 2 and 3, while step 1 to 5 are considered as *new product development*. But more generally, product development can be viewed as a sub-step or phase in the overall lifetime of a product. In fact, some authors not only consider the product development process but also the full product lifetime. For example, Li et al. [28] indicates that there are three phases in the lifetime of a product.

1. **Beginning of life (product design and production)**: Marketing research is performed to find out what are the customers wants and needs. Then a product is created that meet these needs. Then, production must be prepared by choosing suppliers (procurement). During production, the quality of products and of the manufacturing process are assessed and the manufacturing equipment is managed to ensure efficiency (in terms of time, energy and other criteria).

2. **Middle of life:** This includes tasks for logistics (including managing inventory, ordering process, and product transportation), as well as customer service, product support and maintenance (preventive and corrective).
3. **End of life:** This includes tasks related to the product end-of-life, that is when a product cease to be useful or when a company decided to stop marketing and selling a product. These tasks involves mainly product recovery and recycling.

Several authors have argued that all the steps of the product lifetime from design to recycling should be considered for product development since they are interrelated [44]. For example, when designing a product one may want to consider questions such as: (1) which supplier or machine will provide/produce the material? (2) how will the product be manufactured, assembled, stored, transported, used, recycled? (3) how much will the product cost? (4) how much profit will it yield? (5) how the product will be marketed? Ignoring these questions during the design phase can cause serious problems. For example, if a designer ignores issues related to production, he may design a product that is too expensive to produce or cannot be produced due to a lack of appropriate machine for production. Such problems may lead to redesigning the product, which may be expensive and time-consuming, and may ultimately cause product delays and other serious issues. Thus, it is reasonable that the design of a product should be guided by expectations for the whole product lifecycle.

Product Evaluation. Another key consideration in product development is product evaluation. A point made by several authors is that products should be evaluated as early as possible in the product development process, to avoid redesigning at a later stage, which may be much more costly. For example, Chan [12] proposed an idea screening module to filter bad ideas before starting to design. Chan also proposed a virtual customer perception model to predict how a customer will react to a given design. These types of techniques can be used early in the design process, rather than just evaluating the final product. In general, potential customers or users, may play at least two important roles. First, before a product is designed, marketing research can be done to know about what the potential customers want in terms of various factors such as function and aesthetics (e.g. [35,42]). For example, one may survey users about their needs/wants in terms of functional requirements or evaluation criteria for products. Second, one may use surveys (or other methods) to evaluate user satisfaction for a prototype or a final product.

3   Methodology

A systematic literature review (SLR) [9] was conducted for the evaluation of recent studies on ML in industrial design. The main reason to use a SLR is that it offers a method-driven, systematic, and replicable approach. The SLR is a valuable tool to create and assess new knowledge as it capable of minimizing various judgment biases by systematically evaluating relevant findings from recent research studies.

We consider the time period from 2006 to 2021 for the publication time span. To prepare this review, the papers related to ML in industrial design have been collected from online databases such as Scopus, Web of Science, DBLP, journals and conferences. Some main keywords that were used to collect related studies are "machine learning, data mining, industrial design, product design, customer satisfaction and parametric design". Moreover, additional keywords were found using synonyms from a thesaurus. Following the guidelines suggested in [15,16], three steps were done to select studies:

1. Identification,
2. Screening, and
3. Inclusion

The related studies and their bibliometrics were collected in step 1. Screening is done in step 2 to identify which documents to select that is closest and relevant to ML in industrial design. Step 3 aimed to select the documents to be analyzed in detail. We collected 150 studies in total. After screening, we found 42 relevant studies in the literature.

We found that out of 42 studies, 37% (15) were published in last three years (2019–2021) and 12% (5) were published in four years (2006–2009). The top three countries that published the highest number of studies were USA, China (along with Italy) and UK respectively. The top 3 venues that published the most studies related to ML in industrial design were *Manufacturing & Service Operations, Expert Systems with Applications* and *Computers in Industry*. Moreover, 14 studies were review/survey studies and the remaining 28 studies were technical studies, case studies and experiments.

4   Machine Learning in Industrial Design

This section first reviews data that can be used for ML in industrial design. Then, recent studies on this topic are reviewed.

4.1   Data

To be able to evaluate product design, data must be collected. In the era of "big data" and "internet of things", huge amount of rich data about the lifetime of a product can be collected and stored in databases at a very small cost. Analyzing this data may provide numerous benefits. However, analyzing data by hand is time consuming. Thus, several researchers have applied data mining, machine learning, or statistical techniques to analyze data collected in general about product development.

Types of Data. Many different types of data can be collected and analyzed during the development or any stage of the lifetime of a product. Some of this data could be analyzed separately or several types of data could be combined to obtain more insights on products. Some data types that can be considered are [25,28,45]:

- data about customer demands (e.g. product function, configuration, quality, cost, brand)
- data about customers (e.g. age, education, travel behavior)
- characteristics of a product and competitor products (e.g. size, weight, color, user manual)
- information related to production (e.g. how parts are assembled, a production plan)
- information related to logistics (e.g. inventory information, how the product will be stored and transported)
- information related to product support (e.g. spare part list, service instructions, customer support data)
- customer feedback about a product (e.g. feedback forms, physiological data, audio, video, location)
- information about how a product is used (e.g. usage environment, usage condition, usage time, failure data)
- information about the manufacturing process (e.g. how machines are used and scheduled to produce product units).
- information about orders, customer transactions, and customer support
- supplier financial data
- sustainability and green practices data
- product inspection results, data about product recycling

There is thus a large amount of data from the life cycle of a product that can be analyzed. This data can be thought in terms of how it is represented. It can include various forms of data such as spatial data, text data, graphs, multimedia data, behaviors, plans, time series, transactions, sequences and relational data.

Where to Obtain Data? A practical question for researchers is how data about industrial design can be obtained. Besides obtaining data directly from the industry, there exists several public dataset related to product design. For example, some public datasets are:

- a car design evaluation database for classification of acceptability of a car design (archive.ics.uci.edu/ml/datasets/Car+Evaluation). The database has 1,728 instances, and six attributes of car: buying, paint, doors, persons, boot, and safety. The target attribute for classification can take four values: very good, good, acceptable and unacceptable. This data was used to construct a model to predict acceptability of a product by users based on its characteristics [30].
- a dataset of Amazon customer review of products (http://www.snap.stanford.edu/data/#amazon) with star ratings. It contains reviews, title and description of products, which products have been purchased together. And it provides 18 years of data, and products are categorized by category.
- a customer spending dataset (archive.ics.uci.edu/ml/datasets/Wholesale+customers) obtained from a wholesale distributor which indicates how much money each customer spend on different categories of product each year.

– A dataset [1] of weekly customers orders for Dell computer products over a three and a half year period (2013–2016). Another dataset [31] contains 187 weeks customers demands information data for Intel microprocessor. And a similar dataset, called the cross-border e-commerce dataset [37], contains weekly orders placed on Amazon Marketplace over a three-year period (January 1, 2015–December 31, 2017).

Besides, some other datasets may be obtained by contacting other researchers, and some datasets can be purchased from companies. It is also possible for a person to create his own dataset. In that case, the advantage is that the person can choose the dataset characteristics.

4.2   Recent Studies

Recent studies have used ML for various tasks related to industrial design. We identified six clusters that can be incorporated into a conceptual framework for the application of ML in industrial design.

Product Acceptability Estimation. Product acceptability estimation deals with estimating the probability of success (or failure) of products. Garces et al. [19] proposed a ML model to predict if users will accept a product early during the product development process. Garces asked several persons to fill a Likert questionnaire about the acceptability of products based on their characteristics. The data was then used to build a Bayesian network. That model can then predict the acceptability of a product based on its characteristics. The model is specific to a type of products (a communicating pen or software). A limitation of that study is that no formal evaluation was made to evaluate if the model is helpful for designers. Similarly, an approach based on Bayesian network and simulated annealing [20] can be used to evaluate an index for users product acceptability and how to improve users product accessibility. However, the proposed approach cannot deliver an exact level of acceptability and the acceptability assessment relies on the users' perception of the proposed solution.

In a related work, Tang et al. [39] studied the relationship between product form design and customer perception. Tang et al. studied the design of mobile phones in terms of several aesthetics parameters such as screen size, width and height. Users were asked to rate 32 mobile phone samples having different parameter values using a 5-point Likert scale from "Smart" to "Clumsy". With this data, an artificial neural network model was trained, which can predict user perception for any combination of parameter values. This model was then combined with a genetic algorithm to automatically generate a large number of designs with various parameters. Each design was tested using the neural network to select an optimal design in terms of user perception. Tang et al. thus went one step further than Garces et al. by not only predicting user perception but also testing numerous designs automatically to find an optimal one. However, the "optimal model" was not tested with users to see if it is really optimal. Moreover, Luo et al. [30] developed an intelligent model to predict consumer acceptability of products. The model applies three feature ranking methods, and three classifiers and their ensembles for prediction. The models were evaluated on a real case study about car evaluation.

Product Development Failure Prediction. Do et al. [17] proposed a method to analyze logs to determine causes of product development failure. To collect data, Do et al. asked 20 students to submit their work on product development over a semester through a website. Students had to upload various documents related to product development such as: product configurations (3D models in CAD format), assembly structures, engineering changes made to prototypes and product views. Then, a Naive Bayes Classifier model was trained with that data to find the most important causes of failures. It was found for example that if product development take more than 44 days, it is more likely to fail. Recently, ML has also been used in [29,47] to detect product defects from social media data and online review, respectively. The work [47] has limitation that it cannot discover those defects that have never occurred before. Similarly, the proposed method [29] requires manual tagging of training data.

A recently proposed ML approach [32] can predict service-level failures a few weeks earlier and thus alerts the planners/designers. A reconfigurable, online, self-managed and scalable learning system based on IoT ML and orchestration framework was proposed in [36] for the detection of failures in surface mount devices during production. The main limitation of this work is that aspects of the developed framework were not described exhaustively. Kang [22] integrated statistical inference methods and ML techniques to build a framework for product warranty prediction during product development. The work has some limitations from the aspects of learning curve, data gathering and cost vs. frequency.

Product Design as an Optimization Problem. Shi et al. [34] presented an optimization framework for product design. The framework was based on nested partitions (NP) method that can construct product profiles from part-worths data obtained from market research. Various well-known heuristics were used in the framework. Numerical results showed that the NP methods can be used in superior product designs. In other studies [6,10] efficient methods were developed based on Lagrangian relaxation for the product line design problems. The work [6] has certain limitations, such as (1) the accuracy measure assumes that the partworths can accurately describe actual behavior of customer and (2) the optimization methodologies do not take into account the competitive response to the introduction of new product. Mosavi et al. [33] considered the design of a product as a problem of finding a design that satisfies multiple objective (constraints), that may be contradictory. As example, they discussed the design of a 3D wing. Using ML, they built models to find variables describing a product that influence the most the attainment of the design objectives. Kwong et al. [26] proposed an AI-based methodology to integrate three processes (affective design, engineering, and marketing) to define design specifications of new products. The methodology can simultaneously consider the concerns from three processes in the early design stage. In the methodology, a fuzzy regression (FR) approach was used to develop customer satisfaction and cost models. A chaos-based FR approach was then used to generate product utility functions. In last, a non-dominated sorting genetic algorithm-II (NSGA-II) was used to solve multi-objective optimization problems. The effectiveness of the proposed methodology was evaluated on a case study that contains electric iron designs.

In another study, Tseng and Ganzoury [42] presented a system to generate design ideas to help designers in the early stages of product design. The user must provide a design specifications in terms of functional attributes and required function (e.g. size, material, weight). Then, the system generate designs by testing different combinations of modules to find a design satisfying the desired function. The system was presented for some relatively simple designs like a car accelerator pedal.

Predictive Manufacturing. Predictive manufacturing requires the utilization of advanced prediction tools with the goal of giving "selfaware" capabilities to machines/systems. Ademujimi et al. [2] reviewed the literature on how machine learning techniques were used in manufacturing fault diagnosis. Lee et al. [27] argued about the importance of data analysis for manufacturing so as to improve productivity and efficiency. In particular, they indicated that monitoring the performance and current condition of machines (e.g. remaining useful life and degradation level) is key to predict failures and plan maintenance, to reduce manufacturing performance loss. Krumeich et al. [24] investigated the concept of event-based process predictions in various business processes. A case study at Saarstahl AG-a German steel producing company- was conducted to see which data the company can collect by its sensor technology for accurate forecasts.

Han and Chi [21] predicted the CNC tool wear compensation offset value by using the support vector regression alongwith various combinations of data pre-processing methods. For Predictive Maintenance (PdM), Susto et al. [38] presented a multiple classifier ML methodology, called *Multiple Classifier (MC) PdM*, for integral type faults. *MC PdM* can deal efficiently with the unbalanced datasets and the classifiers work in parallel to exploit the knowledge of the tool/logistic variables at each process iteration in order to enhance decision making. However, in *MC PdM*, the choice of the fault horizon affects the performance of the corresponding classifier. Khan et al. [23] recently proposed a manufacturing analytics model to predict failures in the production process in heterogeneous streams of data. The comparison with other classification methods, such as SVM, KNN, ANN, on real data showed that the proposed approach can predict product failure with reasonable accuracy.

Data-Driven Design. Product design can take advantage of the huge amount of available data, such as physical and virtual product, external data (information available on Internet), and enterprise data from customer relationship management systems. The review [8] investigated the definitions, uses, and application of data-driven design (DDD) in the concept development process. It was found that from 2008 to 2019, various text mining techniques are used on online and social media reviews. Authors argued that very little focus is given till now on historical data and on real data collected through sensors. Thus, the opportunity provided by the increased use of the Internet of Things (IoT) in cyber physical systems (CPSs) is not exploited fully. Fuge et al. [18] explored the suitableness of various machine learning algorithms in recommending design methods taken from the HCD Connect online community. The work is beneficial for novice designers to quickly select the appropriate recommending design methods for a given problem, leading to more effective product design. A recent review [13] used both qualitative and quantitative approaches to examine the applications of data science (DS) in the engineering design (ED) field. Some 23 challenges were identified that were related to the integration of DS methodologies into the ED process. The studies [11,43] provided conceptual frameworks to understand the design and innovation in the age of digitization, and their impact on the world of design. Authors concluded that data-driven design has interdisciplinary implications and new innovations does not undermine the basic principles of design, but they are intelligently changing design practices.

Design Support Systems. Chan in his PhD thesis [12], proposed an integrated decision support system (iDSS) to support new product development and help companies in making reliable decisions on new product development. The work focused on covering many aspects, including financial aspect, of new product development rather than a single one. However, *iDSS* requires data warehouse for implementation and operation and also requires massive amount of information from different departments. Bedkowski et al. [4] designed a mobile robot that can provide real-time help for spatial design. The system acquires data about an environment and its objects using sensors. Objects and their spatial relationships are then described using an ontology, which can support reasoning. Then, the assistant can provides suggestions about the placements of objects in the environment and check whether constraints are satisfied such as functional requirements. The work [5] extends the mobile robot [4] to perform qualitative reasoning in the security domain and for spatial design support. However, the classification method only uses 3D information of objects. The decision support system (DSS) [3] can improve design using Warranty Data. The input to the system is a database of customers feedbacks related to product warranty failure and defects. The system used an ontology-based text mining based approach to discover hidden important knowledge from the database. Moreover, Self Organizing Maps (SOM) were used to find information from the database to relate it to the manufacturing data. This enabled the system to detect specific defective component. A hybrid approach was proposed in [40] where Pi-Mind technology was used as a mixture of human-expert-driven and AI-driven decision-making approaches for smart manufacturing processes based on AI and ML technologies.

Figure 1 illustrates the aforementioned clusters. From observation obtained after content analysis, each clusters is mapped to most relevant methods and instruments specified in the literature.

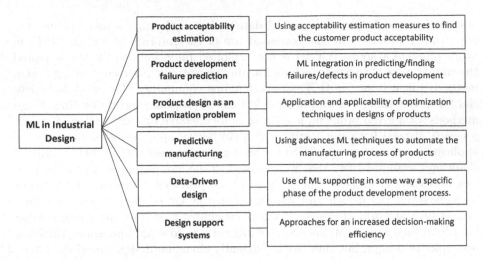

Fig. 1. Conceptual framework for ML in industrial design

5   Research Opportunities

There are many opportunities for applying machine learning and data mining techniques to improve industrial design, as discussed above. Here are some key research opportunities:

Analyzing How User Think or React to Products. This can be done using data collected through sensors, EEG signals, text, feedback forms, etc. A promising topic is to study the influence of emotions on customer satisfaction for products/designs, as well as other reactions such as confusion, motivation and why they occur.

Analyzing How Users Utilize a Product. This can be studied using ML techniques, and by using cognitive models to explain customer behavior. For example, aspects related to spatial cognition such as spatial representations and spatial reasoning can be evaluated. This could be relevant for evaluating the behavior of users in virtual environments, or how user manipulate objects.

Analyzing the User Wants and Needs. ML can be used to analyze customer reviews from websites and other data. This can allows to analyze/ understand/ predict sale data of similar products or characteristics.

Analyzing How Persons Behave as Customers. Some interesting tasks are to predict the return on investment, predict which customer will buy a product, and modelling customer buying behavior.

Analyzing Data to Improve the Manufacturing Processes. Various data may be analyzed such as data from equipment management, fault detection, inspection data and quality monitoring.

Analyzing Data About Suppliers. Data about the performance of suppliers can be modelled as well as other aspects.

Discovering and Analyzing Customers Interest from Online Data: Customers use social media platforms such as Facebook and Twitter to share their opinions. Moreover, companies now store the customers inquires, suggestions, feedbacks and complaints in a database. ML can be used on such online dataset to infer customers interest related to specific products. Moreover, industries/companies can identify potential customers by analyzing online user-generated contents with ML.

Automating Design Practices. Most design practices depend on human decision-making and is a labor-intensive activity. ML techniques such as supervised, unsupervised and reinforcement learning can be used to automate design practices. Moreover, abstract design patterns can be identified with pattern mining that can be applied in the object generation process. Automatic creation and adaptation of design models can increase designers creativity through suggestions of appropriate object shapes. Automation of time-consuming routine tasks will also save time.

Handling Specific Product Types and Development Processes. In this document the term "product" was used to denote any type of products. But for specific types of products, different research challenges are raised. For example, if we loosen the definition of product to consider a virtual environment or mobile phone application as a product, then techniques for evaluating these products may be different from those used for other products, and other challenges may be faced such as the importance of handling spatial designs. Different challenges may also arise by considering various development processes such as: assemble-to-order, make-to-order and store-to-order [25].

Intelligent Design Systems. Another interesting possibility for research is to use the product evaluation techniques to build intelligent design systems. In ML, data is analyzed for two purposes: understanding the past, and predicting the future. This can lead to some interesting research opportunities such as predicting how customers will behave to a hypothetical product, and how they will react to designs. This can lead to interactive design system that could help the designer create designs that are more successful and avoid design problems early. An interactive design system could operate in a continuum that vary from completely manual to fully automatic (parametric design). A more elaborate system equipped with knowledge about design theories could also be used to teach design or recommend design steps to designers. Another interesting area is to use explainable AI in developing hybrid decision support systems.

What Kind of Expertise Is Required? To carry out research on these topics, many kinds of research expertise may be involved such as: ML and Statistics, Design, Sentiment analysis, Opinion mining, Text mining, Planning/Scheduling, Cognitive modeling and User modeling (to better understand the user), Human Computer Interactions, Marketing, Manufacturing (inventory management, suppliers, delivery, cost and feasibility constraints, etc.), and data collection.

6   Conclusion

This paper has provided a detailed survey on the integration of ML in the process of industrial design. The paper has reviewed definitions of industrial design, and the types of data that can be collected and public datasets related to product design. Then, an extensive review of work on the integration of ML in industrial design has been presented. After literature analysis, six clusters were found for the application of ML in industrial design, that are: (1) product acceptability estimation, (2) product development failure prediction (3) product design as an optimization problem, (4) predictive manufacturing, (5) data-driven design and (6) design support systems. Finally, the paper has discussed research opportunities.

This review not only provided a conceptual framework regarding the application of ML in industrial design, but also offers a starting point for further investigation in this area and to suggest more interesting research directions. Practitioners and managers are now more interested in using ML-based methods in industries. We believe that they can use this framework to successfully and efficiently implement state-of-the-art ML-based technologies in industries.

References

1. Acimovic, J., Erize, F., Hu, K., Thomas, D.J., Mieghem, J.A.V.: Product life cycle data set: raw and cleaned data of weekly orders for personal computers. Manuf. Serv. Oper. Manag. **21**(1), 171–176 (2019)
2. Ademujimi, T.T., Brundage, M.P., Prabhu, V.V.: A review of current machine learning techniques used in manufacturing diagnosis. In: Lödding, H., Riedel, R., Thoben, K.-D., von Cieminski, G., Kiritsis, D. (eds.) APMS 2017. IAICT, vol. 513, pp. 407–415. Springer, Cham (2017). https://doi.org/10.1007/978-3-319-66923-6_48
3. Alkahtani, M., Choudhary, A., De, A., Harding, J.A.: A decision support system based on ontology and data mining to improve design using warranty data. Comput. Ind. Eng. **128**, 1027–1039 (2019)
4. Bedkowski, J.: Intelligent mobile assistant for spatial design support. Autom. Constr. **32**, 177–186 (2013)
5. Bedkowski, J., Majek, K., Majek, P., Musialik, P., Pelka, M., Nüchter, A.: Intelligent mobile system for improving spatial design support and security inside buildings. Mob. Netw. Appl. **21**(2), 313–326 (2016)
6. Belloni, A., Freund, R.M., Selove, M., Simester, D.: Optimizing product line designs: efficient methods and comparisons. Manage. Sci. **54**(9), 1544–1552 (2008)
7. Bertolini, M., Mezzogori, D., Neroni, M., Zammori, F.: Machine learning for industrial applications: a comprehensive literature review. Expert Syst. Appl. **175**, 114820 (2021)
8. Bertoni, A.: Data-driven design in concept development: systematic review and missed opportunities. Proc. Des. Soc. Des. Conf. **1**, 100–110 (2020)
9. Booth, A., Sutton, A., Papaioannou, D.: Systematic Approaches to a Successful Literature Review. SAGE Publishing (2016)

10. Camm, J.D., Cochran, J.J., Curry, D.J., Kannan, S.: Conjoint optimization: an exact branch-and-bound algorithm for the share-of-choice problem. Manage. Sci. **52**(3), 435–447 (2006)
11. Cantamessa, M., Montagna, F., Altavilla, S., Casagrande-Seretti, A.: Data-driven design: the new challenges of digitalization on product design and development. Des. Sci. **6**, E27 (2020)
12. Chan, S.L.: An integrated decision support system for new product development with customer satisfaction. Ph.D. thesis, The Hong Kong Polytechnic University (2011)
13. Chiarello, F., Belingheri, P., Fantoni, G.: Data science for engineering design: state of the art and future directions. Comput. Ind. **129**, 103447 (2021)
14. Choudhary, A.K., Harding, J.A., Tiwari, M.K.: Data mining in manufacturing: a review based on the kind of knowledge. J. Intell. Manuf. **20**(5), 501–521 (2009)
15. Cioffi, R., Travaglioni, M., Piscitelli, G., Petrillo, A., De Felice, F.: Artificial intelligence and machine learning applications in smart production: progress, trends, and directions. Sustainability **12**, 492 (2020)
16. Denyer, D., Tranfield, D.: Producing a systematic review. In: The Sage Handbook of Organizational Research Methods, pp. 671–689 (2011)
17. Do, N., Bae, S., Park, C.: Interactive analysis of product development experiments using on-line analytical mining. Comput. Ind. **66**, 52–62 (2015)
18. Fuge, M., Peters, B., Agogino, A.: Machine learning algorithms for recommending design methods. J. Mech. Des. **136**(10), 101103 (2014)
19. Garces, G.A., Rakotondranaivo, A., Bonjour, E.: An acceptability estimation and analysis methodology based on Bayesian networks. Int. J. Ind. Ergon. **53**, 245–256 (2016)
20. Garces, G.A., Rakotondranaivo, A., Bonjour, E.: Improving users' product acceptability: an approach based on Bayesian networks and a simulated annealing algorithm. Int. J. Prod. Res. **54**(17), 5151–5168 (2016)
21. Han, J., Chi, S.: Consideration of manufacturing data to apply machine learning methods for predictive manufacturing. In: Proceedings of ICUFN, pp. 109–113 (2016)
22. Kang, H.R.: Warranty prediction during product development: developing an event generation engine in an engineer-to-order environment. Master's thesis, Rochester Institute of Technology, USA (2011)
23. Khan, A., Schiøler, H., Kulahci, M., Zaki, M., Rasmussen, P.: Predictive manufacturing: a classification strategy to predict product failures. Expert Syst. Appl. (2021)
24. Krumeich, J., Jacobi, S., Werth, D., Loos, P.: Big data analytics for predictive manufacturing control - a case study from process industry. In: Proceedings of Big Data, pp. 530–537 (2014)
25. Kusiak, A., Smith, M.: Data mining in design of products and production systems. Annu. Rev. Control. **31**(1), 147–156 (2007)
26. Kwong, C.K., Jiang, H., Luo, X.: AI-based methodology of integrating affective design, engineering, and marketing for defining design specifications of new products. Eng. Appl. Artif. Intell. **47**, 49–60 (2016)
27. Lee, J., Lapira, E., Bagheri, B., Kao, H.A.: Recent advances and trends in predictive manufacturing systems in big data environment. Manuf. Lett. **1**(1), 38–41 (2013)
28. Li, J., Tao, F., Cheng, Y., Zhao, L.: Big data in product lifecycle management. Int. J. Adv. Manuf. Technol. **81**(1–4), 667–684 (2015)

29. Liu, Y., Jiang, C., Zhao, H.: Using contextual features and multi-view ensemble learning in product defect identification from online discussion forums. Decis. Support Syst. **105**, 1–12 (2018)
30. Luo, S.T., Su, C.T., Lee, W.C.: Constructing intelligent model for acceptability evaluation of a product. Expert Syst. Appl. **38**(11), 13702–13710 (2011)
31. Manary, M.P., Willems, S.P.: Data set: 187 weeks of customer forecasts and orders for microprocessors from intel corporation. Manuf. Serv. Oper. Manag. (2021)
32. Melançon, G.G., Grangier, P., Prescott-Gagnon, E., Sabourin, E., Rousseau, L.: A machine learning-based system for predicting service-level failures in supply chains. INFORMS J. Appl. Anal. **51**(3), 200–212 (2021)
33. Mosavi, A.: Data mining for decision-making in engineering optimal design. J. AI Data Min. **2**(1), 7–14 (2014)
34. Shi, L., Olafsson, S., Chen, Q.: An optimization framework for product design. Manage. Sci. **47**(12), 1681–1692 (2001)
35. Smith, S., Smith, G.C., Jiao, R., Chu, C.-H.: Mass customization in the product life cycle. J. Intell. Manuf. **24**(5), 877–885 (2012). https://doi.org/10.1007/s10845-012-0691-0
36. Soto, J.A.C., Tavakolizadeh, F., Gyulai, D.: An online machine learning framework for early detection of product failures in an industry 4.0 context. Int. J. Comput. Integr. Manuf. **32**(4–5), 452–465 (2019)
37. Sun, L., Lyu, G., Yu, Y., Teo, C.P.: Cross-border e-commerce data set: choosing the right fulfillment option. Manuf. Serv. Oper. Manag. **23**(5), 1297–1313 (2021)
38. Susto, G.A., Schirru, A., Pampuri, S., McLoone, S.F., Beghi, A.: Machine learning for predictive maintenance: a multiple classifier approach. IEEE Trans. Industr. Inf. **11**(3), 812–820 (2015)
39. Tang, C., Fung, K., Lee, E.W., Ho, G.T., Siu, K.W., Mou, W.: Product form design using customer perception evaluation by a combined superellipse fitting and ANN approach. Adv. Eng. Inform. **27**(3), 386–394 (2013)
40. Terziyan, V., Gryshko, S., Golovianko, M.: Patented intelligence: cloning human decision models for industry 4.0. J. Manuf. Syst. **48**, 204–217 (2018)
41. Tjalve, E.: A Short Course in Industrial Design, 1st edn. Elsevier (2015)
42. Tseng, K.C., El-Ganzoury, W.: An intelligent system based on concurrent engineering for innovative product design at the conceptual design stage. Int. J. Adv. Manuf. Technol. **63**(5–8), 421–447 (2012)
43. Verganti, R., Vendraminelli, L., Iansiti, M.: Innovation and design in the age of artificial intelligence. J. Prod. Innov. Manag. **37**, 212–227 (2020)
44. Wang, K., Tong, S., Eynard, B., Roucoules, L., Matta, N.: Review on application of data mining in product design and manufacturing. In: Proceedings of FSKD, vol. 4, pp. 613–618 (2007)
45. Wójcik, W., Gromaszek, K.: Data mining industrial applications. In: Knowledge-Oriented Applications in Data Mining, pp. 431–442. IntechOpen (2011)
46. Woschank, M., Rauch, E., Zsifkovits, H.: A review of further directions for artificial intelligence, machine learning, and deep learning in smart logistics. Sustainability **12**, 3760 (2020)
47. Zheng, L., He, Z., He, S.: A novel probabilistic graphic model to detect product defects from social media data. Decis. Support Syst. **137**, 113369 (2020)

MIning DAta for financial applicationS

6th Workshop on MIning DAta for financial applicationS (MIDAS 2021)

Like the famous King Midas, popularly remembered in Greek mythology for his ability to turn everything he touched with his hand into gold, the wealth of data generated by modern technologies, with widespread presence of computers, users, and media connected by the Internet, is a goldmine for tackling a variety of problems in the financial domain.

Nowadays, people's interactions with technological systems provide us with gargantuan amounts of data documenting collective behavior in a previously unimaginable fashion. Recent research has shown that by properly modeling and analyzing these massive datasets, for instance representing them as network structures, it is possible to gain useful insights into the evolution of the systems considered (i.e., trading, disease spreading, political elections). Investigating the impact of data arising from today's application domains on financial decisions is of paramount importance. Knowledge extracted from data can help gather critical information for trading decisions, reveal early signs of impactful events (such as stock market moves), or anticipate catastrophic events (e.g., financial crises) that result from a combination of actions and affect humans worldwide.

The importance of data-mining tasks in the financial domain has long been recognized. For example, in the Web context, changes in the frequency with which users browse news or look for certain terms on search engines have been correlated with product trends, level of activity in certain industries, unemployment rates, or car and home sales, as well as stock-market trade volumes and price movements. Other core applications include forecasting the stock market, predicting bank bankruptcies, understanding and managing financial risk, trading futures, credit rating, loan management, and bank customer profiling. Despite its well-recognized relevance and some recent related efforts, data mining in finance is still not stably part of the main stream of data-mining conferences. This makes the topic particularly appealing for a workshop proposal, whose small, interactive, and possibly interdisciplinary context provides a unique opportunity to advance research in a stimulating but still quite unexplored field.

The aim of the 6th Workshop on MIning DAta for financial applicationS (MIDAS 2021), held (virtually) in conjunction with the 2021 European Conference on Machine Learning and Principles and Practice of Knowledge Discovery in Databases (ECML PKDD 2021), on September 17, 2021, was to discuss challenges, potentialities, and applications of leveraging data-mining tasks to tackle problems in the financial domain. The workshop provided a premier forum for sharing findings, knowledge, insights, experience, and lessons learned from mining data generated in various domains. The intrinsic interdisciplinary nature of the workshop promoted the interaction between computer scientists, physicists, mathematicians, economists, and financial analysts, thus paving the way for an exciting and stimulating environment involving researchers and practitioners from different areas.

Topics of interest included, among others, forecasting the stock market, trading models, discovering market trends, predictive analytics for financial services, network analytics in finance, planning investment strategies, portfolio management, understanding and managing financial risk, customer/investor profiling, identifying expert investors, financial modeling, measures of success in forecasting, anomaly detection in financial data, fraud detection, discovering patterns and correlations in financial data, text mining and NLP for financial applications, financial network analysis, time series analysis, and pitfall identification.

MIDAS 2021 was structured as a full-day workshop. Owning to the COVID-19 pandemic, MIDAS 2021 was organized as a fully-fledged virtual event. In particular, the workshop followed a "live" mode, where presentations happened in real-time, with organizers, speakers, and attendees remotely joining the event.

We encouraged submissions of regular papers (long or short) and extended abstracts. Regular papers could be up to 15 pages (long papers) or 10 pages (short papers), and reported on novel, unpublished work that might not be mature enough for a conference or journal submission. Extended abstracts could be up to six pages long, and presented work-in-progress, recently published work fitting the workshop topics, or position papers. All submitted papers were peer-reviewed by three reviewers from the Program Committee, and selected on the basis of these reviews. MIDAS 2021 received 10 submissions, among which six papers were accepted (three long papers, one short paper, and two extended abstracts).

In accordance with the reviewers' scores and comments, the paper entitled "Adaptive Supervised Learning for Financial Markets Volatility Targeting Models", authored by Eric Benhamou, David Saltiel, Serge Tabachnik, Corentin Bourdeix, François Chareyron, and Beatrice Guez, was selected as the best paper of the workshop.

The program of the workshop was enriched by an invited speaker: Gianmarco De Francisci Morales from ISI Foundation, who gave a talk titled "How I learned to stop worrying and love the risk".

September 2021

Valerio Bitetta
Ilaria Bordino
Andrea Ferretti
Francesco Gullo
Giovanni Ponti
Lorenzo Severini

Organization

Program Chairs

Valerio Bitetta	UniCredit, Italy
Ilaria Bordino	UniCredit, Italy
Andrea Ferretti	UniCredit, Italy
Francesco Gullo	UniCredit, Italy
Giovanni Ponti	ENEA, Italy
Lorenzo Severini	UniCredit, Italy

Program Committee

Aris Anagnostopoulos	Sapienza University, Italy
Annalisa Appice	University of Bari, Italy
Argimiro Arratia	Universitat Politécnica de Catalunya, Spain
Davide Azzalini	Politecnico of Milan, Italy
Fabio Azzalini	Politecnico of Milan, Italy
Antonia Azzini	C2T, Italy
Xiao Bai	Yahoo Research, USA
Andre Baier	Fraunhofer IEE, Germany
Luca Barbaglia	JRC - European Commission, Italy
Luigi Bellomarini	Banca d'Italia, Italy
Ludovico Boratto	Eurecat, Spain
Cristian Bravo	Western University, Canada
Doug Burdick	IBM Research, USA
Matteo Catena	NTENT, Spain
Jeremy Charlier	National Bank of Canada, Canada
Sergio Consoli	JRC - European Commission, Italy
Carlotta Domeniconi	George Mason University, USA
Wouter Duivesteijn	Eindhoven University of Technology, The Netherlands
Edoardo Galimberti	Independent researcher, Italy
Cuneyt Gurcan Akcora	University of Manitoba, Canada
Roberto Interdonato	CIRAD, France
Anna Krause	University of Wurzburg, Germany
Rajasekar Krishnamurthy	IBM Almaden, USA
Malte Lehna	Fraunhofer IEE, Germany
Domenico Mandaglio	University of Calabria, Italy
Yelena Mejova	ISI Foundation, Italy
Sandra Mitrovic	KU Leuven, Belgium

Davide Mottin	Aarhus University, Denmark
Giulia Preti	ISI Foundation, Italy
Daniel Schloer	University of Wurzburg, Germany
Christoph Scholz	Fraunhofer IEE, Germany
Edoardo Vacchi	Red Hat, Italy
Yongluan Zhou	University of Copenaghen, Denmark

Financial Forecasting with Word Embeddings Extracted from News: A Preliminary Analysis

Luca Barbaglia, Sergio Consoli$^{(\boxtimes)}$, and Susan Wang

European Commission, Joint Research Centre (JRC), Ispra, Italy
{luca.barbaglia,sergio.consoli,susan.wang}@ec.europa.eu

Abstract. News represents a rich source of information about financial agents actions and expectations. We rely on word embedding methods to summarize the daily content of news. We assess the added value of the word embeddings extracted from US news, as a case study, by using different language approaches while forecasting the US S&P500 index by means of DeepAR, an advanced neural forecasting method based on autoregressive Recurrent Neural Networks operating in a probabilistic setting. Although this is currently on-going work, the obtained preliminary results look promising, suggesting an overall validity of the employed methodology.

Keywords: DeepAR · Deep learning · Economic and financial forecasting · Neural forecasting · News analysis · Text analysis · Word embeddings

1 Introduction

Measuring the informational content of text in economic and financial news is useful for market participants to adjust their perception and expectations on the dynamics of financial markets. In this context, the incorporation in forecasting models of economic and financial information coming from news media has already demonstrated great potentials [1–3,5]. Our endeavour is to study the predictive power of news for forecasting financial variables by leveraging on the recent advances in word embeddings [9,21] and deep learning [17,24] models. On the one hand, a large stand of the literature has explored the added value of word embedding technologies for forecasting applications. Shapiro et al. [25], for example, use GloVe [22] and BERT [9] word embeddings to measure economic sentiment, while Xing et al. [27] provide a review of recent works on natural language-based financial forecasting. On the other hand, recent literature has been employing neural networks for volatility forecasting [6,18], where the volatility is a statistical measure of the dispersion of a financial asset's returns. For example, Ramos-Pérez et al. [23] use a stacked artificial neural network to forecast volatility.

In this contribution, in particular, we show our preliminary work focusing on the prediction of the realized variance of the S&P500 index, although the

© The Author(s) 2021
M. Kamp et al. (Eds.): ECML PKDD 2021 Workshops, CCIS 1525, pp. 179–188, 2021.
https://doi.org/10.1007/978-3-030-93733-1_12

adopted methodology can be generalized to other markets and variables. To this end, we rely on word embeddings to summarize the daily content of the news contained in a data set of more than 4 million articles published in US newspapers over the period from 1st of January 2000 until 31st of December 2020. The aim is to evaluate if the combination of a richer information set including the content of economic and financial news with state-of-the-art machine learning can help in such a challenging prediction task. We assess the added value of the extracted word embeddings using different language approaches while forecasting the volatility of the S&P500 index by means of DeepAR [24], an advanced neural forecasting method based on auto-regressive Recurrent Neural Networks (RNNs) operating in a probabilistic setting. The DeepAR model is trained by adopting a rolling-window approach and employed to produce point and density forecasts by using as inputs the past time series values along with the word embeddings as additional regressors. Since our forecasting method calculates the probability attached to each forecast, the output can help investors in their decision making according to their individual risk tolerance. Our preliminary results look promising, suggesting an overall validity of the employed approach.

2 Preliminary Notions

2.1 Word Representation

For deep learning models, the text input needs to be converted to the numerical format. The simplest form is one-hot encoding [28], where each word is represented by a binary vector of size N, the size of the vocabulary, and all values are zero except for the index representing the word, marked as 1. Word embeddings improve upon one-hot-encoding by creating a lower-dimensional representation of the words such that words with similar meaning will be grouped in the vector space [16]. This is based on the idea of "distributional semantics", where a word's meaning is given by the words that frequently appear close by.

Word2Vec [21] and GloVe [22] are two popular algorithms for word embeddings. Word2Vec leverages the concept of a local context window where a target is surrounded by context words. It introduces the Continuous Bag-Of-Words (CBOW) algorithm [8] to predict the current word based on the surrounding context words, and the Skip-gram algorithm to predict surrounding words given the current word [16,21]. GloVe (Global vectors for word representation) combines the concept of global matrix factorization and the local context window methods. Using the intuition that word meaning can be derived from its word co-occurrence probabilities, the model is trained to learn the weights of the word vectors by predicting global word co-occurrence counts [22].

These types of word embeddings are typically trained using a large corpus of data, and their weights are saved for future use in separate tasks. Both embedding types have 300 dimensions, and are context-free, that is, there is a one-to-one mapping between a word and its embedding representation, such that, for instance, the word "bank" has a single embedding representation in the sentence

"I am going to a bank" and "She sits by the river bank". The embeddings for each word are, therefore, static.

2.2 Contextual Word Embeddings

Contextual word embeddings, on the other hand, take the context of each word into account when encoding words in a sentence structure. BERT, Roberta and XLM are popular contextual embedding methods based on the *transformer* architecture [4,9], which is a recent breakthrough in the field of Natural Language Processing (NLP). The transformer was originally introduced as a means of improving neural machine translations [7,29]. Neural machine translation methods typically consist of an encoder-decoder structure to encode a sentence into a fixed-length vector, from which a decoder generates a translation. The encoder-decoder is jointly trained to maximise the probability of a correct translation given a source sentence. Previously this was done in a sequential fashion, using sequence models, such as RNN, LSTM and GRU. The transformer instead uses a layered approach and the "attention" mechanism, to tell the model which part of the sentence to focus on while encoding the word vector. Unlike sequential models, attention can be applied to words in the sentence irrespective of the distance from the position of the word being examined, it also bypasses the need to process the sentence in a sequential manner. As such, the transformer allows sequential data such as texts in sentences to be analyzed in parallel, which not only speeds up the training process but also enables more flexibility as well as improved performance.

BERT (Bidirectional Encoder Representation from Transformer) [9] uses a multi-layer bidirectional transformer encoder architecture, and utilizes a pre-training and fine-tuning approach. Unlike Word2Vec and GloVe embeddings which are extracted and applied to separate downstream models, the most common usage of BERT model is to re-use the entire architecture in the downstream task by adding task-specific output layers and fine-tune the model with task-specific output end-to-end. BERT was the first architecture that achieved deep bi-directionality, by utilizing "Masked Language Model" (MLM) pre-training. A language model pre-training is a technique in NLP where the model is trained to predict the next word in a sentence, with the advantage being that such training does not require labelled data. In a multi-layer environment like the transformer, if a language model is trained from both left-to-right and from right-to-left, the word will inevitably "see itself" in other layers. BERT overcame this by randomly masking 15% of the input text, and train the language model to predict the masked word rather than the next word in the sentence.

DistilRoBERTa and XLM are transformer-based models that support both the fine-tuning and feature-based approaches [4]. As discussed earlier, the fine-tuning approach involves re-using the entire architecture for downstream tasks. For the feature-based approach, weights from one or more layers represent the contextual embeddings, and are extracted from the pre-trained transformer without fine-tuning any parameters. These are used as input to a subsequent deep neural network such as LSTM. Devlin et al. [9] show that the best result for the feature-based approach is obtained by concatenating the top 4 hidden layers of BERT, achieving a result that is only slightly behind the fine-tuning approach.

2.3   Neural Forecasting

Classic techniques in economy and finance do not scale well when data are high-dimensional, noisy, and highly volatile [20]. In this complicated setting, it is not possible to rely upon standard low-dimensional strategies such as hypothesis testing for each individual variable (*t*-tests) or choosing among a small set of candidate models (*F*-test) [20]. In these cases, we are asked to provide "good" answers even if input data are extremely complex, working out of the box to recognize patterns among data and, possibly, to improve the quality of our forecasts. Following this direction, we rely on the DeepAR model [24], a neural forecasting method leveraging on previous work on deep learning and time series data [14,17].

DeepAR's approach is data-driven, that is, it learns a global forecasting model from historical data of all time series under consideration in the data set. The model tailors an RNN architecture into a probabilistic setting, in which predictions are not restricted to point forecasts only, but also density forecasts are produced accordingly to a user-defined distribution (e.g., negative binomial, student *t*, gaussian, etc.). In our case, we choose a student *t*-distribution in order to account for the fat-tail characteristic of the target. The outcome is more robust with respect to point forecasts alone, and uncertainty in the downstream decision-making flow is reduced by minimizing expectations of the loss function (negative log-likelihood) under the forecasting distribution. Probabilistic forecasting methods have been shown to be of crucial importance in various applications, as they -in contrast to point forecasts- enable optimal decision making under uncertainty by minimizing risk functions, that is, expectations of some loss function under the forecast distribution.

Similarly to classic RNNs, DeepAR is able to produce a mapping from input to output considering the time dimension. This mapping, however, is no longer fixed [12]. In addition to providing more accurate forecasts, DeepAR has also other advantages [24]: (i) the model infers the seasonal behavior and time series dependencies, thus reducing the tasks of manual feature engineering; (ii) the probabilistic forecasts are produced in the form of Monte Carlo samples, which are then employed to obtain consistent quantile estimates; (iii) Errors are not assumed to be Gaussian. Besides, the user chooses from a wide range of likelihood functions to better fit the properties of the data in the analysis.

3   Data

The financial time series that we aim to forecast is the annualized daily realized variance of the S&P 500 index sub-sampled from 5 min intra-day observations obtained from the Oxford-Man Institute's realized library[1] [11]. Following [26], we forecast the logarithmic transformation of the realized variance as it enjoys better statistical properties, while ensuring, by construction, the non-negativity of the volatility forecast. Missing data related to weekends are dropped from the target time series, giving a final number of 5,264 data points ranging from January, 3, 2000 until December, 31, 2020.

The source of economic news is obtained from a commercial provider[2]. In our study, we consider a long time period and analyse the entire text contained in the news articles. The data set consists of more than 4 million articles, full-text, for the time period of interest for the following US outlets: The New York Times, The Wall Street Journal, The Washington Post, The Dallas Morning News, The San Francisco Chronicle, and the Chicago Sun-Times.

These newspapers are selected so as to achieve a good national as well as regional coverage. We extract sentences referring to specific economic and financial aspects, by using a keyword-based information extraction procedure with search keywords broadly related to the US economy, monetary and fiscal policies[3]. In order to filter out only sentences referring to US, we also use a location detection heuristic [3] assigning the location to which a sentence is referring as its most frequent named-entity location detected in the news text, and then selecting only sentences with specifically assigned location labels related to US. With this procedure, we obtain a total of over 424,578 sentences. Notice that the bank holidays might occur any day of the week, therefore the retraining step does not necessarily happen on the same day (e.g., every Friday).

4 Experiments Setup

In the first step of our experiment, we compute the word embeddings on the news data set presented in Sect. 3 relying on various embedding techniques. In particular, create a sentence embeddings by averaging individual word embeddings. We use the pre-trained Word2Vec model ("word2vec-google-news-300") from the Python Gensim library[4], where each word is represented by a 300 dimensional vector. The pre-processing steps include tokenisation, lower-casing, punctuation removal, stop-word removal, lemmatisation as well as the removal of out-of-vocabulary words. Then, we retrieve individual word embeddings for each word,

---

[1] The Oxford-Man Institute's realized library is available at https://realized.oxford-man.ox.ac.uk/. The variable in the analysis corresponds to rv5_ss: we refer to the official website for further details on the construction of realized variances, which we employ as volatility measures.

[2] Dow Jones Data, News and Analytics (DNA) platform: https://www.dowjones.com/dna/.

[3] The keywords cover various aspects of the economic activity and policy. For instance, the list includes around 300 terms, such as *inflation, consumer prices, bankruptcy, financial volatility, housing market, competitiveness, debt, employment, etc.*. The complete keyword list can be obtained upon request from the authors.

[4] https://radimrehurek.com/gensim/.

and create sentence embeddings by taking the mean of all the word embeddings in the sentence. Similar pre-processing is applied to get the pre-trained GloVe embeddings from Gensim library. For transformer-based contextual embeddings, we use the sentence transformer library in Python[5]. All the models use mean pooling over word embeddings to obtain fixed 768 dimensional sentence embedding vectors. We consider versions of these models with and without punctuation from the text, and also considering Principal Component Analysis (PCA) over the word embeddings as a feature reduction attempt [15][6].

In the second step of our experiment, we use the daily average of different word embeddings as explanatory features in the DeepAR model to forecast the S&P500 log-realized variance. For our implementation, we make use of the open-source GluonTS library[7], and experimentally adopt an architecture with 2 RNN layers having 40 LSTM cells, 500 training epochs, and a learning rate equal to 0.001[8]. We adopt a rolling window estimation technique for training and validation, with a window length equal to half of the full sample. For each window, we calculate one step-ahead forecasts. We also set a re-training step for the model equal to 5 days, meaning that every 5 consecutive data points the DeepAR model was completely retrained.

5   Preliminary Results

In this section, we show our early empirical findings on the application of DeepAR to the forecasting of the S&P 500 log-realized variance, augmented with the word embedding representation of the US news coming from the different language models presented in Sect. 2. Note that forecasting the log-realized variance of the S&P index is an extremely challenging task, as the series presents large volatility clusters. The goal is to assess whether relevant news content has some predictive power and might help in this difficult job.

Results on the comparison of the considered language models for our forecasting task using DeepAR are shown in Tables 1 and 2 for the point and density forecasts, respectively. For the evaluation, we use common time series prediction metrics, namely: mean square error (MSE), symmetric mean absolute percentage error (sMAPE), mean scaled interval score (MSIS) [19], and mean absolute scaled error (MASE). We always report the model performance relative to the one from the forecasting model without embeddings as additional regressors. Values smaller than unity indicate a better performance relative to the benchmark. On the other hand, values larger than one imply that the baseline model without word embeddings is performing better.

---

[5] https://pypi.org/project/sentence-transformers/.
[6] We consider the first three principal components. Future work shall address the robustness of the results of this choice.
[7] GluonTS, available at: https://ts.gluon.ai/.
[8] Future work shall address the choice of the parameters thoroughly, for instance, relying on time-series cross-validation techniques [13].

Table 1. Mean performance relative to the corresponding forecasting model with no embeddings as additional regressors: values smaller than unity (in bold) indicate a better performance relative to the benchmark.

Horizon	Embeddings	MSE	sMAPE	MSIS	MASE
$h = 1$	*bert_no_punctuation*	**0.990**	**0.978**	1.007	**0.992**
	bert_punctuation	**0.983**	**0.983**	**0.992**	**0.989**
	bert_punctuation_PCA	**0.982**	**0.999**	1.087	**0.992**
	distilroberta_no_punctuation	**0.991**	**0.992**	1.032	**0.999**
	distilroberta_punctuation	**0.993**	**0.989**	1.027	**0.997**
	glove_no_punctuation	1.005	**0.998**	1.025	**0.995**
	xlm_punctuation	1.077	1.023	1.082	1.030

Table 1 reports the forecasting performance across all windows for the point forecasts. From the table, we denote that there is not yet a clear superiority of a word embedding approach with respect to the others. They perform comparably well, providing an added value relative to the corresponding forecasting model without embeddings. There is an exception with *xlm_punctuation*, which attains worse performances relative to the corresponding forecasting model without embeddings regardless of the metric; probably XLM training parameters should be better fine-tuned in future experiments. We can also note that there is not a clear distinction between the word embedding models with and without punctuation, although a slight superiority is obtained when punctuation is considered[9].

From this early experiment, we also see that the feature reduction attempt in BERT using PCA does not provide benefits. We plan to try alternative approaches, like, e.g., employing hierarchical clustering and selecting only embedding features closer to cluster centroids. We believe that feature reduction can provide performance improvements, even though at the moment we are not getting any clear experimental proof. We test the significance of the forecast gains relying on the conditional predictive ability test by Giacomini and White [10], which finds that only the *bert_punctuation* performs significantly better than the benchmark when considering the sMAPE metric at the 90% confidence level.

Table 2 reports the quantile losses at the 0.1, 0.5 and 0.9 quantiles. The best performance for the highest quantiles is obtained by the BERT models with and without punctuation and by XLM, while the rest of the models produce a worse performance with respect to the model without embeddings. This result is something we can expect, given that obtaining results for rare events provided by high quantiles is quite hard and unpredictable. However, BERT models are able to obtain acceptable performance also in these cases, confirming a good generalization capability of the underlying model. As it regards the median forecast,

---

[9] For some models in the table we report indeed only results with punctuation, given their results without punctuation are the same.

186   L. Barbaglia et al.

Table 2. Quantile losses for $\tau = 0.1, 0.5$ and 0.9 quantiles, relative to the corresponding forecasting model with no embeddings as additional regressors: values smaller than unity (in bold) indicate a better performance than the benchmark.

Horizon	Embeddings	$\tau = 0.1$	$\tau = 0.5$	$\tau = 0.9$
$h = 1$	*bert_no_punctuation*	1.023	**0.992**	**0.988**
	bert_punctuation	1.029	**0.989**	**0.966**
	bert_punctuation_PCA	1.064	**0.993**	1.032
	distilroberta_no_punctuation	1.029	**0.999**	1.012
	distilroberta_punctuation	1.022	**0.997**	1.011
	glove_no_punctuation	**0.990**	**0.995**	1.031
	xlm_punctuation	1.067	**0.991**	**0.978**

all models perform better than the benchmark, while only GloVe attains a forecast gain for the lowest quantile. The Giacomini and White [10] test indicates that only *bert_punctuation* attains a significantly better performance than the benchmark when considering a 95% confidence level. The poor performance in the 0.1 quantile might be explained by the logarithmic transformation of the target variable: in future research, we plan to experiment further on this issue.

Word embeddings extracted from economic news generally provide improvements when the DeepAR model is combined with them. This suggests that the content extracted from news contain some predictive power for the target to forecast. When these features are added to the corresponding DeepAR model, the results improve in terms of the considered metrics.

6   Conclusion and Overlook

Word embeddings extracted from news appear to have predictive power for the forecasting exercise of the S&P 500 log-realized variance. DeepAR manages to achieve good prediction results, performing better when the news embeddings are included in the model. We believe that the combination of these cutting-edge technologies has a high potential for economic and financial forecasting applications. The obtained results, although preliminary, look encouraging.

In the future steps of this project, we plan to attempt increasing the forecasting performance of our approach by fine-tuning the pre-trained language models directly with the considered target. In addition, we plan to use other cutting-edge forecasting methods from machine learning in order to have a comparison with respect to the results obtained by the DeepAR model. Future computational experiments will include statistical testing of the significance of the forecast gains. Furthermore, we might also consider novel sentence embedding methods, where a sentence transformer is included and adds a pooling operation to the output of the transformers of the contextual word embedding methods (BERT, RoBERTa or XLM) to derive fixed-size sentence embeddings. The weights of the transformers are shared, so the resulting sentence embeddings are semantically meaningful and can be compared using cosine similarity. Finally, further work might explore the forecasting performance of the proposed methodology when considering the various underlying assets that are included in the S&P500.

References

1. Apergis, N., Lau, M.C.K., Yarovaya, L.: Media sentiment and CDS spread spillovers: evidence from the GIIPS countries. Int. Rev. Financ. Anal. **47**(C), 50–59 (2016)
2. Barbaglia, L., Consoli, S., Manzan, S.: Exploring the predictive power of news and neural machine learning models for economic forecasting. In: Bitetta, V., Bordino, I., Ferretti, A., Gullo, F., Ponti, G., Severini, L. (eds.) MIDAS 2020. LNCS (LNAI), vol. 12591, pp. 135–149. Springer, Cham (2021). https://doi.org/10.1007/978-3-030-66981-2_11
3. Barbaglia, L., Consoli, S., Manzan, S.: Forecasting with economic news. SSRN Working paper 3698121 (2021)
4. Barua, A., Thara, S., Premjith, B., Soman, K.P.: Analysis of contextual and non-contextual word embedding models for Hindi NER with web application for data collection. In: Garg, D., Wong, K., Sarangapani, J., Gupta, S.K. (eds.) IACC 2020. CCIS, vol. 1367, pp. 183–202. Springer, Singapore (2021). https://doi.org/10.1007/978-981-16-0401-0_14
5. Beetsma, R., Giuliodori, M., de Jong, F., Widijanto, D.: Spread the news: the impact of news on the European sovereign bond markets during the crisis. J. Int. Money Financ. **34**, 83–101 (2013)
6. Bucci, A.: Realized volatility forecasting with neural networks. J. Financ. Economet. **18**(3), 502–531 (2020)
7. Clinchant, S., Jung, K.W., Nikoulina, V.: On the use of BERT for neural machine translation. In: Proceedings of the 3rd Workshop on Neural Generation and Translation, pp. 108–117. Association for Computational Linguistics (2019)
8. Csurka, G., Dance, C.R., Willamowski, L.J., Bray, C.: Visual categorization with bags of keypoints. In: Workshop on Statistical Learning in Computer Vision, ECCV, pp. 1–22 (2004)
9. Devlin, J., Chang, M., Lee, K., Toutanova, K.: BERT: pre-training of deep bidirectional transformers for language understanding. In: Proceedings of NAACL-HLT 2019 - The 17th Annual Conference of the North American Chapter of the Association for Computational Linguistics: Human Language Technologies, vol. 1, pp. 4171–4186 (2019)
10. Giacomini, R., White, H.: Tests of conditional predictive ability. Econometrica **74**(6), 1545–1578 (2006)
11. Heber, G., Lunde, A., Shephard, N., Sheppard, K.: Oxford-man institute's realized library. Oxford-Man Institute, University of Oxford, UK (2009). https://realized.oxford-man.ox.ac.uk/
12. Hochreiter, S., Schmidhuber, J.: Long short-term memory. Neural Comput. **9**, 1735–1780 (1997)
13. Hyndman, R.J., Athanasopoulos, G.: Forecasting: Principles and Practice, 3rd edn. OTexts, Melbourne (2021)
14. Januschowski, T., et al.: Criteria for classifying forecasting methods. Int. J. Forecast. **36**(1), 167–177 (2020)
15. Jollife, I.T., Cadima, J.: Principal component analysis: a review and recent developments. Philos. Trans. Roy. Soc. A Math. Phys. Eng. Sci. **374**(2065) (2016)

16. Kusner, M., Sun, Y., Kolkin, N., Weinberger, K.: From word embeddings to document distances. In: 32nd International Conference on Machine Learning, ICML 2015, vol. 2, pp. 957–966 (2015)
17. Lecun, Y., Bengio, Y., Hinton, G.: Deep learning. Nature **521**(7553), 436–444 (2015)
18. Liu, Y.: Novel volatility forecasting using deep learning-long short term memory recurrent neural networks. Expert Syst. Appl. **132**, 99–109 (2019)
19. Makridakis, S., Spiliotis, E., Assimakopoulos, V.: Predicting/hypothesizing the findings of the M4 competition. Int. J. Forecast. **36**(1), 29–36 (2020)
20. Marwala, T.: Economic Modeling Using Artificial Intelligence Methods. Springer, London (2013). https://doi.org/10.1007/978-1-4471-5010-7
21. Mikolov, T., Chen, K., Corrado, G., Dean, J.: Efficient estimation of word representations in vector space. In: 1st International Conference on Learning Representations, ICLR 2013 (2013)
22. Pennington, J., Socher, R., Manning, C.: GloVe: global vectors for word representation. In: Proceedings of EMNLP 2014 - Conference on Empirical Methods in Natural Language Processing, pp. 1532–1543 (2014)
23. Ramos-Pérez, E., Alonso-González, P.J., Núñez-Velázquez, J.J.: Forecasting volatility with a stacked model based on a hybridized artificial neural network. Expert Syst. Appl. **129**, 1–9 (2019)
24. Salinas, D., Flunkert, V., Gasthaus, J., Januschowski, T.: DeepAR: probabilistic forecasting with autoregressive recurrent networks. Int. J. Forecast. **36**(3), 1181–1191 (2020)
25. Shapiro, A.H., Sudhof, M., Wilson, D.J.: Measuring news sentiment. J. Econ. (2020)
26. Wilms, I., Rombouts, J., Croux, C.: Multivariate volatility forecasts for stock market indices. Int. J. Forecast. **37**(2), 484–499 (2021)
27. Xing, F.Z., Cambria, E., Welsch, R.E.: Natural language based financial forecasting: a survey. Artif. Intell. Rev. **50**(1), 49–73 (2017). https://doi.org/10.1007/s10462-017-9588-9
28. Zhang, Y., Jin, R., Zhou, Z.-H.: Understanding bag-of-words model: a statistical framework. Int. J. Mach. Learn. Cybern. **1**(1–4), 43–52 (2010)
29. Zhu, J., et al.: Incorporating BERT into neural machine translation. In: International Conference on Learning Representations (ICLR) (2020)

On Neural Forecasting and News Emotions: The Case of the Spanish Stock Market

Sergio Consoli[1], Matteo Negri[2], Amirhossein Tebbifakhr[2], Elisa Tosetti[3(✉)], and Marco Turchi[2]

[1] European Commission, Joint Research Centre (JRC), Ispra, VA, Italy
`sergio.consoli@ec.europa.eu`
[2] Fondazione Bruno Kessler, Via Sommarive 18, Povo, Trento, Italy
`{negri,atebbifakhr,turchi}@fbk.eu`
[3] Department of Management, Università Ca' Foscari Venezia, Cannaregio 873, Fondamenta San Giobbe, 30121 Venezia, Italy
`elisa.tosetti@unive.it`

Abstract. We provide an overview on the preliminary development of a neural machine translation and deep learning approach to extract the emotional content of economic and financial news from Spanish journals. To this end, we exploit a dataset of over 14 million articles published in Spanish newspapers over the period from 1st of July 1996 until 31st of December 2019. We examine the role of these news-based emotions indicators in forecasting the Spanish IBEX-35 stock market index by using DeepAR [8], an advanced neural forecasting method based on auto-regressive Recurrent Neural Networks operating into a probabilistic setting. The DeepAR model is trained by adopting a rolling-window approach to best accounting for non-linearities in the data, and employed to produce point and density forecasts. After providing an overview of the methodology under current development, some preliminary findings are also given, showing an improvement in the IBEX-35 index fitting when the emotional variables are included in the model, and an overall validity of the employed approach.

Keywords: Economic and financial forecasting · Neural time series forecasting · Deep learning · Recurrent neural networks · Machine translation · Emotion classification · IBEX-35 index · News analysis

1 Introduction

In currently on-going research [3] we are studying the predictive power of news emotions for forecasting economic and financial variables by leveraging on the recent advances on deep learning [7]. News are a promising forecasting tool since they describe current events and trends, and represent the updated expectations of market participants about the future, thus significantly influencing investors' perception and decisions. In this work we focus in particular on the Spanish newspapers and the IBEX-35 stock market index, although the adopted methodology

© Springer Nature Switzerland AG 2021
M. Kamp et al. (Eds.): ECML PKDD 2021 Workshops, CCIS 1525, pp. 189–194, 2021.
https://doi.org/10.1007/978-3-030-93733-1_13

is generalizable to other languages and markets. We first adopt a neural machine translation (NMT) and deep learning approach [9] to extract the emotional content of economic and financial news from the Spanish journals, according to the Ekman's six basic emotions [5]: *fear, anger, joy, sadness, disgust, surprise.*

We then examine the role of these news-based emotion indicators in forecasting the IBEX-35 index, aiming at predicting specifically its daily movements by using as inputs the past time series values along with the daily emotion indicators. The forecasting methodology employed for this task is *DeepAR* [8], an advanced neural forecasting method based on auto-regressive Recurrent Neural Networks (RNNs) operating in a probabilistic setting. This approach produces accurate probabilistic forecasts, based on training an auto-regressive Recurrent Neural Network (RNN) model with feedback connections on a given number of related time series, which in our case are the emotion signals. The aim is to disentangle the improvement in the forecasting power due to the inclusion of the emotions indicators extracted from news within the DeepAR approach. Since our forecasting method calculates the probability attached to each forecast, the output can help investors in their decision making according to their individual risk tolerance.

2   Data

We obtain the historical data of the IBEX-35 index from Yahoo Finance.[1] This is a free-float, capitalization-weighted stock market index that tracks the performance of the 35 most liquid stocks traded on the continuous market on the Bolsa de Madrid. For our study, we consider the close price of the index, that is the price of the stock at the closing time of the market on a given day. Being the IBEX-35 a highly persistent and non-stationary index, we use a log-difference transformation to obtain a stationary series of daily changes representing our prediction target. Missing data related to weekends are dropped from the target time series, giving a final number of 5,950 data points ranging from July, 1, 1996 until December, 31, 2019.

News data is obtained from a commercial provider.[2] The dataset consists of around 14 million articles, full-text, for the time period of interest. Spanish newspapers are selected so as to achieve a good national as well as regional coverage. We extract sentences referring to specific economic and financial aspects, by using a keyword-based information extraction procedure with search keywords broadly related to the Spanish economy, monetary and fiscal policies.[3] In order to filter out only sentences referring to Spain, we also use a location detection heuristic [1] assigning the location to which a sentence is referring as its most frequent named-entity location detected in the news text, and then selecting only sentences with specific assigned location labels related to Spain. With this procedure we obtain a total of over 4.2 million sentences.

---

[1] https://finance.yahoo.com/quote/%5EIBEX.

[2] Dow Jones Data, News and Analytics Platform: https://www.dowjones.com/dna/.

[3] The complete list consists of hundreds of keywords and can be obtained upon request from the authors.

3   Methodology

3.1   Neural Machine Translation

We first train a generic Spanish to English NMT system, built using the freely available parallel data (around 84M parallel sentences) present in the OPUS website,[4] tokenized and encoded using 32K byte-pair codes. To develop the NMT system, we use the Transformer architecture by Vaswani et al. [10] with the original parameter settings. We perform the training step until convergence. For training the NMT system, we use the OpenNMT-tf toolkit.[5] We also embed a pre-trained Spanish BERT model[6] inside the NMT system [11] to give a better representation of the source Spanish text during translation. We then adapt the generic Spanish-English NMT model to the economic domain by fine-tuning it on parallel sentences derived by the news, using two approaches:

1. *Back-translating the English in-domain data.* We automatically translate the English economic sentences back into Spanish. Doing so, we generate translation pairs in which the Spanish source side is the output of the NMT system and the English target side contains human-quality sentences. The Spanish-English sentence pairs are then used to adapt the NMT system.
2. *Selecting in-domain translation pairs from the training data.* We train a language model using the English economic sentences and use it to rank the English side of the 84M parallel sentences from OPUS. A higher rank means, for a given sentence, a higher similarity to the economic sentences. To have a fair comparison, from the top of this parallel ranked list, we select an amount of data equal to the original economic sentences in terms of number of tokens on the English side. The Spanish-English selected sentence pairs are then used to adapt the NMT system.

The fine-tuning is performed continuing the training of the generic model using the economic parallel data created with the two methods, considering them both together and in isolation.

3.2   Emotion Classification

The English classifier is based on a BERT language model [4] adapted to our classification problem. We use in particular one fully-connected neural layer, which maps into the emotion classes. We train the classifier until convergence on a freely available database with English sentences annotated with emotion labels.[7]

---

[4] OPUS, the open parallel corpus. Available at: https://opus.nlpl.eu/.

[5] OpenNMT-tf (v2.0.1), available at: https://github.com/OpenNMT/OpenNMT-tf.

[6] BETO, available at: https://github.com/dccuchile/beto.

[7] The annotated English corpus was taken from the *unified emotion datasets*, available at: https://github.com/sarnthil/unify-emotion-datasets. It is a large English collection of different emotion datasets [2], mapped to a unified set of emotion classes from which we selected the Ekman [5]'s six basic emotions considered in our study. Note that, after some pre-processing, each considered emotion category contained at least 2K samples.

This general model is then further fine-tuned for our emotion detection task by re-training it using a set of 5,100 Spanish economic sentences annotated with the Ekman's six basic emotions [5] by 8 different annotators and translated into English using the European Commission *eTranslation* service.[8] For the annotation task we use the commercial Amazon AWS SageMaker service.[9] In order to realize a unique label for each sample, the following steps are followed: (i) For each sample, we detect the label with the highest vote. In case of equal votes between classes, the priority is given to the least represented class in the dataset; (ii) We select a positive threshold equal to 3 and assign the corresponding label to all the samples with the identified vote higher than this threshold; (iii) The remaining samples are discarded. We then split the labelled data into training (60%), development (10%) and test (30%), obtaining an average F1 classification score on test of nearly 70%, which represents quite an acceptable classification performance for the English classifier. The final emotion annotation of the 4.2M Spanish sentences is then performed by using the NMT system for translating them into English, and then the English classifier to annotate the translated sentences with the considered emotions. The final distribution of emotion labels in the annotated Spanish sentences is: *surprise* = 25%, *joy* = 19%, *sadness* = 0.13%, *anger* = 10%, and *fear* = 9%.[10]

3.3 DeepAR

DeepAR [8] is a neural forecasting method leveraging on previous work on deep learning to time series data [6,7]. The approach is data-driven, that is, DeepAR learns a global forecasting model from historical data of all time series under consideration in the dataset. The model tailors an RNN architecture into a probabilistic setting, in which predictions are not restricted to point forecasts only, but density forecasts are produced accordingly to a user-defined distribution (e.g. negative binomial, student t, gaussian, etc.). In our case, we choose a student t-distribution in order to account for the fat-tail characteristic of the target. The outcome is more robust with respect to point forecasts alone, and uncertainty in the downstream decision making flow is reduced by minimizing expectations of the loss function (negative log-likelihood) under the forecasting distribution.

For our implementation we make use of the open-source GluonTS library[11], and experimentally adopt an architecture with 1 RNN layer having 20 LSTM cells, 500 training epochs, and a learning rate equal to 0.001. We adopt a rolling window estimation technique for training and validation, with a window length equal to half of the full sample, that is 2,975 data points. For each window, we calculate one step-ahead forecasts. We also set a re-training step for the model equal to 7 days, meaning that every 7 consecutive data points the DeepAR model was completely retrained.

---

[8] eTranslation service: https://ec.europa.eu/info/resources-partners/machine-translation-public-administrations-etranslation_en.

[9] Amazon AWS SageMaker, available at: https://aws.amazon.com/sagemaker/.

[10] The remaining 24% of samples are classified as "no emotion" and thus removed.

[11] GluonTS, available at: https://ts.gluon.ai/.

4   Preliminary Findings

We show here our early computational experience on the application of this
methodology to the forecasting of the IBEX-35 daily changes [3]. We consider
an autoregressive-only DeepAR, that is without any covariates included in the
model (*DeepAR-NoCov*), and a DeepAR model including the news emotions
as covariates (*DeepAR-Emotions*). DeepAR is also benchmarked against two
other traditional methods, namely a simple moving average (*Seasonal-MA*) and
a naïve method for random forecasts (*Naïve*). With the moving average method,
the forecasts of all future values are equal to the average (or "mean") of the
historical data. For the naïve forecasts, instead, we simply set all forecasts to be
the value of the last observation for our target. Since naïve forecasts are optimal
when data observations follow a random walk, these are also called random walk
forecasts. The naïve method works well for many economic and financial time
series, as is the case with our IBEX-35 fluctuations data.

Results on the comparison of these methods are shown in Table 1, along with
the loss function values obtained by the methods at different quantiles.[12] For the
evaluation, we use common time series prediction metrics, namely: root mean
square error (RMSE), symmetric mean absolute percentage error (MAPE), and
mean (weighted) quantile loss (mQL), that is the average quantile negative log-
likelihood loss weighted with the density. As the table shows, there is a clear superiority of the DeepAR algorithm with respect to the two other approaches. These
improvements get consistently higher when the DeepAR model is combined with
the news emotions. This suggests that the emotional content extracted from
Spanish news contain a predictive power for our target forecasting. When these
features are added to the *DeepAR-NoCov*, producing the *DeepAR-Emotions*
model, the results clearly improve in terms of all the metrics. These results
look also consistent when we evaluate the models on the different quantiles.
The best performance is obtained again by *DeepAR-Emotions*, followed by the
DeepAR-NoCov model. We also note that the models show higher performance
at high (0.9) and low (0.1) quantiles, with higher weighted quantile losses in
general performing better than the lower quantiles.

Table 1. Results on the comparison of the forecasting algorithms.

metrics	RMSE	MAPE	mQL	$QL_{0.1}$	$QL_{0.3}$	$QL_{0.5}$	$QL_{0.7}$	$QL_{0.9}$
Seasonal-MA	1.206	1.525	1.084	1.069	1.221	1.231	1.204	1.049
Naïve	1.287	1.471	1.179	1.046	1.313	1.424	1.209	0.949
DeepAR-NoCov	1.045	1.450	0.982	0.975	1.159	1.185	1.108	0.868
DeepAR-Emotions	**0.956**	**1.415**	**0.652**	**0.597**	**0.987**	**1.072**	**0.930**	**0.516**

---

[12] The experiments were computed on an Intel(R) Xeon(R) E7 64-bit server having
40 cores at 2.10 GHz and overall 1 TB of shared RAM. The DeepAR model training
required to run for few computational hours in parallel on the available CPU cores.

5   Conclusions

Overall, although preliminary, the obtained results look promising. Emotions extracted from news appear to be relevant for the forecasting exercise of the IBEX-35 fluctuations. DeepAR manages to achieve good trading results, producing better results when the news-based emotions variables are included into the model. We believe that the combination of the cutting-edge technologies used in our approach has high potential for the implementation of effective solutions for the prediction of other economic and financial variables.

References

1. Barbaglia, L., Consoli, S., Manzan, S.: Forecasting with economic news. SSRN Working paper (2020)
2. Bostan, L.-A.-M., Klinger, R.: An analysis of annotated corpora for emotion classification in text. In: Proceedings of the 27th International Conference on Computational Linguistics, pp. 2104–2119 (2018)
3. Consoli, S., Negri, M., Tebbifakhr, A., Tosetti, E., Turchi, M.: Forecasting the IBEX-35 stock index using deep learning and news emotions. In: Proceedings of LOD 2021: The 7th International Conference on Machine Learning, Optimization & Data Science (2021, submitted)
4. Devlin, J., Chang, M.-W., Lee, K., Toutanova, K.: BERT: pre-training of deep bidirectional transformers for language understanding. In: ACL-HLT 2019 Conference Proceedings, vol. 1, pp. 4171–4186 (2019)
5. Ekman, P., Cordaro, D.: What is meant by calling emotions basic. Emot. Rev. **3**(4), 364–370 (2011)
6. Januschowski, T., et al.: Criteria for classifying forecasting methods. Int. J. Forecast. **36**(1), 167–177 (2020)
7. Lecun, Y., Bengio, Y., Hinton, G.: Deep learning. Nature **521**(7553), 436–444 (2015)
8. Salinas, D., Flunkert, V., Gasthaus, J., Januschowski, T.: DeepAR: probabilistic forecasting with autoregressive recurrent networks. Int. J. Forecast. **36**(3), 1181–1191 (2020)
9. Tebbifakhr, A., Bentivogli, L., Negri, M., Turchi, M.: Machine translation for machines: the sentiment classification use case. In: Proceedings of EMNLP-IJCNLP 2019, pp. 1368–1374. ACL (2019)
10. Vaswani, A., et al.: Attention is all you need. In: Advances in Neural Information Processing Systems, pp. 5999–6009 (2017)
11. Zhu, J., et al.: Incorporating BERT into neural machine translation. In: International Conference on Learning Representations (ICLR) (2020)

Adaptive Supervised Learning for Financial Markets Volatility Targeting Models

Eric Benhamou[1,2](✉), David Saltiel[2], Serge Tabachnik[3,4], Corentin Bourdeix[3], François Chareyron[3], and Beatrice Guez[2]

[1] Dauphine University, Paris, France
eric.benhamou@dauphine.eu
[2] Ai for Alpha, Neuilly-sur-Seine, France
[3] Lombard Odier Investment Managers, Geneva, Switzerland
[4] Panthéon-Assas University, Paris, France

Abstract. In the context of risk-based portfolio construction and pro-active risk management, finding robust predictors of future realised volatility is paramount to achieving optimal performance. Volatility has been documented in economics literature to exhibit pronounced persistence with clusters of high or low volatility regimes and to mean-revert to a normal level, underpinning Nobel prize-winning work on Generalized Autoregressive Heteroskedastic (GARCH) models. From a Reinforcement Learning (RL) point of view, this process can be interpreted as a model-based RL approach where the goal of the models is twofold: first, to represent the volatility dynamics and forecast its term structure and second, to compute a resulting allocation to match a given target volatility: hence the name "volatility targeting method for risk-based portfolios". However, the resulting volatility model-based RL approaches are hard to distinguish as each model results in similar performance without a clear dominant one. We therefore present an innovative approach with an additional supervised learning step to predict the best model(s), based on historical performance ordering of RL models. Our contribution shows that adding a supervised learning overlay to decide which model(s) to use provides improvement over a naive benchmark consisting in averaging all RL models. A salient ingredient in this supervised learning task is to adaptively select features based on their significance, thanks to minimum importance filtering. This work extends our previous work on combining model-free and model-based RL. It mixes different types of learning procedures, namely model-based RL and supervised learning opening new doors to combine different machine learning approaches.

Keywords: Volatility targeting · Supervised learning · Best ordering · Model-based · Portfolio allocation · Walk forward · Features selection

© Springer Nature Switzerland AG 2021
M. Kamp et al. (Eds.): ECML PKDD 2021 Workshops, CCIS 1525, pp. 195–209, 2021.
https://doi.org/10.1007/978-3-030-93733-1_14

1 Introduction

Volatility targeting has become popular in the financial industry and academic literature, with the specific objective to design a portfolio, made up of cash and risky assets with a constant predetermined level of portfolio volatility over time. This risk budgeting methodology overcomes the difficulty of inferring future expected performance and covariance structure of the risky assets as required by the traditional mean-variance framework created by Markowitz in 1952 [24]. The strategy, which was first introduced by Qian in 2005 [27], allocates capital between risky and non-risky assets, thanks to volatility forecasts of the risky assets. If the volatility of the risky assets is expected to be high, the weight of the risky asset is reduced and vice versa as presented in [8,11,14,17]. In addition, [15] has shown that left tail risk is significantly reduced thanks to a targeted portfolio's exposure inversely proportional to the forecasted portfolio volatility.

This has motivated the search for a stream of models to forecast volatility based on multiple methodologies that attempt to harness the informational content of this inherently unobservable latent process. These volatility models range from a simple empirical approach leveraging moving averages to more sophisticated ones based on ARCH and GARCH forecasts [9,10], Heterogeneous Autoregressive model of Realized Volatility (HAR-RV), proposed by [13], multivariate high-frequency-based volatility (HEAVY) models [31] and prospective forward-looking measures such as implied volatility [21].

From a modern and machine learning perspective, most of these volatility predictors can be interpreted as model-based reinforcement learning models. They aim to specify the complex structure of volatility and to make specific predictions on which portfolio allocations are sized in inverse proportion to predicted volatility. In certain cases, their parameters are determined to maximize specific performance measures such as the Sharpe ratio of the corresponding strategy. Although initially not formulated as a model-based RL approach, volatility targeting follows its traditional ingredients. The process attempts to identify an evolution of a complex system. Optimal allocation is determined thanks to a cumulative reward. The supervised learning task considered in this paper fulfills specific criteria: the portfolio allocation across the different volatility models. However, because of the complexity and non-stationary behavior of volatility, the appropriate choice of the volatility targeting model remains an open question. Furthermore, the intrinsic high correlation between these volatility models, both in terms of predictors and corresponding performances, present an interesting challenge for classification and supervised learning tasks.

This is precisely the goal of this work. We aim to determine the best allocation for volatility targeting models in order to achieve the maximum *ex post* Sharpe ratio.

1.1 Related Works

Our work can be related to an ever growing body of machine learning literature applied to financial markets. Indeed, with ever increasing competition and data processing speed in the financial markets, robust forecasting methods have become a vital subject for asset managers. The premise of machine learning algorithms - to offer a way to find and model non-linear behaviour in financial time series - has attracted ample attention and efforts that can be traced back to the late 2000's when machine learning research started to pick up in the financial industry. Rather than listing a large related body of work, we will refer to various publications that have reviewed the existing literature in chronological order.

In 2009, [3] surveyed more than 100 related published articles using neural and neuro-fuzzy techniques derived and applied to forecasting stock markets, or discussing classifications of financial market data and forecasting methods. In 2010, [20] conducted a survey on the application of artificial neural networks in forecasting financial market prices, including exchange rates, stock prices, and financial crisis prediction as well as option pricing. In addition, the stream of machine learning publications was not only based on neural network but also on generic and evolutionary algorithms as reviewed in [1].

More recently, [32] reviewed the application of cutting-edge NLP techniques for financial forecasting, using text from financial news or Twitters. [28] covered the wider topic of using machine learning techniques, including deep learning, to financial portfolio allocation and optimization systems. [26] focused on support vector machine and artificial neural networks to forecast prices and regimes based on fundamental and technical analysis. Later, [30] discussed the challenges and research opportunities of machine learning techniques as applied to finance, including issues for algorithmic trading, backtesting and live testing on single stocks and more general predictions of financial markets. Finally in [22], the authors compare machine learning to conventional quantitative research methodologies in finance and discuss the idiosyncrasies of finance and the challenges that financial markets pose to machine learning methodologies. They also examine the opportunities (and applications) that machine learning offers for financial research.

While there are existing studies related to machine learning applied to portfolio optimization, including volatility targeting strategies (e.g. [18,25,33]), the specific problem of volatility model allocation using machine learning in the volatility targeting context is fairly novel. This stems from the two approaches being traditionally very different in spirit: volatility targeting assumes rules while machine learning prides itself on having no a priori or preconceived rules.

Reformulating volatility targeting methods as a model-based RL approach as in [5] opens new doors. In this work, [5] show that using a model free Deep Reinforcement Learning (DRL) approach can help to decide which volatility model(s) to choose. This is underpinned by the fact that DRL appears to be a promising tool to tackle regime changes [4,6] or [7].

However, DRL faces at least two issues. First, DRL can be problematic in financial markets as only one scenario, namely the historical one, can be replayed

198   E. Benhamou et al.

as opposed to games where a simulator can generate many multiples of experiences (such as chess or the game of Go). Second, DRL does not work well when using many features and is still hard to interpret as opposed to a supervised learning method based on decision tree algorithms that can rank and classify specific real features thereby rendering them more tangible and interpretable. In our past specific volatility targeting allocation exercise, choosing the right model(s) in the context of a DRL approach has proven to be a serious challenge [5].

In this study, we are interested in testing a new supervised method that leverages macro data as well as model performance data to select the best volatility targeting model(s). In addition, this new methodology enables a certain understanding of the role of the selected features and the detection of regime shifts thanks to the selected features' changes.

1.2 Contributions

Our contribution is precisely motivated by the shortcomings presented in the aforementioned remarks. We therefore add a supervised learning overlay to decide which model(s) to use. The goal of this supervised learning task is to order all our models and choose the best model or weigh them according to their predicted relative performance. As many data sources are used, we add, in our supervised learning task, a feature filtering step to determine the critical features. The motivation is twofold. Firstly, using too many features tends to add noise to our signal as some features are either non-predictive or redundant with other features. Secondly, we would like to change the selected features when there are regime changes. We therefore add, in our supervised learning step, a filtering selection. We test the salience of this features selection as well as a hyperparameter selection process thanks to a walk-forward approach as described later in the paper.

2 Models Presentation

2.1 Volatility Targeting Models

In our study, we use nine different models to represent and forecast volatility. These models are identical to the ones presented in [5]. They begin with simple concepts such as moving averages, exponential moving averages (RM2006) or a two-step approach as presented in [23] to account for a short memory process. Then, they incorporate more sophisticated and statistically-justified models like the famed GARCH model, as in [12], the Glosten-Jagannathan-Runkle GARCH model as in [16], microstructure-based models like the HEAVY model (which relies on high-frequency data as in [31]), or the HAR model as in [13]. Last but not least, we add two additional prospective implicit models that are based on forward-looking variables such as the VIX. One of them uses Principal Component Analysis to decompose a set of implied volatility indices into the main eigenvectors. The resulting implied volatility proxies are then rescaled to match a realized volatility metric thereby voiding the famous volatility risk premium and Jensen's inequality-related bias. These nine models are quite diverse overall and work alternatively well in various market environments, making the choice of the best model or any type of ranking difficult to tackle.

As presented in [5], volatility targeting is achieved using the volatility forecasts given by the models. If we denote by σ_{target} the target volatility of the strategy and if the model i predicts a future's volatility $\sigma_{t-1}^{i,pred}$, based on information available at time $t-1$, the allocation in the future's model i at time t is given by the ratio between the target volatility and the predicted volatility $b_t^i = \sigma_{target}/\sigma_{t-1}^{i,pred}$.

Hence, we can compute the daily amounts invested in each of the future volatility models and create a corresponding time series of returns $r_t^i = b_t^i \times r_t^{future}$, consisting of investing according to the allocation computed by the volatility targeting model i. This provides n time series of returns r_t^i. The striking point, as illustrated by Fig. 1 is the very high correlation between the different volatility targeting models' returns, thereby motivating the search for a robust method to determine which model(s) to include in the portfolio construction process. As volatility regimes change, the best model varies over time, making the exercise of choosing the best model non-trivial.

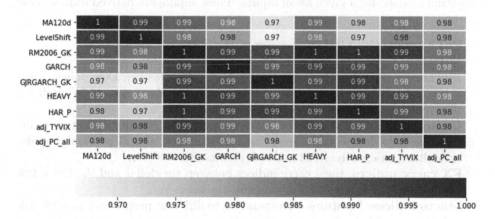

Fig. 1. Correlation between volatility targeting models for the U.S. 10-year Treasury Note futures contract

2.2 Supervised Learning Overlay

In order to identify the best volatility model(s) with a supervised learning task, we use Gradient Boosting Decision Trees (GBDT) to find the model(s) that provide(s) the best next timestep return. More specifically, we selected LightGBM (LGBM) as our framework [19]. The label(s) are for each day the best model(s).

The inputs are various financial and non-financial data that are described at length later in this paper. The specific choices of the GBDT model, in particular LGBM, are motivated by multiple reasons:

- GBDT are the most suitable machine learning methods for small data set classification problems. In particular, they are known to perform better than their state-of-the-art cousins, Deep Learning methods, for small data sets. As a matter of fact, GBDT methods are preferred by Kagglers and have won multiple challenges.
- GBDT methods are less sensitive to data rescaling, compared to logistic regression or penalized methods.
- They can cope with imbalanced data sets.
- They allow for very fast training when using the leaf-wise tree growth (compared to level-wise tree growth).
- Last but not least, among GBDT methods, LGBM is one of the most numerically efficient method, with computing time divided by 2 to 3 compared to XGBoost.

2.3   Features

Our supervised learning task aims to determine the label (the best volatility targeting models) for a given set of inputs. These inputs are derived from several features:

- **PnLs series:** the 9 PnL time series of the different models.
- **Volatility forecasts:** the forecast of the nine volatility models.
- **Market indicators:** the values of the S&P 500, Nasdaq, Dow Jones, Euro Stoxx, FTSE, Nikkei, MSCI World, Emerging Markets and ACWI indices, that represent the most important equity index markets.
- **Commodities indicators:** the prices of several commodity indicators spanning the following sectors: energy markets, industrial and precious metals, agriculture, grains, livestock and soft commodities sectors.
- **FX carry indices:** the 4 carry indices between the dollar and the Euro, the Swiss franc, the Pound sterling and the Japanese Yen.
- **Macro indices:** 5 features corresponding to different proprietary market risk appetites.
- **Bond indicators:** levels of the U.S., U.K., Japan and German 10-year government bonds and the slope computed as the difference between the 10 and 2 years yields.
- **Economic surprises:** economic surprise indices based on the G20 countries, Europe, the U.S., Asia and emerging markets.
- **Implied volatility indicators:** several implied volatility indicators based on FX carry indices, Gold, Crude oil, government bonds and equities indices.
- **Credit spreads:** the TED spreads of the U.S. and the E.U. as well as other international spread indicators.
- **Put/Call ratio:** the put/call ratio for the S&P 500 option market.

Including the volatility model PnL time series, the market indicators, the commodity indicators and the FX carry indices, there is a total of 32 features in a first set. In addition, we compute other statistics such as averages, standard deviations, Sharpe ratios and other related technical indicators, summing up to a total of 416 input features in a second set. Volatility forecasts and macro indices represent another 13 features. We also calculate other statistical figures including short-term moving averages and distance from the average to get an additional 78 inputs. The last 78 macro features are not transformed. In total, we end up with 572 input features in our supervised learning model. We use LightGBM gain as feature importance to select a certain percentage of the most important features, and retrain LightGBM with them to filter the number of features every time the algorithm is trained.

2.4 Walk-Forward Methodology

The whole procedure is summarized in Fig. 2. We use n models to represent the dynamics of the market volatility. We then add other features that provide orthogonal information to the models, such as economic health indices and technical analysis. *In fine*, the most important features are selected. As mentioned previously, LightGBM enables us to rank our various volatility targeting models according to the forecasted return probability of the next timestep. We then construct several strategies using these predictions. In order to test the robustness of our aggregated meta-model out-of-sample, we use the well-known methodology called walk-forward analysis.

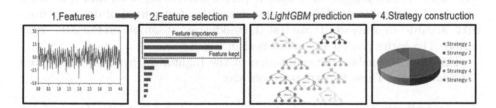

Fig. 2. Overall architecture of the supervised learning task applied to the selection and allocation of volatility targeting strategies

In machine learning, a standard approach is to do k-fold cross-validation. This approach happens to break the chronology of the data and, in certain ill-conceived cases, may potentially use test data in the train set which embodies a blatant case of in-sample optimization. [29] has conducted a comprehensive empirical study of eight common validation schemes and demonstrated that commonly used cross-validation schemes often yield estimates with the largest bias and variance, while forward-validation or walk-forward schemes yield better estimates of the out-of-sample error, even more so in the context of financial time series. We therefore settled on a forward-sliding test set which uses non-overlapping previous past data as the corresponding training sets. In other words, we favor adding incrementally new data in the training set, at each new step, to ensure stability and robustness in the validation process. This method is sometimes referred to as an "anchored walk-forward" validation methodology as we have anchored the training data. Finally, as the test set is always ensuing the training set, the walk-forward analysis creates fewer steps compared with a cross-validation approach which could lead to another source of overfitting.

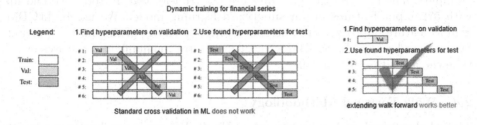

Fig. 3. Overall training, validation and test processes for a walk-forward methodology

In practice, and for our given data sets, we train our models from 2003 to the end of 2010 (giving us at least 7 years of training period), and then use a repetitive validation period of one year from 2011 up to 2016 to determine the best hyperparameters thanks to Optuna. This is a recent open-source Python library developed in 2019 which mixes sampling and pruning algorithms with Bayesian optimization [2]. Once these hyperparameters are determined, we train our model from 2003 to 2016 and use a repetitive test period of one year from 2017 onwards. In other words, we test the model out-of-sample on the 2017–2020 period. The entire process is summarized in Fig. 3.

This method enables the calibration of the LightGBM hyperparameters on a validation set. These hyperparameters are:

- *max_depth*
- *boost_round*
- *min_gain_to_split*
- *feature_fraction*

- *min_sum_hessian_in_leaf*
- *bagging_fraction*
- *lambda_l2*
- *min_importance*

3   Financial Data Experiments

3.1   Market Data

We test our model on two mainstream futures contracts: the continuously rolled CBOT's future on the U.S. 10-year Treasury Note denoted by *TY1* in the rest of the paper, and the continuously rolled CME's E-mini future on the S&P 500 index denoted by *ES1*. As mentioned before, daily data range from 2003 to 2020.

3.2 Hyperparameters Selection and Used Features

Table 1 shows the details of the selected hyperparameters for the two futures contracts *TY1* and *ES1* during the validation period using the Sharpe ratio as the reward function. For *TY1*, the model has a maximum depth of one and selects approximately one hundred features. For *ES1*, the best model is very different. We find that it corresponds to a more complex system with a maximum depth of two, but fewer features are selected, which is somehow intuitive as maximum depth and number of features play similar roles.

For *TY1*, the selected *min_importance* hyperparameter shows that around one hundred features are responsible for 70% of all explanatory information that is used to predict which models have better returns at the next timestep. Then, each year, the model selects the most important features that account for 70% of the total gain. It uses 650 trees with a maximal depth of one. For *ES1*, it is the same logic but with different hyperparameters. Tables 2 and 3 show the 10 most important features selected on the test set from the 572 inputs. Notably, features directly related to volatility models are very often selected. The model focuses on volatility changes and abnormal behaviors using the distance from the average and the percentage change over 10 days. These 10 features are responsible for more than 39% of the total information. They all relate to the volatility of *TY1*.

For both *TY1* and *ES1*, models are retrained each year. Table 2 provides the most important features for *TY1*. Table 4 confirms the stability of the supervised methodology as about 85% of selected features remain identical between two consecutive years. For *ES1*, the conclusion is similar, but we can notice the large presence of volatility features as the model selects the same 24 features each year on average (Table 4).

Table 1. Hyperparameters selected for *TY1* and *ES1* during the validation period (2011–2016)

Hyperparameters	TY1	ES1
max_depth	1	2
boost_round	650	800
min_importance	0.7	0.275
min_sum_hessian_in_leaf	0.125	1.04
min_gain_to_split	0.432	0.028
feature_fraction	0.686	0.834
bagging_fraction	0.49	0.553
lambda_l2	0.184	0.647

Table 2. *TY1* normalized feature importance for the 10 most important features

Feature name	2017	2018	2019	2020	Average
GJR-GARCH_GK_Vol_distance_to_250_MA	**6.10%**	**6.37%**	**6.87%**	**7.67%**	**6.75%**
HEAVY_Vol_distance_to_250_MA	5.91%	5.64%	6.16%	6.01%	5.93%
HAR_P_Vol_distance_to_250_MA	4.58%	5.06%	5.34%	5.50%	5.12%
GARCH_Vol_distance_to_250_MA	4.90%	4.82%	5.19%	4.89%	4.95%
adj_PC_all_std_60	4.65%	4.41%	3.94%	4.43%	4.36%
LevelShift_Vol_pct_change_10	2.99%	2.87%	2.79%	2.93%	2.89%
HEAVY_Vol_pct_change_10	3.03%	2.71%	2.59%	2.48%	2.70%
adj_PC_all_std_125	2.89%	2.63%	2.47%	1.71%	2.43%
GJR-GARCH_GK_std_125	1.80%	2.28%	2.90%	2.24%	2.31%
GJR-GARCH_GK_Vol	1.88%	2.28%	2.47%	1.96%	2.15%

Table 3. *ES1* normalized feature importance of the 10 most important features

Feature name	2017	2018	2019	2020	Average
RAEGARCH_vol_distance_to_250_MA	**10.86%**	**11.76%**	**11.61%**	**12.05%**	**11.57%**
GARCH_vol_distance_to_250_MA	7.49%	7.93%	7.81%	6.71%	7.48%
adj_VIX9D_vol_distance_to_250_MA	5.56%	8.03%	8.32%	7.57%	7.37%
LevelShift_std_60	5.56%	6.74%	7.91%	8.01%	7.05%
adj_VIX9D_vol	7.31%	6.79%	6.51%	6.97%	6.90%
MacroSignal_diff_1	6.90%	6.01%	5.05%	4.67%	5.66%
HEAVY_vol_distance_to_250_MA	4.32%	4.69%	6.19%	5.61%	5.21%
RM2006_GK_vol_pct_change_1	4.12%	4.20%	4.36%	4.31%	4.25%
adj_VIX9D_vol_pct_change_5	4.26%	3.95%	4.22%	4.12%	4.14%
adj_PC_equity_DM_vol_distance_to_250_MA	3.82%	3.64%	4.12%	4.20%	3.95%

Table 4. Number and rates of features kept for *TY1* and *ES1*

Year	Features rate on *TY1*	Features number on *TY1*	Features rate on *ES1*	Features number on *ES1*
2017	/	98	/	26
2018	84%	95	92%	24
2019	87%	93	100%	23
2020	82%	94	88%	24

3.3 Comparison with Benchmark

The model output is a probability for each volatility model to have the highest return at the next timestep. We therefore examine several strategies from these probabilities:

- **Weighted:** the probability of each model is used directly as an allocation,
- **3 best:** only the three best models are taken into account and allocation is computed as the three re-normalized probabilities,
- **Follow the best:** 100% investment in the model with the highest probability.

These strategies are compared to the **benchmark** which is an equally-weighted strategy. Figure 4 shows the allocation of the weighted strategy on *TY1*. The model focuses on few volatility models such as *adjusted TYVIX*, *adjusted Principal Component* and *moving average 120-days*. But the probabilities are not stable which indicates that this strategy exhibits a potentially high turnover. For *ES1*, the model is less stable. This is confirmed by the *weighted* strategy on Fig. 5 as allocations switch frequently between several models.

For *TY1*, the *follow the best* strategy yields better results than the others as it exhibits a better performance with a lower volatility, resulting in a higher Sharpe ratio. Different performances are displayed in Fig. 6. In addition, the *follow the best* strategy has the smallest drawdown which indicates that the model invests in the high-volatility model when markets plummet. However, the turnover is seven times higher than the *benchmark* which implies much larger transaction costs (TC) and reduces the final performance. Note that we have used a heuristic linear 2bps per trade model for transaction costs applied to both the fixed income and equity proxies. From Fig. 4, a large majority of the volatility models do not have a high probability of being the best at the next timestep, hence the allocation between *weighted* and *3 best* strategies are extremely alike and give similar performances. This information is provided in Table 5.

Conversely, Fig. 7 shows that the *follow the best* strategy is riskier than the corresponding *benchmark* for *ES1*. The *weighted* and *3 best* strategies have lower performance than the *benchmark* but are better than *follow the best*. The volatility of the output strategies have a high volatility compared to the *benchmark*, which is due to the frequent changes between volatility models. It is therefore not surprising that these strategies do not exhibit strong returns - the *benchmark* strategy having the best Sharpe ratio. In addition, the supervised model does not seem to work as intended as the *follow the best* strategy has the worst drawdown. We can therefore conclude that the model does not predict well which volatility model will have the best return at the next timestep for *ES1*. Further information is provided in Table 6.

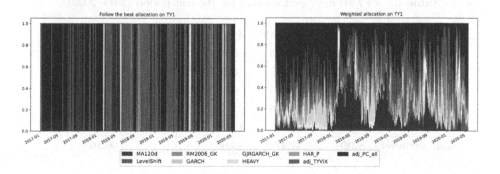

Fig. 4. Allocation of the *weighted* and *follow the best* strategies for *TY1*

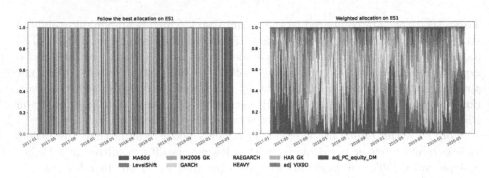

Fig. 5. Allocation of the *weighted* and *follow the best* strategies for *ES1*

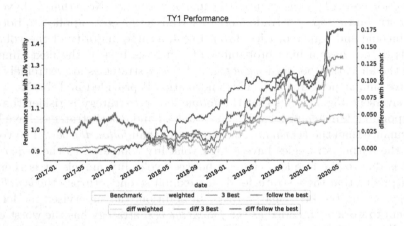

Fig. 6. *TY1* strategy performance on the test set

Table 5. *TY1* strategy performance for the test period (2017–2020)

	Benchmark	Weighted	3 best	FtB w/o. TC	FtB with TC
Ann. ret.	0.068	0.073	0.072	**0.098**	0.083
Ann. vol.	9.0%	8.3%	**8.2%**	8.3%	8.3%
Sharpe ratio	0.759	0.883	0.883	**1.176**	1.001
Sortino	1.177	1.368	1.368	**1.875**	1.601
Drawdown	16.2%	13.5%	13.4%	**12.2%**	13.1%
Ann. turnover	**8.90**	31.47	33.96	66.16	66.16

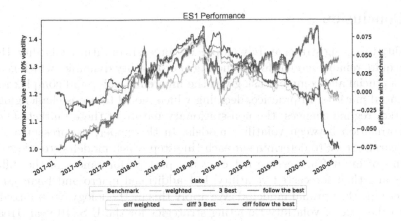

Fig. 7. *ES1* strategy performance on the test set

Table 6. *ES1* strategy performance for the test period (2017–2020)

	Benchmark	Weighted	3 best	FtB w/o. TC	FtB with TC
Ann. ret.	0.088	0.091	**0.094**	0.084	0.071
Ann. vol.	**9.9%**	10.6%	10.8%	12.1%	12.1%
Sharpe ratio	**0.891**	0.861	0.872	0.695	0.583
Sortino	**1.198**	1.147	1.165	0.938	0.802
Drawdown	**14.7%**	15.2%	15.4%	18.4%	18.5%
Ann. turnover	**8.24**	35.98	39.18	62.06	62.06

3.4 Future Works

This study has shown how to construct strategies where the best models are selected by a supervised learning overlay. This adaptive supervised learning methodology leads to good results on the U.S. 10-year Treasury Note futures contract at the cost of a higher turnover. A direct extension of this work is therefore related to explore several techniques that can reduce turnover. In addition, we have found that this approach leads to less efficient results on the E-mini S&P 500 index futures contract. It is therefore worthwhile to better understand the major differences when applying this methodology to stock and bond futures. Finally, these two financial instruments, albeit among the most liquid in the world, represent a very small sample that could be extended to dozens of other financial futures contracts. More conclusive statistics could be reached if applied to a more complete set of generic futures contracts. All these steps are for further exploration in future works.

4   Conclusion

Volatility targeting strategies rely on precise forecasts of future volatility. Hence, they require reliable models for predicting the volatility dynamic, which is, obviously, a crucial and complex task given the inherently noisy and complex nature of financial markets. In practice, deciding which model to use is challenging due to market regime changes, the non-stationary nature of these markets and the high correlation between volatility models. In this paper, we present a supervised learning task to determine at each timestep which model(s) to overweight. In terms of input features, we not only use past performances of the different models and their forecasted volatility, but additional macro and financial data to determine the optimal model(s). We apply this methodology, with mixed success, to the case of volatility targeting strategies for the U.S. 10-year Treasury Note and the E-mini S&P 500 index futures contracts. We show that GBDT is an effective method to predict the best model(s) in the fixed income case while further studies must be conducted for equity indices. We filter our features by importance and observe that the selected features are mostly model-related such as the distance of the volatility forecast to its mean.

References

1. Aguilar-Rivera, R., Valenzuela-Rendón, M., Rodríguez-Ortiz, J.: Genetic algorithms and Darwinian approaches in financial applications: a survey. Expert Syst. Appl. **42**(21), 7684–7697 (2015)
2. Akiba, T., Sano1, S., Yanase1, T., Ohta1, T., Koyama, M.: Optuna: a next-generation hyperparameter optimization framework. arxiv (2019)
3. Atsalakis, G.S., Valavanis, K.P.: Surveying stock market forecasting techniques - part ii: soft computing methods. Exp. Syst. Appl. **36**(3, Part 2), 5932–5941 (2009)
4. Benhamou, E., Saltiel, D., Ohana, J.J., Atif, J., Laraki, R.: Deep reinforcement learning (DRL) for portfolio allocation. In: Dong, Y., Ifrim, G., Mladenić, D., Saunders, C., Van Hoecke, S. (eds.) ECML PKDD 2020. LNCS (LNAI), vol. 12461, pp. 527–531. Springer, Cham (2021). https://doi.org/10.1007/978-3-030-67670-4_32
5. Benhamou, E., Saltiel, D., Tabachnik, S., Wong, S.K., Chareyron, F.: Adaptive learning for financial markets mixing model-based and model-free rl for volatility targeting. In: AAAMAS: ALA. AAAI Press (2021)
6. Benhamou, E., Saltiel, D., Ungari, S., Mukhopadhyay, A.: Bridging the gap between Markowitz planning and deep reinforcement learning. In: Proceedings of the 30th International Conference on Automated Planning and Scheduling (ICAPS): PRL. AAAI Press (2020)
7. Benhamou, E., Saltiel, D., Ungari, S., Mukhopadhyay, A.: Time your hedge with deep reinforcement learning. In: Proceedings of the 30th International Conference on Automated Planning and Scheduling (ICAPS): FinPlan. AAAI Press (2020)
8. Benjamin Bruder, T.R.: Managing risk exposures using the risk budgeting approach. SSRN Electron. J., 2009778 (2012)
9. Bollerslev, T.: Generalized autoregressive conditional heteroskedasticity. J. Econ. **31**, 307–327 (1986)

10. Bollerslev, T., Chou, R.Y., Kroner, K.F.: Arch modeling in finance: a review of the theory and empirical evidence. J. Econ. **52**, 5–59 (1992)
11. Bollerslev, T., Hood, B., Huss, J., Pedersen, L.H.: Risk everywhere: modeling and managing volatility. Rev. Fin. Stud. **31**(7), 2729–2773 (2018)
12. Bollerslev, T., Zhou, H.: Volatility puzzles: a simple framework for gauging return-volatility regressions. J. Econ. **131**, 123–150 (2006)
13. Corsi, F.: A simple approximate long-memory model of realized volatility. J. Financ. Economet. **7**, 174–196 (2009)
14. Chaves, D., Hsu, J., Li, F., Shakernia, O.: Risk parity portfolio vs. other asset allocation heuristic portfolios. J. Investing **20**(1), 108–118 (2011)
15. Dreyer, A.A., Hubrich, S.: Tail-risk mitigation with managed volatility strategies. J. Investment Strat. **8**(2956), 1 (2019)
16. Glosten, L.R., Jagannathan, R., Runkle, D.E.: On the relation between the expected value and the volatility of the nominal excess return on stocks. J. Financ. **48**(5), 1779–1801 (1993)
17. Harvey, C.R., Hoyle, E., Korgaonkar, R., Rattray, S., Sargaison, M., Van Hemert, O.: The impact of volatility targeting. J. Portf. Manag. **45**(1), 14–33 (2018)
18. Jaeger, M., Krügel, S., Marinelli, D., Papenbrock, J., Schwendner, P.: Interpretable machine learning for diversified portfolio construction. J. Financ. Data Sci. (2021)
19. Ke, G., et al.: LightGBM: a highly efficient gradient boosting decision tree. In: Guyon, I., et al. (eds.) Advances in Neural Information Processing Systems, vol. 30, pp. 3146–3154. Curran Associates, Inc. (2017)
20. Li, Y., Ma, W.: Applications of artificial neural networks in financial economics: a survey. In: 2010 International Symposium on Computational Intelligence and Design, vol. 1, pp. 211–214 (2010)
21. Liang, C., Wei, Y., Zhang, Y.: Is implied volatility more informative for forecasting realized volatility: an international perspective. J. Forecast. **39**, 1253–1276 (2020)
22. Lommers, K., Harzli, O.E., Kim, J.: Confronting machine learning with financial research. J. Finan. Data Sci. (2021)
23. Lu, Y.K.: Modeling and forecasting stock return volatility using a random level shift model. J. Empirical Finan. **17**, 138–156 (2009)
24. Markowitz, H.: Portfolio selection. J. Finan. **7**(1), 77–91 (1952)
25. Molyboga, M.: A modified hierarchical risk parity framework for portfolio management. J. Financ. Data Sci. **2**(3), 128–139 (2020)
26. Nti, I.K., Adekoya, A.F., Weyori, B.A.: A systematic review of fundamental and technical analysis of stock market predictions. Artif. Intell. Rev. **53**(4), 3007–3057 (2019). https://doi.org/10.1007/s10462-019-09754-z
27. Qian, E.: Risk parity portfolios. Panagora Asset Managemen (2005)
28. Rundo, F., Trenta, F., di Stallo, A.L., Battiato, S.: Machine learning for quantitative finance applications: a survey. Appl. Sci. **9**(24), 5574 (2019)
29. Schnaubelt, M.: A comparison of machine learning model validation schemes for non-stationary time series data. FAU Discussion Papers in Economics, 42 (2019)
30. Shah, D., Isah, H., Zulkernine, F.: Stock market analysis: a review and taxonomy of prediction techniques. Int. J. Financ. Stud. **7**(2), 26 (2019)
31. Shephard, N., Sheppard, K.: Realising the future: forecasting with high-frequency-based volatility (HEAVY) models. J. Appl. Economet. **25**(2), 197–231 (2010)
32. Xing, F.Z., Cambria, E., Welsch, R.E.: Natural language based financial forecasting: a survey. Artif. Intell. Rev. **50**(1), 49–73 (2017). https://doi.org/10.1007/s10462-017-9588-9
33. Zhang, Z., Zohren, S., Roberts, S.: Deep learning for portfolio optimization. J. Financ. Data Sci. **2**(4), 8–20 (2020)

Efficient Analysis of Transactional Data Using Graph Convolutional Networks

Hamish Hall$^{(\boxtimes)}$, Pedro Baiz, and Philip Nadler

Department of Computing, Imperial College London, London, UK
{hamish.hall19,p.m.baiz,p.nadler}@imperial.ac.uk

Abstract. We show that by transforming financial records into graph structures, Graph-based Deep Learning methods can greatly outperform their conventional Neural Network counterparts by assimilating data latent in the graph structure itself: topology and neighbourhoods. Our resulting approach allows for competitive classification of fraudulent users, even when resampling the data to reinstate the authentic imbalance. When it comes to research and analysis, in the pursuit of safeguarding financial systems, the problem is that transactional datasets are noisy and unstructured, especially with the goal of discerning illicit activity. In this research we demonstrate the powerful capabilities of semi-supervised Graph Convolutional Networks in mining insights out of these large datasets, despite strong imbalances and only partial labelling. Fraud and financial malpractice has always been, and likely will remain ubiquitous. The problems are amplified in the new world of cryptoeconomic financial systems - which are young and unknown, lack regulation and can be confusing for new users. The result is a lucrative playground for scammers, phishers and hackers. However, in this research we have built and describe an effective countermeasure to take on these adversarial actors.

Keywords: Graph data · Graph Neural Networks · Semi-supervised learning · Fraud analysis · Blockchain

1 Introduction

Mining for insights in transactional data is extremely important for money service businesses, both in upkeeping the structural integrity and safety of financial systems, and in the necessity of complying to strict rules for participation. As the quote from US Deputy Attorney General Paul McNulty goes: "If you think compliance is expensive, try non-compliance [21]". Meanwhile financial malpractice has many manifestations: fraud, money laundering, phishing, ponzi schemes, credit fraud, hacked accounts and identity fraud to name a few. Meanwhile in the world of cryptocurrencies: you also have imitation of accounts or addresses, scam lotteries, fake ICOs (coin offerings), malicious contracts, and many more. It is a significant economic problem, said to cost the global economy around £3.89 trillion annually [6].

© Springer Nature Switzerland AG 2021
M. Kamp et al. (Eds.): ECML PKDD 2021 Workshops, CCIS 1525, pp. 210–225, 2021.
https://doi.org/10.1007/978-3-030-93733-1_15

Transactional datasets are sparsely labelled (particularly for public access), overwhelmingly imbalanced and very large in size - there have been over 350 million [5] Ethereum transactions since its conception in 2015, and visa processes around 2,000 transactions per second [1]. When it comes to research and analysis, it is easy for fraudulent transactions to dilute beyond detection. Furthermore, in an evolutionary battle, as attack forensics improve, so do the ingenious camouflage and tactics of scammers and foul players. A recent Ethereum phishing scam involved the masquerading of Elon Musk himself on Twitter, in a ploy to convince users to transfer funds to deviant addresses - over 400 people fell victim.

Fig. 1. An Ethereum phishing scam, as advertised on YouTube.

However, the advent of deep learning has dawned a new world of analysis tool with the power to unearth deeply subtle latent patterns in data. These new algorithms, powerful new hardware and large public datasets, have facilitated a new surge in supervision of fraudulent transactions. It is possible, with the right tuning, to ingest enormous amounts of transactional records and scour for anomalies and odd behaviour.

It must be noted however, despite their power, using deep learning methods as real-world analysis tools can bring associated problems - it is hard to act out the suggestions of a black-box inference engine, without strong ideas of why it has made the prediction it has. This is particularly important for financial forensics as false positives are costly and antithetical to an inclusive global financial system [27], and false negatives allow criminal activity to pass undetected. Therefore it is also important to supplement illicit activity detection models with transparent and detailed explanations. While the libraries to do so are in their infancy, particularly for the Graph Deep Learning tools used in this research, we demonstrate in this paper the insights that can be gained in visualising the results achieved. The contributions of this research are as such:

- We describe and advertise for the modelling of transactional records and systems as graph data, and demonstrate the efficacy of Graph Convolutional Networks to reveal insights not available to conventional Neural Networks.
- We testify the contribution of structural relations and topology to enhance classification success, over features alone.
- We contribute to the furthering of anti-money laundering, and fraud detection techniques, using deep learning tools.

2   Related Work

2.1   Graph Methods and Graph Neural Networks (GNNs)

Traditional methods for mining patterns out of graph data involved transforming graphs into network embeddings, using tools such as matrix factorization as pre-processing for downstream analysis tools (classifiers etc.). GNNs, however, apply the end-to-end feature extraction and analysis of deep learning to graph data. Many models exist and these differ in the way they capture node features, edge features and structural relationships in graphs. Furthermore, graphs typically reach large sizes, so there are different techniques for approximating the graph data while prioritising components most important to the end goal. Graph Convolutional Networks [3,8,9,15,23] generalize the achievements of CNNs for images (regularly spaced grids of pixels) to a domain that can be applied to irregular graph structures, where any node can have any number of connections. They can take one of two approaches: spectral-based, applying the ideas of graph signal processing to analyze node relations using matrix decomposition and harmonic analysis; or spatial-based methods, which aggregate the representations of a nodes neighbours using 'message passing'. The advantage of spatial-based methods is the ability to generalize beyond fixed-shaped graphs [16]. This is imperative for transaction graphs, which come in new shapes every day.

2.2   Fraud Analysis

Some researchers have analyzed the market at scale [12], with some researchers such as Wang et al. [24] recognising that fraud can be better identified by expanding beyond user statistical features, and looking for transaction relationships in graphs. Furthermore, they design a system for node embedding that captures the essence of transactions in a semi-supervised way using graph attention. Expanding on this is the idea of heterogeneous information networks [4,14,31], which aggregate multi-faceted views of data around users. Liang et al. [17] demonstrate the possibility of using GNNs to uncover suspicious activity in the insurance domain - this likely consists of different patterns, but the techniques are worth noting.

In the work of Weber et al. [27] they tackle the large problem of anti money laundering on the Bitcoin network. Particularly exciting, they explore the usage of graph convolutional networks, and in a section dedicated to temporal modelling they use the evolveGCN model deployed by Pareja et al. [23]. Interestingly, also using graph analysis, McGinn et al. [20] have demonstrated and visualized "repeated DNA sequences of transactional behaviour" on the Bitcoin blockchain. Moreover, they do this without relying on "broad and aggretative assumptions", meaning transaction level insights are feasible.

Meanwhile, Ethereum has gained notable popularity and is the closest competitor to Bitcoin for market capitalization. Part of its success leans to the added functionality of smart contracts, and the tokens built upon the platform, but Ethereum is also widely used for account to account transactions. It is also the blockchain that sees the highest number of scam, phishers and ponzi schemes. In their work, Faruggia et al. [10] showed illicit accounts on the Ethereum blockchain could be identified with high accuracy, using decision trees. Not only did they show that illicit accounts have distinguishable characteristics, but they also revealed a list of most important contributing features. The top three being: "time diff between first and last" (i.e. lifespan of an account), "total ether balance" and "min value received". This research proves the possibility of classifying illicit accounts on the Ethereum blockchain - however, in our research we aimed to leverage the graph structure of the transaction data to gather a deeper understanding of the activity of these accounts while they are still active rather than retrospectively.

Other forms of fraud mainly take the form of spam; usually in online reviews of products and services or with fake profiles on social media networks. Many interesting algorithms have been proposed which aim to capture the idiosyncrasies of accounts to catch deviants such as SliceNDice [22], SybilEdge [2], Fraudar [13] and GraphRad [19] for example which mine patterns in user activity graphs. Meanwhile, FdGars [25], GEM [18], ASA [28] and AHIN [30] all achieve impressive results identifying fraudsters using Graph Convolutional Networks. These each involve slight variations in architecture, particularly in how they set up the graph (homogeneous vs. heterogeneous) and the approximations applied (player2vec, struct2vec etc.).

3   Methodology

The proposed methodology is designed to extract useful classification out of large financial datasets, with highly imbalanced class distributions - of which, the positive class of main interest (illicit accounts for example) is heavily diluted. This method is agnostic to the feature engineering pre-processing stage which acts to provide as much information as possible per node. It works to improve classification results, by enriching these node representations with the extended knowledge of the nature of surrounding nodes. Hence, while it seems intuitive to generate and work with directional graphs in an effort to emulate the 'flow' of transactions, this method actually benefits due to the absorption and understanding of a node's wider neighbourhood, so profits from structuring the system using bi-directional graphs. The reason for this will become more obvious in the description of Graph Convolutional Networks, and the message-passing nature of analysis.

3.1 Constructing Transaction Graphs

For the purposes of this research, a set of transactions shall be treated and analyzed as a graph data structure, and this can approached in two possible ways: first, where vertices are accounts and a transaction composes an edge between two of these, or second, a node is itself a transaction, and edges are used to connect funds according to 'flow'. The former is the more conventional approach, while the latter describes how the Elliptic dataset[27] is designed - the key to this analysis is that edges allow information sharing between nodes, so can conceptually abstract multiple connection types. Formally, one of these graphs G consists of a collection V, of vertices, and a collection E, of edges; such that: $G = (V, E)$. Meanwhile, an edge $e \in E$, connects two nodes $u, v \in V$ such that: $e = \langle u, v \rangle$. Graphs can be represented by an adjacency matrix $\mathbf{A}$, whereby a graph with n vertices, and m edges can be represented as a matrix $\mathbf{A} \in \mathbb{R}^{n \times n}$, with $\mathbf{A}[i, j]$ representing the number of edges between u_i and v_j. As most accounts do not interact, these adjacency matrices are very sparse - therefore they are avoided in favour of edge lists E, until required for certain operations. Note, graphs can be directed or un-directed meaning $\mathbf{A}[i, j] \neq \mathbf{A}[j, i]$ or $\mathbf{A}[i, j] = \mathbf{A}[j, i]$ respectively. While a directed graph reflects the nature of transactions, and the flow of funds - an undirected graph does far better in propagating information around the graph. To achieve this, $E = \langle src, dest \rangle$ is represented by a vector of indices u and v: $u = src \parallel dest$ and $v = dest \parallel src$.

Lastly, each node also has a vector representation of features such that $X = \{x_1, x_2 ... x_n\}, x_i \in \mathbb{R}^d$, where d is the vector dimension and, each edge has associated attributes such that $E^a \in \mathbb{R}^{m \times a}$ is the matrix of edge vectors - in a simple case $e_{i,j}^a$ is a scalar value, but analysis can easily be extended to incorporate more edge features such that $e_{i,j}^a \in \mathbb{R}^a$. Therefore, where X is the set of node features and E^a is the set of edge features, transaction graphs used in the analysis of this project can be represented with the set:

$$G = (V, E, E^a, X) \tag{1}$$

Any node in a connected graph, has an optional set of neighbors $\mathcal{N}$, defined as those directly connected with edges. Graphs can be traversed in steps larger than 1, and as such, if nodes i and j are connected by an edge, then the neighbor set of j, $\mathcal{N}(j)$, will feature in the 2-hop neighborhood of i. The neighbor set for a node i, in graph G, as discussed going forward is defined according to:

$$\mathcal{N}(i) = \{j \in V(G) | i \neq j, \exists e \in E(G) : e\langle i, j \rangle\} \tag{2}$$

3.2 Graph Convolutional Networks

In the same way Convolutional Neural Networks revolutionised the analysis of images by aggregating pixel neighborhoods - a similar principle leveraging deep learning can be applied to graphs to assimilate the relationships between nodes. While images and graphs both rely on connections between data points, graphs are non-Euclidean and irregular so the methods that work well on organized grids of pixels can not be transcribed and applied directly.

A message passing scheme is the best choice when required to incorporate more complex systems, with node and edge features. It also allows for the design of models that can be transferred between thematically similar, but structurally different graphs. From the perspective of a single node, as in the central node v of Fig. 2, the intention is to build an output vector h_v^k using an assimilation of information from the previous layer, $k-1$. This information includes vector representations of neighbors, edge features and the previous vector representation of a node.

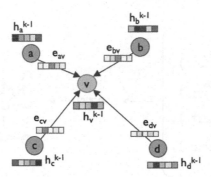

Fig. 2. GNN perspective from a single node v - the state of the system before propagation through a layer.

Generally the formula for progression through a single layer of a message passing neural network is:

$$h_i^k = \phi^k(h_i^{k-1}, A_{j \in \mathcal{N}(i)} M^k(h_i^{k-1}, h_j^{k-1}, e_{i,j})) \tag{3}$$

where ϕ^k represents a differentiable function such as a Multi Layered Perceptron (MLP), with injected non linearity. The superscript k recognises that this function will have a different set of learnable weights for each layer. A and M denote an aggregating function, and message composing function respectively as depicted in the graphic of Fig. 3. The general process for one of these convolutional layers is as such:

1. Compose messages along edges, using some amalgamation of 'sender' vector representation, 'receiver' vector representation, and the corresponding edge features.
2. Propagate messages along the direction of edges, as depicted in the Adjacency matrix.
3. Aggregate neighbor's vectors according to a differentiable aggregator function ('sum', 'mean', 'max', 'min' etc.).
4. Linear transformation via learnable weights, followed by a non-linear activation function (Sigmoid, ReLu etc.).

In Eq. (3), the initial vector representation of a node is its input feature vector: $h_i^0 = x_i$. A GNN is still applicable where nodes have no features, and in this instance the initial vector may be initialized as a vector of zeros, or a one-hot encoding of a given node id. On each subsequent forward pass, the vector output of the previous layer serves as the vector representation going into the next layer, and it is these vectors that are passed between nodes to propagate information through the graph. Hence, the architecture decided upon affects what neighbors, $\mathcal{N}(i)$ a node may 'see'. An undirected graph is less discriminate in information sharing, and more hops gives greater dissemination of information. Nodes are given self-loops such that they do not need to reside in a 2-layer network to receive information about themselves.

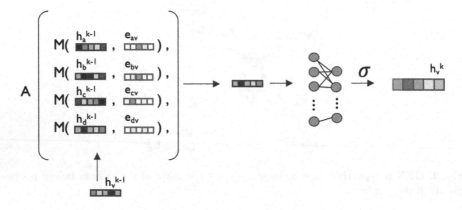

Fig. 3. Information propagation and aggregation in the forward pass of a convolution layer for one node. The result is a dense, latent vector representation.

One of the perks of graph convolutional analysis is its semi-supervised nature. While a dataset may only be partially labelled, a GCN can leverage the information of every node in its learning process. These unlabelled nodes contribute to the characterization of the nodes of interest by acting as part of their neighborhood. Train and test masks are used to tune the loss and backpropagation using the nodes that are labelled, but the information of every node propagates around, and defines the system.

3.3   Parameter Setup

A hyperparameter study revealed an optimal architecture of two graph convolutions, followed by a linear MLP decoding layer. This represents a 2-hop aggregation of neighbourhood information. The first GCN layer maintains input/output ratio, and the second GCN layer fans down to halfway between the number of neurons in the final classification. It was shown that the model profits from maintaining high dimensional node representations for as long as possible. Training is facilitated using a negative log likelihood loss and the model was trained using the Adam optimizer, with a 80/20 train/test split and a learning rate of 0.001. Lastly, proportional class weights are used in the loss calculation stage to assuage the large class imbalance problem.

4   Experiments

While analysis of financial data is important for a myriad of reasons, it is sensitive and valuable in nature - and therefore, not readily available. Fortunately, the last decade has seen the advent of a whole new paradigm of cryptoeconomic system, which rely on pseudo-anonymity and transactional transparency. That is to say, while participants in the system have hidden identities (somewhat), every transaction and interaction is listed publicly, and permanently for as long as the system is live. Meanwhile these cryptocurrencies are fully fledged economic systems and reflect many of the paradigms of conventional fiat systems - payments, trade, investment, exchanges etc. - and they are also vulnerable to a similar arsenal of fraud and attacks. Cryptocurrency transactional data is used as the basis for the analysis in this research as these systems require attack forensics, security measures and user enlightenment just as much as any other financial system, and also work as an open-access sandbox to simulate the larger, conventional financial systems. Ethereum and Bitcoin are chosen as the two largest cryptocurrencies, with the most crowd-sourced data available.

The code for this research can be found at github.com/hachall/ethtxanalysis, including additional results and hyperparameters required to reproduce these results. The GNNs used were built using the libraries: DGL [26] and PyTorch Geometric [11]. Meanwhile the Ethereum datasets produced for this work can be found on Kaggle at kaggle.com/hamishhall/labelled-ethereum-addresses.

4.1   Datasets

Ethereum. Ethereum transactions were retrieved using EtherScan's API using a bespoke method of extraction according to a growing set of addresses initiated around a central set. This method allows the gathering and utilisation of a fraction of transactions, while still providing an authentic 2-hop neighbourhood for this central set of addresses. In doing this, 3 months of transactional data can be reduced to 500,000 relevant transactions, as opposed to the millions that occurred across the whole time window. Statistical features are built per node based on the amounts transacted and the time between transactions, as well as propensity to utilise the different, heterogeneous transaction types afforded on the Ethereum blockchain (such as interaction with tokens). The addresses are then labelled using a combination of data from the crowd-sourced dataset CryptoScamDB and from web-scraping the categories on Etherscan. We have published the extensive dataset of 20,000 labelled Ethereum addresses at the Kaggle link mentioned above. The account statistics obtained, and the nature of the addresses are shown in Tables 1 and 2.

Bitcoin. Bitcoin analysis was undertaken using the Elliptic dataset [27]. This large dataset contains over 200,000 transactions, each equipped with 166 features, and separated over 49 timesteps, spaced a few weeks apart each. The transaction features are a combination of local and aggregated features, normalized for anonymization. The transactions are connected with around 230,000 edges to represent 'flow' of funds. No edges cross between timesteps, so the result is 49 individually connected subgraphs. Rather than separate these and pass them through the model individually, it is easier to treat the whole dataset as a single graph, and allow it to discern the boundaries itself in the process of message-passing. The dataset is labelled as in Table 2d.

Table 1. Transaction graph statistics for the datasets experimented with in this research.

	Nodes	Edges	Features	Class sets
Ethereum	495,392	1,043,020	47	3
Bitcoin	203,769	234,355	166	1

4.2 Node Classification

GNNs can be trained to enrich node feature representations with supplementary information relating to topology and neighborhood. This provides enhanced information to, and improves the success of classifiers intent on discerning the nature of 'users' in a transaction graph. Depending on the dataset there are different opportunities for node analysis. The Ethereum dataset has, with varying degrees of sparsity, three possible approaches for analysis: account type classification, entity recognition and illicit activity analysis. The relative distribution of these classes is shown in Table 2. Meanwhile, the Elliptic dataset is labelled solely on the basis of illicit transactions. Like the Ethereum set, the majority of nodes are unlabelled - these nodes are not ignored however, but rather act as an 'unflagged' node forming a class of its own. This will be important when it comes to analysis - a powerful model must discern important nodes not just from the opposing class, but also the sea of surrounding 'innocuous' neighbors. Luckily, these proffer important information into the convolutional mix so their presence will be shown to be useful.

4.3 Mitigating Imbalance with Downsampling

The overwhelming 'unflagged' class can be diluted for the sake of training using clever masking techniques, to demonstrate the efficacy in classification against these 'layman' accounts - ones that have gone under every public radar thus far for fraud analysis, for example. However, this class imbalance does reflect real-life scenarios and cannot be ignored. Hence it shall be shown, that this large set of unlabelled nodes can be reintroduced to a fully-trained model, and face successful separation, despite their formidable size. Importantly, these nodes are

Table 2. Class distribution according to task

	Wallets	Smart Contracts	Exchanges	Unlabelled
Accounts	156,126	23,341	161	315,545

(a) Ethereum - account types

	Illicit	Licit	Unflagged
Accounts	565	904	495,407

(b) Ethereum - account nature

	DEX	Exchange	ICO	Wallets	Mining	DeFi	Unidentified
Accounts	21	141	59	21	30		496,600

(c) Ethereum - entities

	Illicit	Licit	Unflagged
Transactions	4,545	42,019	157,205

(d) Bitcoin - transaction nature

not removed as they are required for convolution and it is important to maintain an authentic transaction graph - rather they are masked in the loss calculation stage.

5   Results and Discussion

Table 3 demonstrates the superior classification performance, when utilising the neighbourhood aggregation effects of GCNs, against a benchmark MLP pitted at the same task. The MLP is formed of a similar architecture, but receives only the set of node features and undertakes no message passing. Not only does the GCN outperform the MLP in every task, but its model generalizes better to a dataset with reintroduced imbalance.

The relative stability in the recall after resampling indicates the trained model's strength in filtering out the majority unflagged, uninteresting nodes. That said, these classes are so overwhelmingly large that any spill over in predictions drowns out correct predictions of the smaller classes - hence, the drastic drops in precision, as shown in Fig. 4b). In datasets distributed as such, false positives are inevitable - but each of these models has the capacity to filter out, in some cases, well over 90% of irrelevant nodes, while maintaining competitive recalls of important nodes. If incorporated into a tiered forensic analysis system, the results above would amount to a significant reduction in nodes required to process down the pipeline for further scrutiny.

Table 3. Experiment results - with a downsampled majority class and resampled to full population size. Evaluation metrics consist of accuracy, precision/recall and macro-averaged F1 score. The latter being the most significant target when it comes to imbalanced datasets.

Experiment	MLP-downsample			GCN-downsample		
	Accuracy	Prec / Rec	F1	Accuracy	Prec / Rec	F1
Ethereum Account Type Classification	-	-	-	-	-	-
Illicit Account Analysis	0.848	0.8102 / 0.593	0.6848	0.8846	0.8225 / 0.726	**0.7713**
Entity Recognition	0.7564	0.2433 / 0.2657	0.2541	0.8452	0.5787 / 0.5174	**0.5463**
Bitcoin Illicit Activity Analysis	0.8421	0.7967 / 0.8227	0.8095	0.8426	0.8133 / 0.8083	**0.8108**

(a) Results on downsampled data

Experiment	MLP-full			GCN-full		
	Accuracy	Prec / Rec	F1	Accuracy	Prec / Rec	F1
Ethereum Account Type Classification	0.9938	0.6565 / 0.6602	0.6584	0.9932	0.7474 / 0.7596	**0.7535**
Illicit Account Analysis	0.9729	0.375 / 0.5925	0.4593	0.9813	0.4224 / 0.8387	**0.5618**
Entity Recognition	0.9541	0.1678 / 0.2646	0.2054	0.9573	0.1744 / 0.6635	**0.2762**
Bitcoin Illicit Activity Analysis	0.8177	0.6426 / 0.8236	0.7219	0.8359	0.6663 / 0.8086	**0.7306**

(b) Results on resampled data

5.1 Down Sampling

The effect of downsampling is displayed in Fig. 4a. Eventually the accuracy and F1 score for the model part in different directions: a bad sign that the prediction process is defaulting to the disproportionate majority class. Preferentially, models should be trained with up to around 10:1 dilution of the main class. These properly trained models can then be tested for inference on realistically distributed datasets as in Fig. 4b. While the false positives are high - this marks a huge reduction in the nodes required for further analysis.

5.2 Visualization

The effect of graph convolutions can be visualized by observing the contributing significance of initial features and the interconnections of nodes, towards final prediction. Using the state-of-the-art GNNExplainer library [29], it was possible to forensically investigate the reason the model made certain decisions. This tool learns and returns a feature and edge mask, explaining the relative importance of features and edges respectively that contributed greatest to the prediction made. These masks can be learned and calculated for the predictions of every node, and visually laid side by side for comparison. Figure 5 shows a comparison in significant features when making predictions and mispredictions, for Ethereum nodes of illicit, licit and unflagged nature. There are correlations between features for similarly classed nodes, and observing down the columns gives hints at what confused the model into mispredictions.

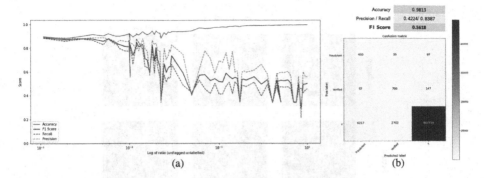

Fig. 4. a) The effect of sample ratio on classification success, and b) the capacity of a downsampled model to still achieve strong success when re-sampling to the overwhelmingly imbalanced case of the real-life data. The confusion matrix represents the results of the model trained to detect illicit activity in the Ethereum network, when incorporating the full dataset.

The threshold based edge masks returned from the explainer library, can then be used to plot the subgraph of significant neighbors for a target node. Figure 6 shows the network visualisation for an Ethereum based phishing scam, and its identification across 5 sites on CryptoScamDB [7]. The weighted edges imply information has been extracted out of the relational data and this is reconciled with the feature information exhibited in Fig. 5. The joint information visually demonstrates that the features are not solely responsible for the success of the model. Evidently, the neighborhood aggregation step of a GCN is also a discerning key.

Meanwhile, these plots can be compared side-by-side to reveal certain recurring patterns that the model has latched on to, aiding in its predictions. Figures 7 and 8 show the subgraphs plotted using NetworkX, using a threshold to filter significant edges based on relative contribution to end prediction. As with the features, where certain columns correlate to reveal the model was depending on a certain feature value - with the visualized subgraphs we can see correlations between nodes of certain classes, and the nodes that were wrongly thought to apply to that class. This is a promising idea that latent topological patterns exist in the transaction networks, which a deep learning model is capable of finding and exploiting for its analysis.

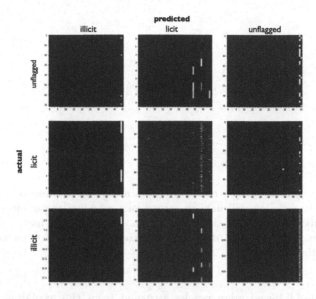

Fig. 5. The resulting confusion matrix after inference on Ethereum accounts for illicit activity analysis, but highlighting the key contributing features as heat maps - in each case using the feature masks produced by GNNExplainer [29]. This can be used as a precursor to investigate certain features further, or the addition of features in a similar domain. Each x-axis represents the 46 available features, and the y-axis depicts each sample being classified. Brighter highlighting indicates where a feature made significant contribution to the classification of the node.

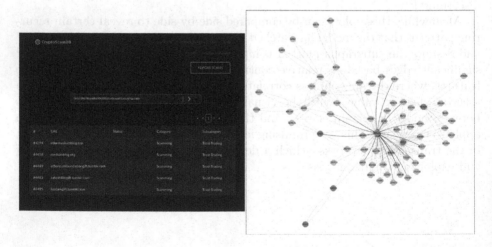

Fig. 6. A correctly identified Ethereum phishing scam address, 0x5208d7f63a089 906889a5a9caed81e9c889e64f8, and its subgraph of significant nodes. The node under scrutiny has the id 86626, in the center. The nodes are coloured as such - pink:unflagged, cyan:illicit and purple:licit.

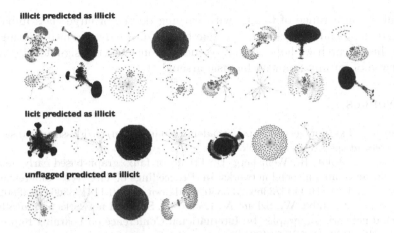

Fig. 7. Comparison of significant subgraphs for nodes predicted as illicit.

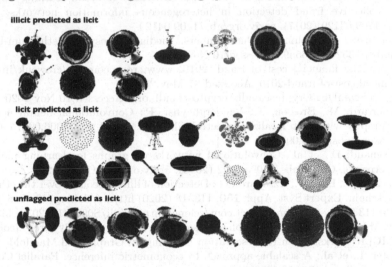

Fig. 8. Comparison of significant subgraphs for nodes predicted as licit.

6 Conclusion

In conclusion, Graph Convolutional Networks are a powerful deep learning tool, with the superior ability to tackle large and highly imbalanced datasets. By modelling transactional data as a graph structure, there is opportunity to supply far more information into a model: topology, patterns of relations, neighborhood characterisation and proximity to revealing nodes. Graph Convolutional Networks have the power to easily incorporate this extra information without reliance on defining it all with arduous feature engineering. Furthermore, the deep learning nature of the model allows the discovery of latent patterns in the data relations, most likely unthought of. The result is superior classification capabilities on a range of tasks - with varying degree of large class imbalance. Taking on financial malpractice can seem like an unwieldy and intimidating task, but in this research we hope to convey and demonstrate the significant power of this new tool for any financial forensic arsenal.

References

1. Binance: Txs per second (tps). academy.binance.com/en/glossary/transactions-per-second-tps. Accessed 16 Nov 2020
2. Breuer, A., Eilat, R., Weinsberg, U.: Friend or faux: graph-based early detection of fake accounts on social networks. In: Proceedings of The Web Conference 2020. https://doi.org/10.1145/3366423.3380204 dx.doi.org/10.1145/3366423.3380204
3. Bruna, J., Zaremba, W., Szlam, A., Lecun, Y.: Spectral networks and locally connected networks on graphs. In: International Conference on Learning Representations (ICLR2014), CBLS, (2014)
4. Cao, B., Mao, M., Viidu, S., Yu, P.S.: Hitfraud: a broad learning approach for collective fraud detection in heterogeneous information networks. CoRR abs/1709.04129 (2017). arxiv.org/abs/1709.04129
5. Consensys: Ethereum by the numbers. media.consensys.net/ethereum-by-the-numbers-3520f44565a9. Accessed 16 Nov 2020
6. Crowe: the financial cost of fraud, 2019. www.crowe.com/uk/croweuk/insights/financial-cost-of-fraud-2019. Accessed 31 May 2020
7. CryptoScamDB: Cryptoscamdb. cryptoscamdb.org. Accessed 10 Nov 2020
8. Defferrard, M., Bresson, X., Vandergheynst, P.: Convolutional neural networks on graphs with fast localized spectral filtering. CoRR abs/1606.09375 (2016). arxiv.org/abs/1606.09375
9. Duvenaud, D., et al.: Convolutional networks on graphs for learning molecular fingerprints. CoRR abs/1509.09292 (2015). arxiv.org/abs/1509.09292
10. Farrugia, S., Ellul, J., Azzopardi, G.: Detection of illicit accounts over the ethereum blockchain. Expert Syst. Appl. **150**, 113318 (2020) https://doi.org/10.1016/j.eswa.2020.113318. www.sciencedirect.com/science/article/pii/S0957417420301433
11. Fey, M., Lenssen, J.E.: Fast graph representation learning with PyTorch Geometric. In: ICLR Workshop on Representation Learning on Graphs and Manifolds (2019)
12. Foster, I., et al.: A scalable approach to econometric inference. Parallel Comput. Technol. Trends **36**, 59 (2020)
13. Hooi, B., Song, H., Beutel, A., Shah, N., Shin, K., Faloutsos, C.: Fraudar: bounding graph fraud in the face of camouflage, pp. 895–904 (2016). https://doi.org/10.1145/2939672.2939747
14. Hu, B., Zhang, Z., Shi, C., Zhou, J., Li, X., Qi, Y.: Cash-out user detection based on attributed heterogeneous information network with a hierarchical attention mechanism (2019)
15. Kipf, T.N., Welling, M.: Semi-supervised classification with graph convolutional networks. CoRR abs/1609.02907 (2016). arxiv.org/abs/1609.02907
16. Li, M., Perrier, E., Xu, C.: Deep hierarchical graph convolution for election prediction from geospatial census data. In: The Thirty-Third AAAI Conference on Artificial Intelligence, AAAI 2019, The Thirty-First Innovative Applications of Artificial Intelligence Conference, IAAI 2019, The Ninth AAAI Symposium on Educational Advances in Artificial Intelligence, EAAI 2019, Honolulu, Hawaii, USA, pp. 647–654. AAAI Press (2019). https://doi.org/10.1609/aaai.v33i01.3301647. doi.org/10.1609/aaai.v33i01.3301647

17. Liang, C., Liu, Z., Liu, B., Zhou, J., Li, X., Yang, S., Qi, Y.: Uncovering insurance fraud conspiracy with network learning. In: Proceedings of the 42nd International ACM SIGIR Conference on Research and Development in Information Retrieval (2019). https://doi.org/10.1145/3331184.3331372
18. Liu, Z., Chen, C., Yang, X., Zhou, J., Li, X., Song, L.: Heterogeneous graph neural networks for malicious account detection. In: Proceedings of the 27th ACM International Conference on Information and Knowledge Management (2018). https://doi.org/10.1145/3269206.3272010
19. Ma, J., Zhang, D.: Graphrad : A graph-based risky account detection system (2018)
20. McGinn, D., McIlwraith, D., Guo, Y.: Toward open data blockchain analytics: a bitcoin perspective. CoRR abs/1802.07523 (2018). arxiv.org/abs/1802.07523
21. McNulty, P.: A tale of two sectors: the challenges of corporate compliance (2009), keynote speech, Compliance Week (2009)
22. Nilforoshan, H., Shah, N.: Slicendice: mining suspicious multi-attribute entity groups with multi-view graphs. In: 2019 IEEE International Conference on Data Science and Advanced Analytics (DSAA) (2019). https://doi.org/10.1109/dsaa.2019.00050
23. Pareja, A., et al.: Evolvegcn: evolving graph convolutional networks for dynamic graphs. CoRR abs/1902.10191 (2019). arxiv.org/abs/1902.10191
24. Wang, D., et al.: A semi-supervised graph attentive network for financial fraud detection. In: 2019 IEEE International Conference on Data Mining (ICDM) (2019). https://doi.org/10.1109/icdm.2019.00070
25. Wang, J., Wen, R., Wu, C., Huang, Y., Xion, J.: Fdgars: fraudster detection via graph convolutional networks in online app review system. In: Companion Proceedings of The 2019 World Wide Web Conference. WWW '19, Association for Computing Machinery, pp. 310–316. New York, NY, USA (2019). https://doi.org/10.1145/3308560.3316586
26. Wang, M., et al.: Deep graph library: a graph-centric, highly-performant package for graph neural networks. arXiv preprint arXiv:1909.01315 (2019)
27. Weber, M., et al.: Anti-money laundering in bitcoin: experimenting with graph convolutional networks for financial forensics (2019)
28. Wen, R., Wang, J., Wu, C., Xiong, J.: Asa: adversary situation awareness via heterogeneous graph convolutional networks, pp. 674–678 (04 2020). https://doi.org/10.1145/3366424.3391266
29. Ying, R., Bourgeois, D., You, J., Zitnik, M., Leskovec, J.: Gnnexplainer: generating explanations for graph neural networks (2019)
30. Zhang, Y., Fan, Y., Ye, Y., Zhao, L., Shi, C.: Key player identification in underground forums over attributed heterogeneous information network embedding framework. In: Proceedings of the 28th ACM International Conference on Information and Knowledge Management. CIKM '19, Association for Computing Machinery, pp. 549–558. New York, NY, USA (2019). https://doi.org/10.1145/3357384.3357876
31. Zhong, Q., Liu, Y., Ao, X., Hu, B., Feng, J., Tang, J., He, Q.: Financial defaulter detection on online credit payment via multi-view attributed heterogeneous information network. In: Proceedings of The Web Conference 2020. WWW '20, Association for Computing Machinery, pp. 785–795. New York, NY, USA (2020). https://doi.org/10.1145/3366423.3380159

A Reasoning Approach to Financial Data Exchange with Statistical Confidentiality

Luigi Bellomarini[1(✉)], Livia Blasi[1], Rosario Laurendi[1], and Emanuel Sallinger[2,3]

[1] Banca d'Italia, Roma, Italy
Luigi.Bellomarini@bancaditalia.it
[2] TU Wien, Vienna, Austria
[3] University of Oxford, Oxford, England

Abstract. Motivated by our experience with the Bank of Italy, in this work we present Vada-SA, a reasoning framework for financial data exchange with statistical confidentiality. By reasoning on the interplay of the features that may lead to identity disclosure, the framework is able to guarantee explainable, declarative, and context-aware confidentiality.

1 Introduction and Problem Setting

Financial data exchange with statistical confidentiality is the problem of safely sharing financial datasets between institutions, preventing the disclosure of the identities referred to in datasets—for instance companies or individuals—while minimizing the amount of lost information. Identity disclosure may be direct, for example due to the leak of an identifying feature, or indirect, if the knowledge of a statistically uncommon n-tuple of features, technically a "quasi-identifier", allows an attacker to make plausible assumptions about the subjects' identity.

This extended abstract of a recently published work [2] is based on our experience with confidential financial data exchange in the business of the Bank of Italy. In particular, a central bank witnesses the problem in multiple sectors, from *banking supervision* to *anti-money laundering*, from *open banking* to *economic and statistical research*. Consider for example an excerpt from a dataset about inflation and growth—used for economic research purposes—in Fig. 1. The *quasi-identifiers* of a dataset (denoted by Q in the figure) are those attributes whose values can jointly disclose the subjects' identity when the dataset is published, by potentially appearing in uncommon combinations. An example is $\{Area, Sector, Employees\}$, in our dataset. The *sampling weight* (W) is an estimation of the representativeness of a tuple in the whole population. If uncommon combinations correspond to low sampling weights, like in row 4, the publication of the record will likely lead to the so-called *statistical disclosure*.

Statistical disclosure control [10] is a broad and relevant topic to which many have contributed especially from the statistics community [4,12,14,16]. Different

---

The views and opinions expressed in this paper are those of the authors and do not necessarily reflect the official policy or position of Banca d'Italia.

M. Kamp et al. (Eds.): ECML PKDD 2021 Workshops, CCIS 1525, pp. 226–231, 2021.
https://doi.org/10.1007/978-3-030-93733-1_16

| | Q | Q | Q | Q | Q | W |
	Area	Sector	Employees	Residential Rev.	Export Rev.	
1	North	Public Service	50-200	0-30	0-30	230
2	South	Commerce	201-1000	0-30	90+	190
3	Center	Commerce	1000+	0-30	30-60	70
4	North	Textiles	1000+	90+	0-30	10
5	North	Construction	1000+	90+	0-30	50
6	North	Other	1000+	0-30	0-30	70
7	North	Other	201-1000	60-90	90+	300
8	North	Textiles	201-1000	60-90	30-60	230
9	South	Public Service	50-200	0-30	0-30	123
10	South	Commerce	1000+	0-30	0-30	145

Fig. 1. A sample of a dataset about inflation and growth.

angles on the problem have been provided within the area of *differential privacy* [6]. Moreover, the importance of the problem witnessed the rise of a number of dedicated software solutions [5, 7, 9, 11, 15]. However, it is our experience that important desiderata are still not covered by existing approaches. In particular, modern solutions are required to be *explainable*, in the sense that the possible confidentiality leaks as well as anonymization countermeasures should be precisely motivated and sustain accountability, *declarative*, as business experts should be only asked to statically classify the dataset features while being relieved from any coding burden, and *context aware*, to intercept identity disclosure as a result of indirect and domain-specific combinations of the features.

In this work we consider these needs and present VADA-SA, a framework for financial data exchange with statistical confidentiality based on a principled combination of logic-based reasoning in the VADALOG System [1] and custom variants of statistical techniques such as risk scoring and anonymization.

2   The VADA-SA Framework

The VADA-SA framework embodies our vision of reasoning-based applications [3]: it is structured as the combination of a *ground extensional component*—the original dataset to anonymize with its basic metadata, an *intensional component*—a formal description of the techniques to assess the disclosure risk and perform the anonymization—expressed with a KRR (*Knowledge Representation and Reasoning*) language—and a *derived extensional component*—obtained as a result of the application of the *reasoning process* to the ground extensional component, to produce the outcome of risk assessment and anonymization.

Figure 2 shows the architecture of VADA-SA. The statistical disclosure control process is handled in VADA-SA through the iterative application of two *reasoning tasks*, jointly named *anonymization cycle*: the *risk analysis*, that estimates the risk of disclosure associated with a dataset, and the *anonymization*, removing the minimum amount of information to fulfill the confidentiality requirements.

The KRR language adopted in VADA-SA is VADALOG [1], a Datalog-based language with a favourable compromise between computational complexity and

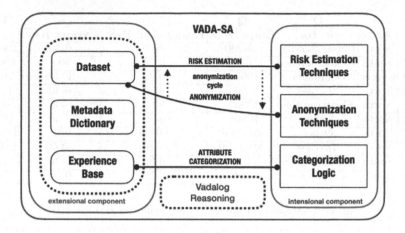

Fig. 2. The VADA-SA architecture.

expressive power. A VADALOG *reasoning task* is formulated through a set of rules, first-order implications of the form $\forall \mathbf{x}\, \phi(\mathbf{x}) \rightarrow \exists \mathbf{z}\, \psi(\mathbf{y}, \mathbf{z})$, where $\phi(\mathbf{x})$ (the *body*) and $\psi(\mathbf{y}, \mathbf{z})$ (the *head*) are conjunctions of atoms over a relational schema and boldface variables denote vectors of variables, with $\mathbf{x} \subseteq \mathbf{y}$. We write these existential rules omitting the universal quantifiers and using commas to denote conjunction of atoms. The semantics of rules is given by the CHASE procedure [8]: intuitively, the chase modifies the extensional component by generating facts until all the reasoning rules are satisfied. The existential quantification in the rule heads is satisfied via the creation of variable data values, known as *labelled nulls*. An implementation of the language is offered by the VADALOG System [1], a state-of-the-art logic-based reasoner. Let us now analyze the reasoning rules encoding the anonymization cycle.

$$\mathrm{Val}(M, I, A, V), \mathrm{Cat}(M, A, C), C = \text{Quasi-identifier},$$
$$\mathrm{VSet} = union((A, V)) \rightarrow \mathrm{Tuple}(M, I, \mathrm{VSet}) \qquad (\alpha)$$
$$\mathrm{Tuple}(M, I, \mathrm{VSet}), \#\mathrm{risk}(I, R), R > T \rightarrow \#\mathrm{anonymize}(I) \qquad (\beta)$$
$$\mathrm{Tuple}(M, I, \mathrm{VSet}), \#\mathrm{risk}(I, R), R \leq T \rightarrow \mathrm{Tuple}_A(M, I, \mathrm{VSet}) \qquad (\gamma)$$

M denotes the dataset to be anonymized. Each tuple has an artificial identifier I. Rule α creates `Tuple` facts for every tuple of M and collects (union) all the attribute-value pairs for the quasi-identifiers of M and the sampling weight into the set variable VSet. Extensional facts of the form `Cat`(dataset, attribute, category) are human-provided metadata storing the category C (i.e., identifier, quasi-identifier, weight, non-identifier, etc.) for an attribute A. If a tuple I violates a risk threshold T, an `anonymize` fact is produced for I, by Rule β.

The atom `#risk` returns the risk R associated to a given tuple I, while `#anonymize` produces new facts for `Tuple`. This mechanism induces a recursion into Rule β, so as to anonymize the tuples that do not pass the risk evaluation. Rule γ copies the validated facts to be returned to `Tuple`$_A$. In the rest of this

		Q	Q	Q		
		Area	**Sector**	**Employees**	**Residential Revenue**	**F**
	1	Roma	Textiles	1000+	0-30	1
	2	Roma	Commerce	1000+	0-30	2
(a)	3	Roma	Commerce	1000+	0-30	2
	4	Roma	Financial	1000+	0-30	2
	5	Roma	Financial	1000+	0-30	2
	6	Milano	Construction	0-200	60-90	1
	7	Torino	Construction	0-200	60-90	1

		Q	Q	Q		
		Area	**Sector**	**Employees**	**Residential Revenue**	**F**
	1	Roma	$\perp_1$	1000+	0-30	5
	2	Roma	Commerce	1000+	0-30	3
(b)	3	Roma	Commerce	1000+	0-30	3
	4	Roma	Financial	1000+	0-30	3
	5	Roma	Financial	1000+	0-30	3
	6	Milano	Construction	0-200	60-90	1
	7	Torino	Construction	0-200	60-90	1

Fig. 3. Local suppression with labelled nulls.

section we show how we model in VADALOG some of the risk evaluation and anonymization techniques offered by VADA-SA.

k-anonymity is a threshold approximation of *re-identification risk estimation* [13]. A set of quasi-identifiers is considered dangerous if the number of occurrences within the dataset is under a threshold k, and safe otherwise.

In Fig. 3a, for the quasi-identifiers *Area* and *Sector*, there is only one occurrence for "Roma" and "Textiles" (tuple 1). We say that the set of pairs $\{\langle \text{Area}, \text{Roma}\rangle, \langle \text{Sector}, \text{Textiles}\rangle\}$, having frequency $f = 1$ violates k-anonymity for $k = 2$. The VADALOG encoding follows (the suffix/prefix "*" denotes a Python-like packing/unpacking operator to turn arguments into name-value sets and vice versa).

$$\text{Tuple}(M, I, \text{VSet}), \text{riskInput}(I), R = count(I, groupBy(*\text{VSet}))$$
$$\rightarrow \text{TupleQ}(R, *\text{VSet}) \quad (\zeta)$$
$$\text{Tuple}(M, I, *\text{VSet}), \text{TupleQ}(R_1, \text{VSet}), R = case\ R_1 < k\ then\ 1\ else\ 0$$
$$\rightarrow \text{riskOutput}(I, R) \quad (\eta)$$

Local Suppression is an anonymization method where dangerous quasi-identifiers are removed to reduce the statistical disclosure risk. In VADA-SA we replace them with labelled nulls and assume that a null can match with any other null or constant. This semantics, which we call *maybe-match*, is a variant of the usual one, where nulls can match only with other nulls having the same label. Figures 3a and 3b show a dataset before and after the local suppression. The n-tuple frequency is on the right. By replacing the value "Textiles" with a null $\perp_1$ in tuple 1, the frequency of many n-tuples of quasi-identifiers increases, reducing the disclosure risk. Our technique is expressed in VADALOG as follows.

$$\text{Tuple}(M, I, \text{VSet}), \text{anonymize}(I)$$
$$\rightarrow \exists Z \; \text{Tuple}(M, I, \{(A, Z)\} \cup (\text{VSet} \setminus \{(A, \_)\})) \tag{ω}$$

3   Experiments

We tested VADA-SA with real-world (R25A4W) and synthetic (R25A4V-U) datasets to assess its *anonymization capability* and *scalability*.

Anonymization Capability. Figure 4a presents the nulls injected by *local suppression* varying the k of k-anonymity. When k is increased, the anonymization cycle is less tolerant. An average real-world dataset requires less than 50 labelled nulls for $25k$ tuples with 5-*anonymity*; unbalanced versions (R25A4V-U) require more labelled nulls. Figure 4b compares the number of nulls injected using our *maybe-match* semantics (in blue) vs. the standard semantics. The *maybe-match* semantics minimizes the number of new nulls, reducing the information loss.

Scalability. Figure 4c shows anonymization times with datasets from $6k$ to $100k$ tuples and different risk estimation techniques, detailed in the full paper [2]. Our approach has a linear trend, with k-anonymity exhibiting a very good behaviour, with elapsed time between 6 and 192 s for $100k$ tuples.

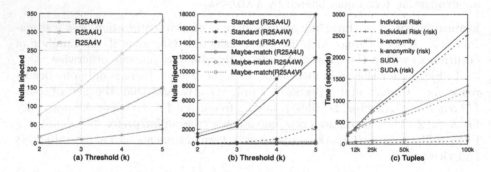

Fig. 4. (a) Nulls injected by k-anonymity threshold. (b) Nulls injected with maybe-matching viz. standard semantics. (c) Execution time by dataset size and risk estimation technique.

4   Conclusion

We presented VADA-SA, a reasoning-based statistical disclosure control framework. The adoption of a fully *declarative* approach conveys *explainability* and business friendliness to our approach, with a logic-based language that is easy to grasp for users. Rules are an ideal means to capture specific business domain notions that may affect confidentiality, maximizing *context awareness*.

References

1. Bellomarini, L., Benedetto, D., Gottlob, G., Sallinger, E.: Vadalog: A modern architecture for automated reasoning with large knowledge graphs. Inf. Syst., 101528 (2020)
2. Bellomarini, L., Blasi, L., Laurendi, R., Sallinger, E.: Financial data exchange with statistical confidentiality: a reasoning-based approach. In: EDBT, pp. 558–569 (2021)
3. Bellomarini, L., Fakhoury, D., Gottlob, G., Sallinger, E.: Knowledge graphs and enterprise AI: the promise of an enabling technology. In: ICDE, pp. 26–37. IEEE (2019)
4. Benedetti, R., Franconi, L.: Statistical and technological solutions for controlled data dissemination. In: Pre-proceedings of New Techniques and Technologies for Statistics. vol. 1, pp. 225–232 (1998)
5. Benschop, T., Machingauta, C., Welch, M.: Statistical disclosure control: a practice guide (2019)
6. Dwork, C.: Differential privacy. In: Bugliesi, M., Preneel, B., Sassone, V., Wegener, I. (eds.) Automata, Languages and Programming, pp. 1–12. Springer Berlin Heidelberg, Heidelberg (2006)
7. Hundepool, A., et al.: τ-argus user's manual, version 3.3. Statistics Netherlands, Voorburg, The Netherlands (2005)
8. Maier, D., Mendelzon, A.O., Sagiv, Y.: Testing implications of data dependencies. TODS 4(4), 455–468 (1979)
9. Manning, A.M., Haglin, D.J., Keane, J.A.: A recursive search algorithm for statistical disclosure assessment. Data Mining Knowl. Discov. 16(2), 165–196 (2008)
10. Matthews, G., Harel, O.: Data confidentiality: a review of methods for statistical disclosure limitation and methods for assessing privacy. Stat. Surv. 5 (2011)
11. Prasser, F., Kohlmayer, F.: Putting statistical disclosure control into practice: the ARX data anonymization tool. In: Gkoulalas-Divanis, A., Loukides, G. (eds.) Medical Data Privacy Handbook. Springer, Cham (2015). https://doi.org/10.1007/978-3-319-23633-9_6
12. Samarati, P.: Protecting respondents identities in microdata release. IEEE Trans. Knowl. Data Eng. 13(6), 1010–1027 (2001)
13. Samarati, P., Sweeney, L.: Protecting privacy when disclosing information: k-anonymity and its enforcement through generalization and suppression (1998)
14. Skinner, C., Marsh, C., Openshaw, S., Wymer, C.: Disclosure control for census microdata. JOS 10(1), 31–51 (1994)
15. Sweeney, L.: Guaranteeing anonymity when sharing medical data, the datafly system. In: Proceedings of AMIA Fall Symposium, pp. 51–55 (1997)
16. Sweeney, L.: Achieving k-anonymity privacy protection using generalization and suppression. Int. J. Uncertain. Fuzziness Knowl. Based Syst. 10(05), 571–588 (2002)

Forecasting Longevity for Financial Applications: A First Experiment with Deep Learning Methods

Jorge M. Bravo[✉] [iD]

NOVA IMS - Universidade Nova de Lisboa, Université Paris-Dauphine PSL, MagIC,
CEFAGE-UE, Lisbon, Portugal
jbravo@novaims.unl.pt

Abstract. Forecasting longevity is essential in multiple research and policy areas,
including the pricing of life insurance contracts, the valuation of capital market solutions for longevity risk management, and pension policy. This paper
empirically investigates the predictive performance of Recurrent Neural Networks
(RNN) with Gated Recurrent Unit (GRU) and Long Short-Term Memory (LSTM)
architectures in jointly modeling and multivariate time series forecasting of age-
specific mortality rates at all ages. We fine-tune the three hidden layers GRU
and LSTM model's hyperparameters for time series forecasting and compare the
model's forecasting accuracy with that produced by traditional Generalised Age-
Period-Cohort (GAPC) stochastic mortality models. The empirical results suggest
that the two RNN architectures generally outperform the GAPC models investigated in both the male and female populations, but the results are sensitive to the
accuracy criteria. The empirical results also show that the RNN-GRU network
slightly outperforms the RNN with an LSTM architecture and can produce mortality schedules that capture relatively well the dynamics of mortality rates across
age and time. Further investigations considering other RNN architectures, calibration procedures, and sample datasets are necessary to confirm the superiority
of RNN in forecasting longevity.

Keywords: Mortality forecasting · RNN · LSTM · GRU · Deep learning ·
Pensions · Insurance

1 Introduction

Forecasts of age-specific mortality and survival rates are essential to understand the
dynamics of human survivorship, for the pricing and risk management of life insurance contracts (e.g., life annuities), for the pricing of novel capital market solutions
for longevity risk management (e.g., longevity bonds, longevity swaps, q-forwards, S-
forwards, K-forwards, longevity caps & floors), to predict the future size and age structure
of the national and/or subnational resident population, to characterize population aging
(Coughlan et al. 2007; Bravo and Silva 2006; Blake et al. 2019; UN 2020; Bravo 2016,
2019, 2021a; Simões et al. 2021).

© Springer Nature Switzerland AG 2021
M. Kamp et al. (Eds.): ECML PKDD 2021 Workshops, CCIS 1525, pp. 232–249, 2021.
https://doi.org/10.1007/978-3-030-93733-1_17

Survival forecasts are fundamental to evaluate the overall health, well-being, and human development of a population, and for assessing the long-term sustainability of national public pension and retirement income schemes. For instance, in recent decades linking earnings-related pension benefits to life expectancy developments observed at retirement ages is one of the major pension reform trends (Bravo and Herce 2020; Ayuso et al. 2021a, 2021b). The link has been established in multiple ways, for instance, automatically indexing the normal (and early) retirement ages to life expectancy (e.g., Italy, The Netherlands, Denmark, Portugal, UK), linking the entry pensions to the so-called sustainability factors (e.g., Finland, Spain) or to life annuity factors or transformation coefficients (e.g., Sweden, Italy, Norway, Poland), connecting the eligibility requirements to the contribution length (e.g., France), introducing longevity-linked life annuities in public and private retirement income schemes (e.g., USA), indexing pension indexation to aging markers (Bovenberg et al. 2015; Bravo and El Mekkaoui 2018; Bravo 2020, 2021). The ongoing COVID-19 pandemic outbreak has highlighted the importance of having good epidemiological, mortality, and life expectancy (Big) data in assessing the impact of public health shocks on health care systems, in quantifying the lost years due to specific causes of death, in planning for proper policy responses, in comparing the effectiveness of containment measures across countries and regions (Ashofteh and Bravo 2020, 2021c; Islam et al. 2021).

In actuarial, financial, and demographic applications, the most common approach to mortality forecasting is to select a unique discrete-time or continuous-time stochastic mortality model from the restricted set of candidate methods using some criteria (e.g., BIC, cross-validation) or procedure (see, e.g., Lee and Carter (1992); Currie (2006); Cairns et al. (2006); Plat (2009); Hyndman et al. (2013); Bravo and Nunes (2021); Li et al. (2021) and references therein). The empirical studies in this area show, however, that it is hard to find (if exists) a single widely accepted mortality forecasting method that performs consistently better across all countries, populations, and time horizons (e.g., Dowd et al. 2010). Because of that, and to consider model risk, a recent competing strand of the literature recommends the use of a Bayesian Model Ensemble (BME) of heterogeneous age-period-cohort stochastic mortality models (Kontis et al. 2017; Bravo et al. 2021; Shang and Haberman 2018; Ayuso et al. 2021b; Ashofteh and Bravo 2021a, 2021b; Bravo and Ayuso, 2020, 2021).

A recent but emerging line of research involves the use of statistical learning, machine learning, and deep learning methods to model and forecast age-specific mortality rates for actuarial and financial applications. The few papers in this area include Deprez et al. (2017) and Hong et al. (2021), who use machine learning techniques to investigate the fitting and forecasting accuracy, Hainaut (2018) who experiments with neural networks to predict mortality rates, Nigri et al. (2019) and Richman and Wüthrich (2019a, 2019b) that combine the classical Lee–Carter model with Recurrent Neural Networks (RNN) to generate forecasts over single or multiple populations, and Bravo (2021c) that preliminary investigates the forecasting accuracy of RNN with LSTM networks using Portuguese data.

Against this background, this paper empirically investigates the predictive performance of Recurrent Neural Networks (RNN) with two popular alternative architectures

— Gated Recurrent Unit (GRU) and Long Short-Term Memory (LSTM) — in multivariate mortality forecasting for financial applications. RNNs are dynamic neural networks extending Feedforward Neural Networks (FNN) to tackle time series problems. RNN incorporates an internal memory to process time series of data as inputs, with the output from the previous iteration being carried forward as input to the current step. Plain vanilla RNN has limited capacity to capture the long-term trends in longevity data and to produce accurate forecasts because of the vanishing effect of gradients when training the network using back-propagation (Bengio et al. 2002). RNNs with GRU or LSTM architecture overcome the short-term memory problem of vanilla RNN considering both the short and long-term dependencies in the data sequences.

The RNN models are calibrated to generate forecasts of age-specific mortality rates for both the male and female populations in a coherent way. We empirically investigate the sensitivity of the forecasting results against alternative hyperparameters choices in three hidden layers GRU and LSTM models (units for each layer, epochs, optimizer, number of hidden neurons). We compare the forecasting accuracy of RNN with that produced by traditional well-known Generalised Age-Period-Cohort (GAPC) stochastic mortality models. The study expands previous analyses in Bravo (2021c) by considering two competing RNN architectures and an extended list of GAPC benchmarks. The selected GAPC benchmarks have proven to fit and forecast well diverse mortality schedules (Dowd et al. 2010). The empirical strategy uses mortality data (deaths and exposure-to-risk classified by sex, age, calendar year, and birth cohort) for Italy from 1960 to 2017 (the latest available year). The data source is the Human Mortality Database (2021). To measure the forecasting accuracy, we use a backtesting approach with a 10-year holding period (test set), common to all models and populations.

The empirical results suggest that the two RNN architectures calibrated to jointly process the male and female age-specific mortality rates generally outperform the four GAPC models investigated in both the male and female populations, but the results are sensitive to the accuracy criteria. The results also show that the RNN-GRU network slightly outperforms the RNN with an LSTM architecture and can produce mortality schedules that capture relatively well the dynamics of mortality rates across age and time, including at younger ages where the increased volatility and the mortality hump make it more difficult to generate consistent and biologically plausible mortality schedules. Further investigation considering alternative RNN architectures, different short and long training sets and look-forward periods, and alternative populations is however required to confirm the robustness of these preliminary results and the superiority of deep learning methods when compared to consolidated GAPC models.

The remainder of the paper is organized as follows. In Sect. 2, we describe the materials and methods used in this study, namely the RNN with LSTM and GRU architecture, the generalised age-period-cohort models used as the benchmark, the methods used to compute period life annuity prices, and the datasets. Section 3 presents and briefly discusses the empirical results. Section 4 concludes and sets up the agenda for further research.

2 Materials and Methods

2.1 Generalised Age-Period-Cohort Stochastic Mortality Models

Following Hunt and Blake (2021) and Bravo (2021a, 2021b), let us denote by $D_{x,t,g}$ the number of deaths observed at age x during calendar year t from the population (country, sex) g initially ($E^0_{x,t,g}$) or centrally ($E^c_{x,t,g}$) exposed-to-risk. GAPC models link a response variable (death probability $q_{x,t,g}$; mortality intensity $\mu_{x,t,g}$) to an appropriate linear predictor $\eta_{x,t,g}$, capturing the systematic effects of age x, time t and year-of-birth (cohort) $c = t - x$, defined as,

$$\eta_{x,t,g} = \alpha_x + \sum_{i=1}^{N} \beta_x^{(i)} \kappa_t^{(i)} + \beta_x^{(0)} \gamma_{t-x}, \tag{1}$$

where $exp(\alpha_x)$ denotes the general shape of the mortality schedule across age, $\beta_x^{(i)} \kappa_t^{(i)}$ is a set of N age-period terms describing the mortality trends, with each time index $\kappa_t^{(i)}$ specifying the general mortality trend and $\beta_x^{(i)}$ capturing its specific effect across ages, the term γ_{t-x} models cohort effects, with $\beta_x^{(0)}$ depicting its effect across ages. In this paper, we consider as benchmarks for the RNN architectures the analytical substructures proposed by Lee and Carter (1992), Currie (2006), Cairns et al. (2006), and Plat (2009), summarized in Table 1.

Table 1. GAPC models: Analytical structure of the linear predictor

Model	Linear predictor analytical structure	Reference
LC	$\eta_{x,t,g} = \alpha_x + \beta_x^{(1)} \kappa_t^{(1)}$	Lee & Carter (1992)
APC	$\eta_{x,t,g} = \alpha_x + \kappa_t^{(1)} + \gamma_{t-x}$	Currie (2006)
CBD	$\eta_{x,t,g} = \kappa_t^{(1)} + (x - \bar{x})\kappa_t^{(2)}$	Cairns et al. (2006)
Plat	$\eta_{x,t,g} = \alpha_x + \kappa_t^{(1)} + (x - \bar{x})\kappa_t^{(2)} + \gamma_{t-x}$	Plat (2009)

Source: Author's preparation

The (canonical) link function $g(\cdot)$ connects the random and the systematic components, i.e., $g\left(\mathbb{E}(D_{x,t,g}/E_{x,t,g})\right) = \eta_{x,t}$. The specification is complemented with assumptions regarding the statistical distribution (Poisson, Binomial) of the number of deaths and a set of parameter constraints to guarantee unique parameter estimates. Estimates of the parameters are obtained via maximum-likelihood methods. To calibrate the models, all GAPC structures are trained on the training set years $T_1^{train} = \{t \in T, 1960 \leq t \leq 2007\}$ and predictive performance was assessed on $T_1^{test} = \{t \in T, 2008 \leq t \leq 2017\}$. To generate mortality forecasts, we proceed as usual and assume that the age-specific vectors $\hat{\alpha}_x$ and $\hat{\beta}_x^{(i)}$ remain constant over time and model $\hat{\kappa}_t^{(i)}$ and $\hat{\gamma}_{t-x}$ using univariate ARIMA(p,d,q) time series methods. We make multi-step 10-year out-of-sample age-specific mortality rate forecasts, from which period life annuity (and life expectancy) prices are computed as follows:

$$a_{x,g}^{P}(t) := \sum_{k=1}^{\omega-x} \left(1 + r_{0,k}\right)^{-k} \times {}_{k}p_{x,t,g}, \tag{2}$$

where $r_{0,k}$ is the spot interest rate for maturity k, ${}_{k}p_{x,t,g}$ is the k-year survival probability for an individual aged x at time t, and ω is the highest attainable age in the life table. For both sexes and all years, we close life tables at the age of 125 years old.

2.2 RNN with LSTM Architecture

Hochreiter and Schmidhuber (1997) developed RNN with an LSTM network considering the short and long-term dependencies in time series of data to overcome the short-term memory problem of vanilla RNN. The network blocks incorporate internal mechanisms (gates) which regulate the flow of information, learning which data in a time series is worthy to keep or to discard at the time of producing forecasts. Following Richman & Wüthrich (2019a), Nigri et al. (2019) and Bravo (2021c), let $(x_1, \ldots, x_T)$ denote a time series of data (age-specific mortality rates) with components $x_t \in \mathbb{R}^{\tau_0}$ observed at times $t = 1, \ldots, T$. Our goal is to use this data as input (explanatory) variables (features) to forecast a given output data $y \in \mathcal{Y} \subset \mathbb{R}$. A typical LSTM unit comprises three gates (an input gate, a forget gate, and an output gate) which control the flow of information into and out of the cell, their interactions, and the subsequent memory cell (Fig. 1). The unit receives as initial information flow the output from the previous short-term memory LSTM unit $h_{t-1} \in \mathbb{R}^h$, with $h \in \mathbb{N}$ denoting the number of LSTM blocks in a hidden layer, the current input $x_t \in \mathbb{R}^{\tau_0}$, and the long-term memory of the previous unit $c_{t-1} \in \mathbb{R}^h$.

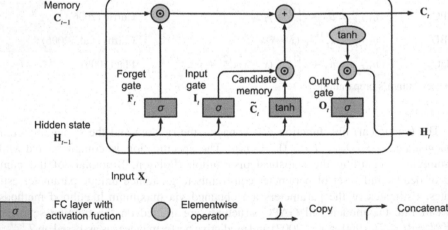

Fig. 1. Schematic representation of a Long Short-Term Memory (LSTM) unit. Source: Zhang et al. (2021).

The data is processed by three gates named forget gate f_t, input gate i_t and output gate o_t, respectively, and auxiliary neural networks assisting in the normalization of the information flow. The forget gate (loss of memory rate) combines the previous unit state h_{t-1} and the current input x_t in a nonlinear way using the sigmoid activation function $\sigma(\cdot)$ to determine how much information from the past c_{t-1} is carried forward to the next units. The input gate (memory update rate) uses the sigmoid function to decide how much input data should be used to update the memory of the network, with the hyperbolic tangent activation function $\phi(\cdot)$ controlling for the importance of the values which are passed. Finally, in the output gate (release of memory information rate) the data input x_t, the new (updated) memory c_t, the previous output h_{t-1} and a bias vector is used to determine the output to the next LSTM unit.

Let $W \in \mathbb{R}^{\tau_0 \times h}$ and $U \in \mathbb{R}^{h \times h}$ denote the weight matrices for the input and the previous short-term result gates, respectively. The RNN with LSTM architecture can be formally described by the following set of equations:

$$f_t = \sigma\left(W_f x_t + U_f h_{t-1} + b_f\right), \tag{3}$$

$$i_t = \sigma(W_i x_t + U_i h_{t-1} + b_i), \tag{4}$$

$$o_t = \sigma(W_o x_t + U_o h_{t-1} + b_o), \tag{5}$$

$$\tilde{c}_t = \phi(W_c x_t + U_c h_{t-1} + b_c), \tag{6}$$

$$c_t = c_{t-1} \circ f_t \circ i_t \circ \tilde{c}_t \tag{7}$$

$$h_t = \phi(c_t) \circ o_t, \tag{8}$$

$$\sigma(x) = \frac{1}{1 + e^{-x}} \in (0, 1), \tag{9}$$

$$\phi(x) = \frac{e^x - e^{-x}}{e^x + e^{-x}} \in (-1, 1), \tag{10}$$

with initial values $c_0 = 0$ and $h_0 = 0$, and where $f_t \in \mathbb{R}^h$, $i_t \in \mathbb{R}^h$, $o_t \in \mathbb{R}^h$ and $z_t \in \mathbb{R}^h$ represent the outputs of the forget gate, input gate, output gate, and the auxiliary-output gate, respectively. The symbol $\circ$ denotes the Hadamard product (element-wise product). The output $h_t \in \mathbb{R}^h$ of the LSTM block is passed to the next layer and became the short memory input for the next instance. We empirically investigate different choices of the hyperparameters of the three hidden layers LSTM model (units for each layer) considering for 10-year forecasting horizons, 500 epochs, the Adaptive Moment Estimation (Adam) optimizer, and the Mean Squared Error (MSE) as loss function.

2.3   RNN with GRU Architecture

Cho et al. (2014) introduced GRU to solve the short-term memory problem of vanilla RNN. GRU share many similarities with LSTM, namely the basic idea of using a gating mechanism (update/reset gate) to learn from long-term dependencies and to decide which and how much past information should be forwarded to the output, but there are some important differences (Fig. 2). First, contrary to LSTM that has three gates, a GRU has only two gates and does not have the output gate that decides how much to reveal of a cell. Second, a GRU does not include an internal memory differing from the exposed hidden state. The input and forget gates are linked by an update gate z_t and the reset gate r_t is applied directly to the previous hidden state. In a GRU, the decision to erase or not a cell (the forget gate in an LSTM) is break up into both z_t and r_t.

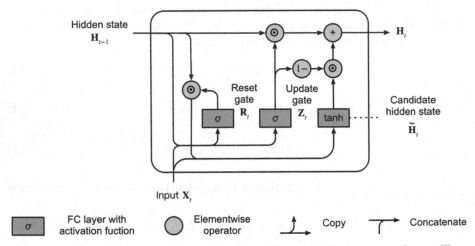

Fig. 2. Schematic representation of a Gated Recurrent Unit (GRU) block structure. Source: Zhang et al. (2021).

The RNN with GRU architecture are formally described by the set of equations:

$$r_t = \sigma(W_r x_t + U_r h_{t-1} + b_r), \tag{11}$$

$$z_t = \sigma(W_z x_t + U_z h_{t-1} + b_z), \tag{12}$$

$$\tilde{h}_t = \phi(W_h x_t + (r_t \circ h_{t-1})U_h + b_h), \tag{13}$$

$$h_t = z_t \circ h_{t-1} + (1 - z_t) \circ \tilde{h}_t. \tag{14}$$

Like in LSTM, we empirically investigate different choices of the hyperparameters of the three hidden layers GRU network considering for 10-year forecasting horizons, 500 epochs, the Adam optimizer, and the MSE as loss function.

2.4 Forecasting Accuracy Metrics

To measure the out-of-sample forecasting error, we use alternative accuracy metrics, namely the Mean Squared Error (MSE), the Mean Absolute Error (MAE), and the Symmetric Mean Absolute Percentage Error (SMAPE), defined as follows:

$$MSE_g = \frac{1}{N} \sum_{t=t_{min}}^{t_{max}} \sum_{x=x_{min}}^{x_{max}} \left(\mu_{x,t,g} - \hat{\mu}_{x,t,g} \right)^2, \tag{15}$$

$$MAE_g = \frac{1}{N} \sum_{t=t_{min}}^{t_{max}} \sum_{x=x_{min}}^{x_{max}} \left| \mu_{x,t,g} - \hat{\mu}_{x,t,g} \right|, \tag{16}$$

$$SMAPE_g = \frac{1}{N} \sum_{x=x_{min}}^{x_{max}} \sum_{t=t_{min}}^{t_{max}} \frac{\left| \hat{\mu}_{x,t,g} - \mu_{x,t,g} \right|}{0.5 \left(\hat{\mu}_{x,t,g} + \mu_{x,t,g} \right)}, \tag{17}$$

with $N = (x_{max} - x_{min} + 1)(t_{max} - t_{min} + 1)$.

2.5 Data

The mortality data used in this study is from the Human Mortality Database (2021). The datasets comprise the number of recorded deaths $D_{x,t,g}$ and the corresponding exposure-to-risk (population counts) $E_{x,t,g}$ by individual age x ($\mathcal{X} = \{x \in \mathbb{N}, 0 \leq x \leq 110+\}$), calendar year $\mathcal{T} = \{t \in \mathbb{N}, 1960 \leq t \leq 2017\}$, year of birth $c = t - x$ and sex for Italy. Figure 3 plots the raw age-specific log-mortality rates $\widehat{m}_{x,t,g}$ by year and sex for selected ages in the range 0 to 90 years old. Figure 4 represents a heatmap and a contour plot of the raw log-mortality rates by age, year, and sex.

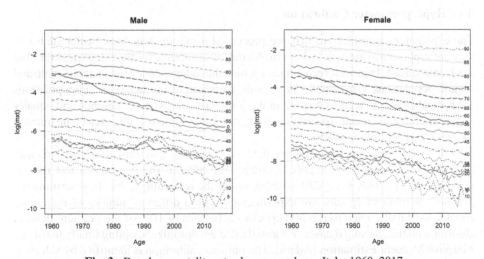

Fig. 3. Raw log-mortality rates by year and sex, Italy, 1960–2017

Mortality trends in Italy in the last 60 years exhibit a clear downward trend at all ages and for both sexes, with more significant longevity improvements observed at younger

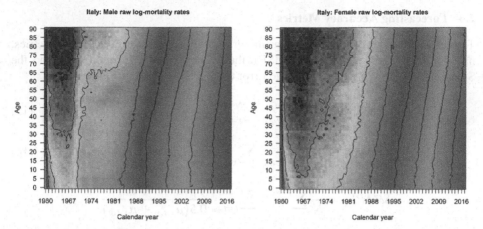

Fig. 4. Heatmap and contour plots of raw log-mortality rates by age and sex, Italy, 1960–2017. Notes: for both sexes, the orange (blue) color represents low (high) mortality rates.

ages and between women. Like in most countries of the world, Italian women have, on average, higher survival prospects than men of all ages. This is also evident in Fig. 4. The marginally upward sloping and diagonal structure of the contour lines and colors in both heatmaps confirms that longevity gains have been shifting steadily from younger ages to adult and old ages.

3   Results

3.1   Hyperparameter Calibration

The explanatory variables are first pre-processed using the Min-Max Scaler such that they are supported in the $[-1;1]$ domain. An indicator variable for the categorical variable sex is introduced. In most forecasting exercises, the independence between the male and female populations is assumed. As a result, forecasts of mortality for subpopulations are not coherent and tend to diverge in the long term. To assure coherence and equally consistent forecasts of age-specific mortality rates, we alternate both sexes in the training dataset when calibrating RNNs.

For model learning, the training data is randomly split into a learning dataset $\left(\mathcal{T}_1^{train} = \{t \in \mathcal{T}, 1960 \leq t \leq 2007\}\right)$ comprising 80% of the data and a test dataset $\left(\mathcal{T}_1^{test} = \{t \in \mathcal{T}, 2008 \leq t \leq 2017\}\right)$ comprising the remaining 20%. To determine the optimum number of epochs, we experimented with a different number of maximum epochs, but finally opted to run 500 epochs (in batches of 100) of the gradient descent algorithm on the learning dataset. We tested different optimizers, opting finally to use the Adaptive Moment Estimation (Adam). The optimal calibration is identified by selecting the lowest MSE loss in the test set using a call-back procedure.

We investigated 72 different three hidden layers GRU and LSTM architectures by exploring all possible combinations in the array $\tau_0 = \{1, 3, 5\}$, $\tau_1 = \{3, 5, 10, 20\}$, $\tau_2 = \{5, 10, 15\}$ and $\tau_3 = \{5, 10\}$. The MSE, MAE, and SMAPE error on $\mathcal{T}_1^{test}$ measure the forecasting accuracy between the alternative GAPC and RNN models tested. The best GRU and LSTM networks (the models with the lowest MSE error) were re-trained on T_1^{train}, and forecasts of $\hat{\mu}_{x,t,g}$ on T_1^{test} were generated. The model fitting, forecasting, and simulation procedures have been implemented using an R software routine.

Table 2 and Table 3 summarize the average fitting and forecasting losses obtained in the joint calibration of both sexes' mortality schedules

Table 2. GRU3: fitting/forecasting loss metrics for different hyperparameter combinations

GRU				MSE (in 10^{-5})			CPU	GRU				MSE (in 10^{-5})			CPU
τ_0	τ_1	τ_2	τ_3	Fit	Men	Wo	time	τ_0	τ_1	τ_2	τ_3	Fit	Men	Wo	time
1	3	5	5	0.56	0.28	0.33	121	1	3	5	10	0.85	1.71	1.28	116
3	3	5	5	1.82	3.80	3.34	129	3	3	5	10	0.56	0.45	0.42	118
5	3	5	5	0.48	0.59	0.76	134	5	3	5	10	0.63	0.31	1.21	117
1	5	5	5	0.57	0.72	0.50	127	1	5	5	10	0.79	0.83	0.70	744
3	5	5	5	0.91	2.60	2.45	129	3	5	5	10	0.66	0.20	0.36	122
5	5	5	5	1.02	1.64	2.05	140	5	5	5	10	0.54	0.45	0.72	127
1	10	5	5	0.79	0.34	0.50	135	1	10	5	10	0.60	0.38	0.46	139
3	10	5	5	0.63	0.91	0.89	132	3	10	5	10	1.27	1.78	1.21	142
5	10	5	5	0.49	0.41	1.41	135	5	10	5	10	0.59	0.20	0.35	144
1	20	5	5	1.01	0.66	0.15	150	1	20	5	10	1.50	0.77	0.13	551
3	20	5	5	0.67	1.75	1.70	152	3	20	5	10	0.49	0.64	0.36	164
5	20	5	5	0.70	3.12	3.84	136	5	20	5	10	1.06	2.52	2.68	885
1	3	10	5	0.57	0.78	0.57	127	1	3	10	10	0.74	0.55	0.38	136
3	3	10	5	0.61	0.78	1.19	124	3	3	10	10	0.48	1.18	1.63	469
5	3	10	5	0.61	0.82	0.95	128	5	3	10	10	0.70	0.93	0.23	139
1	5	10	5	0.45	0.29	0.35	122	1	5	10	10	0.61	0.70	0.51	686
3	5	10	5	1.68	3.07	2.80	118	3	5	10	10	0.65	0.37	0.75	142
5	5	10	5	1.05	2.49	2.33	117	5	5	10	10	2.59	2.96	2.60	357
1	10	10	5	1.06	2.80	1.99	120	1	10	10	10	0.49	1.04	1.04	149
3	10	10	5	0.87	1.63	1.57	119	3	10	10	10	0.41	0.59	0.95	145
5	10	10	5	0.73	0.91	0.83	118	5	10	10	10	0.38	0.55	1.17	184
1	20	10	5	0.46	0.38	0.25	133	1	20	10	10	1.04	1.98	1.01	256
3	20	10	5	0.44	0.59	1.07	132	3	20	10	10	0.72	2.62	1.97	241
5	20	10	5	0.79	2.02	1.57	134	5	20	10	10	0.61	1.59	1.78	247
1	3	15	5	1.40	1.13	0.94	120	1	3	15	10	0.56	0.36	0.14	219
3	3	15	5	0.52	0.52	0.91	121	3	3	15	10	0.55	0.56	0.94	206
5	3	15	5	1.07	1.09	1.73	120	5	3	15	10	0.98	0.20	0.62	188
1	5	15	5	0.69	0.54	0.10	156	1	5	15	10	0.49	0.16	0.15	202
3	5	15	5	0.58	0.43	0.95	121	3	5	15	10	0.45	0.55	0.41	193
5	5	15	5	0.83	1.66	2.18	120	5	5	15	10	0.66	0.27	1.00	175
1	10	15	5	0.66	1.29	1.30	122	1	10	15	10	0.48	1.01	0.89	178
3	10	15	5	0.46	0.59	1.04	121	3	10	15	10	0.46	0.73	0.60	161
5	10	15	5	1.82	4.17	3.20	122	5	10	15	10	0.46	0.97	2.14	150
1	20	15	5	0.50	0.53	0.43	137	1	20	15	10	1.05	1.96	1.05	164
3	20	15	5	0.96	0.43	0.20	144	3	20	15	10	0.48	0.42	0.72	185
5	20	15	5	0.39	0.56	1.21	141	5	20	15	10	1.00	2.52	2.04	186

Notes: τ_0, τ_1, τ_2 and τ_3 denote the number of hidden neurons in the hidden GRU layers; Run times measured in seconds on a personal laptop with Intel(R) Core(TM) i7-10510U CPU @ 2.30GHz with 16GB RAM; Average results for the joint calibration of the male and female populations obtained considering for 10-year fitting (lookback) and forecasting horizons, 500 epochs (for batch sizes 100), and the Adaptive Moment Estimation (Adam) optimizer for all the GRU and LSTM hyperparameter combinations. The results show that the RNN-$GRU_3(\tau_0 = 1; \tau_1 = 5; \tau_2 = 15; \tau_3 = 10)$ and the RNN-$LSTM_3(\tau_0 = 1; \tau_1 = 20; \tau_2 = 10; \tau_3 = 10)$ produced the best forecasting error results.

Table 3. LSTM3: fitting/forecasting loss metrics for different hyperparameter combinations

τ_0	τ_1	τ_2	τ_3	Fit	Men	Wo	CPU time	τ_0	τ_1	τ_2	τ_3	Fit	Men	Wo	CPU time
	LSTM			MSE (in 10^{-5})					LSTM			MSE (in 10^{-5})			
1	3	5	5	0.67	0.56	0.61	96	1	3	5	10	1.05	0.86	0.87	106
3	3	5	5	1.18	1.61	1.22	102	3	3	5	10	0.73	0.41	0.61	99
5	3	5	5	1.28	1.17	1.03	96	5	3	5	10	1.22	0.51	0.78	96
1	5	5	5	0.94	1.00	0.98	101	1	5	5	10	1.14	2.15	1.61	97
3	5	5	5	0.79	1.00	1.32	100	3	5	5	10	1.04	1.18	1.60	97
5	5	5	5	1.02	1.77	2.46	93	5	5	5	10	0.70	0.78	1.01	97
1	10	5	5	1.17	1.04	1.08	108	1	10	5	10	0.60	0.47	0.44	98
3	10	5	5	0.93	0.76	0.59	111	3	10	5	10	0.65	0.19	0.42	98
5	10	5	5	0.83	0.92	1.08	98	5	10	5	10	0.73	0.52	0.79	116
1	20	5	5	0.78	0.70	0.67	111	1	20	5	10	1.74	2.60	1.29	108
3	20	5	5	1.65	2.14	2.04	115	3	20	5	10	0.84	1.92	1.75	110
5	20	5	5	0.70	0.24	0.71	109	5	20	5	10	1.20	0.87	0.78	111
1	3	10	5	0.66	0.19	0.26	101	1	3	10	10	0.90	1.08	0.90	99
3	3	10	5	0.96	1.37	0.92	107	3	3	10	10	0.70	0.50	0.93	98
5	3	10	5	0.66	0.68	0.99	111	5	3	10	10	0.91	1.16	1.45	98
1	5	10	5	1.22	1.76	1.18	113	1	5	10	10	0.99	1.31	1.05	99
3	5	10	5	0.86	1.47	1.67	108	3	5	10	10	2.05	3.10	2.40	98
5	5	10	5	0.93	1.02	1.71	113	5	5	10	10	1.03	1.80	1.94	113
1	10	10	5	0.75	0.24	0.42	126	1	10	10	10	0.67	0.54	0.64	164
3	10	10	5	1.44	2.08	1.68	114	3	10	10	10	0.62	0.35	0.64	252
5	10	10	5	0.70	0.45	0.95	107	5	10	10	10	0.71	0.49	0.28	251
1	20	10	5	0.72	0.58	0.56	109	1	20	10	10	0.63	0.17	0.16	288
3	20	10	5	1.26	0.83	1.00	110	3	20	10	10	0.80	1.52	1.37	312
5	20	10	5	1.08	2.03	1.57	113	5	20	10	10	0.56	0.38	0.64	321
1	3	15	5	0.83	0.65	0.69	113	1	3	15	10	0.68	0.26	0.33	296
3	3	15	5	1.75	1.76	0.93	115	3	3	15	10	1.00	1.63	2.28	298
5	3	15	5	1.00	0.30	0.20	107	5	3	15	10	0.83	0.97	1.76	295
1	5	15	5	0.86	0.72	0.58	107	1	5	15	10	0.76	0.56	0.80	298
3	5	15	5	1.20	1.33	1.12	105	3	5	15	10	0.78	0.31	0.67	298
5	5	15	5	0.92	0.52	1.15	105	5	5	15	10	0.59	0.50	0.91	261
1	10	15	5	0.64	0.64	0.36	112	1	10	15	10	0.88	0.54	0.52	279
3	10	15	5	0.89	0.89	0.84	115	3	10	15	10	0.53	0.72	1.16	273
5	10	15	5	0.65	0.40	0.71	105	5	10	15	10	0.64	0.92	1.61	279
1	20	15	5	0.76	0.96	0.77	121	1	20	15	10	1.07	1.49	1.06	306
3	20	15	5	0.92	0.24	0.87	129	3	20	15	10	1.20	1.88	1.63	299
5	20	15	5	0.68	0.49	0.77	130	5	20	15	10	0.91	1.04	1.05	308

Notes: τ_0, τ_1, τ_2 and τ_3 denote the number of hidden neurons in the hidden LSTM layers; Run times measured in seconds on a personal laptop with Intel(R) Core(TM) i7-10510U CPU@2.30GHz with 16GB RAM; Average results for the joint calibration of the male and female populations obtained considering for 10-year fitting (lookback) and forecasting horizons, 500 epochs (for batch sizes 100), and the Adaptive Moment Estimation (Adam) optimizer

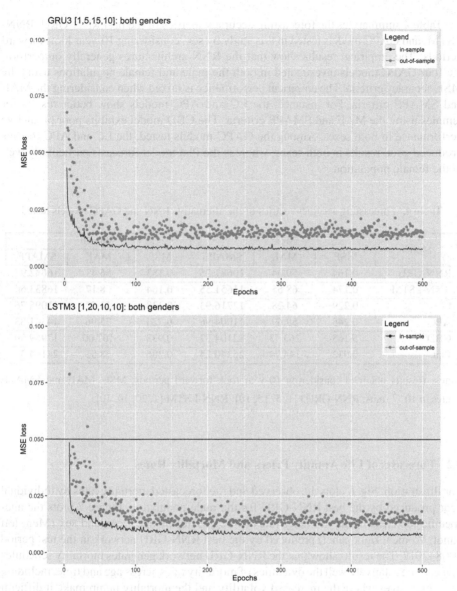

Fig. 5. Best RNN architectures: Early stopping in-sample MSE loss (cyan color) and out-of-sample loss (coral color) (Color figure online)

Figure 5 illustrates the learning strategy on the best RNN GRU and LSTM architectures, plotting the early stopping in-sample and the out-of-sample loss on the test dataset.

Table 4 summarizes the forecasting accuracy metrics of the best RNN-GRU, RNN-LSTM, and GAPC models tested in this study by sex, considering 10-year look-forward periods. The empirical results show that the RNN architectures generally outperform the four GAPC models investigated in both the male and female populations using the MSE accuracy criteria. The empirical performance is mixed when considering the MAE and SMAPE criteria. For instance, the LC and APC models show better results for females using the MAE and SMAPE criteria. The CBD model exhibits poor predictive performance in both sexes. Among the GAPC models tested, the LC and APC models produced good results in both sexes, whereas the Plat model forecasts particularly well in the female population.

Table 4. Forecasting accuracy metrics of the alternative RNN and GAPC models tested

Model	Men			Women		
	MSE	MAE	SMAPE	MSE	MAE	SMAPE
RNN-GRU	0.164	59.04	10681.25	0.153	56.43	16642.97
RNN-LSTM	0.174	68.65	11651.55	0.164	58.17	16833.64
LC	0.229	64.28	12716.93	0.338	53.57	11095.76
APC	0.245	59.69	11004.96	0.724	75.96	14341.83
CBD	5.165	263.73	12104.37	0.933	107.00	17969.50
Plat	0.932	144.74	25340.24	0.206	58.53	24114.35

Notes: Results obtained considering 10-year look-forward periods; MSE, MAE and SMAPE values in 10^{-5} units; RNN-GRU3 [1, 5, 15, 10]; RNN-LSTM [1, 20, 10, 10]

3.2 Forecasts of Life Annuity Prices and Mortality Rates

For illustration, Fig. 6 plots the observed and the forecasted mortality rates by individual year produced by the best RNN-GRU for the male population. Figure 7 plots the age-specific forecasts of the mortality rates (in log scale) by age, year, and sex (Men, left panel; Women, right panel) produced by the best RNN-GRU network in the test period 2008–2017. The results show that the RNN-GRU network generates mortality schedules that capture relatively well the dynamics of mortality rates across age and time, including at younger ages where the increased volatility and the mortality hump make it difficult to generate consistent and biologically plausible mortality schedules.

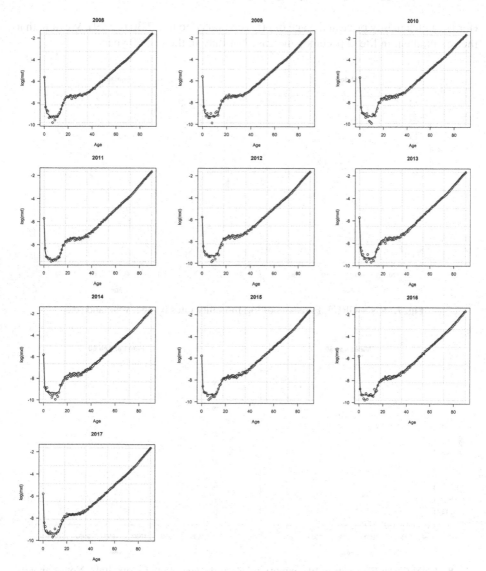

Fig. 6. RNN-GRU3: Forecasts of log-mortality rates by age and year, male population, Italy

Figure 8 represents the estimates of the life annuity prices at the benchmark retirement age of 60 ($x = 60$) by sex, from 1960 to 2017, computed from the survival curves forecasted using the RNN with GRU architecture. The vertical dotted line marks the split between the training and test datasets. The results highlight the long-term positive trends in period life annuity (and life expectancy) at retirement ages. As of 1960, the male (female) life annuity price at the age of 60 is estimated to be 12.99 (14.84). The forecast (and observed) results suggest that longevity increases will maintain a positive (almost linear) trend. This translates into higher annuity prices. As of 2017, the male (female) life annuity price at the age of 60 is estimated to be 17.30 (19.79). We note that the sex gradient in life expectancy increased in Italy in the last 60 years.

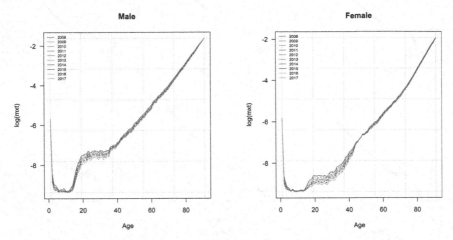

Fig. 7. RNN-GRU3: Forecasts of log-mortality rates by age, year, and sex

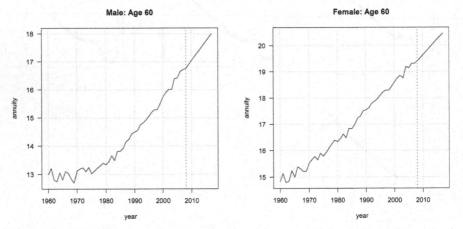

Fig. 8. RNN-GRU: Forecasts of life annuity prices at the age of 60, by sex, Italy. Notes: annuity prices computed assuming a flat yield curve at 2%.

4 Conclusion

Model selection and model combination are currently the two competing approaches when modelling and forecasting mortality, often using statistical learning methods. Yet, little research has been conducted to investigate the comparative forecasting accuracy of traditional GAPC models against novel deep learning methods. In this paper, we conducted a preliminary investigation on the predictive performance of RNN with GRU and LSTM architectures in jointly modelling age- and sex-specific mortality using data for Italy and compared results with that produced by GAPC models. The empirical results suggest that the two RNN architectures investigated produce mortality schedules that capture relatively well the dynamics of mortality rates across age and time, outperforming the benchmark GAPC models, but the results are sensitive to the accuracy criteria. The RNN-GRU network slightly outperforms the RNN with an LSTM architecture in the training data. Further research investigating other RNN designs, other populations, alternative calibration procedures, is however needed to confirm or reject the superiority of RNN models in modelling longevity trends. Extensions to modeling mortality by socioeconomic group are particularly interesting because of the increasing attention to life expectancy gradients by income or education group, and the need to correct for actuarial unfairness in public pension schemes (see, e.g., Bravo et al., 2021; Ayuso et al., 2021a). Extension to multiple state mortality models with longevity heterogeneity considering Markov-ageing approaches is also important to the fair pricing of mortality-linked products (Chamboko and Bravo 2016, 2020). Despite the high predictive power of RNN against GAPC models, the lack or insufficient interpretability of neural networks in mortality modeling is one of the main barriers of deep learning techniques in its wide acceptance by the financial industry in applications such as life insurance pricing of longevity risk management. For instance, European Union regulations now offer individuals impacted by (e.g., personalised pricing) algorithms the right to receive a justification for why a model makes a particular decision under specific circumstances, and the chance to benefit from fair algorithmic competition.

References

Ashofteh, A., Bravo, J.M.: A study on the quality of Novel Coronavirus (Covid-19) official datasets. Stat. J. IAOS **36**(2), 291–301 (2020). https://doi.org/10.3233/SJI-200674

Ashofteh, A., Bravo, J. M.: A conservative approach for online credit scoring. Expert Syst. Appl. **176**, 1–16, (2021a). 114835. https://doi.org/10.1016/j.eswa.2021.114835

Ashofteh, A., Bravo, J.M.: Life table forecasting in COVID-19 times: an ensemble learning approach. In: 2021 16th Iberian Conference on Information Systems and Technologies (CISTI), 2021, pp. 1–6 (2021b). https://doi.org/10.23919/CISTI52073.2021.9476583. https://ieeexplore.ieee.org/document/9476583

Ashofteh, A., Bravo, J.M.: Data science training for official statistics: a new scientific paradigm of information and knowledge development in national statistical systems. Stat. J. IAOS **37**(3), 771–789 (2021c). https://doi.org/10.3233/SJI-210841

Ayuso, M., Bravo, J.M., Holzmann, R.: Getting life expectancy estimates right for pension policy: period versus cohort approach. J. Pens. Econ. Finan. **20**(2), 212–231 (2021). https://doi.org/10.1017/S1474747220000050

Ayuso, M., Bravo, J.M., Holzmann, R., Palmer, E.: Automatic indexation of pension age to life expectancy: when policy design matters. Risks **9**(5), 96 (2021). https://doi.org/10.3390/risks9050096

Bengio, Y., Simard, P.Y., Frasconi, P.: Learning long-term dependencies with gradient descent is difficult. IEEE Trans. Neur. Netw. **5**, 157–166 (2002)

Blake, D., Cairns, A.J.G., Dowd, K., Kessler, A.R.: Still living with mortality: the longevity risk transfer market after one decade. Br. Actuar. J. **24**, 1–80 (2019)

Bovenberg, L., Bilsen, S., Mehlkopf, R.: Personal pensions with risk sharing affordable, adequate and stable private pensions in Europe. Netspar Discussion Paper Series 03–2015 (2015)

Bravo, J.M.: Taxation of pensions in portugal: a semi-dual income tax system. CESifo DICE Rep. J. Inst. Comp. **14**(1), 14–23 (2016)

Bravo, J.M.: Funding for longer lives: retirement wallet and risk-sharing annuities. Ekonomiaz **96**(2), 268–291 (2019)

Bravo, J.M.: Longevity-linked life annuities: a bayesian model ensemble pricing approach. In: CAPSI 2020 Proceedings, 29 (Atas da 20ª Conferência da Associação Portuguesa de Sistemas de Informação 2020). (2020). https://aisel.aisnet.org/capsi2020/29

Bravo, J.M.: Pricing participating longevity-linked life annuities: a Bayesian Model ensemble approach. Europ. Act. J. (2021a). https://doi.org/10.1007/s13385-021-00279-w

Bravo, J.M.: Pricing survivor bonds with affine-jump diffusion stochastic mortality models. In: 2021 The 5th International Conference on E-commerce, E-Business and E-Government (ICEEG 2021). Association for Computing Machinery (ACM), New York, NY, USA. (2021b). https://doi.org/10.1145/3466029.3466037

Bravo, J.M.: Forecasting mortality rates with recurrent neural networks: a preliminary investigation using Portuguese data. In: CAPSI 2021 Proceedings (Atas da 21ª Conferência da Associação Portuguesa de Sistemas de Informação 2021), in press (2021c)

Bravo, J.M., Ayuso, M.: Mortality and life expectancy forecasts using bayesian model combinations: An application to the portuguese population. RISTI - Revista Ibérica de Sistemas e Tecnologias de Informação, E40, pp. 128–144 (2020). https://doi.org/10.17013/risti.40.128-145

Bravo, J.M., Ayuso, M.: Forecasting the retirement age: a bayesian model ensemble approach. In: Rocha, Á., Adeli, H., Dzemyda, G., Moreira, F., Ramalho Correia, A.M. (eds.) WorldCIST 2021. AISC, vol. 1365, pp. 123–135. Springer, Cham (2021). https://doi.org/10.1007/978-3-030-72657-7_12

Bravo, J.M., El Mekkaoui de Freitas, N.: Valuation of longevity-linked life annuities. Insur. Math. Econ. **78**, 212–229 (2018)

Bravo, J.M., Herce, J.A.: Career breaks, broken pensions? long-run effects of early and late-career unemployment spells on pension entitlements. J. Pens. Econ. Finan. 1–27 (2020). https://doi.org/10.1017/S1474747220000189

Bravo, J.M., Nunes, J.P.V.: Pricing longevity derivatives via fourier transforms. Insur. Math. Econ. **96**, 81–97 (2021)

Bravo, J.M., Silva, C.: Immunization using a stochastic process independent multifactor model: the portuguese experience. J. Bank. Finan. **30**(1), 133–156 (2006)

Bravo, J.M., Ayuso, M., Holzmann, R., Palmer, E.: Addressing the life expectancy gap in pension policy. Insur. Math. Econ. **99**, 200–221 (2021). https://doi.org/10.1016/j.insmatheco.2021.03.025

Chamboko, R., Bravo, J.M.: On the modelling of prognosis from delinquency to normal performance on retail consumer loans. Risk Manage. **18**(4), 264–287 (2016)

Chamboko, R., Bravo, J.M.: A multi-state approach to modelling intermediate events and multiple mortgage loan outcomes. Risks **8**, 64 (2020). https://doi.org/10.3390/risks8020064

Cho, K., Van Merriënboer, B., Bahdanau, D., Bengio, Y.: On the properties of neural machine translation: encoder-decoder approaches. arXiv preprint (2014). arXiv:1409.1259

Coughlan, G.D., Epstein, D., Honig, P.: Q-forwards: derivatives for transferring longevity and mortality risks. Working Paper, J. P. Morgan Pension Advisory Group, London (2007)

Currie, I.: Smoothing and forecasting mortality rates with p-splines. Institute and Faculty of Actuaries, London (2006). https://www.actuaries.org.uk/documents/smoothing-and-forecasting-mortality-rates-p-splines-handouts. Accessed on 20 Jul 2018

Deprez, P., Shevchenko, P.V., Wüthrich, M.V.: Machine learning techniques for mortality modeling. Eur. Actuar. J. **7**(2), 337–352 (2017). https://doi.org/10.1007/s13385-017-0152-4

Dowd, K., Cairns, A., Blake, D., Coughlan, G., Epstein, D., Khalaf-Allah, M.: Backtesting stochastic mortality models. North Am. Act. J. **14**(3), 281–298 (2010)

Hainaut, D.: A neural-network analyzer for mortality forecast. Astin Bull. **48**, 481–508 (2018)

Hochreiter, S., Schmidhuber, J.: Long short-term memory. Neural Comput. **9**(8), 1735–1780 (1997)

Hong, W.H., Yap, J.H., Selvachandran, G., et al.: Forecasting mortality rates using hybrid Lee-Carter model, artificial neural network and random forest. Comp. Intell. Syst. **7**, 163–189 (2021)

Hunt, A., Blake, D.: On the structure and classification of mortality models. North Am. Act. J. **25**(sup1), S215–S234 (2021)

Hyndman, R.J., Booth, H., Yasmeen, F.: Coherent mortality forecasting: the product-ratio method with functional time series models. Demography **50**(1), 261–283 (2013)

Islam, N., et al.: Excess deaths associated with covid-19 pandemic in 2020: age and sex disaggregated time series analysis in 29 high income countries, BMJ, 373, n1137 (2021)

Kontis, V., Bennett, J., Mathers, C., Li, G., Foreman, K., Ezzati, M.: Future life expectancy in 35 industrialised countries: projections with a Bayesian model ensemble. Lancet **389**(10076), 1323–1335 (2017)

Lee, R.D., Carter, L.: Modeling and forecasting U.S. mortality. J. Am. Stat. Assoc. **87**, 659–671 (1992)

Li, H., Tan, K.S., Tuljapurkar, S., Zhu, W.: Gompertz law revisited: forecasting mortality with a multi-factor exponential model. Insur. Math. Econ. **99**, 268–281 (2021)

Nigri, A., Levantesi, S., Marino, M., Scognamiglio, S., Perla, F.: A deep learning integrated lee-carter model. Risks **7**(1), 33 (2019). https://doi.org/10.3390/risks7010033

Richman, R., Wüthrich, M.: A neural network extension of the Lee-Carter model to multiple populations. Ann. Act. Sci. **15**(2), 1–21 (2019). https://doi.org/10.1017/S1748499519000071

Richman, R., Wüthrich, M.: Lee and Carter go Machine Learning: Recurrent Neural Networks (2019b). https://ssrn.com/abstract=3441030. Accessed on 10 Jan 2021

Simões, C., Oliveira, L., Bravo, J.M.: Immunization strategies for funding multiple inflation-linked retirement income benefits. Risks **9**(4), 60 (2021). https://doi.org/10.3390/risks9040060

United Nations: Human Development Report 2020. United Nations Development Programme, Washington (2020)

Zhang, A., Lipton, Z., Li, M., Smola, A.: Dive into deep learning. arXiv:2106.11342 (2021)

Sixth Workshop on Data Science for Social Good (SoGood 2021)

Workshop on Data Science for Social Good (SoGood 2021)

The Sixth Workshop on Data Science for Social Good (SoGood 2021) was held in conjunction with the European Conference on Machine Learning and Principles and Practice of Knowledge Discovery in Databases (ECML PKDD 2021) on September 18, 2021. The conference and workshop were scheduled to take place in Bilbao (Basque Country, Spain), but due to the COVID-19 pandemic they were held fully virtually. The previous five editions of the workshop were also held jointly with ECML PKDD in 2016–2020.

The possibilities of using data science for contributing to social, common, or public good are often not sufficiently perceived by the public at large. Data science applications are already helping people at the bottom of the economic pyramid or people with special needs, improving healthcare systems, reinforcing international cooperation, and dealing with environmental problems, disasters, and climate change. In regular conferences and journals, papers on these topics are often scattered among sessions with names that hide their common nature (such as "social networks", "predictive models" or the catch-all term "applications"). Additionally, such forums tend to have a strong bias for papers that are novel in the strictly technical sense (new algorithms, new kinds of data analysis, new technologies) rather than novel in terms of social impact of the application.

This workshop aims to attract papers presenting applications of data science for social good (which may or may not require new methods), or applications that consider social aspects of data science methods and techniques. It also aims to bring together researchers, students, and practitioners to share their experience and foster discussion about the possible applications, challenges, and open research problems, and to continue building a research community in the area of data science for social good.

There are numerous application domains; the call for papers included the following non-exclusive list of topics:

- Government transparency and IT against corruption
- Public safety and disaster relief
- Public policies in epidemic growth and related issues
- Access to food, water, and utilities
- Efficiency and sustainability
- Data journalism
- Economic, social, and personal development
- Transportation
- Energy
- Smart city services
- Education
- Social services, unemployment, and homelessness
- Healthcare
- Ethical issues, fairness, and accountability

- Trustability and interpretability
- Topics aligned with the UN Sustainable Development Goals:

http://www.un.org/sustainabledevelopment/sustainable-development-goals/

The workshop papers were selected through a peer-review process in which each submitted paper was assigned to three members of the Program Committee. The main selection criteria were the novelty of the application and its social impact. Eight papers were accepted for presentation.

The SoGood 2021 Best Paper Award was awarded to Sónia Teixeira, Guilherme Londres, Bruno Veloso, Rita P. Ribeiro, and João Gama for their paper "Improving Smart Waste Collection using AutoML". The best paper award committee included Geoff Holmes (University of Waikato, New Zealand), Emma Tonkin (University of Bristol, UK), and Cèsar Ferri (Technical University of Valencia, Spain).

The program included two keynotes:

- "The Humane AI Vision of AI for Social Good" by Paul Lukowicz (German Research Center for Artificial Intelligence (DFKI) and Technical University of Kaiserslautern, Germany)
- "The Personal and Social Dimensions of Human-centered AI" by Fosca Giannotti (Information Science and Technology Institute "A. Faedo", National Research Council, Pisa, Italy) and Dino Pedreschi (University of Pisa, Italy)

More information about the workshop, including the slides of the keynote talks, can be found on the workshop website: https://sites.google.com/view/ecmlpkddsogood2021/.

Many people contributed to making this workshop a successful event. We would like to thank Paul Lukowicz, Fosca Giannotti, and Dino Pedreschi for their excellent talks, the Program Committee members for their detailed and constructive reviews, the authors for their well-prepared presentations, all workshop attendees for their engagement and participation, and the University of Porto for providing partial support for the keynote speakers.

September 2021

Rita P. Ribeiro
Irena Koprinska
João Gama
Ricard Gavaldà

Organization

Workshop Co-chairs

Ricard Gavaldà	UPC BarcelonaTech, Spain
Irena Koprinska	University of Sydney, Australia
João Gama	University of Porto, Portugal
Rita P. Ribeiro	University of Porto, Portugal

Program Committee

Marta Arias	UPC BarcelonaTech, Spain
José Del Campo-Ávila	University of Málaga, Spain
Andre de Carvalho	University of São Paulo, Brazil
Elaine Faria	Federal University of Uberlandia, Brazil
Calros Ferreira	University of Porto, Portugal
Cèsar Ferri	Technical University of Valencia, Spain
Geoffrey Holmes	University of Waikato, New Zealand
Konstantin Kutzkov	Amalfi Analytics, Spain
Ana Lorena	Technological Institute of Aeronautics, Brazil
Rafael Morales-Bueno	University of Malaga, Spain
Nuno Moniz	University of Porto, Portugal
Ana Nogueira	INESC TEC, Portugal
Maria Pedroto	INESC TEC, Portugal
Sónia Teixeira	INESC TEC, Portugal
Emma Tonkin	University of Bristol, UK
Alicia Troncoso	University Pablo de Olavide, Spain
Martí Zamora	UPC BarcelonaTech, Spain

SoGood 2021 Keynote Talks

The Personal and Social Dimensions of Human-Centered AI

Fosca Giannotti[1] and Dino Pedreschi[2]

[1] Information Science and Technology Institute "A. Faedo", National Research Council (ISTI-CNR), Pisa, Italy
[2] University of Pisa, Italy

Abstract. The future of AI lies in enabling people to collaborate with machines to solve complex problems. Like any efficient collaboration, this requires good communication, trust, clarity, and understanding. On the other side, this also reveals a social dimension of AI, as increasingly complex socio-technical systems emerge, made by interacting people and intelligent agents. The talk will address both the individual and social dimension of such collaboration with a focus on: i) "Explainable AI" providing a reasoned introduction to the work and the research challenges to the work of Explainable AI for Decision Making (XAI); ii) the undesired emerging network effects of social AI systems, as well as the design of transparent mechanisms for decentralized collaboration and decentralized personal data ecosystems that help toward desired aggregate outcomes, e.g. toward the realization of the agreed set of values and objectives at collective levels, such as accessible and sustainable mobility in cities, diversity, and pluralism in the public, fair distribution of economic resources environmental sustainability, a fair and inclusive job market.

Biography

Fosca Giannotti is a director of research of computer science at the Information Science and Technology Institute "A. Faedo" of the National Research Council, Pisa, Italy. Fosca Giannotti is a pioneering scientist in mobility data mining, social network analysis and privacy-preserving data mining. Fosca leads the Pisa KDD Lab - Knowledge Discovery and Data Mining Laboratory, a joint research initiative of the University of Pisa and ISTI-CNR, founded in 1994 as one of the earliest research lab on data mining. Fosca's research focus is on social mining from big data: smart cities, human dynamics, social and economic networks, ethics and trust, diffusion of innovations. She is author of more than 300 papers. She has coordinated tens of European projects and industrial collaborations. Fosca is currently the coordinator of SoBigData, the European research infrastructure on Big Data Analytics and Social

Mining, an ecosystem of ten cutting edge European research centers providing an open platform for interdisciplinary data science and data-driven innovation. Recently she became the recipient of a prestigious ERC Advanced Grant entitled "XAI – Science and technology for the explanation of AI decision making"..

Dino Pedreschi is a Professor of Computer Science at the University of Pisa, and a pioneering scientist in mobility data mining, social network mining and privacy-preserving data mining. He co-leads with Fosca Giannotti the Pisa KDD Lab - Knowledge Discovery and Data Mining Laboratory, a joint research initiative of the University of Pisa and the Information Science and Technology Institute of the Italian National Research Council, one of the earliest research labs centered on data mining. His research focus is on big data analytics and mining and their impact on society. He is a founder of the Business Informatics MSc program at the University of Pisa, a course targeted at the education of interdisciplinary data scientists. Dino has been a visiting scientist at Barabasi Lab (Center for Complex Network Research) of Northeastern University, Boston (2009–2010), and earlier at the University of Texas at Austin (1989–1990), CWI Amsterdam (1993) and UCLA (1995). In 2009, Dino received a Google Research Award for his research on privacy-preserving data mining.

The Humane AI Vision of AI for Social Good

Paul Lukowicz

German Research Center for Artificial Intelligence (DFKI) and Technical
University of Kaiserslautern, Germany

Abstract. This talk presents the Humane AI project, the vision, challenges and
initial solutions in designing AI for social good.

Biography

Prof. Dr. Paul Lukowicz is both Scientific Director of
the German Research Center for Artificial Intelligence
(DFKI GmbH) in Kaiserslautern and Chair of
Embedded Intelligence in the Computer Science
Department at the TU of Kaiserslautern (TUK) since
2012. His main research areas are in context-specific,
wearable recognition systems which include pattern
recognition, system architectures, models, complex
self-organising systems and their applications.

Ensuring the Inclusive Use of NLP in the Global Response to COVID-19

Alexandra Sasha Luccioni[1,2(✉)], Katherine Hoffmann Pham[1,3], Cynthia Sin Nga Lam[1], Joseph Aylett-Bullock[1,4], and Miguel Luengo-Oroz[1]

[1] United Nations Global Pulse, Newyork, UK
{sasha,katherine,cynthia,joseph,miguel}@unglobalpulse.org
[2] Mila Québec Artificial Intelligence Institute, Université de Montréal, Montreal, Canada
[3] NYU Stern School of Business, New York, USA
[4] Institute for Data Science, Durham University, Durham, United Kingdom

Abstract. Natural language processing (NLP) plays a significant role in tools for the COVID-19 pandemic response, from detecting misinformation on social media to helping to provide accurate clinical information or summarizing scientific research. However, the approaches developed thus far have not benefited all populations, regions or languages equally. We discuss ways in which current and future NLP approaches can be made more inclusive by covering low-resource languages, including alternative modalities, leveraging out-of-the-box tools and forming meaningful partnerships. We suggest several future directions for researchers interested in maximizing the positive societal impacts of NLP.

1 Introduction and Context

The COVID-19 pandemic has changed the way we live, work, and travel. In their response to the pandemic, governments and organizations have grappled with pandemic response, deploying numerous tools and initiatives, many of which leverage novel technologies to guide decision-making and build more resilient communities. Textual resources in particular have been critical in pandemic response, facilitating access to scientific information to guide research and enabling the detection of misinformation in the midst of the COVID-19 'infodemic' [6, 14]. Going forward, there is a continuing need for the use of NLP to facilitate the search for and dissemination of accurate information and to counter false narratives and vaccine skepticism. However, the availability, accessibility and use of these resources has been unequal, prioritizing certain languages and benefiting some communities more than others, exacerbating existing inequalities and widening the gap between those who have access to advanced digital technologies and those who do not [4].

To ensure the inclusive use of NLP in the global response to the COVID-19 pandemic, we argue that it is paramount to develop NLP tools that are both comprehensive and accessible, and to apply them in ways that maximize positive impact and minimize potential risks. In this commentary, we identify four areas that we find to be particularly important to achieving this goal: covering low-resource languages, including alternative modalities such as audio or video, using out-of-the-box tools where appropriate and forming meaningful partnerships to broaden access to technical and local expertise,

M. Kamp et al. (Eds.): ECML PKDD 2021 Workshops, CCIS 1525, pp. 259–266, 2021.
https://doi.org/10.1007/978-3-030-93733-1_18

as well as data and tools. We discuss each of these themes below, and conclude with a series of observations and considerations for future research.

2 Low-Resource Languages

While the exact number of existing languages is debated, estimates range anywhere from 6,000 to 7,000 [13]. However, current NLP technologies such as language models, datasets and tool kits have predominantly been developed for a limited number of 'high-resource' languages, which can leave large parts of the world behind. In the context of the COVID-19 pandemic response, where fighting the infodemic of misinformation and fake news has become a top priority, low-resource languages may also suffer a disadvantage since accurate information from verifiable sources can arrive with delays and gaps. Furthermore, while setting up a simple pipeline for detecting misinformation in English or French can take a few days using pre-trained models and tools, it can quickly become a multi-month, resource-intensive endeavor for underrepresented languages [7]. Finally although research initiatives for misinformation detection in low-resource languages do exist (e.g. [10, 18]), there have not been, to our knowledge, tools deployed for this purpose in the context of the COVID-19 pandemic.

There are many challenges to developing NLP tools for low-resource languages, ranging from regional variants that are hard to represent using standard language models (e.g. Arabic), to languages with predominantly oral traditions that have little or no written texts (e.g. Métis). However, the biggest bottleneck for developing language models and tools for low-resource languages remains data availability. For example, mainstream NLP approaches such as word embeddings and large language models are difficult to implement since there are few pre-compiled large text corpora available [24]. This has spurred promising research on NLP in low-data scenarios, with approaches ranging from few-shot and transfer learning [19,21,35] to data augmentation [15] and cross-lingual language models [8]. However, many languages remain under-served in terms of NLP resources and datasets, especially in the context of misinformation detection, which often requires customizing neural language models to encompass specific contexts and topics. In addition to further research developments in this area, it is important to promote the work of those teams compiling large datasets for previously low-resource languages [29,33]. Overall, the state of available resources for languages that are not mainstream is unfortunate and makes it difficult to deploy scalable NLP systems for these languages. Finally, more transparency should be established between existing commercial endeavors to detect fake news (such as those deployed by major social media websites) and researchers, since releasing datasets that have been flagged as misinformation by human moderators can help train NLP models to mimic this behavior.

3 Alternative Modalities

In addition to improving the coverage of underrepresented languages, analyzing data from a broader range of modalities could also help to expand the scope of NLP research. Given the need for rapid response to the COVID-19 pandemic, there has been a bias towards analysis of text or multimedia data sources that are easy to mine, such as Twitter. However, these types of content are created and consumed by only a fraction of the world's population, and are biased towards those with ready access to the internet. In other contexts, alternative channels such as radio, television, or messaging applications might be more common sources of information [27].

Radio in particular is a promising channel for studying opinions and discussions of emerging topics such as COVID-19. There are an estimated 44,000 radio stations worldwide (see e.g. http://radio.garden for a sample), and in the developing world radio stations typically have far wider and more consistent coverage than high-speed internet, with radios available to 75% of households [38]. Even in the United States, radios were estimated to reach 92% of adult listeners on a weekly basis as of 2019, exceeding the reach of any other channel [28]. Radio shows disseminate news, discuss current events, debate rumors, record spontaneous expressions of local opinions and capture information-seeking behavior. In the face of crises or natural disasters, radio may be one of the quickest and most reliable sources of information about the situation on the ground [25].

During the COVID-19 pandemic, researchers at the United Nations (UN) have used radio mining techniques in Uganda to monitor discussions relating to outbreaks and health system capacity, rumors and misinformation, and the socioeconomic impacts of COVID-19 [16]. Developing a radio-based NLP pipeline poses a number of distinct challenges. These include engineering challenges such as capturing and recording radio streams; efficiently managing the high volume of data collected; and transcribing audio recordings to text for further analysis. They also include technical challenges such as speaker disambiguation when multiple individuals are interacting in conversation; filtering out irrelevant content (e.g. commercials, news, and music); and identifying topic-relevant discussions through approximate keyword searches (for example, transcription may introduce new keyword variants – such as "Koby" and "cobi" when "COVID" is said by Spanish speakers). Given the relative lack of prior research on radio data, these challenges might pose fruitful areas for innovation in the NLP community.

Radio is just one of several possible alternative modalities; as noted above, other data sources of interest include television and informal messaging channels or even SMS-based question-and-answer forums. In addition to original research analyzing these channels, another potential direction for future work involves the creation of tools to better enable on-the-ground practitioners to engage with the NLP pipeline in order to analyze alternative data sources. Since much of the content on these alternative channels may involve informal language, local dialects, and context-specific references, allowing practitioners to filter, explore, and improve the output of NLP algorithms is particularly important in this setting. While original research is of vital importance, the use of out-of-the-box tools in NLP pipelines can avoid the duplication of efforts and provide operationally-ready interfaces for practitioners to interact with, which we discuss in further detail below. Some out-of-the box tools have already implemented such functionality for social media sources such as Twitter, as we discuss in further detail below.

4   Out-of-the-Box Tools for Infodemic Management

Social listening is an important means for gaining fast insights into public perceptions and information needs as well as detecting misinformation. This is especially important during crises like the COVID-19 pandemic, where there is an overwhelming volume of data, intertwined with conflicting information [32, 34]. In response to these growing needs, many commercially available machine learning-driven monitoring tools have been developed to public health practitioners, information and communications practitioners and researchers [2]. These out-of-the-box tools built by different companies vary in purpose, data input, capabilities, models, workflow management and output [36]. However, while these tools present tremendous value, they also come with novel risks.

Crises strain resources, and sufficient financial, time and personnel resources are not always available to local public health authorities to invest in social media strategies to begin with [1]. Devoting staff time to processing, analyzing and real-time monitoring of abundant social media data from scratch can be a luxury to organizations that lack the necessary resources and skills [22]. Out-of-the-box tools can simplify the data gathering, cleaning, analysis and presentation processes to low- or no-code [20], providing user-friendly interfaces that facilitate more efficient storage and analysis of data, and offering AI-powered automation for sentiment analysis and continuous monitoring. While in some cases these tools can provide end-to-end insights, they can also be used by technical experts to form one component of a custom-designed NLP pipeline.

Nevertheless, these tools are not without shortcomings. First, the integrity of social media metrics and the ambiguity of their definitions are obstacles for both data analysts and the audience of their reports. 'Visible' social media metrics such as the numbers of likes and followers are inherently fallible due to the lack of context (e.g. 'liking' a post can be driven by many different motives and emotions) as well as the commercialization of fake followers and metrics [3, 9]. The further processed metrics presented in social media listening tools, such as 'reach' and 'impressions', suffer from another layer of uncertainty. Often the tools do not fully disclose how the metrics are being calculated, and the definition of each metric may not be standardized across tools, making it even harder for users and readers to contextualize the information.

Furthermore, the accuracy of built-in classifiers for sentiment analysis is questionable [31]. Studies that compare manual sentiment coding with automatic sentiment analysis have shown that there is not only a poor correlation between the manual coding and the tool-generated results [11], but also a lack of agreement between the tools [5, 41]. It is challenging for researchers to independently investigate why this disagreement occurs, as the proprietary nature of the out-of-the-box tools prevents any external assessment of the integrity of their models. This is further complicated by the fact that language models trained prior to COVID-19 might not fully reflect the current reality because of the emergence of Out-of-Vocabulary words [42].

Some tools attempt to address these problems by implementing human-in-the-loop machine learning, enabling users to correct wrongly classified information [36] or train custom classifiers adapted to users' own context. This highlights the value of versatility in out-of-the-box tools – predicting changes in the global landscape of communications might not be always possible, but by making these tools more adaptable by design, it is possible to cater to more diverse, novel use cases.

5   Importance of Partnerships

To unlock the full potential of NLP methodologies and tools to address crises such as COVID-19, it is important that these techniques are appropriately tailored to each particular application setting; this should be part of any system design thinking. Partnerships with domain experts, end users and other beneficiaries can serve as a crucial resource to help direct research and to ensure meaningful and effective deployment.

In the case of using NLP for the COVID-19 response, productive partnerships could include stakeholders with technical and contextual expertise, data providers and tool developers. In many research settings, methods are developed first and possible applications found later. While this approach is useful for developing theoretical concepts and frameworks, in order to maximize social impact in crisis response scenarios the aims of the application should drive research, with meaningful objectives jointly determined by researchers and implementing partners. Giving greater agency to users of the tools will encourage long-lasting use.

Engaging with partners from different disciplines can be challenging. Often, research agendas and funding cycles require different timelines than the deployment of a tool, sometimes resulting in projects ending prematurely. In the case of many recent projects to tackle COVID-19, it has been difficult to quickly reach the level of maturity needed to operationalize projects and systems at scale [23]. It is therefore essential to establish agendas which accommodate the different time constraints of all stakeholders from the beginning of any project.

In many of the examples mentioned above, partnership development can help NLP researchers, who may be working in geographies which are removed from the application setting of interest, to understand the questions which need to be answered as well as the relevant modalities. For example, in the case of Uganda discussed in Sect. 3, local entities could inform researchers that radio streams are a dominant linguistic modality for reliable information and opinion tracking, thereby redirecting effort away from developing social media-related listening strategies. Similarly, partnerships can provide access to relevant data sources, as well as pre-designed tools (see Sect. 4).

6   Conclusion

To advance the inclusive use of NLP approaches in the COVID-19 response, we have identified the following focus areas:

Data – High-quality data helps build high-quality models and guides research priorities and makes it possible to establish benchmarks. A major challenge with many of the approaches mentioned above is the need for more inclusive large-scale public datasets to allow NLP researchers to explore and work with low-resource languages and alternative modalities. There are promising endeavors to curate datasets of misinformation such as the Fakeddit dataset [26], Poynter and COVIDLies [17], as well as as large community modeling efforts such as the FastAI Model Zoo, which could be expanded to cover a wider range of regions and languages. Similarly, efforts to build datasets from a wider range of sources – e.g., via the creation of radio transcription pipelines – could encourage researchers to work with data from alternative modalities. Partnerships can also serve as a key source for localized and relevant datasets. Finally, evaluation would be facilitated by the creation of multilingual COVID-related datasets, as well as a set of benchmarks for how well models perform on certain tasks (e.g. detecting misinformation).

Adaptation and Flexibility – There are many existing NLP tools, models and approaches that can be (re-)used in the context of pandemic response. While these tools bring convenience and efficiency to social listening in a crisis like COVID-19, one size does not fit all. Different tools are designed for different purposes and use cases, and modifications are often necessary to adapt them to specific contexts. It is necessary to evaluate the quality of the tools and their algorithms as much as possible to avoid making decisions based on flawed data or analysis [30]. These tools should be seen as supports for decision making and cannot be relied upon alone; manual validation of the results in context is always crucial [5]. For instance, one potential strategy for addressing the limitations of these tools involves the use of human-in-the-loop machine learning to ensure human oversight of ultimate decision-making.

Incentives and Frameworks – Beyond the specific context of the pandemic response, the research opportunities described above present challenges that are both academically well-motivated (as many understudied research questions remain to be explored) and likely to make a real-world impact (given the urgency and unprecedented nature of the pandemic). Even as the market for NLP tools for high-resource languages is becoming increasingly saturated, digital inclusion is creating new markets within communities that currently have few or no customized NLP resources and a large demand for them. There is a need to translate between technical and domain expertise and to bridge the gap between current technological capabilities and the needs of stakeholders. Many resources exist to assist in developing data-driven partnerships across different domains [12,37] – for instance, the UN Sustainable Development Goals and their associated targets can act as a common framework for setting aims and objectives, which is shared among institutions on a global level and can guide the response to and recovery from the COVID-19 pandemic [39,40]. As such, they can assist in the coordination and prioritization of tasks, help with the development of a common language between institutions, and outline effective areas for contributions by the NLP community.

References

1. Avery, E.: Public information officers' social media monitoring during the Zika virus crisis, a global health threat surrounded by public uncertainty. Public Relations Rev. **43** (2017). https://doi.org/10.1016/j.pubrev.2017.02.018
2. Batrinca, B., Treleaven, P.: Social media analytics: a survey of techniques, tools and platforms. AI and Soc. **30**, 89–116 (2014). https://doi.org/10.1007/s00146-014-0549-4
3. Baym, N.: Data not seen: the uses and shortcomings of social media metrics. First Monday **18** (2013). https://doi.org/10.5210/fm.v18i10.4873
4. Beaunoyer, E., Dupéré, S., Guitton, M.J.: COVID-19 and digital inequalities: reciprocal impacts and mitigation strategies. Comput. Human Behav., 106424 (2020)

5. Boukes, M., Velde, B., Araujo, T., Vliegenthart, R.: What's the tone? Easy doesn't do it: analyzing performance and agreement between off-the-shelf sentiment analysis tools. Commun. Methods Meas. **14**, 1–22 (10 2019). https://doi.org/10.1080/19312458.2019.1671966
6. Bullock, J., Luccioni, A., Pham, K.H., Lam, C.S.N., Luengo-Oroz, M., et al.: Mapping the landscape of Artificial Intelligence applications against COVID-19. J. Artif. Intell. Res. **69**, 807–845 (2020)
7. Bullock, J., Luengo-Oroz, M.: Automated speech generation from UN General assembly statements: Mapping risks in AI generated texts. In: International Conference on Machine Learning AI for Social Good Workshop (2019)
8. Conneau, A., Baevski, A., Collobert, R., Mohamed, A., Auli, M.: Unsupervised cross-lingual representation learning for speech recognition. arXiv preprint arXiv:2006.13979 (2020)
9. Cresci, S., Di Pietro, R., Petrocchi, M., Spognardi, A., Tesconi, M.: Fame for sale: edetection of fake Twitter followers. Decision Support Syst. **80**, 56–71 (2015) https://doi.org/10.1016/j.dss.2015.09.003
10. Cruz, J.C.B., Tan, J.A., Cheng, C.: Localization of fake news detection via multitask transfer learning. arXiv preprint arXiv:1910.09295 (2019)
11. Deiner, M.S., et al.: Facebook and Twitter vaccine sentiment in response to measles outbreaks. Health Inf. J. **25**(3), 1116–1132 (2019) https://doi.org/10.1177/1460458217740723, pMID: 29148313
12. DSEG: A framework for the ethical use of advanced data science methods in the humanitarian sector (2020)
13. Eberhard, D.M., Simons, G.F., Fennig, C.D.E.: Ethnologue: lof the world. twenty-third edition, online version (2020). www.ethnologue.com
14. Eysenbach, G.: How to fight an infodemic: the four pillars of infodemic management. J. Med. Internet Res. **22**, e21820 (2020). https://doi.org/10.2196/21820
15. Fadaee, M., Bisazza, A., Monz, C.: Data augmentation for low-resource neural machine translation. arXiv preprint arXiv:1705.00440 (2017)
16. Hidalgo-Sanchis, P.: Using speech-to-text technology to support response to the COVID-19 pandemic. https://www.unglobalpulse.org/2020/05/using-speech-to-text-technology-to-support-response-to-the-covid-19-pandemic/ (May 2020)
17. Hossain, T., Logan , R.L., Ugarte, A., Matsubara, Y., Young, S., Singh, S.: COVIDLIES: detecting COVID-19 misinformation on social media. In: Proceedings of the 1st Workshop on NLP for COVID-19 (Part 2) at EMNLP 2020 (2020)
18. Hossain, Z., Rahman, A., Islam, S., Kar, S.: BanFakeNews: A dataset for detecting fake news in Bangla. arXiv preprint arXiv:2004.08789 (2020)
19. Johnson, M., et al.: Google's multilingual neural machine translation system: enabling zero-shot translation. Trans. Assoc. Comput. Linguist. **5**, 339–351 (2017)
20. Lee, I.: Social media analytics for enterprises: typology, methods, and processes. Business Horizon. **61** (2017). https://doi.org/10.1016/j.bushor.2017.11.002
21. Levy, S., Wang, W.Y.: Cross-lingual transfer learning for COVID-19 outbreak alignment. arXiv preprint arXiv:2006.03202 (2020)
22. Lindsay, B.R.: Social media and disasters: current uses, future options, and policy considerations (2011)
23. Luengo-Oroz, M., et al.: Artificial intelligence cooperation to support the global response to COVID-19. Nat. Mach. Intell. **2**(6) (2020)
24. Magueresse, A., Carles, V., Heetderks, E.: Low-resource languages: a review of past work and future challenges. arXiv preprint arXiv:2006.07264 (2020)
25. Munro, R.: Crowdsourcing and the crisis-affected community. Inf. Retrieval **16**(2), 210–266 (2013). https://doi.org/10.1007/s10791-012-9203-2
26. Nakamura, K., Levy, S., Wang, W.Y.: r/fakeddit: a new multimodal benchmark dataset for fine-grained fake news detection. arXiv preprint arXiv:1911.03854 (2019)

27. Newman, L., Hutchinson, P., Meekers, D.: Key findings of the 3-2-1 service COVID-19 surveys: Information (Wave 1) (2020). viamo.io/wp-content/uploads/2020/09/Updated/3/2/1/Service/COVID-19/Survey/Information/1.pdf

28. Nielsen: The steady reach of radio: winning consumer attention (2019). www.nielsen.com/us/en/insights/article/2019/the-steady-reach-of-radio-winning-consumers-attention/

29. Orife, I., et al.: Masakhane - Machine translation for Africa. arXiv preprint arXiv:2003.11529 (2020)

30. Rai, A.: Explainable AI: from black box to glass box. J. Acad. Market. Sci. 48 (2019). https://doi.org/10.1007/s11747-019-00710-5

31. Rappaport, S.: Listening solutions: a marketer's guide to software and services. J. Advert. Res. - JAR 50 (2010). https://doi.org/10.2501/S002184991009135X

32. Ruggiero, A., Vos, M.: Social media monitoring for crisis communication: process, methods and trends in the scientific literature. Online J. Commun. Media Technol.4, 103–130 (2014). https://doi.org/10.29333/ojcmt/2457

33. Scannell, K.P.: The Crúbadán Project: corpus building for under-resourced languages. In: Building and Exploring Web Corpora: Proceedings of the 3rd Web as Corpus Workshop. vol. 4, pp. 5–15 (2007)

34. Sheppard, B.: Mitigating terror and avoidance behavior through the risk perception matrix to augment resilience. J. Homeland Secur. Emergency Manage. 8 (2011). https://doi.org/10.2202/1547-7355.1840

35. Spangher, A., Peng, N., May, J., Ferrara, E.: Enabling low-resource transfer learning across COVID-19 corpora by combining event-extraction and co-training. In: Proceedings of the 1st Workshop on NLP for COVID-19 at ACL 2020 (2020)

36. Stavrakantonakis, I., Gagiu, A.E., Kasper, H., Toma, I., Thalhammer, A.: An approach for evaluation of social media monitoring tools (2012)

37. UNDP, UN Global Pulse: A guide to data innovation for development: from idea to proof of concept (2016)

38. UNESCO: Statistics on Radio (2013). www.unesco.org/new/en/unesco/events/prizes-and-celebrations/celebrations/international-days/world-radio-day-2013/statistics-on-radio/

39. United Nations: 17 goals to transform our world. www.un.org/sustainabledevelopment/

40. Vinuesa, R., et al.: The role of Artificial Intelligence in achieving the sustainable development goals. Nat. Commun. 11(1) (2020)

41. Young, L., Soroka, S.: Affective news: the automated coding of sentiment in political texts. Political Commun. 29, 205–231 (2012). https://doi.org/10.1080/10584609.2012.671234

42. Zheng, X., Liu, Y., Gunceler, D., Willett, D.: Using synthetic audio to improve the recognition of out-of-vocabulary words in end-to-end ASR systems (2020)

A Framework for Building *pro-bono* Data for Good Projects

Miguel José Monteiro[(⊠)] and Paulo Maia

DSSG - Portuguese Association of Data Science for Social Good, Rua da Holanda 1,
Carcavelos, Portugal
{miguel,paulo}@dssg.pt

Abstract. Initiatives relying on data science for social good - non-commercial projects that deliver socially beneficial outcomes - have been on the rise in the last years. The area of Data for Good has several specific challenges, one of which is the definition of a formal framework for the design, conception, prioritization, development and impact measurement of such applications. All over the world, volunteers are organized in local/regional initiatives that provide voluntary support to social good organizations in the development of Data for Good projects. Each of these initiatives follows specific internal frameworks that are not standardized within the community, with information-sharing efforts just starting to appear. Sharing these frameworks could lead to an increase in the amount of successful data for good projects, delivering concrete value in the daily operations of social good institutions. In this paper, the framework that was created and is being followed with success at Data Science for Social Good Portugal (DSSG PT), an open community of data enthusiasts working *pro-bono* in Data for Good projects, is shared. This includes all processes regarding structural organization and management, communication between stakeholders, project scoping and project development that are being followed. It also presents a methodology for social impact measurement of projects and ensuring of ethical standards, such as data privacy and fairness.

Keywords: Data science · Project framework · Data for Good ·
Sustainability · Social impact

1 Introduction

Initiatives relying on data science for social good (Data for Good) can be defined as non-commercial projects leveraging data science technologies to deliver socially beneficial outcomes [2]. For many people working in Data for Good, the 17 United Nations Sustainable Development Goals (UN SDG) [5] are used as an assessment benchmark. More concretely, the objective of a project is evaluated in terms of its impact in one or more of the UN SDGs.

Data for Good Projects have specific challenges when compared to commercial Data Science solutions [4]. There is typically a lack of data literacy in the

© Springer Nature Switzerland AG 2021
M. Kamp et al. (Eds.): ECML PKDD 2021 Workshops, CCIS 1525, pp. 267–282, 2021.
https://doi.org/10.1007/978-3-030-93733-1_19

social institutions, which usually focus their efforts on its core competences, with little to no attention to technical or data infrastructure required for a successful project. Besides this, many organizations do not have access to IT resources or the budget to do so. Finally, facing political, cultural, ethical and legal barriers is common, due to the sensitive nature of the data.

Within the challenges in Data for Good applications, determining the opportunities, risks, principles and recommendations when developing Data for Good applications is a topic of interest in the literature (e.g. related with bias in model deployment or privacy concerns) [1]. Concrete recommendations have been offered to assess, develop, encourage and support Data Science for Good applications [1,3].

The rise of Data Science in the past few years has lead to a surplus of technically-capable and ethically-aligned individuals all over the world who want to apply their skills beyond the traditional business areas of application - in areas where the social impact can be greater [6]. Moreover, several Data for Good initiatives have recently appeared, such as DSSGx (Berlin, Portugal, Salzburg, Florida, Washington and CMU), DSSG Fellowship (Chicago), Data for Good (Denmark, France, Poland and Spain), Correlaid (Germany and France) and DataKind (UK and US).

Even though all these initiatives have a similar goal - to empower social good organization with data - they all tackle that problem from different angles. For example, some initiatives are summer programmes, others are event-based (such as workshops or meetups) and others are project-based. DSSG PT is a project-based initiative and therefore it has its own framework for developing projects. A project-based framework comprises all the processes related with the structural organization and management, communication between stakeholders, project scoping, project development and social impact measurement.

Frameworks are crucial because without them, the knowledge that comes from data enthusiasts and Data for Good initiatives remains untapped or below its potential for delivering concrete value in the daily operations of social good institutions. To the best of the authors' knowledge, no work has been shared regarding practical frameworks for project development in Data for Good applications. Sharing standardized frameworks achieved by years of experience from associations that have already gone through the process is crucial in spreading the Data for Good movement across borders. In turn, this can lead to the creation of new associations and to an increase in data literacy for social good purposes.

Advancing the success of Data for Good will require a multidisciplinary approach, with a deeper investigation of projects in locations and communities where they are both developed and deployed [2]. To advance the knowledge on these applications, in this paper, the framework regarding project scoping and development that is being followed in Data Science for Social Good Portugal (DSSG PT) is shared. DSSG PT is an open community of *pro-bono* data scientists, data lovers and data enthusiasts who tackle social problems using data. The association's goal is to connect people with data experience to institutions that work in social good Projects - such as non-profits and public administration. This framework has been refined during the development of 9 distinct projects since the beginning of the movement. During this time, DSSG PT has worked with 4 social good organizations and 43 volunteers in total, as well as on projects with open data.

The following paper is organized as follows:

- Sect. 2, Stakeholders - this section describes the different stakeholders of the DSSG PT framework and how they relate to each other.
- Sect. 3, Project - this section is where the project roles and lifecycle are described.
- Sect. 4, Sustainability of the Framework - this section describes how DSSG PT partners with other institutions in order to make the framework sustainable, namely on a financial level.
- Sect. 5, Future Improvements - this section presents the identified points of improvement on the framework.

2   Stakeholders

The following section describes the stakeholders involved in the framework of DSSG PT: Beneficiary, Volunteers, DSSG PT Lead Team and Ethics Committee (Fig. 1).

Fig. 1. Diagram of the different stakeholders

2.1   Beneficiary

A Beneficiary is a public or private, governmental or non-governmental, non-profit institution working for social good. Some examples of Beneficiaries are, but not limited to: charities, local governments, schools, non-governmental organizations (NGOs), and non-profits.

A Beneficiary is expected to have collected data (or potential to collect), availability to collaborate in a short-term project (less than 6 months duration) and be at a state of maturity where it can derive value from data for good solutions. DSSG PT works together with Beneficiaries in order to create Data for Good projects, helping them optimize resources, maximize efficiency and increase impact.

An important point is the fact that many Beneficiaries do not have employed or full-time collaborators - some will only have part-time or even volunteer collaborators. This is a major factor to take into account when considering the engagement of the organization with the initiative, which has to be managed along with the core competences and responsibilities of the Beneficiary.

2.2   Volunteers

Volunteers are all people who become part of the teams that will develop the social good Projects for Beneficiaries. Any person can become a Volunteer and they can have several types of background (both technical or non-technical), depending on the requirements of the Project they are working on. They are expected to work on the Data for Good projects from start to end, with a pre-defined weekly time commitment.

Volunteers usually engage in Projects due to a combination of several factors - helping a cause of interest to them, leveraging their technical skills in a volunteering context, refine/acquire new technical skills through a real-world experience and be part of a team of like-minded individuals regarding the societal potential of Data Science.

2.3   DSSG PT Lead Team

The DSSG PT Lead Team (or alternatively, DSSG PT) corresponds to the group of people responsible for managing the growth and strategic planning of DSSG PT. They serve as the facilitator between Beneficiaries and Volunteers, by providing all necessary resources and managing communication and expectations from both sides. This team is ultimately responsible for the success of the project and is the connective tissue between all stakeholders. It is organized in 4 different sub-teams:

Beneficiary Management. The Beneficiary Management Team is responsible for managing the relationship between DSSG PT and its Beneficiaries. They build the Beneficiary portfolio by managing Beneficiary leads and they do requirement analysis for defining the scope of the social good Projects. This team also follows the progress of the Project and meets with the Beneficiary to make sure that it receives timely feedback on how everything is going. In the end of the Project, it follows up with the Beneficiary in order to measure the impact of the initiative.

Moreover, the Beneficiary Management Team is an extremely multidisciplinary group, comprised of members with an understanding of data and data science, who also understand the reality of being a Beneficiary. Having people that combine some data expertise with specific domain knowledge of the area where the Beneficiaries operate is recommended.

Volunteer Management. The Volunteer Management Team is responsible for managing the relationship between DSSG PT and its Volunteers. They build the database of Volunteers and gather relevant information, such as skill-set, experience level and time availability.

The members also manage the recruitment process for the project teams and oversee the communication between volunteers. They are ultimately responsible for the happiness, success and motivation of the Volunteers during the project and they make sure the team stays connected and delivers within the deadlines. This team is also responsible for making sure the Volunteers have all the necessary resources, which includes work location for occasional in-person working session, software licenses and tooling, tools and platform for team collaboration and development, hosting for software solutions, among others.

Image and Communication. The Image & Communication Team is responsible for managing the external communication of everything related to the Projects. This external communication must be tailored to two very different target audiences - on one hand the Volunteers, who are usually tech-savvy individuals and on the other hand the Beneficiaries, who come from the social good field and usually lack expertise in data.

Their work consists of producing media content, such as videos and images, to integrate in communication materials. The team is also in charge of content management and of producing and updating the Project's webpage, where all information is made available to the public.

Sponsors and Partners. The Sponsors & Partners Team is responsible for managing the financial sustainability and partnerships of DSSG PT. They build the sponsor and partner portfolios by approaching new entities and presenting the different opportunities of supporting DSSG PT. More details about those opportunities and types of support are discussed in Sect. 4.

2.4   Ethics Committee

The Ethics Committee is an independent, multidisciplinary, consultation entity. It is fully dedicated to promoting and ensuring ethical standards in the Projects launched by DSSG PT. Every time a Project Scoping phase (Sect. 3.2) is finished, this entity is consulted, with the following responsibilities:

- Review the Project Scope document, focusing on requirements in terms of bias and fairness;

- Examine the available data to make sure all privacy regulations are being respected;
- Evaluate the mission of the Beneficiary and ensure a true social good problem is being solved;
- Suggest and enforce changes to the Project Scope document;
- Give the final seal of approval on the Project Scope.

3   Project

The main objective of DSSG PT is the development of Projects with the goal of increasing the impact of a Beneficiary using data. A Project is defined as an initiative designed by DSSG PT together with a Beneficiary, accomplished by a team of Volunteers. Most of the times, Projects are aligned with one or more UN SDGs.

3.1   Project Roles and Responsibilities

The next sections describe the different project roles and responsibilities (displayed in Fig. 2).

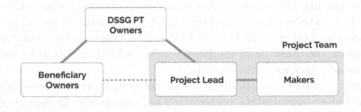

Fig. 2. Diagram of the different roles in a project.

DSSG PT Owners. In this framework, DSSG PT has the main purpose of serving as a bridge between the Beneficiary and the Volunteers. In other words, it is the role of DSSG PT to guarantee that the developed project has quality and relevant impact for the Beneficiary, but also to ensure that the Volunteers have a positive and enriching experience.

To enable this, at the start of each Project, two members of DSSG PT are appointed Owners of the Project and these are the people that ultimately represent DSSG PT throughout the Project. These two members must come one from the Beneficiary Management Team and one from the Volunteer Management Team.

The tasks of the Beneficiary Management Owner are:

- Write the Project Scope document, during the Project Scoping phase;
- Facilitate the process of review and validation of the Project Scope from the Ethics Committee;

- Ensure all necessary formalities of the project related to the Beneficiary;
- Measure the metrics at the start of the Project;
- Mediate the communication between the Project Team and the Beneficiary Owner (Sect. 3.1), whenever there are questions, data and/or feedback to transmit;
- Participate in the fortnightly status report meetings and ensure the participation of the Beneficiary Owners;
- Communicate all updates from the Beneficiary to the second DSSG PT Owner, from the Volunteer Management Team;
- Periodically report the progress of the Project to the rest of the members of DSSG PT;
- Deliver the final output of the Project to the Beneficiary Owner and collect feedback;
- Perform the Social Impact Measurement (Sect. 3.2).

The tasks of the Volunteer Management Owner are:

- Conduct the recruitment process, guaranteeing a match between the technical needs of the Project and the skills of the Volunteers;
- Onboard the project team and kick-off the project;
- Act as manager of people, which includes: ensuring happiness and a good work environment among the Project Team (Sect. 3.1), detect and solve conflicts and encourage the participation of all Volunteers;
- Follow the contributions of each Volunteer throughout the different phases of development in order to understand the level of enthusiasm, through a fortnightly video-call;
- Verify the Project code and repository periodically as a method of quality control of the work that is being developed;
- Communicate all updates from the Volunteers to the second DSSG PT Owner, from the Beneficiary Management Team;
- Periodically report the progress of the project to the rest of the members of DSSG PT;

Beneficiary Owners. On the side of the Beneficiary, the same structure applies. At the start of the Project, two members of the Beneficiary are appointed Owners and these are the people that ultimately represent the Beneficiary throughout the Project. The Beneficiary Owners must have the necessary domain knowledge in order to guide the Volunteers into developing what is truly needed for their association. They must also have access to the necessary resources, such as data and infrastructure from the Beneficiary. Lastly, they must have available time to dedicate to the project, which is part of the reason why two members are chosen. Moreover, engaging two Owners on the Beneficiary side has proven to be critical, as many organizations have fluctuating presence, availability and enthusiasm throughout the Project.

The tasks of the Beneficiary Owners are:

- Collaborate in defining the Project Scope;
- Provide all data necessary to the Project;
- Guide the Volunteers during Project development, by providing domain knowledge and answering product and usability questions;
- Participate in the fortnightly status report meetings with the DSSG PT Owners and the volunteers;
- Serve as the spokesperson inside the Beneficiary and communicate progress report to their fellow collaborators;
- Help with the Project deployment by facilitating access to the technical infrastructure of the Beneficiary;
- Participate in the Social Impact Measurement phase.

Project Team. The Project Team is composed of Volunteers. Each Project Team has two types of roles: one Project Lead and a group of Makers, whose number varies according to the project complexity and duration.

The Project Lead can be seen as an all-encompassing role in the Project, because it includes both technical project management, as well as development itself. This person must have the hard technical skills that are necessary to develop the project and preferably several years of experience working with data projects. On the other hand, the Project Lead is also responsible for representing the Project Team at all moments, acting as a spokesperson. The Project Lead must report progress and communicate regularly with the DSSG PT Owners and must also be present at the fortnightly status report meetings with DSSG PT and the Beneficiary.

The Makers are in charge of project development and deliverables. They can perform different types of tasks, which can be technical, such as, but not limited to, programming code, testing code, building software infrastructure, analyzing data, building models, or non-technical, such as, but not limited to, designing media, communicating results, reading literature, providing consultancy in social good areas. For this reason, the group of Makers must have different backgrounds, depending on the project relevance, in order to truly be a cross-functional team.

3.2   Project Lifecycle

The following subsections describe the steps taken by the team to ensure that the project is developed end-to-end (represented in Fig. 3).

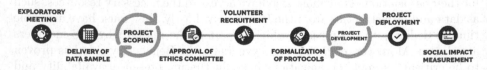

Fig. 3. Diagram of the several steps in the project lifecycle

Exploratory Meeting. The exploratory meeting is the first step of the framework and it marks the first contact between the Beneficiary and DSSG PT. In this meeting, the goal is for both parties to understand what each other does and how both are positioned in the social good scene. Since DSSG PT works with any type of social good entity, it is crucial to understand how the Beneficiary is creating impact, who their target audience is, what are their daily operations and their technological maturity level.

During the meeting, the aim revolves around compiling a list of several initiatives or tasks that the Beneficiary has and then defining several problems associated with those tasks that can be solved with data. After prioritizing those problems with the Beneficiary, the focus then is understanding their data literacy and what data has already been collected or has the potential to be collected. This way it is possible to identify real problems for which a solution would impact the Beneficiary in a positive way, but also assess how realistic the solution can be, considering data and other technical limitations.

The meeting flow is purposely unstructured and it follows the lines of a brainstorming session. The reason for that is that DSSG PT does not want the Beneficiary to feel like it is being interviewed and that there are right and wrong answers or that it is lacking enough knowledge to understand the Project. Instead, the purpose is the opposite: to make the Beneficiary feel like they are as crucial for the Project as DSSG PT, since they are the only ones who have the domain knowledge and they are the ones who will use it. Depending on the Beneficiary's technological maturity level and needs, it might be that no project is developed, and therefore the framework advances no further.

In the end of the meeting, the information is recorded in a standardized format that can be easily shared inside DSSG PT, with the following fields:

- Name of Beneficiary;
- Area of social impact and UN SDG;
- Number of employees and volunteers;
- Mission statement;
- Projects being developed to achieve that mission;
- Problems and obstacles in those projects;
- Collected data and associated format.

Delivery of a Data Sample. After the first meeting and before the project can be conceptualized, a sample of the data must be delivered by the Beneficiary. This step is critical for identifying the existing data and its format and ascertaining how accessible it is.

At this point, a quick first analysis on this data sample must be done by DSSG PT in order to understand its potential. This helps understand if and how this dataset in specific can be leveraged to solve the problem. Moreover, the type of deliverable must also be discussed, in order to avoid too much technical complexity on the final product. The priority of any Project is always to deliver something that the Beneficiary understands and that can deliver value quickly.

The data sample provided by the Beneficiary is also helpful in identifying if more data needs to be collected, both in terms of size and feature dimensionality, especially in the cases where open data may be able to complement the existing one. Besides this, by having the Beneficiary deliver a data sample, DSSG PT can evaluate more concretely how easy it is for the Beneficiary to obtain its own data and interact with digital/data products. This is crucial because it enables DSSG PT to understand how quickly can more data be expected for the remainder of the project and it also gives a real perspective on the data literacy of the Beneficiary. For example, if this step already gets delayed, then this might be a bottleneck later on and it is a risk that will therefore need to be mitigated fast.

Project Scoping. After receiving and analyzing the data sample, it is possible to start drafting the Project Scope. This document will serve as the basis for the whole project and it is where all objectives, descriptions and deliverables are identified. Examples are a written report, a cloud-based application, an AI model, interactive visualizations, among others.

The Project Scope document also describes the metrics that will be used to measure the social impact of the project, so these must be quantifiable, improvable, and appropriate. Lastly, it includes the rules and minimum requirements in terms of expectations from the Beneficiary, which are: to transmit all necessary data, to answer domain questions and to participate in meetings.

This phase is an iterative process between the Beneficiary and DSSG PT, until a final project scope is achieved and agreed. Both DSSG PT and the Beneficiary must answer all questions necessary from each other until both are able to fully understand the scope of the Project and draft the final version of the document.

This document must include the following records:

- Title of Project;
- Estimated date of start and end;
- Area of social impact and UN SDG;
- Name of the Owners, from Beneficiary and DSSG PT;
- Description of Beneficiary;
- Description of the social good mission;
- Objectives of Project, starting by general objective and splitting into specific;
- Description of Project, giving context on the problem and high-level solution;
- Available data, with data dictionary and descriptions;
- Estimate of the necessary resources (number of Volunteers and their skill-set, time allocation, necessary software, etc.)
- Final deliverables;
- Metrics for impact analysis (at least 3);
- Statement of commitment.

Approval from the Ethics Committee. The next step is a review from the Ethics Committee (Sect. 2.4). This phase is critical for the start of the Project and thus, without validation from the Ethics Committee, the Project goes back to the previous phase and the Project Scope is adjusted.

Volunteer Recruitment. Once the Project Scope is officially closed, the recruitment process starts. An open call is made publicly available for anyone, where the Project is presented and the process for application is explained, along with the deadlines. The name of the Beneficiary is purposely not mentioned on the call, but instead only the field of work, in order to discourage people from applying based only on who the Beneficiary is.

After the applications close, the interviews are scheduled with all applicants. Firstly, the Project Lead is recruited. Due to their relevance as the connection between Makers, DSSG PT and the Beneficiary, this recruitment process is made separately to guarantee the best fit possible. For a Project Lead, the priorities are a strong technical background combined with project and product management skills, strong communication and leadership abilities. After the Project Lead is chosen and onboarded, he participates together with DSSG PT in the interviews for Makers. Maker selection usually tries to bring in people with the specific development and execution skills required for this specific data Project.

The interview process comprises reviewing a CV, a small motivation text and an interview. In this interview, besides evaluating specific technical skills, work style and motivation to join both the Data for Good movement and this specific project are assessed. As the end goal is to assemble a team of 3–5 people (Project Lead included), and with the growing popularity of the Data for Good movement, more often than not there are more candidates than available spots. Selection criteria is therefore needed, which includes: technical skills/potential, seniority level, motivation, working style and short to mid term availability.

The goal of this recruitment process is to assemble a motivated team spearheaded by a capable, empathetic and hands-on Project Lead, which combines the technical skills required to execute the Project with different seniority levels, so that intra-team mentorship and learning can take place. While the specifics of this process make it time-consuming, DSSG PT has learned that spending the extra time during recruiting frequently pays off in later stages of the Project.

Formalization of Protocols and Onboarding. With both the Project Scope finalized and the Project Team assembled, all protocols are signed, followed by onboarding. These protocols are signed between DSSG PT and the Beneficiary and DSSG PT and the Volunteers. They aim at establishing and describing the specific terms of collaboration between all parties involved in the project, such as intellectual property, responsibilities, confidentiality, data privacy and objectives.

Project Development. This phase is also iterative and corresponds to the longest phase of the Framework. It corresponds to the actual development of the tasks identified in the Project Scope document.

From the Project Scope document, the Project Lead identifies and describes the tasks of the Project and allocates the Makers to specific tasks, supporting them technically. The Project Team collaborates with DSSG PT and the Beneficiaries by continuously reporting and showcasing the intermediary Project results to all involved parties and gathering feedback. This can be done either online or in-person. This reporting is done fortnightly during a dedicated meeting between the Project Lead, the DSSG PT Owners and the Beneficiary Owners.

DSSG PT provides several tools for the Project Team to work with, such as code versioning platforms, task management application, access to software, among others. DSSG PT does not determine a specific work methodology or schedule but instead leaves it to the Project Team to self-organize according to their preference. The objective of DSSG PT is to purposely give the Project Team maximum ownership over the Project.

Project Delivery and Retrospective. When the Project is finished, the developed code and all the deliverables are handed over to the Beneficiary Owners in an adequate format. In some cases, an in-house installation might be necessary and thus DSSG PT must articulate with the IT teams of the Beneficiary in order to facilitate the deploy of the final solution by the Project Team.

In parallel, the DSSG PT Owners make another measurement of the social impact metrics identified in the Project Scope document, alongside the Beneficiary Owners. This allows DSSG PT to have two measurements of these metrics from the Beneficiary (one at the beginning of the Project and another one at the end), which will be crucial when the third measurement occurs.

Besides this, in order to collect internal feedback for future improvement of the framework, a retrospective analysis is performed by the DSSG PT Owners regarding the following topics:

- Difference between estimated and real Project duration;
- Project Scoping duration;
- Volunteer Recruitment duration;
- Communication delay, for both the Project Team and Beneficiary Owners;
- Project Team written feedback;

The Project Team is then invited to document their experience in the format of a blog post, which is then reviewed by DSSG PT and shared with the community. This serves as a way of sharing knowledge with the community, even if they did not participate directly in the Project. Moreover, it showcases the work of the Project Team, since the team members can, for instance, share it in their work or personal networks.

Social Impact Measurement. After project delivery, DSSG PT measures the social impact of the delivered solution. For that, the initially defined metrics of the Project Scope document are once again measured and compared to the other two previous measurements. This way, DSSG PT has three independent measurements of the social impact metrics at crucial times, which gives a more representative outlook over their evolution throughout time and also externalizes other unrelated factors that might influence the metrics.

The timing of this step is highly dependent on the availability of the Beneficiary to correctly measure those metrics, which also depends on the project deliverable itself, but it is usually around 6 months after delivering the Project to the Beneficiary.

4   Sustainability of the Framework

For long-term sustainability, volunteer work is not sufficient, as some social good projects have expenses associated to its development [4], such as computational capacity or operational costs. In order to guarantee the sustainability of DSSG PT, the Sponsors & Partners Team has defined a set of sponsorship and partnership tiers. Any institution (either for or non-profit) can be a Sponsor or a Partner or both, simultaneously or not, as long as their mission is aligned with the mission of DSSG PT.

As compensation for the support, the sponsors and partners are advertised on the DSSG PT website, social media and newsletter, in different levels, according to a pre-defined agreement.

4.1   Sponsors

Sponsors are entities that directly support DSSG PT financially. Instead of relying solely on donations - which is always a possibility - DSSG PT introduced the concept of Project Patronage. In short, this is a way for companies and other institutions to become "godfathers" of a project. They are able to choose what social good projects most interest them and directly fund those specific projects, enabling them to directly support development.

During the Project Scoping phase, the Sponsors & Partners Team of DSSG PT approaches companies whose mission is related to the mission of the Beneficiary and invites them to be the Project Patron of that Project. A company can, however, become a Project Patron at any point in the Project lifecycle.

For the sake of transparency and competition fairness, the fee for Project Patronage is a fixed value, regardless of the size of the institution. However, that fee was optimized for the Portuguese market and should therefore be adjusted to the market where the Data for Good initiative is being created. These funds are used for covering the expenses of a Project - such as software and hardware, working space, travel expenses, among others. Moreover, the remainder is kept for ensuring the financial sustainability of DSSG PT and a specific amount may also be donated back to the Beneficiary.

4.2   Partners

Partners are entities that provide other benefits that are not direct financing, and are grouped into four categories: Tech Partners, Data Partners, Event Partners and Knowledge Partners.

Tech Partners. Tech Partners provide technology solutions for DSSG PT and/or the Project Teams, such as cloud computation, data visualization solutions, MLOps/Data Engineering services, among others. Tech Partners have the opportunity to test new developments in real-world applications and share solutions with a big community of data scientists.

Data Partners. Data Partners supply DSSG PT with relevant data that can be used for the purpose of a project, for enriching the developed solutions. In cases where the quality of a project can be improved by adding more data, DSSG PT will approach institutions in order gather more data that might not be open to the public or that might be proprietary. If the institutions are in agreement, a data sharing protocol is formalized and the data is given to the project team to work with.

Event Partners. Event Partners provide resources for the events that DSSG PT organizes. These resources can be venue and support amenities (digital or physical), coffee-break services, audio-visuals, among others. It serves as a way for companies to help DSSG PT gain more visibility and increase the size and reach of the community.

Knowledge Partners. Knowledge Partners collaborate with DSSG PT with the aim of creating and sharing knowledge with the community. They assist DSSG PT by not only providing speakers to events such as workshops and meetups but also by training volunteers in the project teams.

5   Future Improvements

Although this framework is already the result of a considerable amount of work and experience in social good projects, there are still several points of improvement that were identified by DSSG PT.

5.1   Information Management

Managing the information acquired by DSSG PT, such as volunteer registrations, interviews, interactions and registration in events is done using several external services (spreadsheets, forms, analytical dashboards, etc.). Having information like this enables DSSG PT to make data-driven decisions. However, this information is still not gathered in a structured way, which means it becomes harder to make it actionable. Additionally, it also does not allow for an automatic gathering of such data, which leads to a lot of manual work by DSSG PT.

5.2   Marketing and Communication

Regarding Marketing and Communication, DSSG PT aims to improve the internal and external communication, namely around the public announcement of calls for volunteers and the communication of results of the finished Projects. By doing this it becomes possible to include these practices in the current framework and replicate them across several different projects.

5.3   Volunteer Engagement

Having a considerably bigger number of Volunteers than the available Projects requires creating workflows for maintaining the community engaged. With this in mind, DSSG PT has started considering the possibility of creating smaller initiatives in which more Volunteers can participate, such as contained Mini-Projects with open data (where no Beneficiary is required) and writing blog posts.

5.4   Post-project Maintenance

The issue of providing technical maintenance to finished Projects following its delivery to the Beneficiary is paramount. It is crucial that this framework includes a way of adding small features or fixing errors that appear in the deliverables throughout time. This is specially critical when working with Volunteers allocated for a fixed time period to work in a Project.

6   Conclusions

On this paper, a complete framework for building *pro-bono* data for good projects was presented. This framework includes all the guidelines regarding the organizational structure and stakeholders, processes and rules for the project lifecycle and finally recommendations to guarantee resource sustainability of the framework. However, DSSG PT does not consider this framework without flaws and therefore several future improvements were also identified. This is a work that is still in progress and for which DSSG PT welcomes other opinions and experiences.

The described methodology has some steps in common with CRISP-DM [7]: CRISP DM's Business and Data Understanding are similar to DSSG PT's Exploratory Meeting and Project Scoping, and Project Deployment to Project Delivery. The intermediate steps of CRISP-DM (Modeling, Evaluation and Deployment) can match Project Development for some of the projects, although not all Data for Good Projects follow all these steps, depending on the Beneficiary's needs. However, DSSG PT's framework is more general for Data for Good Projects, while CRISP-DM focuses exclusively on Data Mining.

By sharing this framework and making it publicly available, it is expected that not only more initiatives with the same purpose as DSSG PT appear worldwide but also that these new initiatives are implemented in a structured manner without repeating previous mistakes. This guarantees a transfer of knowledge and good practices between the community. It also enables other institutions to challenge this framework and incentivies other frameworks to be shared with everyone as well.

Acknowledgements. DSSG PT thanks Catarina Farinha, Daniel Rodrigues and Marília Ferreira da Cunha for their extensive review and constructive criticism of this document. DSSG PT also acknowledges Helena Margarida Faria for the work made in the design of the figures.

References

1. Cowls, J., King, T., Taddeo, M., Floridi, L.: Designing AI for social good: seven essential factors. SSRN Electron. J. (2019). https://doi.org/10.2139/ssrn.3388669, https://www.ssrn.com/abstract=3388669
2. Cowls, J., Tsamados, A., Taddeo, M., Floridi, L.: A definition, benchmark and database of AI for social good initiatives. Nature Mach. Intell. **3**(2), 111–115 (2021). https://doi.org/10.1038/s42256-021-00296-0, http://www.nature.com/articles/s42256-021-00296-0
3. Floridi, L., et al.: AI4people-an ethical framework for a good AI society: opportunities, risks, principles, and recommendations. Minds Mach. **28**(4), 689–707 (2018). https://doi.org/10.1007/s11023-018-9482-5
4. Niño, M., et al.: Data projects for "social good": challenges and opportunities. Int. J. Human. Soc. Sci. **11**(5), 1094–1104 (2017). https://publications.waset.org/10006923/data-projects-for-social-good-challenges-and-opportunities
5. United Nations High Commissioner for Refugees: Refworld — transforming our world : the 2030 agenda for sustainable development. https://www.refworld.org/docid/57b6e3e44.html
6. Tomašev, N., et al.: AI for social good: unlocking the opportunity for positive impact. Nature Commun. **11**(1), 2468 (2020).https://doi.org/10.1038/s41467-020-15871-z, https://www.nature.com/articles/s41467-020-15871-z, bandiera_abtest: a Cc_license_type: cc_by Cg_type: Nature Research Journals Number: 1 Primary_atype: Reviews Publisher: Nature Publishing Group Subject_term: Developing world;Ethics Subject_term_id: developing-world;ethics
7. Wirth, R., Hipp, J.: Crisp-DM: towards a standard process model for data mining. In: Proceedings of the 4th International Conference on the Practical Applications of Knowledge Discovery and Data Mining, vol. 1. Springer-Verlag, London, UK (2000)

Improving Smart Waste Collection Using AutoML

Sónia Teixeira[1,3](✉), Guilherme Londres[1], Bruno Veloso[1,2], Rita P. Ribeiro[1,3], and João Gama[1,3]

[1] LIAAD - INESC TEC, Porto, Portugal
{sonia.c.teixeira,jgama}@inesctec.pt
[2] University Portucalense, Porto, Portugal
[3] University of Porto, Porto, Portugal

Abstract. The production and management of urban waste is a growing challenge and a consequence of our day-to-day resources and activities. According to the Portuguese Environment Agency, in 2019, Portugal produced 1% more tons compared to 2018. The proper management of this waste can be co-substantiated by existing policies, namely, national legislation and the Strategic Plan for Urban Waste. Those policies assess and support the amount of waste processed, allowing the recovery of materials. Among the solutions for waste management is the selective collection of waste. We improve the possibility of manage the smart waste collection of Paper, Plastic, and Glass packaging from corporate customers who joined a recycling program. We have data collected since 2017 until 2020. The main objective of this work is to increase the system's predictive performance, without any loss for citizens, but with improvement in the collection management. We analyze two types of problems: (*i*) the presence or absence of containers; and (*ii*) the prediction of the number of containers by type of waste. To carry out the analysis, we applied three machine learning algorithms: XGBoost, Random Forest, and Rpart. Additionally, we also use AutoML for XGBoost and Random Forest algorithms. The results show that with AutoML, generally, it is possible to obtain better results for classifying the presence or absence of containers by type of waste and predict the number of containers.

Keywords: Data mining for social good · Smart cities · Waste collection

1 Introduction

The production and management of urban waste are growing as a consequence of our day-to-day resources and activities. According to the Portuguese Environment Agency, in 2019, Portugal produced 5281 tons of waste. The total waste produced in 2018 corresponds to 5213. This represents (in 2019) more than 1% compared to 2018 [3]. However, the tons of waste collected has been increasing since 2015. In September 2019, in the north of Portugal, 43 050 tons of waste

© Springer Nature Switzerland AG 2021
M. Kamp et al. (Eds.): ECML PKDD 2021 Workshops, CCIS 1525, pp. 283–298, 2021.
https://doi.org/10.1007/978-3-030-93733-1_20

was collected. From those 43 050 only 24% was properly destined to recycle or revaluation [14].

The principle of protection of human health and the environment is in Portuguese legislation [17], in the sense of production, collection, and transport. The same legislation also establishes that waste producers must proceed with the separation. The need for sustainable management has become a matter of citizenship. In this sense, public policies for waste management were implemented with technical, legal, and economic instruments that guarantee safety and without damage to human health or the environment. Some policies intend to encourage waste management, namely the Strategic Plan for Urban Waste (PERSU2020). In other words, with these incentives and legislation to increase the selective collection of waste is intended to contribute to the recovering materials [2].

In Northern Portugal, the organization responsible for collecting and treating the waste offers a service named door-to-door non-residential collection. It consists of delivering three waste-colored bins with a capacity of 120 liter each. Green, blue, and yellow containers intend for a particular type of material, respectively glass, cardboard and paper, and plastic and metal. The list of customers embraces hospitals, restaurants, and shops, where the waste is collected weekly. Once that, costs with fuel are responsible not only for more greenhouse gas emissions but for almost 70% of the collection costs [23], it is relevant to optimize the collection routes of the trucks. Our objective is to design an intelligent based-system that uses machine learning algorithms to increase the system's predictive capacity, without any loss for citizens, but with improvement in collection management.

We can found in the literature several works related to the problem of waste management. The idea of optimizing waste collection routes is not new and is widely reported in the literature as in [5,18,19]. However, these works usually tackle it as a route optimization problem or suggest ways to implement intelligent sensors in waste containers more recently.

In this paper, we applied machine learning algorithms to identify patterns in the habits of industrial and commercial customers. The planning of the waste collection routes can use the previous patterns to minimize the costs. This work is an extension of recent work [11,16], by using a data set that contains a different set of attributes, applies different machine learning algorithms, and adopts AutoML tools to optimize the hyper-parameters of those algorithms. Automated machine learning (AutoML) is a joint optimization task, [12], which involves building machine learning models (ML) efficiently and automatically. This kind of tool facilitates the adoption by people without expertise in the ML domain. To meet our objective, a Random Forest, XGBoost, Rpart, and H2O AutoML tool to optimize the Random Forest and XGBoost are adopted and compared. This work used data of the last years (2017–2020) of waste collection routes.

This paper aims to contribute to:

- Using machine learning algorithms and AutoML for managing environmental issues in Municipalities;

- Comparing the different approaches, in the first problem, to predict if there is a container to be collected and, in the second problem, how many containers will be full enough.

We conclude that with the AutoML approach, it is generally possible to obtain better results for classifying the presence or absence of containers by type of waste and predict the number of containers to predict the number of waste containers. Overall this document is structured as follows: in Sect. 2 we present the related work regarding intelligent waste management; in Sect. 3 we present the proposed methodology; at Sect. 4 we present the results and discussion. Finally, in Sect. 5, we draw the conclusions and the future work.

2 Smart Waste Management

The National Waste Policy includes five waste management plans: national, and by four sectors (urban, hospital, industrial, and agricultural waste category) [17]. The national waste management plan defines fundamental guidelines for waste management, the specific waste management plan, and the multimunicipal, inter-municipal and municipal action plans. Through municipal and inter-municipal action plans, the urban waste management strategy and the actions to be developed by the responsible entity are defined.

Almost as a standard, the traditional way to collect waste is by sending waste collection trucks with big containers to a predefined route. At specific points, it stops, gathers the waste bins repeatedly until the truck gets fully loaded or the route ends. We can found this model replicated in many cities around the world for decades. A paradigm faced by waste companies is how to improve those routes or how to reduce the expenses [4]. Only the fuel consumption of those trucks is responsible for 70% of the whole operation [23]. One of the ways of doing this reformulation is changing the way this collection happens. There are a few different models, [8,21,25], such as the disposal of big waste containers in predefined points in a neighborhood (eco-points). In each of those places, we can find three big colored containers: green (Glass), blue (paper and carton), yellow (metal and Plastic), and an enormous grey container for non-recyclable waste. Periodically, a specific waste collection truck goes to these predefined points to collect the waste. More recently, there is the adoption of smart sensors in the trash bins. This approach allows companies to know when such a container is near its total capacity and ready to be collected. We can use this information as an input for intelligent routing systems. In the literature typically, we found that different optimization algorithms produce these predefined routes [5,18,19,23].

Recent work proposed by Ferrer et al. [10] proposed the combination of the two previous approaches, i.e., the route optimization and the adoption of an intelligent system to predict how full the trash bins would be. Intelligent waste management is searching for new and more efficient ways to tackle it, using new connected sensors to help route management or other technological approaches. Every day the society becomes more active and aware of how vital appropriate waste management is. Therefore, more investment and development are rising in this field not only as government politics but from popular demand [11].

3   Case Study

For this work, we have two key objectives: (*i*) predict the presence or absence of waste to be collected; and (*ii*) predict the quantity of each type of container (Paper, Plastic, and Glass) available for collection.

3.1   Data Set

LIPOR is the company responsible for waste collection, also is the provider of the data sets used for this work. This data was collected over three years, from March 2017 to January 2020, from 534 single customers summing 72 920 observations. In the beginning, the truck driver and his assistant manually register the data; lately, a semi-automated method was adopted, with pre-filled electronic spreadsheets, facilitating and enhancing the quality of acquired data.

The Vila do Conde data set includes 13 features and 34 419 observations. Among the features we can find, for example, the route number, the customer's latitude and longitude, the month of collection, the day of the week, or even the type of activity of the customer. We applied a pre-processing step to the data set. Namely, features with a high number of missing values, as well as features without any variation for all customers (*e.g.*, Collection designation), were removed, which reduces the number of features from 13 to 5. The 5 features are: WeekDay, Month, distance, distanceInterv and Activity. The 5 features selected are presented in the correlation matrix, presented in Fig. 2.

The original data set has 13 features for each record, and some identify the circuit, some identify the customer, such as GPS coordinates and customer ids. However, some of the features are not interesting for the problem: Type of collection, Municipality, Circuit designation are the same for all observations. The original files also include 5 features that directly, or indirectly, translate a period in time, for example, Date in the table, Date-char, Date, WeekDay, and Month. We considered only two features, WeekDay and Month. Another feature that is also not interesting for the problem is the shift period feature because of the high number of missing values.

Vila do Conde waste collection data set is used to classify the presence and absence of waste by type and predict the number of Paper, Plastic, and Glass containers.

3.2   Data Preprocessing

The most critical feature in the data set, which considers Vila do Conde circuit, is the number of Paper, Plastic, and Glass containers, as it is the target of this work to predict those quantities. We used these same features to obtain information regarding the presence or absence of containers. For the first goal, to predict the presence or absence of container, it was necessary to treat all data sets as follows: all entries with more than 1 container for Paper, Plastic, or Glass, independent of the quantity, were converted to 1. This way, a feature was created to translate the presence or absence of container, *i.e.*, the only possible values for the number of containers would be 0 or 1.

The data set was also treated for extreme values, analyzing each customer and their waste production. Customers with less waste production, which coincides with business activities that are subgroups of a broader activity group, were placed in the broader group. The criterion is to have only groups of activities in the Activity feature. The Services class is the one with the most significant number of containers for collection and the activity with more subgroups of activities. Regardless of the reasons that led to the existence of customers with a minimal amount of data, waste collection is always a necessary service.

We can identify the customer by the features corresponding to the GPS coordinates. We can solve this problem using location-based techniques or based on the type of activity performed by each customer (for example, Hospital, Mini-Market, Restaurant, and others). The original data set includes 45 types of business activity. However, some of them we considered in the same class (for example, Pizzeria is in the restaurant class, Florist in the services class, *etc.*). For that reason, the data set considers 19 classes now. We built the distance feature by calculating the distance between the customer's GPS coordinates and the city center's GPS coordinates, which is of a quantitative type. Vila do Conde is a small county. The location of most of the business activities is in the city center; in the vicinity of the center, the activity is residual. For this reason, the option to calculate the distance is from the customer to the city center. Another feature with three classes (Q1, Q2, and Q3) arises from analyzing this new feature, the distance feature. This one is from a qualitative ordinal type. The three partitions are Q1 - from 0 m to 2500 m; Q2 - from 2500 m to 8500 m and Q3 - above 8500 m.

3.3   Exploratory Data Analysis

One crucial characteristic regarding the first objective, to predict the presence or absence of waste to be collected, is that the data is unbalanced. Figure 1, shows the histogram of the two classes and the difference between them, especially in the presence of Plastic containers.

Regarding seasonality of Vila do Conde municipality waste collection, to predict the presence or absence by type of waste, we observe that April is the month with lower values of waste to be collected (*cf.* Table 1). On the other hand, the months between January to March are those with a higher presence of Paper and Plastic waste to be collected. Values in Table 1 represent the number of containers with waste. For example, 2305 is the number of containers with the presence of paper waste in January, as we can observe in the Table 1 The waste distributions for Paper and Plastic exhibit similar behavior, although the values for the waste paper presence are lower than the plastic. On the other hand, the distribution of Glass waste is slightly different, namely May, July, and August, in which it presents the highest values. These observations contradict the founds

288   S. Teixeira et al.

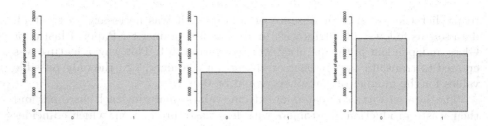

Fig. 1. Absence (0) and Presence (1) of waste containers (left to right: Paper, Plastic and Glass).

of [16], where the author found that the quantity of waste to be collected was higher in the summer months. We can observe in a specific business activity that customers, such as restaurants, present a spike in the middle of the year. However, as [15] mention in his recent work, this trend does not stand.

Table 1. Quantity of containers with presence of waste per month

	Paper	Plastic	Glass
January	2305	2548	1322
February	1900	2299	1203
March	1950	2406	1354
April	1220	1451	838
May	1798	2234	1447
June	1495	1936	1310
July	1686	2046	1525
August	1505	1877	1542
September	1281	1642	1246
October	1585	2006	1242
November	1575	2077	1169
December	1450	1743	1016

The 5 features selected are presented in the correlation matrix, depicted in Fig. 2. Through the obtained correlation matrix between the features, presence, and type of waste, it is possible to slightly suggest that there will be Plastic containers when there are Paper containers to be collected as the correlation index is slightly above 0.5 (*cf.* Fig. 2). Plastic has a weak positive correlation with presence (0.24). On the other hand, Activity has a weak negative relationship with distanceInterv (−0.13). Also, Month feature and WeekDay feature have a weak relationship with the waste types. In the case of WeekDay feature, it has a weak negative relationship with Paper, Plastic, and Glass. Most features have a weak relationship once their values are very close to zero.

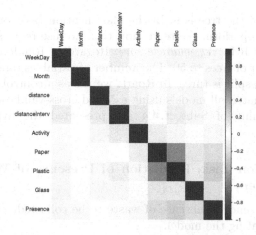

Fig. 2. Correlation matrix between the 5 attributes, the type of waste and the presence of waste.

4 Experimental Results and Discussion

In this section, we start by presenting our experimental setup. We then discuss the obtained results for the classification problem, *i.e.*, the prediction of presence or absence of containers by type. Next, we present the results for the regression problem, *i.e.*, the prediction of the number of containers available for collection. Lastly, we've solved the same problems with AutoML (this is, for classification and regression task).

4.1 Experimental Setup

The models chosen were Random Forest [13], gradient boosting with XGBoost [6] and Rpart [24]. All development was made with R [22]. For AutoML models we use H2O package [1], also from R.

Regarding the models' nomenclature:

- XGB – represents XGBoost;
- RF – represents Random Forest;
- A – is representative of use AutoML;
- 50 – is representative of the boosted rounds (for XGB) or number of trees (for RF);
- g – represents grid search.

Example: RF_50 represents that Random Forest is performed with 50 trees; AXGB_2 represents AutoML XGBoost with 2 number of boosting rounds.

In Subsect. 4.2 and Subsect. 4.3, XGBoost is performed with 50 rounds. For the classification and the regression task, we use the default parameters, which are: number of threads used for training are 2, each step size is 0.3, and the maximum depth of the tree is 6. In the classification task, our objective function is *softmax*. To perform the regression task, we use regression with squared loss (designated at R by *reg:squarederror*). Regarding Random Forest (RF), we defined the number of trees to 50. The number of variables randomly sampled as candidates at each split is three. In Rpart, we use as a control experiment equal to 0.001. We evaluated all models using a 5-fold cross-validation approach.

At the beginning of Subsect. 4.4 are presented the hyperparameters of AutoML.

4.2   Classification Task: Prediction of Presence of Waste in Containers

To predict the presence or absence of waste to be collected, we use accuracy as a metric for evaluating the model.

Obtained Results. Although the data is unbalanced, what is relevant for the analysis of our problem is the existence of containers for collection - the majority class - and not precisely their absence. The focus is to achieve a good performance in the classification of existence. So, this would bring the possibility of the collection being carried out with high certainty, bringing cost reduction without any loss for the citizens. Therefore, in this perspective, to assess how good our model is, we intend to evaluate among all the examples classified as existing collection containers the quantity of correctly classified examples. Assuming that we are in the presence of containers, there is no difference if there were 2, 3, or more containers to be collected, once that all of them reducing to 1, *i.e.*, converted to symbolize the presence of a single container.

Table 2 shows that the average accuracy of Rpart is, in general, the highest between types of waste containers. Among the best results for XGB_50 and RF_50, the classifier with high accuracy for predicting the presence of Paper, Plastic, and Glass containers is XGB_50. Table 3 shows that XGB_50 has the best results for predicting presence of Paper and Plastic. Rpart has the best result for predicting presence of Glass.

Table 2. Accuracy obtained by XGBoost, RF and Rpart for best results.

	XGB_50	RF_50	Rpart
Paper	0.6028 ± 0.0118	0.5683 ± 0.0112	0.7340 ± 0.0012
Plastic	0.7511 ± 0.0052	0.7162 ± 0.7162	0.7852 ± 0.0074
Glass	0.6746 ± 0.0158	0.6632 ± 0.0160	0.7457 ± 0.0347

We can visualize the model characteristics through the ROC curves, containing the true positive rate (sensitivity) and the false positive rate (1-specificity). These curves allow an overview of the classifier. As we can observe in Fig. 3 the classifiers are very close on their best results.

Table 3. AUC obtained by XGBoost, RF and Rpart best results

	XGB_50	RF_50	Rpart
Paper	0.7748	0.7661	0.7740
Plastic	0.7548	0.7268	0.7407
Glass	0.8037	0.8047	0.8128

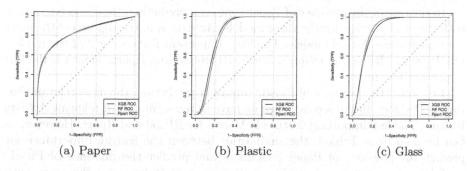

(a) Paper   (b) Plastic   (c) Glass

Fig. 3. ROC curves for the prediction of presence of waste in the containers.

Models Comparison. To assess the goodness of each classifier, we decided to use the critical difference diagram [9]. Figure 4 presents a comparison of all three classifiers, which visually inspects whether there is a statistical difference between the results of the classifiers.

In the first objective (classification of the presence of Paper, Plastic, and Glass containers), the classifiers are statistically indistinguishable, as we can observe in Fig. 4, *i.e.*, the distance is inferior to the critical distance. The data is not enough to conclude if they have the same performance.

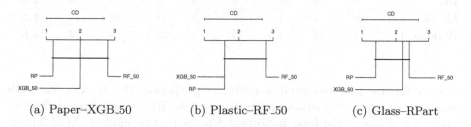

(a) Paper–XGB_50   (b) Plastic–RF_50   (c) Glass–RPart

Fig. 4. Critical difference diagrams for the prediction of presence of waste in the containers.

Feature Importance. A relevant aspect in the analysis is the feature importance for this classification task. The feature importance is according to the gain function described in [7] for XGBoost, and this is a "fractional contribution of each feature to the model based on the total gain of this features splits" [7]. In

Random Forest, the difference between the prediction error for each tree and the error after permuting each predictor variable is averaged over all trees [13], this is the feature importance considers the mean decrease in the accuracy overall classes, according to the described in [13]. Feature importance in Rpart is the "sum of the goodness of split measures for each split" according to [24]. In all cases is considered the importance of the global model considering the feature under analysis. Table 4 presents the results.

In the case of the presence of Paper container prediction, the *Distance* feature is the most important for the three models. *Activity* is in the top two of the most relevant features for all models. The least important feature for 2 of the models (XGB_50 and RF_50) is *DistanceInterv*, DI. Regarding Rpart, *Month* is the less important feature.

Regarding the presence of Plastic container prediction, the most relevant feature is *Distance* and in second place we have as the second most relevant *Activity* feature. The less important feature is Month for RF_50 and Rpart. However, as can be seen from Table 4, the similarities between the feature importance for predict the presence of Paper containers and predict the presence of Plastic containers are pretty evident. The most important features are the same, with only slight changes in the less relevant features. XGB_50 has no change in their positions when comparing both predictions, the presence of Paper and Plastic containers.

Table 4. Rank of feature importance for the prediction of presence of waste in the containers.

	Paper			Plastic			Glass			Avg.
	XGB_50	RF__50	Rpart	XGB_50	RF__50	Rpart	XGB_50	RF__50	Rpart	rank
Activity	2	2	2	2	2	2	2	1	1	1.78
Distance	1	1	1	1	1	1	1	2	2	1.22
DI	5	5	3	5	4	3	5	5	4	4.33
Month	3	4	5	3	5	5	4	4	5	4.22
WeekDay	4	3	4	4	3	4	3	3	3	3.44

Regarding the presence of Glass container prediction, the Activity feature is considered the most important in the two models (RP_50 and Rpart). The DI feature is considered the least important feature by two models (XGB_50 and RF_50). Comparing the rank of feature importance of Paper and Plastic with Glass, the last has a less similar rank distribution with the two other cases (Paper and Plastic). In Glass, XGB_50 presents a slight change in the third and fourth positions compared with Paper and Plastic results. Rank of feature importance for the presence of Glass containers for RF_50 and Rpart, especially in the most important features, is not coincident with the prediction for Paper and Plastic containers.

Finally, observing the average ranks for each feature, we see that the most relevant feature is the distance. That is, the lowest rank value corresponds to the most important feature. The least important feature, on average, is DistanceInterv.

4.3   Regression Task: Prediction of Quantity of Containers with Waste

Predicting the quantity of each type of container to be collected is our second objective of this work. Paper, Plastic, and Glass are better divided between classes than the containers' global presence or absence.

Obtained Results. Since our target is a discrete quantitative variable, this predicts the number of waste containers, MAE (Mean Absolute Error) was considered the metric for evaluating the models. Table 5 presents all MAE results.

Table 5. MAE estimates obtained by XGBoost, RF and Rpart for the prediction of quantity of containers with waste.

	XGB_50	RF_50	Rpart
Paper_MAE	0.7466	0.9887	1.0384
Plastic_MAE	0.5848	0.7571	0.7680
Glass_MAE	0.3486	0.5111	0.4676

Models Comparison. In order to compare the three models, we built the critical difference diagram for each type of waste (*cf.* Fig. 5). The distance between models is lower or equal to the critical distance, so they are statistically indistinguishable. As in the classification task, also in the regression task, it is not possible to make conclusions about performance.

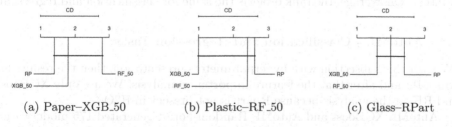

(a) Paper–XGB_50   (b) Plastic–RF_50   (c) Glass–RPart

Fig. 5. Critical difference diagram for the prediction of quantity of containers with waste.

Table 6. Rank of feature importance for the prediction of quantity of containers with waste.

| | Paper | | | Plastic | | | Glass | | | Avg. |
	XGB_50	RF_50	Rpart	XGB_50	RF_50	Rpart	XGB_50	RF_50	Rpart	rank
Activity	2	1	3	2	1	1	2	2	2	1.78
Distance	1	3	2	1	2	2	1	1	1	1.56
DI	5	4	4	5	5	5	5	4	5	4.67
Month	3	5	5	3	4	4	4	5	4	4.11
WeekDay	4	2	1	4	3	3	3	3	3	2.89

Feature Importance. Similar to what we have done in the classification task, we carried a feature importance analysis for this regression task also see Table 6.

Regarding the prediction of the number of Paper containers with waste, the feature importance illustrates that XGBoost and Random Forest models do not explain this in the same way. That is, the importance given to features varies from model to model. Activity and Distance are the most important features for predicting waste Paper containers (at RF_50 and XGB_50, respectively). There is no consensus in models about feature importance rank positions. However, Month is the less relevant feature for RF_50 and Rpart.

For Plastic, we can observe that Activity is the most important feature for decision in RF_50 and Rpart. Although the Activity feature remains between the first positions, it is not the most important at XGB_50. That position occupied by Distance. RF_50 and Rpart have a consensus in all important feature orders. XGB_50 agree with RF_50 and Rpart in the less important feature (DI).

The consensus among models regarding the importance of features seems possible in Glass prediction. The Distance is considered the most important feature, followed by Activity (at XGB_50, RF_50 and Rpart). Also, the third position is consensual between models regarding the WeekDay.

Observing the average ranks for each feature, present in Table 6, the most important feature is the distance. That is, the lowest rank value corresponds to the most important feature. The least important feature, on average, is DistanceInterv. On average, the rank order is the same for classification and regression.

4.4   AutoML - Classification and Regression Tasks

We start this subsection with hyperparameters presentation, then the results for AutoML, and after that the feature importance analysis. We use only XGBoost and RF on the analysis because Rpart is not present in H2O.

AutoML XGBoost and AutoML Random Forest generated 175 model variations. We present the three best results for each type of waste for each task.

Hyperparameters. In AutoML all models consider 0.3 as the step size for boosting steps. The number of threads is four, and the growing policy is depthwise. We evaluated all models using a 5-fold cross-validation approach. In the classification task, the objective function is *binary:logistic* and in the regression task is *reg:squarederror*. The maximum depth of the tree is ten. The only exception is to predict the number of Paper containers for the regression task. In this case, the maximum depth is twenty. The number of rounds and the number of trees is equal between them but varies according to the model. For the classification task, the number of rounds is 38 for Paper, 55 for Plastic and 56 for Glass. For the regression task, the lower number of rounds is 50 for Plastic, 61 for Paper and 98 for Glass. All models which present their nomenclature "g" represent that they performed with grid search.

Obtained Results. Comparing Table 7 with Table 2, we can observe that the selected metric for classification is better in the case of classification with AutoML. Not only for XGBoost, but for all classifiers presented at Table 2.

Table 7. Metrics - classification task using AutoML

	Accuracy
AXGB_g_38 (Paper)	0.7710 ± 0.0033
AXGB_g_55 (Plastic)	0.8458 ± 0.0045
AXGB_g_56 (Glass)	0.8712 ± 0.0061

In case of prediction of the number of containers, when we compare Table 8 with Table 5, we observe that the only result in which AutoML does not perform better is in predicting the number of Glass waste containers. This is, when the MAE is high with AutoML.

Table 8. Metrics - regression task using AutoML

	MAE
AXGB_g_61 (Paper)	0.6774 ± 0.0108
AXGB_50 (Plastic)	0.4755 ± 0.0080
AXGB_g_98 (Glass)	0.4434 ± 0.0049

Generally, AutoML improves the results on predicting each type of waste container and the prediction of the number of waste containers.

Feature Importance. Feature importance is computed considering gains of the respective loss functions for XGBoost, in the case of Random Forest is calculated by the relative influence of each variable (as described in [20]). The best classifiers (for Paper, Plastic and Glass) consider *distance* as the most important feature (cf. Table 9). *Activity*, namely, *Activity.Other* is the second most important for predict the presence of Paper and Glass. The other features are different and depend on the type of prediction (for containers) under analysis. AutoML indicates not only the feature but also the class of feature selected for the feature importance.

Table 9. Rank of feature importance - classification task using AutoML

	AXGB_g_38 (Pap)	AXGB_g_55 (Pla)	AXGB_g_56 (Gla)	Avg. rank
Distance	1	1	1	1
Activity.Other	2	–	2	2
WeekDay.Thursday	–	–	3	3
Activity.TakeAway	–	–	4	4
Activity.MiniMarket	–	–	5	5
Activity.Coffee	–	2	–	2
Month.August	–	3	–	3
distanceInterv.QQ2	–	4	–	4
Activity.Other	–	5	–	5
Activity.PastryShop	3	–	–	3
Activity.Bakery	4	–	–	4
WeekDay.Monday	5	–	–	5

In the case of the regression (cf. Table 10), *Distance* remains the most important feature in all container number predictions. The *Activity*, in particular, *Activity.Other* is the second most important for the prediction of Glass containers. In the case of Paper, it occupies the fifth position. Contrary to the classification case, the most important features are relevant for predicting the number of containers in different types of waste.

Table 10. Rank of feature importance - regression task using AutoML

	AXGB_g_61 (Pap)	AXGB_50 (Pla)	AXGB_g_98 (Gla)	Avg. rank
Distance	1	1	1	1
Activity.Other	5	–	2	3.5
WeekDay.Wednesday	–	3	–	3
Month.August	–	–	4	4
WeekDay.Monday	–	2	3	2.5
WeekDay.Friday	–	4	5	4.5
Activity.HOTEL	2	–	–	2
Activity.Services	3	–	–	3
Activity.Restaurant	4	5	–	4.5

5   Conclusions

In this work, we use three Machine Learning algorithms (XGBoost, Random Forest and Rpart) to predict the presence or absence of containers and predict the number of containers. Both tasks by type of waste. Later we used AutoML for XGBoost and Random Forest to increase the system's predictive performance in classification and regression tasks, without losses for citizens, but with improvements in waste collection.

It is possible to conclude that different models produce different explanations and return features with different importance. This result happens even when the overall results of the models are very similar and statistically indistinguishable. The differences occur due to a principal fact: the choice of the machine learning algorithm. For the first analysis, we fixed the model parameters. In a second analysis, we resort to AutoML to train and tune several models. The number of rounds and the number of trees seems to have been enough for AutoML to improve the results. XGboost presents the best results for AutoML in both tasks. Generally, AutoML improves the results on predicting each type of waste container and the prediction of the number of waste containers. This aspect allowed us to find a sharp difference between the features that explain the presence of containers by type of waste. The same is true for the regression task, although some features are common in their importance for predicting the number of containers.

We intend to enhance a route optimization system in future work, indicating whether or not the truck should stop. This way, we are looking for efficient and valuable solutions that promote more intelligent and more sustainable ecosystems. Strategies that make life in cities healthier and happier for everyone.

Acknowledgments. The research reported in this work was partially supported by the European Commission funded project "Humane AI: Toward AI Systems That Augment and Empower Humans by Understanding Us, our Society and the World Around Us" (grant #820437). The support is gratefully acknowledged.

References

1. H2O: R interface for H2O (2020). http://www.h2o.ai
2. APA: Produção e gestão de resíduos urbanos (2019)
3. APA: Relatório anual de resíduos urbanos (2019)
4. Arribas, C.A., Blazquez, C.A., L.A.: Urban solid waste collection system using mathematical modelling and tools of geographic information systems. Waste Manage. Res. **28**, 355–363 (2010)
5. Calabró, P.S., Komilis, D.: A standardized inspection methodology to evaluate municipal solid waste collection performance. J. Environ. Manage. **246**, 184–191 (2019)
6. Chen, T., Guestrin, C.: Xgboost: A scalable tree boosting system. In: Proceedings of the 22nd ACM SIGKDD International Conference on Knowledge Discovery and Data Mining, KDD 2016, pp. 785–794. ACM, New York (2016)

7. Chen, T., et al.: Xgboost: Extreme gradient Boosting (2021). https://CRAN.R-project.org/package=xgboost r package version 1.4.1.1
8. Dat, L., Linh, D., Chou, S., Yu, V.: Optimizing reverse logistic costs for recycling end-of-life electrical and electronic products. Expert Syst. Appl. **39**(7), 6380–6387 (2012)
9. Demsar, J.: Statistical comparisons of classifiers over multiple data sets. J. Mach. Learn. Res. **7**, 1–30 (2006)
10. Ferrer, J., Alba, E.: BIN-CT: urban waste collection based on predicting the container fill level. Biosystems **186**, 103962 (2019)
11. Filipe, N.: Smart cities - agendamento dinamico de recolhas de residuos porta-a-porta, master thesis. University of Porto (2018)
12. Kotthoff, L., Thornton, C., Hoos, H.H., Hutter, F., Leyton-Brown, K.: Auto-WEKA: automatic model selection and hyperparameter optimization in WEKA. In: Hutter, F., Kotthoff, L., Vanschoren, J. (eds.) Automated Machine Learning. TSSCML, pp. 81–95. Springer, Cham (2019). https://doi.org/10.1007/978-3-030-05318-5_4
13. Liaw, A., Wiener, M.: Classification and regression by randomforest. R News **2**(3), 18–22 (2002). https://CRAN.R-project.org/doc/Rnews/
14. LIPOR: Monthly reports. Tech. rep., LIPOR, September 2019
15. Londres, G.: Using data science to optimize waste collection, master thesis. University of Porto (2020)
16. Londres, G., Filipe, N., Gama, J.: Optimizing waste collection: a data mining approach. In: Cellier, P., Driessens, K. (eds.) ECML PKDD 2019. CCIS, vol. 1167, pp. 570–578. Springer, Cham (2020). https://doi.org/10.1007/978-3-030-43823-4_45
17. MAOTDR: Regime geral da gestão de resíduos, September 2006. decreto-Lei n.o 178/2006
18. Martinho, G., et al.: A case study of packaging waste collection systems in Portugal - part I: performance and operation analysis. Waste Manage. **61**, 96–107 (2017)
19. Navghane, S.S., Killedar, M.S., Rohokale, V.M.: IoT based smart garbage and waste collection bin. Int. J. Adv. Res. Electron. Commun. Eng. (IJARECE) **5**(5), 1576–1578 (2016)
20. Rifkin, R., Klautau, A.: In defense of one-vs-all classification. J. Mach. Learn. Res **5**, 101–141 (2004). http://www.jmlr.org/papers/v5/rifkin04a.html
21. Sniezek, J., Bodin, L.: Using mixed integer programming for solving the capacitated arc routing problem with vehicle/site dependencies with an application to the routing of residential sanitation collection vehicles. Ann. Oper. Res. **144**(1), 33–58 (2006)
22. Team, R.C.: R: A Language and Environment for Statistical Computing. R Foundation for Statistical Computing, Vienna (2020)
23. Teixeira, J., Antunes, A.P., de Sousa, J.P.: Recyclable waste collection planning-a case study. Eur. J. Oper. Res. **158**(3), 543–554 (2004)
24. Therneau, T., Atkinson, B.: RPART: recursive partitioning and regression trees (2019). https://CRAN.R-project.org/package=rpart r package version 4.1-15
25. Tung, D.V., Pinnoi, A.: Vehicle routing-scheduling for waste collection in Hanoi. Eur. J. Oper. Res. **125**(3), 449–468 (2000)

Applying Machine Learning for Traffic Forecasting in Porto, Portugal

Paulo Maia[1]([✉]) [iD], Joana Morgado[2,3] [iD], Tiago Gonçalves[2,4] [iD],
and Tomé Albuquerque[2,4] [iD]

[1] NILG.AI, Porto, Portugal
paulo.maia@nilg.ai
[2] INESC TEC - Institute for Systems and Computer Engineering,
Technology and Science, Porto, Portugal
{tiago.f.goncalves,tome.m.albuquerque,joana.p.morgado}@inesctec.pt
[3] Faculty of Sciences (FCUP), University of Porto, Porto, Portugal
[4] Faculty of Engineering (FEUP), University of Porto, Porto, Portugal

Abstract. Pollutant emissions from passenger cars give rise to harmful effects on human health and the environment. Predicting traffic flow is a challenging problem, but essential to understand what factors influence car traffic and what measures should be taken to reduce carbon dioxide emissions. In this work, we developed a predictive model to forecast traffic flow in several locations in the city of Porto for 24 h later, *i.e.*, the next day at the same time. We trained a XGBoost Regressor with multi-modal data from 2018 and 2019 obtained from traffic and weather sensors of the city of Porto and the geographic location of several points of interest. The proposed model achieved a mean absolute error, mean square error, Spearman's rank correlation coefficient, and Pearson correlation coefficient equal to 80.59, 65395, 0.9162, and 0.7816, respectively, when tested on the test set. The developed model makes it possible to analyse which areas of the city of Porto will have more traffic the next day and take measures to optimise this increasing flow of cars. One of the ideas present in the literature is to develop intelligent traffic lights that change their timers according to the expected traffic in the area. This system could help decrease the levels of carbon dioxide emitted and therefore decrease its harmful effects on the health of the population and the environment.

Keywords: Traffic flow forecasting · Smart cities · Sustainability

1 Introduction

The successful deployment of intelligent transportation systems (ITS) in the next generation of smart cities depends on accurate and timely traffic flow information since it has the potential to help road users make better travel decisions,

Supported by World Data League and the City Hall of Porto.

alleviate traffic congestion, reduce carbon emissions, and improve traffic operation efficiency [7]. For instance, according to the European Environment Agency (EEA), passenger cars are a significant polluter, accounting for 60.7% of total carbon dioxide emissions from road transport in Europe [9]. Moreover, pollutant emissions caused by the traffic (*e.g.*, direct exhaust emissions or non-exhaust emissions originating from tire, brake wear, road surface and engine wear, evaporative emissions, and re-suspended crystal and street dust particles) negatively impact human health [11]. Congested cities are a significant contributor to this.

A precise prediction of the traffic flow in the city along with a comprehensive understanding of the factors that influence the traffic, will support decision-makers to take action into reducing carbon dioxide emissions, improve operational efficiency and contribute to better health quality of the citizens [11,13]. Therefore, tackling this problem is of interest to several stakeholders such as individual travellers, business sectors, and government agencies [19].

Predicting traffic flow is a challenging problem due to *spatial dependencies* (*e.g.*, outflow in a region affects inflow in another), *temporal dependencies* (*e.g.*, traffic congestion at 8am affects typical traffic at 9am, people's routine changes throughout the year) or *environmental factors* (*e.g.*, the weather) [17]. Current methodologies address this task by leveraging multi-modal data and deep learning algorithms [12].

In this work we propose the jointly use of multi-modal data obtained from several sensors of the city of Porto (Portugal) and the geographic location of several points of interest to train an XGBoost Regressor which forecasts the traffic flow for 24 h later. As we are entering a new era of data-driven transportation management and control, powered by the availability and access to new emerging traffic sensor technologies [2,18], we argue that this applied research work may unveil interesting lines of research for the city of Porto, towards sustainability and innovation.

Besides this introduction, the remainder of the paper is organised as follows: Sect. 2 presents the methodology and data that were used to address this challenge; Sect. 3 presents the results; Sect. 4 provides a brief discussion; and Sect. 5 concludes the paper with the main contributions and proposes future work directions.

The code related to this paper is publicly available in a GitLab repository[1].

2   Methodology

2.1   Data Set Description

The city of Porto has been registering car counts at several locations with Inductive Loop sensors since 2015. In the 2021 edition of World Data League[2], a

---

[1] https://gitlab.com/worlddataleague/wdl-solutions/-/tree/main/WDL_2021/Stage_2_Traffic/Challenge_1_Predicting_traffic_flow_in_a_city_using_induction_loop_sensors/Tech\%20Moguls.

[2] https://www.worlddataleague.com.

programming competition which aims to find the best data scientists by solving social-oriented problems, the City Hall of Porto[3] granted access to traffic-related data sources to the participants:

- Sensor data from induction loop sensors: a set of 129 sensors periodically recorded with the number of cars that pass it. Data is available from January 2015 to April 2021 with 4.15 M data points at 15 min sampling.
- Weather conditions: a set of 26 sensors periodically measuring barometric pressure, dew point, relative humidity, solar radiation, temperature, wind direction and wind speed. Data is available from January 2018 to April 2021 with 1.77 M data points and irregular sampling (i.e., it is currently undefined by the data providers).
- Points of interest: a list of 1910 points of interest in the city of Porto, containing the location - latitude and longitude - and the category (e.g., stores, restaurants, apartments, among many others).

Figure 1 shows the locations of sensors throughout the city of Porto.

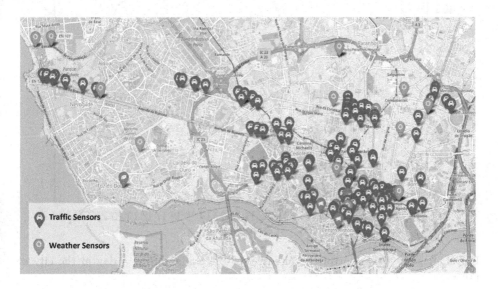

Fig. 1. Sensors distribution by type in the city of Porto.

2.2   Exploratory Data Analysis

We started by doing an exploratory analysis of the data to gain intuition about the problem and define a strategy to solve the problem. We framed our analysis on the types of sensors that ended up being essential to the predictive problem: traffic sensors and weather sensors. Regarding traffic sensors, we noticed that in

---

[3] https://www.porto.pt/pt.

the area of Foz and Campanhã, there seems to be less traffic sensors compared to the remaining major areas of Porto (*i.e.*, Boavista, Antas, Baixa (Downtown) and Bonfim). On the other hand, weather sensors seem to have a relevant amount of coverage throughout the city.

To understand which traffic sensors should be included in our training set, we had to perform a data visualisation. Traffic intensity per sensor was averaged for each hour of the day. Sensors where a manual analysis showed patterns that were contrary to common knowledge (e.g. higher intensity in 00:00-04:00 than rush hours) were removed, after confirming with the data provider that some timestamps had abnormal behaviour.

Figure 2 shows the regular behaviour of the intensity of the traffic during a day in the city of Porto.

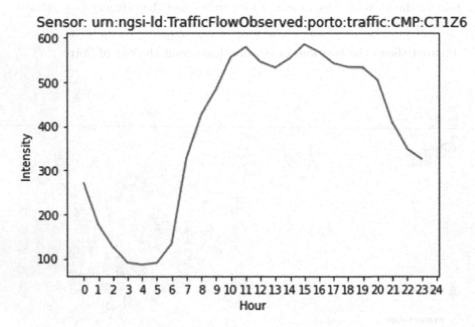

Fig. 2. Regular behaviour of the intensity of the traffic during a day in the city of Porto.

Starting the analysis at 00:00, we realise that the traffic intensity decreases during the night. The intensity starts to increase around 04:00/05:00, which marks the time-points when people start their working routine. It then increases until 10:00/11:00 and keeps an approximately stable behaviour until the end of the working hours, 18:00/19:00, starting to decrease afterwards.

2.3   Target Definition

Initially, we considered that the target of our model should be the value in the next hour since we wanted to develop an actionable system in a more immediate way, such as in the next hour, rather than 24 h later. However, the reality is that data may not be available immediately, and may, for example, be stored and transmitted at the end of the day. Thus, to avoid data integration lags, we decided to build a model that would make the forecast for the next day at the same time.

Figure 3 shows the target distribution in log scale.

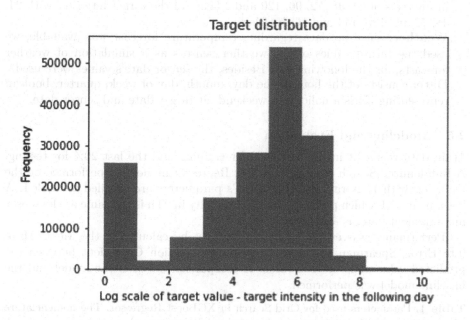

Fig. 3. Target distribution.

2.4   Data Processing and Feature Extraction

To create an equitative interval for the data points and reduce the computational complexity, both weather and sensor data were resampled to an hourly period. Data from 2018 and 2019 was used, which is a common period between both datasets and before the start of the COVID-19 pandemic restrictions. This decision is based on the impact that the pandemic caused in the natural flow of traffic, which would make our analysis less generalisable. After this resampling procedure, traffic data and weather data contain 1.8 M and 108 k samples, respectively.

It is important to take into account that weather data, which is very important for predicting traffic, has no direct mapping to the traffic sensors' location. Therefore, as the sensor distribution is in a small radius, the weather features were averaged per hour.

Given a pair *(sensor id, timestamp)*, we have computed the following features:

- **Sensor location:** consists of the distance to the centroid of the sensors' location. This is an encoding of latitude and longitude that represents the similarity between sensors.
- **Sensor traffic intensity:** consists of the current value, the aggregate statistics (mean, max, min and standard deviation) of rolling windows of intensity in intervals of 24, 48, 72, 96, 120 and 144 h and the target intensity with 24, 48, 72, 96, 120, 144 and 168 h of lag.
- **Weather:** since no data regarding temperature forecast was available, we used the future values of the weather sensors as a simulation of weather forecasts, for the following day. Besides, the sensor date's values were used.
- **Date:** consists of the hour of the day, month, day of week, quarter, boolean representing if it's a holiday or weekend, at target date and sensor date.

2.5   Modeling and Evaluation

Train data was split in the first 80% for training and the last 20% for testing. A Randomized Search with an XGBoost Regressor model was performed on the train set, with 15 iterations. The model's parameters are detailed in Table 1. A baseline model, which predicts that the intensity in 24 h is the same as the sensor measurement date, is also done.

Performance was evaluated on the test set by calculating the Mean Absolute Error, Spearman Rank and Pearson Correlation Coefficient between the predicted value and the true value. A comparison between the model and the baseline model was performed.

Table 1. Parameters used for Grid Search in XGBoost Regressor. The nomenclature of range presented below is (start_value, end_value, increment).

n_estimators	Range (100, 400, 100)
max_depth	Range (3, 10, 2)
min_child_weight	Range (1, 6, 2)
gamma	Range (0.1, 0.5, 0.1)

3   Results

Table 2 compares the model performance on the test set with a baseline model.

Figure 4 presents a SHAP Plot (based on the *Tree Explainer* available in SHAP (SHapley Additive exPlanations) package[4]) that shows us the model focuses mostly on lagged features and month features (correlated with seasonality and weather).

---

[4] https://github.com/slundberg/shap.

Table 2. Results obtained with the baseline and the proposal model. MAE refers to the mean absolute error, MSE to the mean square error, Spearman Rank to the Spearman's rank correlation coefficient, and Pearson rank to the Pearson correlation coefficient.

Model	MAE	RMSE	Spearman rank	Pearson rank
Baseline	93.22	324	0.9012	0.6867
Proposal	**80.59**	**256**	**0.9162**	**0.7816**

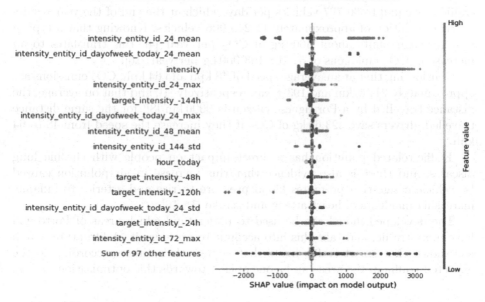

Fig. 4. SHAP plot obtained for our model.

Please note that the model is giving high importance to the temporal features (e.g., intensity_entity_id_dayofweek_today_24_mean). This may be due to: 1) the fact that we have more temporal features in our feature subset (hence, these features end up getting more weight in the decision), or 2) the features obtained from the other sensors are not enough (e.g., it would be interesting to have more air quality sensors throughout the city, to have meaningful features of this parameter related to each region).

As expected, intensity is one of the most important features and is very relevant for predicting traffic. High intensity values increase the predicted traffic for the next day. The target intensities 144 h, 120 h, 48 h and 24 h before the forecast time the next day are also very relevant for traffic forecasting.

4   Discussion

The impact of tourism and the economic growth that has taken place in Porto translates into an increase in the number of cars in circulation [10].

Per year, there has been a 4.1% increase in the number of vehicles (*i.e.*, essentially cars) in circulation in the Greater Porto region, and this increase does not seem to be slowing down [15].

Let's take the year 2019 as an example. In 2019, the annual average daily traffic was equal to 30 797 vehicles per day, which at the end of the year results in the circulation of approximately 11 240 905 vehicles. Knowing that a typical passenger car emits about 4600 kg of CO_2 per year [4], this translates to an increase in CO_2 emissions of 51 708 163 000 kg per year [15]!

Considering that at an average speed of 48 kph and 64 kph, CO_2 emissions are approximately 217 g/km and 193 g/km, respectively [1], and that on average, the distance travelled by a Portuguese citizen is 9000 km [8], for the same distance travelled, drivers save 223.69 kg of CO_2 if they increase the speed from 48 to 64 kph.

Traffic-related pollution has a direct impact on people with chronic lung diseases, and there is also evidence that this increase in air pollution caused by vehicle congestion promotes blood pressure to rise and arteries to inflame, increasing incidents of heart attack and stroke [14,16].

The developed model can be used to understand which areas of Porto will have more traffic, and take this into account to optimise it. A literature search has shown that smart traffic lights that change their timers according to the expected traffic in the area can be one option towards this optimisation [3,5,6].

5   Conclusion and Future Work

In this work, we have developed a forecasting model for predicting traffic intensity in several locations in the city of Porto. There is no direct comparison with model performance in the literature as this data set has not been used before.

The novelty of this work is in the development of a practical application specifically for the city of Porto. The used methods and calculated features follow literature practices.

Future work should be devoted to an extensive comparison of methods for traffic forecasting published in the literature. Moreover, alternative models can be used, such as convolutional neural networks (CNNs) and Long Short Term Memory Networks (LSTMs) which employ traffic intensity as image channels, and predict the intensity for each pixel (latitude/longitude). This may achieve better results than the current approach.

Considering the option of developing smart traffic lights, there are a couple of extra data that would be relevant to have:

- Data regarding the position of traffic lights: We need data regarding the traffic lights positions because it would allows us to have a more precise model.

Please note that the geographic data we used in this work is obtained from traffic intensity detection sensors, which may not be in the real location.
– The average speed of cars in that location: We intend to increase the average speed of cars in order to increase the air quality. However, we acknowledge that our assumptions would be better if we had access to data regarding the speed of cars in the City of Porto, obtained in the spot.

Acknowledgements. This work was developed in the context of World Data League, which is a global competition that aims to solve problems socially-oriented problems by using data. The data was kindly provided by the City Hall of Porto.

References

1. Barth, M., Boriboonsomsin, K.: Real-world carbon dioxide impacts of traffic congestion. Transp. Res. Rec. **2058**(1), 163–171 (2008)
2. Chen, C.P., Zhang, C.Y.: Data-intensive applications, challenges, techniques and technologies: a survey on big data. Inf. Sci. **275**, 314–347 (2014)
3. Díaz, N., Guerra, J., Nicola, J.: Smart traffic light control system. In: 2018 IEEE Third Ecuador Technical Chapters Meeting (ETCM), pp. 1–4. IEEE (2018)
4. The U.S. Environmental Protection Agency: Greenhouse gas emissions from a typical passenger vehicle (2005)
5. Hartanti, D., Aziza, R.N., Siswipraptini, P.C.: Optimization of smart traffic lights to prevent traffic congestion using fuzzy logic. TELKOMNIKA Telecommun. Comput. Electron. Control **17**(1), 320–327 (2019)
6. Kanungo, A., Sharma, A., Singla, C.: Smart traffic lights switching and traffic density calculation using video processing. In: 2014 recent advances in Engineering and computational sciences (RAECS), pp. 1–6. IEEE (2014)
7. Lv, Y., Duan, Y., Kang, W., Li, Z., Wang, F.Y.: Traffic flow prediction with big data: a deep learning approach. IEEE Trans. Intell. Transp. Syst. **16**(2), 865–873 (2014)
8. Observatório, A.: Estudo condutor português (2018)
9. Parliament, E.: CO2 emissions from cars: facts and figures (infographics). https://www.europarl.europa.eu/news/en/headlines/society/20190313STO31218/co2-emissions-from-cars-facts-and-figures-infographics (2019). Accessed 16 June 2021
10. Portugala, A.A.D.: Estatísticas do sector automóvel (2018)
11. Sanchez, K.A., et al.: Urban policy interventions to reduce traffic emissions and traffic-related air pollution: protocol for a systematic evidence map. Environ. Int. **142**, 105826 (2020)
12. Schimbinschi, F., Nguyen, X.V., Bailey, J., Leckie, C., Vu, H., Kotagiri, R.: Traffic forecasting in complex urban networks: leveraging big data and machine learning. In: 2015 IEEE International Conference on Big Data (Big Data), pp. 1019–1024. IEEE (2015)
13. Shahid, N., Shah, M.A., Khan, A., Maple, C., Jeon, G.: Towards greener smart cities and road traffic forecasting using air pollution data. Sustain. Cities Soc. **72**, 103062 (2021)
14. Sydbom, A., Blomberg, A., Parnia, S., Stenfors, N., Sandström, T., Dahlen, S.: Health effects of diesel exhaust emissions. Eur. Respir. J. **17**(4), 733–746 (2001)
15. Instituto de Mobilidade e dos Transportes (IMT): Anuário estatístico de mobilidade e dos transportes (2019)

16. Vimercati, L., et al.: Traffic related air pollution and respiratory morbidity. Lung India **28**(4), 238 (2011)
17. Zhang, J., Zheng, Y., Qi, D.: Deep spatio-temporal residual networks for city-wide crowd flows prediction. In: Proceedings of the AAAI Conference on Artificial Intelligence, vol. 31 (2017)
18. Zhang, J., Wang, F.Y., Wang, K., Lin, W.H., Xu, X., Chen, C.: Data-driven intelligent transportation systems: a survey. IEEE Trans. Intell. Transp. Syst. **12**(4), 1624–1639 (2011)
19. Zhang, N., Wang, F.Y., Zhu, F., Zhao, D., Tang, S.: Dynacas: computational experiments and decision support for its. IEEE Intell. Syst. **23**(6), 19–23 (2008)

IRLCov19: A Large COVID-19 Multilingual Twitter Dataset of Indian Regional Languages

Deepak Uniyal[1](✉) and Amit Agarwal[2]

[1] Graphic Era University, Dehradun, India
[2] IIT Roorkee, Roorkee, India
aagarwal3@cs.iitr.ac.in

Abstract. Emerged in Wuhan city of China in December 2019, COVID-19 continues to spread rapidly across the world despite authorities having made available a number of vaccines. While the coronavirus has been around for a significant period of time, people and authorities still feel the need for awareness due to the mutating nature of the virus and therefore varying symptoms and prevention strategies. People and authorities resort to social media platforms the most to share awareness information and voice out their opinions due to their massive outreach in spreading the word in practically no time. People use a number of languages to communicate over social media platforms based on their familiarity, language outreach, and availability on social media platforms. The entire world has been hit by the coronavirus and India is the second worst-hit country in terms of the number of active coronavirus cases. India, being a multilingual country, offers a great opportunity to study the outreach of various languages that have been actively used across social media platforms. In this study, we aim to study the dataset related to COVID-19 collected in the period between February 2020 to July 2020 specifically for regional languages in India. This could be helpful for the Government of India, various state governments, NGOs, researchers, and policymakers in studying different issues related to the pandemic. We found that English has been the mode of communication in over 64% of tweets while as many as twelve regional languages in India account for approximately 4.77% of tweets.

Keywords: COVID-19 · Twitter · Indian Regional Languages · Natural Language Processing

1 Introduction

The novel coronavirus that erupted in December 2019 from Wuhan, China marked the beginning of the COVID-19 pandemic. With COVID-19 insurgence around the world, people are heavily dependent on social media platforms (SMPs) like Twitter to post their opinions, raise awareness among the general public, show their fear, ask for help, and communicate with fellow citizens.

D. Uniyal and A. Agarwal—Equal contribution.

© Springer Nature Switzerland AG 2021
M. Kamp et al. (Eds.): ECML PKDD 2021 Workshops, CCIS 1525, pp. 309–324, 2021.
https://doi.org/10.1007/978-3-030-93733-1_22

Studies show that SMPs like Twitter has the potential to track emergencies in real-time that can be utilized by health officials, government agencies, and NGOs to respond quickly and more effectively [1, 2].

Since the outbreak of the COVID-19 pandemic, most countries around the world have enforced several preventive and control measures to limit the spread of the virus. The measures range from early screening, isolation of patients, school and workplace closures, curfews, limited numbers of people in social gatherings, travel restrictions, social distancing to even complete lockdown in chosen cities or country as a whole [3, 4]. The success of these preventive measures would effectively imply people maintaining social distance as far as possible and use technology to interact and fulfill their day-to-day needs. In scenarios like this, SMPs like Twitter, Facebook, YouTube, Instagram, Snapchat, Reddit, Pinterest, and LinkedIn, etc. play a vital role by allowing individuals to interact thus helping them to alleviate social isolation. Contrary to the studies which suggest increased loneliness in people by excessive use of social media [5], SMPs have rather emerged as a friend to reduce isolation and boredom during the COVID-19 pandemic [6].

Social media users may use a global or regional language to communicate on the platform based on their understanding of the language and ease of communication with other users producing a lot of data. With a plethora of unstructured data available on social media, it becomes crucial as to how one comprehends the information and uses it effectively to combat COVID-19. India, the second-most populous country in the world, has 23 constitutionally recognized official languages which people may use to communicate. According to a census in 2001, Hindi is the most widely used language in India and is spoken by 53.6% of the Indian population as their first language [7].

A major portion of the social media studies available today is based on the datasets in English. However, to better understand the information posted in the low-resource languages of the largest democracy in the world, we need to study the communication revolving around various Indian languages. Therefore, in this study, we have presented *IRLCov19*, a large COVID-19 Twitter dataset on various Indian regional languages which we collected between 01 February 2020 to 31 July 2020 [8]. We collected nearly 330 million tweets irrespective of the language used and refined it further to remove tweets with duplicate IDs to make the final tweet count to 280 million. We subsequently identified more than 13 million tweets in twelve Indian Regional Languages (*IRL*) from the dataset collected. This dataset can be advantageous for researchers, Government authorities, and policymakers in studying the pandemic from a varied perspective as listed below [9–14]:

– **Public health strategies:** People post the situational information or content on social media corresponding to the need or availability of resources related to various emergency services such as medical supply, bed availability, blood or plasma donation, etc. The dataset we provided, can be used in developing suitable information publishing strategies by studying situational information to effectively respond in a pandemic situation.

- **Identification of echo chambers in social media:** Misinformation or rumors are said to be escalated by a group of users having similar ideologies or interests, known as an echo chamber of social media. This kind of dataset can be of great help in the identification and investigation of the characteristics or social properties of echo chambers which can be helpful in preventing rumor propagation in the early stage.
- **Understanding public reactions and opinions:** Public post their reactions, sentiments, and opinions on the various events, announcements, and actual implementation of fiscal and monetary policies initiated by the government during or after the pandemic. This kind of dataset can be used to study the pandemic from a social perspective, as well as analyzing the public opinions, human behavior, and information spreading pattern across the network.
- **Individual reaction on different policies roll-out by government:** The Reserve Bank of India, along with the government of India and other regulatory bodies, announced various fiscal and monetary measures to aid businesses during the lockdown. Several fiscal benefits by the government include cash transfers to lower-income households, wage support and employment provision to low-wage workers, and insurance coverage for workers in the healthcare sector etc. The monetary benefits include a reduction in the repo and the reverse repo rate by RBI. The government also announced several measures to ease the tax compliance burden such as postponing the tax and GST fillings. The analysis of the Twitter dataset can help gauze the public sentiment related to these policies. This would also help the government and authorities review how strategically the policies were implemented and were able to provide relief to the public.
- **Early detection and surveillance of the pandemic:** Early detection of the pandemic can be helpful in preventing the further spread of the disease and loss of casualties. The analysis of Twitter data can help in the identification of content where masses may report their symptoms, reports, and localities, etc. which can be further used to identify the disease hot spots for prioritizing the further course of actions.
- **Identification of local or global leaders:** Identification of leaders or influencers is very significant during various emergency situations or natural disasters [15] such as Covid-19, earthquake, glacier outbursts, floods, landslides, and wildfires, etc. because of their wide network, reach, popularity, or popular links. Such kind of users could use their remarkable network to spread the awareness information, debunk the misinformation or rumors as quickly as possible, ask for or provide help to the needy, communicate to authorities more effectively during the pandemic.
- **Tracking and debunking misinformation:** During critical and emergency situations it's of utmost importance to identify the misinformation, fake news, propaganda, or rumors and curb them as quickly as possible. It has been observed in the past studies that such kind of information spreads more

quickly than the correct and factual information and therefore it becomes more important to identify and debunk such kind of unverifiable content that endangers public safety at a time when awareness and suitable preventive measures are of utmost importance and avoid any kind of panic in the public.

The rest of the paper is organized as follows. In the next Sect. 2, we describe COVID-19 related studies and datasets. In Sect. 3, we provide the data collection and description in detail. Section 4 is about geo-spatial analysis of tweets and Sect. 5 is about identification and analysis of user influence over the Twittersphere. Section 6 and Sect. 7 explains a way to access dataset and conclusion respectively.

2   Related Work

There are a number of studies related to COVID-19 analysis of social media data being focused on various aspects such as human behavior and reactions analysis [16,17], preparedness for emergency management [10], identifying and debunking conspiracy theories, misinformation, propaganda and fake news [18–21]. Many other studies have collected and shared the COVID-19 related datasets from various social media platforms such as Twitter [22], Instagram [23], Weibo [24] etc. Some of the studies have released datasets belonging to single language such as Arabic [4,25], while others include multilingual datasets [26–30].

The largest available dataset contains 800 million tweets that are collected from 1 Jan 2020 to 8 Nov 2020 [22]. The clean version of the dataset with no retweets is also provided which contains around 194 million tweets. Another large dataset that is collected from 1st Feb 2020 to 1st May 2020 contains 524 million multilingual tweets [26]. It also provides location information in the form of GPS coordinates and places information for some of the tweets as per the availability. The longest-running dataset is of Arabic language [25] which is collected between 27 Jan 2020 to 31 Jan 2021. It also provides information related to propagation networks of the most-retweeted and most-liked tweets that include retweets and conversational threads i.e. threads of replies. However, none of the above datasets focus on the *IRL* and their research implications. We have included 12 Indian languages in our dataset, *IRLCov19* which also includes location information with a subset of tweets depending on the availability of information. We have also analyzed the dataset to compute the local or regional influencers or leaders on the basis of various influencing measures such as *followers*, *retweet count*, *favourite count* and number of *mentions*, which is discussed in detail in Sect. 5.

3   Data Collection and Description

We collected Twitter datasets on COVID-19 during the period from Feb 01 2020 to July 31 2020 using publicly available Twitter streaming API. To download the dataset we utilized a list of trending keywords and hashtags such as *corona*, *Covid-19*, *#COVID19*, *#COVID2019*, *#Covid_19*, *#CoronaVirusUpdates* etc. We kept updating the list of keywords and hashtags as and when they were available daily.

Table 1. Language wise tweets distribution

Language	Percentage	Language	Percentage	Language	Percentage	Language	Percentage
English	64.11	**Marathi**	0.19	Danish	0.018	Latvian	0.003
Spanish	14.08	Greek	0.14	**Malayalam**	0.017	**Sindhi**	0.003
French	5.003	**Telugu**	0.11	Swedish	0.017	Hebrew	0.002
Hindi	3.36	Chinese	0.101	Finnish	0.017	Maldivian	0.001
Italian	2.1	Tagalog	0.09	Basque	0.0127	Amharic	0.001
Thai	1.8	Polish	0.09	Slovenian	0.012	Icelandic	0.001
Undefined	1.76	**Gujarati**	0.071	Czech	0.0106	Bulgarian	0.001
Portuguese	1.45	Persian	0.07	**Punjabi**	0.01	Sorani Kurdish	0.001
German	0.96	**Kannada**	0.059	Sinhala	0.01	Armenian	0.0001
Turkish	0.87	Russian	0.05	Ukrainian	0.007	Burmese	0.0001
Indonesian	0.71	Estonian	0.04	Welsh	0.006	Georgian	0.00005
Tamil	0.55	**Bengali**	0.028	Serbian	0.005	Khmer	0.00004
Catalan	0.5	Haitian Creole	0.025	Lithuanian	0.005	Laotian Lao	0.00004
Arabic	0.42	Romanian	0.023	Norwegian	0.005	Uyghur	0.00003
Urdu	0.36	Korean	0.02	Hungarian	0.005	Tibetan	0.00002
Dutch	0.33	**Oriya**	0.02	Pashto	0.005		
Japanese	0.29	Nepali	0.019	Vietnamese	0.003		

Initially, we collected a dataset of nearly 330 million tweets irrespective of the language of communication. The Table 1 gives the percentage-wise distribution of tweets collected between a given time period. The downloaded tweets may be redundant as a tweet may contain multiple search keywords and therefore get downloaded multiple times for each such keyword. It is imperative to remove such occurrences for a more robust dataset. We pruned the dataset to remove the redundant tweets to result in over 280 million final tweets. We extracted the tweets specific to 12 Indian languages marked in bold in Table 1. Owing to a small percentage, we could infer from the dataset that not many people were using regional languages for communicating on Twitter. Another reason for this could be that the hashtags or mentioned used by regional languages' users could not find a place in the trending list of keywords. We have utilized trending hashtags or keywords and hence the latter could be a strong possibility. It is evident from the dataset that people have used various global, national or regional languages to voice out their opinions on varying matters. English comprises 64.11% of the total tweets out of all 65 languages in the dataset.

In this study, we have focussed on studying the dataset on *IRL* that constitute approximately 13 Million (1,33,63,294) tweets which are about 4.77% of the total collected tweets. The daily distribution of the tweets corresponding to various regional languages is shown in Fig. 1 on a logarithmic scale. It represents the volume of tweets against each language for a period of six months starting Feb 01 2020 to July 31 2020. The data in the table shows that tweets in the Hindi language are consistently high in numbers compared to other *IRL*. The findings coincide with the fact that Hindi is the most spoken language in the country. The high spikes in the graph after mid-March mark the beginning of a voluntary public curfew on March 22 2020. As evident from the plot, this was followed by a 21-day nationwide

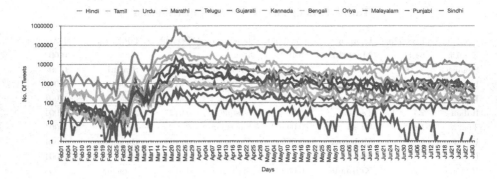

Fig. 1. Day wise tweets distribution for Indian Regional Languages on logarithmic scale

lockdown starting from March 25 2020, which resulted in masses expressing themselves on various SMPs. Table 2 has the count of users with original as well as retweeted tweets. The data shows that a total of 14,28,876 unique users were involved in exchanging thoughts and opinions in *IRL*. While most of these users are non-verified users, a little less than 1% are verified.

The dataset prepared is for research and non-profit uses and includes keywords used for dataset extraction, unique tweet IDs, and everyday language-wise tweet count. We first removed all duplicate entries by keeping the first instance of a tweet and kept a list of tweets corresponding to each language for all days. Later, we identified the location information from each tweet using the metadata in a tweet.

Identification of Location Information From Tweets. The location information in a tweet can be identified in three different ways i.e. by extracting the location information in the form of GPS coordinates from the downloaded JSON Twitter data, using the place or location information from the Tweet object [31–33] and extracting the location information from the textual content [34]. The previous studies show that only 1% of the tweets contain GPS coordinates despite Twitter providing an option to capture the exact location of Tweet by enabling geolocation service on mobile devices. We can also deduce the location from the place and location fields in the JSON data. It can correctly identify the approximate location of the user but not the location of the tweet in all cases. Not all the values in these fields are valid locations; for example, *Universe, Moon, Planet Earth, Heaven etc.* Invalid locations can be handled by transforming them to coordinates i.e. latitude and longitude, by using a python library called GeoPy. It returns coordinates for only valid locations by discarding invalid locations. The library may not always correctly classify valid locations due to misspellings or other possible errors in the text. This inhibits its ability to correctly map the geocode from a given location and such scenarios have been handled manually. The location of a tweet can also be deduced by exploiting the information in the text or by looking at its network of followers or friends. This method of capturing locations can be explored further in future works.

Table 2. Users details corresponding to Indian Regional Languages (*IRLCov19*)

Unique	Count			
	Verified	Non-verified	Total	Verified %
Original users	3498	437339	440837	0.79%
Retweet users	4146	1178347	1182493	0.35%
All users	5284	1423592	1428876	0.37%

In this study, we have used two parsers i.e. $P1$ and $P2$ to extract the location information from Tweets. The extracted location could be in terms of the GPS coordinates or place and location fields as extracted from the profile information. Parser ($P1$) looks for the geo-coordinates that comprise both latitude and longitude in a tweet. Parser ($P2$), however, extracts the place and location fields from the JSON data of the tweet in case ($P1$) could not find geo-coordinates. A retweet contains the profile information of both the original user, known as the source of the tweet, and of the user who retweeted it. Parser $P2$ prioritizes the information of retweeting users over original users while searching for a place or location information as multiple retweets are possible for a tweet across the globe.

4   Geo-Spatial Analysis of Tweets

Geo-Spatial analysis of tweets during emergencies, such as pandemics and natural disasters, plays a vital role in identifying the pattern of information propagation in the affected areas of the leaders involved in the communication. Therefore, the information gathered can be helpful for various regional, national, and global organizations to evaluate the circumstances and develop a strategy to combat the crises. Notably, it can be utilized to identify the prominent leaders around a region working as spreaders of information or misinformation on the social network. This could essentially be used in numerous ways like disseminating the awareness information, communicating the policies or schemes launched by Governments, reaching out to needy people promptly, and tracking down the source of misinformation to put measures in place, etc.

To analyse the locations of *IRLCov19* dataset with respect to each language, we have transformed identified valid locations to their corresponding geo-coordinates with the help of GeoPy [35] - A Python client for several popular geocoding web services, that includes geocoder classes for the *OpenStreetMap Nominatim, Google Geocoding API (V3)*, and many other geocoding services. We have used *Nominatim*, for:

1. *Geocoding* - the process of obtaining GPS coordinates corresponding to a valid location.
2. *Reverse Geocoding* - the process of obtaining location names using GPS coordinates.

316   D. Uniyal and A. Agarwal

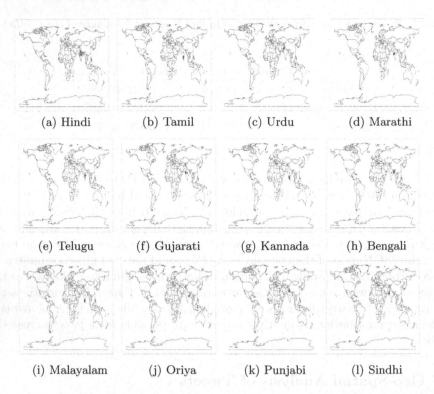

(a) Hindi   (b) Tamil   (c) Urdu   (d) Marathi

(e) Telugu   (f) Gujarati   (g) Kannada   (h) Bengali

(i) Malayalam   (j) Oriya   (k) Punjabi   (l) Sindhi

Fig. 2. Visualization of locations from Indian Regional Languages Tweets (Color figure online)

Firstly, we listed all the locations and coordinates along with their number of occurrences corresponding to each language. Given that some of these locations were already in the form of coordinates, we transformed the remaining locations available in the textual format into coordinates using geocoding service of *Nominatim*. We plotted the coordinates over a world map where the size of a RED dot is directly proportional to the frequency or number of tweets done around that location as shown in Fig. 2. The map shows that most of the tweets corresponding to each language have originated from the region of the country where the language is accepted as a regional language. In certain cases, tweets of an otherwise regional language could also originate from a location around the globe based on where the users of the language reside.

Tweets that mention India as their location are by default mapped to the common latitude and longitude coordinates *22.3511148, 78.6677428* and can be seen marked in red in most of the maps. The distribution of state-wise tweets is also shown in Fig. 3. The colour intensity shows the frequency of tweets with the maximum intensity denoting the highest frequency.

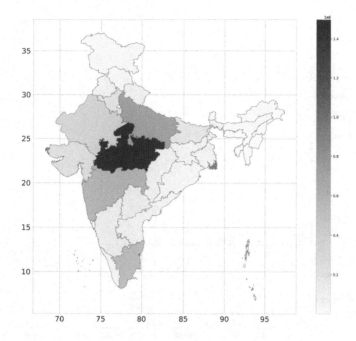

Fig. 3. State wise tweets distribution

5   Identification and Analysis of User Influence over the Twittersphere

There are multiple ways to identify a user's influence over the network, such as In-degree (number of followers), number of retweets, number of favourites (likes) received by the user on tweets, and number of mentions for the user in related discussions over a period of time. The metrics, *In-degree*, *retweets*, *favorites*, and *mentions*, in the aforementioned order, represent the user's popularity, content value, the preference among followers, and the user's name value. These metrics are collectively called influencing measures [9] and is crucial in identifying the influence of a user over the network. Studies suggest that having millions of followers doesn't necessarily prove the influence of the user over the network and is known as *A millions followers fallacy* [36]. Rather, an active audience who mentions a user, likes, and retweets his or her tweets, makes more contribution to the user's influence.

Methodology for Comparing User Influence. We evaluated the influence measure for each user and used the relative order of ranks as a measure of comparison for all 440,837 original users from the dataset. We sorted the users in decreasing order of their *influence measure* where rank 1 indicated a user with the highest influence. The ranks assigned to measures were further used to analyze how ranks varied across various influencing measures and which categories of users were the top influencer for a measure.

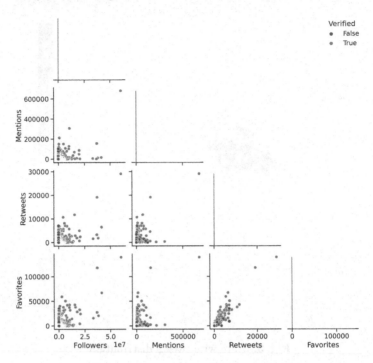

Fig. 4. Scatterplots of influencing variables

We can utilise both the Pearson correlation coefficient or Spearman rank correlation coefficient to measure the strength of an association between two variables. Spearman rank correlation is preferred over Pearson correlation as it can capture the non-linear association between two variables while the latter can only capture the linear relation. Also, Pearson correlation works better on normally distributed data which is quite not the scenarios as visible in Fig. 4. The Spearman does not require data to be normally distributed and is better suited to the need. Spearman correlation coefficient can be calculated by using Eq. 1 where X_i and Y_i are the ranks of users based on two different influence measures in a dataset of N users. A perfect positive correlation of $+1$ or a negative correlation of -1 occurs when each of the variables is a perfect monotone function of the other.

$$\rho = 1 - \frac{6\Sigma(X_i - Y_i)^2}{N(N^2 - 1)} \tag{1}$$

To investigate the correlation between four influencing measures for 4,40,837 original users, we calculated the Spearman rank correlation coefficient between each pair of measures for each regional language as well as for all languages combined as shown in Table 3. A moderately high correlation (above 0.5) exists across the combinations of *mention*, *retweet*, and *favourite* measures. It indicates that, in general, the users who are mentioned and liked more often are most retweeted. While there is a positive correlation of *followers* with the other three

Table 3. Spearman's rank-order correlation coefficients

Language Codes: Hindi - hi, Tamil - ta, Urdu - ur, Marathi - mr, Telugu - te, Gujarati - gu
Kannada - kn, Bengali - bn, Malayalam - ml, Oriya - or, Punjabi - pa, Sindhi - sd, All Languages - all

Correlation	Language												
	hi	ta	ur	mr	te	gu	kn	bn	ml	or	pa	sd	all
Follow-favorite	0.388	0.492	0.471	0.453	0.587	0.427	0.58	0.51	0.561	0.579	0.395	0.501	0.41
Follow-retweet	0.37	0.476	0.447	0.427	0.539	0.399	0.502	0.355	0.282	0.48	0.384	0.449	0.393
Follow-mention	0.462	0.524	0.492	0.498	0.586	0.475	0.563	0.445	0.384	0.591	0.458	0.502	0.477
Favorite-retweet	0.641	0.769	0.696	0.67	0.745	0.677	0.756	0.578	0.601	0.664	0.647	0.707	0.657
Favorite-mention	0.591	0.711	0.649	0.648	0.712	0.657	0.734	0.573	0.614	0.672	0.607	0.697	0.61
Retweet-mention	0.782	0.843	0.834	0.807	0.855	0.82	0.852	0.778	0.807	0.744	0.782	0.84	0.791

Table 4. Influencers category and corresponding frequency

O - Overall Count, Fo - Followers, M - Mentions, R - Retweets, Fa - Favorite

Categories	O, Fo, M, R, Fa	Categories	O, Fo, M, R, Fa
Politics	65,32,28,29,30	Religious	5,0,4,1,1
Media Org.	54,18,40,2,1	Sports	4,2,0,2,0
Media Person	29,9,13,20,18	NA	4,0,1,2,1
Entertainment	26,8,4,15,17	Others	2,0,1,1,0
Actor	20,12,0,12,15	Advocate	2,0,1,2,1
Cricket	15,14,0,3,8	YouTuber	1,1,0,0,0
Law	8,2,3,3,4	Suspend	1,0,0,1,0
Health	6,0,4,2,1	NGO	1,0,1,0,0
Corporate	6,2,0,4,2	Activist	1,0,0,1,1

measures, it doesn't appear to be as prominent as with a combination of the other three measures. This indicates that users with the most followers are not necessarily most mentioned. Also, they may not always produce content that is liked or retweeted most often. Effectively, the users with the most connections may not necessarily be the most influential people in terms of engaging the audience and having a significant outreach to the masses.

The influential users may fall into various categories of people or organizations based on their profession. We collected the Twitter profiles of the top 100 users of each measure to identify the category where the most influential users might belong. These users were categorized into high-level categories such as *people*, or *organizations* belonging to *politics, media, entertainment, and sports, etc.* The data from Table 4 shows that most users across influencing categories belong to people or organizations related to politics (*Narendra Modi, PMO India, Amit Shah, Rahul Gandhi, Arvind Kejriwal, etc.*), sports and entertainment industry such as comedian, musicians, actors, cricketers (*Salman Khan, Virat Kohli, Kapil Sharma, Kumar Vishwas, Filmfare, Saloni Gaur, etc.*), media persons or organizations (*NDTV, Times of India, Aaj Tak, ABP News, Rajat Sharma, Sweta Singh, Sudhir Chaudhary, etc.*). Most of the users in the top 100 across measures are verified.

Users with a large number of followers get a lot of public attention owing to the fact they are directly connected to people in large number. Those with a relatively higher number of retweets or favourites have more engaging content that people tend to like or even retweet to propagate information further. On the other hand, users mentioned are notably political dignitaries such as the prime minister and union ministers of the country, chief ministers of various states and media persons or organizations. This indicates a deeper level of engagement or communication among users. It could be in response to the various government policies enacted during the pandemic, people voicing their opinions on the latest policy updates or advisories issued by the government or health organizations, or seeking help from individuals or organizations in emergencies.

We extracted the top 20 frequently occurring mentions from the *IRLCov19* as shown in Table 5. The findings show that people who post content in their regional languages generally prefer to mention regional media channels, local or state leaders and authorities. The analysis could be useful to identify local leaders and authorities that could eventually help raise awareness and propagate help to the masses during the pandemic. The data further shows that most of the users mentioned are political dignitaries, be it regional ministers, chief ministers of states, prime minister of the country, along with the media persons or organizations. A significant portion of the mentioned users is verified, while those retweeting or posting the tweets are mostly non-verified.

The top influential users, across all four influential measures, are mostly pre-eminent public figures. Further, the top 100 users in each category show a significant overlap with one or the other. A combined list of the top 100 users from each category contains just 250 unique users. We exploited the inference drawn earlier about the three influential measures - *mention, retweet* and *favorite* showing the highest correlation among them to pick up the top twenty mentions across various regional languages as shown in Table 5. The data shows that local leaders dominate in their corresponding region as per the regional language spoken. We have categorized these mentions in various categories as indicated on the top of the table. Each user in the table belongs to the category as indicated by the symbol in () and a verified tag, used as subscript v, corresponding to a verified Twitter profile. The prime ministers of countries and those related to the prime minister's office are shown in ***bold italics***. The chief ministers, deputy chief ministers and their offices are shown in **bold only**. For example - ***narendramodi*** (P_v) indicates that the user *narendramodi* is a PM, has a verified Twitter profile and is related to politics.

6   Dataset Access

The dataset is accessible on GitHub [8]. However, to comply with Twitter's content redistribution policy [37], we are distributing only the IDs of the collected tweets. Tools such as Hydrator [38] can be used to retrieve the full tweet object.

Table 5. Top 20 mentions corresponding to Indian Regional Languages (*IRLCov19*)

P - Related to Politics, MP/MO - Media Person/Org., HP/HO - Health Person/Org.
G/O - Govt. Org./Org., A - Artist, L - Related to Law, C - Corporate Person, R - Related to Religion
N - NGO, S - Account Suspended, W - Account Withheld, NA - Account Doesn't Exist, OT - Others

Hindi	Tamil	Urdu	Marathi
narendramodi (P$_v$)	pttvonlinenews (MO$_v$)	siasatpk (MO$_v$)	rajeshtope11 (HP$_v$)
aajtak (MO$_v$)	news7tamil (MO$_v$)	dawn_news (MO$_v$)	mahadgipr (G$_v$)
zeenews (MO$_v$)	thatstamil (MO$_v$)	urduvoa (MO$_v$)	**cmomaharashtra** (P$_v$)
dchaurasia2312 (MP$_v$)	**cmotamilnadu** (P$_v$)	bolnetwork (MO$_v$)	abpmajhatv (MO$_v$)
pmoindia (P$_v$)	polimernews (MO$_v$)	nabthedentist (HP)	pawarspeaks (P$_v$)
abpnews (MO$_v$)	mkstalin (P$_v$)	arynewsud (MO$_v$)	mataonline (MO$_v$)
1stindianews (MO)	sunnewstamil (P$_v$)	maizahameed (P)	dev_fadnavis (P$_v$)
lambaalka (P$_v$)	news18tamilnadu (MO$_v$)	dunyanews (MO$_v$)	**officeout** (P$_v$)
chouhanshivraj (P$_v$)	thanthitv (MO$_v$)	sheikhsafina (A)	zee24taasnews (MO$_v$)
opindia_in (MO)	ishatamil (N)	maleehahashmey (MP$_v$)	loksattalive (MO$_v$)
myogiadityanath (P$_v$)	kalaignarnews (MO)	*imrankhanpti* (P$_v$)	supriya_sule (P$_v$)
mohfw_india (HO$_v$)	tamilthehindu (MO$_v$)	gnnhdofficial (MO)	marathi_rash (MP)
ndtvindia (MO$_v$)	jayapluschannel (MO$_v$)	ptiofficial (P$_v$)	bbcnewsmarathi (MO$_v$)
drharshvardha (HP$_v$)	dinakaranonline (MO$_v$)	dr_firdouspti (P$_v$)	dgpmaharashtra (L$_v$)
ashokgehlot51 (P$_v$)	drramadoss (P$_v$)	fawadchaudhry (P$_v$)	*narendramodi* (P$_v$)
arvindkejriwal (P$_v$)	rajinikanth (A$_v$)	hamidmirpak (MP$_v$)	anildeshmukhncp (P$_v$)
vikasbhaabp (NA)	vikatan (MP$_v$)	bbcurdu (MP$_v$)	smartpune (O)
drkumarvishwas (A$_v$)	aloor_shanavasP$_v$)	psppakistan (P$_v$)	milokmat (MO$_v$)
ashutosh83b (MP$_v$)	*narendramodi* (P$_v$)	*pakpmo* (P$_v$)	**ajitpawarspeaks** (P$_v$)
sardanarohit (MP$_v$)	arjunsaravanan5 (L)	tahirulqadriur (R)	*pmoindia* (P$_v$)
Telugu	Gujarati	Kannada	Bengali
ntvjustin (MO)	vtvgujarati (MO)	**bsybjp** (P$_v$)	banglargorbomb (P$_v$)
arogyaandhra (HO$_v$)	**vijayrupanibjp** (P$_v$)	**cmofkarnataka** (P$_v$)	abpanandatv (MO$_v$)
janasenaparty (P$_v$)	news18guj (MO$_v$)	siddaramaiah (P$_v$)	bbcbangla (MO$_v$)
bbcnewstelugu (MO$_v$)	*narendramodi* (P$_v$)	srisamsthana (R)	bjp4bengal (P$_v$)
ysjagan (P$_v$)	cmoguj (P$_v$)	sriramulubjp (P$_v$)	ei_samay (MO$_v$)
pawankalyan (P$_v$)	sandeshnews (MO)	publictvnews (MO$_v$)	didikebolo (P$_v$)
telanganacmo (P$_v$)	ddnewsgujarati (MO$_v$)	suvarn (OT)	**mamataofficial** (P$_v$)
tarak9999 (A$_v$)	divya_bhaskar (MO$_v$)	kumarishobakka (S)	dailystarnews (MO$_v$)
jaitdp (P$_v$)	bsnl_gj (G$_v$)	prajavani (MO$_v$)	airnews_ghy (MO$_v$)
urstrulymahesh (A$_v$)	jitu_vaghani (P$_v$)	*narendramodi* (P$_v$)	cpkolkata (L$_v$)
narendramodi (P$_v$)	zee24kalak (MO$_v$)	kicchasudeep (A$_v$)	cpim_westbengal (P$_v$)
jspveeramahila (P)	tv9gujarati (MO$_v$)	shakunthalahs (P)	aitcofficial (P$_v$)
bharatysrcp (P$_v$)	pibahmedabad (MO$_v$)	bjp4karnataka (P$_v$)	dw_bengali (MO$_v$)
tv9telugu (MO$_v$)	gujaratpolice (L$_v$)	oneindiakannada (MO$_v$)	news18bengali (MO$_v$)
bolisetti_satya (P)	**nitinbhai_patel** (P$_v$)	vijaykarnataka (MO$_v$)	*narendramodi* (P$_v$)
jspshatagniteam (MP)	aravindchaudhri (MP$_v$)	news18kannada (MO$_v$)	kpeastsubndiv (L$_v$)
uttarandhranow (MO)	bjp4gujarat (P$_v$)	inckarnataka (P$_v$)	pib_india (MO$_v$)
ncbn(P$_v$)	sanjayezhava (MP)	anilkumble1074 (A$_v$)	myanandabazar (MO$_v$)
manvidad (OT)	gujratsamachar (MO$_v$)	puneethrajkumar (A$_v$)	dailyittefaq (MO)
ktrtrs (P$_v$)	collectorbk (L)	bbmpcomm (L$_v$)	mohfw_india (HO$_v$)

(continued)

Table 5. (*continued*)

P - Related to Politics, MP/MO - Media Person/Org., HP/HO - Health Person/Org.
G/O - Govt. Org./Org., A - Artist, L - Related to Law, C - Corporate Person, R - Related to Religion
N - NGO, S - Account Suspended, W - Account Withheld, NA - Account Doesn't Exist, OT - Others

ORIYA	MALAYALAM	PUNJABI	SINDHI
kanak_news (MO$_v$)	cmokerala (P$_v$)	jagbanionline (MO$_v$)	khalidkoree (OT)
news18odia (MO)	asianetnewstv (NA)	dailyajitnews (MO)	muradalishahppp (P)
sambad_odisha (MO)	vijayanpinarayi (P$_v$)	capt_amarinder (P$_v$)	sialrabail (S)
otvkhabar (MO)	manukumarjain (C$_v$)	ptc_network (MO$_v$)	mukhtar_soomro (OT)
naveen_odisha (P$_v$)	pibtvpm (MO$_v$)	ptcnews (MO)	mahamsindhi (MP)
cmo_odisha (P$_v$)	thekeralapolice (L$_v$)	ishehnaaz_gill (A$_v$)	faraz_aligg (OT)
hfwodisha (HO$_v$)	manoramaonline (MO$_v$)	punjabpmc (P$_v$)	bbhuttozardari (P$_v$)
odishareporter (MO$_v$)	nishthvanth (OT)	punjabgovtindia (G$_v$)	ayazlatifpalijo (P$_v$)
narendramodi (P$_v$)	news18kerala (MO$_v$)	pib_india (MO$_v$)	dadu_plus (S)
ipr_odisha (MO$_v$)	sathyamaanu (OT)	mib_india (MO$_v$)	drhamadwassan (OT)
drgynaec (OT)	thatsmalayalam (MO$_v$)	gurmeetramrahim (W)	ahtishamqhala (OT)
anandstdas (MP)	ddnewsmalayalam (MO$_v$)	narendramodi (P$_v$)	abbasimehwish (OT)
dpradhanbjp (P$_v$)	zhmalayalam (MO)	newscheckerin (MO$_v$)	sindhcmhouse (P)
nandighoshatv (MO)	mfwaikerala (OT)	cmopb (P$_v$)	sindhikhabroon (MO)
zeeodisha (MO)	vikramanmuthu (OT)	pibchandigarh (MO$_v$)	najeebabro2 (P)
pmoindia (P$_v$)	avs_ind (OT)	incpunjab (P$_v$)	sangrisaeed (OT)
skilledinodisha (C)	comrademallu (P)	harsimratbadal_ (P$_V$)	sama4newz (NA)
bjd_odisha (P$_v$)	ambath (OT)	punjabpoliceind (L$_v$)	mnavax (OT)
satyaparida01 (OT)	kavyasree19941 (NA)	sportsperson5 (OT)	chandio_gs (MP)
theargus_in (NA)	manoramanews (MO$_v$)	derasachasauda (W)	sindhicongress (N)

7   Conclusion and Future Work

This paper presents *IRLCov19* - a Twitter dataset of Indian regional languages on the Covid-19 pandemic. The dataset has been collected over a period of 6 months between Feb 01, 2020, to July 31, 2020, and consists of over 13 million multilingual tweets. The tweets in the *IRLCov19* are from more than 1.4 million Twitter users that includes more than 5k verified users. The tweets in the dataset span 12 different Indian regional languages. The dataset can be advantageous for researchers, Government authorities, and policymakers in studying the pandemic from a varied perspective such as understanding public reactions and opinions, early detection and surveillance of the pandemic etc.

Identifying influencers and their locations is a crucial task amid a crisis or emergency. It paves the way for disease hotspot detection, employing suitable and effective information publishing strategies, and tracking and debunking misinformation floating in the network. We utilized GeoPy, a python library, to extract the location of a tweet and use it to collect relevant tweets from the identified location. We further exploited the collected information to identify the top local leaders or influencers and the profiles to which influencers belong. We plan to update the dataset with more paradigms about the COVID-19 dataset related to

Indian Regional Languages. Future studies could explore the information-sharing behaviour among the users and how different groups respond to the pandemic.

References

1. Broniatowski, D.A., Paul, M.J., Dredze, M.: National and local influenza surveillance through Twitter: an analysis of the 2012–2013 influenza epidemic. PLoS ONE **8**(12), e83672 (2013)
2. Vieweg, S., Hughes, A.L., Starbird, K., Palen, L.: Microblogging during two natural hazards events: what twitter may contribute to situational awareness. In: Proceedings of the SIGCHI Conference on Human Factors in Computing Systems, pp. 1079–1088 (2010)
3. Güner, H.R., Hasanoğlu, I., Aktaş, F.: COVID-19: prevention and control measures in community. Turk. J. Med. Sci. **50**(SI-1), 571–577 (2020)
4. Alqurashi, S., Alhindi, A., Alanazi, E.: Large Arabic Twitter dataset on COVID-19. arXiv preprint arXiv:2004.04315 (2020)
5. Primack, B.A., et al.: Social media use and perceived social isolation among young adults in the us. Am. J. Prev. Med. **53**(1), 1–8 (2017)
6. González-Padilla, D.A., Tortolero-Blanco, L.: Social media influence in the COVID-19 pandemic. Int. braz j urol **46**, 120–124 (2020)
7. Census (2021). https://en.wikipedia.org/wiki/2001_Census_of_India. Accessed 1 Apr 2021
8. Github (2021). https://github.com/deepakuniyaliit/Covid19IRLTDataset. Accessed 1 Apr 2021
9. Cha, M., Haddadi, H., Benevenuto, F., Gummadi, K.: Measuring user influence in Twitter: the million follower fallacy. In: Proceedings of the International AAAI Conference on Web and Social Media, vol. 4 (2010)
10. Li, L., et al.: Characterizing the propagation of situational information in social media during COVID-19 epidemic: a case study on Weibo. IEEE Trans. Comput. Soc. Syst. **7**(2), 556–562 (2020)
11. Agarwal, A., Uniyal, D., Toshniwal, D., Deb, D.: Dense vector embedding based approach to identify prominent disseminators from Twitter data amid COVID-19 outbreak. IEEE Trans. Emerg. Top. Comput. Intell. **5**(3), 308–320 (2021)
12. Kouzy, R., et al.: Coronavirus goes viral: quantifying the COVID-19 misinformation epidemic on Twitter. Cureus **12**(3), e7255 (2020)
13. Choi, D., Chun, S., Hyunchul, O., Han, J., et al.: Rumor propagation is amplified by echo chambers in social media. Sci. Rep. **10**(1), 1–10 (2020)
14. Alharbi, A., Lee, M.: Kawarith: an Arabic Twitter corpus for crisis events. In: Proceedings of the Sixth Arabic Natural Language Processing Workshop, pp. 42–52 (2021)
15. Agarwal, A., Toshniwal, D.: Identifying leadership characteristics from social media data during natural hazards using personality traits. Sci. Rep. **10**(1), 1–15 (2020)
16. Barkur, G., Vibha, G.B.K.: Sentiment analysis of nationwide lockdown due to COVID 19 outbreak: evidence from India. Asian J. Psychiatr. **51**, 102089 (2020)
17. Han, X., Wang, J., Zhang, M., Wang, X.: Using social media to mine and analyze public opinion related to COVID-19 in China. Int. J. Environ. Res. Public Health **17**(8), 2788 (2020)
18. Ferrara, E.: What types of COVID-19 conspiracies are populated by Twitter bots? First Monday (2020)

19. Sharma, K., Seo, S., Meng, C., Rambhatla, S., Liu, Y.: COVID-19 on social media: analyzing misinformation in Twitter conversations. arXiv:2003.12309 (2020)
20. Brennen, J.S., Simon, F., Howard, P.N., Nielsen, R.K.: Types, sources, and claims of COVID-19 misinformation. Reuters Inst. **7**(3), 1 (2020)
21. Gupta, L., Gasparyan, A.Y., Misra, D.P., Agarwal, V., Zimba, O., Yessirkepov, M.: Information and misinformation on COVID-19: a cross-sectional survey study. J. Korean Med. Sci. **35**(27), e256 (2020)
22. Banda, J.M., et al.: A large-scale COVID-19 Twitter chatter dataset for open scientific research-an international collaboration. arXiv preprint arXiv:2004.03688 (2020)
23. Zarei, K., Farahbakhsh, R., Crespi, N., Tyson, G.: A first Instagram dataset on COVID-19. arXiv preprint arXiv:2004.12226 (2020)
24. Hu, Y., Huang, H., Chen, A., Mao, X.L.: Weibo-COV: a large-scale COVID-19 social media dataset from Weibo (2020)
25. Haouari, F., Hasanain, M., Suwaileh, R., Elsayed, T.: ArCOV-19: the first Arabic COVID-19 twitter dataset with propagation networks. In: Proceedings of the Sixth Arabic Natural Language Processing Workshop, pp. 82–91 (2021)
26. Qazi, U., Imran, M., Ofli, F.: GeoCoV19: a dataset of hundreds of millions of multilingual COVID-19 tweets with location information. SIGSPATIAL Spec. **12**(1), 6–15 (2020)
27. Gao, Z., Yada, S., Wakamiya, S., Aramaki, E.: NAIST COVID: multilingual COVID-19 Twitter and Weibo dataset. arXiv preprint arXiv:2004.08145 (2020)
28. Aguilar-Gallegos, N., Romero-García, L.E., Martínez-González, E.G., Iván García-Sánchez, E., Aguilar-Ávila, J.: Dataset on dynamics of coronavirus on Twitter. Data Brief **30**, 105684 (2020)
29. Shahi, G.K., Nandini, D.: FakeCovid-a multilingual cross-domain fact check news dataset for COVID-19. arXiv preprint arXiv:2006.11343 (2020)
30. Chen, E., Lerman, K., Ferrara, E.: Tracking social media discourse about the COVID-19 pandemic: development of a public coronavirus Twitter data set. JMIR Public Health Surveill. **6**(2), e19273 (2020)
31. Uniyal, D., Rai, A.: Citizens' emotion on GST: a spatio-temporal analysis over Twitter data. arXiv preprint arXiv:1906.08693 (2019)
32. Uniyal, D., Uniyal, S.: Social media emerging as a third eye!! Decoding users' sentiment on government policy: a case study of GST. In: 2020 Fourth World Conference on Smart Trends in Systems, Security and Sustainability (WorldS4), pp. 116–122. IEEE (2020)
33. Agarwal, A., Singh, R., Toshniwal, D.: Geospatial sentiment analysis using twitter data for UK-EU referendum. J. Inf. Optim. Sci. **39**(1), 303–317 (2018)
34. Agarwal, A., Toshniwal, D.: Face off: travel habits, road conditions and traffic city characteristics bared using Twitter. IEEE Access **7**, 66536–66552 (2019)
35. Geopy (2021). https://geopy.readthedocs.io/en/stable/. Accessed 8 Apr 2021
36. Cataldi, M., Aufaure, M.-A.: The 10 million follower fallacy: audience size does not prove domain-influence on Twitter. Knowl. Inf. Syst. **44**(3), 559–580 (2014). https://doi.org/10.1007/s10115-014-0773-8
37. Twitter Developer Policy (2021). https://developer.twitter.com/en/developer-terms/agreement-and-policy. Accessed 1 Apr 2021
38. Hydrator (2021). https://github.com/DocNow/hydrator. Accessed 1 Apr 2021

Automated ESG Report Analysis by Joint Entity and Relation Extraction

Adrien Ehrhardt[1,2](✉) 🆔 and Minh Tuan Nguyen[1,2]

[1] Groupe de Recherche Opérationnelle, Groupe Crédit Agricole, Montrouge, France
adrien.ehrhardt@credit-agricole-sa.fr
[2] École Polytechnique, Saclay, France

Abstract. The banking industry has lately been under pressure, notably from regulators and NGOs, to report various Environmental, Societal and Governance (ESG) metrics (*e.g.*, the carbon footprint of loans). For years at Crédit Agricole, a specialized division examined ESG and Corporate Social Responsibility (CSR) reports to ensure, *e.g.*, the bank's commitment to de-fund coal activities, and companies with social or environmental issues. With both an intensification of the aforementioned exterior pressure, and of the number of companies making such reports publicly available, the tedious process of going through each report has become unsustainable.

In this work, we present two adaptations of previously published models for joint entity and relation extraction. We train them on a private dataset consisting in ESG and CSR reports annotated internally at Crédit Agricole. We show that we are able to effectively detect entities such as coal activities and environmental or social issues, as well as relations between these entities, thus enabling the financial industry to quickly grasp the creditworthiness of clients and prospects w.r.t. ESG criteria. The resulting model is provided at https://github.com/adimajo/renard_joint.

Keywords: Named Entity Recognition · Relation extraction · NLP

1 Introduction

By deciding which projects and companies to fund, Corporate and Investment banks have many responsibilities, of which environmental concerns are among the latest, and stir passion.

For example, regulatory authorities (see *e.g.* [6]) and NGOs (see *e.g.* [14]) regularly push the industry towards more transparency in that regard.

For years at Crédit Agricole, a specialized division examined, among others, approx. 4,000 ESG and CSR reports each year from clients and prospects to ensure, *e.g.*, the bank's commitment to de-fund coal activities, and companies

Supported by Groupe Crédit Agricole; analyses and opinions of the authors expressed in this work are their own. The authors wish to thank the ESG team at CACIB for the document annotations and their valuable comments.

M. Kamp et al. (Eds.): ECML PKDD 2021 Workshops, CCIS 1525, pp. 325–340, 2021.
https://doi.org/10.1007/978-3-030-93733-1_23

326   A. Ehrhardt and M. T. Nguyen

with social or environmental issues[1]. With an intensification of the aforementioned exterior pressure, signs of intricate relations between ESG metrics and creditworthiness (see *e.g.* [3]), the rise of "sustainable banking"[2], and of the number of companies making such reports publicly available, the tedious process of going through each report has become unsustainable.

The ClimLL Dataset. Following this situation, a random sample (not only current clients) of 31 ESG and CSR reports were annotated internally at Crédit Agricole. These include for example ArcelorMittal[3] and PSA[4]. We refer to this (private) dataset as ClimLL. Using this dataset, our aim is to derive a joint entity and relation extraction model able to replicate this manual annotation on unseen reports so as to accelerate their reading by analysts. Three annotators worked on these reports with 100% overlap at first. Once they reliably reached over 80% interrater reliability, this overlap was progressively reduced.

Data Model. A crucial part of any NLP project is the data model: deciding which concepts to label as entities and relations, such that each have a precise definition, and every annotator can unambiguously annotate the dataset. The data model for ClimLL is displayed on Fig. 1: there are 8 entity types, among which "Coal Activity", "Environmental" and "Social Issues", as well as 5 relation types. This data model is likely to evolve rapidly in the coming years as the ESG metrics of interest will evolve. However, we feel it is a strong basis to build on.

Descriptive Statistics. More than 7,500 sentences from 372 paragraphs are split into a training and a test set containing 280 and 92 paragraphs respectively. All paragraphs from a given report belong to the same split. Sentence lengths range from 2 to 251 words (Fig. 2 - left). In total, there are 28,751 entities and 5,864 relations (Fig. 2 - center and right resp.). A sample sentence extracted from the dataset is displayed on Fig. 3.

Proprietary Model. Using proprietary tools developed by IBM, a joint entity and relation extraction was "trained", which will serve as a baseline (see Sect. 3.4). This model was also used to determine that annotating these 31 reports was sufficient, as the F1 score on the test set stopped improving (see Appendix A).

---

[1] Some of these reports are becoming mandatory, *e.g.* in France as part of the "document d'enregistrement universel" required by the regulating authority, and audited.

[2] The incorporation of ESG criteria alongside traditional financial metrics; see *e.g.* https://www.unepfi.org/banking/bankingprinciples/, https://www.ca-cib.com/our-solutions/sustainable-banking.

[3] Available at https://corporate.arcelormittal.com/corporate-library.

[4] Available at https://www.groupe-psa.com/en/newsroom/corporate-en/groupe-psa-publishes-its-csr-report/.

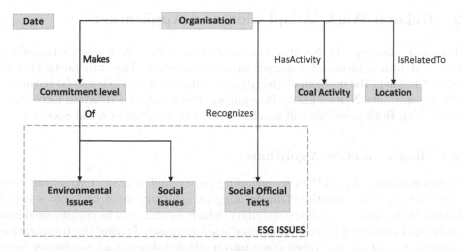

Fig. 1. The data model used to produce ClimLL (entities in boxes, relations as arrows).

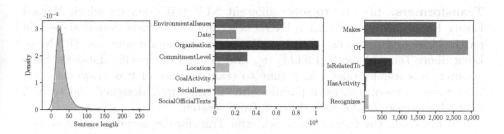

Fig. 2. Distribution of sentence length (left), entities (center) and relations (right).

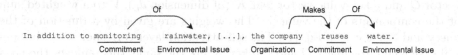

Fig. 3. A sample sentence from ClimLL.

In the next section, we present, adapt and implement two published works to solve this joint entity and relation extraction task. Section 3 is devoted to numerical experiments. We conclude this work in Sect. 4.

2   Related Work: Adaptation and Application

The first challenge in Natural Language Processing (NLP) is to transform raw text into a meaningful numerical representation. This will be tackled in Sect. 2.1. Then, the problem of identifying entities and relations can be naturally decomposed into Named Entity Recognition (Sect. 2.2) and Relation Extraction (Sect. 2.3). Both problems will finally be tackled simultaneously in Sect. 2.4.

2.1   Representation Algorithms

Tokenization. An NLP task, including entity and relation extraction, usually starts with tokenization: transforming an arbitrary input text into a list of tokens from a fixed set, called vocabulary, which, in turn, can be transformed into embedded numerical vectors for computation purposes. During the tokenization process, a word can be broken down into multiple tokens (*e.g.*, "rainwater" $\longrightarrow$ ["rain", "##water"]) or transformed (e.g. to lowercase, lemmatization, stemming, etc.).

Transformers. In order to solve different NLP tasks, among which Named Entity Recognition and Relation Extraction, different models were designed, in particular neural networks, often based on recurrent neural networks (RNN) or Long Short-Term Memory (LSTM) [8], and trained on specific datasets. Such architectures usually take a long time to train because of two drawbacks: (1) they cannot process tokens in parallel and (2) they were designed and trained for each use-case, *i.e.* for each dataset, from scratch.

To overcome the former drawback, the Transformer architecture was proposed [18]. It is a neural network with an encoder and a decoder. Each encoder layer contains a multi-headed self-attention and a feed-forward sub-layer. Each decoder layer contains a masked multi-headed self-attention, a multi-headed attention, and a feed-forward sub-layer. An attention is a map from a query vector Q and a key-value vector pair K (of dimension d_k), V to a weighted sum of the components of the value V. The weights are given by a function of the query and the key as in Eq. (1). The self-attention layer corresponds to the special case where the query Q and the key K are the same: this removes the need for a recurrent neural network and enables parallel computation. Furthermore, the self-attention layer offers shorter paths between long-distance dependencies in text.

$$\text{Attention}(Q, K, V) := \text{softmax}\left(\frac{QK^T}{\sqrt{d_k}}\right) \cdot V. \tag{1}$$

BERT. To overcome the latter drawback of RNNs (retraining on each dataset), the Bidirectional Encoder Representations from Transformer (BERT) model was proposed [4] and trained on the Masked Language Modeling (MLM) [17] and the Next Sentence Prediction (NSP) tasks. During training, BERT takes two tokenized sentences as input, where some tokens are masked, along with "special" tokens ([CLS] at the beginning and [SEP] at the end of each sentence, see Fig. 4). Through MLM, the model learns to predict the masked tokens and, through NSP, the representation of the [CLS] token is used to predict whether two input sentences are consecutive in the original document. Hence, through these two tasks, the model is able to learn the context surrounding each token and across sentences instead of only one direction.

Fig. 4. An example of BERT input in MLM.

Subsequently, by taking the result of its last hidden layer, BERT is used as a representation algorithm: an input sentence is transformed into the consecutive 768-dimensional numerical representation of its tokens. Simple models are then used after this transformation to solve "downstream" NLP tasks [4].

2.2 Named Entity Recognition (NER)

One of these downstream tasks is NER: classifying words into pre-defined classes; for example the "Organization" class is said to "span" over the two words "the company" in Fig. 3.

The approaches range from grammar-based or vocabulary-based to machine learning (see *e.g.* [4,12,15]). In particular, the numerical representation of the first token of each word, given by BERT, can be used as an input to a simple classifier, *e.g.* logistic regression [4]: we will focus on this approach in what follows.

First, the input sentence is tokenized into token ids using the tokenizer provided by BERT, *e.g.*, "rainwater" $\longrightarrow$ ["rain", "##water"] $\longrightarrow$ [4458, 4669]).

For entity recognition, the BERT representation of the first token id of each word serves as an observation w.r.t. the aforementioned simple classifier, while the entity of this word ("Environmental Issue") is the class label, straightforwardly providing a design matrix and allowing the estimation of this classifier. Figure 5 (left) provides an illustration of the tokenization and NER processes. The different formats for providing entity labels are discussed in Appendix B.

2.3 Relation Extraction (RE)

Following the same approach for RE, we implemented the one-pass Multiple Relation Extraction (MRE, see Appendix C) model [21], where the tokens' BERT representation and the true entities serve as input. The average BERT representation of all tokens of each entity span is computed. Each pair of "averaged" entities is then classified into a relation or marked as "not a relation" using a softmax (Fig. 5 - right).

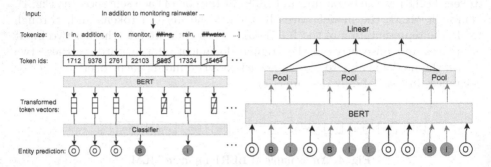

Fig. 5. Tokenization and NER illustration (left), MRE model [21] (right).

2.4   Joint Entity and Relation Extraction (Joint NER & RE)

NER-RE Pipeline. To combine both previous tasks, the "natural" idea is to use a pipeline where the entities are identified first before extracting the relations. Thus, the predicted entities from the NER model described in Sect. 2.2 are given as input to the RE model described in Sect. 2.3 in place of the true entities.

Consequently, this two-stage procedure is vulnerable to compound error and does not consider the connection between entities and relations.

Joint Extraction. Indeed, entities are sometimes defined by the types of relations they are in, as exemplified by these two article titles from CNN: "Bloomberg buys BusinessWeek" and "Bloomberg will sell his company if elected, adviser says". Based on the relations mentioned in the titles, the former "Bloomberg" is a company while the latter refers to a person. Hence, to overcome the disadvantages of the NER-RE pipeline, there have been various studies on alternative methods for joint entity and relation extraction. The Hierarchical Framework [16] consists of two levels of reinforcement learning. The higher level traverses the text to extract and classify relations while the lower level identifies entities within each extracted relation. The Encoder-Decoder architecture [13] implements multiple bidirectional LSTM. However, both methods only detect whether or not a token is part of an entity and do not classify the entity type. Other approaches which are able to extract and classify both entities and relations are, for example, a reinforcement learning multi-turn question answering model [9] or DYGIE [11]. Nevertheless, these methods depend on heavily-engineered architectures and require a lot of resources to train.

Recently, the popularity of BERT-based methods for joint entity and relation extraction has risen. DYGIE++ [20] and Span-based joint entity and relation extraction (SpERT) [5] both make use of BERT. These methods can extract multiple relations from the input sentence while SpERT is span-based and can thus also extract overlapping entities (see Appendix B). It achieved high performance on public joint entity and relation extraction datasets. We focus on the latter in what follows.

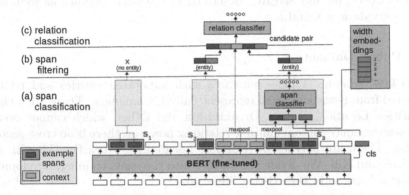

Fig. 6. The SpERT architecture [5], shared under CC BY-NC 4.0.

SpERT. First, similar to the NER-RE pipeline described above, the input sentence is tokenized and passed through BERT. Next, token representations from "candidate" entity spans (see below) are max-pooled (the maximum value per coordinate), concatenated with a trainable width-embedding vector and the representation of the [CLS] token. A softmax layer classifies the concatenated vectors into entity classes or non-entity. Spans classified as non-entity are filtered out. Then, pairs of classified entity spans are once again max-pooled and concatenated with the width-embedding vector for relation classification. The representations of the words between the two entities are also max-pooled and concatenated, which act as a context. The relation classifier is a sigmoid layer and a filter threshold, such that, potentially, multiple relations can be predicted per pair of predicted entities. The whole process is displayed on Fig. 6.

Candidates. During the training process, undersampling is performed such that candidate entity spans and relations consist in the true ones and a fixed number of negative spans generated randomly. On the other hand, during prediction and evaluation, candidate entities are all spans within the sentence and candidate relations are all pairs of predicted entity spans. In order to reduce complexity, the length of the spans is limited to 10 words.

It is worth noting that even though entity spans are spans on lists of tokens, and words may be tokenized into several tokens, the candidate entity spans must contain all tokens of each word.

3   Numerical Experiments

First, we experiment with the entity recognition (see Sect. 2.2) and relation extraction (see Sect. 2.3) models of the NER-RE pipeline separately in Sects. 3.2 and 3.3 respectively. Then, we combine them, as suggested in Sect. 2.4, and compare the performance with our implementation of SpERT (we describe in Appendix D how it differs from the original implementation) on the public datasets CoNLL04 and SciERC (described in the next section), as well as our proprietary dataset ClimLL.

3.1   Public Datasets

CoNLL04 contains 1,400+ sentences with annotated entities and relations extracted from news sources to represent daily life language. There are 4 classes of entities: Location, Person, Organization and Other, which cannot overlap. Each sentence may contain multiple relations; however, there is no cross-sentence relation. There are 5 types of relations: Located_In, Work_For, Live_In, Org-Based_In, and Kill. We divide the dataset into the same training, development, and test subsets as in the existing literature [2].

SciERC focuses on scientific language extracted from paper abstracts. It contains 500 annotated paragraphs with 2,500+ sentences. There can be multiple relations within a sentence but not across sentences. The entities are span-based, which means different entities can overlap. There are 6 entity classes (Task, Method, Metric, Material, Generic, OtherScientificTerm) and 7 relation classes (Conjunction, Feature-of, Hyponym-of, Used-for, Part-of, Compare, Evaluate-for). We use the same training, development and test subsets provided by the dataset authors [10].

3.2   Named Entity Recognition

In this section, the NER model (Fig. 5 - left) is trained on the ClimLL dataset. We used 5 different classifiers: k-nearest neighbor (5 neighbors), decision tree (unlimited depth), random forest (20 trees with unlimited depth), and two neural networks with 1 hidden layer of size 512 and 1024 respectively.

Furthermore, BERT has an input size limit of 512 tokens and was pre-trained mostly on inputs of size less than 128. Since ClimLL offers input paragraphs which are typically tokenized into more than 512 tokens, we experimented with two separation methods to breakdown these paragraphs: (1) split the paragraphs sentence by sentence and pass them to BERT one by one or (2) break the input paragraphs down into chunks of 128 tokens and pass to BERT.

Results are displayed in Table 1. The top-performing classifiers are the k-nearest neighbor and the two neural networks. Even though random forest achieved the highest precision, it has a much lower recall and, thus, a lower

Table 1. NER results on ClimLL (test set, micro-average).

Classifier	(1) Sentence-by-sentence			(2) 128-by-128		
	Precision	Recall	F1	Precision	Recall	F1
k-nearest neighbor	0.79	**0.80**	**0.79**	0.79	**0.80**	**0.79**
Decision tree	0.42	0.46	0.44	0.43	0.47	0.45
Random forest	**0.94**	0.39	0.52	**0.93**	0.40	0.53
Neural network (512)	0.80	0.75	0.77	0.84	0.74	0.78
Neural network (1024)	0.81	0.76	**0.79**	0.83	0.75	0.78
IBM	0.87	0.70	0.78			

F1 score compared to the others. Furthermore, we can see that the entity recognition model produced similar results compared to the IBM model.

It is rather surprising that the 128-by-128 separation achieves similar performance compared to the sentence-by-sentence approach because these 128-token chunks are cutting through the sentences. This result led us to believe that neighboring sentences may carry useful information to detect entities in a given sentence. In what follows, we will use sentence-by-sentence separation.

Also, the results of this section are already overwhelming: using now standard and open-source NLP tools such as BERT and very simple supervised classification models thereafter, we are able to detect the concepts of interest, *e.g.*, coal activities, which could already prove useful to the financial industry.

3.3 Multiple Relation Extraction

For relation extraction, we trained the MRE model [21] (Fig. 5 - right) on CoNLL04 and ClimLL, where sentences and true entities are passed as input. The model was trained for 100 epochs on each dataset. We did not fine-tune any other hyper-parameters. The micro-averaged and macro-averaged results are shown in Table 2. They are inferior to state-of-the-art [5] (0.74 macro F1 with SpERT[5]), due to limitations pointed out in Sect. 2.4.

3.4 Joint Entity and Relation Extraction

After experimenting with the NER and RE tasks, we combined the NER model with a neural network (1 hidden layer of size 1024) classifier and the MRE model to create a NER-RE pipeline for joint entity and relation extraction as described in Sect. 2.4. We benchmarked this pipeline and SpERT on CoNLL04 and ClimLL. On SciERC, we could only test SpERT because the dataset contains overlapping entities. For SpERT, we chose a learning rate of $5e^{-6}$ on ClimLL and $5e^{-5}$ on the other two public datasets. The rest of the hyper-parameters are the same as suggested by the authors [5]. Some training metrics are made available in Appendix E.

---

[5] https://paperswithcode.com/sota/relation-extraction-on-conll04.

Table 2. MRE results on test set.

Dataset	Average	Precision	Recall	F1
ClimLL	Micro	0.61	0.54	0.57
	Macro	0.55	0.54	0.54
CoNLL04	Micro	0.65	0.58	0.61
	Macro	0.66	0.61	0.63

During the evaluation, an entity is considered correct if its span (the begin and end position) and its predicted type match its true value. A relation is considered correct if both of its entities (spans and types) together with the predicted relation type are all correct.

The evaluation results are presented in Table 3. Overall, SpERT outperformed the NER-RE pipeline as predicted. The performance of SpERT on public datasets matches the results shown in the original paper (See footnote 5).

Table 3. Joint entity and relation extraction results on test set.

Dataset	Average	Model	NER			Joint NER & RE		
			Precision	Recall	F1	Precision	Recall	F1
CoNLL04	Micro	NER-RE	0.75	0.80	0.77	0.36	0.47	0.41
		SpERT	**0.86**	**0.91**	**0.89**	**0.71**	**0.70**	**0.70**
	Macro	NER-RE	0.71	0.74	0.73	0.41	0.51	0.45
		SpERT	**0.84**	**0.88**	**0.86**	**0.72**	**0.71**	**0.71**
SciERC	Micro	SpERT	0.64	0.72	0.68	0.31	0.45	0.37
	Macro	SpERT	0.65	0.71	0.68	0.34	0.41	0.35
ClimLL	Micro	NER-RE	0.67	0.68	0.68	0.23	0.18	0.20
		SpERT	**0.75**	**0.79**	**0.77**	**0.36**	**0.44**	**0.40**
	Macro	NER-RE	0.63	0.67	0.64	0.21	0.22	0.21
		SpERT	**0.75**	**0.78**	**0.77**	**0.46**	**0.58**	**0.50**

However, we can also observe that the performance on ClimLL and SciERC cannot match the performance on CoNLL04. This may be because BERT was trained on a general language vocabulary. A much better performance was achieved on SciERC using SciBERT [5], which is a version of BERT pre-trained on scientific vocabulary. Since the ESG reports annotated in ClimLL were most likely also written with a different, more formal language, future work may improve the model performance on ClimLL by fine-tuning BERT and/or pre-training it on a specialized vocabulary.

Comparison with IBM Model. We also compare the performance of SpERT on ClimLL with the IBM model. In order to do this, we evaluate the entity prediction at the word-level (each word is predicted to be either non-entity or an entity type if it is part of a span of this entity type), since this is how the IBM model is evaluated. The results in Table 4 show that SpERT outperformed the IBM model (+4 % in NER and +7 % in Joint NER & RE).

Table 4. Comparison with IBM model (test set, micro-average).

Model	NER			Joint NER & RE		
	Precision	Recall	F1	Precision	Recall	F1
IBM	**0.87**	0.70	0.78	**0.52**	0.24	0.33
SpERT	0.80	**0.84**	**0.82**	0.36	**0.44**	**0.40**

4   Conclusion

With little human and computational resources, we were able to annotate a sufficiently large dataset of ESG and CSR reports and to train two open-source joint entity and relation extraction models. The SpERT model yields superior performance than the current proprietary model at Crédit Agricole and is now used daily, allowing analysts to go through more reports and concentrate on their most useful parts, participating in a broader awareness of the bank's environmental and societal role.

Both models discussed in this work, as well as code to reproduce the results on the public datasets, are publicly available at https://github.com/adimajo/renard_joint. We hope this will empower other institutions to incorporate (further) ESG criteria in their decisions.

Finally, we identified future research directions which may improve the performance of SpERT on ClimLL: incorporating the context of neighboring sentences into its input and pre-training BERT on a specialized vocabulary set, as exemplified by SciBERT.

A   Evolution of Test F1 for the IBM Model

The annotation of 372 paragraphs (see Sect. 1) was deemed sufficient as the F1 scores for NER and Joint NER & RE stopped improving using the IBM proprietary model, as can be seen in Fig. 7.

B   Named Entity Recognition Representation

A popular output representation of NER is BIO (Begin, In, Out) embedding, where each word is marked as the beginning, inside, or outside of an entity (see *e.g.* [19,22]); however, this representation does not allow overlapping entities. On the other hand, span-based methods [5], which classify spans of words, can extract the spans of these overlapping entities. Figure 8 gives examples of BIO and span-based entity representations.

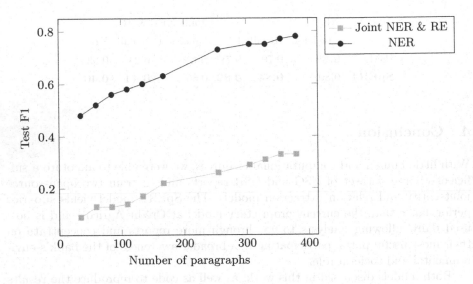

Fig. 7. Evolution of F1 scores w.r.t. the number of paragraphs.

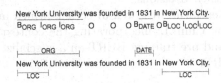

Fig. 8. Examples of BIO (above) and span-based (below) representations.

In the ClimLL dataset, even though the entities are presented in the span-based format in the dataset, there is no overlapping entity. Thus, it is also possible to convert to BIO format. Multiple relations can exist in the same sentence but relations cannot span across sentences. This facilitates splitting the paragraphs by sentence.

C   Single versus Multiple Relation Extraction

Relation extraction algorithms are divided into two categories: Single Relation Extraction [1] (SRE) algorithms which expect only one relation per input sentence and multiple relation extraction [7,21] (MRE) where multiple relations may exist in a single input sentence (Fig. 9).

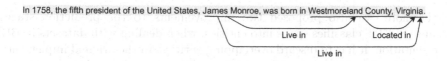

Fig. 9. Multiple relations example.

In this work, multiple relations are considered.

D   SpERT

D.1   Address a Shortcoming in Evaluation

While re-implementing the model, we noticed that, in the evaluation process, SpERT considers an incorrectly predicted entity span or relation as two negative observations. An example is presented in Fig. 10, where the model returns a set of predicted entities with "SpaceX" incorrectly classified as a person. In this case, the original evaluation process would iterate through the union of the true entity and the predicted entity sets. If an entity (including its span and type) is only presented in one of the sets, then it is considered to be classified as non-entity in the other. With this approach, "SpaceX" is considered to be incorrectly classified twice.

Input   SpaceX was founded by Elon Musk in 2002.

Prediction

True entities	Predicted entities
(SpaceX, Organization)	(SpaceX, Person)
(Elon Musk, Person)	(Elon Musk, Person)

Evaluation

Original

Entities	True entities	Predicted entities
SpaceX	Organization	No entity
SpaceX	No entity	Person
Elon Musk	Person	Person

Our version

Entities	True entities	Predicted entities
SpaceX	Organization	Person
Elon Musk	Person	Person

Accuracy   0.33   0.5

Fig. 10. Illustration of a better evaluation process for SpERT.

Thus, instead of iterating through the union of the true entity and predicted entity sets that include both entity spans and types, we only consider the union of the true entity spans with the predicted entity spans. Similarly for relations, we only take the union of the true and predicted spans of the source and target entity pair. As a result, we obtain a more accurate evaluation step.

D.2   Proposed Improvements

Furthermore, we also proposed two improvements to the prediction stages. Because SpERT classifies spans into entities, when dealing with datasets in BIO representation, it has to discard overlapping entities. In the original implementation, predicted entity spans are looped through in no specific order and any span that overlaps with previous spans is discarded. We suggest, instead, prioritizing discarding spans with low classification confidence.

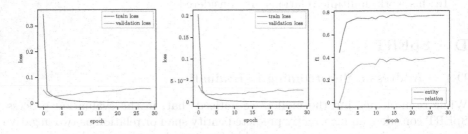

Fig. 11. Entity loss (left), relation loss (center) and F1-score on ClimLL w.r.t. training epochs (right).

Secondly, we noticed that the true pairs of entity types are not considered in the relation prediction stage of the original SpERT: For example, the model can only predict that an entity pair has a "live in" relation if the source entity is a person and the target entity is a location, irrespective of the probability given by the relation prediction stage. Thus, we modified the model so that it only predicts a relation if this relation fits the types of the source and target entities.

E   Evolution of Loss Functions

The entity and relation losses as well as the F1 score on the validation set throughout the training process (30 epochs) of SpERT on ClimLL are displayed on Fig. 11. Both entity and relation losses reached their minimum after only a few epochs while the validation F1 score kept improving.

References

1. Baldini Soares, L., FitzGerald, N., Ling, J., Kwiatkowski, T.: Matching the blanks: Distributional similarity for relation learning. In: Proceedings of the 57th Annual Meeting of the Association for Computational Linguistics, pp. 2895–2905. Association for Computational Linguistics, Florence, Italy, July 2019. https://doi.org/10.18653/v1/P19-1279, https://www.aclweb.org/anthology/P19-1279

2. Bekoulis, G., Deleu, J., Demeester, T., Develder, C.: Joint entity recognition and relation extraction as a multi-head selection problem. Expert Syst. Appl. **114**, 34–45 (2018)

3. Devalle, A., Fiandrino, S., Cantino, V.: The linkage between ESG performance and credit ratings: a firm-level perspective analysis. Int. J. Bus. Manage. **12**, 53 (2017). https://doi.org/10.5539/ijbm.v12n9p53

4. Devlin, J., Chang, M.W., Lee, K., Toutanova, K.: BERT: pre-training of deep bidirectional transformers for language understanding. arXiv preprint arXiv:1810.04805 (2018)

5. Eberts, M., Ulges, A.: Span-based joint entity and relation extraction with transformer pre-training. In: 24th European Conference on Artificial Intelligence (2020)

6. de Guindos, L.: Shining a light on climate risks: the ECB's economy-wide climate stress test (2021). https://www.ecb.europa.eu/press/blog/date/2021/html/ecb.blog210318~3bbc68ffc5.en.html

7. Han, X., Wang, L.: A novel document-level relation extraction method based on BERT and entity information. IEEE Access **8**, 96912–96919 (2020)

8. Hochreiter, S., Schmidhuber, J.: Long short-term memory. Neural Comput. **9**(8), 1735–1780 (1997)

9. Li, X., et al.: Entity-relation extraction as multi-turn question answering. In: Proceedings of the 57th Annual Meeting of the Association for Computational Linguistics, pp. 1340–1350. Association for Computational Linguistics, Florence, Italy, July 2019. https://doi.org/10.18653/v1/P19-1129, https://www.aclweb.org/anthology/P19-1129

10. Luan, Y., He, L., Ostendorf, M., Hajishirzi, H.: Multi-task identification of entities, relations, and coreference for scientific knowledge graph construction. In: Proceedings of Conference on Empirical Methods Natural Language Processing (EMNLP) (2018)

11. Luan, Y., Wadden, D., He, L., Shah, A., Ostendorf, M., Hajishirzi, H.: A general framework for information extraction using dynamic span graphs. In: Proceedings of the 2019 Conference of the North American Chapter of the Association for Computational Linguistics: Human Language Technologies, Volume 1 (Long and Short Papers), pp. 3036–3046. Association for Computational Linguistics, Minneapolis, Minnesota, June 2019. https://doi.org/10.18653/v1/N19-1308, https://www.aclweb.org/anthology/N19-1308

12. Martins, P.H., Marinho, Z., Martins, A.F.T.: Joint learning of named entity recognition and entity linking. In: Proceedings of the 57th Annual Meeting of the Association for Computational Linguistics: Student Research Workshop, pp. 190–196. Association for Computational Linguistics, Florence, Italy, July 2019. https://doi.org/10.18653/v1/P19-2026, https://www.aclweb.org/anthology/P19-2026

13. Nayak, T., Ng, H.T.: Effective modeling of encoder-decoder architecture for joint entity and relation extraction. In: Proceedings of the AAAI Conference on Artificial Intelligence, vol. 34, pp. 8528–8535 (2020)

14. Poidatz, A.: Banques : des engagements climat à prendre au 4ème degré (2020). https://www.oxfamfrance.org/rapports/banques-des-engagements-climat-a-prendre-au-4eme-degre/
15. Straková, J., Straka, M., Hajic, J.: Neural architectures for nested NER through linearization. In: Proceedings of the 57th Annual Meeting of the Association for Computational Linguistics, pp. 5326–5331. Association for Computational Linguistics, Florence, Italy, July 2019. https://doi.org/10.18653/v1/P19-1527, https://www.aclweb.org/anthology/P19-1527
16. Takanobu, R., Zhang, T., Liu, J., Huang, M.: A hierarchical framework for relation extraction with reinforcement learning. In: Proceedings of the AAAI Conference on Artificial Intelligence, vol. 33, pp. 7072–7079 (2019)
17. Taylor, W.L.: "Cloze procedure": a new tool for measuring readability. Journalism Q. **30**(4), 415–433 (1953)
18. Vaswani, A., et al.: Attention is all you need. In: Guyon, I. et al. (eds.) Advances in Neural Information Processing Systems, vol. 30. Curran Associates, Inc. (2017). https://proceedings.neurips.cc/paper/2017/file/3f5ee243547dee91fbd053c1c4a845aa-Paper.pdf
19. Verga, P., Strubell, E., McCallum, A.: Simultaneously self-attending to all mentions for full-abstract biological relation extraction. In: Proceedings of the 2018 Conference of the North American Chapter of the Association for Computational Linguistics: Human Language Technologies, Volume 1 (Long Papers), pp. 872–884. Association for Computational Linguistics, New Orleans, Louisiana, June 2018. https://doi.org/10.18653/v1/N18-1080, https://www.aclweb.org/anthology/N18-1080
20. Wadden, D., Wennberg, U., Luan, Y., Hajishirzi, H.: Entity, relation, and event extraction with contextualized span representations. In: Proceedings of the 2019 Conference on Empirical Methods in Natural Language Processing and the 9th International Joint Conference on Natural Language Processing (EMNLP-IJCNLP), pp. 5784–5789. Association for Computational Linguistics, Hong Kong, China, November 2019. https://doi.org/10.18653/v1/D19-1585, https://www.aclweb.org/anthology/D19-1585
21. Wang, H., et al.: Extracting multiple-relations in one-pass with pre-trained transformers. In: Proceedings of the 57th Annual Meeting of the Association for Computational Linguistics, pp. 1371–1377. Association for Computational Linguistics, Florence, Italy, July 2019. https://doi.org/10.18653/v1/P19-1132, https://www.aclweb.org/anthology/P19-1132
22. Wang, J., Lu, W.: Two are better than one: joint entity and relation extraction with table-sequence encoders. In: Proceedings of the 2020 Conference on Empirical Methods in Natural Language Processing (EMNLP), pp. 1706–1721. Association for Computational Linguistics, Online, November 2020. https://doi.org/10.18653/v1/2020.emnlp-main.133, https://www.aclweb.org/anthology/2020.emnlp-main.133

Hate Speech Detection in Clubhouse

Hadi Mansourifar[1]([✉]), Dana Alsagheer[1], Reza Fathi[1], Weidong Shi[1], Lan Ni[2], and Yan Huang[2]

[1] Computer Science Department, University of Houston, Houston, TX 77004, USA
{hmansour,dralsagh,rfathi,wshi3}@central.uh.edu
[2] Valenti School of Communication, University of Houston, Houston, TX 77004, USA
{lni2,yhuang63}@central.uh.edu

Abstract. With the rise of voice chat rooms, a gigantic resource of data can be exposed to the research community for natural language processing tasks. Moderators in voice chat rooms actively monitor the discussions and remove the participants with offensive language. However, it makes the hate speech detection even more difficult since some participants try to find creative ways to articulate hate speech. This makes the hate speech detection challenging in new social media like Clubhouse. To the best of our knowledge, all the hate speech datasets have been collected from text resources like Twitter. In this paper, we take the first step to collect a significant dataset from Clubhouse as the rising star in social media industry. We analyze the collected instances from statistical point of view using the Google Perspective Scores. Our experiments show that, the Perspective Scores can outperform Bag of Words and Word2Vec as high level text features.

Keywords: Counter hate speech · Clubhouse · Social computing

1 Introduction

"The explosive growth of Clubhouse [1], an audio-based social network buoyed by appearances from tech celebrities like Elon Musk and Mark Zuckerberg, has drawn scrutiny over how the app will handle problematic content, from hate speech to harassment and misinformation" [10]. However, in most of crowded rooms with presence of intellectual people, it's very hard to find overt act of aggressive speech since the moderators monitor and remove the impolite speakers. Consequently, hate speech is uttered in more articulated ways which is not compatible with traditional datasets already published in this domain. Beyond that, Audio presents a fundamentally different set of challenges for moderation than text-based communication. It's more ephemeral and it's harder to research and action," said Discord's chief legal officer, Clint Smith, in an interview [10]. Although the definition of hate speech [6,12,14,28–30] is still the same as any communication that disparages a person or a group on the basis of some characteristic such as race, color, ethnicity, gender, sexual orientation, nationality, religion or other characteristic [12,13,18,19,21,25,29], some people may convey

M. Kamp et al. (Eds.): ECML PKDD 2021 Workshops, CCIS 1525, pp. 341–351, 2021.
https://doi.org/10.1007/978-3-030-93733-1_24

it via more sophisticated ways. This issue is more frequently seen in voice-based social media in which people try to appear polite and educated. To the best of our knowledge, all the hate speech datasets have been collected from text resources like Twitter and audio resources are totally ignored so far. With the rise of voice chat rooms, a gigantic resource of data can be exposed to the research community for offensive language and hate speech detection. In this paper, we investigate the challenges of hate speech detection in Clubhouse. Following Israel-Palestine conflict in May 2021, an extensive discussions broke out about various aspects of this conflict from history and economy to religion and philosophy in number of Clubhouse rooms. Due to huge controversy surrounding this issue, the possibility of finding various instances of hate speech in such discussions was very likely. Recording more than 50 h of discussions related to Israel-Palestine conflict in Clubhouse confirmed our initial assumption. Although the collected dataset is very imbalanced, positive instances include wide range of hate speech samples from highly toxic to seemingly polite ones. This diverse range of hate speech instances can provide the research community with a valuable resource for hate speech analysis in the future. Our collected data show that, a controversial topic can bring together many participants from across the globe in the Clubhouse. Although self-identification is very rare, we found 12 different nationalities among those who disclosed their identities. Also, we observed that such hot discussions in Clubhouse can encompass a wide range of themes from history to philosophy surrounding an international conflict. First, we extracted the text features using three different methods including Bag of Words [16], Word2Vec [17] and Perspective Scores [2]. Second, we used two different base classifiers including XGB [9] and LR [26] to compare the significance of extracted features. To extract the Perspective Scores we used Google Perspective API [2] and we investigated the significance of each score using ANOVA test for the task of binary classification. Our statistical analysis show that, some Perspective Scores including TOXICITY and IDENTITY-ATTACK have a significant impact on hate speech detection. Our contributions are as follows.

- We use voice-based social media to collect significant hate speech data.
- We publish a labelled dataset containing a diverse range of hate speech instances collected from the Clubhouse.
- Our experiments show that, Perspective Scores can play a crucial role in hate speech detection at voice-based social media.

The rest of paper is organized as follows. Section 2 reviews related works. Section 3 demonstrates data collection and annotation. Section 4 presents methodology. Section 5 provides the experimental results and finally Sect. 6 concludes the paper.

2 Related Work

Our research contribution is to collect a new dataset from voice-based social media. To the best of our knowledge all the hate speech datasets [7,24] have

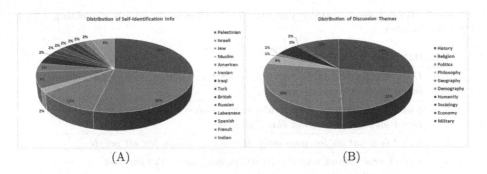

Fig. 1. (A) Distribution of participants' identity according to self-identification info. (B) Distribution of discussions themes.

been collected from text-based resources. In this section, we review some of the well known resources [20] and their characteristics.

- DAVIDSON Dataset [11]: The dataset contains 24,802 tweets in English (5.77% labelled as hate speech, 77.43% as Offensive and 16.80% as Neither) and was published in raw text format. They report collecting this data from Twitter using a lexicon from HateBase containing hateful words and phrases.
- WARNER Dataset [29]: The constituent data was collected from Yahoo News Group and URLs from the American Jewish Society. It contains 9000 paragraphs, manually annotated into seven (7) categories (anti-semitic, anti-black, anti-Asian, anti-woman, anti-Muslim, anti-immigrant or other hate(anti-gay and anti-white)). The dataset is not publicly available.
- DJURIC Dataset [12]: This dataset was collected comments from the Yahoo Finance website. 56,280 comments were labeled as hateful while 895,456 labeled as clean from 209,776 users.
- QIAN Dataset [23]: This dataset was collected from Reddit and Gab including intervention responses written by humans. Their data preserves the conversational thread as a way to provide context. From Reddit, they collected 5,020 conversations which includes a total of 22,324 comments labelled as hate or non-hate. 76.6% of the conversations contain hate speech while only 23.5% of the comments are labelled as hateful. They also collected 11,825 conversations containing 33,776 posts. 94.5% of the conversations contained hate speech while about 43.2% of the comments are labelled as hateful.
- BENIKOVA Dataset [5]: contains 36 German tweets with 33% labelled as hate speech and 67% as non-hate speech.

3   Data Collection and Annotation

At the midst of Israel-Palestine conflict in May 2021, a wide range of discussions broke out from history to politics about various aspects of this conflict in number of Clubhouse rooms. Figure 1 shows the fraction of all sentences which directly

Table 1. Hate speech samples collected from Clubhouse rooms discussing Israel-Palestine conflict.

Ex.	Hate speech
1	*Do you support Israel's right to exist? So, um that doesn't seem to me like a reasonable question*
2	*I would just propose that Arabs sorry, Palestinians who are citizens of Israel uh they are second class citizens*
3	*Israel is a nation for jews only, it's not a nation for all people*
4	*I don't understand why the Israeli people, we can't hear you, you're cutting off*
5	*When Palestinians are given freedom and more rights, that suddenly it's going to be chaos and there's gonna be a lot of violence*
6	*Well look how the Arabs treat each other, how they treat their women as if kind of saying*

pointing to one of these aspects including history, religion, politics, etc. Also, less than 1% of participants in the discussions self-identified themselves as Jew, Muslim, Palestinian, Israeli, Arab, etc. The distribution of identities is reported in part (a) of Fig. 1. To collect the dataset about this topic, more than 50 h of voice was recorded from 5 different rooms all discussing the Israel-Palestine conflict . Afterwards, all the voice data converted to the text format using Amazon Transcribe [30]. The raw text contains more than 11000 sentences. We labelled 468 instances including 122 hate speech instances and 346 normal instances. The annotation was done by two independent individuals and labels assigned with full agreement of both annotators.

Table 2. ANOVA test results on perspective scores of collected dataset. Signif. codes: 0 '***' 0.001 '**' 0.01 '*' 0.05 '.' 0.1 ' ' 1

	Df	Sum Sq	Mean Sq	F value	p-value
TOXICITY	1	56.66	56.66	1088.12	$2e-16$***
SEVERE_TOXICITY	1	0.39	0.39	7.41	0.0067**
IDENTITY_ATTACK	1	7.77	7.77	149.13	$2e-16$***
INSULT	1	0.54	0.54	10.35	0.0014**
PROFANITY	1	0.06	0.06	1.13	0.2880
THREAT	1	0.85	0.85	16.29	$6.37e-05$***
SEXUALLY_EXPLICIT	1	0.00	0.00	0.00	0.9666
OBSCENE	1	0.00	0.00	0.04	0.8364
SPAM	1	0.06	0.06	1.23	0.2677
Residuals	457	23.80	0.05		

3.1 What is in the Data?

During the annotation, we understood that, some individuals articulate the hate speech in very sophisticated ways such that, the moderators could not find enough evidences to remove the participant from the room. Table 1 shows some of the hate speech instances collected from Clubhouse. We also observed that, the collected comments encompass a wide range of topics from history to economy as shown in part (b) of Fig. 1. According to this chart, the most discussed topics are related to history, religion and politics. Surprisingly, we can find topics related to philosophy and economy in the comments which proves the capability of voice-based social media to bring together people from different backgrounds and point of views. We also observed that, such hot discussions over a controversial topic can attract people from different nationalities. Although less than 1% of participants disclosed their nationalities, limited self-identification info show a long list of nationalities as shown in part(a) of Fig. 1.

3.2 Public Dataset

Our labelled dataset is publicly available in [3] but the raw text dataset which includes more than 11000 sentences is not publicly available. The raw text dataset is provided to valid academic requests submitted to the first author of this paper. Note that, the original voices would not be published to public and private requests.

3.3 Challenges of Collecting Data from Clubhouse

In this section, we report number of challenges of collecting data from Clubhouse.

- It's not that easy to find the target rooms discussing a specific topic. First, a number of active individuals must be followed to get access to a range of available rooms. Finding the target people and rooms is a time consuming process.
- In crowded rooms most of the participants trying to be polite and educated. As a consequence, offensive language is very rare in the rooms with many participants.
- Presence of active moderators is a great hurdle for some individuals who wants to use offensive language.

Table 3. ANOVA test results on interaction of collected dataset's Perspective Scores.

	Df	Sum Sq	Mean Sq	F value	p-value
TOXICITY	1	56.66	56.66	1167.20	$2e-16$***
SEVERE_TOXICITY	1	0.39	0.39	7.95	0.0050**
IDENTITY_ATTACK	1	7.77	7.77	159.97	$2e-16$***
INSULT	1	0.54	0.54	11.10	0.0009***
PROFANITY	1	0.06	0.06	1.21	0.2711
THREAT	1	0.85	0.85	17.47	$3.50e-05$***
SEXUALLY_EXPLICIT	1	0.00	0.00	0.00	0.9654
OBSCENE	1	0.00	0.00	0.05	0.8306
SPAM	1	0.06	0.06	1.32	0.2510
TOXICITY:IDENTITY_ATTACK	1	0.24	0.24	4.95	0.0266*
TOXICITY:SPAM	1	1.45	1.45	29.77	$8.03e-08$***
TOXICITY:THREAT	1	0.06	0.06	1.16	0.2813
TOXICITY:INSULT	1	0.06	0.06	1.33	0.2492
Residuals	453	21.99	0.05		

4 Methodology

In this section, we present our approaches to analyse the collected data and train classifiers for hate speech detection. We used three different approaches as feature extraction including Bag of Words [16], Word2vec [17,22] and Perspective Scores [1]. Since Perspective Scores are less well-known comparing to traditional text features we demonstrate them in following section.

4.1 Perspective Scores

In order to extract high level features from hate speech instances, we use Perspective API [1]. Perspective API developed by Jigsaw and Google's Counter Abuse Technology team as a part of the Conversation-AI project. The API provides several pre-trained models to compute several scores between 0 and 1 for different categories as follows [13].

- toxicity is a "rude, disrespectful, or unreasonable comment that is likely to make people leave a discussion."
- severe toxicity is a "very hateful, aggressive, disrespectful comment or otherwise very likely to make a user leave a discussion or give up on sharing their perspective."
- identity attack are "negative or hateful comments targeting someone because of their identity."
- insult is an "insulting, inflammatory, or negative comment towards a person or a group of people."
- profanity are "swear words, curse words, or other obscene or profane language"
- threat "describes an intention to inflict pain, injury, or violence against an individual or group."

All the trained models use Convolutional Neural Networks (CNNs), trained with GloVe word embeddings [22] and fine-tuned during training on data from online sources such as Wikipedia and The New York Times [13].

Analysis of Variance for Regression. Analysis of Variance (ANOVA) consists of calculations that provide information about levels of variability within a regression model and form a basis for tests of significance [27]. We investigated the significance of Perspective Scores on hate speech detection task using ANOVA test. Our experiments show that, TOXICITY and IDENTITY-ATTACK scores have significant impact on hate speech detection as shown in Table 2. Furthermore, we examine the significance of features interaction. Table 3 shows that, there is a significant interaction between TOXICITY and IDENTITY-ATTACK.

5   Experiments

In this section, we review the detail settings of our experiments including base classifiers, feature extraction and performance measures.

5.1   Feature Extraction

We used three different feature extraction methods as follows.

- Bag of words [16,31]: The 'bag of words' is the word vector for each instance in the dataset which is a simple word count for each instance where each position of the vector represents a word. We used ngram range of (1,2) which means that each vector is divided into single words and also pairs of consecutive words. We also set the max size of the word vector to 10,000 words.
- Word2vec : Word2Vec [17,22] is one of the most popular techniques to learn word embeddings using shallow neural network. It was developed by Tomas Mikolov in 2013 at Google. As the pre-trained model we used Google News corpus trained on 3 million words and phrases. this model provides 300-dimensional vectors as the transferred data.
- Perspective Scores: They are high level features calculated by different trained classifiers. We passed all the records to Google Perspective API and collected 9 Perspective Scores per input vector as mentioned in previous section. We applied based classifiers without over-sampling [4,8,15] on the transferred vectors.

5.2   Base Classifiers

- XGB [9]: XGBoost is an implementation of gradient boosted decision trees designed for speed and performance. It has become popular in applied machine learning and Kaggle competitions in recent years.
- LR [26]: It is commonly used for many binary classification tasks which uses logistic function and log odds to perform a binary classification task.

5.3   Performance Measures

Classifier performance metrics are typically evaluated by a confusion matrix, as shown in following table. The rows are actual classes, and the columns are detected classes. TP (True Positive) is the number of correctly classified positive instances. FN (False Negative) is the number of incorrectly classified positive instances. FP (False Positive) is the number of incorrectly classified negative instances. TN (True Negative) is the number of correctly classified negative instances. The three performance measures including precision, recall and F1 are defined by following formulae.

	Detected positive	Detected negative
Actual positive	TP	FN
Actual negative	FP	TN

Recall $=$ TP/(TP+ FN)
Precision $=$ TP/(TP+ FP)
F1 $= (2*$ Recall $*$ Precision$) /($ Recall+ Precision$)$

5.4   Implementation

To implement the feature extraction methods and base classifiers, we used python libraries including Sklearn, Pandas, etc. All the codes and three versions of labelled data corresponding to three types of extracted features including Bag of Word, Word2vec and Perspective Scores can be found in [3].

5.5   Results

In this section, we report the experimental results as shown in Table 4 where the best results are shown in bold per each performance measure . We tested two different base classifiers on features extracted from collected dataset using three different feature extraction methods. The experimental results can be summarized as follows.

- In both classifiers, the best results belong to Perspective Scores as the feature extraction method in terms of all performance measures.
- XGB as base classifier and Perspective Score as feature extraction show the best results in terms of Accuracy, Recall and F1 score.
- LR as base classifier and Perspective Score as feature extraction show the best results in terms of Precision.

Table 4. Experimental results on collected dataset using 2 base classifiers and three feature extraction methods. Bold values represent the best results.

Classifier	Features	Performance measure			
		Accuracy	Precision	Recall	F1
XGB	*Bag of words*	0.848	0.7905	0.5879	0.6634
	Word2Vec	0.8586	0.7991	0.5923	0.6684
	Perspective scores	**0.9528**	0.9183	**0.9052**	**0.9089**
LR	*Bag of words*	0.8543	0.7918	0.61	0.6753
	Word2Vec	0.8629	0.7424	0.7233	0.7255
	Perspective scores	0.9463	**0.9452**	0.8783	0.9057

6   Conclusion

In this paper, we introduced a significant dataset collected from an un-investigated media. We showed that, a voice-based social media like Clubhouse has incredible potential to expose very diverse range of data which embrace a wide range of themes from philosophy to military. It proves that, voice-based chat rooms would become a hub for collecting data for many researchers from different branches of natural language processing. According to self-identification info, participants from 12 different nationalities joined the discussions related to recent Israel-Palestine conflict. We observed that, participants avoid offensive language to utter the hate speech and try to come up with more sophisticated comments to express hate speech. That's why the hate speech detection in Clubhouse is challenging. We tested three different feature extraction methods using two different base classifiers. Our experimental results showed that, Google Perspective Scores outperform the traditional feature extraction methods including Bag of Words and Word2Vec in terms of all tested performance measures.

Acknowledgement. This research is supported by University of Houston President's Grants to Enhance Research on Racism (2020).

References

1. https://www.clubhouse.co/
2. https://www.perspectiveapi.com/
3. https://github.com/hadimansouorifar/HSD-Clubhouse
4. Barua, S., Monirul Islam, M., Yao, X., Murase, K.: MWMOTE-majority weighted minority oversampling technique for imbalanced data set learning. IEEE Trans. knowl. Data Eng. **26**(2), 405–425 (2012)
5. Benikova, D., Wojatzki, M., Zesch, T.: What does this imply? Examining the impact of implicitness on the perception of hate speech. In: Rehm, G., Declerck, T. (eds.) GSCL 2017. LNCS (LNAI), vol. 10713, pp. 171–179. Springer, Cham (2018). https://doi.org/10.1007/978-3-319-73706-5_14

6. Burnap, P., Williams, M.L.: Cyber hate speech on twitter: an application of machine classification and statistical modeling for policy and decision making. Policy Internet **7**(2), 223–242 (2015)

7. Burnap, P., Williams, M.L.: Hate speech, machine classification and statistical modelling of information flows on twitter: Interpretation and communication for policy decision making (2014)

8. Chawla, N.V., Bowyer, K.W., Hall, L.O., Kegelmeyer, W.P.: Smote synthetic minority over-sampling technique. J. Artif. Intell. Res. **16**, 321–357 (2002)

9. Chen, T., et al.: XGBOOST: extreme gradient boosting. R. Pack. Version 0.4-2 **1**(4), 1–4 (2015)

10. Culliford, E.: From Clubhouse to Twitter Spaces, social media grapples with live audio moderation (2021). https://www.reuters.com/article/us-clubhouse-moderation-focus-idINKBN2AP1J2

11. Davidson, T., Warmsley, D., Macy, M., Weber, I.: Automated hate speech detection and the problem of offensive language. In: Proceedings of the International AAAI Conference on Web and Social Media, vol. 11 (2017)

12. Djuric, N., Zhou, J., Morris, R., Grbovic, M., Radosavljevic, V., Bhamidipati, N.: Hate speech detection with comment embeddings. In: Proceedings of the 24th International Conference on World Wide Web, pp. 29–30 (2015)

13. Fortuna, P., Soler, J., Wanner, L.: Toxic, hateful, offensive or abusive? what are we really classifying? an empirical analysis of hate speech datasets. In Proceedings of the 12th Language Resources and Evaluation Conference, pp. 6786–6794 (2020)

14. Gitari, N.D., Zuping, Z., Damien, H., Long, J.: A lexicon-based approach for hate speech detection. Int. J. Multimed. Ubiquit. Eng. **10**(4), 215–230 (2015)

15. Han, H., Wang, W.-Y., Mao, B.-H.: Borderline-SMOTE: a new over-sampling method in imbalanced data sets learning. In: Huang, D.-S., Zhang, X.-P., Huang, G.-B. (eds.) ICIC 2005. LNCS, vol. 3644, pp. 878–887. Springer, Heidelberg (2005). https://doi.org/10.1007/11538059_91

16. Jiang, H., Xiao, Y., Wang, W.: Explaining a bag of words with hierarchical conceptual labels. World Wide Web. **23**, 1–21 (2020)

17. Kim, S., Park, H., Lee, J.: Word2vec-based latent semantic analysis (W2V-LSA) for topic modeling: a study on blockchain technology trend analysis. Expert Syst. App. **152**, 113401 (2020)

18. Kumar, S., Pranesh, R.R., Pandey, S.C.: TweetBLM: A hate speech dataset and analysis of black lives matter-related microblogs on twitter

19. Kwok, I., Wang, Y.: Locate the hate: detecting tweets against blacks. In: Twenty-Seventh AAAI Conference on Artificial Intelligence (2013)

20. Naseem, U., Razzak, I., Eklund, P.W.: A survey of pre-processing techniques to improve short-text quality: a case study on hate speech detection on twitter. Multimed. Tools. App. **80**, 1–28 (2020)

21. Nockleyby, J.: Hate speech in encyclopedia of the American constitution. Electron. J. Acad. Spec. libr. (2000)

22. Pennington, J., Socher, R., Manning, C.D.: Glove: global vectors for word representation. In: Proceedings of the 2014 Conference on Empirical Methods in Natural Language Processing (EMNLP), pp. 1532–1543 (2014)

23. Qian, J., Bethke, A., Liu, Y., Belding, E., Wang, W.Y.: A benchmark dataset for learning to intervene in online hate speech (2019). arXiv preprint arXiv:1909.04251

24. Ross, B., Rist, M., Carbonell, G., Cabrera, B., Kurowsky, N., Wojatzki, M.: Measuring the reliability of hate speech annotations: the case of the European refugee crisis (2017). arXiv preprint arXiv:1701.08118

25. Schmidt, A., Wiegand, M.: A survey on hate speech detection using natural language processing. In: Proceedings of the Fifth International Workshop on Natural Language Processing For Social Media, pp. 1–10 (2017)

26. Shah, K., Patel, H., Sanghvi, D., Shah, M.: A comparative analysis of logistic regression, random forest and knn models for the text classification. Augment. Human Res. **5**(1), 1–16 (2020)

27. Uyanık, G.K., Guler, N.: A study on multiple linear regression analysis. Proc. Soc. Behav. Sci. **106**, 234–240 (2013)

28. Wang, W., Chen, L., Thirunarayan, K., Sheth, A.P.: Cursing in English on twitter. In: Proceedings of the 17th ACM Conference on Computer Supported Cooperative Work & Social Computing, pp. 415–425 (2014)

29. Warner, W., Hirschberg, J.: Detecting hate speech on the world wide web. In: Proceedings of the Second Workshop on Language in Social Media, pp. 19–26 (2012)

30. Waseem, Z., Hovy, D.: Hateful symbols or hateful people? Predictive features for hate speech detection on twitter. In: Proceedings of the NAACL Student Research Workshop, pp. 88–93 (2016)

31. Zhang, Y., Jin, R., Zhou, Z.-H.: Understanding bag-of-words model: a statistical framework. Int. J. Mach. Learn. Cybern. **1**(1–4), 43–52 (2010)

Error Variance, Fairness, and the Curse on Minorities

Emma Beauxis-Aussalet[✉]

Vrije Universiteit Amsterdam, De Boelelaan 1111, Amsterdam, The Netherlands
e.m.a.l.beauxisaussalet@vu.nl

Abstract. Machine learning systems can make more errors for certain populations and not others, and thus create discriminations. To assess such fairness issue, errors are typically compared across populations. We argue that we also need to account for the variability of errors in practice, as the errors measured in test data may not be exactly the same in real-life data (called *target* data). We first introduce statistical methods for estimating random error variance in machine learning problems. The methods estimate how often errors would exceed certain magnitudes, and how often the errors of a population would exceed that of another (e.g., by more than a certain range). The methods are based on well-established sampling theory, and the recently introduced Sample-to-Sample estimation. The latter shows that small target samples yield high error variance, even if the test sample is very large. We demonstrate that, in practice, minorities are bound to bear higher variance, thus amplified error and bias. This can occur even if the test and training sets are accurate, representative, and extremely large. We call this statistical phenomenon the curse on minorities, and we show examples of its impact with basic classification and regression problems. Finally, we outline potential approaches to protect minorities from such curse, and to develop variance-aware fairness assessments.

Keywords: Fairness · Transparency · Error variance · Discrimination

1 Introduction

Machine learning systems have been shown to make systematically more errors for certain populations, thus discriminating them [2,12]. Such fairness issues are part of larger societal issues, and cannot be fully addressed by technical solutions [17]. Yet technical solutions for measuring machine learning errors enable a variety of fairness assessments [9,16] but not without concerns about their appropriate use [6]. For instance, the choice of error metrics and sampling approach must be adapted to the domain and context.

In this position paper, we focus on bias defined as systematic error differences among populations. We discuss the statistical methods for estimating the range of error and bias to expect in practice, among random samples (e.g., to audit a model before deployment). We only discuss random error variance, i.e., the error

© Springer Nature Switzerland AG 2021
M. Kamp et al. (Eds.): ECML PKDD 2021 Workshops, CCIS 1525, pp. 352–365, 2021.
https://doi.org/10.1007/978-3-030-93733-1_25

variations that are solely due to the effect of randomly sampling the test data and the real-life data samples.

However narrow or well-know random variance may be, we show its implications for high-level fairness and transparency issues. We argue that i) error variance should be considered as another dimension of fairness, ii) algorithm audits should use appropriate statistics to make error variance transparent, and iii) regulations should adopt variance-aware approaches when setting limitations on error and bias.

We first review prior work on error and bias metrics, and their variance estimation (Sect. 2) before outlining their application to machine learning problems (Sect. 3). We then argue that error variance is an important dimension of fairness issues (Sect. 4).

We demonstrate that unequal variance amplifies bias, and increases the frequency of large error discrepancies. Minorities are by definition smaller populations, and we demonstrate the higher variance and bias that ensue. Such statistical phenomenon occurs regardless of the quality of test or training data, and can be considered as a curse on minorities. We finally outline potential approaches for mitigating such curse, and for informing stakeholders, users, or policy makers.

2 Statistical Theory

We review essential work on error and bias metrics (Sect. 2.1) and their random sample variance (Sects. 2.2) for classification and regression problems.

2.1 Error and Bias Metrics

The errors measured using *test data* are used to estimate of the errors to expect in the *target data* processed in real life.[1] Such error estimation relies on the assumption that the test data is representative of the target data, i.e., test and target data are randomly sampled from the same population. We distinguish two assumptions: simple random sampling, and stratified random sampling. The strata can be protected populations (e.g., potentially discriminated by higher errors) and/or any class of interest (e.g., in classification problems).

In practice, it is often the case that the target data should be considered as drawn from stratified randomly sampling. For instance, certain classes or protected populations can be larger at certain time periods or locations (e.g., more binational citizens at certain zip codes, or more unemployed females in times of crisis). In this case, we must assume that the target data is drawn from a stratified sampling, with strata for each class or sub-population.

In the sections below, we outline which error metrics are not applicable if the target data follows a stratified sampling, and not a simple random sampling.

---

[1] In this paper, the *target data* is the real-life data processed in practice, not the target variables to predict. The *training data* is not discussed as it is irrelevant for estimating the errors in the target data. Only the *test data* is relevant, and the model may also be semi- or self-supervised.

Classification Problems. Different metrics of classification errors have been established, and address different needs and use cases [8, 13, 14]. We distinguish three kinds of basic error rates, depending on their denominator (Table 1).

– **Actual class size** $n_{x.}$ as denominator: θ_{xy} (1), e.g., True Positive rates θ_{11}
– **Predicted class size** $n_{.y}$ as denominator: e_{xy} (2), e.g., Precision e_{11}
– **Total sample size** $n_{..}$ as denominator: Accuracy A (3), with the correct classifications n_{xx} as numerator

The latter two (e.g., Precision and Accuracy) are biased estimators if the target data can have highly varying class proportions (e.g., for stratified target samples, with strata of data points from the same true class, with highly varying class sizes). In such case, the error rates θ_{xy} should be used [1].

Table 1. Notation and basic variables of error metrics.

n_{xy}	Number of data points actually belonging to class x and classified as class y (errors if $x \neq y$). In binary problems, n_{11} are True Positives, n_{00} are True Negatives, n_{01} are False Positives, and n_{10} are False Negatives
n_{xx}	Number of correct classifications for class x
$n_{x.}$	Total number of data points actually belonging to class x (i.e., $\sum_y n_{xy} = n_{x.}$)
$n_{.y}$	Total number of data points classified as class y (i.e., $\sum_x n_{xy} = n_{.y}$)
$n_{..}$	Total number of data points (i.e., $\sum_x n_{x.} = \sum_y n_{.y} = n_{..}$)
θ_{xy}	Rate of error n_{xy} on actual class size $n_{x.}$ (1) (e.g., True Positive Rate if $x = y$)
e_{xy}	Rate of error n_{xy} on predicted class size $n_{.y}$ (2) (e.g., Precision if $x = y$)
A	Accuracy (3), i.e., rate of correct classification on total sample size

$$\theta_{xy} = \frac{n_{xy}}{n_{x.}} \quad (1) \qquad e_{xy} = \frac{n_{xy}}{n_{.y}} \quad (2) \qquad A = \frac{\sum_x n_{xx}}{n_{..}} \quad (3)$$

These three kinds of error rates at the core of a variety of bias metrics [16]. Metrics θ_{xy} (1) with actual class size as denominator apply to:

– Predictive Equality or False Positive Rate Balance (with $x = 0$ and $y = 1$).
– Equal Opportunity or False Negative Rate Balance (with $x = 1$ and $y = 0$).
– Equalized Odds, Conditional Procedure Accuracy Equality, or Disparate Mistreatment (with $y = 1$).

Metrics e_{xy} (2) with predicted class size as denominator apply to:

– Predictive Parity or Outcome Test (with $x = 1$ and $y = 1$).
– Condition Use Accuracy Equality (with $x \neq y$).

Finally, accuracy A (3), with total sample size as denominator, applies to Overall Accuracy Equality.

Regression Problems. Metrics of regression errors basically rely on residuals, i.e., the difference between the true and predicted values for a data point i ($r_i = y_i - \hat{y}_i$). Residuals are typically averaged over data points, and using the absolute or squared values ($|r_i|$ or r_i^2) to avoid signed values. The latter's mean typically tend to zero in regression problems, as an effect of how regressions are fitted by machine learning systems (or other statistical methods). On the contrary, the mean absolute error (MAE $= 1/n_{..} \sum_i |r_i|$), the mean squared error (MSE $= 1/n_{..} \sum_i r_i^2$), or the root mean squared error (RMSE $= \sqrt{1/n_{..} \sum_i r_i^2}$) have non-null values that represent the range of residuals to expect in a data sample (i.e., error variance MSE and standard deviation RMSE).

Comparing MAE, MSE, or RMSE across protected populations is already a method for considering fairness issues arising from error variance. In this paper, we will introduce additional methods to account for the size and composition of the target samples.

2.2   Estimating Variance

In this section, we first discuss random variance in classification problems, before introducing the Sample-to-Sample method applied to both regression and classification problems.

Classification Problems. Sampling theory defines the random variance of a rate [5] and is applicable to error rates in classification problems. In essence, the smaller the sample, the larger the variance. Applied to the three kinds of errors rates θ_{xy}, e_{xy}, A (1)–(3), simple formulas can estimate the variance of random samples. With specific sampling assumptions, the formulas below can be applied.

$$V\left(\theta_{xy}^{(x,\cdot)}\right) = \frac{\theta_{xy}^*(1-\theta_{xy}^*)}{n_{x.}} \tag{4}$$

$$V\left(e_{xy}^{(\cdot y)}\right) = \frac{e_{xy}^*(1-e_{xy}^*)}{n_{.y}} \tag{5}$$

$$V\left(A^{(\cdot\cdot)}\right) = \frac{A^*(1-A^*)}{n_{..}} \tag{6}$$

These formulas concern infinite populations or infinite stratum population ($n_{x.}^* \to \infty$, $n_{.y}^* \to \infty$, $n_{..}^* \to \infty$) and do not apply finite population correction.

For **errors rates θ_{xy}** (4), the formula concerns random samples of size $n_{x.}$ drawn from the stratum of data points that actually belong to class x, and denoted with upperscript $(x.)$. The stratum's error rate is θ_{xy}^* (e.g., when $n_{x.} \to \infty$).

For **errors rates e_{xy}** (5), the formula concerns random samples of size $n_{.y}$ drawn from the stratum of data points that are classified as class y, denoted with upperscript $(\cdot y)$. The stratum's error rate is e_{xy}^* (e.g., when $n_{.y} \to \infty$).

For **accuracy A** (6), the formula concerns simple random samples of size $n_{..}$ drawn from a population of all classes, denoted with upperscript $(\cdot\cdot)$. The population accuracy is A^* (e.g., when $n_{..} \to \infty$).

Sample-to-Sample Estimation. When the errors in a test sample are used to estimate the errors in a target sample, one sample's error rate is used as an estimator of another sample's error rate. Such estimators, called *Sample-to-Sample* [1], are impacted by the random variance in both test and target samples. We detail this estimation method using **prime symbols** (e.g., n'_{xy}) when referring to the target sample, and **no prime** when referring to the test sample.

The error differences between the test and target samples vary as the difference of two random variables does (e.g., $\theta_{xy} - \theta'_{xy}$). We assume that the test and target samples are independent (e.g., no overlap) with null covariance, e.g., $V(\theta_{xy} - \theta'_{xy}) = V(\theta_{xy}) + V(\theta'_{xy})$.

Hence when estimating the error rates in a target sample from the error rates measured in a test sample, the variance of such Sample-to-Sample estimates is the sum of both test and target sample variance (7)–(9). Thus error estimates for small target sets can have large variance, even if the test sample is very large.

$$V(\widehat{\theta'^{(x.)}_{xy}}) = V(\theta^{(x.)}_{xy}) + V(\theta'^{(x.)}_{xy}) = \frac{\theta^*_{xy}(1-\theta^*_{xy})}{n_x.} + \frac{\theta^*_{xy}(1-\theta^*_{xy})}{n'_x.} \tag{7}$$

$$V(\widehat{e'^{(.y)}_{xy}}) = V(e^{(.y)}_{xy}) + V(e'^{(.y)}_{xy}) = \frac{e^*_{xy}(1-e^*_{xy})}{n_{.y}} + \frac{e^*_{xy}(1-e^*_{xy})}{n'_{.y}} \tag{8}$$

$$V(\widehat{A'^{(..)}}) = V(A^{(..)}) + V(A'^{(..)}) = \frac{A^*(1-A^*)}{n_{..}} + \frac{A^*(1-A^*)}{n'_{.}} \tag{9}$$

It is important to mention, as in Sect. 2.1, that estimates for $\widehat{e'^{(.y)}_{xy}}$ and $\widehat{A'^{(..)}}$ are not applicable if class proportions largely vary among target samples.

Sample-to-Sample in Regression Problems. Sample-to-Sample originally addressed classification problems. Prior work mentions the issue of error variance for regression fairness, but without investigating random sample variance in target samples [7,15]. We thus briefly investigate how residuals in target samples may randomly vary from those measured in a test sample (since the latter is used to estimate the former, i.e., $\widehat{MSE'} = MSE$). The variance of mean squared errors (MSE) is the variance of a mean. According to the central limit theorem, we assume that MSE are normally distributed with $V(\boldsymbol{MSE}) = MSE^{*2}(1/n_{..})$ and $V(\boldsymbol{MSE'}) = MSE^{*2}(1/n'_{..})$.

The error differences between the test and target samples vary as the difference of two random variables (e.g., $\boldsymbol{MSE'} - \boldsymbol{MSE}$). We assume that test and target samples are independent with null covariance, thus $V(\boldsymbol{MSE} - \boldsymbol{MSE'}) = V(\boldsymbol{MSE}) + V(\boldsymbol{MSE'}) = MSE^{*2}(1/n_{..} + 1/n'_{..})$.

In practice, the population MSE^* can be estimated from the test set, i.e., $\widehat{MSE^*} = MSE$. Thus we may apply Sample-to-Sample estimates as in (10), and we evaluate this approach in Sect. 4. Meanwhile, in Sect. 3 we focus on classification problems.

$$\widehat{V}(\boldsymbol{MSE'}) = MSE^2(1/n'_{..} + 1/n_{..}) \tag{10}$$

3   Estimating Variance in Practice

The theory for variance estimation is based on the overall population error rates $(\theta^*_{xy}, e^*_{xy}, A^*)$ which are unknown. In practice, the error rates from the test data can be used to estimate the population error rates [1].

$$\widehat{\theta^*_{xy}} = \theta_{xy} \qquad\qquad \widehat{e^*_{xy}} = e_{xy} \qquad\qquad \widehat{A^*} = A \qquad\qquad (11)$$

We can then compute the variance estimates of error rates (Sect. 3.1) and error differences among sub-populations (Sect. 3.2). Using these methods, we demonstrate the practical impacts of variance on minorities, i.e., larger ranges of error and bias occur for smaller sub-populations (Sect. 3.3). Finally, we outline methods for drawing confidence intervals, to visualise the range of error and bias to expect in practice (Sect. 3.4).

3.1   Estimating Error Variance

We can estimate error variance in target samples using equations (7–9) and (11).

$$\widehat{V(\theta'^{(x.)}_{xy})} = \theta_{xy}(1-\theta_{xy})\left(\frac{1}{n_{x.}} + \frac{1}{\widehat{n'_{x.}}}\right) \qquad\qquad (12)$$

$$\widehat{V(e'^{(.y)}_{xy})} = e_{xy}(1-e_{xy})\left(\frac{1}{n_{.y}} + \frac{1}{n'_{.y}}\right) \qquad\qquad (13)$$

$$\widehat{V(A'^{(..)})} = A(1-A)\left(\frac{1}{n_{..}} + \frac{1}{n'_{..}}\right) \qquad\qquad (14)$$

For error rates θ'_{xy} (12) the true class sizes $n'_{x.}$ are unknown. They can be derived as $\widehat{n'_{x.}} = \sum_y e_{xy} n'_{.y}$ but only if class proportions are stable (i.e., test and target data are random samples from the same class distribution). Otherwise $n'_{x.}$ can be estimated using a system of linear equations, which solution is given by inverting the matrix of error rates θ_{xy} and multiplying it with the vector of predicted class sizes $n'_{.y}$ (15). This is called the matrix inversion method [1,3]. Applying it adds another component of variance, which is worth investigating in future research (e.g., many error rates θ_{xy} are involved).

$$\begin{pmatrix} \widehat{n'_{1.}} \\ \widehat{n'_{2.}} \\ \vdots \\ \widehat{n'_{x.}} \end{pmatrix} = \begin{pmatrix} \theta_{11} & \theta_{21} & \cdots & \theta_{x1} \\ \theta_{12} & \theta_{22} & \cdots & \theta_{x2} \\ \vdots & \vdots & \ddots & \vdots \\ \theta_{1x} & \theta_{2x} & \cdots & \theta_{xx} \end{pmatrix}^{-1} \begin{pmatrix} n'_{.1} \\ n'_{.2} \\ \vdots \\ n'_{.x} \end{pmatrix} \qquad (15)$$

3.2   Estimating Bias Variance

So far, we focused on estimating the variance of a single error rate. Now we estimate the variance of bias arising from error discrepancies among protected populations, i.e., the range of error rate differences to expect in practice.

Our notation uses subscripts α and β to represent the populations to compare (e.g., $n'_{..|\alpha}$ is the target sample size for population α and $\theta_{xy|\beta}$ is the error rate for population β). We assume that the error rates of each population are independent (e.g., populations α and β are distinct with no overlap) thus with null covariance, e.g., $V(\theta_{xy|\alpha} - \theta_{xy|\beta}) = V(\theta_{xy|\alpha}) + V(\theta_{xy|\beta})$. Thus the target sample sizes of both populations α and β impact the variance of error differences (16).

$$\widehat{V}(\theta'^{(x.|\alpha)}_{xy|\alpha} - \theta'^{(x.|\beta)}_{xy|\beta}) = (\theta_{xy|\alpha} - \theta^2_{xy|\alpha})\left(\frac{1}{n_{x.|\alpha}} + \frac{1}{n'_{x.|\alpha}}\right) + (\theta_{xy|\beta} - \theta^2_{xy|\beta})\left(\frac{1}{n_{x.|\beta}} + \frac{1}{n'_{x.|\beta}}\right)$$

$$\widehat{V}(e'^{(.y|\alpha)}_{xy|\alpha} - e'^{(.y|\beta)}_{xy|\beta}) = (e_{xy|\alpha} - e^2_{xy|\alpha})\left(\frac{1}{n_{.y|\alpha}} + \frac{1}{n'_{.y|\alpha}}\right) + (e_{xy|\beta} - e^2_{xy|\beta})\left(\frac{1}{n_{.y|\beta}} + \frac{1}{n'_{.y|\beta}}\right)$$

$$\widehat{V}(A'^{(..)}_{\alpha} - A'^{(..)}_{\alpha}) = (A_\alpha - A^2_\alpha)\left(\frac{1}{n_{..|\alpha}} + \frac{1}{n'_{..|\alpha}}\right) + (A_\beta - A^2_\beta)\left(\frac{1}{n_{..|\beta}} + \frac{1}{n'_{..|\beta}}\right) \tag{16}$$

3.3   The Case of Minorities

The formulas above show that the variance of bias (i.e., of error differences) depends on the sample sizes of both populations α and β. If a population α is a minority, its size is smaller than a population β. Thus the bias to expect may have larger variance than if α and β had similar sizes.

For example, we can easily show a case where the bias variance is larger if one population is a minority, compared to populations of equal sizes (unless circumstances are unrealistic, e.g., extremely different or low accuracy). Let's consider accuracy in a target set of $n' = 1000$ data points with 2 sub-populations. The variance due to the test set is considered null (e.g., $n_{..} \to \infty$) and we use $a = A'_\alpha - A'^2_\alpha$ and $b = A'_\beta - A'^2_\beta$.

- For a minority/majority split into $n'_{..|\alpha} = 100$ and $n'_{..|\beta} = 900$, the random variance from the target sample is approximately $0.01a + 0.0011b$.
- For an equal split into $n'_{..|\alpha} = n'_{..|\beta} = 500$, the variance is $0.002a + 0.002b$.
- If $a = b$, there is more variance in the case of a minority ($0.011a > 0.004a$).
- In general, there is more variance in case of a minority unless $b > 98a$. This is unrealistic since $b < 1$ and $a < 1$, so accuracies would be extremely low. And accuracies would be so different that a fairness issue is already blatant.

This demonstration may not hold for all error rates and population sizes. Future work is needed to formally specify the conditions under which the presence of a minority implies higher bias than more balanced populations. However, we can already observe that the presence of a minority can have significant impacts on the range of bias to expect in practice.

3.4   Confidence Intervals

To communicate how frequently certain magnitudes of error can occur, we can use confidence intervals (CI). Such intervals represent a range of values to expect for a specific proportion of the data samples (having the same sample sizes). For examples, with a confidence level of 50%, the interval represents the range of errors that occur in about 50% of the random samples. Errors are lower than the lower bound in 25% of data samples, and higher than the lower bound in the other 75%.

For example, in Fig. 1 we draw confidence intervals with various confidence levels. They show how frequently certain ranges of error occur among random samples. In this example, True Positive rates lower than 0.89 occur in 25% of female samples (lower bound of 50% CI) but only in 5% of male samples (lower bound of 90% CI). This can be considered as unfair.

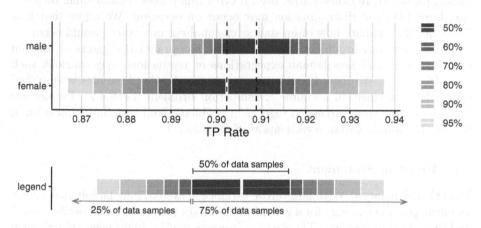

Fig. 1. Example of True Positive (TP) rates θ_{11} compared for female and male populations, with confidence intervals showing the range of error to expect in practice (e.g., 50% intervals show ranges expected for 50% of data samples). We show 50% to 95% CI drawn with the normal approximation and $z \in \{0.67, 0.84, 1.04, 1.28, 1.64, 1.96\}$. *(We acknowledge that this figure omits other genders, and shows only two for simplicity.)*

Specific statistical methods have been established to draw confidence intervals for error rates [11] or differences between error rates [10]. The normal approximation is the simplest method: $\theta'_{xy} \pm z\sqrt{V(\theta'_{xy})}$ e.g., with $z = 1$ for 68% CI, and $z = 1.96$ for 95% CI.

The normal approximation may be the most understandable, e.g., to non-experts. But it is unreliable for small samples (e.g., $n'_x < 30$) and extreme error rates (e.g., $\theta_{xy} \to 0$). In such cases, more complex methods are required such as Wilson scores or Clopper-Pearson estimates [4,18].

Note that in the case of target samples with highly varying class proportions (i.e., stratified sampling), it is complex to account for the variance of estimated class sizes $\widehat{n'_x}$ when the matrix inversion method is required (15). Binary problems can be solved algebraically and Fieller's theorem is applicable [1]. But formulas are complex to derive for multiclass problems, and bootstrapping methods are recommended [3].

4   Error Variance and Fairness

We argue that fairness assessments must consider random error variance, or they may fail to assess the practical risks of bias. Without information on variance, small error differences may seem negligible. However, random error variance makes it possible for large error differences to occur frequently (e.g., depending on sample sizes). In other words, even if error differences remain small on average, large bias and discrimination may occur on occasion. We argue that it is important to estimate how often such occasional circumstances would occur.

To support our argument, we first outline the practical impacts of random error variance, and how human expectations or regulations may overlook such issue (Sect. 4.1). We then discuss a practical case showing how bias is amplified by random variance, in a simple classification problem (Sect. 4.2). Finally, we discuss variance and fairness in regression problems, and test the application of Sample-to-Sample variance estimation (Sect. 4.3).

4.1   Problem Statement

Practical Impacts. With large error variance, a system may largely misclassify an entire population, e.g., for a given batch of data processed at a specific month and at a specific location. The societal impacts can be high: even though such circumstances occur at random, their occurrence can have significant repercussions at the scale of a society. For instance, the medical tests of a hospital could massively fail in a given month. Should an epidemic also strike at the same time, the impacts would be critical.

Minorities, by definition, have smaller populations sizes, and thus larger error variance than a majority group would. In practice, with minorities we run the risk of impacting entire communities, e.g., a local community in a given neighbourhood, at a given period of time. For example, frauds could be massively over-estimated in a local community, which may already suffer from other discriminations for being a minority. Large error discrepancies may be random, but they can have significant repercussions at the scale of a small community, and may not be as rare as expected.

In essence, higher error variance implies higher risks of discrimination, and minorities naturally have higher error variance than majorities. Thus estimating the random variance of errors is needed to inform impact assessments, to prevent discriminations, and to make systems more transparent.

Variance-Aware Human Expectations. It is important that the humans who use, manage, or audit AI systems are aware of the range of errors to expect, especially for small data samples. Stakeholders and decision-makers may not be aware that errors can be much larger than measured on a test sample. Humans may not expect such phenomenon, or may believe it is more rare than it actually is, especially if the test sample is very large.

The users and controllers of an AI system should be aware that random error variance can be significant, that it also depends on the size of target samples, and that therefore minorities have larger variance. Furthermore, they should be aware of the precise range of errors to expect, and at which frequency. This information can be estimated from equations (12)–(14) and (16), and visualized using confidence intervals (Sect. 3.4). Provided with these, humans may understand the range of error and bias to expect in practice.

This is a first step towards informing human expectations, but it is not sufficient. Confidence intervals may be relatively intuitive, but they are not self-explanatory: the information, the visualization, or the terminology may be misunderstood. Moreover, many other aspects must be considered to inform fairness assessments (e.g., test set quality, actual demographics, human recourse and intervention). Future work is required to design visualizations and tutorials, and to explore how fairness criteria and regulations can be adapted.

Variance-Aware Regulations. We focus on a form of regulation that uses thresholds for limiting the error to tolerate (e.g., no less than 90% TP rate), or for limiting the error differences between populations (e.g., bias of maximum -1% TP rate). We argue that a single threshold is not enough to limit error and bias in practice, and that error variance should be considered.

A threshold may be met when measuring errors in a single test sample. But in real life, error magnitudes randomly vary from sample to sample. Hence, the threshold may be passed occasionally, for some samples.

We argue that it is important to know at which frequency a limit would be violated, and to regulate such frequency too. For instance, regulations can specify the frequency at which a threshold may be passed, as in the examples below.

- To limit error: *TP Rate should be higher than 0.9 and no more than 5% of data samples (of size $n'_{x.}$) should exceed this limit.*
- To limit bias: *TP Rate differences should not exceed ±0.1 and no more than 5% of data samples (of size $n'_{x.|\alpha} + n'_{x.|\beta}$) should exceed this limit.*
- To limit bias: *The extreme range of error occurring in 5% of male samples (of size $n'_{x.|\alpha}$) should not occur in more than 20% of female samples (of size $n'_{x.|\beta}$).*
- To limit bias: *The 60% CI for females (for sample size $n'_{x.|\beta}$) should be contained within the 90% CI for males (for sample size $n'_{x.|\alpha}$).*

To be applicable, such regulations need to specify the sample sizes of interest (e.g., the target sample size $n'_{x.|\alpha}$ for TP rates). Choosing the sample sizes may be arbitrary, but it is necessary, as one could tweak the sample sizes to escape the regulation (e.g., if a limit is not met for a small sample, it may be met for a larger sample). Future work is required for establishing realistic and meaningful sample sizes, and these decisions highly depend on the domain and context.

Among potential approaches, we could use the typical demographics of the impacted populations. For instance, the typical populations in geographic areas of interest, e.g., at the scale of neighbourhoods, cities, or regions. The sample sizes can also correspond to batches of data that are typically processed within a time period, e.g., monthly, weekly, or daily. In a domain-agnostic approach, we could use sample sizes of 100 to reflect the intuition behind expressing error rates in percentages. We explore the latter in the example below (Sect. 4.2).

4.2 Variance and Fairness in Classification Problems

A Simple Example. Let's consider a classifier that detects high-risk patients in hospitals, and that has been tested on thousands of patients. To prevent high-risk patients from remaining undetected (False Negatives, FN), doctors may decide to re-examine the uncertain cases, e.g., within a daily arrival of patients. To understand how many high-risk patients can remain undetected, doctors should be aware of the error rate, and the frequency at which higher error rates may occur.

The True Positive (TP) rate of 90% may be reliable, with limited random variance due to the test set size (e.g., ± 1 standard deviation). But it does not represent the range of error to expect in practice. For example, it does not mean that about 10 ± 1 patients remain undetected (FN) in a daily batch of 100 high-risk patients. It does not mean either that 10 ± 2 FN occur in 95% of the daily batches of 100 high-risk patients.

Variance in Practice. For daily data samples of 100 high-risk patients,[2] we can expect 7 to 13 undetected patients out of 100 for 68% of the days (about 5 days a week), and **13 to 16 undetected patients out of 100 in about 15% of the days** (about once a week). There would be more than 16 undetected patients in 2.5% of the days (about once a month).

For a minority group of 10 high-risk patients,[3] we can expect up to 2 undetected patients out of 10 (80% TP rates) in about 68% of the days[4], and **2 to 3 undetected patients out of 10 (70–80% TP rates) in about 15% of the days** (about once a week).

---

[2] Sample-to-Sample estimation: $(0.1 \times 0.9)/100 = 0.0009$ and $\sqrt{0.0009 + 0.01^2} \approx 0.03$. So the 68% CI is about 10 ± 3 FN patients out of 100, and the 95% CI is 10 ± 6.

[3] $(0.1 \times 0.9)/10 = 0.009$ and $\sqrt{0.009 + 0.01^2} \approx 0.1$. So the 68% CI is about 1 ± 1 FN patients out of 10, and the 95% CI is 1 ± 2.

[4] The normal approximation of CI is not exact with so few items, especially for the lower bound (e.g., reaching negative values). This higher bound is still informative.

This is **much more than stated in the test results** where the standard deviation for the test sample alone is $\pm 1\%$. The standard deviations for samples of 100 and 10 high-risk patients are $\pm 3\%$ and $\pm 10\%$ respectively.

Humans may not expect such magnitudes of error to occur so frequently, as it exceeds what is stated in the test results. Furthermore, it illustrates a fairness issue that is inherent to random variance: larger error rates occur more often for a minority than for a majority, and this too is unfair.

4.3   Variance and Fairness in Regression Problems

We evaluated Sample-to-Sample applied to regression problems with the approach in equation (10), Sect. 2.

We simulated a simple regression problem with a single feature $x \in [0, 10]$ with $y_i = 2x + 1 + \epsilon$ and $\widehat{y}_i = 2x + 1$. The noise ϵ is normally distributed $\epsilon \sim N(0, \sigma)$ with $\sigma \in \{1, 1.5, 2\}$. It generates population residuals with mean squared error $MSE^* \in \{1, 2.25, 4\}$.

We used test samples with $n_{..} \in \{1\,000, 10\,000\}$ and target samples with $n'_{..} \in \{100, 1\,000\}$. To compare the residuals in test and target samples, we drew $10\,000$ pairs of test and target samples of both sizes ($40\,000$ pairs in total).

We assumed that larger range of MSE and differences $MSE - MSE'$ occur with smaller target samples. Our results are consistent with this assumption, but not with the formulas we proposed (10).

The actual residuals did not follow $V(\boldsymbol{MSE'}) = MSE^{*2}(1/n'_{..})$ and instead we observed $V(\boldsymbol{MSE'}) \approx 2\,MSE^{*2}\,(1/n'_{..})$. The estimated residuals $\widehat{\boldsymbol{MSE'}}$ did not follow $\widehat{V}(\widehat{\boldsymbol{MSE'}}) = MSE^2(1/n_{..} + 1/n'_{..})$ and instead we observed $V(\widehat{\boldsymbol{MSE'}}) \approx 2\,MSE^2\,(1/n_{..} + 1/n'_{..})$.

Future work is needed to establish the theory that governs these observations. However, our empirical observations show the same variance issues as for classification problems: the variance estimation for target samples depends on the size of both test and target samples. The variance of residuals is larger for smaller target samples, and thus for minorities.

5   Conclusion

We demonstrated that error variance depends on the size of the data processed in real life (called the target sample). Variance increases as a target sample size decreases, and this particularly impacts minorities, since their sample size is consistently lower than majorities. This statistical phenomenon happens even if the test data is extremely large, or has balanced sample size for minorities and majorities.

For minorities, the error variance is naturally higher in practice. This can be considered as a curse on minorities: it is beyond what humans can control, and it impacts communities that are likely to be discriminated otherwise. Therefore, we argue that error variance is an important aspect of fairness assessment, as it creates and amplifies error discrepancies, and thus potential discriminations.

Thus it is important to estimate error variance and confidence intervals, and to account for the actual composition of the real-life populations (e.g., with target sample sizes that are representative of minorities and majorities). However, future work is required to specify the sample and population sizes that are typically encountered in practice, e.g., depending on the application domain.

We also discussed how fairness criteria could take into account error variance, beyond using thresholds to limit error and bias. We argue that fairness criteria should also consider the frequency at which a given threshold may be violated, due to random error variations. Fairness criteria can also rely on drawing confidence intervals with different confidence levels (Fig. 1), to compare the bounds the frequency of certain ranges of error. However, future work is required to design visualizations that are usable and understandable, and to develop guidelines for applying meaningful criteria.

Finally, we recommend that error variance be made transparent and understandable to all users and controllers of AI systems. Indeed, fair system or not, it is important that all stakeholders understand the actual range of errors to expect in practice.

References

1. Beauxis-Aussalet, E., Hardman, L.: Extended methods to handle classification biases. In: IEEE International Conference on Data Science and Advanced Analytics (DSAA) (2017)
2. Buolamwini, J., Gebru, T.: Gender shades: intersectional accuracy disparities in commercial gender classification. In: Conference on Fairness, Accountability and Transparency, pp. 77–91 (2018)
3. Buonaccorsi, J.P.: Measurement Error: Models. Methods and Applications. CRC Press,Taylor and Francis, Boca Raton (2010)
4. Clopper, C.J., Pearson, E.S.: The use of confidence or fiducial limits illustrated in the case of the binomial. Biometrika **26**(4), 404–413 (1934)
5. Cochran, W.G.: Sampling Techniques. John Wiley & Sons, Hoboken (2007)
6. Corbett-Davies, S., Goel, S.: The measure and mismeasure of fairness: a critical review of fair machine learning (2018). arXiv preprint arXiv:1808.00023
7. Foulds, J.R., Islam, R., Keya, K.N., Pan, S.: Bayesian modeling of intersectional fairness: the variance of bias*. In: Proceedings of the 2020 SIAM International Conference on Data Mining, pp. 424–432. SIAM (2020)
8. Hossin, M., Sulaiman, M.N.: A review on evaluation metrics for data classification evaluations. Int. J. Data Mining Knowl. Manage. Process. IJDKP **5**(2), 1–10 (2015)
9. Mehrabi, N., Morstatter, F., Saxena, N., Lerman, K., Galstyan, A.: A survey on bias and fairness in machine learning (2019). arXiv preprint arXiv:1908.09635
10. Newcombe, R.G.: Interval estimation for the difference between independent proportions: comparison of eleven methods. Statist. Med. **17**(8), 873–890 (1998)
11. Newcombe, R.G.: Two-sided confidence intervals for the single proportion: comparison of seven methods. Statist. Med. **17**(8), 857–872 (1998)
12. Obermeyer, Z., Powers, B., Vogeli, C., Mullainathan, S.: Dissecting racial bias in an algorithm used to manage the health of populations. Science **366**(6464), 447–453 (2019)

13. Sebastiani, F.: An axiomatically derived measure for the evaluation of classification algorithms. In: International Conference on The Theory of Information Retrieval (2015)
14. Sokolova, M., Lapalme, G.: A systematic analysis of performance measures for classification tasks. Inf. Process. Manage. **45**(4), 1–14 (2009)
15. Steinberg, D., Reid, A., O'Callaghan, S., Lattimore, F., McCalman, L., Caetano, T.: Fast fair regression via efficient approximations of mutual information (2020). arXiv preprint arXiv:2002.06200
16. Verma, S., Rubin, J.: Fairness definitions explained. In: 2018 IEEE/ACM International Workshop on Software Fairness (FairWare), pp. 1–7. IEEE (2018)
17. Wieringa, M.: What to account for when accounting for algorithms: a systematic literature review on algorithmic accountability. In: Proceedings of the 2020 Conference on Fairness, Accountability, and Transparency, pp. 1–18 (2020)
18. Wilson, E.B.: Probable inference, the law of succession, and statistical inference. J. Am. Statist. Assoc. **22**(158), 209–212 (1927)

Machine Learning for Pharma and Healthcare Applications

Workshop on Machine Learning for Pharma and Healthcare Applications (PharML 2021)

Advances in machine learning and artificial intelligence could empower us to enhance our understanding of the mechanisms of disease and to create more efficacious therapies for patients. The drug development cycle entails many steps where large amounts of valuable data are collected in the context of clinical trials. Working on this data provides us with potential treatment targets, new biomarkers, and other information that enables us to identify which patients will benefit most from a given treatment. Additionally, safety and efficacy information is collected. After a drug enters the market, further data is generated and collected in the form of electronic medical records, disease registries, health insurance claims, surveys, digital devices, and sensors, among others.

In recent years the availability of healthcare data in large quantities, as well as in diverse data modalities and data sources, has introduced new opportunities but also challenges. In addition, the use of the previously mentioned data sources has steadily increased. Using machine learning-based methodologies could help extract knowledge and enable learning from these increasingly heterogeneous data sources. The use of these innovative methods has shown the potential to revolutionize medical practice and enable us to develop personalized medicines.

This workshop invited experts from both industry and academia to share their research and experience in using artificial intelligence and machine learning methods in pharmaceutical research and development. The contents of the workshop were organized around four main thematic areas:

1. Survival Machine Learning
2. Causal Inference
3. Domain Adaptation and Domain Generalization
4. Federated Learning

Four keynote speakers, from both industry and academia, were invited to present their work and to discuss current and future trends in their fields of research:

- Vince Calhoun (Georgia Tech), "COINSTAC: Federating the future of neuroimaging"
- Lee Cooper (Northwestern University), "ML for time-to-event data, genomics, imaging, and beyond"
- Ryan Copping (Roche): "Strengthening the impact of ML at Roche"
- David Ohlssen (Novartis): "Combining the three cultures of quantitative decision making in drug development"

The program also included 15 presentations of accepted manuscripts in the form of research abstracts or long papers. A double-blind peer-review process was performed to select the manuscripts. Each submission was reviewed by at least two members of the Program Committee.

The original call-for-papers, workshop program, and other additional details can be found at the PharML 2021 website: https://sites.google.com/view/pharml2021.

Organization

Workshop Chairs

Lee Cooper	Northwestern University, USA
Naghmeh Ghazaleh	Roche, Switzerland
Jonas Richiardi	Lausanne University Hospital and University of Lausanne, Switzerland
Damian Roqueiro	ETH Zurich, Switzerland
Diego Saldana	Roche, Switzerland
Konstantinos Sechidis	Novartis, Switzerland

Program Committee

Michael Adamer	ETH Zurich, Switzerland
Laura Azzimonti	IDSIA, Switzerland
Mark Baillie	Novartis, Switzerland
Christian Bock	ETH Zurich, Switzerland
Sarah Brüningk	ETH Zurich, Switzerland
Giovanni d'Ario	Roche, Switzerland
Valeria de Luca	Novartis, Switzerland
Geoffrey Fucile	University of Basel, Switzerland
Matias Callara	Roche, Switzerland
Thibaud Coroller	Novartis, USA
Christophe Freyre	Novartis, Switzerland
Marius Garmhausen	Roche, Switzerland
Lasse Hansen	Aarhus University, Denmark
Max Horn	ETH Zurich, Switzerland
Juliane Klatt	ETH Zurich, Switzerland
Matteo Manica	IBM, Switzerland
Joseph Mellor	University of Edinburgh, UK
Michael Mitchley	Roche, Switzerland
Pooya Mobadersany	Janssen, Johnson and Johnson, USA
Amirhossein Mostajabi	Roche, Switzerland
Georgiana Neculae	BenevolentAI, UK
Nikolaos Nikolaou	AstraZeneca, UK
Marilena Oita	Simply Vision, Switzerland
Jon Parkinson	University of Manchester, UK
Rushabh Patel	Children's Hospital of Philadelphia, USA
Konstantinos Pliakos	KU Leuven, Belgium

Maria Giulia Preti	EPFL, Switzerland
Jonathan Rafael-Patino	CHUV, Switzerland
Bastian Rieck	ETH Zurich, Switzerland
Elizaveta Semenova	AstraZeneca, UK
Cameron Shand	UCL, UK
Mohamed Amgad Tageldin	Northwestern University, USA
Grigorios Tsoumakas	Aristotle University of Thessaloniki, Greece
Lukas A. Widmer	Novartis, Switzerland

Embed Wisely: An Ensemble Approach to Predict ICD Coding

Pavithra Rajendran[1], Alexandros Zenonos[1], Joshua Spear[2(✉)], and Rebecca Pope[3]

[1] KPMG UK, 15 Canada Square, London E14 5GL, UK
{Pavithra.Rajendran,Alexandros.Zenonos}@kpmg.co.uk
[2] Great Ormond Street Hospital for Children NHS Foundation Trust, Great Ormond Street,
London WC1N 3JH, UK
joshua.spear@gosh.nhs.uk
[3] UCL Great Ormond Street Institute of Child Health, 30 Guilford St, London WC1N 1EH, UK
r.pope@ucl.ac.uk

Abstract. International Classification of Diseases (ICD) are the de facto codes used globally for clinical coding. These codes enable healthcare providers to claim reimbursement and facilitate efficient storage and retrieval of diagnostic information. The problem of automatically assigning ICD codes has been previously approached as a multilabel classification problem, using neural models and unstructured data. We utilise an approach for efficiently combining multiple sets of pretrained word embeddings to enhance the performance on ICD code prediction. Using post-processing and meta-embeddings techniques, we exploit the geometric properties of word embeddings and combine different sets of word embeddings into a common dimensional space. We empirically show that infusing information from biomedical articles, whilst preserving the local neighbourhood of the embedding, improves the current state-of-the-art deep learning architectures. Furthermore, we demonstrate the efficacy of this approach for a multimodal setting, using unstructured and structured information.

Keywords: ICD coding · Embeddings · Multimodal

1 Introduction

The International Classification of Diseases (ICD) was created in 1893, when a French doctor named Jacques Bertillon named 179 categories of causes of death. It has been revised every ten years since then and has become an important standard for information exchange in the health care sector. Importantly, it has been endorsed by the World Health Organisation (WHO) and has been widely adopted by physicians and other health care providers for reimbursement, storage and retrieval of diagnostic information.

ICD coding is the process of assigning ICD codes to a patient's condition. This, however, is an extremely complex process for several reasons:

- The label space of codes is large with over 15,000 codes in the ICD-9 taxonomy and 140,000 in the ICD-10-CM/PCS taxonomy. Furthermore, the codes are organised in a hierarchical structure where the top-level codes represent generic disease categories and the bottom-level codes represent more specific diseases.

© Springer Nature Switzerland AG 2021
M. Kamp et al. (Eds.): ECML PKDD 2021 Workshops, CCIS 1525, pp. 371–389, 2021.
https://doi.org/10.1007/978-3-030-93733-1_26

– In order to determine which codes to apply to a patient, a large amount of patient data, spread across different sources needs to be navigated and analysed.

While ICD codes are important for making clinical and financial decisions, for the reasons mentioned above, clinical coding is time-consuming, error-prone and expensive. This clearly motivates the requirement for accurate, automated clinical coding which is explored in this paper.

Prior works exploring automated clinical coding using the MIMIC-III dataset have made use of deep learning methods. Specifically, assigning ICD codes to patients based on discharge summaries [11,17,22]. However, dealing with the clinical text, for example, the text found in discharge summarise is challenging from an NLP perspective, as it includes irrelevant information, has an informal tone, does not necessarily follow correct grammatical conventions, contains a large medical vocabulary and contains texts of highly varied lengths. Furthermore, diagnosis and textual descriptions of ICD codes written by clinicians can be written in differing styles despite referring to the same disease. As a result, ICD code definitions have also been used to enrich the label information which, unlike the summaries, are formally and precisely worded.

In our work, we propose a novel multimodal approach, utilising information present in unstructured data (i.e. discharge summaries) and structured data (such as heart rate, haemoglobin, respiratory rate) and develop a meta-classifier for ensembling the predictions of various models, trained on different modalities of data. Furthermore, we utilise a novel approach for combining multiple sets of pretrained word embeddings to improve performance on unstructured data. We empirically demonstrate that the final ensemble model outperforms the baseline method in the multi-label classification task of ICD 10 and ICD 9 coding.

Pretrained word embeddings have been successfully used in downstream NLP tasks [9] since they capture semantic relationships and provide better text representations. In order to further improve these representations, we consider incorporating external knowledge from separate datasets without increasing the dimensionality of the data used for training (augmenting the dataset). Instead we focused on exploiting the geometric properties of the pretrained word embeddings as well as, combining embeddings trained on external knowledge into a common dimensional space using using meta-embedding techniques [1,4,8]. We hypothesise that this approach would be particularly useful for instances where access to pretrained word embeddings is available but the ability it derive them is not (i.e. through lack of significant compute or lack of access to the underlying raw data). To study the potential advantage of our proposed approach, we consider prior work [11,17] utilising pretrained word embeddings trained on the MIMIC dataset.

The contributions of this paper are as follows:

1. Our first contribution is a simple and effective approach for infusing external knowledge into word embeddings derived from textual summaries, without augmenting the dimensionality of the dataset used for training. The semantic information captured by the textual summaries is not necessarily the same as the semantic information captured by the external knowledge. Therefore, in order to preserve the rich representation from both sources, we focus on techniques for infusing the knowledge of both sources without drastically increasing the complexity of the model.

This is achieved by exploiting the geometric properties of word vectors and combining embeddings trained on external information using meta-embedding techniques. We empirically evaluate different approaches using the top 32 ICD 10 and 50 ICD 9 codes and our results indicate that the best performance is obtained by preserving the local neighbourhood of the word vectors while combining them into meta-embeddings.

2. Our second contribution is an ensemble approach that utilises various modalities, combining both structured and unstructured information. We utilise information from various sources to enrich our dataset with information that is potentially missing from the summaries. Our ensemble model empirically outperforms the baseline methods.

2 Related Work

There has been a growing interest within the field of natural language processing for learning representations of words as vectors, also known as word embeddings. These embeddings have been derived via two core methods, namely count-based and prediction-based methods. The Glove algorithm [18] is a popular count-based approach that makes use of the co-occurrences probabilities of words. The Word2Vec [14] approach is a popular prediction-based approach, in which models are trained based on CBOW (continuous bag of words) or the Skip-Gram approach. A growing interest in topics related to word embeddings is reflected by the numerous papers published in various NLP conferences.

Due to vast amounts of data and compute required to train embedding models, many practitioners have utilised pretrained word embeddings. Pretrained word embeddings (or static word embeddings) refer to word embeddings which do not change in a given context. A new area of interest within word embeddings is to learn *meta-embeddings* from multiple sets of pretrained word vectors without having the underlying text sources on which the embeddings have been trained. One of the simplest approaches proposed has been to use concatenation followed by averaging [4]. Yin et al. [23] was one of the earliest works to investigate meta-embeddings. They used a projection layer known as 1TON for computing the meta-embeddings in a linear transformation. However, few works have studied the use of meta-embeddings for the healthcare domain [3,5]. To the best of our knowledge, the application of meta-embedding techniques for multilabel classification of ICD coding has not yet been investigated. In this work we investigate several different approaches for doing so, in particular, we focus on combining pretrained in-domain word embeddings with pretrained word embeddings derived from external sources such as scientific articles on the Web.

Automatic ICD coding using unstructured text data has been explored by researchers for several years whereby the full breadth of learning approaches have been considered. Koopman et al. [10] utilised a multi-label classification approach and combined SVM classifiers via a hierarchical model to assign ICD codes to patient death certificates, first identifying whether the cause of death was due to cancer, then identifying the type of cancer and associated ICD code. Whilst the final solution performed well, there were two key limitations to the approach. Firstly, the coverage of cancers included in the dataset was very imbalanced resulting in cancer types associated with rarer diseases being harder to predict. Secondly, the cancer identification model was susceptible to false-positives when a patient was cited as having cancer but it was not the primary cause of death.

More recently, the scope of the problem has been extended to include multiple ICD codes and it has been addressed via multi-label methods with researchers more often utilising deep learning approaches, generally centred around CNN and LSTM based architectures. Mullenbach et al. [17] adopted a CNN architecture with a single filter, defining a per-label attention mechanism to identify the relevant parts of the latent space. The CNN architecture [9] has been proven to be useful for sentence classification tasks and in this work, they empirically show that CNN is better for ICD code prediction. The per-label attention provided a means of scanning through the entire document without limiting it to a particular segment of the data. This approach achieved state-of-the-results across several MIMIC datasets. In our approach, we use a similar CNN-based architecture but instead focus on infusing external information via embedding vectors and combining structured features, along with the unstructured information. Both approaches are explained in the paper along with empirical evidence of the improved performance that our proposed approach gives.

Vu et al. [21] proposed a BiLSTM encoder along with a per-label attention mechanism, inspired by the work of Lin et al. [12] and proved it to perform well at generating general sentence embeddings. Here, Vu et al. [21] extended the attention mechanism by generalising it for multilabel classification by performing an attention hop per label.

Xie et al. [22] proposed a text-CNN for modelling unstructured clinician notes however, rather than implement an attention mechanism, the authors extracted features via TF-IDF from the unstructured guidelines provided to professionals when defining the ICD classifications. By including these features along with the convolved CNN layer, the authors mimicked the input that the professionals would get from the ICD coding guidelines. To enrich the predictions of the unstructured data model the authors used an ensemble-based method of three models. Semi-structured data was utilised by embedding the ICD code descriptions in the same latent vector space as the diagnosis descriptions and structured data was utilised through a decision tree model. The imbalance issues in the data were addressed via Label Smoothing Regularization and the resulting model achieved state-of-the-art accuracy, for the time, as well as improving model interpretability. However, they did not disclose what structured data they used specifically and what features were used.

Shi et al. [20] proposed a hierarchical deep learning model with attention mechanism that automatically assigned ICD diagnostic codes given a written diagnosis. They also proposed an attention mechanism that was designed to address the mismatch between diagnosis description number and assigned code number. The results showed that the soft attention mechanism improved performance. However, they only focused on the top 50 ICD-9 codes.

3   Proposed Approach

In this section, we explain our proposed multi-label classification approach with discharge summaries (unstructured data) as well the multimodal approach (structured and unstructured data) for automatically predicting the ICD coding (Fig. 1).

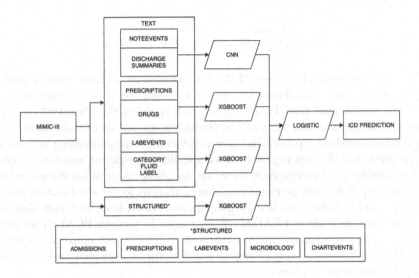

Fig. 1. Multimodal ensemble architecture for ICD prediction

3.1   Unstructured Data

In this subsection, we explain our approaches for classifying unstructured data i.e., discharge summaries. Based on prior work [17], we follow a similar deep learning approach using a convolutional neural network with a per-label attention mechanism that can span across the entire document to identify the portions of the document that correspond to the different labels.

Differing from [17], we propose to study the effect of post-processing word vectors to understand whether we can capture the semantic representations of word embeddings effectively. Furthermore, we investigate the impact of utilising external data from PubMed articles to aid with the ICD classification. However, we propose to infuse this external information into discharge summaries via a meta-embedding technique rather than augmenting the training data with the PubMed articles.

For the rest of the section, we assume that we have access to trained word embeddings from MIMIC discharge summaries using the Word2Vec [14] algorithm as (1) our purpose here is to focus on exploiting as much of the semantic information captured as possible, for better utilisation of embeddings and (2) it serves as a baseline comparison with prior work [17]. The details of the different post-processing steps [16] are described below.

Post-processing Word Vectors. Let us consider a set of words present in a corpus, represented as w $\in$ V, such that each word w is represented by a pretrained word embedding $w_i \in \mathbb{R}^k$ in some k dimensional vector space. We term the first post-processing step [16] as **MeanDiff**. The **MeanDiff** step is implemented by first computing the mean embedding vector, $\hat{w}$, of all words in V and subsequently subtracting $\hat{w}$ from all words in V. The process is defined as follows:

$$\hat{w} = \frac{1}{|V|} \sum_{w \in V} w_w; \quad \tilde{w}_w = w_w - \hat{w}; \forall_{w \in V} \tag{1}$$

Mu and Viswanath [16] observed that the normalised variance ratio of principal components of word embeddings decayed until some top $l \leq d$ components and remained constant after that. They proposed first applying the **MeanDiff** to a set of embedding vectors w_w such that v $\in$ V to obtain a processed set of embedding vectors. They then removed the top l principle components from the embedding vectors, with the hypothesis that the majority of the word specific semantic information is captured in the remaining $d - l$ components. Based on the above observation, the second post-processing step is to apply principal component analysis to the word vectors obtained using Eq. 1 and to remove the first l principal components from each individual word vector. We term this step as **PCADiff** for our usage. To perform **PCADiff** we arrange the word vectors as columns within a matrix $\mathbf{A} \in \mathbb{R}^{k \times |V|}$ and subsequently find the principal component $u_1, \ldots, u_d$. For each word vector w_w, we then remove the first l principal components as follows:

$$w'_w = \tilde{w}_w - \sum_{i=1}^{l} \left(u_i^\top w_w \right) u_i \tag{2}$$

In the above approach, we focus on in-domain trained word embeddings i.e. the word vectors trained on the MIMIC discharge summaries.

The next section discusses the different meta-embedding techniques for combining word vectors trained on external knowledge with the in-domain trained word embeddings. Recent work [23] demonstrated that pretrained word vectors trained on the same source of information but with different algorithms varied in the semantics captured. We propose that the same intuition can be applied to using the same algorithm but on different datasets. In order to capture the semantics from both sets of word embeddings i.e. MIMIC discharge summaries and the PubMed articles, we combine the information in the form of *"meta-embeddings"* i.e. combining the different embeddings into a common meta-embedding space. While there are several approaches to achieve meta-embeddings, in this paper we focus on two methodologies which are described below.

Meta-embeddings. Let us assume, for simplicity, that we have two different sources of information i.e. one based on the discharge summaries and the other based on the PubMed articles. Let us represent the vocabulary of words present in the two sources of information as $\mathcal{S}_1$ and $\mathcal{S}_2$, respectively.

The two methodologies for obtaining meta-embeddings are explained below.

Averaging Meta-embedding. Here, we assume that the words present in S_1 and S_2 are trained with the same algorithm i.e. Word2Vec to produce word vectors. Furthermore, we assume that the vectors belonging to both sources have a common dimensionality, k. Prior work [4] showed that averaging the embedding vectors was a useful meta-embedding technique that achieved comparable results to that of concatenating the vectors.

To understand this, let us consider the meta-embedding of each word, represented by averaging the word vectors from the two sources as follows:

$$\hat{w} = \frac{w_{S_1} + w_{S_2}}{2} \tag{3}$$

In this case, the Euclidean distance between two words $\hat{w}_1$ and $\hat{w}_2$ based on Eq. 3 is given as follows:

$$E_{AVG} = \|\hat{w}_1 - \hat{w}_2\|_2 = \frac{1}{2} \left\| \frac{w_{1S_1} + w_{1S_2}}{2} - \frac{w_{2S_1} + w_{2S_2}}{2} \right\|_2 \tag{4}$$

Coates and Bollegala [4] showed that the source embeddings were approximately orthogonal and hence, averaging captured approximately similar information as concatenation, without increasing the dimensionality. Hence, we use this averaging method for combining the word embeddings as meta-embeddings.

Locally Linear Meta-embedding. In the above method, we find that averaging-based meta-embeddings performs comparably to concatenation [4]. However, one of it's limitations is that it does not capture the variations present within the local neighbourhood of the word vectors in their respective sources. To address this issue, Bollegala et al. [1] constructed meta-embeddings in an unsupervised manner where they considered the mapping of embeddings from different sources to a common meta-embedding space based on the local neighbourhood of a word in each of the sources. Two steps were performed (1) the word embeddings in each source were reconstructed based on their local neighbourhoods (2) these reconstructions were used to project the embeddings into a common meta-embedding space such that the local neighbourhoods were preserved.

Let us assume we have a set of words present in the two sources i.e. S_1 and S_2. Let us also represent their vocabularies as V_1 and V_2 respectively such that, V represents the common set of vocabulary i.e. $V_1 \cap V_2$. Further, for each word $v \in V_1$, we represent the word vector as $v_{V_1} \in \mathbb{R}^{d_1}$. Similarly, for each word $v \in V_2$, we represent the word vector as $v_{V_2} \in \mathbb{R}^{d_2}$. Here, d_1 and d_2 represent the dimensions of the vectors respectively.

In the reconstruction step, for each word $v \in V$ i.e. $v \in V_1 \cap V_2$, we obtain the k nearest neighbours present within the two sources S_1 and S_2. This is carried out using the BallTree algorithm based on prior work [1] since this approximate methodology reduces the time complexity in identifying the approximate k neighbours. Let us denote the neighbours as $\mathcal{N}_{V_1}$ and $\mathcal{N}_{V_2}$ respectively. Furthermore, we denote the neighbours of word v in $\mathcal{N}_{V_i}$ as $\mathcal{N}_{V_i}(v)$.

$$\Psi(\mathbf{W}) = \sum_{i=1}^{2} \sum_{v \in V} \left\| v_{V_i} - \sum_{u \in \mathcal{N}_{V_i}(v)} W_{uv} u_{V_i} \right\|_2^2 \tag{5}$$

where $w_{uv} = 0$; if the words are not k neighbours in either of the sources.

$$\frac{\partial(\Psi(\mathbf{W}))}{\partial w_{uv}} = -2 \sum_{i=1}^{2} \left(v_{\mathcal{V}_i} - \sum_{x \in \mathcal{N}_{\mathcal{V}_i}(x)} w_{vx} x_{\mathcal{V}_i} \right)^{\top} u_{\mathcal{V}_i} \mathbb{I}[u \in \mathcal{N}_{\mathcal{V}_i}(v)] \qquad (6)$$

Given a word $v \in \mathcal{V}$, for each neighbouring word u in $\mathcal{N}_{\mathcal{V}_1}$ and $\mathcal{N}_{\mathcal{V}_2}$, the recontruction weights are learned such that the reconstruction error given in Eq. 5 is minimized i.e. minimizing the sum of the local distortions present in the two sources. To achieve this, the error gradient is computed using Eq. 6.

Based on prior work [1], the weights are uniformly randomly initialized for each k neighbour and optimal weights are obtained using stochastic gradient descent (SGD) with the initial learning rate set as 0.01 and maximum number of iterations set to 100.

The weights are normalized and used in the projection step. The projection step makes use of the normalized reconstructed weights and learns the meta-embeddings of the words u, v $\in \mathcal{V}$ in a common dimensional space $\mathcal{P}$ i.e. $u_{\mathcal{P}}, v_{\mathcal{P}} \in \mathbb{R}^{d_{\mathcal{P}}}$ such that the local neighbourhood from both the sources is preserved. This is done using a truncated eigensolver, minimising the projection cost given below:

$$\Psi(\mathcal{P}) = \sum_{i=1}^{2} \sum_{v \in \mathcal{V}} \left\| v_{\mathcal{P}} - \sum_{u \in \mathcal{N}_{\mathcal{V}_i}(v)} w'_{uv} u_{\mathcal{P}} \right\|_2^2 \qquad (7)$$

where

$$w'_{uv} = w_{uv} \sum_{i=1}^{2} \mathbb{I}[u \in \mathcal{N}_{\mathcal{V}_i}(v)] \qquad (8)$$

such that if x = 1; $\mathbb{I}((x))$ = *True* and *False* otherwise.

The meta-embeddings are obtained by computing the smallest $(d_{\mathcal{P}}+1)$ eigenvectors of the matrix given below.

$$\mathbf{M} = (\mathbf{I} - \mathbf{W}')^{\top}(\mathbf{I} - \mathbf{W}') \qquad (9)$$

such that matrix $\mathbf{W}'$ contains the values computed using Eq. 7.

Different variants of pretrained word embeddings are obtained based on the above discussed methodologies. These different embedding vectors are then fed into a neural model for multilabel classification of ICD codes.

For the purpose of comparison, we use the CNN-based architecture following prior work [17] which is described below.

CNN Encoder. A document is represented as X = $\{x_1, \ldots, x_N\}$ such that each word is represented using a pretrained word vector. A convolutional neural architecture is used to encode the document at each n step as:

$$h_i = \tanh(\mathbf{W}_c * x_{i:i+k-1} + b_c) \qquad (10)$$

where $\mathbf{W}_c \in \mathbb{R}^{k \times d_e \times d_c}$ represents the convolutional filter such that k, d_e, d_c denote filter width, input embedding dimension and filter output size respectively.

Per-label Attention. Following the base representation of the document as $\mathbf{H} = \{h_1, \ldots, h_N\}$, for each label l, a per-label attention vector is computed as follows:

$$a_l = Softmax(\mathbf{H}^T \boldsymbol{u}_l) \tag{11}$$

where $\boldsymbol{u}_l$ represents the vector parameter for each label l. This attention vector is then used for defining the label-based document representations as follows:

$$v_l = \sum_{n=1}^{N} a_{l,n} h_n \tag{12}$$

Classification. The probability per label is computed as follows:

$$\hat{y}_l = \sigma(\alpha_l^\top v_l + b_l) \tag{13}$$

where $\alpha \in \mathbb{R}^{d_c}$ represents the vector containing the prediction weights.

The training objective aims to minimize the binary-cross entropy loss as given below.

$$\text{Loss}(\mathbf{X}, y) = -\sum_{l=1}^{\mathcal{L}} y_l \log(\hat{y}_l) + (1 - y_l) \log(1 - \hat{y}_l) \tag{14}$$

The probability scores per label are further used in combination with structured data to improve the performance of the multilabel classification, which is explained in detail in the following subsection.

3.2 Multimodal Approach

We utilise structured data from the MIMIC-III dataset that is spread across several tables and contains information about a patient's care during their hospital admission as well as some textual information like medication and lab results. The specific information we use relates to admission information, lab reports, prescriptions, vital signs (chart events table) and microbiology test results.

Structured Data

Numeric Data. We aggregate the data up to an admission level and extract statistical properties, i.e., mean, standard deviation, min and max for each numeric value as well as the number of measurements taken per admission. In particular, we utilise the 100 most common items measured across all patients. These include, *heart rate, hemoglobin, respiratory rate, creatine, bun, wbc, magnesium* etc.

Categorical Data. Textual information contained in tables but with no particular meaning, i.e., medication (drugs) and laboratory exams are represented using Term Frequency-Inverse Document Frequency (TF-IDF) based features.

4   Experiments

This section provides a brief overview of the MIMIC-III dataset that we used in our experiments and the different experimental settings for both the unstructured data i.e. discharge summaries and the multimodal data i.e. structured and unstructured information.

4.1   Data and Preprocessing

Table 1. Total number of samples in train, test and dev set based on 32 ICD-10 codes and 50 ICD-9 codes respectively

Data	Train	Dev	Test
32 ICD-10	28201	3134	12430
50 ICD-9	8044	804	1725

In this paper we used the well-known MIMIC-III database for empirically evaluating our approach. The dataset contained electronic health records of 58,976 patients who stayed in the Intensive Care Unit (ICU) of Beth Israel Deaconess Medical Centre from 2001 to 2012 [7]. This included information such as demographics, vital sign measurements, laboratory test results, procedures, medications, caregiver notes and imaging reports. For our purpose, we removed admissions that were not associated with a discharge summary. Also, we removed patient admissions that did not have information on the admission itself (i.e. length of stay), laboratory results and prescriptions, as we required at least some monitoring of the patients health during their stay. The total number of unique admissions after filtering was 44, 765. In this work, our aim was to predict the ICD code classification for each of the admissions we were considering. Even though the MIMIC-III dataset included ICD-9 mappings, we manually mapped those to the new ICD-10 codes and focused on predicting only the top 32, similarly to [22]. Also, for completeness we experimented with the top 50 ICD-9 codes as in previous studies. A discharge summary was considered very useful for understanding what happened during an admission as it included but was not limited to information about the history of illness, past medical history, medication, allergies, family and social history, physical exam at the point of admission, lab result summary, procedures, discharge condition and status as well as discharge medication, follow-up plans, final diagnosis and other discharge instructions. In terms of preprocessing the summaries, we removed symbols and numbers not associated with a text. Table 1 contains the number of samples present within the training, development and test set for experimentation purposes.

4.2 Experimental Settings

Experiments based on both structured and unstructured data were carried out with the top 32 ICD-10 codes and top 50 ICD-codes in order to align with benchmarks in the literature.

Unstructured Data. Experiments based on unstructured information were carried out by extracting the discharge summaries based on the top 32-ICD codes as well as top 50 ICD-9 codes, separately. In addition, we extracted full scientific articles from PubMed, which totalled 672,589 articles [15].

The CNN-based architecture (also known as CAML) [17] served as a baseline for comparison in experiments, since the architecture was used as a base model for all of the experiments we conducted. For the baseline experiment, we initialised the CAML architecture with embeddings trained on the MIMIC train dataset. The hyperparameters set were: embedding dimension as *200*, dropout as *0.5*, filter size as *4*, learning rate as *0.001*, batch size as *16*, filter maps as *50* and patience as *3*. We trained the model for *100* epochs with an early stopping criteria based on the *micro-F1* score such that the training was stopped if the *micro-F1* score did not improve after *3* epochs.

We also experimented with the MultiResCNN architecture using the default hyperparameters [11] aside from embedding size, for which we used 200. Due to the complexity of the model, we reported the scores based on the same epoch as the best epoch achieved using the baseline CNN-architecture (CAML). Based on this, we found the baseline model to perform better. As a result, we used the CAML architecture for the remaining experiments. In order to understand the adaptability of our proposed methodology, we also reported the scores of the most effective meta-embedding technique/MultiResCNN combination that we tried.

The baseline experiment reproduced the results based on prior work i.e. the per-label attention based CNN architecture [17]. To replicate these results, we used Word2Vec to generate word embeddings from the MIMIC training dataset and used them as an input to train the CNN neural network.

We investigated the different techniques explained in Sect. 3.1 to obtain different input embeddings to train the neural model. Word embeddings trained on MIMIC discharge summaries and those trained on PubMed scientific articles are termed as **W2V-MIMIC** and **W2V-PubMed** respectively for our usage.

1. **MeanDiff-Word2Vec-MIMIC.** Mean vector of the vectors in **W2V-MIMIC** removed from individual word vectors (Sect. 3.1).
2. **MeanDiff-PCADiff-Word2Vec-MIMIC.** Above steps followed and extended by computing the principal components and removing the first l principal components from the mean removed word vectors. In our experiments, we considered $l = 2^1$ based on the embedding dimension i.e. 200 which is chosen based on best performance.
3. **Averaging.** Meta-embeddings obtained by combining (**W2V-MIMIC**) and (**W2V-PubMed**) based on the technique explained in Sect. 3.1. Both the vectors had dimensions of 200.

---

[1] Prior work theoretically demonstrated that choosing l depends on the length of the embeddings.

4. **Locally Linear.** Meta-embeddings obtained by combining (**W2V-MIMIC**) and (**W2V-PubMed**) based on the technique explained in Sect. 3.1. The nearest neighbours for each source was set to 1200 since this gave the best result based on prior work [1]. Here, the dimensions were set to 200.
5. **MeanDiff-Averaging.** First, steps in (1) were carried out on **W2V-MIMIC** and **W2V-PubMed** separately and then, combined using the technique explained in (3).
6. **MeanDiff-PCADiff-Averaging.** First, steps in (2) were carried out on **W2V-MIMIC** and **W2V-PubMed** separately and then, combined using the technique (3).
7. **MeanDiff-Locally Linear.** First, steps in (1) were carried out on **W2V-MIMIC** and **W2V-PubMed** separately and then, combined using the technique (4).
8. **MeanDiff-PCADiff-Locally Linear.** First, steps in (2) were carried out on **W2V-MIMIC** and **W2V -PubMed** separately and then, combined using the technique (4).

Experiments were conducted using the same hyperparameters to train the baseline approach to benchmark our results against prior work.

Multimodal Data. For each experiment utilising structured data we trained 3 separate XGBoost models that utilised the different structured datasets available. For each experiment, we ran a randomised search for the best hyperparameters in a crossvalidation fashion. Their corresponding values are shown in Table 2.

1. **XGBoost Numeric Data.** This model utilised only numeric information available in the structured data.
2. **XGBoost Prescription Data.** This model utilised only information from the prescription table in the MIMIC-III dataset. In particular, we aggregated the drugs a patient received during an admission to a single row and applied TF-IDF to extract features.
3. **XGBoost Lab Exam Data.** This model utilised only lab exam data from the MIMIC-III dataset. Similar to the prescription data, we aggregated the data to a single row and applied TF-IDF to extract features.

All three models were trained separately but on data concerning the same patients. All models made predictions on the same Test set as shown in Table 1.

Meta Data. As illustrated by Table 1, we split the MIMIC dataset into three sets. The Train set was used for training the unstructured neural model, and the three structured XGBoost models in the multimodel experiments. The Dev set was used to perform early stopping during the training of the neural model. In the experiments that only concerned unstructured data, the Test set was used for reporting our final results, as shown in Tables 3 and 5. However, in the multimodel experiments, we performed 5-Fold cross validation on the Test set in order to train the meta classifier and report our final results. For each iteration of the k-fold procedure, predictions were made by the base models on 4 of the 5 folds which were subsequently used to train the meta-classifier. The trained meta-classifer then made predictions on the unseen 5th fold. The

Table 2. Hyperparameters used for the XGBoost Algorithm for the top 32 ICD-10 and top 50 ICD-9 experiments

Hyperparameter	32 ICD-10	50 ICD-9)
Colsample by tree	0.85	0.98
Gamma	0.86	0.78
Subsample	0.66	0.67
Number of estimators	2000	2000
Max depth	5	7
Min child weight	5	4
Learning rate	0.15	0.19

meta classifier's predictions on each of the 5 unseen holdout sets were then averaged and used to report the results in Tables 4 and 6. This approach was taken to ensure that the meta-classifier was trained using data that was unseen by the base models and therefore reduced the potential of overfitting. It also meant that the results reported for the multimodel experiments were still generated using unseen data.

5   Results

Table 3 contains the results of experiments aimed at multilabel classification of the top 32 ICD-10 codes using unstructured data (Sect. 3.1). The results indicated that the baseline performance of CAML [17] was better than the more complex MultiResCNN [11] (when training on less epochs than those reported in the original MultiResCNN paper. Refer to Sects. 4.2 for further discussion). As a result, all remaining experiments utilised the CAML architecture as the base neural model. However, we did observe that the MultiResCNN underwent a significant increase in performance when post-processing was applied to the input embeddings. However, further analysis was required to understand the root cause, which was not in scope for this paper. We propose using an ablation study of the MultiResCNN architecture to understand the causes of the performance increase.

The best performance was achieved by applying the post-processing technique **MeanDiff** to the PubMed and MIMIC embeddings and then combining them using the the locally linear meta-embedding technique [1]. However, we hypothesised that the post processing step was only effective for the PubMed embeddings and not the MIMIC embeddings. This conclusion was drawn by comparing the baseline experiment (Word2Vec-MIMIC (CAML [17])) with the one that only used post-processed MIMIC embeddings (MeanDiff-Word2Vec-MIMIC), and comparing the experiment utilising meta-embeddings without post-processing (Locally-linear) against the one using meta-embeddings and post-processing (MeanDiff + Locally Linear). In the former i.e. Word2Vec-MIMIC (CAML [17]) vs MeanDiff-Word2Vec-MIMIC we observed no incremental performance, thus we concluded that post-processing the MIMIC embeddings provided no performance gain. However, when comparing the results of

Table 3. Micro and macro results are presented for multilabel classification of 32 ICD-10 CODES on the test set. *Input Embedding* refers to the different input embedding vectors that are fed into the CNN-based architecture.

Input embedding	Dim	Macro		Micro		
		F1	AUC	F1	AUC	P@8
BASELINE						
Word2Vec-MIMIC (CAML [17])	200	0.5554	0.8767	0.6749	0.9218	0.4034
Word2Vec-MIMIC-MultiResCNN [11]	200	0.2519	0.7195	0.4225	0.8126	0.3151
POST-PROCESSED EMBEDDINGS						
MeanDiff-Word2Vec-MIMIC	200	0.5525	0.8749	0.6714	0.9205	0.4011
MeanDiff-PCADiff-Word2Vec-MIMIC	200	0.5325	0.8726	0.6749	0.9214	0.4021
META-EMBEDDING: Word2Vec-MIMIC, Word2Vec-PubMed						
Averaging	200	0.5750	0.8852	0.6819	0.9248	0.4074
Locally-linear	200	**0.5957**	**0.8940**	**0.6840**	**0.9280**	**0.4088**
Locally-linear (MultiResCNN)	200	0.4061	0.8139	0.5678	0.8813	0.3695
META-EMBEDDINGS on POST-PROCESSED EMBEDDINGS						
MeanDiff + Averaging	200	0.6144	0.9043	0.6923	0.9336	0.4135
MeanDiff-PCADiff + Averaging	200	0.6059	0.9004	0.6988	0.9341	0.4132
MeanDiff + Locally Linear	200	**0.6212**	**0.9096**	**0.7043**	**0.9381**	**0.4163**
MeanDiff-PCADiff + Locally Linear	200	0.6205	0.9080	0.7014	0.9372	0.4160

Table 4. Micro and Macro results are presented for the multimodal multilabel classification of 32 ICD-10 codes.

Unstructured data features	Macro		Micro	
	F1	AUC	F1	AUC
BASELINE				
–	0.33211	0.6078	0.4521	0.6608
Word2Vec-MIMIC	0.5557	0.7294	0.6771	0.7921
META-EMBEDDING: Word2Vec-MIMIC, Word2Vec-PubMed				
Locally linear meta-embedding	0.5826	0.7972	0.6821	0.7436
	± 0.0083	± 0.0028	± 0.0023	± 0.0017
MeanDiff + Locally Linear	**0.6080**	**0.7593**	**0.7057**	**0.8120**
	± 0.0073	± 0.0022	± 0.0022	± 0.0016
MeanDiff-DiffPCA + Locally Linear	0.6047	0.7577	0.7030	0.8103
	± 0.0039	± 0.0013	± 0.0025	± 0.0019

Table 5. Micro and macro results are presented for multilabel classification of 50 ICD-9 CODES on the test set. *Input Embedding* refers to the different input embedding vectors that are fed into the CNN-based architecture.

Input embedding	Dim	Macro		Micro		
		F1	AUC	F1	AUC	P@5
BASELINE						
Word2Vec-MIMIC (CAML [17])	200	0.5571	0.8693	0.6084	0.8910	0.5829
Word2Vec-MIMIC-MultiResCNN ([11])	200	0.3616	0.7643	0.5425	0.8492	0.3415
POST-PROCESSED EMBEDDINGS						
MeanDiff-Word2Vec-MIMIC	200	0.5597	0.8620	0.5974	0.8848	0.5739
MeanDiff-PCADiff-Word2Vec-MIMIC	200	0.5544	0.8577	0.6022	0.8799	0.5730
META-EMBEDDING: Word2Vec-MIMIC,						
Word2Vec-PubMed						
Averaging	200	0.5663	0.8642	0.6132	0.8894	0.5882
Locally-linear	200	**0.5709**	**0.8666**	**0.6161**	**0.8914**	**0.5919**
Locally-linear (MultiResCNN)	200	0.4475	0.8159	0.5761	0.8849	0.3716
META-EMBEDDINGS on POST-PROCESSED						
EMBEDDINGS						
MeanDiff + Averaging	200	0.5665	0.8719	0.6079	0.8937	0.5863
MeanDiff-DiffPCA + Averaging	200	0.5489	0.8685	0.6049	0.8948	0.5631
MeanDiff + Locally Linear	200	0.5730	0.8758	**0.6224**	**0.9011**	**0.5732**
MeanDiff-DiffPCA + Locally Linear	200	**0.5740**	**0.8760**	0.6183	0.8967	0.5661

Table 6. Micro and Macro results are presented for the multimodal multilabel classification of 50 ICD-9 codes.

Unstructured data features	Macro		Micro	
	F1	AUC	F1	AUC
BASELINE				
–	0.3940	0.6679	0.4662	0.6417
Word2Vec-MIMIC	0.5457	0.7179	0.6078	0.7499
META-EMBEDDING:				
Word2Vec-MIMIC, Word2Vec-PubMed				
Locally linear meta-embedding	0.5416	0.7182	0.6077	0.7506
	± 0.012	± 0.0046	± 0.0096	± 0.0051
MeanDiff + Locally Linear	**0.5495**	**0.7528**	**0.6122**	**0.7528**
	± 0.0088	± 0.0059	± 0.012	± 0.0074
MeanDiff-DiffPCA + Locally Linear	0.5530	0.7215	0.6113	0.7523
	± 0.010	± 0.0054	± 0.0113	± 0.0076

Locally-linear vs MeanDiff + Locally Linear we did observe an incremental performance. This lead us to two possible conclusions:

- **MeanDiff** was only effective for enhancing the performance of meta-embedding techniques
- **MeanDiff** was only effective when applied to the PubMed embeddings

In the case of the latter, we hypothesised this was caused by the inaccurate grammatical and semantic structure of discharge summaries in MIMIC dataset however, validating this was out of scope for the paper. Furthermore, the results indicated that the information captured by the local neighbourhood in both sources was important for boosting the performance. We found that post-processing word embeddings by removing principal components did not provide any improvement. However, investigating the reasons for this was out of scope for this paper.

We found that the meta-embeddings were able to capture the different semantic information from the different sources i.e. the discharge summaries and the external knowledge from PubMed articles. Meta-embedding techniques do not require the raw data used to originally train the embeddings. Instead, they only require the embeddings for training. This provided an efficient way of improving the performance without adding to the complexity of the model.

Similar to Tables 3 and 5 contains the results of experiments aimed at multilabel classification of the top 50 ICD-9 codes using unstructured data (Sect. 3.1). We found a similar trend in performance with regard to the different post-processing and meta embeddings combinations. Critically, the highest performing combination for the classification of ICD 10 codes was also the highest performing for the classification of ICD 9 codes. Overall, our proposed approach clearly outperforms the baseline.

Table 4 contains the results of experiments aimed at multilabel classification of the top 32 ICD-10 codes via a multimodel approach (as outlined in Sect. 3.2). Based on these results, we found that utilising the structured information on its own did not provide good performance in comparison with the baseline. Similarly, the results in Table 6 indicated that the structured data alone had poor performance but was improved when ensembling with predictions from other models. Crucially, the results indicated that ensembling the structured data with a CNN model using MIMIC and PubMed embeddings that have been processed via **MeanDiff** and then combined via the locally linear meta-embeddings technique, provided the highest performance of all ensemble models tested.

Our aim was to understand whether we could enhance the prediction of structured information by using our proposed approach for unstructured information. Overall, the results based on the unstructured data indicated that our proposed approach is effective and outperforms the baseline approach. In addition, the results from our proposed approach enhances the performance of the multimodal multi-label classification.

6   Limitations

In this work, we did not focus on the interpretability of the results but rather we refer the reader to related work. Specifically, we would like to refer to [17] for predictions based on unstructured texts and [19,22] for multimodal data. Since, these interpretability methods have been shown to be useful, we make an assumption that their validation results hold for our experiments as well. Furthermore, in this paper we did not attempt to improve the current architecture [17] but rather focused on investigating the benefit of utilising better features as well as structured data.

We did not explore the use of BERT-based models but refer to prior work [2], which indicated why it was not effective to use BERT on the MIMIC dataset. The paper noted a few reasons why BERT models were not effective when applied to the MIMIC dataset namely, the constraint on the word limits i.e. BERT only accepts 512 tokens and, most of the biomedical terms in MIMIC are over fragmented. However, in the future we would like to explore the use of meta-embedding techniques when applied to contextualised word embeddings.

We did not experiment with the full set of ICD codes since these have not been widely used in the current literature. Rather, the top 32 ICD 10 and top 50 ICD 9 codes have been used to report performance. This is a result of the high imbalance of ICD codes present in the MIMIC dataset. Therefore, given the high amount of data required to train ICD classification models, we would not expect models to perform well on ICD codes which rarely appear in the dataset.

7   Conclusion and Future Work

In this paper, we presented a novel multimodal approach for predicting ICD codes using unstructured and structured information. In particular, we studied the effect of infusing external knowledge for enhancing the performance of the current state-of-the-art model using unstructured information by effectively exploiting the geometric properties of pre-trained word embeddings as well as, combining external knowledge using meta-embedding techniques. We empirically showed that our proposed approach can enhance the performance of current state-of-the-art approaches used for multilabel classification of discharge summaries in the MIMIC-III dataset without relying on more complex architectures or using additional knowledge from the descriptions of ICD codes. In particular, post-processing word vectors and then, combining different pre-trained word embeddings using locally-linear meta-embeddings provided the best performance. In addition, we empirically showed that unstructured information enhanced the performance of the multimodal multi-label classification.

In the future, we would like to investigate softer-measures of performing post-processing of pre-trained word embeddings such as using concept negators [13]. We would also like to investigate the potential to exploit the hierarchical structure of the text present in discharge summaries using hyperbolic-based embedding vectors [13] and also, combine different hyperbolic-based embeddings using meta-embedding techniques [6]. Finally, we will experiment with more statistical features and other machine learning algorithms to assess whether we can further improve performance from the structured data.

References

1. Bollegala, D., Hayashi, K., Kawarabayashi, K.: Think globally, embed locally - locally linear meta-embedding of words. In: Proceedings of IJCAI, pp. 3970–3976 (2018)
2. Chalkidis, I., Fergadiotis, M., Kotitsas, S., Malakasiotis, P., Aletras, N., Androutsopoulos, I.: An empirical study on large-scale multi-label text classification including few and zero-shot labels. In: Webber, B., Cohn, T., He, Y., Liu, Y. (eds.) Proceedings of the 2020 Conference on Empirical Methods in Natural Language Processing, EMNLP 2020, Online, November 16–20, 2020. pp. 7503–7515. Association for Computational Linguistics (2020). https://doi.org/10.18653/v1/2020.emnlp-main.607
3. Chowdhury, S., Zhang, C., Yu, P.S., Luo, Y.: Med2meta: Learning representations of medical concepts with meta-embeddings. In: Proceedings of HEALTHINF, pp. 369–376 (2020)
4. Coates, J., Bollegala, D.: Frustratingly easy meta-embedding - computing meta-embeddings by averaging source word embeddings. In: Proceedings of NAACL-HLT, pp. 194–198 (2018)
5. El Boukkouri, H., Ferret, O., Lavergne, T., Zweigenbaum, P.: Embedding strategies for specialized domains: application to clinical entity recognition. In: Proceedings of ACL, pp. 295–301 (2019)
6. Jawanpuria, P., Dev, N.T.V.S., Kunchukuttan, A., Mishra, B.: Learning geometric word meta-embeddings. In: Proceedings of RepL4NLP@ACL, pp. 39–44 (2020)
7. Johnson, A.E., et al.: MIMIC-III, a freely accessible critical care database. Sci. Data 3, 160035 (2016)
8. Kiela, D., Wang, C., Cho, K.: Dynamic meta-embeddings for improved sentence representations. In: Proceedings of EMNLP, pp. 1466–1477 (2018)
9. Kim, Y.: Convolutional neural networks for sentence classification. In: Proceedings of EMNLP, pp. 1746–1751 (2014)
10. Koopman, B., Zuccon, G., Nguyen, A., Bergheim, A., Grayson, N.: Automatic ICD-10 classification of cancers from free-text death certificates. Int. J. Med. Inf. **84**(11), 956–965 (2015)
11. Li, F., Yu, H.: ICD coding from clinical text using multi-filter residual convolutional neural network. In: Proceedings of AAAI, pp. 8180–8187 (2020)
12. Lin, Z., et al.: A structured self-attentive sentence embedding. In: Proceedings of ICLR (2017)
13. Liu, T., Ungar, L., Sedoc, J.: Unsupervised post-processing of word vectors via conceptor negation. In: Proceedings of AAAI, pp. 6778–6785 (2019)
14. Mikolov, T., Sutskever, I., Chen, K., Corrado, G.S., Dean, J.: Distributed representations of words and phrases and their compositionality. In: Proceedings of NIPS, pp. 3111–3119 (2013)
15. Moen, S., Ananiadou, T.S.S.: Distributional semantics resources for biomedical text processing. In: Proceedings of LBM, pp. 39–44 (2013)
16. Mu, J., Viswanath, P.: All-but-the-top: Simple and effective postprocessing for word representations. In: Proceedings of ICLR (2018)
17. Mullenbach, J., Wiegreffe, S., Duke, J., Sun, J., Eisenstein, J.: Explainable prediction of medical codes from clinical text. In: Proceedings of NAACL-HLT, pp. 1101–1111 (2018)
18. Pennington, J., Socher, R., Manning, C.D.: Glove: global vectors for word representation. In: Proceedings of EMNLP, pp. 1532–1543 (2014)
19. Scheurwegs, E., Luyckx, K., Luyten, L., Daelemans, W., Van den Bulcke, T.: Data integration of structured and unstructured sources for assigning clinical codes to patient stays. J. Am. Med. Inf. Assoc. **23**(e1), e11–e19 (2016)
20. Shi, H., Xie, P., Hu, Z., Zhang, M., Xing, E.: Towards automated ICD coding using deep learning. ArXiv abs/1711.04075 (2017)

21. Vu, T., Nguyen, D.Q., Nguyen, A.: A label attention model for ICD coding from clinical text. In: Proceedings of IJCAI, pp. 3335–3341 (2020)
22. Xu, K., et al.: Multimodal machine learning for automated ICD coding. In: Proceedings of Machine Learning for Healthcare Conference, pp. 197–215 (2019)
23. Yin, W., Schütze, H.: Learning word meta-embeddings. In: Proceedings of ACL, pp. 1351–1360 (2016)

L$_1$-Regularized Neural Ranking for Risk Stratification and Its Application to Prediction of Time to Distant Metastasis in Luminal Node Negative Chemotherapy Naïve Breast Cancer Patients

Fayyaz Minhas[1]([⊠]) [iD], Michael S. Toss[2], Noor ul Wahab[1], Emad Rakha[2], and Nasir M. Rajpoot[1] [iD]

[1] Department of Computer Science, Tissue Image Analytics (TIA) Centre, University of Warwick, Coventry, UK
{fayyaz.minhas,noorul.wahab,n.m.rajpoot}@warwick.ac.uk
[2] Nottingham Breast Cancer Research Centre, University of Nottingham, Nottingham, UK
{michael.toss,emad.rakha}@nottingham.ac.uk

Abstract. *"Can we predict if an early stage cancer patient is at high risk of developing distant metastasis and what clinicopathological factors are associated with such a risk?"* In this paper, we propose a ranking based censoring-aware machine learning model for answering such questions. The proposed model is able to generate an interpretable formula for risk stratification using a minimal number of clinicopathological covariates through L$_1$-regulrization. Using this approach, we analyze the association of time to distant metastasis (TTDM) with various clinical parameters for early stage, luminal (ER + /HER2-) breast cancer patients who received endocrine therapy but no chemotherapy (n = 728). The TTDM risk stratification formula obtained using the proposed approach is primarily based on mitotic score, histological tumor type and lymphovascular invasion. These findings corroborate with the known role of these covariates in increased risk for distant metastasis. Our analysis shows that the proposed risk stratification formula can discriminate between cases with high and low risk of distant metastasis (*p*-value < 0.005) and can also rank cases based on their time to distant metastasis with a concordance-index of 0.73.

Keywords: Survival analysis · Survival ranking · Neural networks · Luminal breast cancer

1 Introduction

Using survival data for identification of important biomarkers or clinicopathological factors associated with survival and/or other clinically important events such as time to distant metastasis lies at the heart of clinical research [1–3]. Outcome based survival analysis is key for patient stratification into various subgroups for selection of personalized treatment options and analyzing the impact of therapeutic interventions [4, 5].

© Springer Nature Switzerland AG 2021
M. Kamp et al. (Eds.): ECML PKDD 2021 Workshops, CCIS 1525, pp. 390–400, 2021.
https://doi.org/10.1007/978-3-030-93733-1_27

For this purpose, the most widely used approach is the Cox-Proportional Hazards model (Cox-PH) which relies on the assumption that each covariate has a multiplicative effect in the hazards function that is constant over time [6]. Regularization approaches for handling high dimensional covariates with the Cox-PH model have also been developed [7]. Alternative techniques such as regression or ranking based survival support vector machines (SSVMs) use L2 regularization of the weights and a squared error function which makes these models vulnerable to scaling issues and outliers in the data [8, 9]. Furthermore, mining survival data for extraction of a risk stratification formula based on a minimal set of covariates is complicated due to this regularization. Due to the structure of the loss function in regression based survival support vector machines, these models can potentially lead to over-estimation of survival times in censored cases. In the recent years, a large number of deep learning based survival prediction models have been developed [10–18]. However, difficulties associated with interpretability of these models makes identification of statistically significant markers for survival analysis and construction of risk stratification scores challenging [19]. In this work, we propose a simple ranking based formulation that uses L_1-regularization to obtain a minimal set of covariates to produce a risk stratification formula through bootstrap analysis. We demonstrate the effectiveness of the proposed approach over a dataset of Stage-1, luminal (ER + /HER2-) breast cancer patients who had been given endocrine therapy but no chemotherapy. Effective risk stratification of these patients can lead to personalized therapeutic interventions such as chemotherapy for these patients [20–22]. This cohort of patients is of significant clinical interest due to the differences in the impact of hormone therapy, chemotherapy and immunotherapy for these patients [23].

2 Materials and Methods

2.1 Dataset and Data Representation

The dataset used in this study was obtained from University of Nottingham with a total of 1300 patients which included $n = 728$ Stage-1 (Lymph Node Negative or LN0), ER + /HER2- patients that received endocrine therapy but no chemotherapy. The dataset contains, for each case, a set of clinicopathological covariates which include Multifocality, Invasive Tumor Size (in cms), the Nottingham Histological Grade and its components (Tubule Formation (T), Pleomorphism Score (P) and Mitosis Score (M)), Lymphovascular invasion (LVI), Associated DCIS and LCIS, Number of Positive Lymph nodes, Nottingham Prognostic Index (NPI), Stage, Estrogen Receptor (ER), Progesterone Receptor (PgR) and human epidermal growth factor receptor 2 (HER2) Status, Menopausal status and Patient age. In addition to these, the histological tumor type (HTT) of each case was assigned and grouped by a pathologist to be one of the 7 distinct prognostic types – HTT_1: No special type/NST (57.3% of all cases), HTT_2: Invasive Lobular Carcinoma (7.7%), HTT_3: Tubular and Tubular Mixed Carcinoma (17.1%), HTT_4: Mixed NST and Special Type carcinoma (10.2%), HTT_5: Other Special (Mucinous, Papillary, Micropapillary, Cribiform and Adenoid-Cystic Carcinoma, 2.0%), HTT_6: Mixed Lobular Carcinoma (4.5%) and HTT_7: Metaplastic Carcinoma (1.1%). We used one-hot-encoding to represent each histological tumor type as an indicator variable, resulting in a total of 23 clinicopathological variables. We are also given the time to distant metastasis (TTDM) (in months) for these patients with a 15 + year follow-up (censored at 180 months) with a median follow-up time of 150 months.

2.2 Model Formulation and Implementation

For survival prediction, we assume a discovery subset $D = \{(x'_i, T_i, \delta_i), i = 1 \ldots |D|\}$ such that, for each case in it, we are given a vector of (un-scaled) covariates x'_i, an event indicator variable (δ_i) which indicates whether the event of interest (such as distant metastasis or death) has taken place $(\delta_i = 1)$ or not $(\delta_i = 0)$ and the time T_i to event (if $\delta_i = 1$) or censoring (if $\delta_i = 0$). All variables in the covariate set are scaled to the range [0,1] to eliminate effects of differences in their ranges to yield a vector x_i for a given patient. This scaling also ensures that there are no prior assumptions on the importance of different covariates in terms of their impact on survival. Using the discovery set, we aim to obtain a prediction score $f(x; w) = \sigma(w^T x)$ for a given vector of covariates (x) using a weight vector w where $\sigma(\cdot)$ is the bipolar sigmoid activation function. In order to train the proposed model, we first develop a dataset $P(D) = \{(i,j)|\delta_j = 1, T_i > T_j, \forall i, j = 1 \ldots |D|\}$ which contains pairs of comparable cases, i.e., all possible pairs of patients in the discovery set such that the event of patient with the shorter survival or censoring time has taken place. The weight vector is then obtained by solving the following optimization problem which generates a penalty if the predictor produces a higher score for a case with shorter survival time:

$$\min_{w} Q(w; D) = \lambda \|w\|_1 + \frac{1}{|P(D)|} \sum_{(i,j) \in P(D)} max\big(0, 1 - \big(f(x_i; w) - f(x_j; w)\big)\big)$$

where $\lambda \geq 0$ is a hyperparameter of the model (set to 0.01 for results in this paper) which controls the compromise between the degree of L_1-regularization and the average ranking loss over all comparable pairs. Note that this formulation differs from the classical ranking based survival support vector machine (SSVM) as it uses L_1-regularization which allows a smaller number set of covariates to have non zero weight values in comparison to L2-regularization used in SSVMs. Also, classical SSVMs uses a squared loss function which makes them vulnerable to outliers and survival time scaling issues. In contrast, the proposed model uses simple pairwise ranking hinge loss. The proposed model can be extended for use with non-linear kernel machines or deep learning models in which the prediction function $f(x; \theta)$ can be non-linear with lumped learnable parameters θ. The above optimization problem can be optimized using gradient descent $(w \leftarrow w - \alpha \nabla_w Q(w; D))$. We have implemented this model in PyTorch with adaptive momentum based optimization (Adam) which allows easy integration into deep learning pipelines as well.

2.3 Bootstrap Estimation and Risk Stratification

In order to get reliable risk stratification, we used a bootstrap estimation approach. Specifically, in each bootstrap run $(b = 1, 2, \ldots, B)$, the given dataset is randomly divided into two subsets with event based stratification: a discovery subset (consisting of 60% cases) and a validation subset (consisting of 40% cases) such that the proportion of cases with events is the same in the two sets. In each bootstrap run, the discovery dataset is used to estimate model weights and rank cases in the validation set based on their survival times. The median of the predicted scores (of the training/discovery set) is used as a cut-off threshold to stratify cases in the validation set into risk categories. The log-rank test is used to estimate the p-value in each bootstrap run [24]. In order to combine multiple p-values from all runs, we have used the estimate $p_B = 2p_{50}$ where p_{50} is the median of the p-values of the log-rank test across all bootstrap runs. This provides a conservative estimate of the overall p-value and, consequently, minimizes the chances of false discovery [25]. The concordance index of each run is also calculated as a metric for the quality of ranking based on time to distant metastasis [26]. An ideal ranking model will have a concordance index of 1.0 whereas a completely random one will have a concordance index of 0.5.

In order to obtain a score for risk stratification, the weight parameters from each bootstrap run $\{w^{(b)}, b = 1 \ldots B\}$ are rescaled with respect to their L₁-norm $\left(\frac{w^{(b)}}{\|w^{(b)}\|_1}\right)$ and the median of each element in the weight vector is used to rank different covariates. This yields a bootstrap estimate of the weight vector and all but the top-K weights (based on their magnitude) are set to zero. Inverse scaling is then applied to yield the final weight vector w_K^* to adjust for the effect of the original range scaling and to convert the prediction scores $f(x_i; w)$, which are high (low) for high (low) survival times, to risk scores $r(x'; w_K^*)$ which are high for high risk (i.e., low survival) by multiplying the weights by -1.0 and adding an appropriate bias. The final weights can be used directly with unscaled covariates x'. Once the bootstrap estimate of the risk function is obtained, it is expressed as a simple equation leading to risk stratification and elucidation of the role of different covariates.

3 Results and Discussion

3.1 Bootstrap Analysis

The results of the bootstrap analysis (with $B = 1000$ runs) are shown in Fig. 1 and Table 1 which shows the distribution of the p-values along with the combined p-value ($p_B \ll 0.05$) and the concordance indices (mean c-index $= 0.70$). Figure 2 shows the distribution of weight values of all covariates in bootstrap runs in the form of violin plots. It is important to note that the magnitude of the median weight of the Mitosis score (M) is the highest in comparison to all other covariates. The negative value of the weight indicates that a high value of the mitosis score is negatively associated with time to distant metastasis. Thus, increased mitosis score is associated with higher risks of distant metastasis. Other clinicopathological parameters with high magnitude of weights are Lymphovascular invasion (LVI) and histological tumor type 6 (Mixed Lobular Carcinoma). Due to the use of L₁ regularization in the proposed method, most of the weight coefficients are close to zero. After rescaling, this analysis allows us to write a simplified scoring formula for risk of developing distant metastasis as: $R_{DM} = 0.26M + 0.48LVI + 0.38T_{MLC}$. This indicates that the risk of an individual is higher or equivalently the time to distant metastasis is shorter if their mitotic score ($M \in \{1, 2, 3\}$) is high or there is lymphovascular invasion $LVI \in \{0, 1\}$ and/or if their histological tumor type is Mixed Lobular Carcinoma (Histological Tumor Type HTT 6, $T_{MLC} \in \{0, 1\}$). Since the percentage of patients with MLC in our dataset is small (4.5%), the major contributors to the risk can be attributed to mitosis score and LVI.

3.2   Risk Stratification Index for Distant Metastasis and Its Biological Interpretability

The resulting risk stratification function when applied to the whole cohort leads to very good risk stratification ($p \ll 0.05$) for time to distant metastasis as shown in Fig. 3. The concordance index based on the risk function is 0.73. There is significant difference in the confidence intervals (shaded areas) of the survival probability curves for the high and low risk categories. This is also reflected in the number of events in each group at all time steps. Furthermore, using all covariates in the dataset has minimal impact on improving the concordance index in comparison to using only top 3 covariates (from 0.73 to 0.75).

The three variables involved in the risk stratification formula are known to have a significant impact on survival with a number of publications reporting the increased risk of distant metastasis associated with increased mitotic score [20], LVI [21] and mixed lobular carcinoma [27, 28] in this cohort. The reported formula provides a simplified expression for risk stratification based on these parameters.

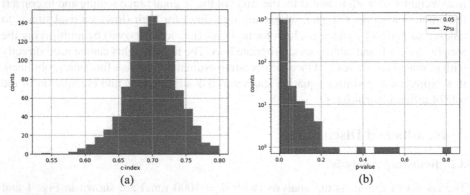

(a)   (b)

Fig. 1. Distributions of (a) concordance index and (b) p-values across bootstrap runs (note logarithmic y-axis in (b) to highlight low counts). The significance p-value cut-off of 0.05 (orange line) and the combined p-value ($2p_{50}$) of 0.002 (green line) are shown in (b). (Color figure online)

Table 1. Result of bootstrap analysis of different methods with the combined p-value ($2p_{50}$) and average concordance index (standard deviation) of 1,000 bootstrap runs.

Method	Combined p-value	Concordance Index (std)
L_1 Cox-PH	0.007	0.68 (0.03)
Ranking SSVM	0.010	0.68 (0.03)
Proposed	**0.002**	**0.70 (0.03)**

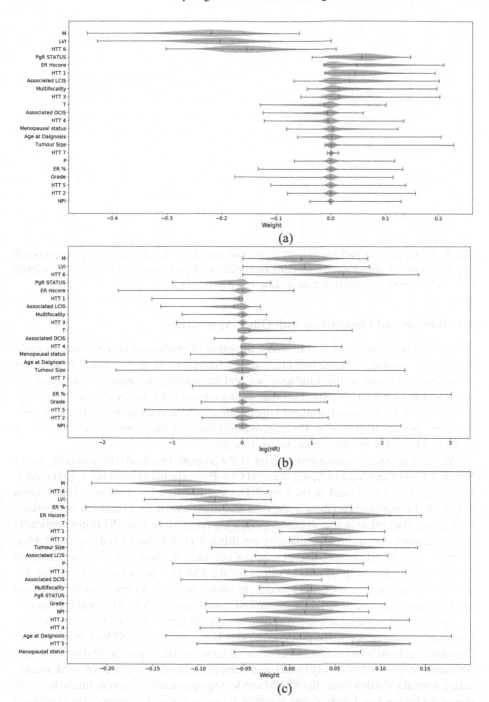

Fig. 2. Distributions of (a) weight values of the proposed model, (b) logarithm of the hazard ratios (HR) from L$_1$ regularized Cox-PH model and (c) weights of the ranking based survival SVM model for all covariates across bootstrap runs. All parameters ordered by importance.

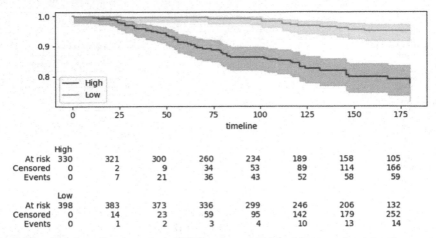

Fig. 3. Stratification of patients (n = 728) into low and high risk categories using the proposed risk stratification function and the resulting probability of distant metastasis free survival (y-axis) over time (months) (x-axis) (log-rank p-value $= 9.1 \times 10^{-11}$).

3.3 Baseline and Comparison with Other Approaches

As concordance index can lead to over-estimation of prediction performance in cases with high censoring, we have first obtained a reference baseline by randomly shuffling event times of cases in the validation set and calculating the expected concordance index across all bootstrap runs. This results in a concordance index of 0.66 and can be interpreted as the expected minimal concordance of a model that predicts completely uninformative survival scores. The concordance index of the proposed model (0.73) is significantly higher in comparison to this baseline.

We have also performed a comparison of the proposed method with a ranking based Survival-SVM (SSVM) and L_1-regularized Cox-Proportional Hazard (Cox-PH) model. L_1 regularization was used in the Cox-PH model to avoid low-rank matrix inversion issues due to indicator variables in the data and to provide a direct and fair comparison with L_1-regularization in the proposed model. Un-regularized Cox-PH is not applicable for this dataset due to high collinearity resulting from the use of indicator variables. In order to avoid differences due to data scaling, each method was given the rescaled dataset. The distributions of weight values for the SSVM and the hazard ratios for different covariates from the Cox-PH model are shown in Fig. 2. In line with the proposed model, both these models have also identified mitosis score, LVI and mixed lobular carcinoma (HTT 6) as the most important factors in prediction of time to distant metastasis. However, in comparison to the proposed model, both Cox-PH and SSVM show possible contributions from a larger number of other variables (relative to their scaling of hazard ratios and weights, respectively) which can complicate the development of a risk stratification formula. Furthermore, the SSVM model requires scaling of event times due to its use of the square loss function which makes it very sensitive to outliers. The combined p-value and c-index of the bootstrap runs are reported in table-1 which shows that the proposed method can potentially reduce false discovery rate (lower combined p-values) and improve ranking quality (higher concordance indices).

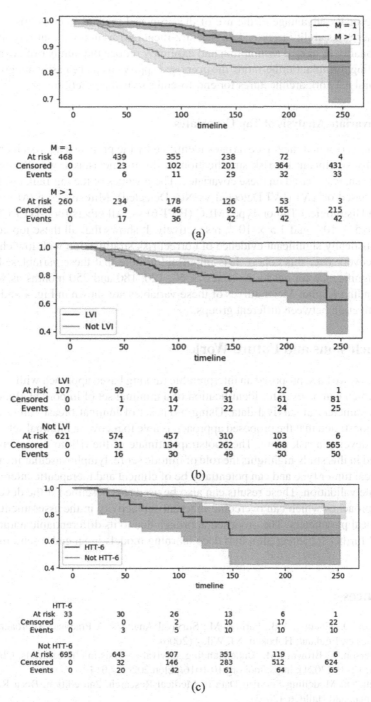

Fig. 4. Results of univariate analysis with (a) mitosis score, (b, LVI (middle) and (c) Histological Tumor Type 6 (MLC). Each curve shows the probability of distant metastasis free survival (y-axis) across time (months) (x-axis).

The primary advantage of the use of the proposed method in comparison to these approaches is its ability to provide a risk stratification formula without relying on any proportionality of hazard assumption and explicitly reduce the number of covariates in the resulting formula. Furthermore, the proposed approach can be easily integrated with deep neural network architectures for end-to-end survival prediction.

3.4 Univariate Analysis of Top Covariates

In order to verify that the top covariates identified by the proposed approach are indeed statistically significant for risk stratification of distant metastasis, we also performed univariate analysis based on these covariates. The p-values of the log-rank test for stratification based on LVI (LVI Detected vs Not Detected), Mitosis score (M = 1 vs. M > 1) and Histological Tumor Type (MLC (HTT-6) vs. All others (non-HTT-6)) are 9.6×10^{-5}, 6.5×10^{-6} and 1.5×10^{-4}, respectively. It shows that all these top covariates show statistically significant evidence of correct risk stratification with low chances of false discovery over this cohort. It is important to note that these variables show statistical significance for censoring times of 60, 120, 180 and 250 months as well. The corresponding Kaplan-Meier curves of these variables are shown in Fig. 4 and indicate clear distinction between different groups.

4 Conclusions and Future Work

In this work, we have proposed an interpretable ranking based approach with L_1 regularization which can be used for identification of a minimal set of important clinicopathological parameters in survival data. Using a dataset of luminal breast carcinomas, we have demonstrated that the proposed approach is able to recover a minimal set of covariates and develop a risk score. The bootstrap estimate of the risk to distant metastasis developed in this study highlights the role of mitotic score, lymphovascular invasion and histological tumor type and can potentially be of clinical and therapeutic interest after a large-scale validation. These results can also be used as a baseline for the development of AI approaches which can overcome inherent subjectivity in the assessment of these pathological parameters. The proposed approach due to its differentiable nature can be extended further for integration into deep learning models in an end-to-end manner as well.

References

1. Machin, D., Cheung, Y.B., Parmar, M.: Survival Analysis: A Practical Approach, 2nd ed. Chichester, England; Hoboken, NJ, Wiley (2006)
2. Emmerson, J., Brown, J.M.: Understanding survival analysis in clinical trials. Clin. Oncol. 33(1), 12–14 (2021). https://doi.org/10.1016/j.clon.2020.07.014
3. Collett, D.: Modelling Survival Data in Medical Research, 2nd edition. Boca Raton, Fla: Chapman and Hall/Crc (2003)
4. Ma, J., Hobbs, B.P., Stingo, F.C.: Statistical methods for establishing personalized treatment rules in oncology. BioMed Res. Int. **2015**, e670691 (2015). https://doi.org/10.1155/2015/670691

5. Rossi, A., Torri, V., Garassino, M.C., Porcu, L., Galetta, D.: The impact of personalized medicine on survival: comparisons of results in metastatic breast, colorectal and non-small-cell lung cancers. Cancer Treat. Rev. **40**(4), 485–494 (2014). https://doi.org/10.1016/j.ctrv.2013.09.012

6. Cox, D.R.: Regression models and life-tables. J. R. Stat. Soc. Ser. B Methodol. **34**(2), 187–220 (1972)

7. Witten, D.M., Tibshirani, R.: Survival analysis with high-dimensional covariates. Stat. Methods Med. Res. **19**(1), 29–51 (2010). https://doi.org/10.1177/0962280209105024

8. Khan, F.M., Zubek, V.B.: Support vector regression for censored data (SVRc): a novel tool for survival analysis. In: 2008 Eighth IEEE International Conference on Data Mining, pp. 863–868 (2008). https://doi.org/10.1109/ICDM.2008.50

9. Pölsterl, S., Navab, N., Katouzian, A.: Fast training of support vector machines for survival analysis. In: Appice, A., Rodrigues, P.P., Santos Costa, V., Gama, J., Jorge, A., Soares, C. (eds.) ECML PKDD 2015. LNCS (LNAI), vol. 9285, pp. 243–259. Springer, Cham (2015). https://doi.org/10.1007/978-3-319-23525-7_15

10. Katzman, J.L., Shaham, U., Cloninger, A., Bates, J., Jiang, T., Kluger, Y.: DeepSurv: personalized treatment recommender system using a Cox proportional hazards deep neural network. BMC Med. Res. Methodol. **18**(1), 24 (2018). https://doi.org/10.1186/s12874-018-0482-1

11. Di, D., Li, S., Zhang, J., Gao, Y.: Ranking-based survival prediction on histopathological whole-slide images. In: Martel, A.L., et al. (eds.) MICCAI 2020. LNCS, vol. 12265, pp. 428–438. Springer, Cham (2020). https://doi.org/10.1007/978-3-030-59722-1_41

12. Wulczyn, E., et al.: Deep learning-based survival prediction for multiple cancer types using histopathology images. ArXiv191207354 Cs Eess Q-Bio (2019). http://arxiv.org/abs/1912.07354. Accessed 22 Dec 2019

13. Li, R., Yao, J., Zhu, X., Li, Y., Huang, J.: Graph CNN for survival analysis on whole slide pathological images. In: Frangi, A.F., Schnabel, J.A., Davatzikos, C., Alberola-López, C., Fichtinger, G. (eds.) MICCAI 2018. LNCS, vol. 11071, pp. 174–182. Springer, Cham (2018). https://doi.org/10.1007/978-3-030-00934-2_20

14. Zhao, L., Feng, D.: DNNSurv: deep neural networks for survival analysis using pseudo values. ArXiv190802337 Cs Stat, (2020). http://arxiv.org/abs/1908.02337. Accessed 22 Jun 2021

15. Kvamme, H., Borgan, Ø., Scheel, I.: Time-to-event prediction with neural networks and cox regression. J. Mach. Learn. Res. **20**(129), 1–30 (2019)

16. Lee, C., Zame, W., Yoon, J., van der Schaar, M.: DeepHit: a deep learning approach to survival analysis with competing risks. Proc. AAAI Conf. Artif. Intell. **32**(1), Art. no. 1 (2018). https://ojs.aaai.org/index.php/AAAI/article/view/11842. Accessed 2 Jul 2021

17. Gensheimer, M.F., Narasimhan, B.: A scalable discrete-time survival model for neural networks (2018). https://doi.org/10.7717/peerj.6257

18. Fotso, S.: Deep Neural Networks for Survival Analysis Based on a Multi-Task Framework. ArXiv180105512 Cs Stat, (2018). http://arxiv.org/abs/1801.05512. Accessed 30 Apr 2021

19. Utkin, L.V., Kovalev, M.S., Kasimov, E.M.: SurvLIME-Inf: a simplified modification of SurvLIME for explanation of machine learning survival models (2020). https://arxiv.org/abs/2005.02387v1. Accessed 02 Jul 2021

20. Rakha, E.A., et al.: Prognostic stratification of oestrogen receptor-positive HER2-negative lymph node-negative class of breast cancer. Histopathology **70**(4), 622–631 (2017). https://doi.org/10.1111/his.13108

21. Makower, D., Lin, J., Xue, X., Sparano, J.A.: Lymphovascular invasion, race, and the 21-gene recurrence score in early estrogen receptor-positive breast cancer. NPJ Breast Cancer **7**(1), 1–7 (2021). https://doi.org/10.1038/s41523-021-00231-x

22. Ignatiadis, M., Sotiriou, C.: Luminal breast cancer: from biology to treatment. Nat. Rev. Clin. Oncol. **10**(9), 494–506 (2013). https://doi.org/10.1038/nrclinonc.2013.124

23. Goldberg, J., et al.: The immunology of hormone receptor positive breast cancer. Front. Immunol., **12**, 674192 (2021). https://doi.org/10.3389/fimmu.2021.674192
24. Bland, J.M., Altman, D.G.: The logrank test. BMJ **328**(7447), 1073 (2004)
25. Romano, J.P., DiCiccio, C.: Multiple Data Splitting for testing. Technical Report No. 2019–03, Stanford University. https://statistics.stanford.edu/sites/g/files/sbiybj6031/f/2019-03.pdf
26. Raykar, V.C., Steck, H., Krishnapuram, B., Dehing-Oberije, C., Lambin, P.: On ranking in survival analysis: bounds on the concordance index. In: Proceedings of the 20th International Conference on Neural Information Processing Systems, Red Hook, NY, USA, pp. 1209–1216 (2007)
27. Duraker, N., Hot, S., Akan, A., Nayır, P.Ö.: A comparison of the clinicopathological features, metastasis sites and survival outcomes of invasive lobular, invasive ductal and mixed invasive ductal and lobular breast carcinoma. Eur. J. Breast Health **16**(1), 22–31 (2020). https://doi.org/10.5152/ejbh.2019.5004
28. Lobbezoo, D., et al.: The role of histological subtype in hormone receptor positive metastatic breast cancer: similar survival but different therapeutic approaches. Oncotarget **7**(20), 29412–29419 (2016). https://doi.org/10.18632/oncotarget.8838

Extracting Multilingual Relations
with Joint Learning of Language Models

Nuria García-Santa[✉] and Kendrick Cetina

Fujitsu Research of Europe (FRE), Camino Cerro de los Gamos 1,
28224 Pozuelo de Alarcón, Madrid, Spain
{nuria.garcia.uk,kendrick.cetina}@fujitsu.com

Abstract. The open access to annotated text for supervised learning
problems is currently an important topic in Machine Learning. For specialized domains, such as healthcare and pharmacological, public annotated documents are subject to restrictions to safeguard patients' privacy. This issue is exacerbated for languages with scarce training data
such as Japanese. To develop accurate solutions despite this situation,
we propose a joint learning network of pre-trained Language Models for
Natural Language Processing tasks, where each model focuses in one specific language. We present a preliminary evaluation that shows improved
performance over baseline network.

Keywords: Natural Language Processing (NLP) · Deep learning ·
Language models · Joint learning · Ensemble architecture · Healthcare

1 Introduction

Annotated data scarcity is a major Machine Learning problem in Natural Language Processing (NLP), ever so evident in healthcare domain where English language constitutes the majority of benchmark datasets in compared with other languages, such as Japanese, with scarcer data. Besides, Japanese carries the issue of
mixing English concepts in its medical documents. Therefore, real-world industry requirements expect NLP systems to deal with multilingual data. These problems reduce scope and coverage of Machine Learning technologies since companies
demand high-accuracy services that are also trusted for healthcare applications.

To mitigate annotated data scarcity, the healthcare community has made
efforts to make datasets publicly available. Many of these datasets were published under the scope of specific benchmarks. But, most of such datasets are
focused in English language, increasing the size gap between English datasets
and other languages. Several of the most popular biomedical domain datasets
are BioCreative[1] for English texts, the CLEF eHealth[2] with special interest in
non-English languages (French, Italian, Hungarian, German and Spanish) along

---

[1] https://biocreative.bioinformatics.udel.edu/tasks/.
[2] https://clefehealth.imag.fr/.

© Springer Nature Switzerland AG 2021
M. Kamp et al. (Eds.): ECML PKDD 2021 Workshops, CCIS 1525, pp. 401–407, 2021.
https://doi.org/10.1007/978-3-030-93733-1_28

the last four years, and, the i2b2/n2c2 NLP challenge[3] mainly for English texts. For Japanese, we can find an instance of biomedical challenge to extract several named entities such as diseases or treatments [1].

Recently, the appearance of large pre-trained Language Models (LMs) in NLP has entailed a big disruption in the field, overcoming most of current highest performances [10]. Nowadays, popular LMs like ELMo [9], BERT [5] and GPT [11] are focused on learning contextual word embeddings. In this work, we focus mainly on two LMs: Multilingual BERT (mBERT)[4] because it covers 104 languages including Japanese, and, BioBERT [7] because it is fine-tuned with biomedical data.

1.1 Ensemble Approaches in Healthcare

Research exploiting ensemble approaches for Machine Learning has increased in the last decades. The work of [3] is a reference in the extraction of gene-disease relationships achieving one of the highest performances nowadays. The authors employed a supervised learning approach in which a rich feature set jointly learned with word embeddings are trained using ensemble Support Vector Machines (SVM). Nevertheless, the system under-performs in presence of long complex sentences requiring strong feature engineering. Deep learning approaches like [12] present healthcare text classification ensemble architectures and in [4] and [6] the authors used pre-trained BERT language model for joint learning of named entities with their relations to analyse clinical documents. [8] proposed a distributed ensemble to extract healthcare data from structured and non-structured sources while preserving patients' privacy. Their ensemble classifier is based on a weighted combination of local base classifiers.

To the best of our knowledge, there is no solution of joint learning in healthcare domain capable of dealing with data in minority benchmark languages. To this end, we propose a novel ensemble architecture of pre-trained language model sub-networks, where each sub-network is specialized in one language and the whole network benefits of the joint learning. Our ensemble architecture can be fine-tuned for specific NLP tasks. We present a proof of concept for Relation Classification of Japanese clinical texts with English terms mixed along Japanese words.

2   Methodology: Joint Learning Architecture

We designed a joint learning network by assembling of several Language Models (LMs). Our proposed method is able to tackle multi-class learning problems in any NLP task and is capable of meeting the needs of current multilingual data challenges where model performance depends on its ability to process data with combined languages (e.g. Japanese with English).

The workflow of our joint learning architecture comprises LMs as sub-networks concatenated to form a larger network. The sub-networks learn together

---

[3] https://portal.dbmi.hms.harvard.edu/projects/n2c2-nlp/.

[4] https://github.com/google-research/bert/blob/master/multilingual.md.

the best combined classification, retrieving an ensemble model. This architecture allows weight update of LMs sub-networks jointly. For each NLP task, the network is fine-tuned with its respective task datasets. The Fig. 1 depicts our proposed joint learning architecture.

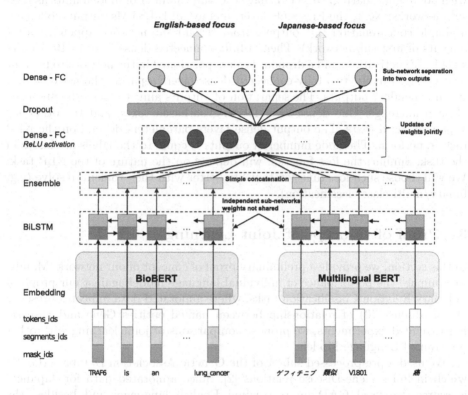

Fig. 1. Joint learning neural network architecture. The ensemble layer concatenates two sub-networks, BioBERT (focused on English texts) and Multilingual BERT (focused in Japanese texts), into a fully connected (FC) dense layer. The final layer separates the network back into two dense layers outputs, each one specialized in one specific language.

First, we load the LMs sub-networks separately. In our biomedical use case, we apply Multilingual BERT, granting the network capability to process Japanese data, and BioBERT, providing a layer of domain specialization thanks to its biomedical fine-tuning in English language. Each sub-network requires previous processing of its corresponding datasets to adapt inputs accordingly. After data preparation, for each language model, the corresponding pre-processed data is inputted to its associated language model to be encoded into an embedding layer. Matrix dimensions of the inputs of each BERT-based LM component, containing weights corresponding to each word that belongs to the sentence, are (row × column), where row is the number of input sample sentences (each sample is a sentence), column is the maximum sentence length. Customarily, each sample has target class that is a column vector.

Outputs of each LM sub-network are connected to Bidirectional Long-Short Term Memory layers (BiLSTMs), still this layer sub-networks remain separated with no weights sharing. BiLSTMs have the same number of hidden units as LMs sub-networks. Next, the Ensemble layer, merges all BiLSTMs outputs following a simple concatenation (i.e. outputs from second sub-network appended after outputs of first sub-network). Then, a fully-connected dense layer of 1024 units with ReLU activation, and a dropout layer is positioned in the network to prevent over-fitting. Finally, two fully-connected dense layers separate the network into two independent outputs. The separation of outputs aims to focus the fine-tune of each language. One dense layer for English-based texts, and the other for Japanese-based texts. The output dense layers parameters depend on the NLP task to perform. The node number of outputs is equal to the labels or classes in the task. Similar, the loss function will depend on the nature of the NLP task. We will choose such loss function that fits better with the problem to solve (e.g. binary/multi-class classification).

3   Proof of Concept of Joint Learning

In this section, we provide a preliminary proof of concept of our network. Mainly, we compare the performance of individual language model against our proposal in binary Relation Classification tasks, where annotated data indicates presence (1) or absence (0) of relationship between named entities Gene and Disease. For extended experiments, we propose comparisons of joint learning with other pre-trained Language Models.

We used a pre-processed subset of the Genetic Association Database (GAD) which includes Gene-Disease relations [2]. Since annotated data for Japanese is scarce, we used GAD in its original English language, and besides, the Japanese translation of said dataset. To translate samples of GAD from English to Japanese, we used the Python tool of *Argos Translate*[5] and *Zinrai Translation Service*[6] [13]. The translated text was later reviewed by Japanese native speakers. And, as mentioned previously, Japanese biomedical texts usually include English words mixed with Japanese words.

As baseline network we fine-tuned Multilingual BERT (mBERT) for our Relation Classification task. Here, we concatenated the GAD English texts and the GAD Japanese-translated texts in one single corpus for the input.

For our proposed architecture, we fine-tuned the joint learning network for the same task, using the GAD English texts as input of the BioBERT sub-network, and, the GAD Japanese-translated texts as input of the Multilingual BERT sub-network. Since we have a binary classification problem, we use binary cross-entropy as loss function, and, sigmoid activation in the last dense layers.

---

[5] https://github.com/argosopentech/argos-translate.

[6] https://www.fujitsu.com/jp/solutions/business-technology/ai/ai-zinrai/translation/index.html.

In the joint learning network, we split independent train sets for Japanese and English to be the inputs of each sub-network (4619 samples each one). While, in the baseline, we used as train set a unified corpus with 9238 Japanese and English samples together. For evaluation fairness, we compared separate test sets of Japanese and English (538 samples each one) for both architectures.

As extension of the experiments we compared more architectures of joint learning using other pre-trained LMs, but, with the same configuration of our proposal, described in the above paragraph. In such experiments we evaluated other three joint learning networks:

- Joint learning of Japanese-BERT (JapBERT) sub-network for GAD Japanese-translated texts with BioBERT sub-network for GAD English texts
- Joint learning of Multilingual BERT sub-network for GAD Japanese-translated texts with GPT-2 sub-network for GAD English texts
- Joint learning of Japanese-BERT sub-network for GAD Japanese-translated texts with GPT-2 sub-network for GAD English texts

Table 1. Performances of the experiments. We present statistical measures running with different epochs. The results are evaluated comparing separate test sets by language (one test set focused in Japanese; other test set focused in English).

Neural network	Japanese			English		
	Precision	Recall	F-score	Precision	Recall	F-score
4 epochs						
Fine-tuning mBERT (baseline)	0.70	0.69	0.69	0.79	0.77	0.76
JapBERT/BioBERT	0.70	0.69	0.69	0.81	0.81	0.81
mBERT/GPT-2	0.69	0.68	0.68	0.51	0.55	0.41
JapBERT/GPT-2	0.66	0.66	0.66	0.50	0.50	0.50
Ours (mBERT/BioBERT)	**0.71**	**0.70**	**0.70**	**0.82**	**0.82**	**0.82**
6 epochs						
Fine-tuning mBERT (baseline)	0.67	0.67	0.67	0.75	0.74	0.74
JapBERT/BioBERT	0.66	0.66	0.65	0.81	0.80	0.80
mBERT/GPT-2	0.70	0.70	0.70	0.51	0.52	0.51
JapBERT/GPT-2	0.68	0.68	0.68	0.52	0.52	0.52
Ours (mBERT/BioBERT)	0.70	0.69	0.69	0.80	0.80	0.80

Performance results of the experiment are included in the Table 1. Results show that our joint learning network overcomes the baseline and other architectures for both languages. The improvement obtained for English data is higher than data in Japanese where the performance increase from the baseline is lower. This is because, in our network, the BioBERT sub-network, which is focused in English language and biomedical vocabulary, together with the Multilingual BERT sub-network, which also deals with English besides Japanese, achieves a big push of improvement for the English-based samples when the weights during training are updated jointly. Such multilingual feature provides better performance than the joint architecture with only Japanese-BERT focused. And, the joint learning with GPT-2 sub-network decreases considerably the performance, moreover, for English language. We can ascribe this result to GPT-2 low fill-mask support needed for relation extraction tasks, penalizing the whole network. Results also show 6 training epochs decreased performance across executions in general, except for joint learning with GPT-2, although its performance is still far from good balanced results. This problem is expected since the low number of training samples prompts over-fitting issues, that incurs in lower performance. Despite this behavior, Table 1 shows that our proposal has less decrease than the other architectures, keeping balanced the numbers for both languages. Such results demonstrate the robustness of our joint learning network for Japanese language.

Qualitative analysis of results show frequent cases of wrong classifications by the baseline but correctly classified by our architecture, where there are English biomedical terms within the Japanese sentence. Table 2 shows four of these cases. This situation reinforces the benefits that BioBERT sub-network provides in the workflow of our joint learning network.

Table 2. Examples of qualitative results with English terms inside Japanese texts, wrong classified by baseline but correctly by ours. RA = Relation Absent, RP = Relation Present

Text	Label	Baseline	Ours
GENEの上流領域では**schizophrenia**と**SNPs**の間に有意な相関は認められず、これらの**SNP**は、明らかに日本人におけるschizophreniaのDISEASEで重要な役割を担っていない。	RA	RP	RA
DISEASEおよびGENEの多型およびハプロタイプと**AIDS**進行との間に統計的に有意な関連は認められなかった。	RA	RP	RA
GSTT1 0/0 **genotype**またはGENE 0/0-**GSTM1** 0/0の複合**genotype**を有する個人は、特に男性および若年キャリアで、DISEASEへの感受性が高い。	RP	RA	RP
GENEの**C2 allele**は、DISEASE、特に結腸がんの感受性因子であり、感受性遺伝子型と塩漬け食品の間には遺伝子環境の明らかな相互作用がある。	RP	RA	RP

4 Conclusions and Future Work

In this paper we presented a novel ensemble architecture through Joint Learning of independent Language Models for dealing with non-English languages and improve results in NLP use cases which need multilingual support. Thanks to our preliminary evaluation, we conclude that our approach offers a promising line of research since the Joint Learning of Language Models over different languages achieved higher performance than learning with a single model which combines English and Japanese samples in one dataset.

For future work, we would like to extend the testing over benchmark datasets along with specialized Language Models for Japanese and other languages with less representation of benchmark data.

References

1. Aramaki, E., Morita, M., Kano, Y., Ohkuma, T.: Overview of the NTCIR-12 MedNLPDoc task. In: NTCIR (2016)
2. Becker, K.G., Barnes, K.C., Bright, T.J., Wang, S.A.: The genetic association database. Nat. Genet. **36**(5), 431–432 (2004)
3. Bhasuran, B., Natarajan, J.: Automatic extraction of gene-disease associations from literature using joint ensemble learning. PLoS ONE **13**(7), e0200699 (2018)
4. Chen, M., Lan, G., Du, F., Lobanov, V.: Joint learning with pre-trained transformer on named entity recognition and relation extraction tasks for clinical analytics. In: Proceedings of the 3rd Clinical Natural Language Processing Workshop, pp. 234–242 (2020)
5. Devlin, J., Chang, M.W., Lee, K., Toutanova, K.: BERT: pre-training of deep bidirectional transformers for language understanding. In: NAACL-HLT (1) (2019)
6. Giorgi, J., Wang, X., Sahar, N., Shin, W.Y., Bader, G.D., Wang, B.: End-to-end Named Entity Recognition and Relation Extraction using Pre-trained Language Models. arXiv e-prints pp. arXiv-1912 (2019)
7. Lee, J., et al.: BioBERT: a pre-trained biomedical language representation model for biomedical text mining. Bioinformatics **36**(4), 1234–1240 (2020)
8. Li, Y., Bai, C., Reddy, C.K.: A distributed ensemble approach for mining healthcare data under privacy constraints. Inf. Sci. **330**, 245–259 (2016)
9. Peters, M., et al.: Deep contextualized word representations. In: Proceedings of the 2018 Conference of the North American Chapter of the Association for Computational Linguistics: Human Language Technologies, vol. 1 (Long Papers), pp. 2227–2237 (2018)
10. Qiu, X., Sun, T., Xu, Y., Shao, Y., Dai, N., Huang, X.: Pre-trained models for natural language processing: a survey. Sci. China Technol. Sci. **63**, 1872–1897 (2020). https://doi.org/10.1007/s11431-020-1647-3
11. Radford, A., Narasimhan, K., Salimans, T., Sutskever, I.: Improving Language Understanding by Generative Pre-Training (2018)
12. Saib, W., Sengeh, D., Dlamini, G., Singh, E.: Hierarchical Deep Learning Ensemble to Automate the Classification of Breast Cancer Pathology Reports by ICD-O Topography. arXiv preprint arXiv:2008.12571 (2020)
13. Tsuchiya, S., Abe, Y., Tanimoto, R., Iwasaki, Y., Morii, R.: Zinrai platform service to accelerate digital innovations for customer businesses. Fujitsu Sci. Tech. J. **55**(2), 38–44 (2019)

Supervised Clustering for Subgroup Discovery: An Application to COVID-19 Symptomatology

Aidan Cooper$^{(\boxtimes)}$ (ID), Orla Doyle (ID), and Alison Bourke (ID)

IQVIA, London, UK
{aidan.cooper,orla.doyle,alison.bourke}@iqvia.com

Abstract. Subgroup discovery is a data mining technique that attempts to find interesting relationships between different instances in a dataset with respect to a property of interest. Cluster analysis is a popular method for extracting homogeneous groups from a heterogeneous population, however, it often yields results that are challenging to interpret and action. In this work, we propose a novel, multi-step clustering methodology based on SHAP (SHapley Additive exPlanation) values and dimensionality reduction, for the purpose of subgroup discovery. Our method produces well-separated clusters that can be readily differentiated by simple decision rules, to yield interpretable subgroups in relation to a target variable. We illustrate our approach using self-reported COVID-19 symptom data across 2,479 participants who tested positive for COVID-19, resulting in the identification of 16 distinct symptom presentations. Future work will investigate common demographic and clinical features exhibited by each cluster cohort, and map clusters to outcomes to better understand the clinical presentation, risk factors and prognosis in COVID-19, as a timely and impactful application of this methodology.

Keywords: COVID-19 · Clustering · Subgroup discovery · SHAP

1 Introduction

One of the main goals of data mining is to discover meaningful patterns in data that can be interpreted and understood in order to extract knowledge. Subgroup discovery (SD) is a broadly applicable technique that aims to find interesting relationships between different instances in a dataset with respect to a property of interest [2,11,12]. Clustering is one approach to SD that involves partitioning unlabelled data into clusters or groups based on their similarity [21,25]. It has wide-ranging applications that span subgroup analysis, outlier detection, data visualisation and numerous others. A routine problem for the clustering practitioner, however, is deriving meaningful interpretations of clustered data that can be understood and actioned.

In clinical data science, the diverse symptom presentations of many diseases are often poorly understood, and symptom cluster research is considered to

© Springer Nature Switzerland AG 2021
M. Kamp et al. (Eds.): ECML PKDD 2021 Workshops, CCIS 1525, pp. 408–422, 2021.
https://doi.org/10.1007/978-3-030-93733-1_29

be an underexplored field that could provide new targets for interventions [19]. Recently, clustering of COVID-19 symptoms has been a topic of significant interest since the onset of the global pandemic, due to the variable symptom presentations that have been observed [9]. There have been various efforts to group COVID-19 patients based on their symptoms, although these segmentations typically have significant symptom overlap, such that the differences between clusters can be difficult to recognise [22,24]. Previous work studying infectious disease epidemics has shown that self-reported symptom data mined from web-based surveillance systems and social media platforms can be used to monitor and detect symptom trends [10,13,14].

In this paper, we present a multi-step clustering methodology that is specifically designed to produce interpretable clusters in a two-dimensional space, for the purpose of SD. We describe these clusters with simple yet highly discriminative decision rules, that are human-readable and appropriate for use in practical, real-world applications.

1.1 Related Work

Our work draws upon established concepts in SD, as well as a variety of recent supervised and unsupervised machine learning techniques in application to clustering. Numerous SD algorithms have been proposed, including some specifically for clinical data analysis, which typically involve statistics-based methods for identifying 'interesting' subgroups that possess unusual distributional properties [4,7,11]. However, these often produce large and overlapping rule sets [2]. Hierarchical clustering has been shown as a way to mitigate high instance-overlap in sets of rules [21]. We augment this approach by conducting significant preprocessing of the data to improve the effectiveness of clustering and subsequent SD.

Central to our methodology is the use of SHAP values as the basis for clustering. This idea is conceptually similar to other approaches that attempt to remove noise-information from datasets such that only the structure important to clustering remains [23]. In their paper for efficient tree ensemble SHAP value computation, Lundberg et al. introduce the concept of "supervised clustering", where instead of applying clustering directly to feature data in a fully-unsupervised manner, clustering is run on feature SHAP values [16]. This confers a number of interesting and desirable properties, most notably weighting features by a measure of importance that emphasises the most informative features whilst minimising the effect of fluctuations in feature values that have little impact on the outcome of interest. SHAP also serves as a pre-processing step that rescales feature data into common units that are the same as the output of the supervised prediction model. Moreover, it is acknowledged as a tool for interpretable clustering by Molnar [20]. Gramegna and Giudici compared clustering on the data directly versus the SHAP values to characterise the buying behaviours of insurance customers and found that clusters were better differentiated using the SHAP-based approach [8]. While our methodology has some similarities, we augment the performance and interpretability by reducing the SHAP values to two-dimensions prior to clustering using Uniform Manifold Approximation and

Projection (UMAP) which has been proposed as an effective pre-processing step for boosting the performance of density-based clustering [18]. UMAP's major advantage is that it preserves the local and global structure of the data, which in our methodology ensures that clusters close in space are close in characteristics, further enhancing the interpretability of our approach by enabling subgroup visualisation.

Finally, rather than characterise clusters using descriptive statistics based on the outcome and feature data, we construct discriminative decision-rules that identify and differentiate the clusters, forming our subgroup descriptions. Decision rules are a popular supervised machine learning technique where interpretability is paramount, and are fundamental to most SD algorithms [20]. They have also been applied successfully in clustering applications as a way to segment data [3]. We show that the dense, well-separated clusters generated in the previous steps of our methodology yield a set of complementary decision rules that are highly discriminative in identifying and differentiating our data, whilst adhering to human-readable levels of complexity.

1.2   Our Contributions

The primary contribution of our work is marrying together multiple sub-fields of clustering into a cohesive methodology for SD. Our approach produces highly discriminative subgroup rules, addressing the commonly encountered challenge in SD - particularly in clinical settings - of large and overlapping rule sets that require subsequent manual filtering and adjustment by experts. Furthermore, the ability to naturally visualise clusters distinguishes our approach from traditional statistics-based SD techniques, addressing another recognised challenge of comprehensive subgroup visualisation [2].

In application to COVID-19, we've demonstrated the feasibility of our method for producing an intuitive two-dimensional mapping of the symptom space, comprised of meaningful regions of symptomatology and well-characterised individual clusters, with respect to not only the presence or absence of different symptoms, but their severity also.

2   Methods

2.1   COVID-19 Active Research Experience (CARE)

We obtained data from participants in a community-based COVID-19 registry known as CARE (https://www.helpstopcovid19.com/). This registry is based in the US and is open to anyone who believes they have been exposed to COVID-19. Via a web platform, participants can report their experience, including symptoms and severity, as well as risk factors, and treatment of COVID-19. The registry also captures any results of viral COVID-19 testing. To date, over 20,000 people have enrolled into CARE, and for this analysis we used symptom reports from US participants who had COVID-19 test results and entered symptom information between 30 July 2020 and 19 January 2021.

Participants recorded the presence or absence of 21 symptoms (including *fatigue, cough, fever* and *decreased smell*) and were also able to grade the severity of each of their symptoms as "Very Mild", "Mild", "Moderate", or "Severe". For each of the 21 symptoms, we combined the presence/absence flag and severity rating into a single ordinal score between 0–5, where 0 corresponds to the absence of a symptom, 1 means the symptom was reported but not rated, and scores of 2–5 correspond to the symptom being reported and rated on the 4-point severity scale with 2 being "Very Mild" up to 5 as "Severe". In addition to the 21 individual symptom variables, we also include an overall count of the number of symptoms reported by the participants in our analysis.

2.2 Clustering and Subgroup Discovery Methodology

Our clustering methodology comprises a sequence of steps, shown in overview in Fig. 1, and outlined in depth below. In summary, we use explainable supervised machine learning to emphasise contributions that help discriminate between classes (e.g., positive vs negative COVID-19 test), i.e., we transform the data to represent the discriminatory question of interest. We then embed the participants who tested positive for COVID-19 in a two-dimensional space, where we look for structure using clustering. Finally, we adopt a rules-based approach for describing and differentiating these clusters, yielding subgroups of COVID-19 symptomatology.

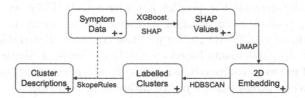

Fig. 1. Conceptual diagram of our multi-step subgroup discovery methodology. Each step is annotated with + and − icons to denote the inclusion of COVID-positive and COVID-negative participants, respectively.

To evaluate this approach of clustering in the discriminative space, we compare the results of our methodology against an equivalent clustering procedure that bypasses the supervised machine learning and SHAP stages, and instead clusters directly on the embedded symptom data in a manner akin to conventional clustering analysis.

COVID-19 Test Outcome Prediction Model. The role of the supervised machine learning model is primarily to serve as a means for obtaining SHAP (SHapley Additive exPlanations) values, which describe the discriminative profile for participants with a positive test for COVID-19.

For supervised machine learning, an XGBoost classification algorithm was trained to predict the COVID-19 test outcome for the 4,063 tested participants [6]. We selected XGBoost for its non-parametric properties, ability to learn interactions between variables, and its compatibility with the SHAP methodology that provides a participant-level view of feature importance for predicting a positive COVID-19 test.

The feature set for XGBoost comprised 21 symptom scores and the count of unique symptoms as input variables, with the outcome of the COVID-19 test (positive encoded as 1, negative as 0) used as the classification label. Hyperparameters were selected by 10-fold cross-validation, using a random search methodology. Cross-validated scores were calculated for the Area Under the Curve of the Receiver Operating Characteristic (AUCROC) and accuracy.

Symptom Variable SHAP Values. SHAP values were calculated for the trained XGBoost model, to determine the contribution of each variable towards the model's COVID-19 test outcome predictions for each individual instance [15]. In this analysis, instances where a variable has a SHAP value greater than zero indicates that the variable is associated with a prediction of a positive COVID-19 test result, and SHAP values less than zero indicate that the variable is associated with a negative COVID-19 test prediction. SHAP values can be thought of as a latent representation of the symptom data that emphasises the variables that are most influential for the COVID-19 test outcome predictions. The resulting SHAP values for COVID-positive participants can be clustered in terms of the similarity of the drivers that predict a positive COVID-19 test. In doing so, the clustering process is encouraged to focus on the symptom variables that are most pertinent to COVID-19, rather than consider all variables equally and potentially group participants based on similarity across irrelevant factors.

SHAP values were computed using the TreeExplainer explanation method under the *interventional* feature perturbation approach [15].

Dimensionality Reduction with UMAP. Uniform Manifold Approximation and Projection (UMAP) was used to reduce the COVID-positive SHAP data to two dimensions [18]. The use of UMAP has two purposes: (i) as a pre-processing step for clustering in order to enhance the performance [1] and (ii) to aid data visualisation. One notable advantage of using UMAP for dimensionality reduction rather than alternatives such as t-SNE, is that it preserves the local and global structure of the data. That is, individual data points are maximally similar within their neighbourhood as well more similar to local neighbourhoods than those that are more distant.

For our use case, the objective is to characterise and segment COVID-19 positive participants and therefore we focus on only these participants in this and subsequent steps. An alternative formulation of the problem - which may or may not be more appropriate for other similar clinical SD tasks - would be to retain both COVID-19 positive and negative participants throughout the analysis. This would ultimately produce clusters that not only segment subgroups of COVID-19 positive participants from each other, but also distinguish them from COVID-19 negative participants. This could be preferred in settings where the intended application is for diagnosis.

The use of UMAP in this COVID-19 setting means that in addition to deriving subgroups of participants that display similar symptomatology, we also obtain regions that encompass multiple clusters with related symptom characteristics.

The UMAP embedding was computed for two components, using a local neighbourhood (*n neighbours*) of 45 data points (three times the default value), and a *minimum distance* between embedded points of zero, enabling data points to be tightly grouped to support the formation of local clusters. This higher than default *n neighbours* value encourages UMAP to produce more general, global neighbourhoods, rather than localised granular structure. Similarly, setting the *minimum distance* value to zero encourages the formation of densely packed, well-separated clusters of embedded data points [18]. These characteristics serve to optimise the clustering results in the next stage.

Density-Based Clustering with HDBSCAN. Hierarchical Density-Based Spatial Clustering of Applications with Noise (HDBSCAN) was used to cluster the two-dimensional UMAP embedding [17]. The HDBSCAN algorithm was selected as it does not require the number of clusters to be specified *a priori* but instead requires that the users specify the minimum size of cluster, which is potentially a more intuitive parameter to work with. Additionally, this approach doesn't force all data points to be assigned to clusters, i.e., samples can remain unassigned to all clusters. Finally, HDBSCAN has been shown to work well with UMAP [1].

HDBSCAN parameters were selected by grid search using ranges that spanned 2–200 for *minimum samples*, 2–200 for *minimum cluster size*, and 0–8 for *cluster selection epsilon*. The set of parameters chosen were those that produced clusters that were maximally separated in the embedding space as measured by the average silhouette coefficient across all instances, subject to the constraint that no more than 3% (an arbitrarily selected threshold) of instances were unassigned by HDBSCAN. Values of 10 for *minimum samples*, 40 for *minimum cluster size* and 0.5 for *cluster selection epsilon* yielded optimal results that maximised the average silhouette coefficient [5].

Rules-Based Cluster Descriptions (Subgroups). A key challenge in the use of clustering methods is the interpretation of the results. We propose to augment the interpretability of our approach by learning rules that identify clusters with high precision and coverage, thus describing our subgroups.

We use the SkopeRules package to describe and differentiate clusters of COVID-positive participants using a one-vs-all methodology [20]. Interpretable rules were found based on the underlying symptomatology data - not the computed SHAP values - for each cluster in turn, by labelling it positively and all other clusters negatively. The resulting rule set serves as our COVID-19 symptomatology subgroup descriptions.

SkopeRules was set to use a *maximum depth* of four, to ensure the rules met the desired level of simplicity of having no more than four terms. *Minimum precision* and *minimum recall* were set at 70%, which was the highest threshold that still enabled rules to be identified for every cluster. For most clusters, the performance of the rules greatly surpassed this.

3   Results

In the following sections, we present results of the clustering and subgroup discovery methodology. We compare the performance against an equivalent procedure applied directly to the unmodified symptom data (Fig. 6 and Table 2).

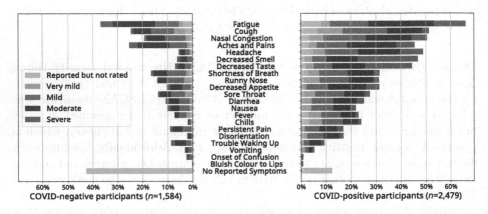

Fig. 2. Reported symptom prevalence in participants tested for COVID-19, ranked by overall prevalence ($n = 4{,}063$).

4,063 participants met the criteria for inclusion (COVID-19 test and entry of symptom information between 30 July 2020 and 19 January 2021). Of these 4,063 participants, 2,479 (61.0%) received a positive COVID-19 test.

The symptom variables are visualised in Fig. 2 for both COVID-positive and negative participants. Non-zero symptom scores are somewhat normally distributed, with ratings of "Mild" or "Moderate" being the most commonly reported severities for all symptoms, with the exception of *decreased smell* and *decreased taste* for which "Severe" was the most frequent severity rating. Scores of 1 (symptom reported but severity not rated) are relatively infrequent. *Fatigue, cough,* and *nasal congestion* were the most common symptoms ($n = 2{,}222$, 1,659, 1,556), whereas *bluish colour to lips, onset of confusion,* and *vomiting* were the least reported symptoms ($n = 24$, 62, 180). The mean number of symptoms reported for the 3,080 participants who reported at least one symptom was 6.71 (SD 4.36). 983 participants reported no symptoms, of whom 307 (31.2%) had positive COVID-19 tests.

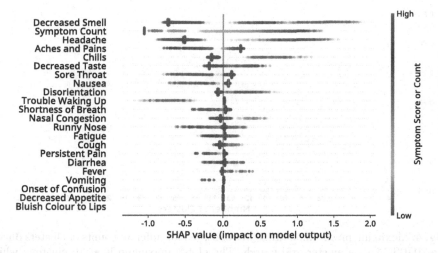

Fig. 3. SHAP values summary plot for the 22 symptom variables used for clustering, ranked by their mean absolute value across all participants with a test result. *Decreased smell, symptom count,* and *headache,* were the three most influential variables for the XGBoost model's predictions, whereas *bluish colour to lips* was the least informative variable.

3.1   COVID-19 Test Outcome Prediction Model

The XGBoost model achieved mean cross-validated scores of 0.825 for Area Under the Curve of the Receiver Operating Characteristic (AUCROC) and 77.1% for accuracy. Qualitatively speaking, these scores indicate that there is a sufficient signal in the symptom scores alone to differentiate between positive and negative participants, albeit with moderate levels of predictive performance.

3.2   Symptom Variable SHAP Values

Figure 3 shows the SHAP values derived from the XGBoost model. For each of the 22 symptom variables, each participant is represented as an individual data point. The symptoms are ordered according to their mean absolute SHAP value (contribution to prediction) and the colour scale represents the symptom severity level. *Decreased smell, headache,* and *aches and pains* were the three most informative symptoms for predicting the COVID-19 test results, as ranked by mean absolute SHAP value. Examining the colours of the individual points reveals that in the first two cases, higher symptom scores are typically associated with positive test result predictions, whereas scores of zero encourage the opposite. A similar trend is seen for other highly ranking symptoms, such as *chills* and *decreased taste,* although the opposite is observed for *aches and pains, sore throat,* and *nausea. Runny nose* and *fatigue* are examples of a mixed cases, where high scores can encourage predictions of positive or negative test outcomes dependent on the presentation of other symptoms.

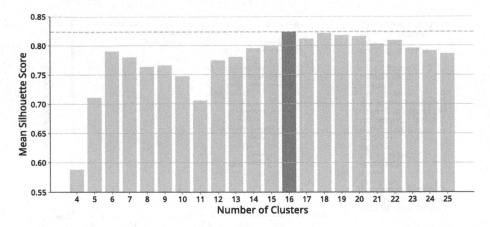

Fig. 4. Maximum mean silhouette scores observed for different counts of clusters during the HDBSCAN parameter grid search. The global maximum is at 16 clusters, which we visualise in Fig. 5 and define subgroups for in Table 1.

Comparison of Fig. 3 with Fig. 2 indicates some correlation between the overall prevalence of symptoms and their influence over the XGBoost model's predictions, although the symptoms that top the SHAP rankings are those that are disproportionately represented in one of the test outcome groups. *Decreased smell* is one such symptom, and has been recognised in other studies as one of the strongest predictors of COVID-19 [10]. Another notable example is *chills*, which ranks 15th by prevalence yet 4th by influence.

The *symptom count* ranks 2nd most informative and shows a linear relationship with test outcome prediction, where the absence of any symptoms leads to a negative test prediction and the presence of many symptoms leads to a positive test prediction.

As is to be expected, the top three most informative variables feature prominently within the rules that describe the resulting clusters.

3.3   Dimensionality Reduction and Clustering

Table 1 shows the counts, descriptions, and rules of the COVID-positive clusters (visualised in Fig. 5). The grid search of HDBSCAN parameters found that a maximum mean silhouette score of 0.822 was achieved by a 16-cluster segmentation. HDBSCAN is not constrained to assign each data points to clusters, and 62 (2.5%) of participants were unassigned. Counts of participants in each cluster vary between 315 in the largest cluster (2, *"headache without chills or decreased smell"*) and 54 in the smallest (8, *"chills without headache or decreased smell"*).

Although it was found that 16 clusters was the optimal number for maximising the mean silhouette score, from the grid search results in Fig. 4, it can be seen that a local maximum also exists for 6 clusters. If a smaller number of coarser clusters with higher instance counts was desired for reasons of clinical

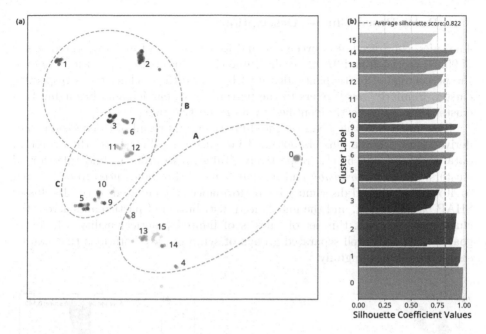

Fig. 5. (a) Visual representation of the clustered, two-dimensional UMAP embedding of COVID-positive participant SHAP values. Regions **A**, **B**, and **C** - identified by examining the rules in Table 1, and selected for their differences with respect to the two most influential symptoms - surround distinct spatial areas of key symptom combinations: no *decreased smell* or *headache* (**A**); *headache* (**B**); *decreased smell* (**C**). (b) Silhouette plot of the 16 identified clusters, with micro-average silhouette score 0.822.

utility, this alternative segmentation could be characterised further. This illustrates the flexibility of our methodology for producing subgroups at the desired level of granularity, by subsuming or dividing clusters within the two-dimensional symptom space through tuning of the HDBSCAN parameters.

Figure 6 shows the equivalent results after clustering on a two-dimensional UMAP embedding obtained directly from the underlying symptom data, bypassing the SHAP value computation stage. Clustering with HDBSCAN on this embedding is highly unstable with respect to small changes in parameters, with results fluctuating between two and over twenty distinct clusters. After careful fine-tuning of parameters, this procedure produces seven clusters with a considerably lower mean silhouette score of 0.140. The majority (68.1%) of the data is assigned to a single, amorphous cluster, largely comprised of data points with negative silhouette coefficients. There were 234 participants (9.4%) without cluster membership, and the five smallest clusters account for only 9.4% of the total data, further evidencing this procedure's limited effectiveness for deriving an interpretable segmentation of this data.

3.4   Rules-Based Cluster Descriptions

The rules, comprised of between one and four terms, had mean weighted scores of 95.3% precision and 97.9% recall (Table 1). In this context, precision refers to the percentage of participants identified by a rule that belong to its respective cluster. Similarly, recall refers to the percentage of participants belonging to a cluster that are correctly identified by its respective rule.

By comparison, the mean weighted precision and recall of the decision rules derived for the seven clusters obtained via clustering directly on the symptom data are 99.1% and 52.5%, respectively (Table 2). In order to find rules for all clusters, *minimum precision* and *minimum recall* thresholds need to be lowered to 40%. The reduced discriminative performance as compared to the 16-cluster SHAP-based variant, and the imbalanced distribution of participants across the clusters, means that this set of rules is of limited practical utility, where the goal is to identify well-separated groups of symptom presentations that can be characterised meaningfully.

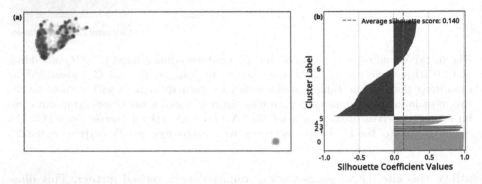

Fig. 6. (a) Visual representation of the clustered, two-dimensional UMAP embedding of COVID-19-positive participants' symptom data (as opposed to SHAP values). (b) Silhouette plot of the 7 identified clusters, with micro-average silhouette score 0.140.

Closer inspection of the rules and their constituent terms shows that they're highly complementary as a set, cleanly segmenting groups of instances by the presence or absence of specific symptoms and their differing levels of severity. The second largest cluster, 0, corresponds to the 12.4% of COVID-positive participants with no reported symptoms.

A benefit of UMAP not afforded by related techniques such as t-SNE, is that clusters close together in the embedded space are more similar than those that are far apart. We illustrate this with three *regions*, A, B, C, which surround clusters that share similar characteristics with respect to the two most influential symptom variables, *decreased smell* and *headache* (Fig. 5). Clusters within Region A explicitly exclude both symptoms, clusters within Region B explicitly include *headache*, and clusters within Region C explicitly include *headache*. Clusters within the overlap of Regions B and C consist of both *decreased taste*

Table 1. Subgroup descriptions and rules for COVID-positive participants, and corresponding rule precision and recall scores.

Cluster	Count (%)	Description	Rule	Precision	Recall
0	307 (12.4%)	Asymptomatic	Symptom count = 0	100.0%	100.0%
1	183 (7.4%)	Headache and chills, without decreased smell	Headache $\geq$ 1, chills $\geq$ 1, decr. smell = 0	100.0%	100.0%
2	315 (12.7%)	Headache, without chills or decreased smell	Headache $\geq$ 1, chills = 0, decr. smell = 0	100.0%	100.0%
3	214 (8.6%)	Headache, severe decreased smell, no/unrated trouble waking up, no chills	Headache $\geq$ 1, trouble waking up $\leq$ 1, chills = 0, decr. smell = 5	100.0%	100.0%
4	65 (2.6%)	1 symptom that isn't decreased smell or mod./severe fatigue	Symptom count = 1, decr. smell = 0, fatigue $\leq$ 3	77.1%	98.5%
5	206 (8.3%)	Severe decreased smell, without headache	Decr. smell = 5, headache = 0	100.0%	99.5%
6	60 (2.4%)	Severe decreased smell, rated trouble waking up, and headache	Decr. smell = 5, headache $\geq$ 1, trouble waking up $\geq$ 2	100.0%	100.0%
7	121 (4.9%)	Severe decreased smell, headache, chills, and no/unrated trouble waking up	Decr. smell = 5, headache $\geq$ 1, chills $\geq$ 1, trouble waking up $\leq$ 1	100.0%	100.0%
8	54 (2.2%)	Chills without headache or decreased smell	Chills $\geq$ 1, headache = 0, decr. smell = 0	100.0%	100.0%
9	68 (2.7%)	Non-severe decreased smell, mild- severe aches and pains, without headache	1 $\leq$ decr. smell $\leq$ 4, aches and pains $\geq$ 3, headache = 0	91.9%	100.0%
10	138 (5.6%)	Non-severe decreased smell, no/unrated/very mild aches and pains without headache	1 $\leq$ decr. smell $\leq$ 4, aches and pains $\leq$ 2, headache = 0	79.6%	96.4%
11	149 (6.0%)	Non-severe decreased smell, with headache and chills	1 $\leq$ decr. smell $\leq$ 4, headache $\geq$ 1, chills $\geq$ 1	98.6%	96.0%
12	167 (6.7%)	Non-severe decreased smell, headache, without chills	1 $\leq$ decr. smell $\leq$ 4, headache $\geq$ 1, chills = 0	95.4%	98.8%
13	150 (6.1%)	3+ symptoms that aren't headache, decreased smell, or mild- severe aches and pains	Symptom count $\geq$ 3, headache = 0, decr. smell = 0, aches and pains $\leq$ 2	73.4%	99.3%
14	66 (2.7%)	2 symptoms that aren't headache or decreased smell	Symptom count = 2, headache = 0, decr. smell = 0	75.9%	100.0%
15	60 (2.4%)	Mild-severe aches and pains, without headache, decreased smell, or rated chills	Aches and pains $\geq$ 3, headache = 0, chills $\leq$ 1, decr. smell = 0	100.0%	77.9%
N/A	62 (2.5%)	Unassigned	–	–	–

and *headache*. Trivially, Region A also encompasses the most universally distant cluster, 0, which corresponds to participants who reported no symptoms. This aligns with clinical intuition that symptomless patients should be far removed from the symptomatic groups. Similar regions can be identified for other prominent symptoms such as *chills*.

Table 2. Cluster results derived from symptom data (as opposed to SHAP values). The *Cluster Descriptions* are interpretations of the *Cluster Rules* derived by SkopeRules, translated into natural language. The *Cluster Rules* are combinations of terms that dictate the presence or absence, and severity of different symptoms. *Rule Precision* quantifies the percentage of COVID-19-positive participants identified by the *Cluster Rule* that truly belong to the respective cluster. *Rule Recall* quantifies the percentage of COVID-19-positive participants that truly belong to a cluster that are successfully identified by its corresponding *Cluster Rule*.

Cluster	Count (%)	Description	Rule	Precision	Recall
0	326 (13.2%)	Asymptomatic	Symptom count = 0	100.0%	94.2%
1	44 (1.8%)	Only fatigue	Symptom count = 1, fatigue $\geq$ 2	100.0%	61.4%
2	24 (1.0%)	Only cough	Symptom count = 1, cough $\geq$ 1	100.0%	62.5%
3	15 (0.6%)	2–3 symptoms that include decreased smell and (very) mild decreased taste	$2 \geq$ symptom count $\leq$ 3, decr. smell $\geq$ 1, $2 \geq$ decr. taste $\leq$ 3	68.2%	100.0%
4	88 (3.5%)	2–6 symptoms that include rated decreased smell and nasal congestion, but not rated decreased taste	$2 \geq$ symptom count $\leq$ 6, decr. smell $\geq$ 2, nasal congestion $\geq$ 2, decr. taste $\leq$ 1	97.7%	47.7%
5	61 (2.5%)	1–3 symptoms that include rated shortness of breath, but not rated nasal congestion	$1 \geq$ symptom count $\leq$ 3, shortness of breath $\geq$ 2, nasal congestion $\leq$ 1	88.6%	50.8%
6	1687 (68.1%)	3+ symptoms that include moderate-severe decreased smell, rated decreased taste, but not severe trouble waking up	Symptom count $\geq$ 3, decr. smell $\geq$ 4, decr. taste $\geq$ 2, trouble waking up $\leq$ 4	99.6%	44.0%
N/A	234 (9.4%)	Unassigned	–	–	–

4   Conclusions and Future Directions

Our methods augment clustering approaches for SD by incorporating SHAP values as a latent representation of the data that is more amenable to clustering with respect to the target of interest. We have shown that compared to a standard methodology that clusters directly on the feature data, our approach yields subgroups that are better distributed and described by interpretable rules with superior discriminative performance. In doing so, we address a common pitfall of SD, by generating a compact and highly accurate rule set with minimal overlap.

We also demonstrate the utility of visualising and identifying subgroups derived from a 2D embedding, as a means for understanding not only the commonalities of instances within a subgroup, but also the similarities of subgroups proximally located in the 2D space. This addresses another challenge in SD of comprehensively visualising subgroups, and for practical purposes, can help elucidate 'regions' that encompass multiple subgroups and encapsulate broader trends in the data.

Having established the potential of this methodology on this experimental dataset, in future work we intend to investigate the different demographic and clinical features exhibited by the clusters produced by this methodology, and map clusters to outcomes to better understand the clinical presentation, risk factors and prognosis in COVID-19. We believe this novel approach to SD, based on a multi-step supervised clustering pipeline, produces a cleaner and better characterised segmentation of COVID-19 symptomatology than a conventional clustering approach, and that this methodology can be applied more widely to other SD problems where interpretability and differentiability of clusters is paramount.

References

1. Allaoui, M., Kherfi, M.L., Cheriet, A.: Considerably improving clustering algorithms using UMAP dimensionality reduction technique: a comparative study. In: El Moataz, A., Mammass, D., Mansouri, A., Nouboud, F. (eds.) Image and Signal Processing, pp. 317–325. Springer International Publishing, Cham (2020)
2. Atzmueller, M.: Subgroup discovery. WIREs Data Mining Knowl. Disc. 5(1), 35–49 (2015)
3. Barbado, A., Corcho, Ó., Benjamins, R.: Rule Extraction in Unsupervised Anomaly Detection for Model Explainability: Application to OneClass SVM (2019). arXiv e-prints arXiv:1911.09315
4. Belfodil, A., Belfodil, A., Bendimerad, A., Lamarre, P., Robardet, C., Kaytoue, M., Plantevit, M.: Fssd - a fast and efficient algorithm for subgroup set discovery. In: 2019 IEEE International Conference on Data Science and Advanced Analytics (DSAA). pp. 91–99 (2019). https://doi.org/10.1109/DSAA.2019.00023
5. Chen, G., Jaradat, S., Banerjee, N., Tanaka, T., Ko, M., Zhang, M.: Evaluation and comparison of clustering algorithms in analyzing ES cell gene expression data. Statistica Sinica 12, 241–262 (2002)
6. Chen, T., Guestrin, C.: XGBoost: A Scalable Tree Boosting System (2016). arXiv e-prints arXiv:1603.02754
7. Esnault, C., Gadonna, M.L., Queyrel, M., Templier, A., Zucker, J.D.: Q-finder: an algorithm for credible subgroup discovery in clinical data analysis - an application to the international diabetes management practice study. Front. Artif. Intell. 3, 83 (2020)
8. Gramegna, A., Giudici, P.: Why to buy insurance? An explainable artificial intelligence approach. Risks 8(4), 1–10 (2020). https://doi.org/10.3390/risks8040137
9. Grant, M.C., Geoghegan, L., Arbyn, M., Mohammed, Z., McGuinness, L., Clarke, E.L., Wade, R.G.: The prevalence of symptoms in 24,410 adults infected by the novel coronavirus (SARS-CoV-2; COVID-19): a systematic review and meta-analysis of 148 studies from 9 countries. PLoS One 15(6), e0234765 (2020)

10. Güemes, A., et al.: A syndromic surveillance tool to detect anomalous clusters of COVID-19 symptoms in the United States. Sci. Rep. **11**(1), 4660 (2021)
11. Helal, S.: Subgroup discovery algorithms: a survey and empirical evaluation. J. Comput. Sci. Technol. **31**, 561–576 (2016). https://doi.org/10.1007/s11390-016-1647-1
12. Herrera, F., Carmona, C.J., González, P., Del Jesus, M.J.: An overview on subgroup discovery: foundations and applications. Knowl. Inf. Syst. **29**, 495–525 (2011). https://doi.org/10.1007/s10115-010-0356-2
13. Kalimeri, K., et al.: Unsupervised extraction of epidemic syndromes from participatory influenza surveillance self-reported symptoms. PLOS Comput. Biol. **15**(4), 1–21 (2019)
14. Lim, S., Tucker, C.S., Kumara, S.: An unsupervised machine learning model for discovering latent infectious diseases using social media data. J. Biomed. Inf. **66**, 82–94 (2017)
15. Lundberg, S.M., et al.: From local explanations to global understanding with explainable AI for trees. Nat. Mach. Intell. **2**(1), 2522–5839 (2020)
16. Lundberg, S.M., Erion, G.G., Lee, S.I.: Consistent Individualized Feature Attribution for Tree Ensembles (2018). arXiv e-prints arXiv:1802.03888
17. McInnes, L., Healy, J., Astels, S.: HDBScan: hierarchical density based clustering. J. Open Source Softw. **2**(11), 1–14 (2017). https://doi.org/10.21105/joss.00205
18. McInnes, L., Healy, J., Melville, J.: UMAP: Uniform Manifold Approximation and Projection for Dimension Reduction (2018). arXiv e-prints arXiv:1802.03426
19. Miaskowski, C., et al.: Advancing symptom science through symptom cluster research: expert panel proceedings and recommendations. J. Natl. Cancer Inst. **109**, 1–10 (2017). https://doi.org/10.1093/jnci/djw253
20. Molnar, C.: Interpretable Machine Learning (2019). https://christophm.github.io/interpretable-ml-book/
21. Niemann, U., Spiliopoulou, M., Preim, B., Ittermann, T., Völzke, H.: Combining subgroup discovery and clustering to identify diverse subpopulations in cohort study data. In: 2017 IEEE 30th International Symposium on Computer-Based Medical Systems (CBMS), pp. 582–587 (2017). https://doi.org/10.1109/CBMS.2017.15
22. Rubio-Rivas, M., et al.: Predicting clinical outcome with phenotypic clusters in COVID-19 pneumonia: An analysis of 12,066 hospitalized patients from the Spanish registry semi-COVID-19. J. Clin. Med. **9**(11), 3488 (2020)
23. Schelling, B., Bauer, L.G.M., Behzadi, S., Plant, C.: Utilizing structure-rich features to improve clustering. In: The European Conference on Machine Learning and Principles and Practice of Knowledge Discovery in Databases 2020 (2020). http://eprints.cs.univie.ac.at/6416/
24. Sudre, C.H., et al.: Symptom clusters in COVID-19: a potential clinical prediction tool from the COVID symptom study app. Sci. Adv. **7**(12), 1–7 (2021). https://doi.org/10.1126/sciadv.abd4177 org/content/7/12/eabd4177
25. Zimmermann, A., De Raedt, L.: Cluster-grouping: from subgroup discovery to clustering. Mach. Learn. **77**, 125–159 (2009). https://doi.org/10.1007/s10994-009-5121-y

Diagnostic Surveillance of High-Grade Gliomas: Towards Automated Change Detection Using Radiology Report Classification

Tommaso Di Noto[1]([✉])(ID), Chirine Atat[1](ID), Eduardo Gamito Teiga[1](ID),
Monika Hegi[2,3,4](ID), Andreas Hottinger[5](ID), Meritxell Bach Cuadra[1,6](ID),
Patric Hagmann[1](ID), and Jonas Richiardi[1](ID)

[1] Department of Radiology, Lausanne University Hospital
and University of Lausanne, Lausanne, Switzerland
tommaso.di-noto@chuv.ch
[2] Neuroscience Research Center, Lausanne University Hospital
and University of Lausanne, Lausanne, Switzerland
[3] Neurosurgery, Lausanne University Hospital and University of Lausanne,
Lausanne, Switzerland
[4] Swiss Cancer Center Léman (SCCL), Lausanne, Switzerland
[5] Department of Clinical Neurosciences; Department of Oncology,
Lausanne University Hospital and University of Lausanne, Lausanne, Switzerland
[6] Medical Image Analysis Laboratory, Center for Biomedical Imaging,
Lausanne, Switzerland

Abstract. Natural Language Processing (NLP) on electronic health records (EHRs) can be used to monitor the evolution of pathologies over time to facilitate diagnosis and improve decision-making. In this study, we designed an NLP pipeline to classify Magnetic Resonance Imaging (MRI) radiology reports of patients with high-grade gliomas. Specifically, we aimed to distinguish reports indicating changes in tumors between one examination and the follow-up examination (treatment response/tumor progression versus stability). A total of 164 patients with 361 associated reports were retrieved from routine imaging, and reports were labeled by one radiologist. First, we assessed which embedding is more suitable when working with limited data, in French, from a specific domain. To do so, we compared a classic embedding techniques, TF-IDF, to a neural embedding technique, Doc2Vec, after hyperparameter optimization for both. A random forest classifier was used to classify the reports into stable (unchanged tumor) or unstable (changed tumor). Second, we applied the post-hoc LIME explainability tool to understand the decisions taken by the model. Overall, classification results obtained in repeated 5-fold cross-validation with TF-IDF reached around 89% AUC and were significantly better than those achieved with Doc2Vec (Wilcoxon signed-rank test, $P = 0.009$). The explainability toolkit run on TF-IDF revealed some interesting patterns: first, words indicating change such as *progression* were rightfully frequent for reports classified as unstable; similarly, words indicating no change such as *not* were frequent for reports classified as stable. Lastly,

© Springer Nature Switzerland AG 2021
M. Kamp et al. (Eds.): ECML PKDD 2021 Workshops, CCIS 1525, pp. 423–436, 2021.
https://doi.org/10.1007/978-3-030-93733-1_30

424   T. Di Noto et al.

the toolkit discovered misleading words such as *T2* which are clearly not directly relevant for the task. All the code used for this study is made available.

Keywords: Natural Language Processing (NLP) · Term Frequency - Inverse Document Frequency (TF-IDF) · Doc2Vec · Diagnostic surveillance · LIME model explainability

1 Introduction

In the last decade, Machine Learning (ML) has reshaped research in radiology. ML models yield state-of-the-art results for numerous medical imaging tasks such as segmentation, anomaly detection, registration, and disease classification [1]. In addition to images, ML models have also been increasingly applied to radiology reports and more generally to data coming from Radiology Information Systems (RIS) [2]. However, even though radiology reports contain valuable, high-level insights from trained physicians, they also come with some associated drawbacks; in particular, most reports are stored as unstructured, free-text documents. Consequently, they exhibit a strong degree of ambiguity, uncertainty and lack of conciseness [3].

Natural Language Processing (NLP) is a branch of ML that helps computers understand, interpret, and manipulate human language [4]. In the case of radiology reports, NLP has the goal of extracting clinically relevant information from unstructured texts. As recently illustrated in one extensive review [5], one frequent application of NLP for radiology reports is diagnostic surveillance. Its objective is to monitor the evolution of a pathology in order to extrapolate useful knowledge and improve decision-making. In line with this trend, our work focuses on oncology patients with high-grade gliomas that are scanned longitudinally for frequent follow-up.

According to [5], the majority (86%) of studies published up until 2019 focused on medical reports written in English, while only 1% of the reviewed studies utilized French reports. This language gap is understandable given that a substantial portion of NLP tools was developed using English texts. Nonetheless, in medical NLP, researchers need to adapt their models to the language of the radiology reports. This entails custom precautions and expedients to take since languages are often syntactically and/or semantically different from English. In this work, we investigate NLP methods for radiology reports written in French.

In addition, [5] concluded that although a growing number of Deep Learning (DL) NLP methods has been applied in recent years, "conventional ML approaches are still prevalent". To assess which technique is more suitable for our dataset, we compare two traditional embedding strategies, namely Term Frequency-Inverse Document Frequency (TF-IDF) [6] and Doc2Vec [7].

The task that we address is binary document classification. Specifically, we aim to identify the main conclusion of the medical reports deciding among the following groups: tumor *stability* vs. tumor *instability*. Details about these classes are provided in Sect. 2.2. The potential applications of our report classifier are twofold: first, it could help referring physicians to focus the attention on the main conclusion of the report, thus accelerating subsequent decisions. Second, the predicted classes could be used as weak labels for a downstream machine learning task (e.g. automated cohort creation). In addition, most clinically relevant images in RIS are associated with a radiology report, and thus offer potential access to several hundred thousands of weakly labelled images in medium to large hospitals.

In this work we also conduct an interpretability analysis of the model's decisions [8,9], based on the post-hoc interpretation technique LIME [10]. Its main objective is to identify the most important words that influenced the final prediction, by creating a surrogate linear model that performs local input perturbation (details in Sect. 2.4).

In summary, this study presents a classifier for French radiology reports in the context of diagnostic surveillance, while comparing two embedding techniques and providing a visual interpretation of the model's decisions.

1.1 Related Works

Here, we present the works most similar to ours. In [11], the authors compared several embedding techniques and five different classifiers for detecting the radiologist's intent in oncologic evaluations. Similarly, [12] investigated a DL model to identify oncologic outcomes from radiology reports. The authors in [13] utilized a combination of ML and rule-based approaches to highlight important changes and identify significant observations that characterize radiology reports. [14] devised a model that extracts radiological measurements and the corresponding core descriptors (e.g. temporality, anatomical entity, ...) from Magnetic Resonance (MR), Computed Tomography (CT) and mammography reports. The work of [15] describes an NLP pipeline that identifies patients with (pre)cancer of the cervix and anus from histopathologic reports. Last, [16] detected thromboembolic diseases and incidental findings from angiography and venography reports.

Among all these works, only [16] used French reports, while the others worked with English documents. Moreover, only [12] addressed the issue of model explainability which we believe is paramount for the ML community, especially in the medical domain.

2   Materials and Methods

2.1   Dataset

We retrospectively included 164 subjects that underwent longitudinal MR glioma follow-up in the university hospital of Lausanne (CHUV) between 2005 and 2019. 71% of the patients in the cohort had Glioblastoma Multiforme (GBM), while the remaining 29% had either an oligoastrocytoma or an oligodendroglioma. At every session, a series of MR scans were performed including structural, perfusion and functional imaging. For the sake of this study, we only focused on the native T1-weighted (T1w) scan, the T2-weighted (T2w) scan and the T1w-gad (post gadolinium injection, a contrast agent). For 25 patients, we collected images and reports across multiple sessions (on average, 9 sessions per subject). For the remaining 139 patients, we only retrieved images and reports from 1 random session. This latter sampling strategy was adopted to increase the chance of having cases of tumor progression and tumor response, since multiple sessions of the same subject mostly showed tumor stability and thus led to a very imbalanced data set. Overall, we ended up with a dataset of 361 radiology reports to use for the NLP pipeline. Every report was written (dictated) during routine clinical practice by a junior radiologist after exploring all sequences of interest. Then, a senior radiologist reviewed each case amending the final report when necessary. The extracted reports have varying length ranging from 114 to 533 words (average 255, standard deviation 68). The MR acquisition parameters for the cohort are provided in Table 1. The protocol of this study was approved by the regional ethics committee; written informed consent was waived.

Table 1. MR acquisition parameters of scans used for the study population.

# sessions ≡ # reports	Vendor	Scanner	Field strength [T]
174	Siemens Healthcare	Skyra	3.0
73	Philips	Intera	3.0
46	Siemens Healthcare	Prisma	3.0
32	Siemens Healthcare	Symphony	1.5
21	Siemens Healthcare	TrioTim	3.0
10	Siemens Healthcare	Aera	1.5
5	Siemens Healthcare	Verio	3.0

2.2 Report Tagging

In order to build a supervised document classifier, one radiologist (4 years of experience in neuroimaging) tagged the reports with labels of interest. For each report, the annotator was instructed to perform two separate tasks: first, she had to assign 3 classes to the reports; one class that indicated the global conclusion of the report, one class to indicate the evolution of the enhanced part of the lesion (T1w conclusion) and the last one to indicate the evolution of the lesion on T2-weighted sequences (T2w conclusion). For each of these three groups, the annotator could choose between the following labels:

– **Stable**: assigned when the tumor did not change significantly with respect to the previous comparative exam.

- **Progression**: assigned when the tumor worsened with respect to the previous comparative exam. This class included cases where the enhanced part of the tumor increased in size or when the T2 signal anomalies surrounding the tumor increased in extension.
- **Response**: assigned when the tumor responded positively to the treatment (either chemotherapy or radiotherapy).
- **Unknown**: used when the annotator was not able to assign any of the three classes above.

The second task of the annotator was to highlight the most recent comparative date in the reports. Since the reports are not structured, this helped linking the current report being tagged with the most meaningful previous one. For simplicity, in this work we only focused on the global conclusion of the reports, and not on the T1 and T2 conclusions. Also, we removed all cases that were tagged as **unknown** (21 reports) and we merged **progression** and **response** into one unique class which we denote as **unstable**. By doing this, we narrowed the task to a binary classification problem where the model tries to distinguish between **stable** and **unstable** reports. After these modifications, we ended up with 191 **stable** reports and 149 **unstable** reports.

To facilitate the annotation process, we utilized the open-source software Dataturks[1]. This provided a graphic interface to the annotator which allowed her to tag, skip, highlight, and review the reports in a user-friendly way. Moreover, it automatically generated machine-readable labels once the annotation process was over. One exemplary report is illustrated in Fig. 1, together with the corresponding annotations.

2.3 Text Preprocessing and Embedding

Several preprocessing steps were carried out to reduce the vocabulary size. First, we removed all proper nouns such as physicians' and patients' names. This was performed using a pre-trained French Part-Of-Speech tagger from the Spacy library (version 3.0.6) [19]. Second, all the words in the reports were converted to lowercase. This operation is typical when there are no words that indicate a specific meaning when expressed with capital letters. Third, we removed punctuation and the most common French stop words, namely ['de', 'la', 'en', 'et', 'du', 'd', 'le', 'l', 'un', 'une', 'les', 'des', 'ces', 'á', 'au', 'aux']. Among these, we ensured to keep the French negation 'pas' (*not*) since it is very frequent in the reports, and reverses the meaning of the sentence. Fourth, all reports were tokenized using the *wordpunct* class of the Natural Language Toolkit framework (version 3.6.1) [20]. As last step, since all the reports contain the three sections *'indications'*, *'description'* and *'conclusion'*, we removed all content before the *'indication'* section, which is either useless (e.g. department phone number) or sensitive (e.g. patient identifier).

---

[1] OpenSource Data Annotation tool - http://github.com/DataTurks/DataTurks.

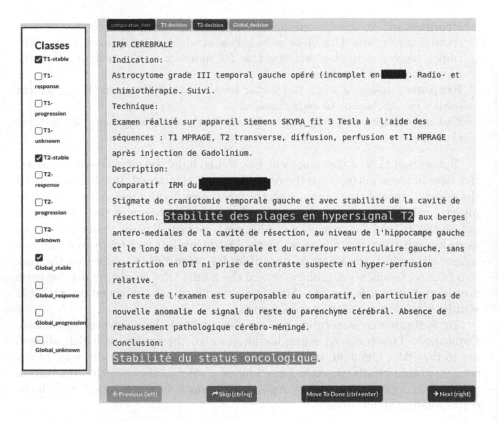

Fig. 1. Dataturks annotation interface. The annotator can select the classes in the left box and highlight the text of interest. Sensitive information has been blacked out for privacy.

A key step in any NLP pipeline is text embedding. This corresponds to the conversion of tokenized text into numerical vectors. Historically, many embedding techniques have been proposed in literature. In this work, we compare two of the most widespread, namely TF-IDF [6] and Doc2Vec [7]. While the former is a standard term-weighting embedding scheme (traditional ML) that preserves the length of the tokenized documents, the latter is a DL-based technique that creates dense vectors which encode word order and context. TF-IDF was performed at the word level with the sklearn package (version 0.24.1) [21], whereas Doc2Vec was performed using the gensim library (version 4.0.1) [22].

2.4   Experiments

All experiments were run in a 5-fold, nested, stratified cross validation (CV). The internal CV was used to tune the hyperparameters of the pipeline with a custom Grid Search algorithm. Instead, the external CV was used to compute results on hold-out test samples. For TF-IDF, two hyperparameters were tuned:

first, the types of retained N-grams were searched in the range [3,5]. Second, the percentage of vocabulary size to use was varied between 100% (all words are used) and 90% (the 10% rarest words are removed). The other parameters were fixed: the minimum document frequency was set to 2 and the maximum document frequency was set to 0.9 (indicating 90% of the documents). For Doc2Vec, the algorithm type (PV-DM or PV-DBOW) and the vector dimensionality [10] were tuned with the validation set. The context window was set to 5 words. Five "noise" negative words were drawn. Words with a total frequency lower than 2 were ignored. The model was trained for 100 epochs. Since stop words are not necessarily useless for Doc2Vec, we also tried to run the Doc2Vec pipeline preserving them.

The stratification of the CV guaranteed that both training and test sets contained approximately the same percentage of reports indicating tumor **stability** and tumor **instability**. To avoid overoptimistic predictions, we also ensured that the reports from multiple sessions of the same subject were not present some in the train set and some in the test set. Furthermore, to reduce the bias introduced by the random choice of patients at each CV split, the whole nested CV was repeated 10 times, each time performing the splitting anew, and results were averaged.

For all experiments, we adopted the Random Forest algorithm [23] to classify the embedded documents, using once again the sklearn package. As hyperparameters, we set a fixed number of 501 trees and we tuned the maximum retained features in the internal CV, choosing between 0.8 (only 80% of the features are used) and 1.0 (all features are used).

To compare the two pipelines (Doc2Vec vs. TF-IDF embedding), we computed all standard classification metrics, namely accuracy, sensitivity, specificity, positive predictive value, negative predictive value and F1-score. Moreover, we also plotted the Receiver Operating Characteristic (ROC) and Precision-Recall (PR) curves. The reports indicating tumor stability were considered as negative samples, whereas those indicating a change in the tumor were considered as positive samples. The classification metrics and the curves were averaged across the 10 runs. To statistically compare the classification results, a Wilcoxon signed-rank test was performed [24]. For simplicity, the test only accounted for the area under the ROC curve (AUC) across the 10 runs. A significance threshold level $\alpha = 0.05$ was set for comparing P values.

The explainability analysis was performed with the LIME toolkit on the TF-IDF pipeline only since it resulted in higher performances (see Table 2). We set the best hyperparameters obtained across the random runs and we ran LIME over all test reports. For each report, the toolkit performs a post-hoc interpretation following a two-step approach: first, it randomly generates neighborhood data in the vicinity of the example being explained; then, it "learns locally weighted linear models on this neighborhood data to explain each of the classes in an interpretable way". The user can choose how many features (words) are shown in the explanation. For this work, we set a maximum of 6 features per document. These weighted features represent the linear model which approximates the behaviour of the random forest classifier in the vicinity of the explained test example.

All the Python 3.6 code developed for this study is available on github[2].

3   Results

3.1   Classification Performances

The nested CV with the Doc2Vec embedding took 50 min per run, while the one with TF-IDF took 2 h. The most frequent hyperparameters chosen in the internal CV for Doc2Vec across the 10 random runs were a vector size of 10 and the PV-DV version of the algorithm. Instead, for TF-IDF, n-grams in the range (1, 3) were the most frequent, and the optimal percentage of vocabulary size was 90%. For the Random Forest classifier, the configuration with 80% of the features was most frequent.

We report in Table 2 the classification results of the two pipelines (TF-IDF vs. Doc2Vec), averaged over the 10 runs. Similarly, Figs. 2 and 3 illustrate the average ROC and PR curves. When comparing the two pipelines across the 10 random runs with the Wilcoxon signed-rank test, the AUC values of TF-IDF were significantly higher than those of Doc2Vec ($P = 0.009$). Last, classification results of the Doc2Vec pipeline run preserving the stop words led to higher results (average AUC $= .85\pm .03$). However, these were still significantly lower than the TF-IDF pipeline.

Table 2. Classification results across the 10 random runs. Values are presented as mean ± standard deviation. Bold values indicate the highest performances. Acc = accuracy; Sens = sensitivity; Spec = specificity; PPV = positive predictive value; NPV = negative predictive value; F1 = F1-score; AUC = area under the ROC curve; AUPR = area under the PR curve.

Embedding	Acc %	Sens %	Spec %	PPV %	NPV %	F1 %	AUC	AUPR
TF-IDF	**88±1**	91±1	**75±0**	**95±0**	**60±2**	**93±0**	**.89±.01**	**.97±.00**
Doc2Vec	86±2	**94±3**	38±10	89±1	57±10	92±1	.83±.05	.96±.01

3.2   Error Analysis and Model Interpretation

To further understand the decisions taken by the random forest algorithm, we applied the LIME post-hoc interpretability toolkit. Specifically, we investigated both the explanations created for the correctly classified reports and for the false positive and false negative reports. Table 3 shows the most frequent words used by the linear classifier created by LIME. We notice that most of the words intuitively make sense for the True Positive and True Negative samples. For instance, words like 'progression', 'augmentation' and 'diminution' that all indicate some

---

[2] https://github.com/connectomicslab/Glioma_NLP.

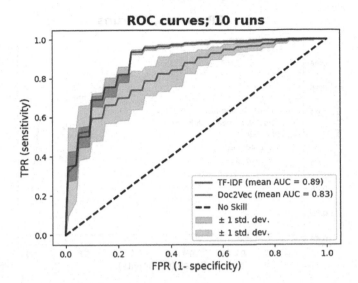

Fig. 2. Receiver operating characteristic (ROC) curves of the two pipelines (TF-IDF vs. Doc2Vec) averaged across the 10 runs.

sort of change are recurrent for predicting TP samples and outweigh the corresponding words indicating tumor stability such as '*sans*' (*without*) or '*récidive*' (*recurrence*). A similar trend can be observed for TN samples where words like '*pas*' (*not*), '*stabilité*' (*stability*) and '*inchangé*' (*unchanged*) outweigh words indicating instability like '*apparition*' (*appearance*). However, the error analysis also highlighted some recurrent mistakes, such as the importance given to the words '*t2*' and '*axial*' in the FN samples or '*2007*' in the FP which ultimately deteriorate the predictions. To have a qualitative idea of the output of the LIME toolkit, we show in Figs. 4 and 5 one TP and one FN example, respectively.

4   Discussion

In this work, we explored the potential of NLP for the task of diagnostic surveillance in patients with high-grade gliomas. As pointed out in [5], and subsequently shown in other works [25,26], traditional ML embedding techniques can lead to comparable results with respect to DL techniques when properly tuned. Moreover, they are still frequent when the dataset size is limited such as in medical imaging applications. Our work confirms this trend since, given the same classifier, the TF-IDF pipeline statistically outperformed the Doc2Vec one. The explainability analysis highlighted interesting trends. For the correctly classified reports, it confirmed that the model is focusing on relevant words.

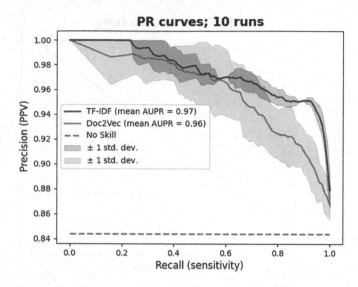

Fig. 3. Precision-Recall (PR) curves of the two pipelines (TF-IDF vs. Doc2Vec) averaged across the 10 runs.

When investigating reports indicating instability, most of the recurrent terms indeed indicate a status of change such as '*diminution*', '*progression*' or '*plus*' (*more*). Similarly, the recurrent words for the reports indicating tumor stability reflect a status of no-change (e.g. '*pas*' (French negation)). Regarding the errors of the model, the LIME toolkit also uncovered some misleading words which obfuscate the final predictions. For instance, the words '*appareil*' (*MR scanner*), '*t2*', '*axial*' or '*transverse*' are recurrent in the explanations of FP and FN even though they are related to the acquisition process rather the status of the tumor.

The following limitations must be acknowledged. First, the annotations were performed by one single radiologist which is not the optimal scenario for ambiguous NLP tasks. Second, the dataset size is still limited with respect to similar studies [11,12,14].

In future works we are planning to enlarge the dataset and add a second annotator to assess inter-rate variability (and ideally intra-rater variability as well). Also, we would like to investigate which part of the report is the most important with respect to the final prediction. For instance, we would like to evaluate classification performances when using only *description* and *conclusion* of the reports, or even just the *conclusion*. In addition, we are planning to

Table 3. Six most frequent features (words) used by the linear model generated by LIME to predict the class of the reports, sorted in descending order. For instance, the word *'progression'* is the most frequent word indicating instability used by the linear classifier for the TP test documents, whereas *'pas'* (French negation) is the most frequent word indicating stability used for the TN test documents. TP = True Positive (i.e. reports indicating tumor instability and predicted as such); TN = True Negative; FP = False Positive; FN = False Negative.

	Stable	Unstable		Stable	Unstable
TP	sans	progression	**FP**	sans	progression
	récidive	augmentation		depuis	axial
	pas	oedème		appareil	diminution
	signe	plus		réalisé	plus
	anomalie	diminution		inchangé	oedème
	ou	spectroscopie		pondération	2007
TN	pas	apparition	**FN**	récidive	apparition
	récidive	augmentation		pas	spectroscopie
	sans	axial		sans	augmentation
	stabilité	spectroscopie		transverse	diminution
	transverse	plus		t2	axial
	inchangé	postérieure		stabilité	dans

experiment different classifiers, or French pre-trained embedding models developed with larger corpora. Next, we will investigate what happens when shifting from a binary problem (*stable* vs. *unstable*) to a more granular task. Last, we will leverage the information extracted by the explainability toolkit to further preprocess the documents, for instance removing terms related to the acquisition protocol.

In conclusion, this work presented an NLP pipeline for the classification of radiology reports for patients with high-grade gliomas. The top-performing model (TF-IDF + Random Forest) attained satisfactory performances (AUC = .89) that lays a good foundation for generating weak labels, and the post-hoc explainability toolkit that we used holds promise for the development of a robust and transparent ML analysis.

Text with highlighted words

glioblastome fronto pariétal gauche avec status post traitement par radiothérapie bilan 5 mois post arrêt traitement description examen réalisé sur appareil 3 aide séquences t1 sagittales t2 axiales perfusion gadolinium t1 sagittales axiales ainsi que spectroscopie comparatif irm████████ on retrouve status post craniotomie fronto pariétale gauche avec cavité exérèse hypersignal t2 bordée hémosidérine sans modification pas modification non plus hypersignal t2 prédominant niveau corona radiata centre semi ovale gauche ainsi qu rétro atrial bilatéral partie lié radiothérapie également sans modification persistance rehaussement prédominant dans portion inférieure interne cavité résection très discrète diminution par rapport comparatif mois ████ séries perfusions qualité sub optimales ne permettant pas interprétation séries spectroscopies montrent discrète augmentation choline associée baisse retrouve quelques hyper intensités signal substance blanche bi hémisphériques nature aspécifique dégénérescence xantho granulomateuse plexus choroïdes citerne optochiasmatique niveau loge sellaire muqueux cadre sinus maxillaire droit sphénoïde droit conclusions discrète diminution prises contraste localisées face inférieure interne cavité exérèse glioblastome fronto pariétal gauche pas autre changement significatif ████████████████████████

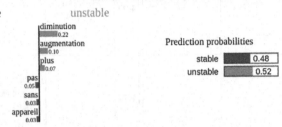

Fig. 4. LIME toolkit explanations for a TP report. Words such as '*diminution*' and '*augmentation*' correctly outweigh words indicating stability like '*pas*' (French negation) or '*sans*' (*without*). Sensitive information has been blacked out for privacy.

Text with highlighted words

suivi évolution glioblastome réséqué████████traité par radio chimiothérapie adjuvante technique examen réalisé sur appareil 3 t avec séquences t1 sagittale t2 transverse dti injection gadolinium suivie perfusion séquences t1 sagittale transverse spectroscopie description examen comparatif████████status post thérapeutique avec résection tumorale frontale droite sans modification taille aspect cavité résection t2 frontal droit extension inchangée pas modification également extension hypersignal frontal controlatéral série injectée démontre apparition nouvelle prise contraste nodulaire frontale antérieure droite arrière partie antéro interne cavité résection tumorale mesurant 10x4 mm allure suspecte surveiller par ailleurs persistance dilatation ventriculaire modérée ainsi que déformation corne frontale droite secondaire status postopératoire sans évolution persistance séquelle hémorragique arrière corne postérieure ventricule latéral droit inchangée conclusions apparition nouvelle prise contraste nodulaire arrière partie antéro interne cavité résection frontale droite suspecte surveiller associé ████████████

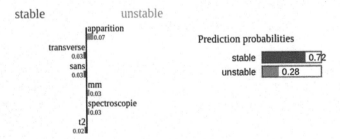

Fig. 5. LIME toolkit explanations for a FN report. Words such as '*sans*' and '*transverse*' incorrectly outweigh the key word indicating instability in this report which is '*apparition*' (*appearance*). Sensitive information has been blacked out for privacy.

References

1. Shen, D., Wu, G., Suk, H.-I.: Deep learning in medical image analysis. Annu. Rev. Biomed. Eng. **19**, 221–248 (2017)
2. Lakhani, P., et al.: Machine learning in radiology: applications beyond image interpretation. J. Am. Coll. Radiol. **15**(2), 350–359 (2018)
3. Schwartz, L.H., et al.: Improving communication of diagnostic radiology findings through structured reporting. Radiology **260**(1), 174–181 (2011)
4. Chowdhury, G.G.: Natural language processing. Annu. Rev. Inf. Sci. Technol. **37**(1), 51–89 (2003)
5. Casey, A., et al.: A Systematic Review of Natural Language Processing Applied to Radiology Reports. arXiv preprint arXiv:2102.09553 (2021)
6. Sammut, C., Webb, G.I. (eds.): Encyclopedia of Machine Learning. Springer, Boston (2011). https://doi.org/10.1007/978-0-387-30164-8
7. Le, Q., Mikolov, T.: Distributed representations of sentences and documents. In: International Conference on Machine Learning. PMLR (2014)
8. Lipton, Z.C.: The mythos of model interpretability: in machine learning, the concept of interpretability is both important and slippery. Queue **16**(3), 31–57 (2018)
9. Doshi-Velez, F., Kim, B.: Towards a rigorous science of interpretable machine learning. arXiv preprint arXiv:1702.08608 (2017)
10. Ribeiro, M.T., Singh, S., Guestrin, C.: "Why should I trust you?" Explaining the predictions of any classifier. In: Proceedings of the 22nd ACM SIGKDD International Conference on Knowledge Discovery and Data Mining (2016)
11. Chen, P.-H., et al.: Integrating natural language processing and machine learning algorithms to categorize oncologic response in radiology reports. J. Digit. Imaging **31**(2), 178–184 (2018)
12. Kehl, K.L., et al.: Assessment of deep natural language processing in ascertaining oncologic outcomes from radiology reports. JAMA Oncol. **5**(10), 1421–1429 (2019)
13. Hassanpour, S., Bay, G., Langlotz, C.P.: Characterization of change and significance for clinical findings in radiology reports through natural language processing. J. Digit. Imaging **30**(3), 314–322 (2017)
14. Bozkurt, S., et al.: Automated detection of measurements and their descriptors in radiology reports using a hybrid natural language processing algorithm. J. Digit. Imaging **32**(4), 544–553 (2019)
15. Oliveira, C.R., et al.: Natural language processing for surveillance of cervical and anal cancer and precancer: algorithm development and split-validation study. JMIR Med. Inform. **8**(11), e20826 (2020)
16. Pham, A.-D., et al.: Natural language processing of radiology reports for the detection of thromboembolic diseases and clinically relevant incidental findings. BMC Bioinform. **15**(1), 1–10 (2014)
17. Carletta, J.: Assessing agreement on classification tasks: the kappa statistic. arXiv preprint arXiv:cmp-lg/9602004 (1996)
18. Gwet, K.L.: Handbook of Inter-Rater Reliability: The Definitive Guide to Measuring the Extent of Agreement Among Raters. Advanced Analytics, LLC (2014)
19. Honnibal, M., Montani, I., et al.: spaCy: industrial-strength natural language processing in Python. Zenodo (2020). https://doi.org/10.5281/zenodo.1212303
20. Bird, S., Klein, E., Loper, E.: Natural Language Processing with Python: Analyzing Text with the Natural Language Toolkit. O'Reilly Media, Inc., Sebastopol (2009)
21. Pedregosa, F., et al.: Scikit-learn: machine learning in Python. J. Mach. Learn. Res. **12**, 2825–2830 (2011)

436   T. Di Noto et al.

22. Rehurek, R., Sojka, P.: Gensim-python framework for vector space modelling. NLP Centre, Faculty of Informatics, Masaryk University, Brno, Czech Republic 3.2 (2011)
23. Breiman, L.: Random forests. Mach. Learn. **45**(1), 5–32 (2001)
24. Wilcoxon, F.: Individual comparisons by ranking methods. In: Kotz, S., Johnson, N.L. (eds.) Breakthroughs in Statistics. Springer Series in Statistics (Perspectives in Statistics), pp. 196–202. Springer, New York (1992). https://doi.org/10.1007/978-1-4612-4380-9_16
25. Dessi, D., et al.: TF-IDF vs word embeddings for morbidity identification in clinical notes: an initial study. arXiv preprint arXiv:2105.09632 (2021)
26. Marcińczuk, M., et al.: Text document clustering: wordnet vs. TF-IDF vs. word embeddings. In: Proceedings of the 11th Global Wordnet Conference (2021)

All You Need is Color: Image Based Spatial Gene Expression Prediction Using Neural Stain Learning

Muhammad Dawood[1] (iD), Kim Branson[2], Nasir M. Rajpoot[1] (iD),
and Fayyaz ul Amir Afsar Minhas[1](✉) (iD)

[1] Department of Computer Science, University of Warwick, Coventry, UK
{Muhammad.Dawood,N.M.Rajpoot,Fayyaz.Minhas}@warwick.ac.uk
[2] GlaxoSmithKline, Artificial Intelligence and Machine Learning, Palo Alto, California, USA
kim.m.branson@gsk.com

Abstract. *"Is it possible to predict expression levels of different genes at a given spatial location in the routine histology image of a tumor section by modeling its stain absorption characteristics?"* In this work, we propose a "stain-aware" machine learning approach for prediction of spatial transcriptomic gene expression profiles using digital pathology image of a routine Hematoxylin & Eosin (H&E) histology section. Unlike recent deep learning methods which are used for gene expression prediction, our proposed approach termed Neural Stain Learning (NSL) explicitly models the association of stain absorption characteristics of the tissue with gene expression patterns in spatial transcriptomics by learning a problem-specific stain deconvolution matrix in an end-to-end manner. The proposed method with only 11 trainable weight parameters outperforms both classical regression models with cellular composition and morphological features as well as deep learning methods. We have found that the gene expression predictions from the proposed approach show higher correlations with true expression values obtained through sequencing for a larger set of genes in comparison to other approaches.

Keywords: Gene expression prediction · Spatial transcriptomics · Stain deconvolution · Computational pathology

1 Introduction

Gene expression quantification plays a key role in understanding cancer genetics and identifying potential targets for novel therapeutics. For example, cancer driver mutations can be identified by comparative analysis of differential gene expression levels across normal and cancerous tissues, which can then be used for targeted therapy [1, 4]. To determine gene expression in a tissue sample, transcriptomic sequencing technologies such as bulk RNA-Seq [5] and single-cell RNA-sequencing (scRNA-seq) [6, 7] are used. Bulk RNA-Seq gives expression of different genes across different cell types, whereas single-cell RNA-Seq estimates gene expression at cellular level. However, both these

© Springer Nature Switzerland AG 2021
M. Kamp et al. (Eds.): ECML PKDD 2021 Workshops, CCIS 1525, pp. 437–450, 2021.
https://doi.org/10.1007/978-3-030-93733-1_32

technologies fail to capture the spatial variations in gene expression profile across a tissue sample, which is crucial when studying tumor heterogeneity [8].

To tackle this dilemma, one potential solution is Spatial Transcriptomics (ST). It is a relatively new technology that measures spatially resolved messenger RNA (mRNA) profile in a tissue section using unique DNA barcodes [9]. These unique DNA barcodes are used to map the expression of thousands of genes at each spot in a tissue slide. For each tissue section, ST methods generate a local spot-level gene expression profile together with a whole slide image (WSI) for the Hematoxylin & Eosin (H&E) stained tissue section. This information can be very beneficial in terms of understanding gene expression variations across different regions in a given tumor sample and has been used to gain valuable insights into the role of various different kinds of cells in the tumor microenvironment (TME) and their impact on response to therapy [10, 11].

An interesting question in this regard is whether, and to what degree, it is possible to predict gene expression profiles from the WSI of H&E stained tumor section alone using the ST data as ground-truth. This association of visual characteristics of the tissue with gene expression profiles can provide new insights into the local mapping of various different kind of cells in the TME and can lead to possible discovery of visual cues associated with expression profiles of different genes [12]. Deep learning has been used to predict genetic mutations [13, 16], gene and RNA-Seq expression profile [17], Microsatellite Instability (MSI) [18, 19], and Tumor Mutation Burden (TMB) [20, 21] from WSIs of H&E sections. Since these methods have been developed using bulk RNA-Seq data, where the target gene expression profile is available at the tissue level and provides a coarse-grained phenotype only, these methods may not be able to uncover exact visual patterns that correlate with a specific gene expression profile. In contrast, the target label in the ST data is available at spot level which provides a more fine-grained local mapping of transcriptomic variation across the tumor tissue. Recently a deep learning method was proposed for predicting spatially resolved gene expression profile from spatial transcriptomic imaging data [22].

A vast majority of existing methods for computational pathology in general, and for image based prediction of local gene expression profiles in particular, use convolutional neural networks such as DenseNet [23], ResNet [24], often pretrained on natural images and finetuned on computational pathology tasks. Most of them fail to explicitly model tissue staining in their design, which is a fundamental aspect of computational pathology images. Pathology images are obtained by staining a given sample with a dye that absorbs incident light depending upon dye concentration and its binding characteristics for different components (e.g., proteins, DNA, etc.) in the sample. Routine stains such as Hematoxylin, Eosin and special stains for antibody-optimized immuno-histochemical (IHC) markers are often used for pathology diagnosis and/or biomarker analysis. Consequently, the image acquisition process in routine histopathology and ST is predominantly based on light absorption. This contrasts with natural images obtained through standard digital cameras, such as those in the widely used ImageNet database, which are unstained and operate on a different lighting and camera model involving reflected, absorbed, and radiated light. Despite this fundamental difference, machine learning models in computational pathology and Spatial Transcriptomics Imaging are not explicitly "stain-aware". Stain normalization and separation [25–29] are used as preprocessing steps in computational pathology algorithms to control variations resulting from differences in slide preparation protocols and digital slide scanning with scanners from different vendors. In recent years, stain and color-based augmentation of images in deep learning models are also used to overcome such variations [30, 31].

In this work, we investigate the contribution of stain information contained in WSIs of routine H&E stained tissue sections with associated ST data for image based local gene expression prediction directly without using computationally intensive deep learning approaches. We propose a novel neural stain deconvolution layer that can model stain deconvolution in an end-to-end manner. We show that the proposed neural stain learning (NSL) can model the prediction of local gene expression and lead to statistically significant correlation scores between true and predicted expression levels for a larger number of genes in comparison to existing methods using deep convolutional networks or cellular composition or cellular morphology based regression. The simplicity of our NSL method is underscored by the fact that the number of trainable weight parameters in the proposed scheme is significantly smaller (11 per gene), as compared to millions of learnable parameters in the case of a convolutional network.

2   Materials and Methods

The workflow of the proposed approach for image based local gene expression prediction from WSI of routine H&E tumor section with associated ST data is shown in Fig. 1. We take an image patch corresponding to an ST spot as input and generate gene expression prediction from visual information contained in the image patch. The model is trained using WSIs and associated local gene expression data from ST experiments. Below we provide details about the dataset and pre-processing, problem modeling and model training and evaluation.

2.1   Dataset and Preprocessing

We used a publicly available dataset [32], consisting of 36 tissue histology slides acquired from eight Human Epidermal growth factor Receptor 2 (HER2) positive breast cancer patients. WSIs in this dataset were obtained by sectioning frozen tissue sample at $16 \, \mu m$, after staining with H&E and scanning at $20 \times$ objective. Each WSI contains multiple spots arranged in a grid like pattern for measurement of spatial gene expression profiles of 11,880 genes. On average, there are 378 spots per slide with a total of $13,620$ spots in the dataset. Gene expression data was normalized using regularized negative binomial regression method. From each WSI, patches of size 256×256 pixels (corresponding to a tissue area of $170 \times 170 \, \mu m^2$) were taken from the center of each spot, making the tissue region captured by the cropped image slightly larger than the actual spot size ($100 \times 100 \, \mu m^2$). Genes at each spot were filtered based on their median expression level and the top 250 genes with significant expression across all spots were analyzed. As the gene expression data distribution was highly skewed (some values were too high and some of them were zero), we transformed the gene expression data using a logarithmic transformation after addition of a pseudo-count value.

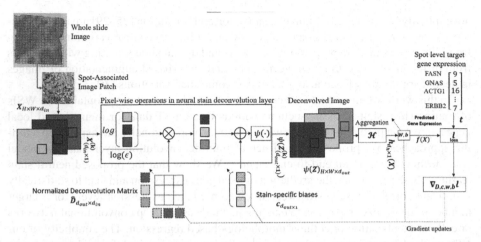

Fig. 1. Workflow of the proposed approach for gene expression prediction task. From each WSI, image patches corresponding to all ST spots are extracted using spatial coordinate data, and the spot level gene expression profile was used as a target label for learning problem-specific stain matrix. Deconvolved pixels values for the image patch are then aggregated to get a single patch-level feature for the gene expression prediction task.

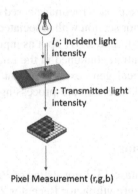

Fig. 2. Simplified diagram of whole slide image scanning of a stained histological sample.

2.2 Prediction of Spatial Gene Expression Using Neural Stain Learning

In order to model the problem of predicting gene expression levels of a number of genes at a given spot from the corresponding RGB image as a learning problem, consider a training dataset $\mathcal{B} = \{(\mathbf{X_i}, \mathbf{t_i}) | i = 1 \ldots N\}$ comprising of N spots and their associated gene expression profiles. We denote the image patch corresponding to a spot by $\mathbf{X_i}$ and its associated target vector of normalized gene expression scores for a number G of genes by $\mathbf{t_i} \in \mathfrak{R}^G$. The objective of the learning problem is to estimate learnable parameters θ of a predictor $y_i = f(X_i; \theta)$ such that the output of the function f matches target gene expression levels for test images. Several recent methods for image based local gene expression prediction tend to obtain the prediction function using deep neural network models. In this work, we modelled this problem as a stain estimation problem based on the hypothesis that the gene expression level of a gene at a spot affects the degree of staining/dye absorption in the tissue leading to changes in pixel values in the corresponding image. Therefore, if we can estimate the association between stain variations in an image and the corresponding gene expression patterns of a gene using a training dataset, it would then be possible to infer gene expression levels of a gene for a test image. The underlying concept for this approach is shown in Fig. 2. The observed RGB intensity value at a pixel in the scanned image of a tissue sample at a given spot is dependent upon light absorption characteristics of the dye used to stain the tissue sample, the amount of stain or dye absorbed by the tissue sample as well as the intensity of incident light [25]. Based on the Beer-Lambert law, the vector of stain intensities z at a given pixel can be estimated from the corresponding RGB pixel values x by the relation $z = -D\log(x)$ where D is a stain deconvolution matrix which determines how different stains in the given image correspond to color pixel intensities [26]. The deconvolution matrix corresponding to standard stains such as Hematoxylin, Eosin and DAB are available in the literature along with a number of methods for estimating the prevalent stain vectors and normalizing stain variations in images [25–29].

In this work, our goal is to estimate the deconvolution matrix in such a way that the resulting stain intensities can explain variations in gene expression patterns. Figure 1 shows the general framework of the proposed approach called Neural Stain Learning (NSL). NSL assumes a randomly initialized stain deconvolution matrix. It takes an input image corresponding to a spot and deconvolves each pixel value in the input image to generate a vector of stain intensities which form the deconvolved image. This stain deconvolved image is then used to regress the gene expression profile corresponding to a given spot. The gradient of the difference between predicted and target gene expression values in the training dataset is used to update the elements of the deconvolution matrix and parameters of the regressor in an end-to-end manner using gradient descent optimization.

More formally, assume that $X^{(k)}$ is a column vector of RGB values corresponding to a single pixel $k = 1 \ldots K$ in input image X with each pixel value in the range $[\epsilon, 1]$ (with small $\epsilon > 0$). Also, assume that $\widehat{D}$ is a row-normalized form of the randomly initialized de-convolution matrix D, i.e., for each row j, $\widehat{D}_j = \frac{D_j}{\|D_j\|}$. The corresponding stain intensities in the stain deconvolved image Z can thus be obtained as: $Z^{(k)} = \widehat{D}\frac{\log(X^k)}{\log(\epsilon)}$. As discussed earlier, the goal of NSL is to obtain an optimal "pseudo"-deconvolution matrix D^* that allows prediction of target values of the training images. We denote the overall prediction function by $f(X; D, \theta)$ which has two sets of learnable parameters – the deconvolution matrix D which is used to produce stain intensities at each pixel in the image and weight parameters θ that are used to predict gene expression levels based on these stain intensities. The overall learning problem can be written as the following empirical risk minimization with the loss functional $l(\cdot, \cdot)$:

$$\mathbf{D}^*, \theta^* = \underset{\mathbf{D}, \theta}{\arg\min} \, L(f; \mathcal{B}) = \sum_i l(f(X_i; D, \theta), t_i)$$

In this work, we have used the simple mean squared error loss function. As a minimal learning example and without loss of generality, we can assume a single downstream neuron which operates on aggregated stain intensities of the input image to predict the expression of a single gene. More specifically, the predictor can be written as follows:

$$f(X; D, \theta = (w, b, c)) = w\mathcal{H}_{k=1...K}\left\{\psi\left(\widehat{D}\frac{\log(X^{(k)})}{\log(\epsilon)} + c\right)\right\} + b$$

where c is an (optional) 3×1 vector of "stain" -wise learnable bias parameters such that c_j is added to the jth channel of $Z^{(k)} = \widehat{D}\frac{\log(X^k)}{\log(\epsilon)}$. $\psi(\cdot)$ is an activation function (bipolar sigmoid) that operates on the deconvolved stain output $Z^{(k)}$ and $\mathcal{H}_{k=1...K}$ is an operator that aggregates the transformed stain values via simple averaging:

$$\mathcal{H}_{k=1...K}\left\{\psi\left(Z^{(k)}\right)\right\} = \frac{1}{K}\sum_{k=1}^{K} 1_3^T \psi\left(Z^{(k)}\right).$$

The output of the aggregation is then fed into a single neuron with weights w and bias b which generates a prediction corresponding to a single gene. The proposed architecture can be implemented with any automatic differentiation package such as PyTorch or TensorFlow by computing the gradient $\nabla L(f; \mathcal{B})$ of the loss function with respect to all learnable parameters in the above model. At each optimization step, the deconvolution matrix is row-normalized to yield $\widehat{D}$. It is important to note that $\psi\left(\widehat{D}\frac{\log(X^{(k)})}{\log(\epsilon)} + c\right)$ in the proposed model can be thought of as a general neural stain deconvolution layer with a single neuron with 3 inputs and 3 outputs whose weights constitute the normalized stain deconvolution matrix $\widehat{D}$. These weights are shared across the pixels of all training images. This results in a very small number of learnable weight parameters (11 per gene – 6 independent weights in the row-normalized 3×3 matrix $\widehat{D}$, 3 optional stain-wise biases and a weight and bias parameter for the neuron used for generating the gene level output) for the overall prediction model which is much smaller than the millions of weights used in classical deep learning architectures. Furthermore, the proposed architecture is not specific to any particular type of learning problem and can be applied to other learning problems in absorption microscopy.

2.3   Model Training and Evaluation

The generalization performance of the proposed model was evaluated using leave one patient out cross-validation, i.e., data for one patient was held out for testing and training was performed on the remaining patients. For the test patient, we calculated the Pearson correlation coefficient of the predicted and true/target gene expression (from the corresponding ST spot) with its associated p-value. In order to analyze the predictive accuracy of the proposed method, we used the median correlation score of a gene across all patients as a performance metric. The p-values associated with the correlation score of a given gene across multiple cross-validation runs were combined by calculating the median p-value (p_{50}) and using $2p_{50}$ as a conservative estimate for significance [33]. In each cross-validation run, the model was trained for 250 epochs using the adaptive momentum based optimizer [34] with a learning rate of 0.001 and batch size of 128.

2.4 Comparison with Other Approaches

We compared the performance of the proposed model with methods that use deep learning or cellular features for gene expression prediction. In this section, we describe details of experiments for comparative performance evaluation.

Comparison with DenseNet121

To compare our results with deep learning methods, we fine-tuned ImageNet [35] pretrained DenseNet121 [23] on spatial transcriptomic data using adaptive momentum based optimizer [34] with a batch size of 32 and initial learning rate of 0.001. Moreover, to limit model overfitting, the model training was stopped early if performance over validation set did not increase across 5 consecutive epochs [36].

Comparison with Cellular Composition and Morphological Features

In order to understand the association between various types of cells in a given spot and the corresponding gene expression patterns, we used cellular composition (counts of neoplastic, epithelial, connective, inflammatory, and necrotic) and nuclei morphological features for predicting spot level gene expression profile [37]. The nuclei were segmented and classified using a nuclear segmentation and classification model called HoVer-Net [38] pretrained on PanNuke dataset [39, 40]. HoVer-Net cellular boundaries prediction were then used for computing cellular counts, and shape-based (major and minor axis length, and major-to-minor axis length ratio) and color-based (RGB channel-wise mean) morphological features for each nucleus. Patch level features were obtained by computing the mean and standard deviation of nuclei-level features. We trained XGboost [41], Random Forest [42], Multi-Layer Perceptron [43], and Ordinary least squared regressor (OLS) over these features, but OLS outperformed and we used their results for performance comparison.

3   Results and Discussion

3.1 Visual Results

In order to assess the quality of predictions of gene expression levels using the proposed approach, we show the results of spot-level predictions overlaid on top of various test images together with their true gene expression levels for a number of genes in Fig. 3. It can be observed that the predicted expression shows significant correlation with true expression for these images. For each image, the Pearson correlation coefficient for a given gene in shown in the figure. The correlation scores of predicted and true gene expression for both GNAS and ACTG1 is 0.82 whereas for FASN and ERBB2 the correlation coefficient is 0.64. It is important to mention here that the predicted expression is generated using spot level image information only, and the correlation is expected to improve further by averaging the predicted expression across neighboring spots.

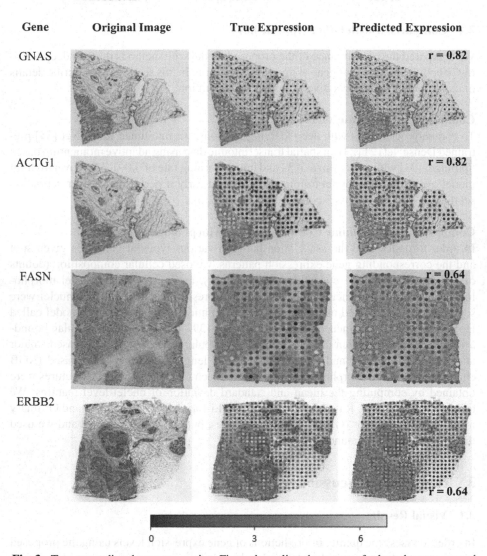

Fig. 3. True vs predicted gene expression. First column lists the names of selected genes; second columns show the original WSI consisting of multiple spots; third column shows a visualization of true spatial expression of a given gene at each spot; finally, the last column shows visualization of the predicted expression for a given gene at each spot. For two genes (GNAS and ACTG1), the Pearson correlation (r) is 0.82, while for two other genes FASN and ERBB2 the correlation is 0.64.

3.2 Quantitative Results

The median Pearson correlation coefficient between true and predicted gene expression levels for all 250 genes used in our analysis across all patients is shown in Fig. 4a together with their combined p-value. From the plot, it can be seen that the proposed NSL model has predicted the expression of 215 (out of 250) genes with a significant p-value. Moreover, the model has predicted 12-genes with a median Pearson correlation greater than 0.5. These genes include FASN, GNAS, ACTG1, ACTB, ERBB2, PSAP, TMSB10, PSMD3, PRDX1, EIF4G2, HSP90AB1, S100A11 and PFN1. Table 1 provides the median correlation coefficients of different genes along with the counts of genes whose expression was predicted with a high correlation score and significant p-values.

3.3 Gene Set Enrichment and Pathway Analysis

In order to understand the role of genes whose expression was predicted with high correlation using the proposed method, we performed gene set and pathway analysis using DAVID [44, 45]. Based on this analysis, we found that out of 215 genes with statistically significant correlation, 54, 56, 43, and 42 genes are respectively involved in cancer, pharmacogenomics, immune, and infections pathways [44, 45]. Among the genes whose expression was predicted with high (>0.5) correlation, ERBB2, FASN, GNAS, ACTB, and PSAP are considered as biomarkers for breast, gastric and prostate cancers.

The most interesting aspect of our pathway analysis results in the context of our proposed approach is that genes whose expression was predicted with high correlation are involved in cell adhesion and tumor formation which is expected to have the most significant association on light absorption and hematoxylin binding in the tissue. This analysis clearly shows that the proposed approach of neural stain learning is able to learn tissue specific absorption characteristics and use them to predict gene expression levels in an effective manner.

3.4 Comparisons with DenseNet-121

Figure 4(b) and Table 1 show the performance of DenseNet-121 in terms of p-value and median correlation score. From the plot, it can be seen that DenseNet-121 was able to predict the expression of only 170 genes with a significant p-value, but for the entire gene set the median Pearson correlation is less than 0.5.

3.5 Comparison with Cellular Composition and Morphological Features

Figure 4(c) and Table 1 show the prediction accuracy of a model that uses cellular composition and morphological features for gene expression prediction. From the plot, it can be seen that the model was able to predict the expression of 209 genes with a significant p-value, however, only 4 genes are predicted with a median correlation coefficient greater than 0.5. This shows that NSL greatly outperforms other compared approaches. Moreover, computing these features is laborious and computationally demanding.

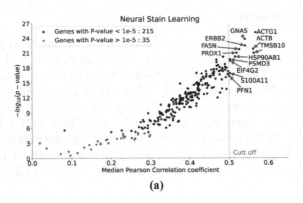

(a)

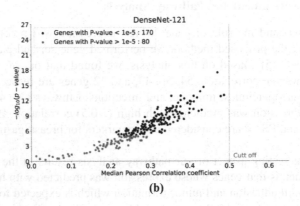

(b)

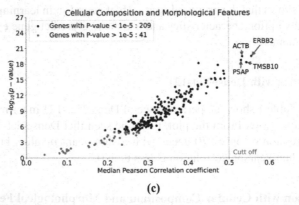

(c)

Fig. 4. Gene Expression vs *p*-value plots for (a) proposed neural stain learning model, (b) DenseNet-121 and (c) Cellular Composition and Morphological Feature based regression. Black dots show genes predicted with significant (*p*-value < 10^{-5}) while red dots show genes predicted with insignificant *p*-value. The vertical red line represents the cut-off threshold (genes predicted with correlation greater than 0.5).

Table 1. Median value of the correlation coefficient between predicted and true expression levels of selected genes and the total number of genes predicted with a median correlation score $r > 0.5$ and the total number of genes predicted with statistically significant correlation scores for different predictors.

Gene/Method	GNAS	FASN	ACTG1	ACTB	ERBB2	PFN1	# Genes with $r > 0.5$	# Genes with $p < 10^{-5}$
DenseNet	0.42	0.40	0.36	0.42	0.47	0.29	0	170
CC + MF	0.48	0.43	0.44	0.53	**0.55**	0.48	4	209
NSL	**0.54**	**0.52**	**0.58**	**0.56**	0.54	**0.50**	12	**215**

4 Conclusions and Future Work

In this work, we investigated the contribution of stain information contained in histopathology images for image base gene expression prediction task in ST data. Handling the deficiency of previously proposed methods of not explicitly handling fundamental aspects of pathology images, i.e., histological staining, we proposed a novel neural stain deconvolution layer, which exploits tissue stain information for the gene expression prediction task. We have shown that for the gene expression prediction task, the proposed neural stain learning method significantly outperformed compared to methods using standard cellular features and deep learning based methods. Although morphometry may be informative for prediction, we have shown that gene expression of certain genes can be predicted using color information alone. Furthermore, the output of the proposed stain deconvolution layer can also be fed as input to a deep network. Apart from this, it can also be used for any other learning problem (classification, ranking, etc.) as long as a loss function can be formulated for it. We hope this study will open new ways of investigating the contribution of stain information to other computational pathology tasks, and assess stain layer performance when coupled with deep neural networks.

Acknowledgments. MD would like to acknowledge the PhD studentship support from Glaxo-SmithKline. FM and NR supported by the PathLAKE digital pathology consortium which is funded from the Data to Early Diagnosis and Precision Medicine strand of the government's Industrial Strategy Challenge Fund, managed and delivered by UK Research and Innovation (UKRI).

References

1. Segal, E., Friedman, N., Kaminski, N., Regev, A., Koller, D.: From signatures to models: understanding cancer using microarrays. Nat. Genet. **37**(Suppl), S38-45 (2005). https://doi.org/10.1038/ng1561
2. Lander, E.S.: Array of hope. Nat. Genet. **21**(1), 3–4 (1999). https://doi.org/10.1038/4427
3. Braman, N., Gordon, J.W.H., Goossens, E.T., Willis, C., Stumpe, M.C., Venkataraman, J.: Deep orthogonal fusion: multimodal prognostic biomarker discovery integrating radiology, pathology, genomic, and clinical data. In: de Bruijne, M., Cattin, P.C., Cotin, S., Padoy, N.,

Speidel, S., Zheng, Y., Essert, C. (eds.) MICCAI 2021. LNCS, vol. 12905, pp. 667–677. Springer, Cham (2021). https://doi.org/10.1007/978-3-030-87240-3_64

4. Bilal, M., et al.: Novel deep learning algorithm predicts the status of molecular pathways and key mutations in colorectal cancer from routine histology images. medRxiv (2021). https://doi.org/10.1101/2021.01.19.21250122

5. Wang, Z., Gerstein, M., Snyder, M.: RNA-Seq: a revolutionary tool for transcriptomics. Nat. Rev. Genet. **10**(1), 57–63 (2009). https://doi.org/10.1038/nrg2484

6. Tang, F., et al.: mRNA-Seq whole-transcriptome analysis of a single cell. Nat. Methods **6**(5), 377–382 (2009). https://doi.org/10.1038/nmeth.1315

7. Picelli, S., et al.: Smart-seq2 for sensitive full-length transcriptome profiling in single cells. Nat. Methods **10**(11), 1096–1098 (2013). https://doi.org/10.1038/nmeth.2639

8. Gerlinger, M., et al.: Intratumor heterogeneity and branched evolution revealed by multiregion sequencing. N. Engl. J. Med. **366**(10), 883–892 (2012). https://doi.org/10.1056/NEJMoa1113205

9. Ståhl, P.L., et al.: Visualization and analysis of gene expression in tissue sections by spatial transcriptomics. Science **353**(6294), 78–82 (2016). https://doi.org/10.1126/science.aaf2403

10. Berglund, E., et al.: Spatial maps of prostate cancer transcriptomes reveal an unexplored landscape of heterogeneity. Nat. Commun. **9**(1), 2419 (2018). https://doi.org/10.1038/s41467-018-04724-5

11. Thrane, K., Eriksson, H., Maaskola, J., Hansson, J., Lundeberg, J.: Spatially resolved transcriptomics enables dissection of genetic heterogeneity in stage iii cutaneous malignant melanoma. Cancer Res. **78**(20), 5970–5979 (2018). https://doi.org/10.1158/0008-5472.CAN-18-0747

12. Echle, A., et al.: Deep learning in cancer pathology: a new generation of clinical biomarkers. Br. J. Cancer **124**(4), 686–696 (2021). https://doi.org/10.1038/s41416-020-01122-x

13. Chen, M., et al.: Classification and mutation prediction based on histopathology H&E images in liver cancer using deep learning. NPJ Precis. Oncol. **4**(1), Art. no. 1, (2020). https://doi.org/10.1038/s41698-020-0120-3

14. Velmahos, C.S., Badgeley, M., Lo, Y.-C.: Using deep learning to identify bladder cancers with FGFR-activating mutations from histology images. Cancer Med. **10**(14), 4805–4813. https://doi.org/10.1002/cam4.4044

15. Wulczyn, E., et al.: Predicting prostate cancer specific-mortality with artificial intelligence-based gleason grading. Commun. Med. **1**(1), 1–8 (2021). https://doi.org/10.1038/s43856-021-00005-3

16. Lu, W., Graham, S., Bilal, M., Rajpoot, N., Minhas, F.: Capturing cellular topology in multi-gigapixel pathology images. In: 2020 IEEE/CVF Conference on Computer Vision and Pattern Recognition Workshops (CVPRW), pp. 1049–1058 (2020). https://doi.org/10.1109/CVPRW50498.2020.00138

17. Schmauch, B., et al.: A deep learning model to predict RNA-Seq expression of tumours from whole slide images. Nat. Commun. **11**, 1 (2020). https://doi.org/10.1038/s41467-020-17678-4

18. Kather, J.N., et al.: Deep learning can predict microsatellite instability directly from histology in gastrointestinal cancer. Nat. Med. **25**(7), 1054–1056 (2019). https://doi.org/10.1038/s41591-019-0462-y

19. Cao, R., et al.: Development and interpretation of a pathomics-based model for the prediction of microsatellite instability in Colorectal cancer. Theranostics **10**(24), 11080–11091 (2020). https://doi.org/10.7150/thno.49864

20. Jain, M.S., Massoud, T.F., Massoud, T.F.: Predicting tumour mutational burden from histopathological images using multiscale deep learning. Nat. Mach. Intell. **2**(6), 356–362 (2020). https://doi.org/10.1038/s42256-020-0190-5

21. Wang, L., Jiao, Y., Qiao, Y., Zeng, N., Yu, R.: A novel approach combined transfer learning and deep learning to predict TMB from histology image. Pattern Recognit. Lett. **135**, 244–248 (2020). https://doi.org/10.1016/j.patrec.2020.04.008

22. He, B., et al.: Integrating spatial gene expression and breast tumour morphology via deep learning. Nat. Biomed. Eng. **4**(8), 827–834 (2020). https://doi.org/10.1038/s41551-020-0578-x

23. Huang, G., Liu, Z., Van Der Maaten, L., Weinberger, K.Q.: Densely connected convolutional networks. In: 2017 IEEE Conference on Computer Vision and Pattern Recognition (CVPR), Honolulu, HI, pp. 2261–2269 (2017). https://doi.org/10.1109/CVPR.2017.243

24. He, K., Zhang, X., Ren, S., Sun, J.: Deep residual learning for image recognition. In: 2016 IEEE Conference on Computer Vision and Pattern Recognition (CVPR), pp. 770–778 (2016). https://doi.org/10.1109/CVPR.2016.90

25. Reinhard, E., Adhikhmin, M., Gooch, B., Shirley, P.: Color transfer between images. IEEE Comput. Graph. Appl. **21**(5), 34–41 (2001). https://doi.org/10.1109/38.946629

26. Ruifrok, A.C., Johnston, D.A.: Quantification of histochemical staining by color deconvolution. Anal. Quant. Cytol. Histol. **23**(4), 291–299 (2001)

27. Macenko, M., et al.: A method for normalizing histology slides for quantitative analysis. In: 2009 IEEE International Symposium on Biomedical Imaging: From Nano to Macro, pp. 1107–1110 (2009). https://doi.org/10.1109/ISBI.2009.5193250

28. Khan, A.M., Rajpoot, N., Treanor, D., Magee, D.: A nonlinear mapping approach to stain normalization in digital histopathology images using image-specific color deconvolution. IEEE Trans. Biomed. Eng. **61**(6), 1729–1738 (2014). https://doi.org/10.1109/TBME.2014.2303294

29. Alsubaie, N., Trahearn, N., Raza, S.E.A., Snead, D., Rajpoot, N.M.: Stain deconvolution using statistical analysis of multi-resolution stain colour representation. PLoS ONE **12**(1), e0169875 (2017). https://doi.org/10.1371/journal.pone.0169875

30. Zanjani, F.G., Zinger, S., Bejnordi, B.E., van der Laak, J.A.W.M., de With, P.H.N.: Stain normalization of histopathology images using generative adversarial networks. In: 2018 IEEE 15th International Symposium on Biomedical Imaging (ISBI 2018), pp. 573–577 (2018). https://doi.org/10.1109/ISBI.2018.8363641

31. Tellez, D., et al.: Quantifying the effects of data augmentation and stain color normalization in convolutional neural networks for computational pathology. Med. Image Anal. **58**, 101544 (2019). https://doi.org/10.1016/j.media.2019.101544

32. Andersson, A., et al.: Spatial deconvolution of her2-positive breast tumors reveals novel intercellular relationships. *bioRxiv*, p. 2020.07.14.200600 (2020). https://doi.org/10.1101/2020.07.14.200600

33. DiCiccio, C.J., DiCiccio, T.J., Romano, J.P.: Exact tests via multiple data splitting. Stat. Probab. Lett. **166**, 108865 (2020). https://doi.org/10.1016/j.spl.2020.108865

34. Kingma, D.P., Ba, J.: Adam: A Method for Stochastic Optimization. CoRR (2014). https://arxiv.org/abs/1412.6980v9. Accessed 4 May 2019

35. Russakovsky, O., et al.: ImageNet large scale visual recognition challenge. Int. J. Comput. Vision **115**(3), 211–252 (2015). https://doi.org/10.1007/s11263-015-0816-y

36. Prechelt, L.: Early stopping — but when? In: Montavon, G., Orr, G.B., Müller, K.-R. (eds.) Neural Networks: Tricks of the Trade. LNCS, vol. 7700, pp. 53–67. Springer, Heidelberg (2012). https://doi.org/10.1007/978-3-642-35289-8_5

37. Cheng, J., et al.: Integrative analysis of histopathological images and genomic data predicts clear cell renal cell carcinoma prognosis. Cancer Res. **77**(21), e91–e100 (2017). https://doi.org/10.1158/0008-5472.CAN-17-0313

38. Graham, S., et al.: Hover-Net: Simultaneous segmentation and classification of nuclei in multi-tissue histology images. Med. Image Anal. **58**, 101563 (2019). https://doi.org/10.1016/j.media.2019.101563

39. Gamper, J., Alemi Koohbanani, N., Benet, K., Khuram, A., Rajpoot, N.: PanNuke: an open pan-cancer histology dataset for nuclei instance segmentation and classification. In: Reyes-Aldasoro, C.C., Janowczyk, A., Veta, M., Bankhead, P., Sirinukunwattana, K. (eds.) ECDP 2019. LNCS, vol. 11435, pp. 11–19. Springer, Cham (2019). https://doi.org/10.1007/978-3-030-23937-4_2

40. Gamper, J., et al.: PanNuke dataset extension, insights and baselines. ArXiv (2020)

41. Chen, T., Guestrin, C.: XGBoost: a scalable tree boosting system. In: Proceedings of the 22nd ACM SIGKDD International Conference on Knowledge Discovery and Data Mining, New York, NY, USA, pp. 785–794 (2016). https://doi.org/10.1145/2939672.2939785

42. Breiman, L.: Random forests. Mach. Learn. 45(1), 5–32 (2001). https://doi.org/10.1023/A:1010933404324

43. Murtagh, F.: Multilayer perceptrons for classification and regression. Neurocomputing 2(5), 183–197 (1991). https://doi.org/10.1016/0925-2312(91)90023-5

44. Huang, D.W., Sherman, B.T., Lempicki, R.A.: Bioinformatics enrichment tools: paths toward the comprehensive functional analysis of large gene lists. Nucleic Acids Res. 37(1), 1–13 (2009). https://doi.org/10.1093/nar/gkn923

45. Huang, D.W., Sherman, B.T., Lempicki, R.A.: Systematic and integrative analysis of large gene lists using DAVID bioinformatics resources. Nat. Protoc. 4(1), 44–57 (2009). https://doi.org/10.1038/nprot.2008.211

Explaining a Random Survival Forest by Extracting Prototype Rules

Klest Dedja[1,2(✉)], Felipe Kenji Nakano[1,2], Konstantinos Pliakos[1,2], and Celine Vens[1,2]

[1] Department of Public Health and Primary Care, KU Leuven, Kortrijk, Belgium
{klest.dedja,felipekenji.nakano,konstantinos.pliakos,
celine.vens}@kuleuven.be
[2] ITEC - imec and KU Leuven, Kortrijk, Belgium

Abstract. Tree-ensemble algorithms and specifically Random Survival Forests (RSF) have emerged as prominently powerful methods for survival data analysis. Tree-ensembles are very accurate, robust, resilient to overfitting, and can naturally handle missing values as well as categorical data. However, since they consist of multiple models, they are not as interpretable as single decision trees. In this work, we propose a method that learns to extract a limited number of representative rulesets from the ensemble providing explanations of the ensemble model's outcome. We propose a local approach, focusing on explaining predictions for a specific sample, and is mainly divided into three parts; tree-filtering, low dimensional representation, and prototype ruleset extraction. Here, we employ RSF as the ensemble model but our approach is generalised to other settings as well. We conducted preliminary experiments on both binary classification using relevant data as well as time-to-event predictions in a survival analysis context. The obtained results demonstrate that our approach performs comparably well to the original Random (Survival) Forest that it explains, while based only on few trees from the whole forest.

Keywords: Explainable AI · Random Forest · Survival analysis

1 Introduction

Nowadays, machine learning (ML) models have many applications and are employed in various domains with magnificent predictive performance. Nevertheless, their predictions are not interpretable by humans, something that causes mistrust and constrains the applicability of ML, especially in sectors where accountability is crucial. Consequently, there is a great interest in interpretable ML models. This is nevertheless not easy, as there is often a trade-off between interpretability and predictive performance. This has led the ML community to also focus on building tools for explaining "black-box" models and their predictions.

Relevant studies include agnostic post-hoc explainers such as SHAP [1] and LIME [2]. Moreover, other approaches are designed explicitly for some models,

© Springer Nature Switzerland AG 2021
M. Kamp et al. (Eds.): ECML PKDD 2021 Workshops, CCIS 1525, pp. 451–458, 2021.
https://doi.org/10.1007/978-3-030-93733-1_33

such as iForest [3] which has been developed to leverage the interpretability of the Random Forest (RF) algorithm. Finally, another example is [4], where the authors studied different tree-distance measures as well as an approach for extracting a few trees from a forest.

Several explainability methods, such as [4] follow a *global* approach. This means that the focus is on explaining the model as a whole rather than providing an explanation to the sample under analysis. Other tools like [1] and [2] follow a *local* approach, where the explanation is instance-based. In local approaches the focus is on finding the reasons driving the particular prediction, and in analysing the behaviour of the model on similar instances.

Different from other methods which most often deal with binary classification, our work also focuses on time-to-event predictions. These predictions differ from the standard classification or regression tasks since the information about the (time-to) outcome is not always present: some observations are *censored*, which means that only a lower or upper bound of the true time is available (right or left censoring, respectively). To properly handle such observations, a *survival analysis* approach is mandatory, and ML algorithms are adapted to solve this different task. When it comes to the Random Forest (RF) algorithm, a survival counterpart called Random Survival Forest (RSF) [5] has been proposed.

In this work, we propose a local explainability approach for tree-ensemble models and specifically RSF, where just a few decision rules or trees are mined and shown to the end user as an explanation. The goal of our work is to propose a model that locally approximates the performance of a tree-ensemble model while providing an explanation of the prediction through a limited set of rules. Our method consists of three main parts. First, a subset of trees is selected based on how close are their predictions to the ones of the original forest. Next, we build a low-dimensional representation of trees mining the tree structure. Last, we perform clustering on this representation to extract only a few prototype rulesets. The interpretation of a model gets compromised when this model consists of hundreds of rules, however, it is relatively easy to explain a prediction if this is based only on a few rules instead. To the best of our knowledge, this is the first time that such a method is proposed in the context of survival data analysis.

2   Method

Let $\mathcal{L}$ be a typical random survival forest that is built on a training set. Our method first extracts λ trees $\mathcal{L}_i \in \mathcal{L}$ that generate the most similar predictions to the whole ensemble model $\mathcal{L}$. More specifically, given a sample x and its ensemble prediction $\hat{y}$, we select the λ trees whose predictions are closest in value to $\hat{y}$. Next, we represent each of the selected $\mathcal{L}_i$ as a vector based on the tree structure. We propose two approaches to generate such vector representations:

- A *path-based* vector representation where the sample of interest x traverses the tree and the input variable used to perform each split is recorded. When the sample reaches a leaf, the process stops and the output vector $[f_1, f_2, \ldots, f_d]$

consists of the number of times that each feature $x_1, x_2, \ldots, x_d$ is selected to perform a split along the path. The path-based representation of the tree is therefore:

$$\mathcal{L}_i(x) \rightarrow v_i = [f_1, f_2, \ldots, f_d], \tag{1}$$

introduced in [4].

- A full *tree-based* vectorisation: here we record the splitting variables used in *every* internal split of the tree; assuming the input features are again $x_1, x_2, \ldots x_d$, we obtain the number of splitting occurrences $g_1, g_2, \ldots g_d$, and the tree representation becomes:

$$\mathcal{L}_i(x) \rightarrow w_i = [g_1, g_2, \ldots, g_d] \tag{2}$$

These procedures can be applied to both a RSF as well as a plain RF.

Next, we transfer this representation to a low-dimensional space using for example PCA or Multidimensional Scaling (MDS). The latter comes with the caveat that a tree or rule distance must be defined first. This way we remove the noise from the representation, improving computational efficiency, and enabling a better visualisation of the clustering result. We use MDS for our experiments and we introduce the chosen tree distance in the next paragraph.

Given two vector representations w_j and w_k of the trees, we use $1 - J_{\mathcal{W}}(w_j, w_k)$ as a distance matrix, where $J_{\mathcal{W}}$ stands for the Jaccard similarity index. MDS is performed on the distance matrix and a low dimensional representation of the trees is obtained. Similarly for the rule-based approach, the distance matrix between rule sets can be build to obtain a low dimensional representation of the decision paths instead. Hereafter, rules and trees vectors will be treated in the same way, and any step referring to a tree vector can also be applied to a rule path vector.

As a next step, we perform clustering on the low-dimensional tree representation using a standard clustering method, such as K-Means. This way the trees are grouped into $k \in \{1, \ldots K\}$ clusters and for each cluster k we define the most similar trees to the cluster centre as representatives for explaining the outcome of the model. We call these trees *final candidates*, and we indicate them as $\bar{\mathcal{L}}_k$; these will be the trees presented to the end-user for explainability purposes. Given the K clusters, the corresponding final candidates $(\bar{\mathcal{L}}_k)$ and an instance x, the final surrogate model prediction $\bar{y}$ is built as follows:

$$\bar{y} = \sum_{k=1}^{K} \beta_k \bar{\mathcal{L}}_k(x) \tag{3}$$

where β_k represents the weight given to the cluster k. We define β_k as the proportion of trees that are part of the cluster. It follows that $\sum \beta_k = 1$, and that the surrogate model is a weighted average of the chosen trees.

Finally, we calculate the *faithfulness* of the surrogate model to the original ensemble, relative to the sample we seek an explanation for. Given an instance x, its original prediction $\hat{y}$ and the new surrogate prediction $\bar{y}$ we define and compute faithfulness $\mathcal{F}(x)$ as $\mathcal{F}(x) = 1 - (\hat{y} - \bar{y})^2$. These values are then used to tune the optimal number of clusters K and other model hyper-parameters such as number of output components d of the PCA or MDS and the number of trees λ to keep in the pre-selection phase. More specifically, the hyper-parameter combination that maximises $\mathcal{F}$ is chosen; alternatively, the parameter values can be determined by the user. In this case, end-users have the possibility to choose, for example, their own values for the number of clusters K, and are allowed to explore the trade-off between having a more interpretable model against one obtaining more explanations for a given example.

3   Experiments

We tested our model across 24 publicly available datasets for binary classification and 12 datasets with survival data. We compared the predictive performance of our surrogate model (tree-based vectorisation: see Eq. 2) against the original ensemble learner and a couple of competing approaches. A detailed report on the performances and additional information on the datasets is available in the Appendix.

Moreover, we computed the dissimilarity of the trees extracted from our model following both a tree-based as well as path-based vectorisation and compared it, when relevant, to the competing approaches. The goal in this case was to verify that no redundant trees are shown to the end-user and that the clustering step worked as intended: extremely similar trees should indeed fall in the same cluster and not be extracted together as a final explanation. In contrast, trees shown to the end-user should come from different clusters and therefore be somewhat dissimilar.

Results of both performance and dissimilarity are reported using 5-fold train/validation/test splits, where the test sample size is limited to contain at most 50 entries for computational reasons. The remaining samples are split between train and validation with a 3:1 ratio. To evaluate performance, the Area Under the ROC is used as a metric for binary classification, while the C-Index is used for the survival data. As for the dissimilarity metric, we use the average Jaccard index measured across the final selected trees.

We compare our proposed "Local explainer" method against the following competing set-ups:

- a single Decision Tree (DT) learner and survival counterpart SDT, as a baseline from an interpretable model.
- a small RF/RSF model, where the number of learners equals the number of selected clusters K from the Local explainer.
- the Cox Proportional-Hazard model (Cox PH) with regularisation. Survival set-up only.
- the original RF/RSF, generated with 100 trees.

For our experiments the full-tree-based approach is used and MDS is the chosen dimensionality-reduction technique; in order to build the dissimilarity matrix, we choose the previously introduced $1 - J_{\mathcal{W}}$ operator. The maximum number of clusters K is set to 4, and their exact number is tuned by maximising faithfulness $\mathcal{F}$. Similarly, we tune the number of output dimensions d using MDS, with the choice between $d = 2$ and d equal to the original number of components. Additionally, we tune the number of pre-selected trees λ choosing among $10, 15$ and 20. In our runs, we observed that reducing the maximum number of clusters K to 2 reduces performance of both the Local Explainer and the Small Trees methods, which was to be expected. On the other side, changing the values of λ and d has no effect on performance and a small, negative effect on dissimilarity, this latter aspect will be further analysed.

Table 1. Average predictive performance on binary classification and survival data. In bold, the best performances with ones that are not significantly worse. Our proposed method's performance is shown under the name "Local explainer".

Set-up (# datasets)	(S)DT learner	Small R(S)F	Cox PH	Local explainer	original R(S)F
Binary (24)	0.748	0.804	—	**0.838**	**0.854**
Survival (12)	0.642	0.649	**0.684**	**0.708**	**0.710**

We share the results in Table 1. The comparison shows that the proposed model outperforms all the other competing methods; moreover, its performance is close to both RF and RSF despite the limited number of trees used. In addition, a more detailed analysis is performed by means of a post-hoc Friedman-Nemenyi test for comparing the performance of ML algorithms over multiple datasets [6] and Fig. 1 shows the results. Here, the average rank of the method across all datasets is visible on the scale, and methods that are not statistically significantly different in performance at $\alpha = .05$ are connected by segments whose length is at most equal to the Critical Distance (CD) as computed by the test. In both set-ups, our method statistically significantly outperforms (S)DT

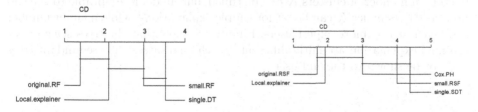

Fig. 1. Friedman-Nemenyi test, results on binary data (left) and survival (right).

learners and Small R(S)F, moreover, it is considerably better than Cox PH. As for the dissimilarities among the trees, we run our comparison by computing the average among-tree distance generated by the MDS representation of the final candidates, both with the *tree-based* and the *rule-based* dissimilarity indices. The results are summarised in Table 2.

Table 2. Average ruleset dissimilarities for binary classification and survival set-up, comparing the proposed local method with a small R(S)F with the same amount of trees.

	Rule type	Small RF	Local explainer		Rule type	Small RSF	Local explainer
Binary	Rule path	0.802	0.835	Survival	Rule path	0.772	0.770
	Full tree	0.691	0.725		Full tree	0.558	0.569

The table shows that the trees selected in the final step are reasonably diverse. In fact, they are at least as diverse as the ones generated by a R(S)F with a comparable number of learners. The data also reveals that the dissimilarity scores tend to be higher in general when considering rule path. We believe that this is due to the increased sparsity of the generated vectors.

4 Conclusion

Our proposed model extracts a small number of prototype rules, locally explaining predictions for a specific sample while maintaining the predictive performance of the original ensemble model. Although we focus on the context of survival data analysis, we have manifested that our approach is applicable and rather effective to other tasks as well, such as binary classification. In particular, the model is capable of significantly outperforming RF/RSF generated by the same number of learners, and its performance is still competitive to the original ensemble of trees despite using no more than four trees. Additionally, since the maximum number of clusters K can be tuned, our model is adaptable to the end user needs: a smaller K can be set for simple explanations, while a larger number can be chosen by more expert users. Finally, we show that the trees selected for the final explanation are fairly different, which guarantees that redundant trees will not be shown to the end user.

Future work will include investigation of the structure of the extracted rule sets to assess whether they are not only accurate and diverse, but also relevant. Furthermore, we could consider tasks with several outputs (multi-target and multi-event survival analysis) and different tree representations. Finally, the application of different measures of (dis)similarity between trees or between extracted rule-paths would also be an interesting topic of future research.

Acknowledgements. This research received funding from the Flemish Government (AI Research Program) and the Research Fund Flanders (project G080118N).

A   Appendix

Here we provide further details about the datasets used for this study, in addition to details about the achieved performance of the methods (Tables 3 and 4).

Table 3. Overview of the survival datasets, 12 datasets in total

			C-index				
	data size (obs., vars.)	censoring rate	single SDT	small RSF	Local explainer	original RSF	Cox P.H.
addicts	(238, 3)	37%	0.6187	0.6221	0.6507	0.6501	0.6239
ALS[a]	(5324, 76)	67%	0.7298	0.7594	0.7962	0.7997	0.5562
breast-cancer-surv.	(198, 80)	74%	0.5079	0.4896	0.635	0.6383	0.6476
DBCD	(295, 4919)	73%	0.5553	0.6309	0.7497	0.7519	0.7342
DLBCL	(240, 7399)	42%	0.5158	0.5504	0.6036	0.6217	0.6312
echocardiogram	(130, 9)	32%	0.5403	0.4347	0.4629	0.4627	0.5305
gbsg2	(686, 8)	56%	0.6224	0.6864	0.7135	0.7216	0.7017
lung	(228, 8)	28%	0.5429	0.5763	0.6034	0.6041	0.5774
cirrhosis	(403, 19)	56%	0.7733	0.8096	0.8571	0.8564	0.8469
rotterdam-1[b]	(2982, 11)	57%	0.7537	0.7832	0.794	0.7933	0.7522
rotterdam-2[c]	(2982, 12)	57%	0.8229	0.8715	0.894	0.901	0.8938
veteran	(137, 9)	7%	0.7113	0.5343	0.7343	0.7257	0.7146
whas500	(500, 14)	57%	0.6519	0.6861	0.7036	0.7052	0.6841
avg. performance			0.642	0.649	0.708	0.710	0.6842

[a]After dropping rows and columns with more than 30% missing data and imputing the remaining missing values,
[b]After dropping recurr variable, highly correlated with time-to-event
[c]Keeping recurr variable

Table 4. Overview of the binary classification datasets, 24 datasets in total

		AUROC			
	data size	single DT	small RF	Local explainer	original RF
blood	(748, 4)	0.6564	0.6925	0.7485	0.7513
bc_diagnostic	(569, 30)	0.9364	0.9711	0.9806	0.9791
bc_original	(699, 10)	1	1	1	1
bc_prognostic	(198, 33)	0.5632	0.5389	0.5315	0.5378
bc_coimba	(116, 9)	0.6779	0.6323	0.7185	0.7692
Colonoscopy_green	(98, 62)	0.6398	0.7897	0.8949	0.9
Colonoscopy_hinsel.	(97, 62)	0.4777	0.525	0.5354	0.575
Colonoscopy_schiller	(92, 62)	0.6284	0.5892	0.6108	0.6123
divorce	(170, 54)	0.9806	0.9567	0.9588	1
Flowmeters	(87, 36)	0.9095	0.9029	0.9629	0.9686
haberman	(306, 3)	0.5636	0.6802	0.7056	0.7037
hcc-survival	(165, 49)	0.608	0.7727	0.8342	0.8408
ionosphere	(351, 34)	0.8797	0.9651	0.9771	0.9788
LSVT_voice_rehab	(126, 310)	0.7421	0.8162	0.8404	0.8779
mamographic	(961, 5)	0.8124	0.8702	0.8721	0.8704
musk	(476, 166)	0.7754	0.8575	0.9252	0.9328
parkinson	(756, 753)	0.7172	0.8628	0.9301	0.9374
risk_factors	(858, 35)	0.8386	0.9879	0.9539	0.966
simulation_crashes	(540, 18)	0.7606	0.7924	0.7799	0.8967
sonar	(208, 60)	0.6882	0.8435	0.8809	0.9
SPECT	(267, 22)	0.735	0.75	0.7922	0.792
SPECTF	(267, 44)	0.6333	0.745	0.7735	0.8065
vertebral_column	(310, 6)	0.819	0.8447	0.9467	0.9504
wholesale	(440, 7)	0.9003	0.9035	0.9506	0.9596
avg. performance		0.7476	0.8038	0.8377	0.8544

References

1. Lundberg, S., Lee, S.: A unified approach to interpreting model predictions. In: Advances in Neural Information Processing Systems, pp. 4766–4775 (2017)
2. Ribeiro, M.T., et al.: Why should i trust you? Explaining the predictions of any classifier. In: Proceedings of the 22nd ACM SIGKDD International Conference on Knowledge Discovery and Data Mining, pp. 1135–1144 (2016)
3. Zhao, X., et al.: iForest: interpreting random forests via visual analytics. IEEE Trans. Visu. Comput. Graph. **25**(1), 407–416 (2019)
4. Sies, A., Van Mechelen, I.: C443: a methodology to see a forest for the trees. J. Classif. **37**(3), 730–753 (2020)
5. Ishwaran, H., et al.: Random survival forests. Ann. Appl. Stat. **2**(3), 841–860 (2008)
6. Demšar, J.: Statistical comparisons of classifiers over multiple data sets. J. Mach. Learn. Res. **7**, 1–30 (2006)

Federated Learning of Oligonucleotide Drug Molecule Thermodynamics with Differentially Private ADMM-Based SVM

Shirin Tavara[1](✉), Alexander Schliep[1], and Debabrota Basu[2]

[1] CSE, University of Gothenburg | Chalmers University of Technology,
Gothenburg, Sweden
tavara@chalmers.se
[2] Équipe Scool, Inria, UMR 9189-CRIStAL, CNRS, Univ. Lille, Centrale Lille,
Lille, France

Abstract. A crucial step to assure drug safety is predicting off-target binding. For oligonucleotide drugs this requires learning the relevant thermodynamics from often large-scale data distributed across different organisations. This process will respect data privacy if distributed and private learning under limited and private communication between local nodes is used. We propose an ADMM-based SVM with differential privacy for this purpose. We empirically show that this approach achieves accuracy comparable to the non-private one, i.e. ~86%, while yielding tight empirical privacy guarantees even after convergence.

Keywords: Differential privacy · Distributed learning · Federated learning · Oligonucleotide drug molecules · ADMM · SVM

1 Introduction

Machine learning (ML) and AI have been a remarkable success in improving small molecule drug discovery over the past decade. Advanced ML models have been applied to generate novel molecular structures, suggest synthesis pathways, or predict biochemical properties or interactions of those molecules [6,15,16]. The advances have led to open-source software [3] and cross-industry co-operations centered around federated learning [20]. While small molecules interacting with proteins are the most frequently used drug modality, alternatives are explored to address unmet clinical needs. In particular, advances in chemistry for the novel class of drugs based on antisense oligonucleotides (ASOs) have shown promise to deliver successful therapies to the clinic [2]. In ASOs, similar to modalities like small interfering RNAs (siRNAs), the fundamental reaction is one of hybridization, or binding, of two oligonucleotides. The main difference to most small molecule drugs is that oligonucleotide-based drugs modulate the expression of genes post transcription by leveraging inter-cellular mechanisms to degrade the

M. Kamp et al. (Eds.): ECML PKDD 2021 Workshops, CCIS 1525, pp. 459–467, 2021.
https://doi.org/10.1007/978-3-030-93733-1_34

gene's transcript, i.e. its mRNA, before it is translated to a protein. Thermodynamics of oligonucleotides, i.e. structure formation of individual RNA molecules, and hybridization of two oligonucleotides, have been studied extensively: the former to improve understanding of RNA molecules, and the latter partly because DNA microarrays, the main platform for gene expression measurements before the advent of high-throughput sequencing, rely on hybridization. Consequently, there is a wide range of data sets, biophysical models and software available [19].

Thermodynamics are a crucial factor *both* in drug efficacy—binding to the intended target—and drug safety—assuring no binding to unintended targets [33]. These models however do not reflect the many different chemical modifications proposed for ASOs, which often have a stabilizing effect [22] and thus alter the binding energy even without changes to the oligonucleotide sequences. Experiments to elucidate the binding energies are performed by many pharmaceutical companies and academic laboratories, but due to intellectual property interests in both oligonucleotide sequences and gene targets, this information cannot be shared easily. This suggests that a privacy-preserving federated learning approach would allow development of improved ML models for prediction of thermodynamics from the entirety of data, while protecting respective IP rights.

For our proof of concept, the machine learning task we consider is that of predicting off-target hybridization between an oligonucleotide and an mRNA binding site with mismatches in its sequence. We consider the free energy as the indicator of hybridization [33]. The mismatches are represented as features capturing different aspects of sequence dissimilarity. In lieu of experimental data, we use the widely popular nearest-neighbor model [38] as implemented in the Vienna RNA package [19] to simulate data.

We propose to use an SVM [24] to classify the occurrence of binding and non-binding, and an ADMM-based [29] framework to train in a distributed manner. We adopt a differentially private mechanism [9] that respects privacy of individual nodes and local data while learning and communicating the final SVM model (Sect. 3). This conglomeration allows us to operate over a large number of nodes and data, while experimentally achieving comparable accuracy as the non-private SVM and a reasonably tight privacy after global convergence (Sect. 4).

2 Background

In this section, we provide a brief overview of the methods: SVM, ADMM, and Differential Privacy, which are essential for developing our methodology.

Support Vector Machines (SVM). Support vector machines (SVM) are a supervised machine learning framework to solve classification [24,30,32,36] and regression problems [7,11,26]. Let us consider a binary classification problem with dataset D, i.e. training samples $\{x_i\}_{i=1}^N$ and corresponding class labels $\{y_i\}_{i=1}^N \in \{+1, -1\}^N$. SVMs separate two classes of training data by finding a *hyperplane*, $h(x) \triangleq w^T \Phi(x) + b$, with the maximum distance, or *margin*, from the closest points on either side of $h(x)$. In training, a primal optimization problem as in Eq. (1) is solved to determine the hyperplane with the maximum margin.

$$\min_{\mathbf{w},b} \frac{1}{2}||\mathbf{w}||^2 + C\sum_{i=1}^{N} \xi_i \quad \text{s.t. } y_i(\mathbf{w}^T\Phi(\mathbf{x}_i) + b) \geq 1 - \xi_i, \xi_i \geq 0, \forall i \in [N]. \quad (1)$$

Here, $\mathbf{w} \in \mathbb{R}^D$ represents the weight vector of the model which is orthogonal to the hyperplane, ξ_i's are the classification error, b is the bias parameter, and $\Phi(\mathbf{x}) : \mathbb{R}^N \rightarrow \mathbb{R}^D$ is a map function. If the training samples are linearly separable, the map function is linear, i.e. $\Phi(\mathbf{x}) = \mathbf{x}$. In more complex and nonlinear scenarios, SVM uses a kernel-based mapping function Φ, e.g. Radial Basis Functions (RBFs), to map training data into a high-dimensional space, where linear separation of data is possible [18,27].

Alternating Direction Method of Multipliers (ADMM). In many real-life applications, including the application we consider, the data is often large and distributed across different organisations at different locations. This naturally calls for incorporating a distributed framework to train the SVM where local models are built in different local servers and the local servers internally communicate to form a global model. ADMM [13,29] provides a robust, scalable, and parallelizable framework to train SVM models on such distributed data, where each node has limited access to the local datasets $\{D_i\}_{i=1}^{M}$ and can only communicate to certain neighbouring nodes[1]. In this case, an individual node $i \in [M]$ solves a local problem

$$\min_{\mathbf{w}_i} f_i(\mathbf{w}_i) \quad \text{s.t. } \mathbf{w}_i - \mathbf{w}_j = 0, \forall i \in \mathcal{N}_i, \quad (2)$$

such that the global objective function to optimize is $f(\mathbf{w}) \triangleq \sum_{i=1}^{M} f_i(\mathbf{w}_i)$, and $\mathcal{N}_i$ is the set of one-hop neighboring nodes of the node i. The constraints in (2) require that local variables $\mathbf{w}_i$'s should agree across one-hop neighbors $\mathbf{w}_j$'s. This asks for communication between neighbouring nodes. Detailed information regarding convergence and robustness of ADMM can be found in [4,12]. ADMM's dependence on the network between nodes and their communications can be found in [29,31]. We use ADMM to train our SVM model over distributed data.

Differential Privacy (DP). The final SVM model learnt using ADMM and the internal communication between nodes during the interactive procedure of ADMM posit new challenges for protecting data privacy of involved users. Specially, considering privacy is imperative if the data contains sensitive and classified information such as financial, medical records etc. [37], which should be protected against unauthorized disclosure. DP [10] is a widely-studied and scalably deployed statistical framework that enables data privacy. A differentially private algorithm aims to generate outputs that remain almost indistinguishable when an individual's data is added or deleted from the training dataset [14].

Definition 1 $(((\epsilon, \delta) - DP)$ [10]). *A randomized algorithm $\mathcal{M}$ is (ϵ, δ)-differential private if for any two neighboring datasets $\mathcal{D}$ and $\mathcal{D}'$ that only differ at most in one data point, and for any subset of output $O \in Range(\mathcal{M})$, the*

---

[1] Here, M is the number of nodes across which the data is distributed and $M \leq N$.

following holds, $\Pr[\mathcal{M}(\mathcal{D}) = O] \leq e^{\epsilon}\Pr[\mathcal{M}(\mathcal{D}') = O] + \delta$, *given privacy level* $\epsilon \geq 0$, *slack* $\delta \geq 0$.

The lower the privacy level ϵ, the harder it is to distinguish the neighbouring datasets, and thus a higher degree of DP is ensured. DP has been used to publicly release medical and genetic data while respecting the data privacy of involved individuals [25, 28, 34]. This motivates the use of DP as the privacy framework for distributed learning of the hybridization prediction.

3   Methodology

In this section, we present the differentially private ADMM-based SVM algorithm and the thermodynamics data that it is used to learn.

ADMM-Based Training of SVM. We use the ADMM-based SVM algorithm proposed by Forero et al. [12] as the non-private base algorithm. The communication model in the algorithm is decentralized such that each node computes the local optimization problem (Eq. (2)) and then broadcasts the local results to all the one-hop neighboring nodes ($\mathcal{N}_i$). In the aggregation phase, each node receives and gathers the neighboring results to conduct the corresponding updates. The process continues until the result of all nodes reach the consensus defined by the constraints in (2). For further details, please check [31].

Differentially Private ADMM-Based SVM (DP-ADMM-SVM). To incorporate differential privacy (DP) into the ADMM-based SVM algorithm, we adopt the PP-ADMM algorithm [9]. Following PP-ADMM, we add calibrated Gaussian noise into the local objective function $f_i(\mathbf{w}_i)$ at each ADMM iteration. Specifically, each node i generates a random vector η_{i1} from a Gaussian distribution $\mathcal{N}(\mathbf{0}, \sigma_{i1}^2 \mathbf{I}_d)$ and adds $(\eta_{i1})^T \mathbf{w}_i$ into the local objective function and obtains an approximated solution $\hat{\mathbf{w}}_i^t$ at iteration t. While communicating the local model $\hat{\mathbf{w}}_i^t$ to the neighboring nodes, another random noise vector η_{i2} is generated from a Gaussian distribution $\mathcal{N}(\mathbf{0}, \sigma_{i2}^2 \mathbf{I}_d)$ and added to the approximate solution of the perturbed objective function, i.e., $\mathbf{w}_i^t = \hat{\mathbf{w}}_i^t + \eta_{i2}$. Here, σ_{i1}^2 and σ_{i2}^2 are proportional to ϵ^{-2}, where ϵ is the desired privacy level at every iteration. For further details regarding noise variances σ_{i1} and σ_{i2}, we refer to [9].

Algorithm 1. DP-ADMM-SVM

1: **Input:** Dataset $\{D_i\}_{i=1}^M$, initial models $\mathbf{w}_i^0$, privacy parameters ϵ, an optimizer
2: **Initialization:** Compute noise variances σ_{i1}^2 & σ_{i2}^2, regularization parameters
3: **while** #Iterations $\leq$ MAX_ITER **do**
4:     For each node, add noise $\eta_{i1} \sim \mathcal{N}(\mathbf{0}, \sigma_{i1}^2 \mathbf{I}_d)$ to the local objective $f_i(\mathbf{w}_i)$
5:     For each node, use the optimizer to obtain updated model $\hat{\mathbf{w}}_i^{t+1}$
6:     For each node, add noise $\eta_{i2} \sim \mathcal{N}(\mathbf{0}, \sigma_{i2}^2 \mathbf{I}_d)$ to $\hat{\mathbf{w}}_i^{t+1}$ & get the local model $\mathbf{w}_i^{t+1}$
7:     For each node, broadcast the local model $\mathbf{w}_i^{t+1}$ to neighbours $\mathcal{N}_i$
8:     Update local models of each node using the communicated neighbouring models
9: **end while**

---

4   Experimental Analysis: Results and Discussions

In order to establish that the proposed methodology can scale to a large number of academic and industrial participants, we have decided to use the relatively large number of 224 entities with private data, which maps directly to the available computational resources. In order to study the privacy and accuracy of DP-ADMM-SVM, we conducted three experiments on 479,136 data points privately distributed over 224 nodes. We implemented DP-ADMM-SVM in C++ and performed the computations on 224 nodes provided by Tetralith, the Swedish National Supercomputer Centre's largest HPC cluster at Linköping University [21]. In this section, we describe the data under investigation, and corresponding insights from the experimental results.

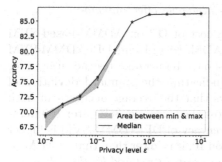
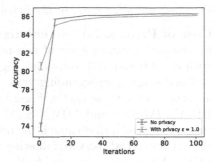

Fig. 1. Accuracy of 10 runs for ADMM algorithm with 50 iterations in logarithmic scale. The grey area shows the area between the minimum and maximum accuracy of 10 runs and the black line is the median accuracy of 10 runs.

Fig. 2. Average of accuracy per iteration for distributed ADMM-based SVM using 224 nodes, $\epsilon = 1.0$ and 50 ADMM iterations with and without privacy. The error bars show the standard deviation of accuracy.

Data Description. We sample 10,000 binding sites of length 15, i.e. 15-mers, uniformly from the Human transcriptome, i.e. the set of all expressed sequences (GRCh38 reference genome). Their perfect Watson-Crick complements define the oligonucleotides. For each oligo, we simulate 50 binding sites at an edit distance to the perfect match site of up to 5. Note that larger edit distances are highly unlikely to lead to binding. We compute the difference in Gibbs free energy $\Delta G°$ between the perfect match duplex and the mismatch duplex using RNAcofold [19]. We use $\Delta G° < \tau$ as the binary indicator variable for the hybridization with $\tau = 7$. The sequence dissimilarity was represented through the following features: edit distance, length of longest common factor, 2- and 3-gram distance, Jaquard distance on 2- and 3-grams, and weighted versions of the q-gram distances, with weights[2] derived from the nearest neighbor model [38]. Randomly

---

[2] E.g. the 3-gram "GCG" has larger weight due to higher binding affinity than "ATA".

selecting data for each of the 224 nodes resulted in a total of 479,136 data points in the training data set.

Accuracy vs. Privacy Trade-Off. In order to study the effect of privacy on accuracy of DP-ADMM-SVM, we compute the test accuracy of DP-ADMM-SVM after 50 ADMM iterations and repeat 10 times. In each run, we fix $\delta = 10^{-4}$ and vary the privacy level ϵ logarithmically (with base 10) in $[0.01, 10]$. Figure 1 shows the average accuracy of 10 runs on 224 nodes containing a grey area, which is the area between the minimum and maximum average accuracy along with the median of average accuracy of 10 runs in logarithmic scale. Figure 1 shows that the accuracy increases with increase in ϵ for $0.01 \le \epsilon \le 1.0$.[3] For $1.0 \le \epsilon \le 10.0$, the accuracy remains stable around 86%. Figure 1 also illustrates that the grey area between the maximum and minimum average accuracy over 224 nodes gets tighter as ϵ increases. *This experiment shows that accuracy increases as privacy decreases but after $\epsilon = 1.0$, the privacy has negligible effect anymore.*

Cost of Privacy. Now we investigate the cost of DP on ADMM-based SVM by comparing convergence of non-private ADMM-SVM and DP–ADMM-SVM with $\epsilon = 1.0$ over 100 iterations. Figure 2 shows the average test accuracy over 224 nodes and corresponding error bars indicating the standard deviation of accuracies over these nodes. Figure 2 shows that the average accuracy of both DP-ADMM-SVM and ADMM-SVM is almost the same, i.e. 86% after 100 iterations. We observe that though the initial accuracy of DP-ADMM-SVM is higher than that of ADMM-SVM, following iteration 10, it is lower than that of ADMM-SVM. *Both of these are due to the randomization introduced by the DP mechanism. This leads to model stability over iterations and lower accuracy after convergence* [23].

Empirical Estimate of Privacy Level. From the naïve [10] and adaptive [17] composition theorems of differential privacy, we know that the effective DP decreases, i.e. the effective privacy level of the ML model increases, as the number of iterations increase. Following the invent of moment accountant [1], we know that often the privacy level achieved by the dataset under experiment is much tighter than that of these data-independent and worst-case composition theorems. In order to investigate the increase in effective privacy level of DP-ADMM-SVM with increasing number of iterations, we plot the privacy levels ϵ computed using naive and adaptive compositions and a budget accountant as

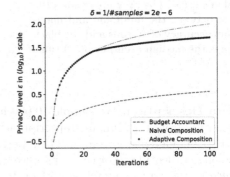

Fig. 3. Data-dependent (Budget Accountant) and data-independent (Naive and Adaptive Composition) privacy levels achieved per iteration.

---

[3] Increase in privacy level ϵ indicates decrease in differential privacy.

a function of the number of ADMM iterations. We fix the ϵ per-step, i.e. the ϵ used to calibrate the noise, as 1, and $\delta = 1/N$, where the number of samples $N = 479,136$ [5]. Figure 3 shows that the naïve and adaptive compositions predict the worst-case privacy level of the SVM model obtained after 100 iterations as 100.0 and 51.15 respectively. In contrast, *while considering the data, the empirical privacy level of the SVM model is 3.59, which is significantly tighter and indicates moderate loss (i.e. $\epsilon \in [1, 10]$) in DP.*

5   Conclusion

We propose to use Differentially Private ADMM-based SVM to learn the thermodynamics of oligonucleotide drug molecules from data distributed across multiple nodes and with communication limited to immediate neighbours. We show that DP-ADMM-SVM achieves $\sim 86\%$ accuracy for privacy level $\epsilon = 1$ at predicting off-target hybridization, a determinant of drug safety. This accuracy level is comparable with that of non-private ADMM-based SVM and does not improve for lower DP, i.e. $\epsilon \geq 1$. We empirically show that the data-dependent privacy level of the final SVM model is $(3.59, 1/\#\text{samples})$. This is significantly tight as a global privacy level where a distributed learning problem over 224 nodes and $479,136$ data points evolves over iterations. In future work we want to improve the present DP mechanism such that it is not worst-case [8], does gradient perturbation [35], and is affected and gets stronger by the network between nodes.

Acknowledgments. SSF Strategic Mobility Grant "Drug Discovery for Antisense Oligos" (A.S.), Swedish National Supercomputer Centre (A.S. & S.T.).

References

1. Abadi, M., et al.: Deep learning with differential privacy. In: Proceedings of the 2016 ACM SIGSAC Conference on Computer and Communications Security, pp. 308–318 (2016)
2. Bennett, C.F.: Therapeutic antisense oligonucleotides are coming of age. Annu. Rev. Med. **70**, 307–321 (2019)
3. Blaschke, T., et al.: Reinvent 2.0: an AI tool for de novo drug design. J. Chem. Inf. Mod. **60**(12), 5918–5922 (2020)
4. Boyd, S., Parikh, N., Chu, E., Peleato, B., Eckstein, J.: Distributed optimization and statistical learning via the alternating direction method of multipliers. Found. Trends® Mach. Learn. **3**(1), 1–122 (2011)
5. Canonne, C.: What is δ, and what δ difference does it make? DifferentialPrivacy.org, March 2021. https://differentialprivacy.org/flavoursofdelta/
6. Chen, H., Engkvist, O., Wang, Y., Olivecrona, M., Blaschke, T.: The rise of deep learning in drug discovery. Drug Discov. Today **23**(6), 1241–1250 (2018)
7. Collobert, R., Bengio, S.: Svmtorch: support vector machines for large-scale regression problems. J. Mach. Learn. Res. **1**, 143–160 (2001)
8. Dandekar, A., Basu, D., Bressan, S.: Differential privacy at risk: bridging randomness and privacy budget. In: Proceedings on Privacy Enhancing Technologies, vol. 1, pp. 64–84 (2021)

9. Ding, J., Wang, J., Liang, G., Bi, J., Pan, M.: Towards plausible differentially private ADMM based distributed machine learning. In: Proceedings of the 29th ACM International Conference on Information & Knowledge Management, pp. 285–294 (2020)

10. Dwork, C., McSherry, F., Nissim, K., Smith, A.: Calibrating noise to sensitivity in private data analysis. In: Halevi, S., Rabin, T. (eds.) TCC 2006. LNCS, vol. 3876, pp. 265–284. Springer, Heidelberg (2006). https://doi.org/10.1007/11681878_14

11. Flake, G.W., Lawrence, S.: Efficient SVM regression training with SMO. Mach. Learn. **46**(1), 271–290 (2002)

12. Forero, P.A., Cano, A., Giannakis, G.B.: Consensus-based distributed support vector machines. J. Mach. Learn. Res. **11**, 1663–1707 (2010)

13. França, G., Bento, J.: How is distributed ADMM affected by network topology? ArXiv e-prints, October 2017

14. Harvard: Differential privacy (2021). https://privacytools.seas.harvard.edu/differential-privacy

15. Johansson, S., et al.: AI-assisted synthesis prediction. Drug Discov. Today Technol. **32–33**, 65–72 (2020)

16. Johansson, S.V., et al.: Using active learning to develop machine learning models for reaction yield prediction. ChemRxiv (2021). https://doi.org/10.33774/chemrxiv-2021-bpv0c. Under review

17. Kairouz, P., Oh, S., Viswanath, P.: The composition theorem for differential privacy. In: International Conference on Machine Learning, pp. 1376–1385. PMLR (2015)

18. Leslie, C., Eskin, E., Noble, W.S.: The spectrum kernel: a string kernel for SVM protein classification. In: Biocomputing 2002, pp. 564–575. World Scientific (2001)

19. Lorenz, R., et al.: ViennaRNA package 2.0. Algorithms Mol. Biol. **6**(1), 1–14 (2011)

20. Martin, E.J., Zhu, X.W.: Collaborative profile-QSAR: a natural platform for building collaborative models among competing companies. J. Chem. Inf. Mod. **61**(4), 1603–1616 (2021)

21. NSC: Tetralith (2021). https://www.nsc.liu.se/systems/tetralith/, https://www.nsc.liu.se/systems/tetralith/

22. Papargyri, N., Pontoppidan, M., Andersen, M.R., Koch, T., Hagedorn, P.H.: Chemical diversity of locked nucleic acid-modified antisense oligonucleotides allows optimization of pharmaceutical properties. Mol. Ther. Nucleic Acids **19**, 706–717 (2020)

23. Pinot, R., Yger, F., Gouy-Pailler, C., Atif, J.: A unified view on differential privacy and robustness to adversarial examples (2019)

24. Platt, J.: Sequential minimal optimization: A fast algorithm for training support vector machines. Technical Report MSR-TR-98-14, Microsoft Research, April 1998

25. Raisaro, J.L., et al.: Protecting privacy and security of genomic data in i2b2 with homomorphic encryption and differential privacy. IEEE/ACM Trans. Comput. Biol. Bioinform. **15**(5), 1413–1426 (2018)

26. Shevade, S.K., Keerthi, S.S., Bhattacharyya, C., Murthy, K.R.K.: Improvements to the SMO algorithm for SVM regression. IEEE Trans. Neural Netw. **11**(5), 1188–1193 (2000)

27. Soman, K., Loganathan, R., Ajay, V.: Machine learning with SVM and other kernel methods. PHI Learning Pvt. Ltd. (2009)

28. Sun, Z., Wang, Y., Shu, M., Liu, R., Zhao, H.: Differential privacy for data and model publishing of medical data. IEEE Access **7**, 152103–152114 (2019)

29. Tavara, S.: Parallel computing of support vector machines: a survey. ACM Comput. Surv. (CSUR) **51**(6), 1–38 (2019)

30. Tavara, S., Schliep, A.: Effect of network topology on the performance of ADMM-based SVMs. In: 2018 30th International Symposium on Computer Architecture and High Performance Computing (SBAC-PAD), pp. 388–393. IEEE (2018)
31. Tavara, S., Schliep, A.: Effects of network topology on the performance of consensus and distributed learning of SVMs using ADMM. PeerJ Comput. Sci. **7**, e397 (2021)
32. Tavara, S., Sundell, H., Dahlbom, A.: Empirical study of time efficiency and accuracy of support vector machines using an improved version of PSVM. In: Proceedings of the International Conference on Parallel and Distributed Processing Techniques and Applications (PDPTA), p. 177. The Steering Committee of The World Congress in Computer Science, Computer (2015)
33. Watt, A.T., Swayze, G., Swayze, E.E., Freier, S.M.: Likelihood of nonspecific activity of gapmer antisense oligonucleotides is associated with relative hybridization free energy. Nucleic Acid Ther. **30**(4), 215–228 (2020)
34. Wei, J., Lin, Y., Yao, X., Zhang, J., Liu, X.: Differential privacy-based genetic matching in personalized medicine. IEEE Trans. Emerg. Top. Comput. (2020)
35. Yu, D., Zhang, H., Chen, W., Liu, T.Y., Yin, J.: Gradient perturbation is underrated for differentially private convex optimization. arXiv preprint arXiv:1911.11363 (2019)
36. Zhang, R., Ma, J.: An improved SVM method P-SVM for classification of remotely sensed data. Int. J. Remote Sens. **29**(20), 6029–6036 (2008)
37. Zhang, X., Khalili, M.M., Liu, M.: Improving the privacy and accuracy of ADMM-based distributed algorithms. In: International Conference on Machine Learning, pp. 5796–5805. PMLR (2018)
38. Zuker, M., Mathews, D.H., Turner, D.H.: Algorithms and thermodynamics for RNA secondary structure prediction: a practical guide. In: Barciszewski, J., Clark, B.F.C. (eds.) RNA Biochemistry and Biotechnology. NATO Science Series (Series 3: High Technology), vol. 70, pp. 11–43. Springer, Dordrecht (1999). https://doi.org/10.1007/978-94-011-4485-8_2

Mining Medication-Effect Relations from Twitter Data Using Pre-trained Transformer Language Model

Keyuan Jiang[1](✉) (iD), Dingkai Zhang[2], and Gordon R. Bernard[3]

[1] Purdue University Northwest, Hammond, IN 46323, USA
kjiang@pnw.edu
[2] Ningbo City College of Vocational Technology, Ningbo, Zhejiang, China
[3] Vanderbilt University, Nashville, TN 37232, USA
gordon.bernard@vanderbilt.edu

Abstract. Pharmacovigilance aims to promote safe use of pharmaceutical products by continuously assessing the safety of marketed medications. Lately, an active area of this endeavor is to use social media such as Twitter as an alternative data source to gather patient-reported experience with medication use. Published work focused on identifying expressions of adverse effects in social media data while giving little attention to understanding the relationship between a mentioned medication and any mentioned effect expressions. In this study, we investigated the discovery of medication-effect relations from Twitter text using BERT, a transformer-based language model, with fine-tuning. Our results on a corpus of 9,516 annotated tweets show that the overall performance of our method is superior to the 4 baseline approaches studied. The outcome of this work may help automate and accelerate the process of discovering potentially unreported medication effects from patient-reported experiences documented in the sheer amount of social media data.

Keywords: Medication effect relations · Relation extraction · Twitter · Transformer language model · Pharmacovigilance

1 Introduction

Advancement of biomedicine has yielded a great number of medications for therapeutic treatment. These medications come with a wide variety of effects, beneficial and/or adverse. Although a large number of drug safety and efficacy tests have been conducted in various phases of clinical trials during the drug development process, there are differences in the application scenarios such as off-label uses [1] and disease states of the drug due to differences in the individual [2]. Therefore, studying medication effects after they were put on market has become an important research effort for pharmacovigilance, which aims to reduce and prevent the harm and risk to patients in the clinical care process while improving the beneficial effects.

© Springer Nature Switzerland AG 2021
M. Kamp et al. (Eds.): ECML PKDD 2021 Workshops, CCIS 1525, pp. 468–478, 2021.
https://doi.org/10.1007/978-3-030-93733-1_35

Emergence of social media has made mass communication much easier, and users can freely post any topics imaginable and share their personal experiences, including those pertaining to their use of medications. The wealthy information of personal medication experiences on social media has driven many research efforts of considering social media as an alternative, supplementary data source for pharmacovigilance. In writing their systematic review in 2015, Golder et al. [3] collected more than 3,000 publications related to pharmacovigilance and social media. A comprehensive review of utilizing social media data for pharmacovigilance was written by Sarker et al. [4] in which the authors discussed the status, challenges and issues of this active research. Although research efforts in this direction had continued to grow, most of them mainly focused on detecting mentions of adverse reactions or effects, which is an entity recognition task in information retrieval. A recent work along this direction can be found in [5] in which the authors presented their effort of developing an end-to-end ADE (adverse drug events) and normalization pipeline for Twitter data.

Little has been done in finding the relation between a medication and any mentions of effects within the context of social media data, partially due to the unique characteristics of social media which are noisy and contain informal writing, especially on general purpose social media such as Twitter. Extracting medication effect relations largely remains a manual process as described in the recent work of discovering potentially unreported effects of Humira and opioids from Twitter data [6, 7].

There exist a number of relations of word pairs, ranging from class-inclusion, part-whole, contrast, to cause-purpose, and they have been used for relation extraction tasks in shared tasks such as SemEval [8]. Many of such relations are irrelevant to our interest of studying medication-effect relations. In the medical domain, there also exist a number of semantic relations. The U.S. National Library of Medicine (NLM) compiled a list of hierarchical semantic relations[1] in its Unified Medical Language System® (UMLS®), and many of the UMLS Semantic Relations pertain to medication-effect relations, such as *treats*, *causes*, and *produces*. The SemRep software, developed by the U.S. NLM, extracts the predicates from the text of biomedical literature and map them to these normalized semantic relations [9]. A predicate is considered as a relation between two biomedical concepts in a subject-predicate-object triple. In the world of social media data, Twitter data in particular, formal linguistic rules are not followed closely, and thus identifying predicates correctly in tweet text is a challenging task.

Various efforts have been attempted in extracting drug-related relations in biomedical field, including machine learning-based methods [10–12], dependency tree-based approaches [13–16], and kernel-based methods [17–19]. These methods were developed mainly for processing formal writings of scientific literature. On the other hand, there is a lack of relation extraction tools for Twitter data even though there are published works on information extraction from Twitter data [20–22] which focused on entity recognition.

Yu et al. attempted to extract drug-effect relations from Twitter data [23]. They treated the drug-effect relation as the cause-effect relation, and investigated the supervised approach of 6 conventional classifiers on a corpus of 200 tweets, with human-engineered

---

[1] https://www.nlm.nih.gov/research/umls/META3_current_relations.html.

features including n-grams and part-of-speech (POS) tags. Their methods achieved accuracies ranging from 52.64% to 76.90%, but no results of other classification performance measures were provided. In addition, the example tweets shown in their work do not pertain to drug effects. Adrover et al. [24] studied identification of adverse effects of HIV treatment from Twitter posts. They also used the supervised method with conventional classifiers which were trained with 4,000 annotated tweets. Although a total of 1642 tweets was identified to have personal experience (effects) of HIV treatment, no standard performance measure data were reported.

Owning to their abundance, Twitter data were considered for this study. Twitter data are known for their noisiness, and may contain creative short texts to include the needed information within the limited space, incomplete sentences, and they do not follow grammatical and spelling rules. All these make conventional approaches developed for formal writings perform poorly in accurately identifying relations.

The uniqueness of Twitter data calls for two separate tasks of data processing: (1) differentiating noisy tweets from relevant ones which describe the medication-effect relations, and (2) determining the type of medication-effect relations from relevant tweets, a task of relation extraction. To simplify the processing, noisy or irrelevant Twitter instances were treated as a separate class of *no relation* in this study, and hence our task became a multi-class classification problem.

In identifying relations in Twitter posts pertaining to medication effects, three types of relation between a medication and effect expression were defined: side effect (s), indication (i) (for beneficial relation), and no relation (n). This simplification of effects as side effects and indications was inspired by the SIDER database [25] which was used in gathering and cleaning our Twitter data. The SIDER database, hosted at European Molecular Biology Laboratory (EMBL), is a resource of side effects of the marketed pharmaceutical products. Examples of the 3 relations are as follows (medications are in boldface and effects are underscored):

"I was in ellis hospital a year ago. The **seroquel** gave me a minor <u>hallucination</u> at one point." (s)
"The other day I had a <u>head ache</u> and took some **aspirin**. My <u>head ache</u> went away." (i)
"Tf when you gotta take **vyvanse** and drink four loko to get you through the <u>painful</u> hours of studying" (n)

The first tweet describes the side effect (hallucination, CUI: C0018524 – CUI stands for Concept Unique Identifier, a unique identifier for UMLS Metathesaurus concept to which strings with the same meaning are linked [31]) due to the use of Seroquel. The second tweet states that Aspirin treats the user's headache (CUI: C0018681), which is an indication. In the last tweet, word *painful* is figurative to decorate *hours of studying*, and not used to describe the painful (CUI: C0030193) experience due to use of Vyvanse.

In this study, we treated the relation discovery as a supervised classification problem and investigated the classification performance of representing Twitter data using the pretrained transformer language model, BERT (Bidirectional Encoder Representations from Transformers) [26], which was developed by Google Research and had achieved the record-breaking results in 18 natural language processing (NLP) tasks [26]. Unlike other word embedding techniques such as word2vec [27] which is based upon term co-occurrences, the BERT model uses bidirectional training and embeds semantics of the words more accurately from the context. The same word can be represented differently based upon the context. The BERT language model also provides a mechanism of classification through fine-tuning (FT).

In addition to comparing our proposed method with baseline approaches, two commonly used software programs, Open IE and SemRep, were investigated to understand how well each of them behaves with Twitter data. Open IE [29] is a relation extraction program for open domain (as opposed to a specific domain), and SemRep [9], developed by the U.S. National Library Medicine, is a tool to interpret semantic relations in biomedical literature.

Both Open IE and SemRep do not directly output medication-effect relations. Open IE outputs relations in triples each containing two entities and a relation between them, and a SemRep's output includes biomedical concepts and a normalized predicate relating the concepts. Outputs from both tools (relations and predicates) were mapped to three medication-effect relations.

Open IE occasionally yielded phrase entities which contain an effect concept. For example, it considered "me super shaky" as an entity in its output: (*Adderall, makes, me super shaky*), when processing "Adderall always makes me super shaky," even though it generated another output of (*Adderall, makes, shaky*). We treated the former as a subword relation, and the later a whole-word relation. In evaluation, both sub-word and whole-word cases were studied.

2   Method

The pipeline of data processing and analysis is shown in Fig. 1. After initial processing of Twitter data, which is described in the Data section, a corpus of tweets containing at least a medication and one or more effect expressions was generated. This corpus was annotated and later used by both baseline methods and the proposed transformer-based approach. Classification performance of each method was collected and evaluated. Finally, a statistical analysis was conducted to confirm the differences in classification performance between the baseline methods and the proposed method.

2.1   Baseline Methods

Word embedding has been used in many biomedical NLP applications, thanks to its ability to capture semantics properties and linguistic relationships between terms [28]. For this reason, four word embedding-based methods were chosen as the baseline methods to evaluate the performance of the proposed approach. Two word embedding techniques (BOW and TF-IDF - BOW: bag of words, TF-IDF: term frequency–inverse document frequency) and two classifiers (support vector machine (SVM) and deep neural network (DNN)) were combined to form 4 word embedding-based methods: TF-IDF with SVM classifier, BOW with SVM classifier, TF-IDF with DNN classifier, and BOW with DNN classifier. The SVM was selected as it achieved the highest accuracy in a prior effort for the same task [23]. The DNN classifier was configured to have 5 hidden layers with 1,500 nodes in each layer.

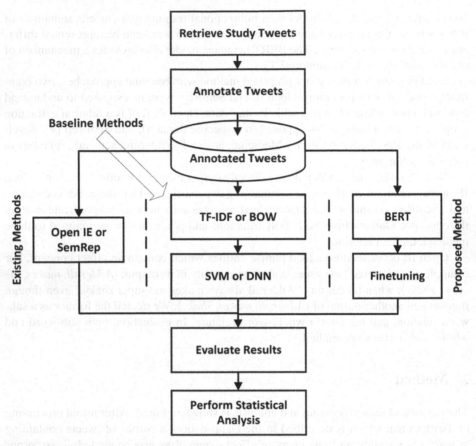

Fig. 1. Pipeline of data processing and analysis.

2.2 Transformer-Based Model Fine-Tuning

In our study, the pretrained BERT base model, which can be configured as a classifier with fine-tuning, was used for our 3-class prediction task. In the BERT base model, trained with a corpus of 3.3 billion words from the BooksCorpus and English Wikipedia, there are 768 inputs, 12 layers, and 12 attention heads. One of the model output tokens [CLS] which is for "the aggregate sequence representation for classification tasks" [26], was used for our classification. A dropout layer with a dropout rate of 0.1, and a dense layer were added to pool output of the model as the classification outcome.

Each tweet was treated as a sequence of 64 tokens, and a special token was applied to pad tweets shorter than 64 tokens. To avoid performing attention on padding tokens, an attention mask was applied to the input data. For each tweet, a 0 mask was for tokens which should be masked, whereas a 1 mask was for those that are not masked.

2.3   Data

A collection of 53 million tweets related to 100 medications was gathered using a Web crawler developed by our team in compliance with the Twitter.com access policy. Pre-processing the 53 million raw tweets generated 12 million "clean" tweets which are English only, non-duplicating, and not re-tweets. Furthermore, the "clean" tweets were filtered with effect terms obtained from the SIDER database, and their variations in consumer health vocabulary (CHV) [30], yielding a corpus of 3.6 million tweets which were used to infer the pairs of medication and effect based upon relational similarity [6]. Finally, 300 pairs were randomly selected and 9,516 tweets containing these pairs of medication and effect were retrieved from the collection of 3.6 million tweets. This random sampling was intended not to overwhelm our team with annotating the entire collection of 3.6 million tweets due to the time and resource constraints.

Table 1. Composition of the annotated tweet corpus

Class	# of Tweets
Side effect (s)	2,470
Indication (i)	2,290
No relation (n)	4,747
Total	9,516

The 9,516 selected tweets were annotated by two annotators according to an annotation guideline. The guideline defines each class of the effects, and lists examples of each class. The two annotators were first trained to annotate 100 tweets. The outcome of their work was evaluated and shared with them to ensure that both understand the annotation task. Afterwards, they continue to annotate the remaining tweets. Any disagreement due to subjectivity and ambiguity in the annotation was resolved by another researcher. The annotated corpus of tweets is shared on the GitHub[2]. Table 1 lists the composition of the annotated tweet corpus.

2.4   Evaluation

Both baseline and proposed methods in this study were evaluated with 10-fold cross-validation. The annotated tweet corpus was partitioned into the same 10 folds for all the methods – that is, each partition contains the same set of instances for different methods. The average value was calculated for each performance measure.

To determine whether or not the differences in classification performance between the transformer-based method and each baseline approach are due to chance, we conducted a hypothesis test on each performance measure for each pair of the proposed method and a baseline method (H_0: *no* difference in performance measure exists, and H_a: difference in performance measure *does* exist). Each time, the same data partition was used. The

---

[2] https://github.com/medeffects/tweet_corpora.

Wilcoxon Signed-Rank Test [32], a nonparametric paired difference test, was chosen, because the test does not require any assumptions regarding the data distribution. A difference in performance was considered in existence if the corresponding signed-rank is less than or equal to the critical value of the given α and n (0.05 and 10 respectively in our case).

3   Results

Table 2 lists the results of classification performance, among which the top 3 rows are for Open IE and SemRep, the following 4 rows are for baseline methods and the last row is for the transformer-based approach. The highest value of each measure for the baseline and proposed methods is in boldface.

Table 2. Classification performance results. sw for sub-word, ww for whole-word, s for side effect, i for indication, n for no relation, w for weighted, and BERT+FT for BERT+Fine-Tuning. Boldface figures are the highest values within the bottom 5 rows.

Method	Acc.	Prec (s)	Prec (i)	Prec (n)	Rec (s)	Rec (i)	Rec (n)	F1 (w)
Open IE (sw)	.508	.570	.731	.504	.021	.038	.988	.361
Open IE (ww)	.501	.450	.778	.500	.007	.009	.995	.340
SemRep	.503	.447	.531	.503	.014	.071	.967	.367
BOW+SVM	.681	.693	.567	.716	.707	.445	.779	.663
TF-IDF+SVM	.679	.706	.570	.700	.693	.399	**.802**	.667
BOW+DNN	.682	.677	.553	.738	.718	.511	.742	.678
TF-IDF+DNN	.671	.688	.535	.712	.696	.458	.755	.664
BERT+FT	**.717**	**.720**	**.612**	**.772**	**.789**	**.544**	.760	**.711**

Shown in Table 3 are the results of Wilcoxon Signed-Rank Test between each pair of a baseline method and the transformer-based method for each performance measure. A test result is considered *significant* if the corresponding signed-rank is less than or equal to the critical value for $\alpha = 0.05$ and $n = 10$ which is for 10 folds of tweets. The critical value table is from [33]. In other words, the test result is *significant* if the difference of the measure between the two methods *does exist*.

4   Discussion

It can be observed from Table 2 that both Open IE and SemRep performed in a strange manner on our study tweets. Both achieved an accuracy of 50%. For precision, both performed best on i class. For recall, both methods behaved poorly on both s and i classes, leaving out most true positives from the predicted results – most of the predicted tweets are not those belong to the corresponding class. On the contrary, their recalls on n class are extremely high but with 0.500 precisions, indicating that half of their

Table 3. Wilcoxon signed-rank test results for $\alpha = 0.05$ and $n = 10$. Sig: significant, Not Sig: not significant. A significant test result indicates that the difference of the performance measure between a baseline method and the proposed method *does* exist. F1 (w): weighted F1.

	Acc.	Prec (s)	Prec (i)	Prec (n)	Rec (s)	Rec (i)	Rec (n)	F1 (w)
Bow+SVM	Sig	Not Sig	Not Sig	Sig	Sig	Sig	Sig	Sig
TF-IDF+SVM	Sig	Not Sig	Not Sig	Sig	Sig	Sig	Sig	Sig
Bow+DNN	Sig	Sig	Sig	Not Sig	Sig	Sig	Not Sig	Sig
TF-IDF+DNN	Sig	Not Sig	Sig	Sig	Sig	Sig	Sig	Sig

predications are false positives (*s* and *i* instances). In short, the results of both methods on our study tweets confirm that both methods, developed for formal writing, do not perform satisfactorily, making both unusable for our task.

In comparison with the baseline methods, our transformer-based method achieved the highest values in 7 out of 8 performance measures. Our statistical analysis (Wilcoxon Signed-Rank Test) results in Table 3 support that there exist the differences (*significant*) in accuracy, recalls on *s* and *i* classes, and weighted F1 scores, between the transformer-based method and each of the baseline methods.

For precisions, the transformer-based method performed either better than or equally well with the baseline methods, showing that the predicted results of our proposed method include more true positives than false positives of each corresponding class.

Both BOW-SVM and TF-IDF+SVM method achieved the higher values in recall on *n* class (.779 and .802 respectively), and our statistical analysis *does* show the existence of differences between each of them and BERT+FT. This could indicate that our method may leave out some true positives from the prediction of the *n* class. In practical applications, our focus will be on understanding the medication effects of both *s* and *i* classes, and hence, a relatively lower recall on *n* class is not a concern. In addition, the weighted F1 score of the transformer-based method is better than that of each and every baseline method, supported by the hypothesis test. As such, the transformer-based approach is a superior choice.

In summary, the overall performance of the transformer-based method is better than any single baseline method tested in this study, and it should be the choice of our task should a single method be considered.

Our study data contain both tweets which are statements of the fact (e.g. therapeutic or side effect) and those that are descriptions of one's personal experience. For post-marketing surveillance, the latter is of most importance. One of the future directions is to combine this relation discovery method with our method of identifying personal experience tweets [34], in order to automate the process of identifying medication effects reported by Twitter users, from ever-growing amount of available Twitter data.

5 Conclusions

In this study, the transformer-based language model was investigated to discover medication-effect relations expressed in Twitter data, and its overall performance was compared with 4 baseline methods. The results of the transformer-based method on a corpus of 9,516 annotated tweets showed that its overall performance is superior to any single baseline method with statistical support, exhibiting the utility of this transformer-based approach for discovering the description of medication-effect relations in Twitter posts. The outcome of this work may help automate and accelerate discovery of potentially unknown medication effects from patient-reported experiences mentioned in the sheer amount of social media data. It is conceivable that the proposed method may be applicable to other relation extraction tasks in health-related fields, such as the disease-symptom relation.

Acknowledgement. Authors wish to thank anonymous reviewers for their critiques and constructive comments which improved this manuscript.

References

1. Ramos-Casals, M., et al.: Off-label use of rituximab in 196 patients with severe, refractory systemic autoimmune diseases. Clin. Exp. Rheumatol. **28**, 468–476 (2010)
2. Effinger, A., O'Driscoll, C.M., McAllister, M., Fotaki, N.: Impact of gastrointestinal disease states on oral drug absorption–implications for formulation design–a PEARRL review. J. Pharm. Pharmacol. **71**, 674–698 (2019)
3. Golder, S., Norman, G., Loke, Y.: Systematic review on the prevalence, frequency and comparative value of adverse events data in social media. Br. J. Clin. Pharmacol. **80**, 878–888 (2015)
4. Sarker, A., et al.: Utilizing social media data for pharmacovigilance: a review. J. Biomed. Inform. **54**, 202–212 (2015)
5. Magge, A., et al.: DeepADEMiner: a deep learning pharmacovigilance pipeline for extraction and normalization of adverse drug effect mentions on twitter. medRxiv (2020)
6. Jiang, K., Huang, L., Chen, T., Karbaschi, G., Zhang, D., Bernard, G.R.: Mining potentially unreported effects from Twitter posts through relational similarity: a case for opioids. In: 2020 IEEE International Conference on Bioinformatics and Biomedicine (BIBM), pp. 2603–2609 (2020)
7. Jiang, K., Feng, S., Huang, L., Chen, T., Bernard, G.R.: Mining potential effects of HUMIRA in Twitter posts through relational similarity. Stud. Health Technol. Inf. **270**, 874–878 (2020)
8. Jurgens, D., Mohammad, S., Turney, P., Holyoak, K.: Semeval-2012 task 2: measuring degrees of relational similarity. In: SEM 2012: The First Joint Conference on Lexical and Computational Semantics–Volume 1: Proceedings of the Main Conference and the Shared Task, and Volume 2: Proceedings of the Sixth International Workshop on Semantic Evaluation (SemEval 2012), pp. 356–364 (2012)
9. Rindflesch, T.C., Fiszman, M.: The interaction of domain knowledge and linguistic structure in natural language processing: interpreting hypernymic propositions in biomedical text. J. Biomed. Inform. **36**, 462–477 (2003)
10. Aramaki, E., et al.: Extraction of adverse drug effects from clinical records. Medinfo **160**, 739–743 (2010)

11. Gurulingappa, H., Rajput, A.M., Roberts, A., Fluck, J., Hofmann-Apitius, M., Toldo, L.: Development of a benchmark corpus to support the automatic extraction of drug-related adverse effects from medical case reports. J. Biomed. Inform. **45**, 885–892 (2012)

12. Zhang, Y., Lu, Z.: Exploring semi-supervised variational autoencoders for biomedical relation extraction. Methods **166**, 112–119 (2019)

13. Rindflesch, T.C., Fiszman, M.: The interaction of domain knowledge and linguistic structure in natural language processing: interpreting hypernymic propositions in biomedical text. J. Biomed. Inform. **36**(6), 462–477 (2003)

14. Culotta, A., Sorensen, J.: Dependency tree kernels for relation extraction. In: Proceedings of the 42nd Annual Meeting of the Association for Computational Linguistics (ACL-04), Barcelona, pp. 423–429 (2004)

15. Wang, C., James, F.: Medical relation extraction with manifold models. In: Proceedings of the 52nd Annual Meeting of the Association for Computational Linguistics, pp. 828–838 (2014)

16. Song, M., Won, K.C., Dahee, L., Go, E.H., Keun, Y.K.: PKDE4J: entity and relation extraction for public knowledge discovery. J. Biomed. Inform. **57**, 320–332 (2015)

17. Segura-Bedmar, I., Martínez, P., de Pablo-Sánchez, C.: Using a shallow linguistic kernel for drug–drug interaction extraction. J. Biomed. Inform. **44**, 789–804 (2011)

18. Kim, S., Liu, H., Yeganova, L., Wilbur, W.: Extracting drug–drug interactions from literature using a rich feature-based linear kernel approach. J. Biomed. Inform. **55**, 23–30 (2015)

19. Giuliano, C., Lavelli, A., Roman, L.: Exploiting shallow linguistic information for relation extraction from biomedical literature. In: 11th Conference of the European Chapter of the Association for Computational Linguistics, Trento (2006)

20. Kalina, B., Derczynski, L., Funk, A., Greenwood, M., Maynard, D., Aswani, N.: Twitie: an open-source information extraction pipeline for microblog text. In: Proceedings of the International Conference Recent Advances in Natural Language Processing RANLP 2013, Hissar, pp. 83–90 (2013)

21. Hasby, M., Khodra, M.L.: Optimal path finding based on traffic information extraction from Twitter. In: International Conference on ICT for Smart Society, Jakarta, pp. 1–5 (2013)

22. Anggareska, D., Purwarianti, A.: Information extraction of public complaints on Twitter text for bandung government. In: 2014 International Conference on Data and Software Engineering (ICODSE), Bandung, pp. 1–6 (2014)

23. Yu, F., Moh, M., Moh, T.S.: Towards extracting drug-effect relation from Twitter: a supervised learning approach. In: IEEE 2nd International Conference on Big Data Security on Cloud (BigDataSecurity), High Performance and Smart Computing (HPSC), and Intelligent Data and Security (IDS), pp. 339–344. IEEE (2016)

24. Adrover, C., Bodnar, T., Huang, Z., Telenti, A., Salathé, M.: Identifying adverse effects of HIV drug treatment and associated sentiments using Twitter. JMIR Publ. Health Surveill. **1**, e7 (2015)

25. Kuhn, M., Letunic, I., Jensen, L.J., Bork, P.: The SIDER database of drugs and side effects. Nucleic Acids Res. **44**, D1075–D1079 (2015)

26. Devlin, J., Chang, M.W., Lee, K., Toutanova, K.: Bert: pre-training of deep bidirectional transformers for language understanding (2018). https://arxiv.org/abs/1810.04805

27. Mikolov, T., Chen, K., Corrado, G., Dean, J.: Efficient estimation of word representations in vector space. In: Proceedings of Workshop at ICLR, Scottsdale (2013)

28. Wang, Y., et al.: A comparison of word embeddings for the biomedical natural language processing. J. Biomed. Inform. **87**, 12–20 (2018)

29. Angeli, G., Premkumar, M.J., Manning, C.D.: Leveraging linguistic structure for open domain information extraction. In: Proceedings of the 53rd Annual Meeting of the Association for Computational Linguistics and the 7th International Joint Conference on Natural Language Processing, vol. 1, pp. 344–354 (2015)

30. Zeng, Q.T., Tse, T.: Exploring and developing consumer health vocabularies. J. Am. Med. Inform. Assoc. **13**, 24–29 (2006)
31. National Library of Medicine. Unified Medical Language System® (UMLS®) Glossary (2016). https://www.nlm.nih.gov/research/umls/new_users/glossary.html
32. Scheff, S.W.: Nonparametric statistics. In: Fundamental Statistical Principles for the Neurobiologist. Academic Press, New York (2016)
33. Sani, F., Todman, J.: Experimental design and statistics for psychology: a first course. In: Appendix 1: Statistical Tables, pp. 183–196. John Wiley & Sons, New York (2006)
34. Jiang, K., Feng, S., Song, Q., Calix, R.A., Gupta, M., Bernard, G.R.: Identifying tweets of personal health experience through word embedding and LSTM neural network. BMC Bioinformatics **19**(8), 67–74 (2018)

A Scalable AI Approach for Clinical Trial Cohort Optimization

Xiong Liu[1(✉)], Cheng Shi[2], Uday Deore[3], Yingbo Wang[4], Myah Tran[4], Iya Khalil[1], and Murthy Devarakonda[1]

[1] AI Innovation Center, Novartis, Cambridge, MA, USA
[2] Novartis Pharmaceuticals, East Hanover, NJ, USA
[3] Global Drug Development, Novartis, East Hanover, NJ, USA
[4] Global Drug Development, Novartis, Basel, Switzerland

Abstract. FDA has been promoting enrollment practices that could enhance the diversity of clinical trial populations by broadening eligibility criteria. However, how to broaden eligibility remains a significant challenge. We propose an AI approach to Cohort Optimization (AICO) through transformer-based natural language processing of the eligibility criteria and evaluation of the criteria using real-world data. The method can extract common eligibility criteria variables from a large set of relevant trials and measure the generalizability of trial designs to real-world patients. It overcomes the scalability limits of existing manual methods and enables rapid simulation of eligibility criteria design for a disease of interest. A case study on breast cancer trial design demonstrates the utility of the method in improving trial generalizability.

Keywords: Clinical trial · Natural language processing · Real-world data · Cohort optimization · Generalizability

1 Introduction

Previous studies have shown that randomized clinical trials (RCTs) are often selective and not fully representative of the real-world patients [8,15]. Overly restrictive patient selection could lead to low enrollment and compromise study generalizability [7]. Therefore, FDA has been promoting enrollment practices that could lead to enhanced diversity in clinical trials through broadening eligibility criteria [2].

Eligibility criteria play an essential role in defining the study population. The quality of criteria directly affects patient enrollment and study generalizability. The trial-and-error approach to define criteria often leads to many protocol amendments [15]. Data-driven tools are needed to help clinical trial teams discover potential patient pool that was left out before and make better eligibility criteria choices [13].

Clinical trial data are increasingly available through public registries (e.g., ClinicalTrials.gov). Meanwhile, real world data (RWD), such as electronic health

© Springer Nature Switzerland AG 2021
M. Kamp et al. (Eds.): ECML PKDD 2021 Workshops, CCIS 1525, pp. 479–489, 2021.
https://doi.org/10.1007/978-3-030-93733-1_36

records (EHRs), claims and billing data, are increasingly being used in drug development [3]. Combining trial designs (e.g., different eligibility criteria) with RWD could provide insights on the impact of study design in the real-world patient population and hence its generalizability post approval of the drug.

Recently, several eligibility criteria design tools based on RWD have been developed for cohort optimization. For example, Liu et al. developed a computational framework called Trial Pathfinder to systematically evaluate the effect of different eligibility criteria on cancer trial populations and outcomes using RWD [10]. They showed that relaxing criteria in non-small cell lung cancer trials doubled the number of eligible patients while maintaining similar hazard ratio of the overall survival in comparison to more stringent trials. Kim et al. investigated the impact of eligibility criteria on recruitment and clinical outcomes of COVID-19 clinical trials using EHR data [9]. They found that adjusting the thresholds of common eligibility criteria in COVID-19 trials could generate more outcome events with fewer patients. Similarly, Chen et al. used real-world data to simulate clinical trials of Alzheimer's disease. They followed the study protocol of one Alzheimer's disease trial to identify the study population and considered different scenarios for simulating both intervention and control arms. The result showed that trial simulation using RWD is feasible for safety evaluation [4].

However, current methods still face the challenge of scalability. Trial Pathfinder by Liu et al. is based on manual encoding of the eligibility criteria, where they developed rules to encode 10 non-small cell lung cancer trials to select patients. In the study by Kim et al., two researchers manually annotated eligibility criteria from a set of 32 trials using the OMOP data model. These methods are only effective to a small number of trials and are not scalable to hundreds or even thousands of trials.

In addition, current methods focused on outcome events without an explicit measure of trial generalizability. There is a need for quantifying the study cohort representativeness with respect to the real-world patient population. Previous definitions of generalizability, such as the Generalizability Index for Study Trait (GIST) [6], are based on the collective population representativeness of a set of trials measured by quantitative eligibility features. However, these definitions do not capture the cohort representativeness for a single study.

We propose a scalable AI framework for Cohort Optimization, thus called AICO, to automatically extract common eligibility criteria from a large set of clinical trials and evaluate the effect of these eligibility criteria on trial generalizability. Our design is based up on the recent AI advances in transformer-based natural language processing (NLP). Pre-trained language models, such as Bidirectional Encoder Representations from Transformers (BERT), have demonstrated superior performance over previous baseline models across NLP tasks such as question answering and language inference [5]. In the clinical trial domain, a BERT-based model called CT-BERT [12] was recently introduced for named entity (or variable) extraction from the eligibility criteria. CT-BERT was built on ClinicalTrials.gov data by fine-tuning pre-trained BERT models. Previous study on eligibility criteria extraction [12] compared CT-BERT with other baseline models including the

Attention-based Bidirectional LSTM (Att-BiLSTM) model [11] and the Conditional Random Field (CRF) model. The F1 scores for CT-BERT, Att-BiLSTM and CRF were 0.844, 0.802 and 0.804, respectively [12]. This shows the advantage of BERT-based NLP in eligibility criteria extraction. Getting high accuracy makes automatic AI-driven trial design feasible.

We apply CT-BERT to extract quantitative eligibility criteria variables for a set of relevant trials (up to hundreds or thousands) for a disease of interest. We then use the RWD database Optum to evaluate the generalizability of the study cohort defined by the extracted eligibility variables. We introduce a generalizability score for a single trial to measure the representativeness of the study cohort by calculating the percentage of eligible real-world patients. We also include a design capability called "what-if" analysis that allows the trial designer to adjust the thresholds of eligibility variables (e.g., clinical variables) to evaluate how different eligibility criteria designs could impact the study cohort generalizability.

We demonstrated the utility of AICO in designing the eligibility criteria of HR+ HER2- breast cancer trials. We selected an example trial with the ClinicalTrials.gov ID NCT02513394, which is a phase III double blinded, parallel-group trial. We followed the criteria of the study to identify the study population, target population and calculate the generalizability score of the trial. We adjusted the thresholds of two clinical variables of the trial: Absolute neutrophil count and Hemoglobin. The result showed that the generalizability improved by 7% without changing other criteria.

Our contributions include: 1) automatic extraction of common eligibility criteria variables from unstructured eligibility criteria using advanced NLP; 2) identification of eligible patients from RWD (i.e., EHRs) based on the extracted eligibility criteria variables; 3) calculation of clinical trial generalizability score based on the matching between eligibility criteria and EHRs; and 4) a use case in breast cancer which shows that broadening the thresholds of clinical variables improves trial generalizability.

2 Methods

We propose a new approach, called AICO, to enable cohort optimization. Figure 1 shows the AICO framework, which includes BERT NLP-based extraction of eligibility variables and RWD analysis to identify cohorts and optimize trial generalizability. The details are described below.

2.1 Data Sources

Clinical Trial Data Source: Clinical trial protocols for a disease of interest are retrieved from the ClinicalTrials.gov. The data includes metadata (e.g., title, indication, phase, year) and the eligibility criteria text.

RWD Source: Cohort of the disease is identified and assessed from the Optum de-identified EHR database.

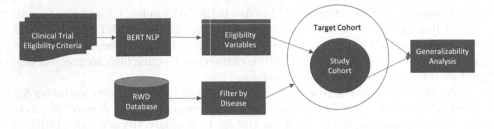

Fig. 1. AICO framework for generalizability analysis and cohort optimization.

2.2   NLP Extraction of Eligibility Criteria

Eligibility criteria are documented as unstructured text, which is not readily suitable for automated cohort definition and knowledge sharing. We apply a deep learning NLP model called CT-BERT [12] to extract variables from the eligibility criteria. CT-BERT is trained by fine-tuning pre-trained BERT models on eligibility criteria. It defines 15 entity (or variable) types in clinical trial text, such as cancer, chronic disease, treatment, and clinical variable. Previous study on a 10-trial benchmark data set shows that CT-BERT achieved F1 of 0.844 and outperformed other baseline models including attention-based BiLSTM and CRF [12].

Given a set of trials for an indication or disease, we use CT-BERT to transform the eligibility criteria text into a set of structured eligibility variables. We then identify the most frequent variables in each variable type. These frequent variables are used to identify real-world patients from the RWD.

2.3   Cohort Identification in RWD

From the Optum database, we identified 2 populations: the target cohort and the study cohort. The target cohort are those who will benefit from the treatment, and thus should be broader as patients with the given disease in general. The study cohort are patients who meet the eligibility criteria based on the eligibility variables in the clinical trial.

The target cohort is identified based on the ICD10 code for the given indication. For example, in the case of metastatic breast cancer, the target cohort is identified using the ICD-10 code C50.

The study cohort is identified by filtering the target cohort. Based on the common variables returned by the CT-BERT NLP model, we convert them to the corresponding variables available in the Optum database. The available variables in Optum are called "computable" eligibility variables, while the unavailable ones are filtered. We then use the computable eligibility variables to identify the study cohort.

2.4 Definition of Trial Generalizability

Previous definitions of trial generalizability, e.g., GIST [6], are based on a set of trials and not applicable to individual eligibility criteria design. We define a new generalizability score for a single trial design by measuring the percentage of study cohort (SC) among the target cohort (TC):

$$Generalizability(T_i) = SC/TC = P(V_1, V_2, \ldots, V_n | I_j)/P(I_j)$$

Where T_i is the ith trial design, $P()$ is the patient count, V_1, V_2, and V_n are the computable eligibility criteria variables, and I_j is the jth indication. If V_n is a continuous variable (e.g., age, BMI), the value range of V_n is determined by the lower bound and upper bound of the variable; if V_n is discrete (e.g., cancer stage), its value is determined by a single value.

The implementation of $P()$ for TC is based on the ICD-10 code or proxy for the given indication. The detailed implementation of $P()$ for SC is based on a relational patient model, where each patient is represented as a vector of the computable variables. Given a specific design, we convert the values for all the computable variables into a structured query over the patient model and retrieve the patient count.

2.5 Evaluating the Impact of Criteria Design

AICO provides the capability to evaluate the criteria design for a given indication based on the computable variables. We call this capability "what-if" analysis because the user can adjust the values of the computable variables and see the generalizability score for the design. By manually adjusting the thresholds of computable variables, the user can either evaluate the generalizability of a completed trial or estimate the generalizability for a new trial design.

3 Results

3.1 Breast Cancer Trials

In this study we focused on the eligibility criteria design for HR+ HER2- breast cancer trials. The relevant trials were identified by search the condition or disease field of ClinicalTrials.gov using the search term 'HR+ HER2- breast cancer'. A total of 125 trials were identified as of March 1, 2021.

3.2 NLP Extraction of Eligibility Criteria

Using CT-BERT, we extracted 11,709 entities from 3,572 criteria sentences in the 125 breast cancer trials. Table 1 shows some examples of the extracted entities and associated entity types. CT-BERT can recognize complex entity types with high accuracy. For example, it can extract "hemoglobin" as clinical variable and "9 g/dl" as its lower bound in a simple criterion (1st criterion). It can

Table 1. Examples of extracted entities from the eligibility criteria of breast cancer trials

Eligibility	Criterion	Entity	Type
Inclusion	Hemoglobin >= 9 g/dL (90 g/L)	Hemoglobin	Clinical variable
		9 g/dL (90 g/L)	Lower bound
Inclusion	Absolute neutrophil count >= 1,500/mcL; platelets >= 100,000/mcL; total bilirubin within 1.25 x normal institutional limits	Absolute neutrophil count	Clinical variable
		1,500/mcL	Lower bound
		platelets	Clinical variable
		100,000/mcL	Lower bound
		Total bilirubin	Clinical variable
		1.25 x normal institutional limits	Upper bound
Exclusion	History of liver disease, such as cirrhosis or chronic active hepatitis B and C	Liver disease	Disease
		Cirrhosis	Disease
		Chronic active hepatitis b and c	Disease
Exclusion	Food or drugs that are known to be CYP3A4 inhibitors	CYP3A4 inhibitors	Treatment

also extract multiple variables such as "absolute neutrophil count", "platelets", and "total bilirubin" and associated value ranges in more complex criterion (2nd criterion). Other variables such as prior disease and treatment are also extracted. The extracted variable names are standardized using a rule-based method to facilitate the follow-up analysis. For example, "ANC" and "absolute neutrophil count (ANC)" are standardized to the same concept of "absolute neutrophil count".

3.3   Common Eligibility Criteria in Breast Cancer Trials

We identified common eligibility criteria variables based on their frequency in the 125 trials. The most frequent variables across all types include demographic variables (e.g., women, age), disease variables (e.g., breast cancer, metastatic disease), treatment variables (e.g., chemotherapy, endocrine therapy), and clinical variables (e.g., ECOG, platelets, creatinine).

Figure 2 shows the most frequent clinical variables ranked by the number of unique trials. The top 5 variables include ECOG, platelets, creatinine, bilirubin, and hemoglobin. 85 trials considered ECOG in the eligibility criteria, making it the most common clinical variable.

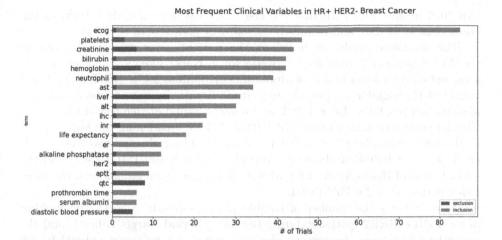

Fig. 2. Top 20 clinical variables in the eligibility criteria of breast cancer trials.

3.4 The Target Cohort and Study Cohort in RWD

We identified the target cohort of HR+ HER2- breast cancer patients based on ICD-10 code C50. We did not consider sub-cohort by HR or HER2 status because it is not available in ICD-10. A better method to estimate HR and HER2 status [14] shall be developed in the future. In addition, we used the overall index period as 2009–2021 based on the start dates of the 125 trials. In total, we identified 199,169 patients in the Optum database during the overall index period.

For simplification, we used the most common clinical variables to define the study cohort. We then identified the 'computable' variables available in Optum, including ALT, AST, bilirubin, creatinine, hemoglobin, and neutrophil. All the values for the variables were cleaned and normalized with the standard unit. The same set of variables were also used to characterize the target cohort.

3.5 Cohort Optimization Study

We studied the impact of the thresholds of the clinical variables on generalizability for three clinical trials, including one real trial (NCT02513394) and two simulated trials.

The NCT02513394 trial is a Phase III study evaluating the addition of 2 years of Palbociclib to standard adjuvant endocrine therapy for patients with HR+/HER2- early breast cancer (EBC). It has the following inclusion criteria using 4 common clinical variables: 1) Absolute neutrophil count $>= 1.5\ 109$/L; 2) Hemoglobin $>= 10$ g/dl; 3) Total Bilirubin $<= 3$ x ULN; and 4) AST $<= 1.5$ x ULN. We selected the ULN for total bilirubin as 1.2 mg/dL and the ULN for AST as 24 units per liter. The enrollment start date was Aug 26, 2015 and end date Feb 11, 2019. We selected the index period for real-world patients as

Jan 2014 to Jan 2019 such that the last diagnosis date is within 2 year of the enrollment start date and before the enrollment end date of the trial.

The simulated trials are based on the patient event grade definitions in the NCI Common Terminology Criteria for Adverse Events [1], where Grade 1 patients have a lower bound of absolute neutrophil as $1.5 \times 109/L$ and a lower bound of Hemoglobin as $10\,g/dl$, and Grade 2 patients have a lower bound of absolute neutrophil as $1.0 \times 109/L$ and a lower bound of Hemoglobin as $8\,g/dl$. The 1st simulated trial modified NCT02513394 by broadening the lower bound of absolute neutrophil to $1.0 \times 109/L$ (Grade 2). The 2nd simulated trial broadened the lower bound of absolute neutrophil to $1.0 \times 109/L$ (Grade 2) and the lower bound of Hemoglobin to $8\,g/dl$ (Grade 2). Both simulations used the same index period as in NCT02513394.

Table 2 shows the number of eligible patients (study cohort), the number of total HR+ HER2- patients during the index period (target cohort), and the generalizability score (percentage of study cohort among target cohort) for all trials. The real trial has a generalizability score of 80.15%, the 1st simulated trial improved the generalizability to 80.90% by broadening only absolute neutrophil, and the 2nd simulated trial further improved the generalizability to 85.70% by reducing the hemoglobin level threshold. This demonstrates that relaxing the thresholds of clinical variables can improve the trial generalizability up to 7% (80.15% vs 85.70%).

4   Discussion

4.1   AICO Advantages

AICO has several distinctive features. First, it can automatically process a large number of relevant trials to identify common eligibility criteria variables. This provides improvement over other methods which are manual and limited to a small number of trials. Although manual extraction of eligibility criteria ensures accuracy, it faces a scalability issue at the same time. Our method leverages the cutting-edge BERT-based models (i.e., CT-BERT) to extract eligibility criteria variables. Previous study has shown that CT-BERT achieved a F1 score of 0.844 and outperformed other baselines based on a 10-trial benchmark data set. We did not measure the F1 score for the current breast cancer study due to the lack of benchmark data. Visual inspection of the extraction results showed that their quality is sufficient to enable downstream RWD analysis. In fact, the common eligibility variables shown in Fig. 2 confirmed our prior knowledge about breast cancer trials.

Table 2. The number of patients and trial generalizability in breast cancer trials

Trial	Eligibility criteria	Study cohort	Target cohort	Generalizability
Real trial (NCT02513394)	• Absolute neutrophil ≥ 1.5 109/L • Hemoglobin ≥ 10 g/dl • Total Bilirubin ≤ 3 x ULN • AST ≤ 1.5 x ULN	75,432	94,114	80.15%
Simulated trial 1	• Absolute neutrophil ≥ 1.0 109/L • Hemoglobin ≥ 10 g/dl • Total Bilirubin ≤ 3 x ULN • AST ≤ 1.5 x ULN	76,132	94,114	80.90%
Simulated trial 2	• Absolute neutrophil ≥ 1.0 109/L • Hemoglobin ≥ 8 g/dl • Total Bilirubin ≤ 3 x ULN • AST ≤ 1.5 x ULN	80,655	94,114	85.70%

Second, AICO defines an intuitive generalizability score for each trial design by comparing the study cohort with the target cohort in RWD. Previous cohort optimization methods focused on evaluating outcome events instead of measuring the trial generalizability. Also, previous generalizability studies defined generalizability for a set of trials, which is not applicable to a single trial design. Our generalizability definition not only connects the common eligibility variables with the RWD patients but also measures the representativeness of study cohort.

Third, AICO enables cohort optimization through what-if analysis. Our case study in breast cancer shows that adjusting the thresholds of clinical variables improved the generalizability. Although the threshold adjustment is still a manual process, it is possible to incorporate domain knowledge about the trials to make more meaningful adjustment. For example, we adjusted the lower bounds of absolute neutrophil and hemoglobin for NCT02513394 (a phase III trial on Palbociclib) based on the event grades defined in the NCI Common Terminology Criteria for Adverse Events [1]. So the adjusted thresholds should not be totally arbitrary.

4.2 Limitations

This study also has several limitations. First, we leveraged the existing entity or variable type definition in CT-BERT without considering disease or trial specific entities. CT-BERT includes 15 entity types in clinical text such as disease, treatment, clinical variables, and value ranges. However, more fine-grained types such as mutation status, biopsy and histology are still needed for oncology trials.

Second, the study cohort definition is based on common eligibility criteria variables across relevant trials. Less common or frequent variable types were not used, which could miss unique features for individual trials. However, it is possible to combine common variables and trial-specific variables to better define the cohort for a specific trial.

Third, we only performed case studies using the Optum database. Although Optum provides comprehensive EHRs, it may not include all variables identified by the CT-BERT NLP model. That is why we introduced 'computable' variables to only include available variables in Optum RWD. To enable more computable variables, more RWD databases such as Flatiron will need to be explored.

5 Conclusions

We present AICO, a new framework for scalable cohort optimization based on advanced NLP and RWD assessment of trial generalizability. It facilitates eligibility criteria design for a given clinical trial of interest, allowing possibility for the study to enroll faster and to enroll patients who are most likely to receive the drug if approved. We performed a case study in HR+ HER2- breast cancer to automatically extract eligibility variables from hundreds of relevant trials to enable cohort definition and identification. We then experimented how different eligibility criteria choices may impact the size of the study cohort and the trial generalizability. We found that broadening the thresholds of clinical variables could improve the generalizability through trial simulations. Thus, our approach overcomes the scalability limits of previous manual methods and enables rapid simulation of trial design towards better generalizability.

Future work will include 1) identifying and extracting new variable types that are not covered by existing NLP models, 2) refining study cohort definition to include both common and trial-specific variables, 3) strategies to map eligibility variables to more 'computable' variables in RWD by exploring more RWD databases, and 4) developing more use cases in different disease areas.

References

1. Common Terminology Criteria for Adverse Events (CTCAE) Version 5.0 (2017). https://ctep.cancer.gov/protocoldevelopment/electronic_applications/ctc. htm. Accessed 25 Aug 2021
2. Enhancing the Diversity of Clinical Trial Populations - Eligibility Criteria, Enrollment Practices, and Trial Designs Guidance for Industry (2021). https:// www.fda.gov/regulatory-information/search-fda-guidance-documents/enhancing-diversity-clinical-trial-populations-eligibility-criteria-enrollment-practices-and-trial. Accessed 1 July 2021
3. Chen, Z., Liu, X., Hogan, W., Shenkman, E., Bian, J.: Applications of artificial intelligence in drug development using real-world data. Drug Discov. Today (2020)
4. Chen, Z., et al.: Exploring the feasibility of using real-world data from a large clinical data research network to simulate clinical trials of Alzheimer's disease. NPJ Digit. Med. 4(1), 1–9 (2021)
5. Devlin, J., Chang, M.W., Lee, K., Toutanova, K.: BERT: pre-training of deep bidirectional transformers for language understanding. arXiv preprint arXiv:1810.04805 (2018)
6. He, Z., Chandar, P., Ryan, P., Weng, C.: Simulation-based evaluation of the generalizability index for study traits. In: AMIA Annual Symposium Proceedings, vol. 2015, p. 594. American Medical Informatics Association (2015)
7. He, Z., et al.: Clinical trial generalizability assessment in the big data era: a review. Clin. Transl. Sci. 13(4), 675–684 (2020)

8. Kennedy-Martin, T., Curtis, S., Faries, D., Robinson, S., Johnston, J.: A literature review on the representativeness of randomized controlled trial samples and implications for the external validity of trial results. Trials **16**(1), 1–14 (2015)

9. Kim, J.H., et al.: Towards clinical data-driven eligibility criteria optimization for interventional COVID-19 clinical trials. J. Am. Med. Inform. Assoc. **28**(1), 14–22 (2021)

10. Liu, R., et al.: Evaluating eligibility criteria of oncology trials using real-world data and AI. Nature **592**(7855), 629–633 (2021)

11. Liu, X., Finelli, L.A., Hersch, G.L., Khalil, I.: Attention-based LSTM network for COVID-19 clinical trial parsing. In: 2020 IEEE International Conference on Big Data (Big Data), pp. 3761–3766. IEEE (2020)

12. Liu, X., Hersch, G., Khalil, I., Devarakonda, M.: Clinical trial information extraction with BERT. In: IEEE International Conference on Healthcare Informatics (2021)

13. Sharma, N.S.: Patient centric approach for clinical trials: current trend and new opportunities. Perspect. Clin. Res. **6**(3), 134 (2015)

14. Twelves, C., et al.: Systemic treatment of hormone receptor positive, human epidermal growth factor 2 negative metastatic breast cancer: retrospective analysis from leeds cancer centre. BMC Cancer **20**(1), 1–12 (2020)

15. Weng, C.: Optimizing clinical research participant selection with informatics. Trends Pharmacol. Sci. **36**(11), 706–709 (2015)

Private Cross-Silo Federated Learning
for Extracting Vaccine Adverse Event Mentions

Pallika Kanani[1](✉), Virendra J. Marathe[2], Daniel Peterson[3], Rave Harpaz[4],
and Steve Bright[5]

[1] Oracle Labs, Burlington, MO, USA
pallika.kanani@oracle.com
[2] Oracle Labs, Nashua, NH, USA
virendra.marathe@oracle.com
[3] Oracle Labs, Broomfield, CO, USA
daniel.peterson@oracle.com
[4] Oracle, New York, NY, USA
rave.harpaz@oracle.com
[5] Oracle, Las Vegas, NY, USA
steve.bright@oracle.com

Abstract. Federated Learning (FL) is quickly becoming a goto distributed training paradigm for users to jointly train a global model without physically sharing their data. Users can indirectly contribute to, and directly benefit from a much larger aggregate data corpus used to train the global model. However, literature on successful application of FL in real-world problem settings is somewhat sparse. In this paper, we describe our experience applying a FL based solution to the Named Entity Recognition (NER) task for an adverse event detection application in the context of mass scale vaccination programs. We present a comprehensive empirical analysis of various dimensions of benefits gained with FL based training. Furthermore, we investigate effects of tighter *Differential Privacy (DP)* constraints in highly sensitive settings where federation users must enforce DP to ensure strict privacy guarantees. We show that DP can severely cripple the global model's prediction accuracy, thus disincentivizing users from participating in the federation. In response, we demonstrate how recent innovation in *personalization* methods can help significantly recover the lost accuracy.

1 Introduction

Federated Learning (FL) is a distributed ML paradigm that enables multiple users to jointly train a shared model without sharing their data with any other users [4,30], offering advantages in both scale and privacy. In FL, multiple users wish to perform essentially the same task using ML, with a model architecture that is agreed upon in advance. Each user wants the best possible model for their individual use, but often has a limited budget for labeling their own data. Pooling the data of multiple users could improve model accuracy, because accuracy generally increases with increased training data. However user data cannot be shipped to a common model training facility due to bandwidth limitations or data privacy concerns. As a result, users locally train the

M. Kamp et al. (Eds.): ECML PKDD 2021 Workshops, CCIS 1525, pp. 490–505, 2021.
https://doi.org/10.1007/978-3-030-93733-1_37

shared (global) model on their local data, and thereafter send the updated model to the *federation server*. The federation server aggregates updates received from its users to improve the global model for all users.

Although the initial focus of FL has been on targeting millions of mobile devices [4], also called *cross-device FL*, the benefits of its architecture are evident even for institutional settings, also called *cross-silo FL* [28]. While cross-device FL is concerned with both bandwidth consumption and data privacy, cross-silo federations and their users are considered well equipped with resources to handle bandwidth concerns, and data privacy is the primary objective. Our work focuses on the cross-silo FL setting.

Today our world grapples with safely rolling out massive scale vaccination programs to end a pandemic. Understanding adverse events related to these vaccines is critically important. These adverse events are often expressed in free text form, such as social media posts and reports provided to health care agencies and pharmaceutical companies. Currently, mentions of specific adverse events are extracted and coded manually, which is a time consuming, expensive and non-scalable process. Therefore, Machine Learning (ML) based methods to extract named entities (adverse events) automatically from such unstructured data are highly desirable.

Typically, more training data yield more accurate models. Unfortunately, collecting human annotations for building such Named Entity Recognition (NER) models is expensive, and particularly challenging given the need to maintain privacy of health records. One way to overcome this data scarcity issue would be for various agencies to share their data to build a joint model with combined data. However, privacy concerns, government regulation and data use agreements might not allow the data to leave individual organizational or geographical silos. Sharing user data with other users is absolutely not an option in these settings.

Cross-silo FL makes perfect sense to address such problems. Each vaccine provider's data remains in its private *silo*. At the same time, the provider can collaborate with other providers on a FL framework to collectively improve the NER model used for adverse event detection. Everyone benefits without violating data privacy. More specifically, for institutions participating in a federation as users, restricting data movement helps fulfill contractual obligations with their customers and comply with legal regulatory constraints on data movement [6, 17].

However, restricting the provider's training data to its private silo does not guarantee complete privacy. Recent works have demonstrated that the data can indirectly leak out through model updates shipped by users to the federation server [3, 42, 44]. To combat this problem, researchers have proposed the addition of Differential Privacy (DP) [12–14] to FL [1, 19, 31, 41].

Informally, DP aims to provide a bound on the variation in the model's output based on the inclusion or exclusion of a single data point used in its training set. This is done by introducing precisely calibrated noise in the training process. The method of noise calibration and injection varies between implementations [1, 41], but is always structured to enforce the precise formal DP guarantee, which we define in Sect. 2. We will refer to this process as "DP inducing noise injection" henceforth. This noise makes it difficult, even impossible, to determine whether any particular data point was used to train the model.

In settings where the federation server is trusted, DP enforcement is delegated to the federation server [41]. However, in settings where users do not trust even the federation server, DP may need to be enforced by the users locally [29]. While all this noise is structured to enforce formally provable privacy guarantees for each training data point [13], it can significantly degrade accuracy of model predictions. This degradation may happen to an extent that disincentivizes users from participating in the federation – the global (noisy) model performs worse than a user-resident local model trained just on the user's dataset, which we call the *individual* model.

Another instance where the global model may perform worse than the individual model for a user is when the user's data distribution is different from most of the users, or the users collectively have non-IID training data [25,37]. There is a rapidly growing body of FL *Personalization* literature to address this problem [11,15,38,39,45,52], a handful of which addresses model degradation due to DP induced noise [45,52].

We are interested in applying this body of work to real-world problem settings. The health care sector is one such application domain that can leverage FL in significant ways. Indeed there is rapidly growing awareness and investment in FL at world-wide scale including consortiums [43] and public-private partnerships [26]. This is accompanied by the beginnings of applied research in this sector [36].

In this paper, we case study application of FL to the problem of vaccine adverse event detection, the first of its kind to the best of our knowledge. Importance of such a study cannot be understated in today's pandemic stricken world. Given the unprecedented speed at which new vaccines have been rolled out, it is crucial to automatically extract mentions of adverse events related to these vaccines from patient reports. We study implications of applying FL to train a Named Entity Recognition (NER) model on the Vaccine Adverse Event Reporting System (VAERS) dataset that we have annotated and partitioned by vaccine manufacturers. Each vaccine manufacturer acts as a federation user whose dataset is *siloed* in its private sandbox; all these sandboxes participate in our FL framework over multiple training rounds.

Our experiments reveal several interesting insights including general effectiveness of FL on model performance, effects of DP enforcement on model performance, and the value of personalization techniques to incentivize users to participate in FL. In particular, we show that FL improves average F1 value by 37.43% over the individual model, while enforcement of DP (DP-FL) degrades the FL model's average F1 by 25.17%. For one of the users, this degradation is so severe that the private FL model F1 is worse by 45.55% when compared with the individual model F1. This clearly makes DP-FL a non-starter for some users to join the federation. We study FL with *Fine-Tuning* (FT-FL) [52], a personalization approach that fine-tunes the global model at each user *after* the entire FL training process completes. Interestingly, contrary to prior work [52], simply augmenting fine-tuning to FL does not result in prediction accuracy improvement for the federation users. Instead, user accuracy degrades in most cases. However, somewhat surprisingly, fine-tuning in the presence of DP (FT-DP-FL) boosts user accuracy by 24.88%, compared to the individual model, to strongly incentivize users to join and stay with the federation. We also observe that vaccine reports related to different manufacturers have slightly different vocabulary (e.g. mentions of different vaccine names), and different distributions of adverse events, which aid FT-DP-FL in effectively recovering lost accuracy.

Even more interestingly, our findings indicate a unique *incentive structure* for users to join the federation. In particular, we find that users with small amount of training data, a.k.a. *small* users, have a strong incentive to join and stay with the federation even when DP is enforced without fine-tuning. This is because the user's private dataset is so small that any locally trained individual model performs poorly. Furthermore, even the global model that is degraded because of DP inducing noise performs significantly better than the user's individual model. In short, small users have virtually no incentive to leave the federation, and may not require additional layers of personalization to improve the global model as long as there are enough participants in the federation.

For users with larger amount of data, the narrative is quite different. In particular, we observe that the global model's degradation due to DP inducing noise is significant enough to disincentivize those users from participating in the federation. As a result, if they opt for the additional layer of privacy through DP, the importance of personalization based enhancements, which salvage the accuracy lost due to DP inducing noise, cannot be understated.

In summary, this paper makes the following contributions:

- We present the first comprehensive study, to the best of our knowledge, on application of FL to the vaccine adverse event detection task in the field of pharmacoviligence on real-world data – the **VAERS** dataset.
- Our study examines benefits of FL based training, along with its robustness to user participation.
- We examine challenges posed by enforcement of differential privacy, to the extent that may disincentivize users from participating in a federation.
- We show that, unlike prior work [52], simply augmenting FL with personalization techniques, such as the aforementioned fine-tuning (FT-FL), does not necessarily improve prediction accuracy for FL users. In fact, it degrades prediction accuracy in our experiments. However, somewhat surprisingly, the same techniques (FT-DP-FL) turn out to be highly effective in recovering lost accuracy due to DP inducing noise injection. We furthermore show that personalization is robust to user participation uncertainties (e.g. users dropping out).
- We report an interesting new *incentive structure* amongst users participating in the federation, where users with small amount of training data are strongly incentivized to join and stay with the federation, whereas users with somewhat larger amounts of data require enhancements, such as FT-DP-FL, to overcome the pitfalls of DP inducing noise injection.
- Another surprising finding in our study is that fine-tuning based personalization is highly resilient to increasingly tighter margins for the differential privacy budget ($\epsilon < 1$).

The rest of the paper is structured as follows: We discuss background material and related work in Sect. 2. The VAERS system used as the basis of this study is described in Sect. 3. We describe our NER model used in an adverse event detection system, along with our FL framework and the personalization approach we use in Sect. 4. Our comprehensive experiments and their analysis appears in Sect. 5.

2   Background

Federated Learning (FL). In FL, a federation server initializes a global model and ships it to all participating users thereby initiating distributed training. Training happens over multiple rounds. In each round, each user, on receiving the global model re-trains the model on its private data and sends back the resulting parameter updates to the federation server. The federation server aggregates updates from all users applying them to the global model, and then ships the revised model back to the users. The most widely used method of aggregation is FedAvg [30,40], where user parameter updates are averaged at the federation server and applied to the global model. Formally, FedAvg solves the following optimization problem:

$$\min_{w \in \mathcal{R}^d} f(w) \qquad where, f(w) \stackrel{\text{def}}{=} \frac{1}{n} \sum_{i=1}^{n} f_i(w) \tag{1}$$

The function $f_i = \mathcal{L}(w; x_i, y_i)$ represents the local loss for each of the n federation users on the model w using the user's private data x_i, y_i.

Figure 1 shows the overall FL architecture. Users can dynamically join the federation or drop out. The framework is structured to be resilient to such changes. Noting privacy concerns, more recent work has proposed addition of differential privacy to FL [19,31,40].

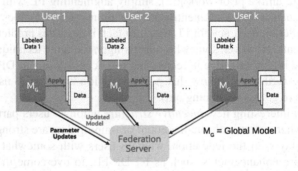

Fig. 1. The Federated Learning setting. M_G is the global model the federation server sends to users, each of which re-trains M_G on its private data and sends the updated model parameters back to the federation server.

Differential Privacy (DP). Differential Privacy [13] is a mathematically quantifiable privacy guarantee for a data set used by a computation that analyzes it. While it originally emerged in the database and data mining communities, triggered by privacy concerns in Machine Learning (ML) [16,24,33,47,49], DP has garnered enormous traction in the ML community over the last decade [1,5,7,9,10].

In DP, the privacy guarantee applies to each individual item in the data set and is formally specified in terms of a pair of data sets that differ in at most one item. Specifically, consider an algorithm A such that $A : D \mapsto R$, where D and R are respectively the domain and range of A. Now consider two data sets d and d' that differ from each other in exactly one data item. Such data sets are considered *adjacent* to each other in the DP literature. Algorithm A is said to be (ε, δ)-differentially private if the following condition holds true for all adjacent d and d' and any subset of outputs $O \subseteq R$:

$$P[A(d) \in O] \leq e^\varepsilon P[A(d') \in O] + \delta \qquad (2)$$

Enforcement of DP typically translates into introduction of a "correction" in algorithm A to ensure that the differential privacy bound holds for any two adjacent inputs. This correction is commonly referred to as the *noise* introduced in the algorithm, its input, or output to ensure that the (ε, δ)-differential privacy bound holds. While a disciplined introduction of noise guarantees DP, the noise itself leads to accuracy degradation in the output produced by A. In the context of ML, the algorithm is a model being trained using sensitive private data sets, and accuracy degradation can significantly hamper the model's utility.

Personalization in FL. The basic FL algorithm, FedAvg, assumes IID training data across all FL users. In fact, it is known to be quite effective in practice for such data distributions. However, FedAvg may perform poorly in the presence of non-IID user data [25,37]. A recent flurry of research addresses this problem using *personalization* techniques [11,15,38,39,45,52] that specialize training at each user, typically in the form of training an additional local model, or letting the local copy of the global model "drift" from the global model in a constrained fashion. This enables the local model to fit better to the user's local data distribution thereby delivering a better performing model.

Adverse Event Mention Extraction. By some estimates, adverse drug reactions are among the leading causes of death in the developed world. Reports of adverse events are a critical source of information for tracking and studying adverse events associated with medicinal products. However, portions of the sought information is only available in unstructured format. The use of and necessity of automated methods for extracting mentions of drug adverse events from unstructured text is widely recognized in pharmacovigilance [23]. Several different genres of text are tackled in this line of research, including social media [21,32], biomedical literature [34,50], clinical narratives [22,35] and drug labels [46]. More recently, use of state of the art deep learning technology for NER have been proposed [20].

3   Vaccine Adverse Event Reporting System

Drug and vaccine safety surveillance relies predominantly on spontaneous reporting systems. These systems are comprised of reports of suspected drug/vaccine adverse events (potential side effects) collected from healthcare professionals, consumers, and pharmaceutical companies, and maintained largely by regulatory and health agencies. Among other, these systems are used to detect possible safety problems - called "signals" - that may be related to a vaccination or the consumption of a drug. In the US, the prominent surveillance system for vaccines is the U.S. Centers for Disease Control and Prevention (CDC) and the Food and Drug Administration (FDA) Vaccine Adverse Event Reporting System (VAERS), created in 1990.

The VAERS data (de-identified) is publicly available in structured format. Each VAERS report includes the name of (and additional information about) the administrated vaccine, a list of adverse events related to the vaccine, dates, and limited demographic information about the patient receiving the vaccine (e.g., age, gender). Importantly, the report also includes a textual narrative describing the adverse event. For example,

"Shortly after patient was vaccinated, she started to feel an itching, tingling feeling in her throat. Fearing that it was an allergic reaction, I called 911. The patient remained alert, talking and breathing normally until paramedics arrived, though she stated that she started to feel additional tingling in her arms and chest."

In this example, the following token spans would be annotated as adverse events: "itching", "tingling feeling in her throat", "allergic reaction", "tingling in her arms and chest".

Most of the data collected in VAERS is currently processed by humans for downstream applications. Adverse event reports, whether they're forms, emails, articles, or other source documents, do not arrive in structured format, which means they have to be entered manually into safety systems. This manual data entry can take hours and represents a significant cost to the organization. Free-text narratives take the most time, requiring a manual sift through every sentence to find relevant information and then enter it into the correct field. With the rapidly increasing volume of such data this human effort is becoming prohibitive and calls for the increased use of automated methods such as NER. In addition, pharmacovigilance data such as that available in and similar to VAERS originates from private siloed sources, motivating the need for privacy preserving distributed approaches such as FL.

4   Model and Framework

4.1   NER Based on Recurrent Neural Networks

The recurrent neural network (RNN) architecture we used to perform NER is based on a commonly applied BiLSTM architecture. The architecture consists of three major components: (1) a word representation layer made of word embeddings, (2) two stacked layers of bidirectional long short-term memory (LSTM) cells, and (3) a feedforward layer that performs the final BIO sequence labeling.

Pre-trained word embeddings were used to seed the network's word embedding layer. These were generated using Word2Vec applied to the sentences comprising the VAERS NER dataset described in Sect. 5. Dropout regularization was implemented between each of the three major network components. The dropout rate was 0.4.

The network was implemented on PyTorch6 and trained using stochastic minibatch gradient descent with the Adam optimizer for a pre-defined number of iterations. Each iteration processed a batch of 256 randomly selected sentences. The network was trained for a total of 20 epochs, each epoch consisting of number of sentences in the training set/batch size iterations.

4.2   Federated Learning Framework

We have implemented our own FL simulation framework, on PyTorch6, that hosts the federation server and users on the same computer. The framework supports several federated aggregation protocols, including FedAvg and FedSGD [30], of which we use FedAvg in our evaluation. The framework is extendable to support other custom aggregation protocols [11, 15, 38, 45, 52].

Trust Model Considerations and Differential Privacy. The decision to train a ML model using the FL framework requires careful analysis of privacy considerations for users' data. More specifically, the *meaning* of the term "data privacy" in a given setting needs to be precisely understood since it has profound implications on techniques required to enforce the desired data privacy. For instance, in some settings, simply restricting user data to its private silo is sufficient for the use case. On the other hand, in settings involving highly sensitive private data (e.g. health records of individuals), it may be desirable to ensure that even the parameter updates shipped from the user silo to the federation server cannot be reverse engineered by any means, external to the user, to determine the user's training data records. Ultimately, the level of privacy protection must be agreed upon by all parties involved. While an exhaustive treatment of a taxonomy of such *trust models* in FL is beyond the scope of this paper, we assume that personal health records describing an adverse reaction to a vaccine are highly sensitive private material. Consequently, they must be protected using techniques guaranteeing the strictest data privacy.

In the FL setting, these data records would be hosted in a participating pharmaceutical company's silo. The pharmaceutical company's silo performs the role of a user in the federation. We view Differential Privacy (DP) as an appropriate tool to enforce privacy guarantees to individuals' health records. However, more careful analysis of how DP is enforced in FL settings is required. Other technologies such as secure multi-party computation [51] and homomorphic encryption [18] may be worth considering, but are beyond the scope of this work. Additional security technologies such as end-to-end encryption may be necessary to augument to the DP solution, but is also outside the scope of this work.

We assume a trust model where users do not trust the federation server, and enforce DP *locally* on the parameter updates shipped back to the server. To enforce DP locally, we use the algorithm proposed by Abadi et al. [1] that injects gaussian noise (calculated using their moments accountant algorithm) in parameter gradients during local training at each user. Noisy gradients lead to noisy parameter updates, which are eventually shipped from the user to the federation server.

Interestingly, since users can possess datasets with different sizes, the computed noise, which is a function of the dataset size, varies considerably from user to user. For instance, the noise introduced for a user with a handful of data points is much higher than the noise introduced by a user with a much larger private dataset. However, FedAvg smoothes out the noisy updates through the parameter aggregation process (averaging, in our case). The resulting model that each user receives is much more robust. Note that our implementation of DP covers the privacy of each narrative, but we assume that there is not enough information in the data to link multiple narratives relating to the same person.

Personalization Through Fine Tuning. The main allure of FL for a user is the promise of significant prediction accuracy improvements over a locally trained *individual* model. While parameter aggregation through FL can significantly improve accuracy of the global model, introduction of noise to enforce DP can severely compromise that improvement. The degradation can be severe enough to make users reconsider their decision to join the federation, and deter new users from joining the federation. Furthermore, data distributions across users may have significant side effects on the global model's prediction accuracy: If a user's dataset has a significantly different distribution than most of the federation users, the global model may perform worse than a locally trained individual model. If users of a federation have non-IID data, the resulting global model may be ineffective [37].

Many researchers have recently proposed different forms of *personalization* approaches to remedy the disparate data distribution problem [2,8,27,38,39,45,48,52]. Just two of these works [45,52], to the best of our knowledge, propose personalization approaches as solutions to model degradation due to DP inducing noise. Among the proposed personalization approaches, we focus on FL with *Fine Tuning* [52]: FT-FL for fine tuning on top of plain FL, and FT-DP-FL for fine tuning on top of FL with DP enforcement at the user. In this approach each user continues training, without noise, the local copy of the global differentially private model *after* the FL training process has completed.

The fine tuning based parameter updates are private to each user and are not shared with the federation. As a result, the fine tuned local models may diverge from the global model at varying degrees in order to better fit the users' private data. While endlessly fine tuning the global model can lead to the model converging to a locally trained individual model, care must be taken to ensure that the fine-tuned model does not deteriorate. This can be achieved through standard hyperparameter tuning techniques.

5   Experiments

5.1   Dataset

We used a total of 17,841 narratives submitted to VAERS through the years 2015–2017 to form the NER data set used for this study. The narratives were automatically annotated for adverse event named entities using the list of adverse events supplied with each report. In total the NER data set used for this study comprised of 87,730 sentences and 39,139 annotated adverse event named entities. In our experiments, we split the data randomly into train, validation, tune and test sets in the proportion 60%, 10%, 10%, and 20% respectively. We used the validation set to decide early stopping in the fine tuning algorithm and tuned the rest of parameters on the tune set. We refer to "large manufacturers" as those with more than 1000 VAERS reports in this data and "small manufacturers" as those with fewer reports to reflect the availability of training data in each user's silo. In the rest of this paper, we use the terms 'manufacturer' and 'user' interchangeably.

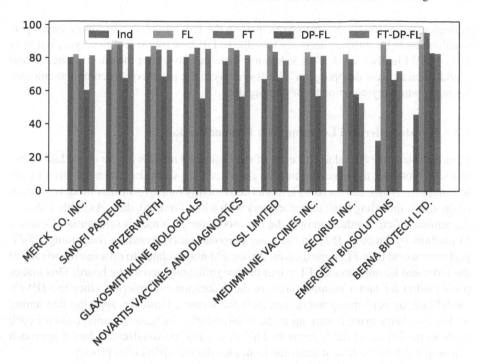

Fig. 2. F1 per manufacturer for different methods for $\epsilon = 2.0$

5.2 Experimental Setup

As the first baseline for our experiments, we train Individual models (*Ind*), i.e. assume that each manufacturer only uses their own training set, and test on their respective test set. This baseline represents the case in which the manufacturer chooses not to partici-pate in the federation at all. *FL* is the federated learning model trained in a collaborative fashion across users using the FedAvg algorithm. This model is then fine tuned for each user using the protocol described in Sect. 4, which yield a set of models, one per manu-facturer, that we call *FT*. Next, we introduce DP to the *FL* model, as described in Sect. 4. We use $\epsilon = 2.0$ for this first set of experiments as it is considered a fairly conservative privacy setting in the literature [1] and calculate the sigma values suitable per user. We call this private federated learning variant *DP-FL*. Finally, we fine tune this private FL model and call it *FT-DP-FL*.

The training parameters for all of these algorithms were tuned using a separate tuning dataset. We use a learning rate of 0.01 and train all the federated models for 20 rounds of FedAvg, with additional 20 epochs for the fine tuning variants at each manufacturer. For evaluation, we compute the precision, recall, and F1 of each token label on a 1-vs-all basis. The values reported are the mean F1 score (henceforth called F1) for the labels at the beginning or inside of an adverse event mention.

We ask the following questions as part of this study. Does *FL* perform better than *Ind* models across users? What happens when differential privacy is introduced? Does personalization help improve accuracy over *FL* and mitigate *DP-FL*'s accuracy loss enough to re-incentivize users to participate in the federation? If fine-tuning based per-sonalization helps mitigate accuracy loss due to DP, how robust is it to varying parame-ters of DP? Finally, we ask if the federation is stable enough for the uncertainties of real world, such as users dropping out? We also analyze the incentive structure that emerges for users with varying amounts of training data.

5.3   Private Federated Learning with Personalization

Figure 2 shows the F1 values for each of the described models on the individual users' test sets. Note that the manufacturers on the x-axis are sorted based on the size of their training sets. As we can see, the FL model consistently outperforms *Ind* models for each of the users, including large manufacturers with a lot of training data. As Table 1 shows, the amount of error reduction over the *Ind* model for each user is substantial. Contrary to findings by Yu et al. [52], in our case, personalization based on fine tuning *FT-FL* performs worse than *FL* in most cases. As we add noise related to differential privacy to the federated learning model, F1 values drop significantly across the board. This makes participation for larger manufacturers in the federation unattractive, since the *DP-FL* model ends up performing worse than their *Ind* models. However, applying fine tuning in this case helps bring it back up to the point, where it is again advantageous for each party to participate in the federation. This shows that personalization based approach can help mitigate the loss of accuracy from introducing differential privacy.

Table 1. F1 and Error Reduction with Federated Learning and Private Federated Learning with Fine Tuning. 'Vaccine Manufacturer' is a field in the public **VAERS** database that identifies the manufacturer of the vaccine reported in the **VAERS** form. There is no relationship between this field and the reporter. 'Num **VAERS** Reports' does not represent the rate of adverse events associ-ated with the manufacturer or its products and cannot be used to estimate such rates. The statistics are based on a sample of reports submitted to **VAERS** between 2015–2017 whose MedDra coded adverse events appeared in the narrative. Because the statistics are based on a carefully selected sample, the distribution of reports shown may not represent the true distribution of reports asso-ciated with different vaccine manufacturers.

Vaccine manufacture	Num reports	Individual F1	FL		FT-DP-FL	
			F1	Error red.	F1	Error red.
Merck Co. Inc.	7638	80.10	82.00	9.55%	81.20	5.53%
Sanofi Pasteur	3352	84.60	90.40	37.66%	88.40	24.68%
Pfizer-Wyeth	2428	80.50	87.00	33.33%	84.60	21.03%
Glaxo-Smithkline Biologicals	2289	80.20	82.20	10.10%	85.30	25.76%
Novartis Vaccines and Diagnostics	1183	77.80	85.80	36.04%	81.50	16.67%
CSL Limited	465	67.10	88.50	65.05%	78.30	34.04%
Medimmune Vaccines Inc.	265	69.30	83.50	46.25%	81.10	38.44%
Seqirus Inc.	111	15.00	82.10	78.94%	52.60	44.24%
Emergent Biosolutions	58	30.10	89.70	85.26%	71.90	59.80%
Berna Biotech Ltd.	52	45.80	95.40	91.51%	82.50	67.71%

It is interesting to note that for small manufacturers, with an exception of one with very small amount of evaluation data, it is always beneficial to participate in the federation, even for *DP-FL*, with or without personalization. For large manufacturers however, the DP is only attractive in the presence of the mitigation offered by fine-tuning based personalization (*FT-DP-FL*).

5.4 Stability of Federation Against Users Leaving

Table 2. Stability of Private FL with Fine Tuning performance when a single user leaves. M1-M10 are manufacturers sorted in descending order by size. Each row represents a manufacturer that is leaving the federation. Each Column represents the difference between F1 values under full federation and this reduced federation for that manufacturer. The table on the left represents FL and the table on the right represents FT-DP-FL

	M1	M2	M3	M4	M5	M6	M7	M8	M9	M10
M1	0.0	0.9	1.8	0.4	1.0	2.1	1.8	0.4	1.0	0.0
M2	−0.3	0.0	0.4	0.5	1.4	1.6	1.6	−0.4	3.2	−1.5
M3	−0.1	0.5	0.0	0.1	0.1	0.9	1.4	1.9	1.0	−1.5
M4	−0.6	0.8	0.2	0.0	2.6	−0.2	3.5	1.3	1.0	0.0
M5	−0.5	−0.1	−0.1	2.9	0.0	0.6	0.6	−1.9	1.0	0.0
M6	−0.8	0.0	0.2	−0.5	−0.4	0.0	1.6	−1.1	2.1	0.0
M7	−0.5	0.5	−0.3	−0.5	0.1	0.7	0.0	0.4	1.0	−1.5
M8	−0.7	0.3	0.3	−0.1	−0.5	0.0	−0.5	0.0	0.8	0.0
M9	−0.4	0.1	0.2	0.0	0.4	0.1	0.9	0.9	0.0	4.5
M10	−1.0	0.0	−0.2	−0.2	−0.2	0.3	−1.3	−1.1	0.0	0.0

	M1	M2	M3	M4	M5	M6	M7	M8	M9	M10
M1	0.0	0.1	0.4	1.9	−2.4	1.4	2.9	−8.3	0.3	15.8
M2	−0.1	0.0	0.6	1.6	−1.5	−1.6	0.5	−2.5	1.4	22.5
M3	0.5	0.5	0.0	2.1	−1.7	0.2	−1.3	−1.2	−1.2	3.7
M4	−0.3	−0.3	0.2	0.0	−0.1	−4.3	0.7	−1.3	−0.4	18.7
M5	−0.1	0.0	−0.3	1.0	0.0	−0.3	−0.3	−1.9	−0.8	0.5
M6	−0.2	−0.5	0.3	1.6	−1.9	0.0	−1.5	−0.3	−0.5	4.2
M7	−0.5	0.1	0.3	2.2	−1.2	−2.8	0.0	−0.5	0.9	28.9
M8	0.5	0.5	0.8	0.6	0.0	−4.0	−0.9	0.0	5.2	15.8
M9	−0.5	−0.5	0.3	1.0	−2.5	−3.3	−3.5	−2.4	0.0	4.1
M10	−0.1	−0.2	1.0	0.9	−1.8	−3.2	−0.1	−1.4	2.2	0.0

Building a federation across organizations can be challenging in the real world due to a variety of factors. For instance, users may discontinue their participation in the federation. We simulate this scenario and study the effect of one of the manufacturers leaving the federation. As we can see from Table 2, both federated learning and private federated learning with fine tuning are fairly stable against such a change, with the exception of a few manufacturers with very small amount of training and test data. In other words, no single manufacturer has disproportionally large impact on the overall accuracy gains from participating in the federation.

5.5 Federation of Small Manufacturers

Another scenario that we simulate is the one where only participants with small amount of training data agree to collaborate. In this case, we do not have the advantage of the large amount of training data from any of the larger manufacturers. To better understand if such a federation is still advantageous, we compare the F1 values for small manufacturers in two different scenarios: one, in which they are a part of a large federation with all manufacturers, and second, in which they are a part of a federation with only the small manufacturers.

Figure 3 shows these comparisons for FL and FT-DP-FL respectively. As is clear from the bar chart, even in the case of a federation with just the small manufacturers, most of the manufacturers benefit significantly from participating. In fact, the performance of all manufacturers in the small federation closely tracks their performance in the large federation, with one exception.

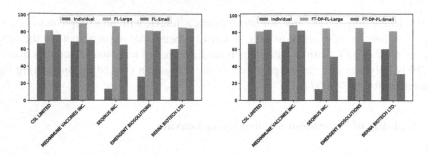

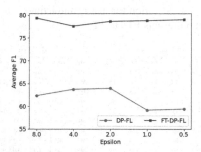

Fig. 3. F1 for small manufacturers when they are a part of a larger federation vs. a federation of only small manufacturers. The graph on left is for FL and the one on right is for FT-DP-FL

Fig. 4. Average F1 across users for the two differentially private FL variants.

5.6 Robustness to Differential Privacy Noise

Next, we study the effectiveness of personalization in recovering from the accuracy loss resulting from differential privacy noise. We vary the parameter ϵ and measure F1 averaged across users for two of the algorithm variants: differentially private federated learning (DP-FL) and the fine tuned differentially private federated learning (FT-DP-FL). As we can see from Fig. 4, average F1 for DP-FL deteriorates significantly for values of ϵ less than 2. However, even in these cases, the personalized version, FT-DP-FL manages to retain its performance. We believe this is an important finding that provides significant latitude to differentially private FL frameworks to further tighten the privacy budget of ϵ without compromising utility.

6 Conclusion

Extracting mentions of vaccine adverse events using machine learning methods is an extremely urgent task right now. Federated Learning is a promising approach for breaking down organizational and geographical barriers to collaboration on building very effective models to solve this problem. Our work demonstrates that the loss of accuracy incurred through adding additional layers of privacy can be mitigated by introducing personalization. We show that manufacturers with dataset of all different sizes can benefit from participating in such a federation and that it is stable to potential real world changes. In the future, we would like to investigate other approaches to personalization applied to this problem domain.

References

1. Abadi, M., et al.: Deep learning with differential privacy. In: Proceedings of the 2016 ACM SIGSAC Conference on Computer and Communications Security, pp. 308–318 (2016)
2. Arivazhagan, M.G., Aggarwal, V., Singh, A.K., Choudhary, S.: Federated learning with personalization layers. CoRR, abs/1912.00818 (2019)
3. Bagdasaryan, E., Veit, A., Hua, Y., Estrin, D., Shmatikov, V.: How to backdoor federated learning. In: The 23rd International Conference on Artificial Intelligence and Statistics, AISTATS 2020, Palermo, Sicily, Italy, 26–28 August 2020, volume 108 of Proceedings of Machine Learning Research, pp. 2938–2948. PMLR (2020)
4. Bonawitz, K., et al.: Towards federated learning at scale: system design. CoRR (2019)
5. Carlini, N., Liu, C., Erlingsson, Ú., Kos, J., Song, D.: The secret sharer: evaluating and testing unintended memorization in neural networks. In: 28th USENIX Security Symposium, pp. 267–284 (2019)
6. California consumer privacy act (CCPA). https://oag.ca.gov/privacy/ccpa
7. Chaudhuri, K., Monteleoni, C., Sarwate, A.D.: Differentially private empirical risk minimization. J. Mach. Learn. Res. 12, 1069–1109 (2011)
8. Deng, Y., Kamani, M.M., Mahdavi, M.: Adaptive personalized federated learning. CoRR, abs/2003.13461 (2020)
9. Differential Privacy Team. Learning with Privacy at Scale (2017). https://machinelearning. apple.com/2017/12/06/learning-with-privacy-at-scale.html
10. Dimitrakakis, C., Nelson, B., Zhang, Z., Mitrokotsa, A., Rubinstein, B.I.P.: Differential privacy for Bayesian inference through posterior sampling. J. Mach. Learn. Res. 18(1), 343–381 (2017)
11. Dinh, C.T., Tran, N.H., Nguyen, T.D.: Personalized federated learning with Moreau envelopes. In: Advances in Neural Information Processing Systems 33: Annual Conference on Neural Information Processing Systems 2020, Virtual (2020)
12. Dwork, C.: Differential privacy. In: 33rd International Colloquium Automata, Languages and Programming, ICALP, pp. 1–12 (2006)
13. Dwork, C., McSherry, F., Nissim, K., Smith, A.: Calibrating noise to sensitivity in private data analysis. In: Halevi, S., Rabin, T. (eds.) TCC 2006. LNCS, vol. 3876, pp. 265–284. Springer, Heidelberg (2006). https://doi.org/10.1007/11681878_14
14. Dwork, C., Roth, A.: The algorithmic foundations of differential privacy. Found. Trends Theor. Comput. Sci. 9(3–4), 211–407 (2014)
15. Fallah, A., Mokhtari, A., Ozdaglar, A.: Personalized federated learning: a meta-learning approach (2020)
16. Fredrikson, M., Jha, S., Ristenpart, T.: Model inversion attacks that exploit confidence information and basic countermeasures. In: Proceedings of the 22nd ACM SIGSAC Conference on Computer and Communications Security, pp. 1322–1333 (2015)
17. General data protection regulation (GDPR). https://gdpr-info.eu/
18. Gentry, C.: Fully homomorphic encryption using ideal lattices. In: Proceedings of the Forty-first Annual ACM Symposium on Theory of Computing, pp. 169–178 (2009)
19. Geyer, R.C., Klein, T., Nabi, M.: Differentially private federated learning: a client level perspective. CoRR, abs/1712.07557 (2017)

20. Giorgi, J.M., Bader, G.D.: Transfer learning for biomedical named entity recognition with neural networks. Bioinformatics **34**(23), 4087–4094 (2018)
21. Gurulingappa, H., Rajput, A.M., Roberts, A., Fluck, J., Hofmann-Apitius, M., Toldo, L.: Development of a benchmark corpus to support the automatic extraction of drug-related adverse effects from medical case reports. J. Biomed. Inform. **45**(5), 885–892 (2012)
22. Haerian, K., Varn, D., Vaidya, S., Ena, L., Chase, H., Friedman, C.: Detection of pharmacovigilance-related adverse events using electronic health records and automated methods. Clin. Pharmacol. Ther. **92**(2), 228–234 (2012)
23. Harpaz, R., et al.: Text mining for adverse drug events: the promise, challenges, and state of the art. Drug Saf. Int. J. Med. Toxicol. Drug Exp. **37**, 777–790 (2014)
24. Hitaj, B., Ateniese, G., Perez-Cruz, F.: Deep models under the GAN: information leakage from collaborative deep learning. In: Proceedings of the 2017 ACM SIGSAC Conference on Computer and Communications Security, pp. 603–618 (2017)
25. Hsieh, K., Phanishayee, A., Mutlu, O., Gibbons, P.B.: The non-IID data quagmire of decentralized machine learning. CoRR, abs/1910.00189 (2019)
26. Innovatice medices initiative: Europe's partnership for health. https://www.imi.europa.eu
27. Jiang, Y., Konecný, J., Rush, K., Kannan, S.: Improving federated learning personalization via model agnostic meta learning. CoRR, abs/1909.12488 (2019)
28. Kairouz, P., et al.: Advances and open problems in federated learning. CoRR, abs/1912.04977 (2019)
29. Kasiviswanathan, S.P., Lee, H.K., Nissim, K., Raskhodnikova, S., Smith, A.D.: What can we learn privately? CoRR, abs/0803.0924 (2008)
30. Konecný, J., McMahan, B., Ramage, D.: Federated optimization: distributed optimization beyond the datacenter. CoRR, abs/1511.03575 (2015)
31. Konecný, J., McMahan, H.B., Ramage, D., Richtárik, P.: Federated optimization: distributed machine learning for on-device intelligence. CoRR, abs/1610.02527 (2016)
32. Korkontzelos, I., Nikfarjam, A., Shardlow, M., Sarker, A., Ananiadou, S., Gonzalez, G.H.: Analysis of the effect of sentiment analysis on extracting adverse drug reactions from tweets and forum posts. J. Biomed. Inform. **62**, 148–158 (2016)
33. Korolova, A.: Privacy violations using microtargeted ads: a case study. In: 2010 IEEE International Conference on Data Mining Workshops, pp. 474–482 (2010)
34. Leaman, R., Wojtulewicz, L., Sullivan, R., Skariah, A., Yang, J., Gonzalez, G.: Towards internet-age pharmacovigilance: extracting adverse drug reactions from user posts in health-related social networks. In: Proceedings of the 2010 Workshop on Biomedical Natural Language Processing, BioNLP@ACL 2010, Uppsala, Sweden, 15 July 2010, pp. 117–125. Association for Computational Linguistics (2010)
35. LePendu, P., et al.: Pharmacovigilance using clinical notes. Clin. Pharmacol. Ther. **93**, 547–555 (2013)
36. Li, X., Gu, Y., Dvornek, N., Staib, L.H., Ventola, P., Duncan, J.S.: Multi-site fMRI analysis using privacy-preserving federated learning and domain adaptation: abide results. Med. Image Anal. **65**, 101765 (2020)
37. Li, X., Huang, K., Yang, W., Wang, S., Zhang, Z.: On the convergence of FedAvg on non-IID data. In: 8th International Conference on Learning Representations, ICLR 2020, Addis Ababa, Ethiopia, 26–30 April 2020. OpenReview.net (2020)
38. Liang, P.P., Liu, T., Liu, Z., Salakhutdinov, R., Morency, L.: Think locally, act globally: federated learning with local and global representations. CoRR, abs/2001.01523 (2020)
39. Mansour, Y., Mohri, M., Ro, J., Suresh, A.T.: Three approaches for personalization with applications to federated learning. CoRR, abs/2002.10619 (2020)
40. McMahan, H.B., Moore, E., Ramage, D., Arcas, B.A.y.: Federated learning of deep networks using model averaging. CoRR, abs/1602.05629 (2016)

41. McMahan, H.B., Ramage, D., Talwar, K., Zhang, L.: Learning differentially private language models without losing accuracy. CoRR, abs/1710.06963 (2017)

42. Melis, L., Song, C., Cristofaro, E.D., Shmatikov, V.: Inference attacks against collaborative learning. CoRR, abs/1805.04049 (2018)

43. New research consortium seeks to accelerate drug discovery using machine learning to unlock maximum potential of pharma industry data. https://www.janssen.com/emea/new-research-consortium-seeks-accelerate-drug-discovery-using-machine-learning-unlock-maximum

44. Nasr, M., Shokri, R., Houmansadr, A.: Comprehensive privacy analysis of deep learning: passive and active white-box inference attacks against centralized and federated learning. In: 2019 IEEE Symposium on Security and Privacy, SP 2019, San Francisco, CA, USA, 19–23 May 2019, pp. 739–753. IEEE (2019)

45. Peterson, D.W., Kanani, P., Marathe, V.J.: Private federated learning with domain adaptation. CoRR, abs/1912.06733 (2019)

46. Roberts, K., Demner-Fushman, D., Tonning, J.M.: Overview of the TAC 2017 adverse reaction extraction from drug labels track. In: Proceedings of the 2017 Text Analysis Conference, TAC 2017, Gaithersburg, Maryland, USA, 13–14 November 2017. NIST (2017)

47. Shokri, R., Stronati, M., Song, C., Shmatikov, V.: Membership inference attacks against machine learning models. In: 2017 IEEE Symposium on Security and Privacy (SP), pp. 3–18 (2017)

48. Smith, V., Chiang, C.-K., Sanjabi, M., Talwalkar, A.: Federated multi-task learning (2017)

49. Tramèr, F., Zhang, F., Juels, A., Reiter, M.K., Ristenpart, T.: Stealing machine learning models via prediction APIs. In: Proceedings of the 25th USENIX Conference on Security Symposium, pp. 601–618 (2016)

50. Winnenburg, R., et al.: Leveraging medline indexing for pharmacovigilance - inherent limitations and mitigation strategies. J. Biomed. Inform. (2015)

51. Yao, A.C.: How to generate and exchange secrets. In: 27th Annual Symposium on Foundations of Computer Science, pp. 162–167 (1986)

52. Yu, T., Bagdasaryan, E., Shmatikov, V.: Salvaging federated learning by local adaptation. CoRR, abs/2002.04758 (2020)

Machine Learning for Buildings Energy Management

Workshop on Machine Learning for Buildings Energy Management (MLBEM 2021)

Increased energy efficiency and decarbonization of the energy system are two primary objectives of the European Energy Union. European buildings remain predominantly inefficient, accounting for 40% of final energy consumption and 36% of the total EU CO_2 emissions. Machine learning is a key enabler of scalable and efficient tools for building energy assessment and for the development of services capable of dealing with the increased complexity of energy management in buildings generated by the electrification of the energy system. The aim of this workshop was to provide energy and machine learning researchers with a forum to exchange and discuss scientific contributions, open challenges, and recent achievements in machine learning and their role in the development of efficient and scalable building energy management systems.

EU targets for 2030 include reaching a 32% share of renewable energy and increasing energy efficiency by at least 32.5%. Due to the scale and complexity of current building energy systems, traditional modeling, simulation, and optimization techniques are not feasible and unable to achieve satisfactory results. To achieve the aforementioned goals, modern buildings require the capabilities of self-assessing and self-optimizing energy resources, of meeting user preferences and requirements, and to contribute to an overall better and sustainable energy system. Based on the recent history, this workshop was organized as a European forum for building's energy and ML researchers and practitioners wishing to discuss the recent developments of ML for developing Building Energy Management (BEM) systems, by paying special attention to solutions rooted in techniques such as pattern mining, neural networks and deep learning, probabilistic inference, stream learning and mining, and big data analytics and visualization.

The ongoing energy transition brings the possibility of real-time energy resource management to building owners/managers and energy operators, with potential benefits for consumers, producers, and the environment. To better tap into this potential, stakeholders must be able to continuously assess the energy performance of building energy systems and appliances, identifying areas where optimization services can be applied. Implementing this assessment and optimization capability requires real-time monitoring and control of the building equipment and major energy consuming appliances. This functionality can be effectively performed by Internet of Things (IoT) enabled sensors and devices coupled to services that can assess and optimize the energy resources in buildings. The capability to analyze and optimize buildings energy resources and energy consuming equipment in useful time is not possible without employing Machine Learning (ML) techniques and big data infrastructures. This gives rise to ML BEM services that can be effective in an increasingly electrified and complex environment with energy flows between the grid, photovoltaic production, electric vehicles, storage batteries, building thermal capacity, and considering changing consumption patterns, occupants comfort, and highly variable user preferences.

The workshop aimed at filling a gap in the EU workshop panorama, providing researchers with a forum to exchange and discuss scientific contributions and open challenges, both theoretical and practical, related to the use of machine-learning approaches in building energy management. We wanted to foster joint work and knowledge exchange between the building's energy community, and researchers and practitioners from the ML area, and its intersection with big data, data science, and visualization. The workshop provided a forum for discussing novel trends and achievements in machine learning and their role in the development of scalable BEM systems and services. It aimed to highlight the latest research trends in machine learning, privacy of data, big data, deep learning, incremental and stream learning, and adversarial learning. In particular, it aimed to promote the application of these emerging ML techniques to buildings energy management.

We hope that the workshop contributed to identifying new application areas as well as open and future research problems related to the application of machine-learning in the building's energy field.

Pedro M. Ferreira
Guilherme Graça

Organization

MLBEM 2021 Chairs

Pedro M. Ferreira   Universidade de Lisboa, Portugal
Guilherme Graça   Universidade de Lisboa, Portugal

Program Committee

Anna Marszal-Pomianowska   Aalborg University, Denmark
Daniel Albuquerque   University of Lisbon, Portugal
Guilherme Graça   University of Lisbon, Portugal
José Domingo Álvarez   University of Almería, Spain
María Del Mar Castilla Nieto University of Almería, Spain
Pedro M. Ferreira   University of Lisbon, Portugal

Building Appliances Energy Performance Assessment

Zygimantas Jasiunas$^{(\boxtimes)}$, Pedro M. Ferreira, and José Cecílio

LASIGE, Faculty of Sciences of the University of Lisbon, Lisbon, Portugal
zjasiunas@fc.ul.pt, {pmferreira,jmcecilio}@ciencias.ulisboa.pt

Abstract. According to the European Union (EU), about 72% of buildings and their equipment are not adapted to be energy efficient. This fact drives the EU countries to implement a new strategy to increase energy efficiency and promote decarbonization. Wrong estimations of real-life energy consumption and energy-consuming equipment are common factors that are degrading energy efficiency. Real-life energy consumption measurements of buildings compared with the predictions may be exceeded by more than 100%. To improve the forecasts and guide the users to configure their appliances right, a system prototype that monitors and acquires data from various appliances and provides fine-grained information about each appliance is proposed. It is designed to understand the real-life consumption of each device and compare it with the laboratory measurements observed and used by the EU energy efficiency labelling system. This work is a part of the "Self Assessment Towards Optimization" (SATO) project, where new energy assessments services are made available. These new services are data-capable and allow to express real-life utilization and life-cycle evolution.

Keywords: Microcontrollers · Sensors · Appliance monitoring · Appliance classification

1 Introduction

Significant carbon dioxide (CO_2) emission is being produced in the European Union (EU) and represents about 40% of final energy consumption [1]. This value is driving the EU to create new approaches to increase energy efficiency and promoting decarbonization. The objective of reaching a 32% share of renewable energy and increasing energy efficiency by at least 32.5% by 2030 compared to 1990 statistics [2] is being discussed and adopted as the goal of the EU energy strategy.

One source of the problem arises from the inefficiency of the EU buildings. About 72% of the existing buildings are not adapted for being energy efficient due to construction issues. Solutions such as demolishing and rebuilding are not economically neither environmentally viable. However, this problem is not only the one that influences energy efficiency. Wrong estimations of real-life energy consumption and energy-consuming equipment are common factors, which also

© Springer Nature Switzerland AG 2021
M. Kamp et al. (Eds.): ECML PKDD 2021 Workshops, CCIS 1525, pp. 511–524, 2021.
https://doi.org/10.1007/978-3-030-93733-1_38

degrades energy efficiency. According to [3], real-life energy consumption measurements of buildings compared with the predictions exceed by more than 100%.

Over past years the energy consumption from plug loads has been consistently rising and consuming up to 33% of all energy in commercial buildings [4] and electricity used for lighting and most electrical appliances represents 14.1% (this excludes the use of electricity for powering the central heating, cooling or cooking systems) [5].

However, to draw a realistic picture of truthful energy consumption, an assessment of real-life energy utilization must be done, including all energy-consuming equipment in a given building. Internet of things (IoT) can monitor the energy consumption of home appliances using sensors, edge devices, and cloud platforms to perform continuous real-time monitoring.

To inform users about electricity consumption EU has introduced energy labels that provide a clear and simple indication of the energy efficiency in products at the point of purchase. These labels come with the comparative scale from "A," which means most efficient, to "G" (least efficient). This approach is a crucial driver for users to choose the appliance that is the most energy-efficient. However, we have manufacturers competing among themselves to create more efficient devices labeled as highly efficient. To determine the efficiency and appropriate labeling of energy efficiency appliances, they are assessed in the laboratory. Studies, such as [6,7] show that appliances used in real-life situations are using more energy than compared with those in a laboratory.

This work proposes an approach that allows recognizing and classifying appliances according to the energy consumption profile and operation characteristics. Our proposal aims to perform an automatic, highly accurate appliance classification based on monitored loads in a household environment. The contribution of this paper is real-time appliance classification with support for multifunctional appliance cycle classification, e.g., washing machine washing cycle recognition. Besides the classification approach, we contribute to a new appliance monitoring dataset and a prototype for energy monitoring and consumption measurement. In this paper, we do not go into detail about prototype creation. However, we are mentioning the prototype's capabilities and the monitored data provided by our approach.

2   Related Work

Many approaches have been proposed in the literature to monitor energy utilization, execute data acquisition and successfully classify electrical appliances. These approaches are falling into two categories, namely intrusive load monitoring (ILM) and non-intrusive load monitoring (NILM) [8,9]. Each of these approaches has its advantages and disadvantages.

NILM approach is based on a single sensor placed at utility energy entry that captures all energy consumption in a household and desegregates the overall energy usage. It works by applying analysis on voltage-current waveform from which power consumption of each load entry can be known [8,10]. One of the advantages is the cheaper installation cost, little interference with the user since monitoring is based on a single sensor [11]. Although it is still possible to recognize actively used appliances using pattern recognition techniques, this data does not provide such fine-grain appliance energy consumption about every device. It is nearly impossible to recognize if a device is on idle mode or completely turned off. Using this approach, measurements are not as detailed, and sensitive data readings are missed.

When every load is being monitored, it is assumed to be ILM. The advantage of such an approach is detailed energy consumption and high precision data of each device [8,12]. Since each appliance will need to have a dedicated current sensor, smart plug, or other consumption measurement device, the cost of this multitude of sensors may be a drawback. Fortunately, nowadays, technology allows us to execute ILM for an affordable price due to the rise of lose-cost sensors with relatively high precision.

In [9] an ILM approach was applied using a plogg - configurable smart plug, acquisition device that was capable of measuring a list of variables and produces a four-dimensional vector of electrical parameters including power (W), reactive power (var), current (A), and phase of voltage relative to current (ϕ). Five classes of appliances were investigated, including laptop, fridge, computer and monitor, phone charger, and coffee machine. For each class, six different models of each class were recorded for a total of 30 appliances. The sensor was programmed to send an acquisition snapshots with a sampling frequency of 10^{-1} Hz (one data acquisition taken each 10 s). For data classification, two algorithms were used, namely k-neared Neighbour (KNN) and Gaussian Mixture Model (GMM). In the experiment, 85% of accuracy was reached for both algorithms.

In [13], a research of real-time device identification of 14 devices data were recorded using a smart plug. Four electrical features were recorded: active power, reactive power, root mean square (RMS) voltage, RMS current, and phase shift. The authors chose the Support Vector Machines, Artificial Neural Network, K-Means, Silhouette, Mean-Shift classification algorithms for the classification propose. According to this publication, Silhouette and K-Means reached 98% accuracy, and the lowest accuracy has been recorded by the Mean Shift algorithm 94%.

For completeness of this section, we created a Table 1 mentioning machine learning algorithms used for appliance classification and references. This table also includes the average accuracy generated based on multiple sources, some of the references in the table are not mentioned in the related work due to similarities of the projects and we wanted to avoid repeatably in the text of related work.

Considering the state-of-the-art, we have implemented a solution that follows the ILM approach with high sensitivity sensors. We are more interested in this solutions because it will provide us with more detailed information about appliance usage, their functioning cycles and additionally water consumption of and washing program classification of washing machines and dishwashers. It would

Table 1. Compiled classification algorithm usage based on revision of related work

Algorithm	Average accuracy	Citation
K-nearest neighbour	87.48%	[4,9,14–16]
Random forest (RF)	94.1%	[4,16–18]
Support-vector machine	94.47%	[13,15,18]
Bagging	94.2%	[4,17,18]
Gaussian mixture models	89.86%	[9,14,19]
Naive Bayes	81.1%	[15,17]

not be possible to recognise this information with NILM approach. Furthermore, due to the low-cost sensors and hardware the implementation is highly viable.

3   Methodology

In this work, we propose an appliance classification and labeling approach for real-life operation monitoring solutions for appliances. The prototype implemented during this work provides us with fine-grained data about each appliance's energy consumption. Each monitoring device includes a micro-controller and is currently attached to it. The data sensed by sensors is collected by the local microcontroller, which will process/compress and send it to the gateway. Upon receiving the data at the gateway, it is formatted according to the cloud platform that will receive it for further processing and device/operation cycle classification. The whole architecture is presented in the next section.

3.1   Sensor Data Acquisition

The sensor data is acquired by a node, composed of an Arduino Nano IoT 33 microcontroller and current sensor (PZEM-004T) (Fig. 2), and sent to the gateway. Each message is wirelessly transferred to the gateway via MQTT protocol, and the gateway collects the data inside the local MongoDB database. This data is also forwarded to a cloud platform, where the classification algorithm runs. The appliance classification approach comprises a set o Machine Learning algorithms deployed on a scalable cloud infrastructure. It includes several contains, which support online classification and model updating.

Each data record that arrives at cloud infrastructure will is forwarded to the MongoDB database, the online classification component, and the model update component. The online classification runs a Machine Learning model that was previously computed based on the data records that are stored in the MongoDB database. We collected records, labeled them, and trained the model to create the first Machine Learning model. An illustration of monitoring and data collection prototype is illustrated in Fig. 1. A classification container is forwarding the classification result to a personal computer (PC) to confirm real-time recognition.

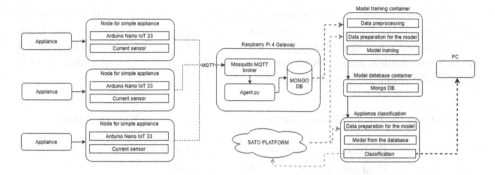

Fig. 1. Our prototype architecture for appliance classification

Fig. 2. Current sensor PZEM-004T inside electricity box

3.2 Data Collection

The data has been collected with a sampling rate 1 Hz (one sample per second). Our prototype provides us with 6-dimensional features: real power, power factor, RMS current, frequency, RMS voltage, and energy. Table 2 describes the list of features that we are capturing, and Table 3 shows the appliances that were recorded. Some appliances have been registered while functioning in different states, e.g., ON or SLEEP. For instance, we recorded an Asus laptop while using it usually (reading email, browsing the internet) and when playing games. Most of the appliances were recorded for 60 min, except the toaster, because it is not suitable to keep it on for such an extended period. Due to this reason, the toaster is underrepresented in the dataset. Exclusively washing machine was recorded with a sampling frequency of 1/2 Hz per second, meaning that every 2 s, a measurement is being taken. Due to long washing cycles, we are experimenting with slightly less frequent samples. Few washing machine cycles have been recorded and labeled as WASHING, and we were also recording it while it was on stand-by mode, just being plugged in the power socket without even being turned on.

Furthermore, we have recorded a few washing machine cycles that we will try to classify. Table 4 presents the washing cycles that have been recorded. Each cycle was recorded three times, one for training the model, the second one for testing the model, and a third one for classifying to use as previously unseen data to the Machine Learning model.

Table 2. List of features captured with our prototype. Source: author.

Feature	Symbol	Unit	Sensor precision
Real power	P	Watts	0.001
Power factor	pf	-	.01
RMS current	I	Ampere	0.001
Frequency	f	Hertz	0.1
RMS Voltage	V	Volt	0.001
Energy	Wh	Watt-hour	1

Table 3. Appliances that have been recorded using our prototype. Source: author.

Type	Model	Release date	State	Session length	N^o of samples
Air purifier	Airfree P100	2019	ON	60 min	3600
Laptop	Asus rog GL503GE	2018	ON	60 min	3600
Laptop	Asus rog GL503GE	2018	GAMING	60 min	3600
Laptop	Laptop HP Pavilion	2012	ON	60 min	3600
Monitor	AOC27B1H	2019	ON	60 min	3600
Monitor	AOC27B1H	2019	SLEEP	60 min	3600
Shaver	Philips S3133	2020	CHARGING	60 min	3600
Smartphone	Huawei Mate 9	2016	CHARGING	60 min	3600
TV	Samsung UE40C6510UW	2010	ON	60 min	3600
TV	Samsung UE40C6510UW	2010	SLEEP	60 min	3600
Tablet	Apple iPad 10.2	2019	CHARGING	60 min	3600
Toothbrush	OralB-Braun	2017	CHARGING	60 min	3600
Washing machine	Aqualtis AQ114D69D	2010	STANDBY	60 min	3600
Washing machine	Aqualtis AQ114D69D	2010	WASHING	360 min	10 800
Toaster	Krups 6330	2010	ON	5 min	300
Total					54 300

3.3   Data Prepossessing

In our database, we do not take into consideration record if $P \leq 0$ and $I \leq 0$, meaning that at the moment of capturing a measurement appliance was consuming no energy (being idle or power-saving) or the sensor was not sensitive enough to be able to capture the power and current traces. This rule was applied only for the dataset that is mentioned in Table 3.

Furthermore, in electricity data, we have some features that have high magnitude values compared to others. For example, power has a substantial magnitude

Table 4. List of monitored washing machine program cycles. Source: author.

Washing cycle	$N°$ of sessions	Session length	$N°$ of samples
Prewashing	3	80 min	2400
Baby clothes	3	120 min	3700
Coloured	3	70 min	2100
Rinsing	3	35 min	1000
Mix	3	40 min	1200
7 day clothes	3	83 min	2500
Delicate clothes	3	60 min	1800
Total			40 500

comparing with the current. It is important to scale these values to avoid this underlying assumption that larger values have a higher impact. For this, we have used a standard scaler from *sklearn.preprocessing* python library [20]. It standardizes features by removing the mean and scaling to unit variance. The standard score of sample x is calculated as:

$$z = (x - u)/s$$

where u is the mean of the training samples or zero if with-mean = False, and s is the standard deviation of the training samples or one if with-std = False.

3.4 Execution Method

The K-fold cross-validation approach is used instead of splitting the data into specific parts (e.g., 80%–20% for training and testing). In cross-validation, we can split data more times. Those splits are called folds. We have used K = 10. Meaning that model will be tested during ten iterations, where nine parts are used for training and one for testing. Using Cross-validation, we will better understand how well the learner will generalize to unseen data.

3.5 Model Development for Appliance Classification

In this work we want to implement a real-life energy assessment. One of the critical parts is highly accurate appliance classification and identification in the grid. For this purpose, we design a set of experiments where the k-nearest neighbors (KNN), random forest (RF), support-vector machine (SVM), and extreme gradient boosting (XGBoost) algorithms were used. In this section, we discuss the development of mentioned algorithms.

K-Nearest Neighbour. In this algorithm, an essential hyperparameter is the value of K, which tells the algorithm how many surrounding neighbors we will consider to make a classification prediction on a given data point. In our experiments, we iteratively provide K from 1 to N, and each time we record the prediction accuracy to choose the best K value.

Random Forest. This algorithm has multiple hyper-parameters, and when adequately tuned, it might increase the model's accuracy. For hyperparameter tuning, the randomized grid search algorithm [21] is used. This algorithm requires a set of parameters, such as grid values, the number of iterations and K folds for cross-validation, and it will try to find randomized parameters from the provided grid by multiple iterations. During the experimentation quite pleasing results were obtained when setting *maxdepth* to 35.

Extreme Gradient Boosting. similarly to RF algorithm, XGBoost has multiple hyper-parameters that needs to be tuned for higher classification accuracy of a model. For grid-search of XGBoost, the following hyper-parameters are chosen:

Support-Vector Machine. SVM also contains multiple hyper-parameters that can be tuned to better the performance of classification. We were experimenting with "C, gamma," and different kernels. C value determines the miss-classifying of each training example, smaller C value is telling SVM to find a larger-margin separating the hyper-plane, whilst higher C value makes can is more prone to be influenced by outliers because the hyperplane might be divided closer towards an opposite class of outlier point leaving smaller margins. *gamma* is used with RBF kernel. In linear or polynomial kernel, gamma is not being used. When trying to divide two clusters, higher gamma means more curvature. In our experiments we are using $C = 1000$, $Gamma = 0.1$, and kernel is *rbf*.

4   Appliance Classification Results

Using our experimental data from Table 4, KNN performed 98% of accuracy, and it takes 1.5 s to train. XGBoost gave us 99% and took 3.8 s to train The SVM accuracy was 99.8%, and the training took 11.3 s, while the RF provides 99.99% of accuracy and takes 1.5 s for training. Execution accuracy that is mentioned here is not including hyper-parameter tuning. We consider the training time when using already tuned parameters. From the results, we can say that the RF algorithm obtained the best accuracy. Moreover, the worst was KNN. Nevertheless, its accuracy is great 98%. In the illustration Fig. 3, we show a confusion matrix from appliance classification experiment using RF classification since it performed best in our results.

4.1   Preparation for Real Time Classification

To classify appliances in real-time, we have saved our trained ML model using object serialization. To do this, we have used a *pickle* python library that helps

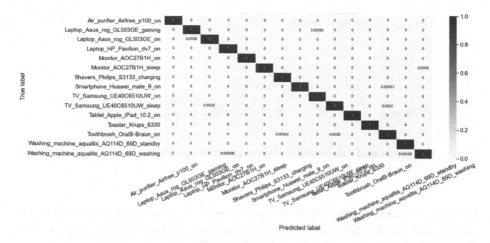

Fig. 3. Confusion matrix using RF algorithm

us to save trained model into a serialized object file *model.pkl*, that can be reused for instantaneous classification without training the model over and over again. We built a docker container solution responsible for data prepossessing, model training, storing the model inside the MongoDB database, and labeling models with timestamps. Additionally, a specific container pulls the latest trained model from the model database. It offers a REST API for online classification, meaning that if we send a request with appliance monitoring data, it replies to us with a classification label. This approach is very flexible and can be implemented for real-time appliance classification.

4.2 Washing Machine Cycle Recognition and Classification

In this experiment we monitored an *Aqualtis AQ114D69D* washing machine during different washing cycles. Cycles that were recorded and used in this experiment are mentioned in Table 4.

The first thing we have tried was using the same approach as appliance classification, labeling the data, and classifying it. This approach gave us abysmal results. KNN reported 33% accuracy, meaning that the washing cycle signal amplitudes are very similar and can not be clustered for differentiation. In Fig. 4 we plot electricity current (*A*) readings of two washing cycles from our sensor to have an idea of how different cycles look. From the Fig. 4 we can tell that the amplitudes are very similar due to this reason, we can not use a traditional classification approach.

Every program cycle produces a slightly different energy consumption pattern during its functioning cycle, meaning that we have to treat this data as a time series observation. Unfortunately, we cannot detect the washing cycle program in real-time due to the nature of time-series data. The classification can be made only after half of the washing cycle or at the end of the cycle. Our approach was

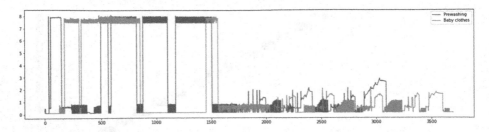

Fig. 4. Comparison of two washing cycles. Blue line - "Prewashing", orange - "Baby clothes" (Color figure online)

to divide a washing cycle in half. We have a water heating pattern on the left side signal, and on the right side, we have an actual washing pattern and perform feature extraction from a time-series signal. To extract multiple features, we have used a TSFEL python feature extraction library [22], which in our case extracted around 325 different features per one time-series signal feature. For feature extraction we have used all our time series features from Table 2. It uses time-series signals and extracts temporal, statistical, and spectral features from a time-series signal. One time series window creates one row with features. In our case, we divide the signal into two parts, meaning that one washing cycle provides us with two rows of features per class. In total, we had 1951 extracted features per single window.

We have extracted features from 7 different washing cycles. Each cycle has been recorded three times. One cycle is used for training, the second one is for testing for the model, and the third is for classification testing to prove that this method works. Washing cycles are described in Table 4.

Our experiment used a KNN algorithm to classify by extracted features from the washing cycle based on recorded patterns. We ran the algorithm with a hyperparameter K = 1. We used all the features that the TSFEL library provided. From obtained results, we can demonstrate that our approach of washing cycle classification works as planned. A confusion matrix is illustrated in Fig. 5. In the future, we will perform automated feature selection to reduce the number of features that possess the least importance.

To test the model with unseen washing cycle data, first, we need to perform feature extraction from the signal and supply extracted features to the ML model. The model was able to recognize a new unseen washing cycle and successfully classify it from our testing.

5   Evaluation of Real Time Classification

For real-time appliance evaluation, we used one of our nodes collecting the electricity consumption patterns every 2 s and sending the message via MQTT to the gateway. Then, the gateway forwards a message to our cloud infrastructure, which then returns the appliance classification. This experiment aims to see if

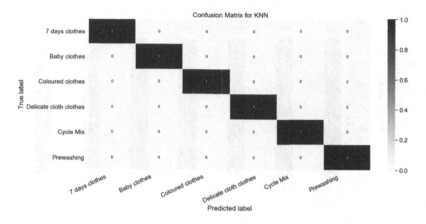

Fig. 5. Feature extraction pipeline using TSFEL library of a single washing cycle.

our solution can handle previously unseen data and the degree of reliability that it offers.

This experiment will monitor appliances in the list from our dataset, although the new incoming data is unseen to the machine learning (ML) model. We will be evaluating the correctness of real-time classification by connecting the appliance to our monitoring node and forwarding the measured data to RF ML model that is running in google cloud platforms virtual machine (VM) server. An appliance will be connected to the monitoring node for 10 min, and we will be logging the classification responses from the cloud application, monitoring node will be capturing the energy consumption data each 2 s. By the end of the experiment we will have 300 responses for each appliance from the VM server. Furthermore, we will count the true positive (TP), and false positive (FP) results. We randomly selected seven appliances for real-time classification. In Fig. 6 we show the obtained results from our experiment. During the monitoring some appliances have been miss-classified during 10 min experiment. While recording the monitor, we had one false positive, which was classified as a washing machine being in stand-by mode. Air-purifier had one false positive which was classified as a washing machine. iPad was mistaken three times with Huawei Mate 9 smartphone. Asus laptop during the normal functioning was miss-classified with Asus laptop during gaming. In this experiment, we had only 0.9% fallacious results based on the responses from the VM server.

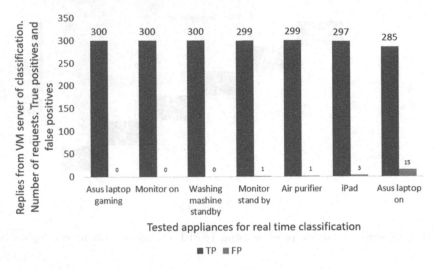

Fig. 6. Real time classification testing results. TP - true positives, FP - false positives

6   Conclusions

We successfully have implemented a low-cost, highly flexible appliance monitoring platform prototype that can simultaneously monitor multiple appliances using multiple nodes. Based on our experiment results, we can claim that we can perform real-time appliance classification with a small error. We were able to classify different washing machine cycles by implementing feature extraction from a time-series signal. Nevertheless, we need to investigate this approach with a more extensive dataset. Results mean that our approach can supply dashboards with critical information about appliances and their energy consumption. We can provide daily, weekly, monthly reports about the energy consumption of each device and even provide the data of energy consumption per washing machine cycle. Using obtained data, we can classify monitored appliances, including devices functioning in multiple states, with excellent accuracy using the Random Forest classification algorithm with an accuracy of 99.1% based on a real-time classification experiment. Although the accuracy of testing the model with training and testing data provided us with 99.99%. We can conclude that we need to grow our dataset with more samples and a longer monitoring time. The next step is to implement an appliance fault prediction and detection based on monitoring time-series data. For this task, we are planning to use pattern recognition approaches using auto-encoders.

Acknowledgements. This work was supported by the European Commission through the Sato project (Grant agreement ID: 957128) and the LASIGE Research Unit, ref. UIDB/00408/2020 and ref. UIDP/00408/2020.

References

1. Pohoryles, D.A., Maduta, C., Bournas, D.A., Kouris, L.A.: Energy performance of existing residential buildings in Europe: a novel approach combining energy with seismic retrofitting. Energy Build. **223**, 110024 (2020)
2. European Commission: Fourth report on the state of the energy union. https://lec.europa.eu/info/publications/4th-state-energy-union_en. Accessed 26 Oct 2021
3. Menezes, A.C., Cripps, A., Bouchlaghem, D., Buswell, R.: Predicted vs. actual energy performance of non-domestic buildings: using post-occupancy evaluation data to reduce the performance gap. Appl. Energy **97**, 355–364 (2012)
4. Tekler, Z.D., Low, R., Zhou, Y., Yuen, C., Blessing, L., Spanos, C.: Near-real-time plug load identification using low-frequency power data in office spaces: experiments and applications. Appl. Energy **275**, 115391 (2020)
5. European Commission. Eurostat: Energy consumption and use by households. https://ec.europa.eu/eurostat/web/products-eurostat-news/-/ddn-20200626-1. Accessed 09 July 2021
6. Biglia, A., Gemmell, A.J., Foster, H.J., Evans, J.A.: Energy performance of domestic cold appliances in laboratory and home environments. Energy **204**, 117932 (2020)
7. Palmer, J., Terry, N., Kane, T.: Further analysis of the household electricity survey. Early Findings: Demand Side Management (2013)
8. Abubakar, I., Khalid, S.N., Mustafa, M.W., Shareef, H., Mustapha, M.: Application of load monitoring in appliances' energy management–a review. Renew. Sustain. Energy Rev. **67**, 235–245 (2017)
9. Zufferey, D., Gisler, C., Khaled, O.A., Hennebert, J.: Machine learning approaches for electric appliance classification, 740–745. IEEE (2012)
10. Zhang, B., Zhao, S., Shi, Q., Zhang, R.: Low-rate non-intrusive appliance load monitoring based on graph signal processing. In: 2019 International Conference on Security, Pattern Analysis, and Cybernetics (SPAC), pp. 11–16. IEEE (2019)
11. Wang, A.L., Chen, B.X., Wang, C.G., Hua, D.: Non-intrusive load monitoring algorithm based on features of V–I trajectory. Electric Pow. Syst. Res. **157**, 134–144 (2018)
12. Ridi, A., Gisler, C., Hennebert, J.: A survey on intrusive load monitoring for appliance recognition. In: 2014 22nd International Conference on Pattern Recognition, pp. 3702–3707. IEEE (2014)
13. Abeykoon, V., Kankanamdurage, N., Senevirathna, A., Ranaweera, P., Udawalpola, R.: Real time identification of electrical devices through power consumption pattern detection. Pervasive Comput. **10**(1), 40–48 (2016)
14. Ridi, A., Gisler, C., Hennebert, J.: Automatic identification of electrical appliances using smart plugs. In: 2013 8th International Workshop on Systems, Signal Processing and Their Applications (WoSSPA), pp. 301–305. IEEE (2013)
15. Reddy, R.S., Keesara, N., Pudi, V., Garg, V.: Plug load identification in educational buildings using machine learning algorithms. In: Proceedings of BS2015: 14th Conference of International Building Performance Simulation Association, Hyderabad, India, pp. 1940–1946 (2015)
16. Mpawenimana, I., Pegatoquet, A., Soe, W.T., Belleudy, C.: Appliances identification for different electrical signatures using moving average as data preparation. In: 2018 Ninth International Green and Sustainable Computing Conference (IGSC), pp. 1–6. IEEE (2018)

17. Reinhardt, A., et al.: On the accuracy of appliance identification based on distributed load metering data. In: 2012 Sustainable Internet and ICT for Sustainability (SustainIT), pp. 1–9. IEEE (2012)
18. Tundis, A., Faizan, A., Mühlhäuser, M.: A feature-based model for the identification of electrical devices in smart environments. Sensors **19**(11), 2611 (2019)
19. Ridi, A., Hennebert, J.: Hidden Markov models for ILM appliance identification. Procedia Comput. Sci. **32**, 1010–1015 (2014)
20. scikit learn.org: sklearn standardscaler. https://scikit-learn.org/stable/modules/generated/sklearn.preprocessing.StandardScaler.html. Accessed 20 July 2021
21. scikit learn.org: sklearn randomizedsearchcv. https://scikit-learn.org/stable/modules/generated/sklearn.model_selection.RandomizedSearchCV.html. Accessed 20 July 2021
22. Barandas, M., et al.: TSFEL: time series feature extraction library. SoftwareX **11**, 100456 (2020)

Drilling a Large Corpus of Document Images of Geological Information Extraction

Jean-Louis Debezia[1]([✉]), Mélodie Boillet[2], Christopher Kermorvant[2],
and Quentin Barral[1]

[1] Geosophy, 155 Bvd de l'Hôpital, 75013 Paris, France
{jean-louis.debezia,quentin.barral}@geosophy.io
[2] TEKLIA, 30 rue Raymond Losserand, 75014 Paris, France
{boillet,kermorvant}@teklia.com
http://www.geosophy.io, http://teklia.com

Abstract. Geo-energy is a resource widely available on Earth that consists in using the first 10–100 meters below the surface where the temperature is low and constant during the year. This 12 to 15 °C is ideal for heat pumps to provide heat and cold with an excellent coefficient of performance. Despite a very high potential, this resource is not often integrated in France. One of the main reasons is the lack of knowledge of rocks capacity to deliver sufficient power on surface. More than 2 millions of scanned documents are available on the french geological survey. We propose a way to classify and analyze them in order to quantify the underground resource.

Keywords: Classification · Neural network · Geo-energy ·
Permeability · Green buildings

1 Introduction

Because the building sector represents 40% of global consumption and 36% of greenhouse gas emissions[1], the EU is seeking sustainable solutions for heating and cooling, adapted to existing constructions. 78% of the EU's population lives in areas where the soil thermal inertia can be useful for both cooling and heating[2], making geothermal heat pumps a highly efficient solution, able to save up to 75% of building consumption and 90% of its carbon emissions compared to gas systems. Today though, it covers only 2% of total heating/cooling consumption while this abundant resource could easily be used ten times more. It is due to: 1) the lack of awareness of the available resources: the feasibility studies being risky, expensive and only performed by rare experts; 2) the uncertainty of the quality of the

---

[1] https://ec.europa.eu/energy/en/topics/energy-efficiency/heating-and-cooling.
[2] https://www.powerengineeringint.com/coal-fired/advances-made-in-eu-geothermal-heating-development/.

© Springer Nature Switzerland AG 2021
M. Kamp et al. (Eds.): ECML PKDD 2021 Workshops, CCIS 1525, pp. 525–530, 2021.
https://doi.org/10.1007/978-3-030-93733-1_39

resource, which determines the output of the system; 3)unknown investment costs and ROI, which prevent it from being planned when it is financially relevant.

In the case of geothermal heat pumps, the operational principle does not rely on heat extraction, but on constant temperature in the subsurface, at depths typically between 10 and 400 m^3. This level generally maintains the same temperature in winter as in summer between 15 and 20 °C.

2 Underground Data

The technical design offices can provide a first approximation of the geo-energy power available in the ground, given either as a water flow rate or a transmissivity/permeability. The proposed value is estimated through neighboring installations: for each new project, the design engineer studies its own data sets and the public data available in the local geological survey (BRGM in France) in order to gather information on nearby wells. From those wells, they propose an estimate for the petrophysical parameters such as porosity, permeability [3] which represents the ability of water to flow in the rocks, thermal conductivity and thermal capacity. There is no global and pre-analyzed database, only raw data are available in France.

Due to the high level on uncertainties of rocks properties (and in particular the permeability), design offices accept to confirm the first approximation only after drilling a well and running pumping tests on it. This induces for the owner a financial risk (the drilling cost is between 20 and 200 k€ depending on the accessibility of the site and the characteristics of the well namely depth, diameter and type of rocks) and a technical risk (potential modifications of the construction plans if the estimated resources are not confirmed after drilling). It is easily understandable that an important number of buildings owners don't go deeper in geo-energy potential analysis due to those risks. It is difficult to perform a market analysis to quantify the impact of the financial and technical risks, but the facts are that only 2,000 heat pumps based on geo-energy were sold in France in 2020 (including all type of buildings, from small independent houses to big office buildings) whereas 812,000 aerothermal heat pumps (classical system) were installed. From a technical point of view, it is not satisfying to impose a invasive testing well when a lot of data are not processed.

3 Automatic Geological Information Extraction in Document Images

3.1 General Document Processing Workflow

More than 800,000 underground structures (geotechnical survey, oil and gas wells, water wells, geo-energy wells,...) are listed in the BRGM database. Associated with

---

[3] https://ericsenergy.com/heating-cooling/learn-more-about-geothermal-heat-pumps/.

them, 2,213,989 scanned documents are available online. They are drilling and tests reports, geological logs, water quality, etc. and contains many key information to model the rocks parameters. The diversity of the documents is such that it is not possible to extract geological information with a single generic procedure. It is necessary to develop several extraction pipelines depending on the typology of the documents: mainly textual, tables, forms, maps or sketches. The different pipelines are presented on Fig. 1. The first stage is common for all the pipelines and consists in an automatic classification of the type of pages. This classification will determine which extraction process has to be applied to the page. We present in this section the training and evaluation of the page classification system.

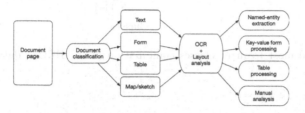

Fig. 1. The different workflows needed to extract the geological information from the scanned documents, depending on their types

3.2 BRGM Dataset Annotated for Classification

The BRGM document data set is composed of 2,213,989 PDF documents, containing multiple pages. Each page can be composed of different elements such as text zones, tables, forms, graphs, maps, photos, logs. Since it is not possible to know in advance which of this structure contains the geological information we are interested in, each page should be labeled with the different types of structure it contains. The classification problem is therefore inherently multi-class and multi-label (cf. Fig. 2).

In order to create a training sample for the automatic document classifier, we sampled 2,000 documents from the complete data set, which represent 2,323 images after splitting the documents into pages. The sample was manually labeled using the document processing platform Arkindex[4]. Seven labels were defined to represent the different elements located in the documents: log – form – graph – map – photo – table – text. Examples of three pages showing the different elements are presented on Fig. 3.

The labeling of the pages was not straightforward. First identifying the different types of structure is sometimes not obvious. For example, a table with only 2 columns could be considered as a form or a simple form containing a lot of text could be considered a plain text zone. Moreover, some structural elements cover only a small part of the page and may not be relevant for the information extraction. However, since we don't know in advance where lies the information, we decided to focus on labeling the different elements present on the page whether they contain an information of interest or not.

---

[4] https://demo.arkindex.org.

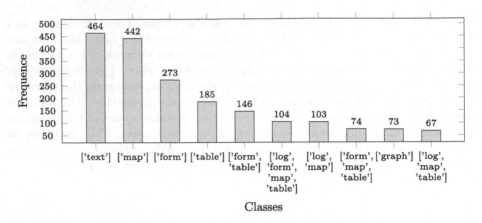

Fig. 2. The 10 most frequent classes combination in the BRGM dataset of scanned documents.

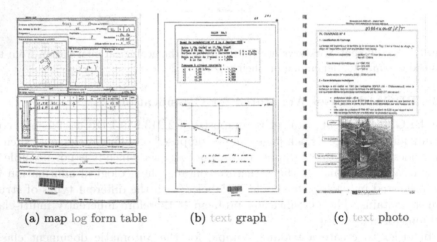

(a) map log form table   (b) text graph   (c) text photo

Fig. 3. Sample images from the BRGM database along with their labels

3.3   Document Classification Model

Training a model from scratch requires a very large amount of data to achieve an accurate classification. Since we had only 2,323 images, we chose to use transfer learning in order to fine-tune a pre-trained model on our images and get accurate classification. We first compared two Deep Neural Network architectures (VGG [4] and ResNet [2]) pre-trained on ImageNet [1] as feature extractor. This latter is followed by layers randomly initialized [Linear-ReLU-Dropout-Linear] to run the classification and a final sigmoid layer to obtain probabilities for each class. Since we have a small number of training sample, the first Linear layer reduces the number of features to 500, which also limits the number of parameters to be computed. To run the experiments, we randomly split the dataset into training, validation and testing sets which respectively corresponds to 1858, 232 and 233 images (80-10-10%). The images are resized to fit the input size of the pre-trained model (224 × 224 RGB for VGG and ResNet), normalized and randomly flipped for data augmentation. The parameters of the VGG and ResNet layers are kept constant during training, only the added classification layers are fully trained on our images. Since each image can belong to multiple classes, the probabilities output by the sigmoid layer are thresholded with $t = 0.5$ to assign the final classes. First, we chose to compare various feature extractors to select the best one before improving the results. These first experiments showed that, under the same conditions, VGG16 yielded better results on our dataset (based on BCELoss and the F1-Score) than the other ResNet and VGG models. For the next experiments, VGG16 pre-trained model is then used as feature extractor.

The second set of experiments consisted in optimizing the model's hyper-parameters: batch size, number of epochs, learning rate and optimizer. We also tested to change the loss to the BCEWithLogitsLoss, however the results were similar to the standard BCELoss. Table 1 shows the ranges of values tested.

Table 1. Ranges of the tested values for VGG16's hyparameters optimization

Hyperparameter	Range
Learning rate	[0.01, 0.005, 0.001, 0.0005, 0.0001]
Batch size	[16, 32, 64]
Number of epochs	[30, 40, 50]
Optimizer	[Adam]

Batch size of 32, 30 epochs and a 0.005 learning rate gave the accurest model whose results are presented in the next section.

3.4 Results and Discussion

The results of the best model are presented on Fig. 4a. The average F1-Score is 0.84 which is a good score considering our data set size and the complexity of the task. When we focus on **form - table - text** classes, 78% of form elements are detected by the model (86% for tables and 87% for text) and only 17% are confused with another element type (8% for tables and 11% for text). The training curve presented on Fig. 4b shows a positive correlation between the F1-Score Micro and the data set size suggesting a potential further increase of the model performance with more labeled data.

One limitation of our approach is that the definition of the different classes is not very precise and subjective so that the manual classification is some-times difficult to achieve. Moreover, this approach does not take into account the proportion of the document for the classification: a small table of 2 lines and 2 columns has the same impact on the manual classification as a full page table. Finally the approach does not provide either the location of the different elements, which will need to be predicted by the following processing steps.

Class	Precision	Recall	F1-Score
Coupe	0.88	0.79	0.83
Form	0.78	0.83	0.80
Graph	0.81	0.52	0.63
Map	0.92	0.83	0.87
Photo	1.0	1.0	1.0
Table	0.86	0.92	0.89
Text	0.87	0.89	0.88
Micro Avg	**0.86**	**0.83**	**0.84**

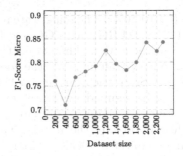

(a) Performance metrics by labels   (b) F1-Score Micro and dataset size correlation

Fig. 4. Results on test set (233 images)

4   Conclusion

We presented the first step of a fully automatic workflow to extract geological information in scanned drilling reports. On a small sample of 200 documents, selected randomly on the entire database, we observed that 3% of the documents contain information on well productivity and rocks capacity. If this ratio is also observed in the entire dataset, it means that more than 60,000 water rates can be found in the documents. As a reference, our geologists team went manually through documents: after three man.months of hard work, 5,000 flow rates have been collected. With more than 60,000 wells identified as water producers and quantified with a water flow rate, the hydro-geological model of the first hundred meters of France will be dense and robust, thus improving the prediction of geo-energy feasibility and selecting properly the right buildings to connect to their underground.

References

1. Deng, J., Dong, W., Socher, R., Li, L.J., Li, K., Li, F.F.: ImageNet: a large-scale hierarchical image database. In: 2009 IEEE Conference on Computer Vision and Pattern Recognition, pp. 248–255, June 2009. https://doi.org/10.1109/CVPR.2009.5206848
2. He, K., Zhang, X., Ren, S., Sun, J.: Deep residual learning for image recognition. In: 2016 IEEE Conference on Computer Vision and Pattern Recognition (CVPR), pp. 770–778 (2016). https://doi.org/10.1109/CVPR.2016.90
3. Lamé, A.: Modélisation hydrogéologique des aquifères de Paris et impacts des aménagements du sous-sol sur les écoulements souterrains. Theses, Ecole Nationale Supérieure des Mines de Paris, December 2013. https://pastel.archives-ouvertes.fr/pastel-00973861
4. Simonyan, K., Zisserman, A.: Very deep convolutional networks for large-scale image recognition. In: Bengio, Y., LeCun, Y. (eds.) 3rd International Conference on Learning Representations, ICLR 2015, San Diego, CA, USA, 7–9 May 2015, Conference Track Proceedings (2015). http://arxiv.org/abs/1409.1556

Data Envelopment Analysis for Energy Audits of Housing Properties

Sushodhan Vaishampayan[(⊠)], Aditi Pawde, Akshada Shinde, Manoj Apte, and Girish Keshav Palshikar

TCS Research, Tata Consultancy Services Ltd., Pune 411013, India
{sushodhan.sv,pawde.aditi,akshada.shinde,manoj.apte,gk.palshikar}@tcs.com

Abstract. Energy audit is a standardized and well-accepted process, consisting of inspection, survey, assessment, and evaluation of residential properties, commercial establishments and industrial plants, using sophisticated instruments as well as human experts. Energy audit of a city consists of inspections of many thousands (or even hundreds of thousands) of properties of varied ages, types, sizes, conditions, occupancy, and usage patterns. In this paper, we demonstrate how data envelopment analysis (DEA) techniques can be used to derive useful insights from energy audit data of a city, as compared to regression-based or anomaly detection based approaches. We also show how DEA can be used to come up with recommendations for reducing energy consumption. We illustrate the approach by analyzing energy audit data of Austin, Texas.

1 Introduction

From 2014 to 2017, the world's primary energy supply increased from 155,481 terawatt-hour (TWh) to 162,494 TWh and global CO_2 emissions rose from 32.3 gigatonnes (Gt) to 32.7 Gt[1]. Given these alarming figures, it has become important to reduce energy consumption by making more effective use of energy without compromising on utility and other benefits. Reduced energy consumption reduces carbon footprint, decreases energy spends, contributes to sustainability and helps in improving the environment. *Energy audit* [1,2] is now a standardized and well-accepted process, consisting of inspection, survey, assessment, and evaluation of residential properties, commercial establishments and industrial plants, using sophisticated instruments as well as human experts. Typical goals of an energy audit are to understand patterns of energy usage, to evaluate operating environment and equipment conditions that affect energy consumption, and to identify opportunities for reducing energy consumption.

Energy audits of large establishments result in a lot of precious data. In this paper, we focus on energy audits of cities and demonstrate how data envelopment analysis (DEA) techniques can be used to derive useful insights from energy audit data. Several cities (e.g., Seattle, Austin in USA) regularly conduct energy audits

---

[1] https://www.iea.org/reports/global-energy-review-2021.

© Springer Nature Switzerland AG 2021
M. Kamp et al. (Eds.): ECML PKDD 2021 Workshops, CCIS 1525, pp. 531–545, 2021.
https://doi.org/10.1007/978-3-030-93733-1_40

and set targets for reducing energy consumptions. Energy audit of a city consists of inspections of many thousands (or even hundreds of thousands) of properties of varied ages, types, sizes, conditions, occupancies, and usage patterns. At first glance, one may feel that energy audit data itself should be directly useful to identify opportunities to reduce energy consumption. While that is somewhat true at the level of an individual property, different insights need to be discovered from the collected audit data of many properties.

Energy (in)efficiency of a property is measured in terms of *Energy Use Intensity (EUI)*, which is computed as the total energy consumed by the property in one year divided by the total floor area of the property ($kWh/m^2/year$). Lower (higher) values of EUI indicate higher (lower) energy efficiency of a property's operations. However, EUI is computed only on the basis of floor area of the property. In reality, the energy consumption is affected by many other variables related to the property: age, condition, occupancy levels, usage patterns etc. Thus, only using EUI to identify energy inefficient properties is inadequate. In that case, the first question is: *how do we define a principled and more general notion of energy efficiency that takes into account other attributes of the property than its floor area?* DEA is a popular approach for evaluating a diverse range of energy efficiency issues; see [3] and [4] for comprehensive surveys. Following this work, we also model the energy efficiency of a property as DEA efficiency, where the input and output variables describing each property are obtained from an energy audit; we refer to this generalized notion as *energy proficiency.*

The second question is: *how do we identify properties with "unusually low" energy proficiency?* Since there is no *gold standard* available for what an ideal energy proficiency value should be, we need methods to identify low energy proficiency properties by comparing similar properties with each other. Answer to this question leads to further questions. *How to identify "personalized" improvements to a particular property P to improve its energy proficiency?* Next is the question of *benchmarking: how to identify an "ideal" target property P' having a much higher energy proficiency than P?* Here, we will use the identified "ideal" property P' to suggest improvements for P. There are other interesting questions that we do not attempt to answer in this paper. For example, given the energy audit data of a city for several years, what insights can be discovered and what changes in patterns of energy consumption can be observed? how to identify sufficiently many properties with low energy proficiency, so that if all (or most) of them are improved in some "specified" ways, then the energy consumption of the city would be reduced by a "required amount", which is often identified as a target by the city government?

The techniques we use to answer these questions are based on the well-known *Data Envelopment Analysis (DEA)*. We use the energy audit data for Austin, Texas to illustrate the solution approaches, which can be easily adapted to other forms of energy audit data. The paper is organized as follows. Section 2 describes some related work. Section 3 describes the real-life dataset of energy audits conducted in the city of Austin, Texas. Section 4 gives a very short summary of DEA. In Sect. 5, we use the DEA methodology to analyze energy audit data of residential properties and to answer some of the above questions. Finally, we provide our conclusions and outline some future work in Sect. 6.

2   Related Work

An audit is a methodical examination of relevant information (equipment, data, documents, objects, processes) within an organization by an external and independent body [5]. Goals of an audit include: (a) detection of non-compliance to policies, standard operating procedures and relevant laws; and (b) evaluation of risk factors from perspectives such as frauds, safety, security, mis-management, impending losses etc. While financial audits are the most common, there are other types of focused audits such as forensic audits, safety audits, energy audits, quality audits, project audits, operations audit, among others. Given the variety and complexity of auditing tasks in various domains, it is not surprising that AI, data mining and machine learning techniques have been found to be useful to assist auditors [6–16]. Broad goals of such work has been to improve the quality and effectiveness of the audits and to reduce the time, efforts involved in audits.

[17] presents a review about how the AI and ML models such as Artificial Neural Networks (ANN), Support Vector Machines, Gaussian-based regressions, clustering etc., are utilized for building energy prediction models and for improving energy performance. It discusses about *benchmarking* - a method to determine whether a building is using more or less energy than its peer facilities with similar occupancies, climates, and sizes etc. It indicates the advantages and drawbacks of each model and their application for benchmarking. In [18] the data of energy audits of 151 existing public buildings of Southern Italy is analysed and used to assess the energy performance of a building using two ANN models. The first ANN model predicts *Primary Energy* (PE) demand with parameters such as climate data, thermophysics and geometrical characteristics, building HVAC systems etc. Based on the outputs of first model, corresponding retrofit actions are suggested for a building using second ANN model by taking cost and economic feasibility into consideration.

Regression, clustering and classification are some of the basic ML techniques that find application in energy conservation. [19] assess the energy performance of schools in Italy using k-means clustering. The most relevant indicators correlated to energy consumption are identified using regression analysis. Buildings having similar indicator values are clustered in the same group. Building with the shortest distance from the centroid of this group is represented as the *reference building*. These reference buildings are useful tools for optimizing retrofit solutions. [20] propose a classifier called falling rule list (FRL) classifier, based on binary features derived from New York City's (NYC) Local Law 87 (LL87) data. It checks the eligibility of a building for Energy Conservation Measures (ECMs) category based on given specific set of building characteristics. These ECM categories such as lighting (Upgrade to LED, Install Occupancy/Vacancy Sensors), Envelope (Sealing – Door, Increase Insulation – Roof), etc. can then be recommended to save energy. The significance of this study is substantial in terms of boosting the adoption of building ECMs, stimulating reductions in energy usage and greenhouse gas (GHG) emissions from buildings.

DEA is a popular approach for evaluating energy efficiency issues in many geographies, countries, regions, sectors and across various application areas such as Environmental Efficiency, Economic and eco-efficiency, Renewable and sustainable energy, water efficiency etc.; see [3] and [4] for comprehensive surveys. [21] have used DEA to evaluate carbon emission performance of 29 Chinese provincial administrative regions by computing potential carbon emission reductions for energy conservation technology and energy structural adjustment. [22] use directional distance functions and DEA to assess eco-efficiency i.e. the ability to create more goods and services with less impact on the environment. They compute indicators of eco-efficiency representing different objectives regarding economic and ecological performance. [23] uses Malmquist CO_2 Emission Performance Index (MCPI) which is obtained by solving multiple DEA models for measuring changes in total factor carbon emission performance over time. MCPI is used to compare performance of the world's top 18 CO_2 emitter countries. Energy saving is crucial for sustainable development. [24] uses energy, labor and capital as inputs and GDP as a single output. DEA is applied to find Energy Savings Target (EST) for APEC economies without reducing the maximum potential Gross Domestic Product (GDP).

Achieving higher energy efficiency is of utmost importance to attain sustainable development. Thus, improved techniques of evaluation of energy efficiency play vital role [25]. Widely accepted definition of energy efficiency, Total Factor Energy Efficiency (TFEE) is given by [26] and defined as ratio of target energy input to actual input required at an output level. This notion states that energy efficiency is an issue relating to economy, energy and environment and thus its computation should involve consideration of factors such as labor and capital as input along with energy input. Different extensions of DEA models are proposed in the literature to cater to dynamic nature of energy efficiency evaluation. Exclusion of undesirable output such as carbon emission in measuring energy efficiency levels tends to overestimation of the energy efficiency level of environmentally friendly countries [27]. The extended model Undesirable DEA is useful in such cases. Energy systems are complex and they defy the basic assumption of DEA where each production system is considered as a 'black box'. An adjusted network DEA model proposed in [28] separates energy producing and energy consuming departments and applies this model to China's industrial sector. The non-parametric Malmquist Productivity Index (MPI), as time series analysis tool, has been extended to DEA models to characterize dynamic changes in efficiency of energy systems because of changes in production technology over time [29]. Game Cross-Efficiency DEA and Meta-Frontier DEA are some other extended DEA models proposed for energy efficiency evaluation [25].

Energy audit is an important tool to assess energy efficiency. Authors of [30] have used energy audit data from Austin Energy to study design and installation issues associated with air conditioning systems. They concluded that upgrading the air conditioning systems could possibly reduce the peak power demand by as much as 205 MW which is about 30% of Austin's Climate protection plan goal of 700 MW peak reduction. [31] is follow up work of [30] and gives similar recommendations. In our knowledge, there is no work that evaluates energy use of residential sector based on energy audit data using DEA.

Benchmarking refers to comparing performance of an entity with the best target in order to define scope of improvement. Level 0 category of energy audit is known as *benchmarking*. This audit analyses energy use of the whole building and compares it with other similar buildings. This provides broader perspective on whether detailed audit is needed or not. We aim at achieving such benchmark properties for an inefficient property and corresponding recommendations using the techniques also confusingly called *benchmarking* in DEA literature. In DEA, *technical inefficiency* is typically measured as the distance between the observed unit and a benchmarking target on the efficiency frontier. Many benchmarking methods are available in DEA; see [32] for a survey. In this paper, we have used three methods, summarized below, two of which are available as R packages.

While finding the relative efficiency of a DMU, it is compared to a hypothetical unit formed by taking the weighted average of DMUs on the frontier, that are closest to the DMU under evaluation. These closest frontier DMUs are called *peers* and their respective weights are called λ-values. The artificial unit which is a λ-weighted average of the peers is actually the projection of the DMU under evaluation on to the frontier [33]. This artificial unit can be directly used as a target for suggesting improvement to the DMU under evaluation. We used *Benchmarking*[2] package in R for finding the peers and λ-values.

Another package *deaR*[3] has an inbuilt function *targets()* which generates target values for an inefficient unit. The function uses a Slack Based Measure (SBM) [34], where input slack s^- and output slack s^+ are found. The input slacks are *input-excesses* and output-slacks are *output-shortfalls*. The target values can be found as follows: for inputs x_o; $x_o \leftarrow x_o - s^-$ and for output y_o; $y_o \leftarrow y_o + s^+$. This operation is called the *SBM-projection*.

The closest projection of a unit on the efficiency frontier and corresponding efficiency can be found by using Euclidean Distance [35]. In this method, a *reference set* of an inefficient DMU is defined as the set of efficient DMUs that are used to compute the projection and the *reference supporting hyperplane* is the hyperplane comprising of these DMUs. Projection of the inefficient DMUs on to this hyperplane is computed by deleting input and augmenting output with the help of Euclidean Distance Based (EDB) scaling factor (ρ). Similarly, EDB measure of efficiency (π) and super-efficiency (γ) is computed for ranking of efficient DMUs.

3   Energy Audit Data for Austin

A broad goal of the city of Austin, Texas is to reduce the peak energy demand of 800 MW by 2020. Towards this, the city released energy audit data of multi-family properties older than 10 years[4]. The data was collected during the energy audits conducted between 22nd Feb 2010 to 2nd Feb 2016 (data last updated:

---

[2] cran.r-project.org/web/packages/Benchmarking/index.html.

[3] cran.r-project.org/web/packages/deaR/index.html.

[4] https://austinenergy.com/ae/energy-efficiency/ecad-ordinance/for-multifamily-properties.

Table 1. Summary statistics for Austin data.

Column	Mean	STDEV	Q2	Q3
p_duct_leakage	30.6	18.9	26.1	43.0
attic_r_value	17.2	8.4	15.0	22.0
age	35.3	14.1	34.0	44.0
total_units	127.6	131.2	69.0	216.0
EUI	10.2	3.1	10.1	12.4

26th Feb, 2016, accessed: 8th Feb, 2021) for 807 propoerties. Out of which 545 properties are with no missing value in any column. Columns in this data are described below.

- p_duct_leakage (X_1): percent leakage in the ducts used for forced air delivery in heating and cooling; higher leakage values lower the energy efficiency.
- attic_r_value (X_2): gives the quality of resistance to heat flow provided by the insulation in the attic; higher values indicate better thermal performance of the insulation.
- age (X_3): of the property in number of years.
- total_units (X_4): the number of flats (units) in the property.
- window_screens (X_5): 0 if the property needs (lacks) window screens; 1 otherwise. 218 properties (40%) had the value of 1.
- common_laundry (X_6): 0 if the property does not have a common laundry facility; 1 otherwise. 390 properties (71.6%) had the value of 1.
- utilities (X_7): 0 indicates only electric and 1 indicates both gas and electric utilities are used in the property. 193 properties (35.4%) had the value of 1.
- community_EUI (Y): This refers to the EUI of the building in $kWh/sqft/year$. Since the data is normalized to range [0,1] before experimentation, converting unit to $kWh/m^2/year$ has no effect.

Table 1 gives the summary statistics for non-Boolean columns.

4   Data Envelopment Analysis

Data Envelopment Analysis (DEA) [36,37] is a well-known optimization-based method for comparing a set of functionally similar *organizational units* (called *decision making units (DMU))* using a generalized notion of relative efficiency. DEA has been applied to evaluate performance of units such as hospitals, universities, banks, ports, production factories etc. Suppose we have a set of N units, each described by a pair of feature vectors $(\mathbf{x}^{(i)}, \mathbf{y}^{(i)})$, $i = 1, \ldots, N$. Here, each $\mathbf{x}^{(i)} = (x_1^{(i)}, x_2^{(i)}, \ldots, x_m^{(i)})$ is an m-vector of *input* values, and each $\mathbf{y}^{(i)} = (y_1^{(i)}, y_2^{(i)}, \ldots, y_n^{(i)})$ is an n-vector of *output* values. Let $(\mathbf{x}^{(0)}, \mathbf{y}^{(0)})$ be another given unit, called the *target unit*. DEA defines ways to compute the relative efficiency of the target unit, given the other N units. *Efficiency* of the target unit is defined as the ratio of a weighted sum of its output values divided by a weighted sum of its input values.

$$h^{(0)} = \frac{b_1^{(0)} \cdot y_1^{(0)} + \ldots + b_n^{(0)} \cdot y_n^{(0)}}{a_1^{(0)} \cdot x_1^{(0)} + \ldots + a_m^{(0)} \cdot x_m^{(0)}} \tag{1}$$

The weights $a_1^{(0)}, \ldots, a_m^{(0)}$ and $b_1^{(0)}, \ldots, b_n^{(0)}$ are computed such that the efficiency of the target unit is maximized and some constraints are satisfied.

$$\text{maximize} \quad \frac{b_1^{(0)} \cdot y_1^{(0)} + \ldots + b_n^{(0)} \cdot y_n^{(0)}}{a_1^{(0)} \cdot x_1^{(0)} + \ldots + a_m^{(0)} \cdot x_m^{(0)}} \tag{2}$$

$$\text{s.t.} \frac{b_1^{(j)} \cdot y_1^{(j)} + \ldots + b_n^{(j)} \cdot y_n^{(j)}}{a_1^{(j)} \cdot x_1^{(j)} + \ldots + a_m^{(j)} \cdot x_m^{(j)}} \leq 1 \ \forall 1 \leq j \leq N \tag{3}$$

$$a_1, \ldots, a_m \geq \epsilon \tag{4}$$

$$b_1, \ldots, b_n \geq \epsilon \tag{5}$$

The objective function and some of the constraints involve ratios of the decision variables (weights). To convert this optimization to a linear programming problem, only the numerator in Eq. (1) is treated as the objective function and the denominator is maintained at some constant value (this is added as a constraint). The constraints in Eq. (3) are rewritten as:

$$\left(\sum_{i=1}^{n} b_i^{(j)} \cdot y_i^{(j)} \right) - \left(\sum_{k=1}^{m} a_k^{(j)} \cdot x_k^{(j)} \right) \leq 0 \ \forall 1 \leq j \leq N \tag{6}$$

There are other formulations of the DEA optimization program, notably the variable-returns-to-scale (VRS).

5   Properties with Low Energy Efficiency

We have earlier identified the questions that need to be answered by mining the energy audit data. The first question is about how to find properties which are *anomalous*, hence interesting, from an energy audit perspective.

5.1   Using Outlier Detection Techniques

An obvious way is to find properties having "very high" EUI, ignoring all other attributes of properties. We use a simple method to find such properties. Quartiles for the EUI column are: $Q_1 = 7.8, Q_2 = 10.06, Q_3 = 12.42$. Then $IQR = Q_3 - Q_1 = 4.62$, and $U = Q_3 + 1.5 \cdot IQR = 19.35$. Only one property (ID = 219437) has EUI value more than U. To use another method, since the EUI column has average $= 10.21$, STDEV $= 3.15$, there is only one property (again, ID = 219437) having EUI more than $10.21 + 3 \cdot 3.15 = 19.76$. Clearly, using only EUI to identify anomalous properties is not very useful. We can apply these methods to identify properties that have "too high" value in another attribute, say *p_duct_leakage*. However, these applications of outlier detection techniques to single columns do not yield a satisfactory output from the energy audit perspective.

Next, we used a set of 16 well-known anomaly detection techniques from the Python library PyOD [38]. Each record in the input data consists of a property having 8 attributes (described earlier). We took top 10 anomalous properties identified as anomalous by each method, and observed that some properties are identified as anomalous by multiple algorithms. Table 2 shows the top 10 properties, along with the count of the algorithms (out of 16) for which these properties occurred in top 10 anomalous properties. Among these, 287617 and 242225 are large with over 300 units and have very high *p_duct_leakage*, 75% and 65% respectively. Property 283288 is over 100 years old. Such properties are susceptible to high usage of energy due to old wiring, outdated equipment, leakages etc. Thus, the anomaly detection algorithms seem to have identified some good candidates for suggesting improvements, though more such properties could be identified. Another issue is that these algorithms do not take into account any explicit notion of energy efficiency. Hence it is hard to explain why a particular property is detected as anomalous (outlier) and what recommendations can be systematically generated to improve its energy efficiency.

Table 2. Top 10 anomalous properties identified by 16 anomaly detection algorithms.

Property	Count	X_1	X_2	X_3	X_4	X_5	X_6	X_7	Y
310468–310472	10	14	15	30	600	0	0	0	11.96
208408	7	9	30	116	5	0	1	0	14.11
522659	7	8.7	17	13	540	1	1	0	9.46
497787	7	50	27	14	550	1	0	1	8.38
R359319	6	52	30	17	518	1	0	1	6.68
203523	6	30	12	111	9	1	0	1	9.06
532172	5	53	30	12	528	1	1	0	6.9
242225	5	65	6	42	409	0	1	1	8.15
283288	5	28	19	108	6	0	1	1	3.87
287617	5	75	19	42	370	1	1	0	5.82

Using Marginal Efficiencies to Identify Anomalous Properties: In another experiment, we tried to identify anomalous properties, where each property was represented by 4 marginal efficiencies:

$$\gamma_1 = (1/Y)/X_1 \tag{7}$$
$$\gamma_2 = (1/Y)/(1/X_2) \tag{8}$$
$$\gamma_3 = (1/Y)/X_3 \tag{9}$$
$$\gamma_4 = (1/Y)/X_4 \tag{10}$$

Marginal efficiencies determine goodness of a property with respect to each attribute. Boolean variables are excluded while computing marginal efficiencies. We expect anomalous properties to have low marginal efficiencies. In order to detect such properties, we applied the *iForest* algorithm from PyOD Python library to this dataset. Top 10 property IDs reported by this method are 223184, 291163, 208147, 312816, 234723, 234724, 234722, 204045, 203419 and 199744. Consider property 223184. Its original attributes are (33, 2, 34, 11, 0, 0, 1, 6.19) and the marginal efficiencies are (0.005, 0.32, 0.005, 0.014). γ_1 is low due to the high (*p_duct_leakage*) i.e. $X_1 = 33\%$ which is ($>Q_2$). Clearly, 3 of its 4 marginal efficiencies are very low, which explains why it is detected as an anomalous property.

A generic issue with the anomaly detection techniques is that they do not employ any notion of energy efficiency and hence it becomes difficult to systematically suggest any recommendations for improving the anomalous properties.

5.2   Using Regression Models

The attributes of each property have a clear categorization: EUI can be considered as *output* and the others as *input*. That is, EUI can be an unknown function of the remaining property attributes. So we built regression models to estimate this function and used them to identify anomalous properties. The results of 5 different regression techniques are given in the Table 3. We also tried Decision Tree regression but it led to extreme overfitting and showed negative R^2 in 5-fold cross validation (negative R^2 means that the model does worse than the one which predicts $\hat{y}$ for every input).

In this table, columns R^2_{best} and MSE_{best} contain the R^2 value and the Mean Squared Error (MSE) of the best performing model among those built with different combinations of inputs. The columns R^2_{full} and MSE_{full} contain the R^2 value and MSE of the model created using all the input variables. For example, for the K-Nearest Neighbors (K-NN) Regression, the regression model built with the numeric variables X_1, X_2, X_3, X_4 and just one boolean variable X_7 was slightly better than the regression model built with all the variables (numeric and boolean).

We considered a property as anomalous (w.r.t. the given regression model) if its actual (signed) prediction error ($y - \hat{y}$) was too large i.e., above a given threshold h_0. Using the histogram of actual errors, we found out that only few properties were having error above 6.0. So we fixed our threshold h_0 to 6.0. A large prediction error for a property indicates that its actual EUI is much higher than the predicted EUI. The number of properties considered anomalous by respective regression techniques is given in the column #anomalies of Table 3.

Table 3. Regressions models for Austin data.

Model	R^2_{best}	MSE_{best}	R^2_{full}	MSE_{full}	#anomalies
Ordinary least squares	0.28	7.14	0.28	7.14	7
Lasso regression	0.28	7.16	0.28	7.17	8
Support vector regression	0.11	8.76	0.11	8.83	15
Partial least squares regression ($n\_components = 4$)	0.28	7.14	0.28	7.14	7
K-NN regression ($K = 5$)	**0.41**	**5.88**	0.40	5.92	3

5.3   Using DEA Efficiency

The main issue with the anomalous properties reported by regression techniques is that the models do not provide any explainable notion of energy efficiency. Also, the number of anomalous properties seems rather low. Hence, we now use the standard notion of DEA-based energy efficiency (which we call energy proficiency), which is more general than EUI and takes into account other attributes of the property than its floor area. If each property is described in terms of input and output variables, then the DEA efficiency of the property corresponds to a more general notion of energy efficiency; higher DEA efficiency can be considered as higher energy proficiency. We map the original variables in Austin data to a new set of variables as follows: $X'_1 = X_1, X'_2 = 1/X_2, X'_3 = X_3, X'_4 = X_4, X'_5 = 1 - X_5, X'_6 = 1 - X_6, X'_7 = 1 - X_7, Y' = 1/Y$. This formulation helps us to match DEA efficiency to *energy proficiency* e.g., reduction in *p_duct_leakage* (X_1) and increase in *attic_r_value* (X_2) should result in decrease in EUI (Y). The input data to DEA techniques is normalized such that all the values fall in the range [0,1]. Solving input oriented model with this formulation for Austin data then leads to 87 properties on the frontier. Examples of properties with low efficiencies are: 242225 (0.24), 310468–310472 (0.26), 155451 (0.26), 262089 (0.27), 239687 (0.28). Suppose we take 100 properties with the lowest efficiencies. Note that not all of these properties have high EUI; out of these 100 properties 26 have EUI below 10.1 (median for EUI), indicating that they are reasonably good from a purely EUI consideration. Thus, the DEA efficiency is identifying them as bad for different reasons.

We generate a candidate explanation for why DEA efficiency of a property P is low as a tuple $(\eta_1, \eta_2, \eta_3, \eta_4)$, where η_i is the *marginal efficiency rank* with respect to i-th input variable. First, we have already defined *marginal efficiency* of a property P with respect to i-th input variable as $\gamma_i = \frac{Y'}{X'_i}$. Let $W^{(P)}$ be the set of peer properties of P including P i.e., $W^{(P)}$ is the set of P and K properties which are nearest to P in terms of the vector of input variables (K is a user-specified constant; e.g., $K = 20$). Then η_i is the rank of the marginal efficiency of P among set of the marginal efficiencies of the properties in $W^{(P)}$. As an example, consider property $P = 242225$ which has the lowest efficiency of 0.24. Original values for the 7 property attributes $X_1, \ldots, X_7$ and EUI of P are $(65.0, 6.0, 42, 409, 0, 1, 1, 8.15)$. Thus the marginal efficiencies of P are $(0.002, 0.736, 0.003, 0.0003)$; e.g., $\gamma_2 = (1/8.15)/(1/6.0) = 0.736$. Now we compute the K ($=20$) nearest neighbors of property P among all properties (the set $W^{(P)}$) and compute the same 4 marginal efficiencies for the properties in $W^{(P)}$. Then, ordering the properties in $W^{(P)}$ in descending order of the marginal efficiency γ_i, η_i is the rank of P in this set. For P, the ranks are $(17, 19, 12, 18)$, showing that P has very low marginal efficiencies as compared to its 20 nearest neighbors, which explains why its overall DEA efficiency is low. Note that this explanation does not make any explicit use of the frontier.

5.4   Recommendations for Improvements

The next task is to come up with a recommendation to improve a property having low DEA efficiency. A recommendation is a suggestion for changing values of some of the input variables. Table 4 shows the recommendation for the 5 least energy proficient properties, as generated using 3 methods: Reco-A, Reco-B and Reco-C, which are the *deaR* package method [34], *Benchmarking* package method [33] and Euclidean distance based method [35] respectively. Once a recommendation is generated, we create a dummy property with these recommended values as input values and run DEA again to get its new efficiency. As seen from the table, methods A and B are able to generate useful recommendations in terms of improving energy proficiency. For example, for property 242225, both methods A and B suggested decreasing X_1 (*p_duct_leakage*), and increasing X_2 (*attic_r_value*), which are useful in improving energy proficiency. Also, the recommendations generated by methods A and B are close to each other. Method C fails to generate any recommendation for three properties. For properties 310468–310472 and 155451, the changes suggested by method C are reasonable but are rather small in magnitude in some cases. We are still analyzing the difference in behavior of method C with other methods. Note that the methods are suggesting changes to *all* inputs; but in reality, some input variables are not modifiable (e.g., age). In another experiment we observed that if we incorporate recommendation for only controllable inputs X_1 and X_2 i.e., *p_duct_leakage* and *attic_r_value* respectively, efficiency of inefficient properties increases and may not reach 1 since not all recommendations are incorporated.

Table 4. Recommendations for 5 least efficient properties.

Property ID		X_1	X_2	X_3	X_4	X_5	X_6	X_7	Y	Efficiency
242225	Original	65	6	42	409	0	1	1	8.15	0.24
	Reco-A	8.71	17.34	17.72	101.7	0.97	1	1	8.15	1
	Reco-B	8.71	17.69	17.72	101.7	0.97	1	1	8.15	1
	Reco-C	–	–	–	–	–	–	–	–	–
310468–310472	Original	14	15	30	600	0	0	0	11.96	0.26
	Reco-A	6.36	31.43	15.16	157.7	0.97	0.97	0.97	9.08	1
	Reco-B	6.36	31.89	15.16	157.7	0.97	0.97	0.97	11.96	1
	Reco-C	13.22	137.02	12.14	599.98	0	0	0	9.78	0.49
155451	Original	39	11	30	280	0	0	0	11.08	0.26
	Reco-A	13.01	24.1	15.27	76.76	0.74	0.74	0.74	8.25	1
	Reco-B	13.01	25.43	15.27	76.76	0.74	0.74	0.74	11.08	1
	Reco-C	38.1	45.56	9.25	279.97	0	0	0	8.94	0.4
262089	Original	18	7	32	384	0	1	0	13.89	0.27
	Reco-A	7.6	26.14	16	107.64	0.73	1	0.73	7.86	1
	Reco-B	7.6	27.82	16	107.64	0.73	1	0.73	13.89	1
	Reco-C	–	–	–	–	–	–	–	–	–
239687	Original	14.5	10	31	503	1	1	0	13.65	0.28
	Reco-A	6.71	27.87	15.86	143.19	1	1	0.97	9.04	1
	Reco-B	6.71	29.31	15.86	143.19	1	1	0.97	13.65	1
	Reco-C	–	–	–	–	–	–	–	–	–

6   Conclusions and Further Work

Identifying low energy proficient properties and providing them recommendations is an important task in an Energy Audit. In this paper, our goal is to identify such properties, find out benchmark or *target* properties for them and provide personalized improvements. We used publicly available energy audit data for multi-families from Austin Energy, Texas. From the data we used percent duct leakage, attic R-value, total units, age (in years), windows screening needed, common laundry and utility type as input variables and community EUI (in $kWh/sqft/year$) as output variable. We first applied 16 Anomaly Detection algorithms considering input and output variables together in their original form to find out anomalous properties with respect to high energy usage and analyzed their ensembles. We then transformed 4 input variables into *marginal efficiencies* and performed Anomaly Detection on this transformed feature set. The results show that there was no overlap in these two sets, though they pointed out some inefficient properties. We also built a regression model using input variables as independent variables and EUI as dependent variable and analyzed properties having very high prediction error as anomalies. Though some inefficient properties are obtained as result, both Anomaly Detection and Regression Analysis techniques do not employ any notion of energy efficiency and hence it becomes difficult to systematically suggest any recommendations for improvement. Moreover, these methods can produce highly non-efficient as well as highly efficient properties as anomalous properties.

We then used Data Envelopment Analysis (DEA) to achieve our goal. We transformed input and output variables before using DEA. Input variables whose values when increased results in decrease in EUI are inverted and others are kept as it is. The output variable EUI is inverted as we are interested in decreased value of EUI. The transformation obtained is in such a way that DEA efficiency of a property should depict energy proficiency and properties with highest energy proficiency should form DEA efficiency frontier. Once such frontier is constructed, ideal targets for the property can be found out in terms of DEA *peers* and recommendations can be generated. We observed that DEA efficiency obtained with newly recommended input variable values increases and in most of the cases reaches 1. Similar effect is observed even when only subset of the recommendations is incorporated. We also generate explanation of why DEA efficiency of a property is low with the help of *marginal efficiency ranks*. Formulating DEA to obtain meaningful recommendations for residential properties from the energy audit perspective is the novel contribution of this paper.

It may not be possible to incorporate all the recommendations obtained from DEA due to presence of non-controllable inputs (e.g., age). We aim at generating final recommendations considering only the controllable inputs in our future work. Specifically, we would like to focus on analyzing the effect of changing only the controllable variables and its impact on the efficiency based on the combination of variables selected. We also plan at analyzing different schemes for changing the input variables based on the cost of changing the variables, the total budget available and the energy savings achieved.

References

1. Krarti, M.: Energy Audit of Building Systems: An Engineering Approach. CRC Press, Boca Raton (2000)
2. Thumann, A.: Handbook of Energy Audits, 9th edn. The Fairmont Press, Lilburn (2012)
3. Mardani, A., Zavadskas, E.K., Streimikiene, D., Jusoh, A., Khoshnoudi, M.: A comprehensive review of data envelopment analysis (DEA) approach in energy efficiency. Renew. Sustain. Energy Rev. **70**, 1298–1322 (2017)
4. Xu, T., You, J., Li, H., Shao, L.: Energy efficiency evaluation based on data envelopment analysis: a literature review. Energies **13**(3548) (2020)
5. Arens, A.A., Loebbecke, J.K.: Auditing: An Integrated Approach, 8th edn. Pearson, London (1999)
6. Dickey, G., Blanke, S., Seaton, L.: Machine learning in auditing: current and future applications. CPA J. **89**(6), 16–21 (2019)
7. Bowling, S., Meyer, C.: How we successfully implemented AI in audit. J. Account. **227**(5), 26–28 (2019)
8. Kokina, J., Davenport, T.H.: The emergence of artificial intelligence: how automation is changing auditing. J. Emerg. Technol. Account. **14**(1), 115–122 (2017)

9. Issa, H., Sun, T., Vasarhelyi, M.A.: Research ideas for artificial intelligence in auditing: the formalization of audit and workforce supplementation. J. Emerg. Technol. Account. **13**(2), 1–20 (2016)
10. Brown-Liburd, H., Issa, H., Lombardi, D.: Behavioral implications of big data's impact on audit judgment and decision making and future research directions. Account. Horiz. **29**(2), 451–468 (2015)
11. Earley, C.E.: Data Analytics in Auditing: Opportunities and Challenges, vol. 58 (2015)
12. Issa, H., Kogan, A.: A predictive ordered logistic regression model as a tool for quality review of control risk assessments. J. Inf. Syst. **28**(2), 209–229 (2014)
13. Hunton, J.E., Rose, J.M.: 21st-century auditing: advancing decision support systems to achieve continuous auditing. Account. Horiz. **24**(2), 297–312 (2010)
14. Omoteso, K., Patel, A., Scott, P.: Information and communications technology and auditing: current implications and future directions. Int. J. Audit. **14**(2), 147–162 (2010)
15. Etheridge, H.L., Sriram, R.S., Hsu, H.K.: A comparison of selected artificial neural networks that help auditors evaluate client financial viability. Decis. Sci. **31**(2), 531–550 (2000)
16. Asarhelyi, M.A.: Artificial intelligence in accounting and auditing: the use of expert systems (1989)
17. Seyedzadeh, S., Rahimian, F.P., Glesk, I., Roper, M.: Machine learning for estimation of building energy consumption and performance: a review. Visual. Eng. **6**(1), 1–20 (2018)
18. Beccali, M., Ciulla, G., Brano, V.L., Galatioto, A., Bonomolo, M.: Artificial neural network decision support tool for assessment of the energy performance and the refurbishment actions for the non-residential building stock in southern Italy. Energy **137**, 1201–1218 (2017)
19. Lara, R.A., Pernigotto, G., Cappelletti, F., Romagnoni, P., Gasparella, A.: Energy audit of schools by means of cluster analysis. Energy Build. **95**, 160–171 (2015)
20. Marasco, D.E., Kontokosta, C.E.: Applications of machine learning methods to identifying and predicting building retrofit opportunities. Energy Build. **128**, 431–441 (2016)
21. Guo, X.-D., Zhu, L., Fan, Y., Xie, B.-C.: Evaluation of potential reductions in carbon emissions in Chinese Provinces based on environmental DEA. Energy Policy **39**(5), 2352–2360 (2011)
22. Picazo-Tadeo, A.J., Beltrán-Esteve, M., Gómez-Limón, J.A.: Assessing eco-efficiency with directional distance functions. Eur. J. Oper. Res. **220**(3), 798–809 (2012)
23. Zhou, P., Ang, B.W., Han, J.Y.: Total factor carbon emission performance: a Malmquist index analysis. Energy Econ. **32**(1), 194–201 (2010)
24. Hu, J.-L., Kao, C.-H.: Efficient energy-saving targets for APEC economies. Energy Policy **35**(1), 373–382 (2007)
25. Song, M., An, Q., Zhang, W., Wang, Z., Jie, W.: Environmental efficiency evaluation based on data envelopment analysis: a review. Renew. Sustain. Energy Rev. **16**(7), 4465–4469 (2012)
26. Hu, J.-L., Wang, S.-C.: Total-factor energy efficiency of regions in China. Energy Policy **34**(17), 3206–3217 (2006)
27. He, P., Sun, Y., Shen, H., Jian, J., Zhongfu, Y.: Does environmental tax affect energy efficiency? An empirical study of energy efficiency in OECD countries based on DEA and logit model. Sustainability **11**(14), 3792 (2019)

28. Liu, Y., Wang, K.: Energy efficiency of China's industry sector: an adjusted network DEA (data envelopment analysis)-based decomposition analysis. Energy **93**, 1328–1337 (2015)

29. Färe, R., Grosskopf, S., Lindgren, B., Roos, P.: Productivity developments in Swedish hospitals: a Malmquist output index approach. In: Charnes, W.W.C., Lewin, A.Y., Seiford, L.M. (eds.) Data Envelopment Analysis: Theory, Methodology, and Applications, pp. 253–272. Springer, Dordrecht (1994). https://doi.org/10.1007/978-94-011-0637-5_13

30. Rhodes, J.D., Stephens, B., Webber, M.E.: Using energy audits to investigate the impacts of common air-conditioning design and installation issues on peak power demand and energy consumption in Austin, Texas. Energy Build. **43**(11), 3271–3278 (2011)

31. Rhodes, J., Stephens, B., Webber, M.E.: Energy audit analysis of residential air-conditioning systems in Austin, Texas. ASHRAE Trans. **118**(1) (2012)

32. Aparicio, J.: A survey on measuring efficiency through the determination of the least distance in data envelopment analysis. J. Centrum Cathedra (2016)

33. Bogetoft, P., Otto, L.: Benchmarking with DEA, SFA, and R, vol. 157. Springer, New York (2010). https://doi.org/10.1007/978-1-4419-7961-2

34. Tone, K.: A slacks-based measure of efficiency in data envelopment analysis. Eur. J. Oper. Res. **130**(3), 498–509 (2001)

35. Amirteimoori, A., Kordrostami, S.: A Euclidean distance-based measure of efficiency in data envelopment analysis. Optimization **59**(7), 985–996 (2010)

36. Charnes, A., Cooper, W.W., Rhodes, E.: Measuring the efficiency of decision making units. Eur. J. Oper. Res. **2**(6), 429–444 (1978)

37. Cooper, W.W., Seiford, L.M., Tone, K.: Data Envelopment Analysis, 2nd edn. Springer, Boston (2007). https://doi.org/10.1007/b109347

38. Zhao, Y., Nasrullah, Z., Li, Z.: PyOD: a Python toolbox for scalable outlier detection. J. Mach. Learn. Res. **20**(96), 1–7 (2019)

A Comparative Study on Machine Learning Algorithms for Assessing Energy Efficiency of Buildings

Christian Nnaemeka Egwim[1]([✉]) [iD], Oluwapelumi Oluwaseun Egunjobi[2] [iD],
Alvaro Gomes[2] [iD], and Hafiz Alaka[1] [iD]

[1] Big Data Technologies and Innovation Laboratory, University of Hertfordshire, Hatfield, UK
c.egwim@herts.ac.uk

[2] Energy for Sustainability (EFS), MIT-Portugal, Universidade de Coimbra, Coimbra, Portugal

Abstract. An increase in energy demand in buildings continues to give rise to air pollution with a consequent impact on human health. To curb this trend, energy efficiency assessment plays a crucial role in helping to understand the energy in buildings and to recommend strategies to improve efficiency. Unfortunately, many existing approaches to assessing the energy efficiency of buildings are failing to do it accurately. Hence, the recommended energy efficiency strategies thereafter are failing to achieve the expected result. One approach in recent times uses data-driven predictive analytics techniques like machine learning (ML) algorithms to assess a building's energy efficiency towards improving its performance. However, as many ML algorithms exist, the selection of the right one is important for a successful assessment. Unfortunately, many of the existing works in this regard have simply adopted an ML algorithm without a justified rationale which may result in poor selection of the good performing ML algorithm. Therefore, in this study, a premise to compare the performance of ML algorithms for the assessment of energy efficiency of buildings was proposed. First, consolidated energy efficiency ratings of buildings from different data sources are used to develop predictive models using several ML algorithms. Thereafter, identification of best performing model was done by comparing evaluation metrics like RMSE, R-Squared, and Adjusted R-Squared. From the comparison, Extra Trees predictive model came top with RMSE, R-Squared, and Adjusted R-Squared of 2.79, 93%, and 93% respectively. This approach helps in the initial selection of suitable and better-performing ML algorithms.

Keywords: Buildings · Energy efficiency · Machine learning

1 Introduction

More than 40% of carbon emissions are attributed to the consumption of energy in buildings [1]. According to Penistone [2], this high energy demand is due to the increasing number of building dwellers with corresponding population growth and growing appetite for energy-consuming appliances. Unfortunately, energy-related carbon emissions give rise to indoor and outdoor air pollution with corresponding negative impacts

© Springer Nature Switzerland AG 2021
M. Kamp et al. (Eds.): ECML PKDD 2021 Workshops, CCIS 1525, pp. 546–566, 2021.
https://doi.org/10.1007/978-3-030-93733-1_41

on human health. For example, Rural Affairs Committee [3] reports that in the UK, a considerable number of deaths are caused by poor air quality from carbon emissions. As such, in recent times several collaborations, policies, and strategies have been introduced by many developed countries to meet this goal. Among these policies are the EU's nearly-zero energy building proposal, requiring buildings from 2021 to have high energy performance. Another is the introduction of the issuance of energy certificates to promote energy efficiency awareness [4].

One strategy of enhancing the energy performance of buildings is improving their energy efficiency. Oliver and Peters [5] state that energy efficiency strategies alone have the potential to save 23.6 metric tons of carbon dioxide per year by 2030. However, despite the interventions by the government and other bodies at improving energy performance, many reports [6–10] indicate insufficient progress. As such, there is an urgent need to introduce new strategies or complement existing ones if building energy performance goals are to be met timely. A crucial step in improving energy efficiency is its assessment. In the light of this, a contemporary trend in research has emerged in which data-driven predictive analytics approaches are used to assess the energy efficiency of buildings towards making better decisions and choices in improving energy performance [11]. The predictive analysis utilizes Artificial Intelligence (AI)/Machine Learning (ML) which has been widely adopted across other industries with records of tremendous successes [12, 13]. For example, it has been successfully employed in the healthcare industry for precise diagnosis and to make the best choice of treatment course from several alternatives. Likewise, in the transportation sector, it seats at the center of decisions for autonomous driving.

AI is a collection of state-of-the-art technologies that permit machines or any computer programme to sense, comprehend, act, and learn [14]. ML on the other hand is a branch of AI that allows computers to learn by a direct route from examples, data and experience. ML approaches to replace the traditional methods of programming that relied on hardcoded step by step rules [15]. This is done by giving the system a huge amount of data to learn from as a task, leaving it to decide how best to achieve the task in form of the desired output. Several ML algorithms such as Genetic Algorithm (GA), Artificial Neural Networks (ANN), Linear Regression (LR), Logistic Regression, Nearest-Neighbour Mapping, Decision Trees (DT), K-Means Clustering, Random Forests, Support Vector Machines, Principal Component Analysis, Singular Value Decomposition, among many others exist for implementation. Many research like [11, 16, 17] have already attempted the use of ML algorithms for predicting the energy efficiency of buildings.

The choice of which ML algorithm to use depends on several factors like ease of use, accuracy, the structure of the dataset, training time, among others. Likewise, outcomes and performances of different ML algorithms vary even when used against the same dataset due to several factors. The main influencing factors being the nature of the underlying ML algorithm, characteristics of the dataset regarding its size, resolution and data type, and the number of selected features. For example, Sha [18] comparative study of the performance of several ML algorithms in predicting cooling and consumption in buildings observed significant performance degradation from changing dataset resolution of training data from one (1) hour to six (6) minutes. In general, the LR algorithm which inherently only supports linear model is likely to perform better than DT when the feature set is many on a small dataset. Similarly, DT which employs non-parametric methods is likely to outperform ANN when the large training dataset is made up of categorical values data type. Therefore, considering the dilemma vis-a-vis the performance of ML algorithms, choosing a suitable ML algorithm is a tough and crucial decision towards its successful.

Unfortunately, many of the existing studies [11, 16, 17] have arbitrarily utilized or simply adopted various ML algorithms from previous research without rationale, resulting in poor performance, bad selection of good performing models or unenhanced generalizability of models developed from these ML algorithms across other regions. As a result, these studies have produced a knowledge vacuum that must be filled. Hence the need for a comparative study that will consolidate and evaluate the application of several ML algorithms in developing predictive models for assessing the energy efficiency of buildings. Thus, this study, therefore, aims to compare and evaluate the application of commonly employed ML algorithms used to develop models for assessing the energy efficiency of buildings. The following objectives will be:

1. Consolidate energy efficiency ratings of domestic and non-domestic buildings from different data sources into one database to establish the most applicable factors affecting the energy efficiency of buildings.
2. Utilize established factors in objective 1 as independent variables for all ML algorithms to develop predictive models.
3. Compare the performance of all ML algorithms against their respective predictive models.

The contribution of this study is therefore to fill the gap in the lack of a rationale in the selection of suitable ML algorithms for assessing the energy efficiency of buildings. For this work, due to availability and ease of access, energy data from the UK is utilized. Consequently, this is novel because the thorough review of the existing body of knowledge indicated that this is the first-time robust ML methods are employed to predict the energy efficiency of buildings in the UK. The same approach can be utilized for energy data from other countries. The outcome of our study will help in the initial choice of suitable ML for further predictive analysis. Furthermore, it will help to guide the decision of building construction managers, building dwellers, government bodies, and other concerned stakeholders in implementing strategies and employing measures for buildings energy performance improvement towards reduced carbon emissions and improved air quality.

2   Related Work

This section examines the aim, methodology, result, and analysis of the most recent related vast body of literature by numerous authors from across the world in the subject of energy consumption and optimization in buildings, as indicated in Table 1, using various or combined individual ML Algorithms.

Table 1. Survey of related literature

Author	ML model	Methodology	Result
Mazzeo [19]	Artificial Neural Network (ANN) with Gargon Algorithm	ANN for flexible power system design to forecast energy performance of an energy community. In the approach, ANN is applied to large data set with dimensionless input variables to estimate energy performance indicators and grid indicator factors for the energy community	The optimized ANN with 20 neurons produced the highest prediction accuracy with a global R of 0.9958 and P of 0.0004 in comparison with lower neurons
Abediniangerabi, Makhmalbaf and Shahandashti [20]	Deep Learning Models, Gradient Boosting Machine, Random Forest, Generalized Linear Regression	ML models for the prediction of the energy performance of building façade system. The façade system considered are fiber reinforced concrete and conventional panels for making decisions to support energy efficient building vis-a-vis energy savings during early design stages. The accuracy of the result obtained was compared with other common prediction models	The Deep Learning models in comparison to others had the best accuracy with MAE of 1.59 and RMSE of 3.48

(*continued*)

Table 1. (*continued*)

Author	ML model	Methodology	Result
Maltais and Gosselin [21]	Artificial Neural Networks (ANN) with optimized parameters	ANN for the prediction of domestic hot water usage. The approach attempts to improve the accuracy of prediction of load demands from domestic water heating systems for the purpose of improving energy efficiency	The ANN models which were tested with data from a 40-unit residential condominium of varying family sizes yielded good results with R2 of 0.88 but produced uncertainties for families with smaller water heating systems
Alishahi, Nik-Bakht and Ouf [22]	Poisson Regression	Poisson Regression to study occupancy behavior in building using WIFI count data. The method attempts to provide an alternative approach as opposed to using sensor information from devices (like heat and ventilation systems) to obtain and integrate occupancy information to adapt to building operation for the purpose of increasing energy savings	The system was validated using data obtained from an academic building in Canada. It produced a good prediction pattern with R2 of 0.98 during the week and 0.81 during weekends

(*continued*)

Table 1. (*continued*)

Author	ML model	Methodology	Result
Sha, Moujahed and Qi [18]	Gradient Tree Boosting (GTB), Linear Regression, Rid Regression, Elastic Net (ELN), Multilayer Perceptron MLP), Recurrent Neural Network (RNN), Long Short-Term Memory (LSTM), Convolutional Neural Network (CNN)	ML for predicting cooling loads and energy consumption in buildings. The work aimed at developing an approach for controlling and evaluating the performance of mechanical ventilators for reducing building cooling loads	Data obtained from Building Automation System (BAS) from a high-rise building in Canada was applied to the ML models developed of which GTB produced the best accuracy with RMSE of 12.3%, 12.4% and 12.7% in 1 h, 30 min and 6 min, respectively
Mulero-Palencia, Álvarez-Díaz and Andrés-Chicote [23]	Decision Tree	Developed a tool for prototype diagnosis during design stage of building renovation. The system which is aimed at reducing emissions during building renovation helps to make critical decision and select better renovation alternatives	The tool developed was tested using renovation buildings for different countries. The result obtained varied from country to country as the building state and government regulations were different from country to country

(*continued*)

Table 1. (*continued*)

Author	ML model	Methodology	Result
Yigit [24]	Evolutionary Algorithm (EA), Gradient Boosting Machine (GBM)	ML to develop an energy simulation tool for optimized thermal design in residential buildings. The tool attempts to shorten the time required in optimization simulation so that simulation for larger buildings can be done faster. GBM was used as a surrogate model and DEAP, an evolutionary algorithm was used for optimization	The surrogate model on test yielded R2 of 0.992 on cross-validation and 0.991 on testing. The result helps to make decision in selecting an alternative optimal energy design approach
Alduailij [25]	Linear Regression, Dynamic Regression, ARIMA Time Series, Exponential Smoothing Time Series, Artificial Neural Network, Deep Neural Network	ML is used to detect consumption peaks in buildings. The system uses historic load demand curves to provides potential insights for making decisions towards energy saving, efficient use of appliances, and identification of demand response possibilities	Data energy and weather data obtained from five (5) government buildings collected over 1 week uninterrupted were applied to the ML models. ARIMA yielded the highest accuracy of 98.91%

(*continued*)

Table 1. (*continued*)

Author	ML model	Methodology	Result
Szul, Tabor and Pancerz [26]	BORUTA on Rough Set Theory (RST)	ML for features selection to forecast the heating energy demand rate of a building. The works aim to emphasize the need for care in the selection of model features. It also aims at providing insight for developing diverse approaches to improving energy efficiency in buildings	The model which was tested using data from 109 multi-family buildings produced a satisfactory result with R2 between 0.81 and 0.85. 14 features were selected by the BORUTA algorithm and a further decrease in the number of features selected yielded no significant difference, hence confirming the feature selection
Amasyali and El-Gohary [27]	Classification and Regression trees (CART), Ensemble Bagging trees (EBT), Artificial Neural Networks (ANN), and Deep Neural Networks (DNN)	ML for predicting energy consumption patterns in buildings while including occupancy behavior. The approach takes into consideration occupancy patterns to attain better accuracy in predicting energy consumption for the purpose of identifying potentials for energy savings	A simulation of the model on EnergyPlus using 3 months of energy, building, weather, occupancy data with reliable performance and high accuracy emphasized the importance of the occupancy variable in the prediction algorithm

(*continued*)

Table 1. (*continued*)

Author	ML model	Methodology	Result
Seyrfar [28]	Back-Propagation Neural Network (BPNN), Extreme Gradient Boosting (XGBoost), Random Forest (RF)	Combines energy, demographic, and socio-economic data to predict energy consumption in buildings. The approach aims at attaining higher accuracy and identify consumption patterns toward implementing energy efficiency measures and reducing carbon emission	The ML models were simulated using data obtained from the United States (US) Consensus Bureau of which XGBoost had better performance with 68% accuracy

3   Research Methodology

To consolidate energy efficiency ratings of domestic and non-domestic buildings as an approach to data collection, this study uses open data from the department of the energy performance of buildings data: England and Wales. Energy Performance Certificates (EPCs) for domestic and non-domestic buildings built, sold, or rented since 2008 were used. These data contain information on the energy efficiency ratings of domestic and non-domestic buildings during the energy assessment process. More precisely, this study uses all datasets from every constituency under the city of London local authority, consisting of property types: flat, bungalow, maisonette, house, and park-home; property total floor area ranging from one meter squared and hundred and ten meters squared; and finally with current EPC rating from A to G, (where A is very efficient, and G is the least efficient) lodged between April 2018 and April 2021. Table 2 describes the major features of this dataset used in this study.

The raw dataset was extracted and downloaded as a comma-separated values file. To achieve the second objective of this study, this raw dataset was pre-processed into a clean dataset and analyzed by carrying out data imputation and outlier detection. Scaling and encoding feature engineering techniques were implemented to enable the selection of features or independent variables (see Table 2) to increase the predictive power (hyperparameter optimization) of the ML algorithms. The resulting clean and pre-processed dataset was split randomly into two in a ratio of 60% to 40% of the training dataset and testing dataset, respectively. Several ML algorithms were imported into a running instance of Jupiter Notebook using Scikit-learn - an integral Python programming language module with a broad spectrum of state-of-the-art algorithms for supervised and unsupervised medium-scale problems [29].

Since these ML algorithms fit independent variables (features) to a known dependent variable (target), supervised modeling taxonomy was undoubtedly chosen in this study.

Table 2. Dataset description

Feature ID	Features	Feature type
F1	Energy consumption	Independent variable
F2	CO2 Emissions	Independent variable
F3	Lightning cost	Independent variable
F4	Heating cost	Independent variable
F5	Hot water cost	Independent variable
F6	Total floor area	Independent variable
F7	Floor level	Independent variable
F8	CO2 emissions per floor area	Independent variable
F9	Number of habitable rooms	Independent variable
F10	Number of heated rooms	Independent variable
F11	Hot water energy efficiency	Independent variable
F12	Hot water environmental efficiency	Independent variable
F13	Windows energy efficiency	Independent variable
F14	Windows environmental efficiency	Independent variable
F15	Walls energy efficiency	Independent variable
F16	Walls environmental efficiency	Independent variable
F17	Main heat energy efficiency	Independent variable
F18	Main heat environmental efficiency	Independent variable
F19	Lighting energy efficiency	Independent variable
F20	Lighting environmental efficiency	Independent variable
F21	**Energy efficiency of buildings**	**Dependent variable**

Additionally, because the target contains numerical data, regression analysis was used. Regression analysis is a type of predictive modeling approach that examines the connection between a target and feature(s) [30]. This is especially useful as it can express the degree to which one or more features have an influence on a target during ML predictions. There are a variety of regression algorithms that can be used to develop predictive models when experimenting with regression analysis. Which one to employ primarily depends on three factors – number of features, type of target, and shape of the regression line. Therefore, to mitigate any form of bias, we rather employed all regression algorithms that are available in scikit-learn version 0.23.1 at the time of this study for experimentations without any constraints on the previously mentioned factors. In concrete, a total of 42 regression algorithms available in this version was employed to develop the individual models using the training dataset (60% of the total dataset). This resulted in 42 developed regression models. Afterward, the unseen test dataset (40% of the total dataset) was used to evaluate the performance of these models that were developed. As the 42 models are all regressors, stratified k-fold, a variant of k-fold that returns stratified folds containing about the same proportion of target class as the initial dataset was used for cross-validation, where k = 10, in order to avoid individual model overfitting on the dataset. Finally, Root Mean Square Error (RMSE), Coefficient of Determination (R-Squared) Adjusted Coefficient of Determination (Adjusted R-Squared) modeling evaluation metrics were employed to measure the several model performances on the testing dataset as shown in Fig. 1.

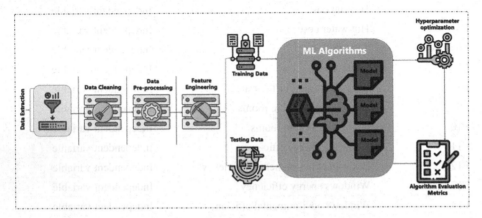

Fig. 1. ML prediction architecture

4   Analysis and Results

An initial investigation on the data through Exploratory Data Analysis (EDA) showed that the data is a two - dimensional array with 826 rows and 21 columns where the 1st to the 20th columns (F1–F20 factor IDs) represent the features/independent variables and the 21st column (F21) represent the target/dependent variable. Outliers and missing values were detected and dropped thus resulting in a final 772 rows and 21 columns. Category columns F11–F20 (see Table 2) were encoded into 1 (Very Poor), 2 (Poor), 3 (Average), 4 (Good), and 5 (Very Good). Furthermore, as a final transformation on the dataset, One-hot encoding (k-1 variant) a categorical encoding technique was used to transform all categorical datasets into a set of binary results (0 or 1). As most ML algorithms assume that any given dataset is normally distributed, with zero mean and unit variance, this study used the standardization feature scaling method to meet this requirement [29, 31]. This method involves subtracting the mean from each feature observation and dividing by the standard deviation as shown in the equation below:

$$X' = \frac{X - \bar{x}}{\sigma} \tag{1}$$

Where X' represents the standardized value; X a given feature observation; $\bar{x}$ the mean and σ the standard deviation. Hence our resulting feature scaled dataset has its variance at 1, centered its mean at 0, and with a varying min-max value. Ultimately, a multivariate filter-based feature selection method called Spearman's rank correlation coefficient was implemented to evaluate the entire feature space, and eliminate obsolete, redundant, and noisy features, boost model accuracy, improve model interpretability, lower computational complexity and enhance generalizability. This Spearman's correlation coefficient is a non-parametric test used to determine the degree of connection between two or more features with a monotonic function, indicating a growing or decreasing relationship. The calculated strength between the features using Spearman's correlation coefficient fluctuates between +1 and 1, which happens when one feature is a perfect monotone function of the other. Thereafter, the dataset was split using the "train_test_split" function of Scikit-learn at a ratio of 60:40 for training and testing, respectively.

Consequently, after the described pre-processing, encoding, and standardization steps were implemented, the resulting training dataset (60% of the entire dataset) was utilized to train individual models in this study by fitting 42 ML algorithms (all regression algorithms available in scikit-learn version 0.23.1) to their respective models using their respective Scikit-learn libraries (see Table 3). This resulted in 42 developed models. Afterward, we used the test dataset (40% of the entire dataset) to evaluate the performance of these models that were developed. To mitigate the potential of these models' overfitting on the test dataset, a stratified 10-fold cross-validation resampling technique was used to evaluate the performance of all the ML models developed using the 42 ML algorithms employed. The main parameters for each model used for hyperparameter optimization are alpha and lambda of values 100 and 10 respectively. These parameters were chosen to control the learning process as a way to apply regularization on each model for the bias-variance trade-off (low bias and low variance). The outcome of these assessments implemented on the test dataset is given as performance evaluation metrics for all models developed in this study (see Table 3). More precisely, it reveals the RMSE, R-Squared, and Adjusted R-Squared computed using the stratified 10-fold cross-validation for the ML algorithms.

RMSE (see Eq. 2) represents the standard deviation of the differences between the model predictions and the true values (training data). The closer the RSME value is to 0 the better the model.

$$RMSE = \sqrt{\frac{1}{n}\sum_{i=1}^{n}(y_i - \hat{y}_i)} \tag{2}$$

R-Squared (see Eq. 3) on the other hand represents the proportion of variance of target (dependent variable) that has been explained by the independent variables in the model. Its values range between 0 and 1 where 1 represent a perfect model and 0 a poor model.

$$R\text{-}Squared = 1 - \frac{\sum_{i=1}^{n}(y_i - \hat{y}_i)^2}{\sum_{i=1}^{n}(y_i - \bar{y})^2} \tag{3}$$

Adjusted R-Squared (see Eq. 4) is a modified and better version of R-Squared that considers the number of predictors (independent variables) in a given model.

$$R\text{-}Squared_{adjusted} = 1 - \left[\frac{(1 - R^2)(n - 1)}{n - k - 1}\right] \tag{4}$$

Table 3. Algorithms, models and their respective performance evaluation metrics implemented on the test dataset.

S/N	Algorithms	Model	Performance evaluation metrics		
			Adjusted R-Squared	R-Squared	RMSE
1	Extra-trees	ExtraTreesRegressor	0.93	0.93	2.79
2	Gradient boosting	GradientBoostingRegressor	0.91	0.92	3.05
3	Extreme gradient boosting	XGBRegressor	0.91	0.92	3.07
4	Histogram-based gradient boosting	HistGradientBoostingRegressor	0.91	0.91	3.15
5	Transformed target	TransformedTargetRegressor	0.90	0.91	3.16
6	Ordinary least square linear regression	LinearRegression	0.90	0.91	3.16
7	Linear least squares (with l2 regularization)	Ridge	0.90	0.91	3.18
8	Lasso linear model (with iterative fitting along a regularization path)	LassoCV	0.90	0.91	3.19
9	Bayesian ridge regression	BayesianRidge	0.90	0.91	3.19
10	Light gradient boosted machine	LGBMRegressor	0.90	0.91	3.19

(continued)

Table 3. (*continued*)

S/N	Algorithms	Model	Performance evaluation metrics		
			Adjusted R-Squared	R-Squared	RMSE
11	Elastic Net model (with iterative fitting along a regularization path)	ElasticNetCV	0.90	0.91	3.22
12	Generalized linear model (with a Poisson distribution)	PoissonRegressor	0.90	0.91	3.26
13	Ridge regression (with built-in cross-validation)	RidgeCV	0.90	0.90	3.27
14	Stochastic gradient descent	SGDRegressor	0.90	0.90	3.28
15	Random forest	RandomForestRegressor	0.88	0.89	3.49
16	Huber linear regression model	HuberRegressor	0.88	0.89	3.59
17	Lasso lars information criterion	LassoLarsIC	0.87	0.88	3.65
18	Least angle regression model (cross-validated (CV))	LarsCV	0.87	0.88	3.72
19	Orthogonal matching pursuit model (OMP-CV)	OrthogonalMatchingPursuitCV	0.86	0.87	3.83
20	Linear support vector regression	LinearSVR	0.86	0.87	3.87
21	Lasso lars (CV)	LassoLarsCV	0.85	0.86	3.97
22	AdaBoost	AdaBoostRegressor	0.85	0.86	4.02
23	Bagging	BaggingRegressor	0.84	0.85	4.07

(*continued*)

Table 3. (*continued*)

S/N	Algorithms	Model	Performance evaluation metrics		
			Adjusted R-Squared	R-Squared	RMSE
24	RANdom SAmple consensus	RANSACRegressor	0.84	0.85	4.12
25	Lasso linear model	Lasso	0.81	0.82	4.47
26	Decision tree	DecisionTreeRegressor	0.79	0.80	4.70
27	Linear regression (with combined L1 and L2 priors as regularizer)	ElasticNet	0.79	0.80	4.74
28	K-nearest neighbors	KNeighborsRegressor	0.78	0.80	4.76
29	Generalized linear model (with a Gamma distribution)	GammaRegressor	0.78	0.79	4.81
30	Generalized linear model	GeneralizedLinearRegressor	0.77	0.78	4.94
31	Generalized linear model (with a Tweedie distribution)	TweedieRegressor	0.77	0.78	4.94
32	Least angle regression model	Lars	0.73	0.75	5.29
33	Passive aggressive machine	PassiveAggressiveRegressor	0.71	0.73	5.53
34	Extremely randomized tree	ExtraTreeRegressor	0.71	0.73	5.53
35	Epsilon-support vector machine	SVR	0.70	0.72	5.59

(*continued*)

Table 3. (*continued*)

S/N	Algorithms	Model	Performance evaluation metrics		
			Adjusted R-Squared	R-Squared	RMSE
36	Orthogonal matching pursuit model (OMP)	OrthogonalMatchingPursuit	0.67	0.70	5.84
37	Nu support vector machine	NuSVR	0.67	0.69	5.86
38	Dummy estimator	DummyRegressor	−0.07	−0.00	10.59
39	Lasso lars	LassoLars	−0.07	−0.00	10.59
40	Multi-layer perceptron	MLPRegressor	−0.89	−0.77	14.08
41	Gaussian process	GaussianProcessRegressor	−12.3	−11.43	37.33
42	Kernel ridge regression	KernelRidge	−44.25	−41.31	68.86

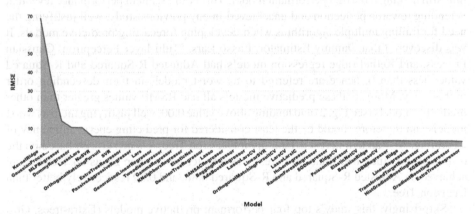

Fig. 2. Predictive models by RSME

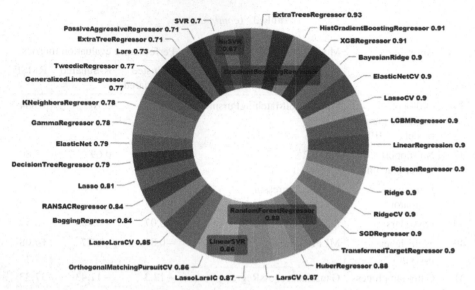

Fig. 3. Predictive models by adjusted R-squared

5   Discussion of Results

Comparatively, looking through Table 3 and Fig. 3, Extra-trees predictive model came out as the top performant model having achieved an Adjusted R-Squared and R-Squared 0.93, and 0.93 respectively higher than the rest of the models. This implies a high correlation between the independent variable (F1 to F20) and the dependent variable F21. Also, Extra-trees's RSME value of 2.79 is the closest value to 0.00 (see Fig. 2), thus still making it the best performant model. This is an excellent performance level that is tending towards perfection and unachieved in any previous study, well justifying the need for trailing multiple algorithms when developing forecasting/predictive models. It was discovered that Dummy Estimator, Lasso Lars, Multi-layer Perceptron, Gaussian Process, and Kernel ridge regression models had Adjusted R-Squared and R-Squared values less than 0, hence are referred to as worst models in their descending order in this study. More so, these predictive models all had RSME values greater than other predictive models (see Fig. 2) and tending above value 0.00, well justifying them as worst models and therefore should be the least considered for predicting energy efficiency of a building. As Random Forest is built upon Decision Tree, it is no surprise based on the results of this study that Random Forest was a better model than Decision Tree having achieved an Adjusted R-Squared and R-Squared 0.88, and 0.89 respectively better than Decision Tree.

Surprisingly, this study's top four performant predictive models (Extra-trees, Gradient boosting, Extreme gradient boosting, and Histogram-based gradient boosting) are all ensemble methods, which are machine learning methods that involve the use of multiple algorithms where the cumulative outcome from them is almost always greater in terms of predictive accuracy relative to the use of a single algorithm as they integrate decisions from different algorithms to maximize their overall performances [32]. Extra-trees belongs to the family of bagging ensemble method where multiple models of the same algorithm are used, however with different subsets of data selected randomly [33]. Gradient boosting, Extreme gradient boosting, and Histogram-based gradient boosting, on the other hand, belongs to the family of boosting ensemble method which is known as a repetitive technique that adapts the weight of the observation to the last grading. If an observation has been falsely categorized, the weight of this observation would be raised and conversely [34]. Thus, this study also proved these assertions. Also, interestingly, Multi-layer Perceptron, a class of feedforward artificial neural network (ANN) and one of the well-known and widely used algorithms by researchers were found among the four non-performing algorithms assessed in this study as the least models to consider for fore-casting building energy efficiency. This is arguably due to the fact that although neural networks have been shown to approximate every continuously differentiable function, there is no assurance that a given network would ever learn this approximation given a specific weights initialization since, for example, the independent variables and the dependent variable used in this study are mostly continuous variables (see Sect. 4). Thus, making their weight matrices susceptible to initial randomization.

Furthermore, in this study, only 20 features from a list of non-exhaustive features were used in the assessment of the energy efficiency of buildings. There are other existing works considering lesser or more features and even other sets of features. For example, Abediniangerabi, Makhmalbaf and Shahandashti [20] considered only six (6) feature classes which included weather and occupancy data asides from heating and cooling data. Feature selection and data representation play a key role in enhancing the performance of ML algorithms and it is being widely explored in representation learning. Similarly, in many cases, the choice of features is dependent on the available dataset obtained directly or computed from sensor data installed in buildings. However, since sensor installation and integration come with a cost, there is usually a trade-off between the number of sensors installed in buildings and the number of classes of data to be obtained. It will be of interest to have additional features like the comfort level indicator of building dwellers since building energy efficiency can only be sustained in a long term within the limits of these comfort levels. Unfortunately, in many buildings, this kind of data is difficult to obtain directly and accurately from sensors because of the ever-dynamic behavior of building occupants. There are several literatures exploring the use of long-term data from building appliances to obtain accurate results in this regard. However, in this study, it can be argued that this data (comfort level indicator) is indirectly encoded in some of the already selected 20-features. Give for instance, a building dweller will adjust operations of heating and cooling appliances to meet needs until at least comfort levels are met. While this argument may seem rational, it will still be important to carry-out comparative studies to evaluate how this feature or other features not included in this study impacts the performance of ML algorithms.

6   Conclusion and Recommendations

The rise in carbon emissions from the caused increase in energy demand from buildings is a major concern as it has continued to cause poor air quality with a consequent negative impact on human health across the globe. More so, efforts at curbing this trend have yielded insufficient results hence necessitating the need for more effective strategies. One of such contemporary strategies employs data-driven predictive analytics techniques to assess building energy efficiency to better explain contributing factors influencing its performance. In this approach that employs ML, the choice of ML algorithm is crucial to obtaining a good result. However, many existing research randomly selects a ML algorithm without justification.

In this study, therefore, a premise to compare the performance of machine learning algorithms for assessing the energy efficiency of buildings was proposed. To begin, this study consolidates energy efficiency ratings of domestic and non-domestic buildings from different data sources into one database as an approach to its quantitative data. The dataset in turn was used to train several ML (43 in number) algorithms to develop predictive models and evaluation metrics were computed. From the comparison of metrics for the different ML algorithms, the Extra Trees predictive model came out top having achieved an RMSE, R-Squared, and Adjusted R-Squared of 2.79, 93%, and 93% respectively.

Thus, this study highly recommends the need for initial predictive analysis for the selection of good performing model and better still the use of ensemble methods in predicting the energy efficiency of buildings. For example, from the result obtained, a choice of Extra Trees predictive model is justified being the best performing algorithm amongst others considered and as such may be further explored for even better result and implementation. Overall, the result from a study of this kind helps to build construction managers, building dwellers, government bodies, and other stakeholders to make better decisions towards improving the energy performance of buildings. However, while the proposed contemporary method of analysis is assumed to be applicable in assessing energy efficiency of buildings within the sector, the unique data transformation employed in this study may not, as typical of any data driven model, be transferable to the data from other regions. Furthermore, to obtain improved outcomes, asides including more features in the selection, representation learning can be employed for features extraction. Similarly, future studies should be targeted at extending the algorithms or optimizing already considered one.

References

1. IEA and UNEP. Global Status Report for Buildings and Construction (2019)
2. Penistone, A.: UK greenhouse gas emissions, provisional figures. In: National Statistic, March 2019, p. 46 (2019). https://assets.publishing.service.gov.uk/government/uploads/system/uploads/attachment_data/file/790626/2018-provisional-emissions-statistics-report.pdf. Accessed 29 Jun 2021
3. R. Affairs Committee. Air Quality and Coronavirus: A Glimpse of a Different Future or Business as Usual Fifth Report of Session 2019–2021 Report, Together with Formal Minutes Relating to the Report (2021). www.parliament.uk. Accessed 29 Jun 2021
4. Ekins, P., Lees, E.: The impact of EU policies on energy use in and the evolution of the UK built environment. Energy Policy 36(12), 4580–4583 (2008). https://doi.org/10.1016/j.enpol.2008.09.006

5. Olivier, J.G.J., Peters, J.A.H.W.: Trends in Global Co 2 and Total Greenhouse Gas Emissions 2019 Report (2020). https://www.pbl.nl/sites/default/files/downloads/pbl-2020-trends-in-global-. Accessed 30 Jun 2021
6. Malinauskaite, J., Jouhara, H., Ahmad, L., Milani, M., Montorsi, L., Venturelli, M.: Energy efficiency in industry: EU and national policies in Italy and the UK. Energy **172**, 255–269 (2019). https://doi.org/10.1016/j.energy.2019.01.130
7. Brooks, E., Law, A., Huang, L.: A comparative analysis of retrofitting historic buildings for energy efficiency in the UK and China. DISP **50**(3), 66–75 (2014). https://doi.org/10.1080/02513625.2014.979044
8. Marshall, E., Steinberger, J.K., Dupont, V., Foxon, T.J.: Combining energy efficiency measure approaches and occupancy patterns in building modelling in the UK residential context. Energy Build. **111**, 98–108 (2016). https://doi.org/10.1016/j.enbuild.2015.11.039
9. Rosenow, J., Guertler, P., Sorrell, S., Eyre, N.: The remaining potential for energy savings in UK households. Energy Policy **121**, 542–552 (2018). https://doi.org/10.1016/j.enpol.2018.06.033
10. Broad, O., Hawker, G., Dodds, P.E.: Decarbonising the UK residential sector: the dependence of national abatement on flexible and local views of the future. Energy Policy **140**, 111321 (2020). https://doi.org/10.1016/j.enpol.2020.111321
11. Benavente-Peces, C., Ibadah, N.: Buildings energy efficiency analysis and classification using various machine learning technique classifiers. Energies **13**(13), 1–24 (2020). https://doi.org/10.3390/en13133497
12. Blanco, J.L., Fuchs, S., Parsons, M., Ribeirinho, M.J.: Artificial intelligence: construction technology's next frontier. In: Mckinsey Co, April 2018, pp. 1–8 (2018). https://www.mckinsey.com/industries/capital-projects-and-infrastructure/our-insights/artificial-intelligence-construction-technologys-next-frontier
13. Marks, M.: Construction: The Next Great Tech Transformation Voices Michael Marks (2017)
14. Goyal, M.: Artificial intelligence: a tool for hyper personalization. Int. J. Manag. Rev. **07**, 2320–7132 (2019)
15. T. Royal Society. Machine Learning: The Power and Promise of Computers that Learn by Example (2017)
16. Bilous, I., Deshko, V., Sukhodub, I.: Parametric analysis of external and internal factors influence on building energy performance using non-linear multivariate regression models. J. Build. Eng. **20**, 327–336 (2018). https://doi.org/10.1016/j.jobe.2018.07.021
17. Goyal, M., Pandey, M., Thakur, R.: Exploratory analysis of machine learning techniques to predict energy efficiency in buildings. In: IEEE 8th International Conference on Reliability, Infocom Technologies and Optimization (Trends and Future Directions), ICRITO 2020, pp. 1033–1037 (2020). https://doi.org/10.1109/ICRITO48877.2020.9197976
18. Sha, H., Moujahed, M., Qi, D.: Machine learning-based cooling load prediction and optimal control for mechanical ventilative cooling in high-rise buildings. Energy Build. **242**, 110980 (2021). https://doi.org/10.1016/j.enbuild.2021.110980
19. Mazzeo, D., et al.: Artificial intelligence application for the performance prediction of a clean energy community. Energy **232**, 120999 (2021). https://doi.org/10.1016/j.energy.2021.120999
20. Abediniangerabi, B., Makhmalbaf, A., Shahandashti, M.: Deep learning for estimating energy savings of early-stage facade design decisions. Energy AI **5**, 100077 (2021). https://doi.org/10.1016/j.egyai.2021.100077
21. Maltais, L.G., Gosselin, L.: Predictability analysis of domestic hot water consumption with neural networks: from single units to large residential buildings. Energy **229**, 120658 (2021). https://doi.org/10.1016/j.energy.2021.120658

22. Alishahi, N., Nik-Bakht, M., Ouf, M.M.: A framework to identify key occupancy indicators for optimizing building operation using WiFi connection count data. Build. Environ. **200**, 107936 (2021). https://doi.org/10.1016/j.buildenv.2021.107936

23. Mulero-Palencia, S., Álvarez-Díaz, S., Andrés-Chicote, M.: Machine learning for the improvement of deep renovation building projects using as-built BIM models. Sustainability **13**(12), 6576 (2021). https://doi.org/10.3390/su13126576

24. Yigit, S.: A machine-learning-based method for thermal design optimization of residential buildings in highly urbanized areas of Turkey. J. Build. Eng. **38**, 102225 (2021). https://doi.org/10.1016/j.jobe.2021.102225

25. Alduailij, M.A., Petri, I., Rana, O., Alduailij, M.A., Aldawood, A.S.: Forecasting peak energy demand for smart buildings. J. Supercomput. **77**(6), 6356–6380 (2020). https://doi.org/10.1007/s11227-020-03540-3

26. Szul, T., Tabor, S., Pancerz, K.: Application of the BORUTA algorithm to input data selection for a model based on rough set theory (RST) to prediction energy consumption for building heating. Energies **14**(10), 2779 (2021). https://doi.org/10.3390/en14102779

27. Amasyali, K., El-Gohary, N.: Machine learning for occupant-behavior-sensitive cooling energy consumption prediction in office buildings. Renew. Sustain. Energy Rev. **142**, 110714 (2021). https://doi.org/10.1016/j.rser.2021.110714

28. Seyrfar, A., Ataei, H., Movahedi, A., Derrible, S.: Data-driven approach for evaluating the energy efficiency in multifamily residential buildings. Pract. Period. Struct. Des. Constr. **26**(2), 04020074 (2021). https://doi.org/10.1061/(asce)sc.1943-5576.0000555

29. Pedregosa, F., et al.: Scikit-learn: machine learning in python. J. Mach. Learn. Res. **12**(85), 2825–2830 (2011). http://scikit-learn.sourceforge.net. Accessed 07 Jan 2021

30. Kuhn, M., Johnson, K.: Applied Predictive Modeling. Springer, New York (2013). https://doi.org/10.1007/978-1-4614-6849-3

31. Alaka, H.A., et al.: Systematic review of bankruptcy prediction models: towards a framework for tool selection. Exp. Syst. Appl. **94**, 164–184 (2018). https://doi.org/10.1016/j.eswa.2017.10.040

32. Badawi, H., Azais, F., Bernard, S., Comte, M., Kerzerho, V., Lefevre, F.: Use of ensemble methods for indirect test of RF circuits: Can it bring benefits? In: 20th IEEE Latin-American Test Symposium – LATS 2019, no. 1 (2019). https://doi.org/10.1109/LATW.2019.8704641

33. Opitz, D., Maclin, R.: Popular ensemble methods: an empirical study. J. Artif. Intell. Res. **11**, 169–198 (1999). https://doi.org/10.1613/jair.614

34. Dietterich, T.G.: Ensemble methods in machine learning. In: Kittler, J., Roli, F. (eds.) MCS 2000. LNCS, vol. 1857, pp. 1–15. Springer, Heidelberg (2000). https://doi.org/10.1007/3-540-45014-9_1

Buildings Occupancy Estimation: Preliminary Results Using Bluetooth Signals and Artificial Neural Networks

Frederico Apolónia[✉], Pedro M. Ferreira, and José Cecílio

LASIGE, Faculdade de Ciências da Universidade de Lisboa, Lisbon, Portugal
fapolonia@lasige.di.fc.ul.pt, {pmf,jmcecilio}@ciencias.ulisboa.pt

Abstract. The energy consumption in the European Union continues to grow above the expected values, and buildings are one of the largest consumers in front of industry and transportation sectors. As buildings have different roles with different requirements and characteristics, new approaches are required to increase the efficiency of new and old buildings to reduce consumption. Locating people inside buildings can be done using cameras, sensors, or radio signal strengths, where their intrusion may vary. In this paper, we present our approach to locating building occupants using Bluetooth Low Energy (BLE) Scanners without previously requiring the fingerprint of the area where the system is deployed. To do it, we created a Machine Learning pipeline to locate the devices. Using our approach, we obtained an average error of 5.68 m. We also demonstrate that rotating the positions of the Scanners while maintaining their distances does not have an impact on the location accuracy.

Keywords: Indoor location · BLE · Energy efficiency · Non-intrusive monitoring

1 Introduction

Building energy consumption in 2004, in the European Union, corresponding to around 37% of all energy consumed, in front of the industry sector (28%) and the transportation sector (32%) [9]. The European Union also states that buildings have a core role in aiding on the path of reducing energy consumption and reducing the ecological footprint via their modernization [4]. As building's energy consumption levels are still high, the search for tools and mechanisms to improve their efficiency levels is a very relevant problem in our day and age. On the scope of the Self Assessment Toward Optimization of Building Energy, the SATO project, a solution is proposed to interconnect multiple smart devices on a single platform to enable, with the generated devices data, the development of new frameworks and solutions for better assessments to aid the building management.

This work was supported by the European Commission through the Sato Project (Grant agreement ID: 957128) and the LASIGE Research Unit, ref. UIDB/00408/2020 and ref. UIDP/00408/2020.

M. Kamp et al. (Eds.): ECML PKDD 2021 Workshops, CCIS 1525, pp. 567–579, 2021.
https://doi.org/10.1007/978-3-030-93733-1_42

With our proposal, we are exploring an indoor location system to locate users and report room occupancy. Our system does not require the installation of any application on the smartphone as it uses Scanners to retrieve signal strengths from the devices. The collected data from the Scanners is anonymized to prevent any future trace back between device locations and users. We are also proposing a real-world deployment that does not require fingerprinting for new locations with the usage of geometrical figures which were previously fingerprinted and with models already trained.

In this paper, we will describe the design, implementation, and usage of multiple Multilayered Perception networks to estimate the indoor location of users on a building and assess the building occupancy. The data used to locate people inside a building is collected via several scanners scattered around a building making continuous monitoring of the surrounding area. The collected data is then sent to a gateway, where it is anonymized and sent to the SATO platform. Upon receiving the data at the SATO platform, an internal process is activated and devices are located.

In this work, we tested different scanners' configurations and machine learning algorithms to analyze the accuracy of the algorithms and the impact of the scanner's position on the final accuracy of the system. The contributions of this work are the detection of indoor occupancy via non-intrusive methods and the design of an architecture of a distributed system to identify the occupancy of indoor spaces. This information can be later used to extract the movement patterns inside buildings, or determine which areas are most used inside buildings.

In the next section, we will describe, in Sect. 3 we describe the architecture of our proposed system. In Sect. 4 we explain how we collected the data and created the multiple datasets and also make a statistical analysis. In Sect. 5, we propose a machine learning pipeline to locate indoor devices independently to the Scanner locations, and in Sect. 6 we show the results obtained with our work. In Sect. 7 we present the conclusions from our work and describe future work related to this paper to improve the obtained results.

2   Related Work

Indoor location systems are used for different application areas, such as localization and navigation, asset tracking, and autonomous vehicle navigation. Typically, those systems are designed for specific contexts and environments, which imposes additional challenges when they are deployed to new areas, applications or environments. The data collection on site is also very exhaustive and time-consuming and can be affected by indoor rearrangements. Because there are multiple smart-devices manufacturers with different configurations, it is not possible to create test sets that contain all these different devices, which will impact the online accuracy [11].

The evaluation of performance can be done using different metrics. Accuracy is given in % and measures how accurate the system is while predicting an unknown location, Precision measures how frequently the system achieves the accuracy, and Recall gives the rate of true positives. The Average Localization Error is the average of all distance errors between the real location and the predicted location, calculated using Euclidean distances. Mean Squared Error (MSE) is the sum of the mean of the squared differences between the real location and the predicted location. Root Mean Squared Error (RMSE) is the squared root of Mean Squared Error.

Currently, Machine Learning approaches are being used to learn from the collected data and extract information from it. Supervised Machine Learning uses labeled data to make predictions, from a label set, defined on the dataset.

kNN, k-Nearest Neighbors, is a classification algorithm where new data is labeled according to the majority class of the k nearest neighbors. It is a simple algorithm to implement and uses only two parameters, the number of neighbors, k, and a distance function. Kriz et al. [5] developed a solution with Bluetooth Low Energy (BLE) beacons and Wi-Fi beacons and used a weighted kNN to predict device locations. In their proposal, BLE beacons are deployed where Wi-Fi Access Points (APs) would not have access to power and they have fingerprinted the area where the system was deployed. They achieved an average error of 1.08 m. Brunato and Battiti [1], to test different fingerprinting location algorithms, collected data from different divisions using Wi-Fi APs. Using kNN with $k = 8$ they achieved an average error of 3.12 m. Li et al. [6] experimented with multiple Wi-Fi APs, from 16 to 132, and with k neighbours from 1 to 6 to determine the kNN average error. With 132 APs and $k = 4$, they achieved an average error of 1,23 m.

K*, k-means clustering, is also a classification algorithm where new data is compared with previously labeled classes and the closest class is assigned to the new values. The difference between K* is that it uses entropy, determined by the probability of transforming an existing entry into another, to define its distance metric. Mascharka et al. [8] fingerprinted an area with Wi-Fi APs and other smartphone sensors and, using K*, obtained an average error of 1.134 m for the x axis and 0.762 m for the y axis.

SVM, Support Vector Machines, classifies new data by using hyperplanes of N-1-dimensions, where N is the number of features, to classify the points. When there is more than one class, the goal is to find an optimal hyperplane that contains the maximum margin between points from each class. Chriki et al. [3] used Wi-Fi fingerprinting with SVM to determine the area where the target is. The multiple areas are the SVM classes. Brunato and Battiti [1] obtained an average error of 3,04 m.

Neural Network is a network of multiple layers with nodes, that are neurons, and it usually has one input layer, at least one hidden layer, and an output layer. During the training phase, the real output is compared with the estimated one and, the given error is calculated. This error is then back-propagated across the network to change the weights between nodes. This process is repeated multiple times, epochs until it reaches an acceptable level of an evaluation metric level. Neural Networks detects non-linear and complex relationships between dependent and independent features and it is within the hidden layer where relationships between input variables are found. Chen et al. [2] used a Generalized Regression Neural Network, which has a faster training process, using Received Radio Signal fingerprinting obtained a RMSE of 0.103 m when a line-of-sight (LOS) exists between the device and the APs and an RMSE of 0.129 m when there is no LOS. Brunato and Battiti [1], using their Wi-Fi APs dataset, obtained an average error of 3,18 m when using MLP.

Bayesian Networks are probabilistic models based on the Bayes theorem and are composed of nodes. These nodes are represented by the variables and edge nodes identify dependencies between two variables. Madigan et al. [7] collected Wi-Fi strength signals and created a Bayesian model to assess indoor locations. The used models require a very low amount of samples. The model has four layers, where the first contains the position variables, the second is composed of distances of the variables from the base stations, the third layer contains the observed signal strengths and the last layer has the base station parameters.

3   Localization Architecture

In this section, we will describe the design and implementation of our proposed indoor location framework. In Fig. 1, we have the representation of the implemented system. The diagram also represents the flow of the data. It is captured on the Scanners and anonymized on the Gateway, then it is sent to the Platform where the data is used to estimate the locations of individuals inside buildings. These locations are then sent to the SATO Platform. In orange, we represent the cyber-physical components that are deployed on-site and belong to the Physical Layer. In green, we distinguish from the previous components and mark the ones that belong to the Processing Layer.

The Physical Layer contains Scanners and Gateways. In this Layer, the devices surrounding the Scanners are sensed and identified along with their Received Signal Strength Indicator (RSSI) value. This collected data is then sent to a Gateway and is anonymized before being sent to the Processing Layer.

When a Scanner turns on, it starts by registering himself on a nearby Gateway. During the registration, the Scanner receives a list of other Scanners' MAC addresses to be filtered during the scanning phase because the Scanners are using BLE to retrieve information from nearby devices. When a device is scanning using BLE, it can be identified by another nearby scanning BLE device. We added the registration phase to prevent this issue, and Scanners will filter themselves so that the system does not identify any Scanner as a building user's device. After the registration, the Scanner also receives from the Gateway what is the current cycle instant. This instant is used to coordinate the Scanners according to time.

Scanners have four different statuses, Scanning, Sending Devices, Sleeping, and Scan Preparation. During the Scanning phase, Scanners will search for nearby devices that emit BLE packets and capture them. For each device captured by the Scanner, the MAC address and the RSSI value are extracted. Before saving the values on a local JSON data structure, the device MAC address is

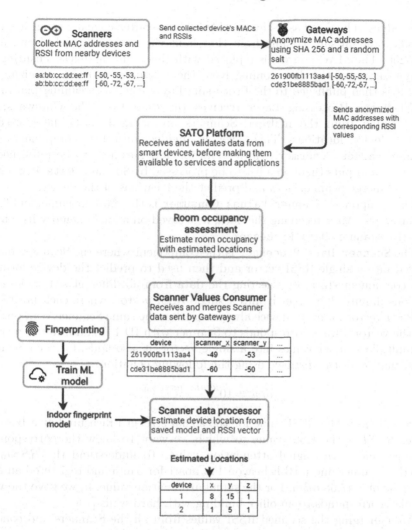

Fig. 1. Diagram of the architecture of the implemented system (Color figure online)

compared with the previous Scanner addresses received during the initial registration. After the Scanning phase, the Scanner will enter the Sleeping phase until it is time to send the collected devices. During the Sending Devices phase, the Scanner will send to a nearby Gateway the JSON containing the collected devices. After sending the devices, the Scanner enters again on the Sleeping stage until it's time to prepare to Scan for nearby devices, where the BLE module is turned on again, so the cycle repeats.

Gateways are used to handle the Scanners registrations and receive data from them. When a Gateway receives the devices from a Scanner, it recreates on its side the JSON dictionary with the MAC addresses associated with the

RSSI values. Then, it hashes every MAC address after concatenating it with a periodic random salt, coming from the cloud via a streaming platform, using SHA-256. The MAC address is replaced with the resulting digest, ensuring the anonymization of the data coming from the Scanners. After anonymizing the data, it is then published to the Processing Layer using a streaming platform.

When the Processing Layer receives the data from the Gateways, the data coming from the multiple Scanners are merged to be later used to predict device locations. This layer is divided into two components, the Scanner Values Consumer, which waits for new messages to be published by Gateways and puts them on a list to be processed by Scanner Data Processor that will merge Scanner data and predict the locations of the devices.

The component Scanner Values Consumer is the data consumer published by Gateways. After receiving the data, it is saved on a local memory list shared with the Scanner Data Processor.

The Scanner Data Processor is the component where the Scanners data is merged into a single RSSI vector and then used to predict the device location. This component starts by selecting the data from all different scanners on the previous minute. It merges it into a single RSSI vector, where each position of the RSSI vector for every device always matches the same Scanner, e.g., position 0 of the vector always corresponds to Scanner with ID 1. In addition to merging the multiple scanner values into a single vector, it also adds, for each Scanner, an estimation of the distance using the following equation:

$$dist = 10^{RSSI_0 - RSSI/10n} \qquad (1)$$

where $RSSI_0$ is the RSSI value for the signal strength measured at a base distance, $RSSI$ is the RSSI value to which we want to know the corresponding distance, and n the signal attenuation value. To understand the $RSSI_0$, we placed a Scanner and a BLE beacon 1 m apart for 5 min and registered an average value of -47.68 dBm. For the signal attenuation value, n, we gave the value 3, which corresponds to an office building with hard walls [10].

After merging the scanned RSSI values from all the Scanners and concatenating the estimated distances, the result is a table such as the one presented in Table 1. These values are then given to our Machine Learning pipeline, Fig. 3, to get the final devices' locations.

Table 1. An example of a row of RSSI values with corresponding distances after merging Scanners data. This row would then be given to the models to predict a device's location.

Scanner 1	Scanner 2	Scanner 3	Scanner 4	Dist 1	Dist 2	Dist 3	Dist 4
−65	−87	−90	−90	3.78	20.44	25.74	25.74

4   Data Collection and Analysis

This section describes how data is collected to create the multiple datasets and configurations deployed in our tests and the representation of the collected data to the Neural Network. We will also compare the real distances to the measured RSSI to check if the model we're using is correct.

The data was captured at the Faculty of Sciences of the University of Lisbon within three rooms. We applied a grid over the layout where each cell is a $2.75\,\text{m} \times 2.75\,\text{m}^2$. Following the application of the grid, we created four different configurations to place the Scanners around the rooms. These configurations are $90°$ rotations of each other, with slight adjustments to put the Scanners within the exact distances. With these rotations we intended to determine if the rotation of the Scanners has an impact on the accuracy whilst maintaining the same distances between the Scanners.

For each configuration, to collect the data, we placed a Raspberry Pi at each position for 5 min. Scanners collected the BLE packets and sent them to the Gateway, where the data was filtered to save the known Raspberry Pi and labeled with the corresponding location. Each Scanner read RSSI value is a feature used on the MLP models to identify the device location. We also added the estimated distances calculated from the read RSSI value during the dataset creation, as explained in Sect. 3. For each configuration we obtained a dataset with the following characteristics:

- Configuration 1–891 entries;
- Configuration 2–876 entries;
- Configuration 3–750 entries;
- Configuration 4–630 entries.

In Fig. 2, we have a comparison between the estimated distances from the Path-loss model and the real distances according to the RSSI values at each point. Real distances were calculated by applying the Pythagoras Theorem, where a is the height (2.2 m) and b the distance between the measurement point and the Scanner location. From the graph analysis, we can see that the model is close to being correct until it reaches $-86\,\text{dBm}$, where it starts measuring the distances much further than what they are.

5   Device Location Approach

In this work, we used a multiple Multilayer Perceptron (MLP) approach to locate the indoor devices. Our approach is represented in Fig. 3. The processing approach begins with the input of the merged Scanner data, within one minute, to the multiple models that will predict the device locations. With all devices predictions, the locations are transformed to the base configuration coordinates. The models are sorted by error and then clustered by the most significant error gaps. The cluster with the most number of models is picked, and their results are averaged.

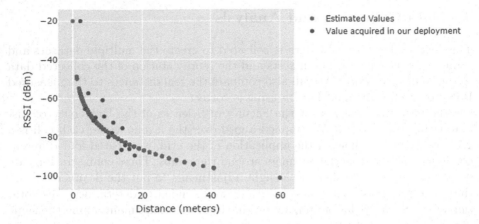

Fig. 2. Comparison between real distances and estimated distances from the RSSI Path-loss model

As we have seen in Sect. 4, Data Collection and Analysis, created four different Scanners configurations. With the four different configurations, and created eight different models. The first four models ($m1$–$m4$) only receive as inputs the four Scanners read values. The last four models ($m5$–$m8$) receive the RSSI values coupled with the estimated distances for each Scanner RSSI value, as seen in Sect. 3, Localization Architecture. Each MLP model was created using Keras[1] with variable input size, two hidden layers using the Rectified Linear Unit (ReLU) activation function, a batch size of 300, and 1000 training epochs. During the model compilation, we used the Adam optimizer with a learning rate of 0.001. To determine what are the best configurations for each model, we used grid-search to determine the following best hyper-parameters:

- Number of input neurons, 4 or 8 for RSSIs only models and 8 or 16 for models with distances;
- Number of neurons on the first and second layers, between 10 and 100 for each layer.

To better evaluate the accuracy of the models we 10-folded cross-validated the models for each dataset, which produced 10 models for each one. In Table 2, we represented the best hyper-parameters obtained for each model, their average training time and the mean-squared error for each model.

With the parameters hyper tuned, we then used the 80 models, from the 10-fold validation, to build a device location estimation represented on the diagram of Fig. 3. These models are associated with their accuracy errors and are all used to locate the devices from the RSSI lists. After obtaining all the resulting locations from the cross-validation models, only the outputs of previously administrator selected models are considered on the deployed system. The outputs

---

[1] https://keras.io/.

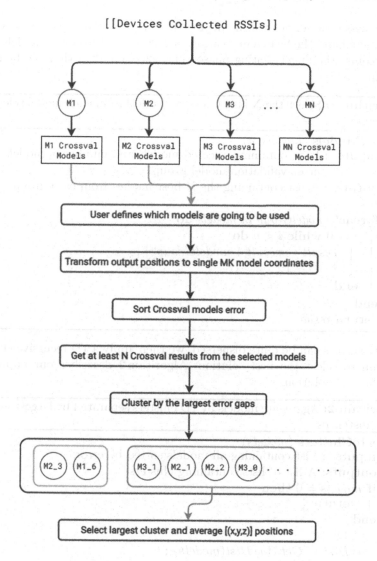

Fig. 3. Indoor devices localization pipeline

coming from all the models except *m1* and *m5* are transformed. The exempted models are not transformed because the configuration used to create the two models is used as the base coordinates. It is done by using simple geometry to convert the x and y abscissas to the correct coordinate plane.

After the transformation has taken place, each cross-validation group of models is sorted by error. Then the N best models from each cross-validation group are selected and added to a list. Besides using this method to avoid giving too much weight to a single model, we also do this to allow the user to use multiple geometrical figures, e.g. squares and triangles, to map the area where the occupation assessment service will be deployed. This way, the deployment area can be abstracted and the Scanners locations are decoupled from the models and no longer require the fingerprinting phase. The selection algorithm can be seen on Algorithm 1.

Algorithm 1: Select the N best Crossval models from each model selected by the user

---

SelectModels $(models, n)$
   inputs : List containing selected models and number of models per cross-validation model group
   outputs: A list containing the N best models from each group
   $result \leftarrow []$;
   foreach $modelGroup$ in $models$ **do**
      $i \leftarrow 0$ **while** $i < n$ **do**
         $result \leftarrow result + modelGroup[i]$;
         $i \leftarrow i + 1$;
      end
   end
   return $result$;

As the errors can be quite dispersed, we then apply a 1D recursive clustering algorithm to select the best solution. Algorithm 2 describes our approach to select the best solution.

Algorithm 2: Aggregate models by 1D clusters separated by largest model errors distances

---

CreateClusters $(models)$
   inputs : List containing all models sorted by error
   outputs: A list of lists containing clusters
   if $models = \emptyset$ **then**
      | **return** []
   end
   $i \leftarrow 0$;
   $maxDist \leftarrow GetMaxDist(models)$;
   while $i < Length(models) - 1$ **do**
      $k \leftarrow i + 1$;
      $dist \leftarrow |models[i].error - models[k].error|$;
      if $dist \geq maxDist$ **then**
         $index \leftarrow i$;
         break ;
      end
      $i \leftarrow i + 1$;
   end
   $leftModels \leftarrow models[: index]$;
   return $CreateClusters(leftModels) + models[index:Length(models)]$;

Following the cross-validation model selections and the clustering, the final location is given by picking the largest cluster, as this is most likely to provide the correct answer. We go through each device and average the locations given and output the results for all the located devices.

6 Results

As we have previously discussed in Sect. 5, we created a model for each configuration. We also created a new dataset for each model with the estimated distances for each scanner, to add more features to the Neural Networks. During this section, we will discuss the results obtained from the models and then discuss the results obtained from the implementation of our pipeline.

Table 2. Hyper-parameters table with the average best distances.

Model	Has distances?	Input layer neurons	First layer neurons	Second layer neurons	Average training time (seconds)	Average error (meters)	Standard deviation
m1	✗	4	10	90	31.25	5.927	5.089
m2	✗	4	10	10	27.08	3.371	3.036
m3	✗	4	10	30	32.96	5.055	5.460
m4	✗	4	10	90	33.51	8.590	11.31
m5	✓	16	10	100	27.01	3.404	3.568
m6	✓	16	10	60	24.50	2.138	1.946
m7	✓	16	10	100	29.28	3.521	3.922
m8	✓	8	90	60	25.98	8.703	11.481

In Table 2, we have represented the best results after training the models. The models $m1$ to $m3$ and $m5$ to $m7$ were created from datasets of the configurations with 4 active Scanners. $m4$ and $m8$ only had 3 available Scanners, as the third configuration didn't have the fourth one. From Table 2, it is visible that with the usage of estimated distances to estimate device locations, the average error of each model is reduced, except for the pair $m4$ and $m8$. As every model is a 90° rotation, when we apply the distances the average error is similar between the different configurations. The differences on the average error can be explained by the different positions of the Scanners on the environment, as they might be affected by different objects and walls. The obtained results with a maximum difference of 1.383 m show us that whilst maintaining the same distances between scanners, their rotations do not have a huge impact on their accuracy.

To evaluate our indoor location proposal, we implemented the proposed pipeline. When testing, we set the administrator parameters to use all models except $m4$ and $m8$, which have the worst errors. The minimum number of models is set to 10, so all of the cross-validation models are used on clustering.

We sent 512 RSSI vectors, randomly picked from the datasets to the pipeline, and received the corresponding location estimations. To evaluate the performance of the pipeline, we measured the distance between the two points (estimated by using our proposal and the real measurements) with Euclidean Distances. The result distance is multiplied by 2.75 m, the width of each grid cell. We obtained an average error of 5.68 m with a standard deviation of 2.61 m. The results obtained are far from the state of the art, in particular the results obtained from Kriz et al. [5], where with the fusion of BLE with Wi-Fi and obtained an average error of 1.08 m.

7   Conclusion

In this paper, we proposed a non-intrusive approach for an indoor location system. The proposed solution does not require the building users to install any software on their smartphones. This system guarantees the privacy of all data collected via its anonymization and by only giving an output of the (x, y) coordinates of all the devices seen by the scanners. Our proposal utilizes the results from multiple models to abstract the deployed area from the fingerprinting, via using geometrical figures approximations.

During the data collection process of our work, we found some problems related to the hardware used. The used Scanners hardware does not provide robustness. This problem could be eased out with more powerful hardware and broader support for more programming languages and different frameworks. The fingerprinting process is also very exhaustive and not very scalable to larger environments.

In future work, we will create datasets with figures of triangles and rectangles. These new datasets would then be applied to a new area with their distances matching the distances of the triangle and rectangle datasets and validate the real-world applicability of our work. We would also like to experiment with the same architecture using different hardware. To try to increase the model accuracy, the system should be deployed with more Scanners and could be fused with other commonly used radio-signal technology, such as Wi-Fi. The datasets could also be trained with unsupervised learning so that other features could be extracted via machine learning.

Acknowledgments. This work was supported by the European Commission through the Sato Project (Grant agreement ID: 957128) and the LASIGE Research Unit, ref. UIDB/00408/2020 and ref. UIDP/00408/2020.

References

1. Brunato, M., Battiti, R.: Statistical learning theory for location fingerprinting in wireless LANs. Comput. Netw. **47**, 825–845 (2005). https://doi.org/10.1016/j.comnet.2004.09.004

2. Chen, Z., Wang, J.: GROF: indoor localization using a multiple-bandwidth general regression neural network and outlier filter. Sensors **18**(11) (2018). https://doi.org/10.3390/s18113723, https://www.mdpi.com/1424-8220/18/11/3723

3. Chriki, A., Touati, H., Snoussi, H.: SVM-based indoor localization in wireless sensor networks. In: 2017 13th International Wireless Communications and Mobile Computing Conference (IWCMC), pp. 1144–1149 (2017). https://doi.org/10.1109/IWCMC.2017.7986446

4. European Commission: Commission Recommendation (EU) 2019/1019 of 7 June 2019 on building modernisation. European Commission (2019). https://eur-lex.europa.eu/eli/reco/2019/1019/oj

5. Kriz, P., Maly, F., Kozel, T.: Improving indoor localization using Bluetooth low energy beacons, April 2016. https://www.hindawi.com/journals/misy/2016/2083094/

6. Li, B., Wang, Y., Lee, H., Dempster, A., Rizos, C.: Method for yielding a database of location fingerprints in WLAN. In: Communications, IEE Proceedings, vol. 152, pp. 580–586, November 2005. https://doi.org/10.1049/ip-com:20050078

7. Madigan, D., Einahrawy, E., Martin, R., Ju, W.H., Krishnan, P., Krishnakumar, A.: Bayesian indoor positioning systems. In: Proceedings IEEE 24th Annual Joint Conference of the IEEE Computer and Communications Societies, vol. 2, pp. 1217–1227 (2005). https://doi.org/10.1109/INFCOM.2005.1498348

8. Mascharka, D., Manley, E.: Machine learning for indoor localization using mobile phone-based sensors, May 2015. https://arxiv.org/abs/1505.06125

9. Pérez-Lombard, L., Ortiz, J., Pout, C.: A review on buildings energy consumption information. Energy Build. **40**(3), 394–398 (2008)

10. Rappaport, T.S.: Wireless Communications: Principles and Practice. Prentice Hall PTR, Hoboken (2002)

11. Roy, P., Chowdhury, C.: A Survey of machine learning techniques for indoor localization and navigation systems (2021). https://doi.org/10.1007/s10846-021-01327-z

Author Index

Printed in the United States
by Baker & Taylor Publisher Services

Printed in the United States
by Baker & Taylor Publisher Services